NEW YORK

JOURNAL OF PHARMACY,

EDITED BY

THOMAS ANTISELL, M.D.,

AIDED BY

PROFESSOR TORREY, M.D., CHARLES ENDERLIN, M.D.,

BENJAMIN CANAVAN.

VOLUME III.

New-York:

PRINTED BY CHARLES SHIELDS,

CORNER OF PLATT AND GOLD STREETS.

1854.

CONTENTS OF VOL. III.

ORIGINAL AND SELECTED.

Fluid Magnesia. By the Editor........ 1
Chemistry of Perfumery........ 2
On the Use of Benzole in the Preparation of Vegetable Alkaloids. By John Williams........ 8
Contributions to the History of the Fatty Bodies. By M. Lefort........ 13
Action of Carbonic Acid on Quinine and Cinchonine; formation of Crystallized Carbonate of Quinine. By M. Langlois........ 19
On the Transformation of Tartaric Acid into Racemic Acid; the Discovery of Inactive Tartaric Acid, &c. By L. Pasteur........ 23
On a New Method for Determining the Commercial Value of Manganese. By A. P. Price, Ph. D., F. C. S........ 27
Exhibition of the Industry of all Nations—Jury Report........ 30
On the Natural Acidity of the Urine. By Lehmann........ 36
On the Connexion between Atomic Constitution and Boiling Points........ 37
Notice of the "California Nutmeg." By Professor J. Torrey, M. D........ 49
On the Introduction of Amygdaline into Pharmacy as a Means of Producing Prussic Acid. By the Editor........ 51
On Veratria. By James Beatson........ 56
On Practical Pharmacy. By Justus Liebig, M. D........ 57
Classification of Medical Substances........ 65
Chemical Relations of the Plants of the order Ericaceæ. By F. Rochleder........ 70
On the Formation and Constitution of Resins. By Dr. Charles Löwig........ 72
On Castor. By E. Weber and C. J. Lehmann........ 75
A Quick Approximitive Method of Estimating Minute Quantities of Iodine. By Thornton J. Herapath........ 80
On the Composition of Essence of Thyme. By M. A. Lallemand........ 82
Preparation of Uric Acid from the Excrements of Pigeons. By A. E. Arppe........ 85
Camphor from Sassafras Oil. By Faltin........ 86
Preparation of Valerianic Acid........ 86
On some of the Eruptive Phenomena of Iceland. By Dr. John Tyndall, F. R. S........ 97
Analysis of Tin Pyrites. By Dr. J. W. Mallet........ 102
Platinizing Copper Vessels........ 104
Condensation of Gases at the Surface of Solid Bodies. By MM. Jamin and A. Bertrand........ 105
On the Toxicology of Bichromate of Potassa. By M. Jaillard........ 106
Remarks on the Structural Condition of Iron. By T. R. V. Fuchs........ 116
New Method of Determining the Quantity of Urea in the Urine. By John W. Draper, M. D........ 119
On the Venom of Serpents. By J. Gilman, A. M., M.D., LL D........ 121
On Practical Pharmacy. By Justus Liebig, M. D........ 125
Action of Carbonic Acid on Quinine and Cinchonine. By M. Langlois........ 131
Medicines Holding Gum Resins Suspended........ 134
Formation of White Lead........ 135
Lac Varnish to Prevent Iron and Steel from Rusting........ 135
On the Pharmacy of the Cimicifuga. By William Procter, Jr........ 145
On the Means of Detecting Fraudulent Alterations in Documents. By MM. Chevallier and Lassaigne........ 147
Amorphous Phosphorus. By A. Puttfarcken........ 153
Benzoic Acid and Tests for its Purity........ 154
On the Composition of Butter. By Prof. Heintz........ 157
Saccharine Carbonate of Iron and Manganese. By T. S. Speer, M. D., of Cheltenham........ 160

On Practical Pharmacy. By Justus Liebig, M. D 162
Bromine and Iodine in Chili Nitre 172
On the Sulphurets Decomposable by Water. By E. Fremy 174
Non-Existence of Aridium 176
On Iron Alum 177
On the Products of the Distillation of Bituminous Shale. By the Editor 176
Purity of Balsam Copaiba 183
Address. By George D. Coggeshall 193
On the Manufacture of Spermaceti and Whale Oils. By George Thompson 200
On the Fatal Effects of, and Impurities in, Chloroform. By the Editor 203
Contributions to Pharmacy. By John Metauer, M. D., LL D 209
On Alexander and Morfit's Process for Organic Analysis. By Charles M. Wetherill, Ph.D., M. D 215
Elimination of Lead by Iodide of Potassium. By J. Outram, Jr 218
On Practical Pharmacy. By Justus Liebig, M. D 220
Iron Ore in the Carboniferous Limestone and Coal Measure of Iowa 233
On the Commercial Test of Soda Ash. By Edward N. Kent 243
Poisoning by Aconite—The Hendrickson Trial 245
On Practical Pharmacy. By Justus Liebig, M. D 254
Pulvis Ferri—Iron by Hydrogen. By William Procter, Jr 259
Researches upon the New Combinations of Salicyl. By Charles Gerhardt 262
The New Metal—"Aluminium" 266
Wheat Flour Deficient in Gluten 268
Analysis of Mineral Waters and Ores in Tennessee. By R. O. Currey, M. D 270
On Soap as a Means of Art. By Ferguson Branson, M. D., Sheffield 272
Condensation of the Gases by Porous Bodies. By MM. Favre and Silbermann 275
Researches on Evaporation. By Professor Marcet, of Geneva 277
The Nature of the Lava from the Eruption of Etna in 1852. By C. Hauer 281
On Creosote and its Products of Decomposition. By M. Von Gorup-Besanez 289
On the Deodorizing and Disinfecting Properties of Charcoal, with the description of a Charcoal Respirator for Purifying the Air by Filtration. By John Stenhouse, LL.D., F. R. S. .300
On Practical Pharmacy. By Justus Liebig, M. D 305
On the Employment of Molybdate of Ammonia for Detecting Arsenic. By H. Struve 310
On the Fluorides. By M. Fremy 313
On the Determination of Iodine. By R. Kersting 316
The Medicinal Plants of Australia. By P. L. Simmonds, Esq 322
Essence for Preston Salts (Mounseys) 326
Separation of Copper from Silver 326
On the Purity of Alcohol. By Edward N. Kent 337
On Concentrated Infusions and Decoctions. By Isaiah Deck, M. D., Chemist 338
On the Ramée, a New Fibre adapted for Textile Manufactures 341
On Quinine. By Dr. Nevins 345
Sympathetic Ink 348
On Lupuline. By J. Personne 349
Detection of Poppy or Nut Oil in Olive Oil. By E. Marchand 350
Urea in its Relations to the General Phenomena of Animal Physiology. By Th. Bischoff 352
On the Use of Hydrogen as a Calorific Agent. By Dr. Henry Hartshorne 358
Prepared Citrate of Magnesia. By Charles Ellis 361
On the Marsh Leeches of Mont Salut (Landes) 362
Iodide of Sodium. By William Procter, Jr 653
Unguentum Hydrargyri Nitratis 367
Pharmaceutical Notes. By Benjamin Canavan 385
On Litho-Photography. By. MM. Barreswil and Davanne 387
On the Acidity, Sweetness, and Strength of Wine, Beer, and Spirits. By H. Bence Jones, M. D., F. R. S 390
On a Subject presenting the Chemical Reaction of Cellulose, found in the Brain and Spinal Cord of Man. By Rudolph Virchow 393
Examination of Gas of the Philadelphia Gas Works. By Charles M. Wetherill, Ph.D., M. D. .398
On the Adulterations of Oils. By F. Crace Calvert, Esq 404

General Table of Reactions. By F. Crace Calvert, Esq....417
On the Employment of Chlorine in Analysis. By MM. Rivot, Beudant and Daguin....418
Analysis of the Mineral Waters of Mont Dore. By M. Thenard....425
Proceedings of the Pharmaceutical Association....433
On Osmotic Force. By Professor Graham....449
On the Different Spirits of Turpentine. By M. Marcellin Berthelot....456
The Metal Aluminium, its probable Use in Pharmacy. By W. Hamilton, M. B....460
Gas Cooking—Galvanic Battery....463
The Mode of Distinguishing Quinine from Quinidine....466
Manufacture and Consumption of Quinine in the United States....467
On the Detection of Blood Spots. By J. Löwe....469
On the Production of Wine, Brandy and Tartar in the Valley of the Ohio. By W. Procter, Jr....471
The Preparation of Sugar of Milk in Bavaria....474
Preparation of Cubebin....476
Extract Cinchoniæ Rubri Fluid. By John Canavan....481
On the Analysis of Rain Water. By M. Martin....482
On the Filtration of Air Considered as a Means of Preserving Organic Substances from Putrefaction. By MM. H. Schröder and Th. De Dusch....489
On the Essential Oil of Osmitopsis Asteriscorides. By M. Gorup Besanez....491
The Identity of Peucedanine with Imperatorine. By M. Wagner....492
On the Action of Solanine upon the Animal Organism. By M. Feaas....492
Analysis of the Shell of Helix Pomatia. By M. Wicke....493
On Red and Black Sulphur. By G. Magnus....494
Arsenic Eaters. By Dr. J. J. Tschudi....496
New Variety of Balsam of Copaiba. By Mr. Charles Lowe....500
On a New Process of Preparing Powder of Iron. By Arthur Morgan, L A.C....502
On a New Variety of Flaxseed. By Wm. Procter, Jr....505
On the Changes Produced in the Blood by the Administration of Cod Liver Oil and Cocoa-Nut Oil. By Theophilus Thompson, M.D., F.R.S....506
On the Preparation of Calomel in the Humid Way. By Prof. Wöhler....507
On the Tincture of Arnica. By M. V. Garnier....508
On the Tincture of Arnica. By M. Pichou....510
Application of Murexide as a Coloring Matter for Wool....511
Introductory Lecture....517
Pharmaceutical Notes and Gleanings....529
American Pharmaceutical Association....531
The Leaves of the Magnolia Tripetala as a Dressing for Blisters. By T. S. Wilson, M.D....542
Decomposition of Phosphate and Sulphate of Lime by Hydrochloric Acid. By M. Cari Mantranet....544
On the Influence of Belladonna in Counteracting Poisonous Effects of Opium. By Thomas Anderson, M.D....545
Soda an Antidote for Snake Bite and the Sting of Poisonous Insects....547
New Mode of Preparing Ointment of Mirate of Mercury....548
Iodine Injections in Leucorrhœa. By Dr. Russell....550
The Salts of Manganese. By E. H. Davis, M.D....554
Purification of Spirits by Filtration. By Mr. W. Schaffer....557
New Process of Procuring Phosphorus. By M. Cari Montrand....558
Polytrichum Juniperinum....559

VARIETIES.

Presence of Iodine in Air and Water. By the Editor 39
On a New Thermostat for Regulating Temperature and Ventilation. By W. Sykes Ward.... 39
Artificial Production of Diamond Powder 39
Red Fire 39
Table for Determining the Nature of Saline Deposits in the Urine by the Microscope. By Dr. Bird 40
Table for Discovering the Nature of Saline Deposits in the Urine by Chemical Reagents. By Dr. Bird 40

Oil a Test for Copper 40
Caustic Baryta from Carbonate 40
Hariety in the Milk of Various Animals 87
Vot-Air Vessel 88
Etherizing Congress 88
Acclimation of the Deodar 89
Artificial Wood 89
Cotton Tree 90
Fertility of Nile Mud 90
On Ethers formed from Acids and Ordinary Ether. By M. Berthelot 90
The Art of Printing from Nature 91
French Prizes 91
On the Import of Sperm and Whale Oil into the United States 91
Tobacco Culture in Connecticut 91
Researches upon the Presence and Quantity of Nitric Acid in Plants. By M. Schesing...... 92
On the Photo-Microscopic Views of the Filaments of Wool, Cotton and Flax Cotton. By M. Bertsch 92
On the Economic Manufacture of Bichromate of Potassa. By M. Jacquelain 92
Review of the New York Drug Market 93
Mode of Determining the Optical Power of a Microscope. By Professor Harting 186
Oleo Resin of Male Fern 188
On the Waters of the Great Salt Lake, Rocky Mountains. By Dr. L. D. Gale 189
On the Waters ot the Warm and Hot Springs of Salt Lake City. By Dr. L. D. Gale 189
Manufacture of Sal-Ammoniac from the Residues sf Gas Works 189
Preparation for the Destruction of Vermin 140
Preparation of Pure Quinine 140
Ether Impregnated with Quinine in the Treatment of Intermittent Fever 141
eparation of Bromine from Iodine 141
Arrificial Silification of Limestones 142
New Varnish for Heliographic Engraving on Steel 142
Photographic Engravings on Glass 143
Detection of Picric Acid in Beer. By J. Lassaigne 143
The Ericsson 143
British Association of Chemists and Druggists 143
The Chiropodist and the Tiger 144
Extraordinary Malaria Visitation 144
French Academy of Medicine 144
Faculty of Medicine of Paris 144
Deville's New Lamp Forge 184
Magnetism of Volcanic Rocks 184
Alcohol from Beet Root 185
Telegraph Insulators 185
Photography 186
Effect of Intense Cold 187
Purity of Milk 188
Determination of Iodine. By M. de Luca 188
Observations on the Constitution of Rain Water 189
New Mode of Detecting Strychnia and its Salts 189
Indigo in the Animal Economy 189
Improvement in Sticking Plaster 190
Medical Use of Strychnia 190
Valerianic Acid from Fusel Oil 190
Preparation of Ferrocyanhydric Acid 190
Vessels for Preserving Fluohydric Acid 191
Dolomite 191
M. Bussy on the Urine and Blood of Persons who died of Yellow Fever 191
External Use of Ipecacuanha 236
Value of Phosphate of Lime 236

New Hæmostatic Agent 236
Deleteriousness of London Gas 237
Poisoning by Arsenious Acid and Chromate of Lead 237
Iodine in Natural Waters. By Chatin 237
Medical Statistics of France 237
Purple-Red Ink for Marking Linen 238
Table of Produce and Gravity of Volatile Oils 282
Red Indigo 282
Improved Method of Manufacturing Liquid Cements, Pigments and Paints. By Mr. George Bell 283
Improved Process for Bleaching Beeswax, and the Fatty Acids. By Mr. G. F. Wilson 283
Improved Method of Manufacturing Epsom Salts. By Dr. Richardson 284
New Variety of Copaiva Balsam 284
Crystalline Hydrate of Oxide of Iron 284
A Delicate Reagent for the Detection of Reducing Bodies. By J. Lowenthal 285
Test for Quinine 285
Preservation of Leeches 285
How Families are Poisoned—Scheele's Green in Baker's Shops. By Alfred S. Taylor, M.D., F. R. S. 327
Detection of Blood-stains on a Knife Covered with Rust 328
Adulteration of Sulphate of Quinine 329
Specific and Latent Effects of Vapors. By MM. Favre and Silbermann.... 331
Oxidized Silver 331
On the Preparation of Copal Varnish. By Professor Heeren 331
Detection of Strychnine in Saccharine Powders. By A. Vogel, Jun. 333
On the Estimation of Tin. By Peter Hart, Manchester 333
Detectiou of Blood-stains on Garments 334
Cast-Iron for Artificial Magnets 334
Saltpetre 335
Dr. Stenhouse's Charcoal Respirator for Purifying the Air by Filtration 369
Preparation of Paraffin and Pure Acetic Acid upon a large scale from the Distillation Products of Wood. By Reinhold V. Reichenbach 372
Responsibiiity of the Pharmaceutical Chemist 373
Manufacture of Alum from the Residuum of the Distillation of Boghead Cannel Coal 374
On the Relative Values of the different kinds of Meat as Food 375
Non-Solubility of Morphia in Chloroform 376
Mode of Using Bi-Sulphate of Soda as a Substitute for Cream of Tartar and Alum 376
Method of Communicating a Dull Black Color to Brass 377
Syrup of Elderberries (Sambucus Canadensis) as a Substitute for the Compound Syrup of Sarsaparilla. By W. H. Worthington 377
Employment of Glycerine in Diseases of the Skin 378
The Seeds of Asparagus a Substitute for Coffee 379
Proceedings of the Pharmaceutical Association 379
Oxide of Carbon as a Poison. By M. Adrieu Cherrot 428
Notice of an Attempt to Poison with Strychnia. By H. F. Fish, of Waterbury, Conn. 429
Syrupus Manganesiæ Phosphatis. By Thomas S. Wiegand 430
On Some Peculiar Reactions of Metals in the Humid Way. By Prof. Wöhler.... 477
Professor Tiedemann 477
Syrupus Calcis Phosphatis 478
Adulteration of Castor Oil 478
Cost of the Electric Light 479
Cheap Substitute for Damp Blue 479
On the Detection of Alcohol in Judiciary Investigations. By Dr. Ed. Strauch 560
Method of Rapidly Bleaching Wax and Purifying Tallow, Oils, &c 562
On the Recognition of Blood-spots upon Linen and Cotton Stuffs. By C. Wiehr 563
Experimental Investigation of the Poisonous Quality of the Oil of Bitter Almonds when freed from Hydrocyanic Acid 564
Poisoning attributed to Vapor of Cyanide of Potassium 565
Recovery after taking a Large Dose of Prussic Acid 565

Poisoning by Darnel Seeds 566
Inhalation of Ether and Chloroform 566
Paris Society of Pharmacy 567
Artesian Wells 567
University of Edinburgh 567

REVIEWS.

The Medical Formulary. By Benjamin Ellis, M.D. 95
Douze Lecons de Photographie. Par M. le Docteur Fau 238
Journals Received 239

EDITORIAL.

Gratulatory 41
American Pharmaceutical Association 42
Local Formulæ 42
Columbia College 42
Book Notices 43
Patent, to J. C. Booth, Philadelphia, for Manufacture of Chromate and Bi-Chromate of Potash from Chrome Iron Ore 43
Table of Imported Drugs 44
General Remarks on Poisoning 94
Meeting of the American Pharmaceutical Association 191
August Laurent 191
Editorial Apologies 192
Blandet's Experiments for Preserving Dead Bodies by Injection 192
Albany Medical College "Working Laboratory" 192
Massachusetts College of Pharmacy 240
Colnmbia College 240
Remarks on Mr. Outram's Determination of Lead in the Urine 240
Remarks on a New Method of Baking 286
Columbia College 286
Paris Prizes 287
Cases of Poisoning 287
Analysis of Diabetic Urine 288
American Pharmaceutical Association 335
Columbia College 336
Dr. Reese on the Hendrickson Trial 336
The London Pharmaceutical Society 338
Dr. Griseler on Rancid Oil 338
Patent Medicine Vendors 383
American Pharmaceutical Association 383
American Medical Association 383
Professor Doremus on Soda Water 384
Remarks on the City Inspector's Report 431
On Fuming or Nordhaussen Oil of Vitriol for the Manufacture of Collodion 479
Discussion on the Proper Pronunciation of the Word "Pharmaceutical" 480
Remarks on the American Pharmaceutical Association 480
Obituary—Death of Dr. Enderlin 568

NEW YORK

JOURNAL OF PHARMACY.

DECEMBER, 1854.

FLUID MAGNESIA.

BY THE EDITOR.

This medicament, introduced to the profession by Sir James Murray, and generally adopted, is at all times manufactured of very variable strength. By Sir J. M., who held a patent for its manufacture in Great Britain and Ireland, it was stated to be furnished at the strength of 14 grains to the ounce. Its manufacture being commenced in this city about a year since, and having received a bottle from the manufacturers, I determined the amount of solid matter and of magnesia which a given quantity would yield.

1. On evaporating one ounce of fluid to dryness, the residue being ignited in a porcelain crucible, weighed 4.50 grains.

2. Digested 1 oz. for an hour to expel the carbonic acid, which precipitated a portion of the magnesia; then added caustic potass until the precipitation ceased; precipitate collected, dried, ignited, and weighed = 4.33.

3. The residue of experiment 1, treated with weak hydrochloric acid, did not wholly dissolve, but left a white gritty powder to 15; this dissolved in boiling hydrochloric acid, and on evaporation to dryness and ignition, it was insoluble in the same acid; this portion was silica.

Now, as 100 parts of ordinary carbonate of magnesia contain 41.6 of caustic magnesia (MgO), so, from experiment 2, 4.33 gr. would supply 10.41 grains of carbonate of magnesia in 1 oz. of liquid. This "American Fluid Magnesia," as it is termed, does not, therefore, contain the full amount of magnesia, which the condensed gas would dissolve, by nearly one-third.

Since the solvent powers of carbonic acid upon the earths have been so happily introduced into medicine, it is worth considering whether a solution of phosphate of lime in carbonic acid might not be used with advantage.

CHEMISTRY OF PERFUMERY.

The subjoined processes for the manufacture of flavoring extracts are so much more full in details than any which have appeared elsewhere that we have been led to abstract them from the pages of the London Journal of the Society of Arts, which has borrowed them from a Wirtemberg periodical. We have added the scale of common temperatures, and to a slight extent condensed the whole.—Ed.

Pineapple Oil.—This product consists of a solution of one part of butyric acid ether in eight or ten parts of spirits of wine. For preparing butyric acid ether pure, butyric acid is required, and this is obtained most readily and in greatest quantity by the fermentation of sugar or of St. John's bread (*siliqua dulcis*). To prepare butyric acid from sugar, M. Bentch takes a solution of 6 lbs. of sugar and half an ounce of Tartaric acid in 26 lbs. of water, which is left to stand for some days; at the same time about one-fourth of a pound of old decayed cheese is diffused in 8 lbs. of sour milk, from which the cream has been removed; and, after this has also stood for some days, it is mixed with the first solution, and the whole is kept from four to six weeks at a temperature about 24° to 28° Reaumer, (86° to 95° F.) water being added from time to time to replace that which is lost by evaporation. After the evolution of gas has entirely ceased, the liquid is dissolved in its own bulk of water, and, finally, 8 lbs. of soda, crystallized, dissolved in 12 to 16 lbs. of water, are added to it. The liquid is then filtered and evaporated till it weighs only 10 lbs., when a quantity of sulphuric acid, (nordhausen) 5½ lbs. diluted with an equal weight of water, is carefully mixed with it, by small portions at a time. The butyric acid in the state of an oily substance will now appear on the surface of the liquid, from which it may be skimmed off; but as the remaining liquid contains more butyric acid it is submitted to distillation, by which means another portion of diluted butyric acid is obtained, which may be concentrated by means of melted chloride of calcium, or by saturating it with carbonate of soda, evaporating and decomposing by sulphuric acid. By this method 1¾ lbs. of butyric acid are obtained from 6 lbs. of sugar.

M. Marson says that the same product may be obtained from St. John's bread (*siliqua dulcis*) by taking 4 lbs. of the mashed bread and mixing it with 10 lbs. of water and 1 lb. of chalk; the liquid matter must be maintained from three to four weeks at a temperature from 25° to 35° Reaumer, (87° to 112° F.) and be often and well stirred, and from time to time the water evaporated must be replaced. After fermentation has ceased, a quantity of water equal to the bulk of the solution is added, and afterwards a concentrated solution of 2½ or 2¾ lbs. of carbonate of soda, when it is finally evaporated. To the concentrated liquid is then added 1½ to 2 lbs. of sulphuric acid, diluted with 2 lbs. of water, and the remainder of the process is performed as already described. By this method a little more than half a pound of colored butyric acid will be obtained. The acid retains a peculiar smell from the St. John's bread, which continues even in the ether prepared from the same, while that prepared from sugar gives an ether of a very pure smell. It will be found advantageous to agitate the oily butyric acid with chloride of calcium, in order to deprive it entirely of moisture.

For preparing butyric acid ether (butyrate of oxide of ethyle) from butyric acid, 1 lb. of butyric acid is dissolved in 1 lb. of rectified alcohol, (95° Tralles) and is mixed with ½ to ¼ of an ounce of concentrated sulphuric acid. The compound is treated for some minutes, when the butyric acid ether will form a thin layer on the top. The whole is then mixed with one-half of its bulk of water, and the upper layer taken off; the remaining liquid being submitted to distillation yields another quantity of butyric ether, which is mixed with that obtained in the first instance, and the whole well agitated with a very dilute solution of soda, in order to deprive it of all the acid, which operation should be repeated several times if a very pure ether is desired to be obtained. Care should be taken to use but small quantities of the soda solution at a time so as not to lose too much ether, the latter being to some extent soluble in water; when large quantities are acted upon, the wash waters should be collected, mixed with an equal quantity of spirits of wine, and distilled, by which means a solution of pure butyric acid ether in spirits of wine is obtained.

Butyric acid ether may also be obtained directly from butyrate of soda, by dissolving one part of this salt in one part of rectified alcohol, adding one part of sulphuric acid, and heating some minutes. The ether collects on the top of the liquid, and is purified by washing with water and with diluted soda solution.

For preparing pineapple oil, 1 lb. of butyric acid ether is dissolved in 8 to 10 lbs. of spirits of wine, which should be previously deprived of its empyreumatic or fusel oil. Pure French spirits of wine will be found best suited for this purpose. According to the purpose for which the pineapple oil is intended, either rectified alcohol, of 80° to 90° Tralles, or brandy, of 40° to 50°, should be used for dissolving the ether. Twenty to twenty-five drops of such an extract will suffice for giving a strong pineapple odor to 1 lb. of the sugar solution, to which some acid, generally tartaric or citric acid, is added.

Bergamot Pear Oil.—What is called pear oil is an alcoholic solution of acetate of oxide of amyle and acetate of oxide of ethyle, prepared from potato fusel oil (the hydrate of oxide of amyle). This fusel oil, or oil of potato spirits, is the compound distilled over toward the end of the first distillation of spirits made from potatoes, and is an oily liquid of a very strong and nauseous odor. This oil, in the state in which it is obtained from large potato brandy distilleries, is never pure, but it may be purified by adding it with a dilute soda solution, when the pure fusel oil collects as an oily layer on the top of the liquid: this oily substance is then submitted to distillation, and that part which distils over at 100° to 112° Reaumer is collected and forms the pure fusil oil.

For preparing acetate of oxide of amyle from this fusel oil, 1 lb. of pure ice vinegar is mixed with an equal quantity of fusel oil, to which is added half a pound of sulphuric acid. The liquid is digested for some hours at about 100°, when the acetate of oxide of amyle separates, particularly when mixed with a small quantity of water. The remaining liquid, when mixed with more water, yields, when submitted to distillation, a further quantity of acetate of oxide of amyle. The entire quantity of acetate thus obtained is agitated several times with water and a little soda solution, so as to deprive it of all free acid.

This acetate may also be obtained by taking one part of fusel oil to 1½ parts of dry acetate of soda, or 2 parts of acetate of potash with 1 to 1½ parts of sulphuric acid. The liquid being kept for some time at a gentle heat, the amyle acetate is separated by adding water and proceeding as above. Fifteen parts of amyle acetate are mixed with 1½ parts of vinegar ether, (vinegar naphtha, acetate of oxide of ethyle) and dissolved in 100 to 120 parts of spirits of wine, as in the case of pineapple extract; an acid, as tartaric or citric, should be added to the sugar solution on making use of the pear extract, which addition makes the flavor of the bergamot pear better distinguishable, and the taste acquires at the same time more of the refreshing qualities of the fruit.

Apple Oil.—What is called apple oil is a solution of valerianate of oxide of amyle in spirits of wine, which may be obtained as a secondary product when fusel oil is distilled with chromate of potash and sulphuric acid for the preparation of valerianic acid. The light solution which collects in the top of the distilled liquid contains valerianate of oxide of amyle, together with the liquids, such as aldehyde, which gives to the product a less agreeable smell and taste. It is, therefore, to be preferred for preparing pure valerianate of oxide of ethyle.

For preparing valerianic acid, 1 part of fusel oil is mixed, by small portions, with 3 parts of sulphuric acid, and afterwards 2 parts of water are added. At the same time, a solution of 2¼ parts of bichromate of potash, in 4½ parts of water, is treated in a tubular retort; the first liquid is then permitted to flow very slowly into the liquid of the retort in such a manner that the boiling goes on very slowly. The liquid which is distilled over is saturated with carbonate of soda, and is evaporated, either to dryness, to obtain valerianate of soda, or to the consistency of syrup, when sulphuric acid is added (about two parts of the concentrated acid, diluted with the same quantity of water for every three parts of crystalline carbonate of soda). The valerianic acid forms an oily layer on the upper part of the liquid, which latter will still yield some valerianic acid on being submitted to distillation.

For preparing valerianate of oxide of amyle, 1 part, by weight, of pure fusel oil is mixed with an equal quantity, by weight, of common sulphuric acid. The resulting solution is added to 1¼ parts of oily valerianic acid or to one and a half parts dry valerianate of soda, and is treated by a water bath, and then mixed with water, by which means the impure valerianate will be separated. This is washed several times with water, then with a solution of carbonate of soda, and finally with water again. In preparing this compound, it is essential that the mixture of sulphuric acid and fusel oil with valerianic acid should not be heated too high, or for too long, as the product will thereby acquire an insufferably pungent smell when required for use. One part of the valerianate is dissolved in 6 or 8 parts of spirits of wine, and acid is added in the same manner as has been before explained in the preparation of other extracts.

Artificial Oil of Bitter Almonds.—When Mitscherlich, in 1834, discovered nitro benzole, he little thought after twenty years to find this body in an exhibition. He certainly at the time pointed out the remarkable resemblance which the odor of nitro benzole had to that of bitter almonds; but the only sources of obtaining benzole at that time, viz., the oil of compressed gas and the distillation of benzoic acid, were much too expensive, and put an end to the idea of substituting nitro benzole for the oil of bitter almonds. Mansfield, however, in 1849, showed that benzole may be produced easily, and in large quantities, from the oil of coal tar, and this discovery has not been lost sight of in the arts. Among the articles of French perfumery in the London Exhibition, with the title of *Artificial Oil of Bitter Almonds* and the fanciful name of *Essence of Mirbane*, there were several specimens of oils which consisted of more or less pure nitro benzole. The apparatus used in the preparation of this substance is that proposed by Mansfield. It consists of a large glass worm, the upper end of which branches into two tubes, which are provided with funnels. A stream of concentrated nitric acid flows slowly through one of these funnels, while the other is for the benzole, which for this purpose need not be absolutely pure; at the points where the tubes of the funnels unite, the two bodies come into contact; the chemical compound formed becomes sufficiently cooled in passing through the worm, and only requires to be washed with water and finally with a weak solution of carbonate of soda to be ready for use. Although the nitro benzole closely resembles oil of bitter almonds in its physical properties, it possesses a somewhat different odor, readily recognized by a practical person. However, it answers well for scenting soap, and would be extensively applicable for confectionery and other culinary purposes. For the latter purpose it has the special advantage over oil of bitter almonds, that it contains no Prussic acid.—*Journal Society of Arts*, Oct., 1853.

ON THE USE OF BENZOLE IN THE PREPARATION OF VEGETABLE ALKALOIDS.*

BY JOHN WILLIAMS.

The application of Benzole to the elimination of various vegetable alkaloids having engaged my attention for some time past, I venture to lay the present paper before you, more in the hope of its receiving practical adaptation from your hands, than from any idea that the subject has been worked out to its fullest extent.

First, then, a few words respecting benzole:

This important and interesting body was first discovered by Faraday, and named by him *bicarburetted hydrogen;* it was afterwards produced by the decomposition of benzoïc acid by heat in presence of lime or baryta, and hence named benzole; it has, however, since been proved to exist in very considerable quantities in coal-tar naphtha, or that portion of the liquid products of the destructive distillation of coal, which floats on water, boils below the temperature of 212° F., and congeals to a solid mass at 32°. The ordinary coal-tar naphtha of commerce is a very impure product; the mode of separating the benzole from it, was, I believe, first pointed out by Mansfield. He took the ordinary naphtha, distilled it in a still with a double head, so constructed that only that portion of the naphtha which distils at the lowest temperature was collected; the product thus obtained was digested with oil of vitriol, which turned it black. I have found it necessary that this part of the process should be repeated at least twice, or the proper degree of purification would not be effected. The benzole thus separated was now washed with water, dried with anhydrous sulphate of soda, and re-distilled; it was then exposed to a freezing temperature, and, when solid, subjected to pressure, when the pure benzole was obtained; but, for the purposes I have to point out, I do not consider this last operation necessary.

---

* Read before the "Chemical Discussion Society," Oct. 27th, 1853.

Benzole, thus obtained, is a clear, volatile liquid, having still a distinct odor of coal gas, but more aromatic; it is quite insoluble in water, and is excessively inflammable; this last property renders great caution necessary in conducting the processes I am about to describe. Benzole, in its powers of solution, may be likened to ether, but, from its low price, and from its not being so volatile as that body, it possesses practical advantages in working, which, I think, will more than counterbalance its disagreeable odor and great imflammability.

The first application of benzole I have to describe is in the preparation of quinine and its allied bases. An acid infusion of the bark was prepared in the usual manner; sufficient caustic potassa was added to render it strongly alkaline; it was then shaken with about one-fourth of its bulk of benzole; the whole of the quinine; quinidine, quinoïdine, &c., was at once yielded to that agent. I found, however, that the cinchonine was not extracted without greater difficulty. The benzole was distilled off, leaving the mixed alkaloids as a slightly yellow, resinous mass, which, when dissolved in weak sulphuric acid, and filtered, yielded a solution from which the white bases were at once precipitated, and separated in the usual manner.

This process, I think, would not answer for manufacturing quinine on a large scale, but I find it is a very elegant, certain, and easy mode of performing the analysis of cinchona barks, for, if moderate care is used, the alkaline liquid remaining after the action of the benzole does not contain the smallest trace of alkaloid.

The next substance acted upon was the quinoïdine or amorphous quinine of commerce, which, as usually found, is a blackish, resinous looking substance, with a peculiar, burnt, empyreumatic odor. When this body is powdered and digested with benzole it yields all its bitter principle to it, the benzole generally separating from the mass almost colorless. By distilling, or dissolving, the residuum in weak sulphuric acid, filtering (which effectually deprives the liquid of any odor of benzole with which it may be contaminated) and precipitating with caustic soda, the quinoïdine or amorphous quinine is obtained of a pale straw color, and when dissolved in weak SO^3 yields a nearly colorless solution. Of course the quantity yielded is comparatively small—rarely more than a drachm from an ounce—but often not nearly so much, thus rendering the real quinoïdine a more expensive body for medicinal use than even quinine itself.

I may here mention one great advantage of the use of benzole in preparing these alkaloids, which is, that the coloring matter contained in the liquid, extract, or powder acted on, is almost invariably left behind, so that with one operation the base is obtained pure, or nearly so, and any odor arising from the benzole is lost when the base is dissolved in acid, filtered, and re-precipitated.

Morphine was the next body to which my attention was directed, but in this instance I failed to obtain a satisfactory result; morphine being but slightly, if at all, soluble in benzole, in which particular benzole again agrees with ether.

With the next alkaloid, however, I was more successful. Nux vomica seeds were taken, softened in boiling water, sliced in a proper machine, and boiled in many successive waters until that menstruum ceased to extract either color or taste from the seeds. It might be advantageous to use weak sulphuric acid in this operation; but, for reasons which it is not necessary to mention, this was not done. The liquids were now boiled down in a copper to a convenient bulk, filtered, and again evaporated to the consistence of thin treacle. To this aqueous extract a strong solution of caustic potassa was added until it was strongly alkaline. It was then mixed with an equal bulk of benzole, well agitated, and kept in a warm stove for about twelve hours. The first benzole was poured off, and a second, but smaller quantity, was added, and left to digest in like manner with the extract, and afterwards the mixed benzoles distilled—the residuum, treated with acetic acid, filtered, and precipitated with caustic soda; the precipitate was white, and consisted of strychnia and brucine. These were dissolved in sulphuric acid and separated in the usual manner. The quantity of strychnine yielded by this process is large; and, when it is dissolved in a little weak alcohol and allowed to crystallize, the base is yielded of great beauty and perfect purity.

The next process I have to describe is one for preparing cantharidine. This substance, though of great use to the medical man, has hitherto, from the great expense of manufacturing it, been comparatively little used in its pure form. Powdered catharides are to be heated to about 150°, with rather more than an equal bulk of benzole; after about an hour's digestion the magma is to be transferred to a percolator; and, when the first portion of benzole has gone through, fresh warm benzole is passed through it. A pound of cantharides requires about from six pints to a gallon of benzole to be thoroughly exhausted. The benzole is now to be distilled. A rather dark colored oily liquid is the result, which is to be poured into an evaporating-basin, and left for, say twelve hours; at the end of which time the liquid will be found studded with magnificent crystals of cantharidine sometimes a quarter of an inch long.

I found some difficulty in purifying these crystals from the mother-liquid, but at length succeeded by washing the whole mass in a beaker-glass with a little cold ether, which dissolved the dark oily liquid freely, but scarcely affected the cantharidine; the crystals subsided to the bottom, and the supernatant liquid being poured off, the crystals were washed once or twice more with very small quantities of ether, and then turned out on bibulous paper; they speedily dried but were not quite white; by dissolving them in a flask of fresh benzole, heating, adding a little charcoal, filtering, and allowing the liquid to cool, they were obtained of perfect whiteness, but not so large as at first. From a pound of cantharides about thirty grains of cantharidine may thus be readily obtained.

I must caution those who may follow this process to beware of the blistering property of the benzole solution of cantharidine in all its stages. Unless great care be used severe blisters will be the painful result.

The following applications of benzole have not yielded quite such satisfactory results as the foregoing, but still such as to encourage us to persevere in the application of this body to delicate chemical manipulation, and to prove that it is an important addition to our means of organic research.

Atropine was obtained, though not in distinct crystals, by the following method. An acqueous extract of belladonna, prepared with great care, *in vacuo*, was rubbed with sufficient water to soften it; then a little very concentrated solution of carbonate of potassa having been incorporated, the benzole was added, and the whole well rubbed together. After two or three quantities of benzole had thus been rubbed with the extract they were mixed and distilled; the dark oily residuum was treated with acetic acid, filtered, and precipitated with ammonia, a white curdy precipitate was formed, which, however, was not yet pure, as it refused to crystallize when dissolved in alcohol and evaporated: a resinous or oily matter still contaminated it, which interfered with its purification. This subject still engages my attention, and I hope at a future opportunity to be able to give a better account of the matter.

Extract of henbane, prepared with equal care, was treated in a similar manner; the acid solution of the oily residuum did not, however, give a curdy precipitate with ammonia, but only a slight opalescence; however, upon shaking the liquid with an equal bulk of ether, separating and allowing the ether to evaporate very slowly, a minute quantity of crystals were on one occasion produced, which burnt perfectly, were soluble in a few drops of dilute acetic acid, and precipitated again as a white cloud by ammonia, which cloud was instantly taken up by being shaken with ether.

I next turned my attention to the so-called sulphate of bebeerine of commerce. It was treated with a solution of caustic potassa, and then with benzole; the benzole being distilled off yielded the bebeerine of a pale straw color, but in very small quantity. It was soluble in acids and precipitated by alkalies, and possessed the usual basic characters. I did not attempt to crystallize it.

Extract of digitalis was tried, and readily yielded its alkaloid.

Extract of conium also, the benzole being washed with weak sulphuric acid, yielded the sulphate of conium, which, afterwards distilled with strong potassa, yielded the coneïne in a state of purity.

Taraxacum, sarsaparilla, and colocynth, were tried, but no active principles could be eliminated from these bodies by this process.

Nut galls, in fine powder, were treated with benzole. Tannin, of good color, was the result of its evaporation; but from the impossibility of perfectly freeing it from the odor of the benzole, I fear that this process will not prove of practical use, unless in the production of tannin on the large scale for use in the arts, when the odor would be of minor importance.

I hope to be able on a future occasion to give you a few more illustrations of the practical use of benzole in operative chemistry.—*Chemist*, December, 1853.

CONTRIBUTIONS TO THE HISTORY OF THE FATTY BODIES.

BY M. LEFORT,

Pharmaceutist at Paris.

I endeavored, in a former memoir, to make known the elementary compcsition of the vegetable fat oils, and the compounds which they produce with chlorine and bromine. I showed, by numerous analyses, that many oils, although proceeding from vegetables which differ very much as to botanical classification, possess an identical composition, and, moreover, that they all contain four equivalents of oxygen—the quantity found in most of the fat acids.

After examining the reactions produced when chlorine, bromine, and iodine are put in contact with the vegetable fatty oils, it became interesting to investigate whether these metalloïds would not react more particularly on one of their components; on oleïne, for example, more than on stearine or margarine, which, united to glycerine, constitute, as is generally admitted, the greater number of the fatty substances.

The following are the results at which I have arrived:—

Iodine—which, as I have shown, only reacts on the fat oils by removing from them a very small portion of their hydrogen —does not appear to me to remove a greater quantity from oleïne than from stearine or margarine. The action which this metalloïd exerts on the oils or their component parts, is not to be compared to those exhibited by chlorine and bromine. It is known from the experiments of M. Pelouze, that glycerine furnishes no peculiar compound with iodine, whereas with chlorine and bromine it gives chloruretted and bromuretted glycerine. Under the influence of the nascent state, would not this substance and iodine form iodised glycerine, or an iodide of glycerine? M. Berthé has already proved that the iodised product obtained with or without the aid of water, differs considerably both in composition and characters.

Chlorine and bromine combine very well with oleïne, margarine, and stearine.

These new substances, to the preparation of which it is unnecessary for me to recur, being all obtained in the same manner as the chloruretted and bromuretted oils, described in my first memoir, are denser than water.

Their consistency presents very remarkable differences. Thus, whereas chloruretted oleïne and bromuretted oleïne are thicker than pure oleïne, the consistency of chloruretted and bromuretted stearine and margarine is not so thick as that of pure stearine and margarine, and moreover, they melt at a much lower temperature.

This fact is very evident with the margarine of olive oil. In fact, from being solid—as it is when carefully prepared—it gives, when combined with chlorine and bromine, two products which have a great resemblance to the corresponding oleïne, to such an extent that we might ask, whether the solid principle of olive oil (which melts at 68° F.—whereas animal margarine melts at 116° F.—considered, by some chemists, as margarine in a peculiar isomeric state, and by MM. Pelouze and Boudet as a combination of margarine and oleïne) is not rather oleïne, under a peculiar modification in combination with the margarine, which exists normally in all vegetable oils, and of solid oleïne, which would pass to the liquid state, under the influence of the haloïd bodies. It is well known that oleïc acid exists in the solid and the liquid states.

No reagent has shown that the metalloïds exist in these combinations in a free state.

Stearine, margarine, and oleïne lose, under the influence of chlorine and bromine, a quantity of hydrogen corresponding to four equivalents in the first,—the only one whose exact composition we know.

I have, in fact, obtained,—

With chloruretted stearine......21.17 and 21.43 Cl.
With bromuretted stearine .....35.97 and 35.99 Br.

The formula $C^{76} H^{66} \left\{ \begin{matrix} Cl^4 \\ Br^4 \end{matrix} \right\} O^8$ requires

Cl ....20·35
Br..............36.52

Chloruretted margarine gave		............19.12 Cl.
Bromuretted margarine	"	............35.12 Br.
Chloruretted oleïne	"	............22.08 Cl.
Bromuretted oleïne	"	............36.69 Br.

Admitting that margarine and oleïne possess compositions differing but little from that of stearine, the chlorine and bromine would likewise be substituted for four equivalents of hydrogen.

To complete this series of researches, I undertook some experiments on the action which the haloïd bodies exert on the fat acids.

Iodine does not react on the fatty acids produced by the saponification of the vegetable fat oils and of the fatty bodies of animal origin.

Chlorine and bromine form no peculiar compounds with

stearic and margaric acids completely deprived of oleïc acid; a small quantity of these metalloïds is dissolved by the fatty acids, but they do not produce hydrochloric and hydrobromic acids.

Oleïc acid, on the contrary, is very subject to the law of substitutions.

The acid used in my experiments proceeded from the treatment of oil of sweet almonds by potassa, and it was purified by the process indicated by M. Gottlieb. It belonged to the liquid variety.

Chloruretted Oleïc Acid ($C^{36}H^{32}Cl^{2}O^{4}$).

This compound and the following were obtained in the same manner as all the chloruretted and bromuretted combinations which I have made known. It is liquid at the ordinary temperature, denser than water, and possesses, no doubt in consequence of the prolonged heat to which it is necessary to subject it for the removal of its water of interposition, a very decided brown tint. It has an acid reaction with litmus paper. Its consistency is rather greater than that of the pure acid; its density at the temperature of 48° F. is 1.082. It boils at 374° F.

The following are the numbers given by its analysis:—

I. 1.374 of matter gave.. 1.173 Cl Ag. or 0.289 Cl.
II. 1.516 " " ...1.239 Cl Ag. or 0.305 Cl.

Or, in hundredths:

		I.	II.	Calculated.
C^{36}	......2700...	"	"	"
H^{32}	...... 400...	"	"	"
Cl^{2}	..... 888...	21.06	20.17	20.23
O^{4}	...... 400...	"	"	"
	4388			

Bromuretted Oleïc Acid ($C^{36}H^{32}Br^{2}O^{4}$).

Bromuretted oleïc acid possesses very nearly the same consistence as the chlorurretted acid, but it has a more marked brown tint. Its density at the temperature of 47° F. is 1.272. It boils at 392° F., and has an acid reaction on litmus paper.

Its analysis gave:

I. 1.1802 of matter gave...1.551 Br. Ag. or 0·651 Br.
II. 1.486 " " ...1.301 Br. Ag. or 0.546 Br.

which represents in hundredths:

		I.	II.	Calculated
C^{36}	......2700...	"	"	"
H^{32}	...... 400...	"	"	"
Br^{2}	.....2000...	36.13	36.76	36.36.
O^{4}	...... 400...	"	"	"
	5500			

Before assigning to the chloruretted and bromuretted oils formulæ which would enable them to be considered as definite compounds, I thought it necessary, knowing the action exerted by sulphuric acid on the fatty bodies, to examine whether chlorine and bromine would not act as oxidising bodies, furnishing chlorides and bromides of glycerine, and chloruretted and bromuretted oleïc and margaric acids. All the experiments which I have tried for this purpose have shown me that glycerine did not separate, and that chlorine and bromine reacted on the fat oils and their components, as on simple bodies.

These experiments come anew, to demonstrate that if, in certain reactions, iodine behaves in the same manner as chlorine and bromine, in others, on the contrary, it differs completely.

Notwithstanding the remarkable works of MM. Braconnot, Chevreul, and Le Canu, on fatty bodies, the peculiar constitution of a great number of them still leaves much to be desired.

Before M. Braconnot, the neutral fatty bodies were considered as formed of one and the same substance. He showed that by subjecting them to pressure at a temperature below 32° F., two matters were obtained, which he called suet and oil. The variable quantities of these two bodies which he obtained with the different oils subjected to examination, led him to imagine that they were not definite compounds. The later researches of MM. Chevreul and Le Canu have put beyond doubt in most vegetable fatty oils, and in many fatty bodies of animal origin, the presence of three different principles, to which have been given the names of stearine, margarine, and oleïne.

The numerous difficulties encountered in trying to isolate perfectly these bodies one from another, have hitherto prevented chemists from making an elementary analysis of them, to determine their equivalents.

On this subject M. Le Canu asked himself whether stearine and margarine, although possessing fusing points which differ a little, had not the same composition: MM. Pelouze and Boudet think, on the contrary, that stearine and oleïne should be placed in the class of isomeric bodies.

If, availing myself of the facts already known, and of those which I have mentioned in this memoir, I compare the reactions which produce stearine, margarine, and oleïne, and their derivatives, stearic, margaric, and oleïc acids, above all, the conversion of stearic acid into margaric acid by distillation; the negative results produced by chlorine and bromine with stearic and margaric acids, whereas the oleïc acid formed a definite compound: I am more disposed to think that the opinion of M. Le Canu should be preferred, and that oleïne is a peculiar principle, which is to the vegetable fat oils what stearine is to fatty matters of animal origin.

It is not only possible that stearine and margarine are isomeric bodies, but it is probable that each of them and oleïne possess isomeric modifications which then permit of explanation:—the physical differences observed when they proceed from the animal or the vegetable kingdom; the ease with which certain fatty oils absorb oxygen from the air and become drying oils; the different manner in which they behave with the alkalies and metallic oxides; finally the identity of composition found between certain vegetable fatty oils, although solidifying at different degrees, and proceeding from very different sources.

Stearine, margarine, and oleïne, made, whether from the animal or vegetable kingdom, may be well compared with fibrine, albumen, legumine, and caseïne, and all substances of similar origin, which with the most different properties, still possess an identical composition.

I think, that by means of the considerations which I have just made public, it is possible to consider the vegetable fatty oils, as compounds in constant definite proportions of oleïne and margarine, susceptible of taking various isomeric modifications; or rather as olëo-margarates of glycerine, which may be separated under the influence of the most feeble forces. They would be to the seeds what the essences are to the flowers, salicine and populine to the barks, finally analogous to many other proximate principles, which chemlsts are daily learning to separate into the most opposite principles.—*Journal de Pharmacie*, August, 1853.

ACTION OF CARBONIC ACID ON QUININE AND CINCHONINE; FORMATION OF CRYSTALLISED CARBONATE OF QUININE.

BY M. LANGLOIS.

We passed a current of carbonic acid gas into water, containing recently precipitated quinine and cinchonine. The prolonged action of carbonic acid gas determines the solution of quinine and cinchonine; but the former is more readily dissolved than the latter. Both solutions exposed to the air, lose a portion of their carbonic acid, and furnish the first crystals of carbonate of quinine, the other cinchonine only. We shall see, as we proceed, to what this difference is owing.

Crystallised carbonate of quinine may easily be obtained by following the directions which we shall give.

Ten grains of sulphate of quinine must be dissolved in distilled water, with the addition of a few drops of sulphuric acid. Ammonia is added in order to precipitate the quinine; the latter is collected on a filter and washed; it is afterwards diffused while moist in a quart of water. The liquid, which has a milky appearance, is put into a test-glass with a foot, into which is passed a stream of well-washed carbonic acid, procured by the decomposition of marble, by means of hydrochloric acid. In less than an hour the quinine is almost entirely dissolved. The liquor, although super-saturated with carbonic acid, always retains an alkaline reäction.

The quinine combines directly with the carbonic acid without dissolving, when it is not diffused in a large quantity of water, by operating, on the contrary, in the way which we have directed, we obtain a complete and very limpid solution, from which are obtained, after exposure to the air, crystals of carbonate of quinine, which increase in size during from twenty to twenty-four hours. After this time no more is deposited, although the liquor still contains some. Spontaneous evaporation furnishes only quinine; the latter is instantly pre. cipitated by ammonia, potassa, and soda which saturate the carbonic acid. Lime water acts in the same way, forming, moreover, a deposit of carbonate of lime.

The solution of this carbonate of quinine furnishes at first, as is evident, crystals, represented by the saline combination; and afterwards, this combination is destroyed, giving rise to carbonic acid and quinine. There is, therefore, a perfect analogy between these phenomena and those produced by a solution of carbonate of cinchonine. This latter never gives crystals, because the salt exists in small quantity in it, which is owing, doubtless, to the solubility of cinchonine in water, increasing very little by the intervention of carbonic acid.

Carbonate of quinine is under the form of transparent, acicular crystals; these crystals promptly effloresce in contact with the air; they are soluble in alcohol, insoluble in ether, and they restore the blue color of reddened litmus paper. In the presence of the acids, they cause a brisk effervesence.

At the temperature of 230° F. they are decomposed; the carbonic acid is disengaged, and the quinine remains without undergoing any alteration. It melts only when the heat reaches 338° F.

We found in the decomposition of carbonate of quinine, at a moderate temperature, an easy means of analysing it. The experiments were repeated several times; but we shall content ourselves with detailing only one.

We took the weight of a glass tube 12 to 15 centimetres long, and closed at one end. We introduced into it 0.399 of carbonate of quinine. It was then put into communication by by means of a cork covered with caoutchouc, with a bent tube, which is passed under a graduated bell glass, placed over mercury contained in a test-glass, with a stand. The extremity of this tube went beyond the surface of the metal, and reached into the empty part of the bell glass, into which the carbonic acid gas was received. The sealed tube containing the salt was heated in an oil bath, into which dipped the bulb of a thermometer. As soon as the temperature of the oil-bath attained 230° F. the carbonate of quinine was decomposed, disengaging carbonic acid, and without undergoing perceptible changes in its physical characters.

I obtained from the 399 milligrammes of salt employed for the experiment, 21.36 of carbonic acid gas at the temperature of 32° F., and at the pressure of 76 centimetres. This volume of gas weighed 0.0422 gr. Carbonic acid ceased to be disengaged a long time before the oil-bath had attained the temperature of 338° F., which is that at which quinine enters into fusion, and at which it is entirely freed from the water which it contains. By means of a few pieces of blotting-paper, the moisture which remained adhering to the sides of the tube was easily removed. The weight of this empty tube being known, I obtained, by weighing it again, that of the quinine contained in it. The weight of the latter was 321 milligrammes. We have thus, on one hand, in this analysis, the proportion of the carbonic acid, and on the other, that of the quinine. The water was estimated by the difference: 0·399 gr. of carbonate of quinine furnished:

	Grammes.
Quinine	0·3210
Carbonic Acid	0·0422
Water	0·0358

These numbers lead us to represent the composition of this salt by the following formula:

$$(C^{20}H^{12}NO^{2}, HO)\ CO^{2}, HO.$$

In fact, we have in hundredths,—

	Theory.	Experiment.
Quinine	80·21	80·45
Carbonic Acid	10·88	10·58
Water	8·91	8·97
	100·00	100·00

Six successive experiments on various quantities of carbonate of quinine gave similar results.

As it must be regarded as neutral, in establishing its composition, we shall also have fixed the cypher of the equivalent of quinine, which corresponds with that admitted by Liebig.

The decomposition of carbonate of quinine at a moderate temperature has enabled us to prove again the non-formation of this salt by double decomposition, that is to say, by treating a saline solution of quinine with carbonate of potassa or soda. The precipitate which is formed contains only quinine, retaining always, notwithstanding repeated washings, a greater or less quantity of the carbonate employed. It is to the presence of the latter, that the precipitate owes the property of effervescing with the acids; but when it is fused in a glass tube, not the smallest trace of carbonic acid is evolved. That which I here say of quinine, applies also to cinchonine, and perhaps even to all the other vegetable bases. We had already given this idea in a note inserted some years ago, in vol. xxxii of the "*Annalen der Chemie*," but then our opinion was founded solely on the results of some reäctions which were not of the value of thosewhich we now obtain by the employment of heat.

Comptes Rendus Nov. 7, 1853.

ON THE TRANSFORMATION OF TARTARIC ACID INTO RACEMIC ACID, THE DISCOVERY OF INACTIVE TARTARIC ACID, AND A NEW METHOD OF SEPARATING RACEMIC ACID INTO DEXTRO- AND LÆVO-TARTARIC ACIDS.

BY L. PASTEUR.

In a memoir recently presented by me to the Academy of Sciences, I showed that all the salts of cinchonine, of quinine, of quinidine and of cinchonidine, when submitted to the action of heat, were capable of being converted into salts of quinicine and cinchonicine, two new organic bases, isomeric respectively with quinine and quinidine, and with cinchonine and cinchonidine. If, in the study of these isomeric metamorphoses, the tartrates of these alkalies be employed, and the action of heat be carried far beyond the point at which cinchonicine and quinicine are produced, the modifying influence of the heat is exerted upon the tartaric acid itself. Thus tartrate of cinchonine, submitted to a gradually increasing temperature, becomes first of all converted into tartrate of cinchonicine. When the heat is continued, the cinchonicine becomes changed; it loses water, acquires a color, and becomes converted into quinoidine. The tartaric acid also undergoes important modifications, and after five or six hours' exposure to a heat of 338° F., a portion of it has been changed into racemic acid. The vessel is then broken, and the black resinous mass contained in it treated repeatedly with boiling water; the liquid is filtered after cooling, and chloride of calcium added to it in excess, by which all the racemic acid is immediately precipitated in the form of racemate of lime, from which the racemic acid is readily extracted.

The principal part played by the cinchonicine in this operation is to give a little stability to the tartaric acid, and to enable it to support, without destruction, a temperature which would change it rapidly in a free state. Cinchonine and cinchonicine, although they are substances which act upon polarized light, play no part in this transformation. Tartaric ether, for example, in which tartaric acid is in combination with an inactive body, which is capable of supporting an elevated temperature without destruction, furnishes considerable quantities of racemic acid by the action of heat.

The racemic acid thus artificially obtained is completely identical both in its physical and chemical properties, with natural racemic acid. It especially possesses the important character of being capable of resolution into dextro and lævo-tartaric acids, exhibiting equal rotatory powers in opposite directions in their combinations with bases.

This resolution of artificial racemic acid into dextro and lævo-tartaric acids leads us to this result, that ordinary dextro-tartaric acid may be artificially converted into its opposite, lævo-tartaric acid, a result which is particularly remarkable in connection with this extraordinary fact, which will no doubt be explained some day, that a product with an active polarity has never, under any circumstances, been obtained by starting from an inactive substance, although nearly all the substances elaborated by nature in the vegetable organism are dissymmetric in the same manner as tartaric acid. What gives to this fact of the transformation of dextro-tartaric acid a particular originality is, that I have ascertained that in the same circumstances lævo-tartaric acid also becomes converted into racemic acid. What a strange tendency is exhibited by these natural organic bodies! a totality of dissymmetric dextro or lævo-molecules becoming half transformed, simply by the influence of an elevated temperature, into inverse molecules, which, when once produced, combine with the first.

During a long period I had regarded the production of racemic acid from tartaric acid as impossible. In fact I supposed that racemic acid was a combination of lævo-tartaric acid with dextro-tartaric acid. The conversion of dextro-tartaric acid into racemic acid is, consequently, of the same nature as that of the transformation of dextro-tartaric acid into lævo-tartaric acid. Now all that can be done with the dextro-tartaric acid can be effected under the same circumstances with the lævo-tartaric acid. If, therefore, any operation performed with the dextro acid changed its direction of rotation to the left, the same operation performed with the lævo-tartaric acid would render it right. The transformation, therefore, appears impossible; at the most, we may arrive at an inactive acid.

Fortunately, experiment has contradicted these theoretical deductions. However, they served me as guides; and the less I was disposed to seek for the conversion of tartaric acid into racemic acid, the more I endeavored to produce inactive tartaric acid. Not only did the existence of this acid appear to me to be theoretically possible, but I also know the intimate connexion between tartaric and malic acids, and I had already obtained inactive malic acid. Now, it is in seeking for inactive tartaric acid that I ascertained the convertibility of tartaric acid into racemic acid. But the same operation, fortunately and singularly, furnished me also with considerable quantities of inactive tartaric acid. In other words, I have obtained, together with racemic acid, a tartaric acid which has no action upon polarized light, and which is, moreover, capable of being resolved, under the same circumstances as racemic acid, into dextro and lævo-tartaric acids: an extremely curious acid, crystallizing readily, and giving salts which yield neither to the tartrates nor to the racemates in beauty or form. I have already said that, after treating tartrate of cinchonine, which had been exposed for several hours to a heat of 338° F., with water, and adding chloride of calcium to the liquid, the racemic acid formed at the expense of tartaric acid is precipitated in the form of racemate of lime. If the liquid be immediately filtered, to separate the racemate, a fresh crystallization is deposited in about twenty-four hours; this consists of pure inactive tartrate of lime, from which the inactive tartaric acid may be readily extracted.

Lastly, I have ascertained that the inactive tartaric acid is produced in the preceding operation entirely at the expense of the racemic acid already formed. This is proved by the fact, that if racemate of cinchonine be kept at a temperature of 338° F. for several hours, a considerable portion of it is converted into this inactive tartaric acid.

We consequently now know four tartaric acids—dextro-tartaric acid; lævo-tartaric acid; the combination of both, or racemic acid; and the inactive acid, which deviates neither to the right nor left, nor is formed by the combination of the dextro and lævo-tartaric acids. There is no doubt that this series of four isomeric tartaric acids is a type round which a multitude of others will range hereafter.

There is, however, a serious difficulty to be found in the ulterior applications of these new results. Thus, to pass from dextro-tartaric acid to lævo-tartaric acid, it is necessary to pass through the racemic acid, which is a combination of the two, and to split this combination. For this purpose I proposed the formation of the double salt of soda and ammonia. The crystals produced are of two sorts; these I separated by hand according to the character of their hemihedric form. This splitting is here accidental. It is, no doubt, a very curious phenomenon, for which, however, we see no proximate cause; besides, it is only one racemate that presents this faculty of splitting; consequently a new racemic acid might be obtained in some other series than the tartaric series, which probably it might be found impossible to resolve, and the inverse of the product started from to obtain it would remain unknown. This was until lately the state of the question; but I have recently found a chemical process, resting on general principles, for the resolution of racemic acid.

In a former memoir, I showed that the absolute identity of the physical and chemical properties of non-superposable right and left bodies ceased to exist when these products were placed in the presence of active bodies. Thus the dextro and lævo-tartrates of the same active organic alkali are quite distinct in crystalline form, solubility, &c. It was to be hoped, therefore, that we might profit by this dissimilarity to isolate the two acids composing racemic acid; and for this purpose, after many fruitless researches, I have found means to render the two bases quinicine and cinchonicine serviceable. When racemate of cinchonicine is prepared, and its solution brought to a certain state of concentration, it always happens that the first crystallization is principally formed of lævo-tartrate of cinchonicine, the dextro-tartrate remaining in the mother-liquor. A similar result is presented with quinicine, only that in this case the dextro-tartrate is the first deposited. When, therefore, it is supposed that an organic product possesses a binary constitution analogous to that of racemic acid, its resolution should be attempted by placing it in contact with an active product, which, by the necessarily dissimilar properties of the combinations which it is capable of forming with the components of the complex group will render the separation of the latter possible.—*London Chem. Gazette*, Nov. 1, 1853, from *Comptes Rendus*, Aug. 1, 1853, p. 162.

ON A NEW METHOD FOR DETERMINING THE COMMERCIAL VALUE OF MANGANESE.

BY ASTLEY PASTON PRICE, PH.D., F.C.S.,

Chemical Assistant in the Laboratory of the Government School of Mines.

It is well known that several methods have been described for determining the commercial value of oxide of manganese, that is to say for estimating the amount of chlorine capable of being obtained from a given sample of manganese.

There are, however, certain practical inconveniences attendant on the employment of many of these processes, most of them demanding an amount of time and manipulation which is most desirable to obviate.

The method I have for some time employed, and which I have found to give accurate results, is based on the conversion of arsenious into arsenic acid, by means of chlorine, and the transformation of arsenious into arsenic acid by the employment of a solution of hypermanganate of potash.

The specimen of manganese under examination is dissolved in a normal hydrochloric acid solution of arsenious acid; and the arsenious acid remaining unchanged into arsenic acid is determined by a standard solution of hypermanganate of potash. In employing a solvent containing a reducing agent, it will be found that the solution of the oxides of manganese is materially facilitated, and may be effected at a low temperature in a very short space of time.

In adopting this method some difficulties presented themselves:

1. On dissolving arsenious acid in hydrochloric acid, terchloride of arsenic is given off, and it becomes difficult to obtain a correct normal solution. This difficulty is avoided by dissolving the arsenious acid in a solution of caustic potash, and then adding the alkaline solution to an access of hydrochloric acid.

Another difficulty occurred in effecting the solution of the oxide of manganese in the arsenical solution, as in proportion to the elevation of temperature does the loss of terchloride of arsenic increase. This source of error is prevented by employing a dilute acid solution of arsenious acid, and adapting one of Will's nitrogen bulbs, containing a solution of potash, to the flask in which the oxide of manganese is dissolved. Any terchloride of arsenic which may pass over is there effectually retained, provided solution be effected at a low temperature. The normal solution of arsenious acid is made by dissolving 113·53 grs. of arsenious acid, corresponding to 100 grs. of peroxide of manganese, in a solution of potash, and then adding hydrochloric acid until the solution occupies 100 measures.

A standard solution of hypermanganate of potash is obtained by diluting, for example, five measures of the normal solution of arsenious acid, corresponding to five grs. of peroxide of manganese, and then determining the number of measures of the solution of hypermanganate of potash that are required to transform the arsenious acid therein contained into arsenic acid.

These two solutions being obtained, an estimation of the

value of a specimen of oxide of manganese may be expeditiously and accurately made.

Ten, or any number of grains of the specimen under examination, are placed in a small flask, to which ten or more measures, of the normal arsenical solution are added, and to the flask is adapted one of Will's nitrogen apparatus, containing a solution of potash. The flask is then placed in a water bath, or a gentle heat is applied until the solution is effected. The contents of the flask, after having been allowed to cool, are, together with the solution of potash, transferred to a larger flask, and diluted with water. The amount of arsenious acid remaining unchanged is then determined by the addition of the stardard solution of hypermanganate of potash, and the quantity thus indicated being deducted from the number of grains of arsenious acid employed in the first instance, will give the value of the specimen submitted to analysis.

In order to obtain correct results by this method, it is, of course, necessary that the hydrochloric acid and the potash employed should be free from sulphurous or nitric acid, or any other reducing or oxidizing impurities.—*Chem. Gazette*, Nov. 1, 1853.

EXHIBITION OF THE INDUSTRY OF ALL NATIONS.

We have selected that portion of the report of the official awards made by the juries of the *Association for the Exhibition of the Industry of all Nations*, which comprises those articles having any bearing upon chemistry or pharmacy and present it to the readers of the journal.

JURY B.

Classes 2, 4, part of Classes, 10, 18, 24, 25.

JURORS:

Professor JOHN TORREY, M. D., Chairman.

H. PLANTEN, Esq., Deputy.

J. H. Currie, Esq.,
Dr. B. W. McCready,
F. L. Talcott, Esq.
H. D. Telkampf, Esq.,
Alexander Oakley, Esq.,
Prof. W. Gibbs.
Dr. David A. Wells.

Dr. J. Bryant Smith,
Acting Secretary.

Silver Medal.

Batchelor, J. M., Gulf Hills, Miss., U. S., for Cotton of staple and best working quality.

Dedovich, Von Lang Oels, Silesia, for the finest specimen of Wool in German Department.

Graux, M., Mauchamp, France, for superior specimen of Combing Wool.

Hoffman, Anthony, Pine Plains, N. Y., U. S., for the finest specimen of Wool in the U. S. Department.

Larderel de, Count, Tuscany, for Boracic Acid.

Pope, John, the Oaks, Tennessee, U. S., for cotton of staple and best working quality.

Bronze Medal and Special Mention.

Gehe & Co., Dresden, Saxony, for series of Mineral, Vegetable, and Animal Productions.

Hellman, W. H., N. Y. City, U. S., for Bronze Powder and Metal Leaf.

Lyles, Polhemus, & Co., N. Y. City, U. S., for specimens of Oils, Spermaceti, Sperm and patent Candles.

Merck, E., Darmstadt, Prussia, for specimens of Alkaloids.

Phalon, E., N. Y. City, U. S., for Cologne Fountains, Choice Extracts, &c.

Phœnix Manufacturing Co., Taunton, Mass., U. S., for Black Lead Crucibles and Stove Polish.

Rimmel, Eugene, London, Great Britain, for Perfumery and Soaps.

Bronze Medal.

Birkner & Hartman, Nurnberg, Germany, for Bronzes and Leaf Metal.

Bazin, Xavier, Philadelphia, U. S., for specimens of fine Toilet Soaps and Perfumery.

Beck & Co., Boston, Mass., U. S., for Babbitt's Toilet Soaps, Shaving Creams, &c.

Brandon, N. D., Amsterdam, Holland, for Stearine Candles and Tapers, Lime Soap, and Stearic Acid.

Batkai, Wenzel, Prague, Bohemia, for various Chemical and Pharmaceutical Productions, and for Chemical and Pharmaceutical Instruments.

Buchner, William, Darmstadt, for Ultramarine, with special approbation.

Bonzel, Freres, Haubordin, Ultramarine, with special approbation.

Colgate, William & Co., New York City, U. S., specimens of Fancy Soaps; also for fine Starch from Indian Corn.

Cleaver, Frederick S., London, England, for Honey, Toilet, and other Soaps.

Curtius, Julius, Duisburg, for Ultramarine.

Des Brosses, Frederick, Manhattanville, U. S., for patent distilled Chemical Sperm Candles.

Estivant & Alberic, France, for Glue.

Fries, C. A., Heidelberg, for Ultramarine, with special approbation.

Guimet, J. B., Lyons, France, Ultramarine.

Godin, M., Chatillon, Dep. Seine, France, for specimens of Merino Combing Wool.

Gerardi, Martini, Turin, Sardinia, for specimens of Vegetable Oils.

Gressler, E., Erfurt, Prussian Saxony, for Chemical and Physical Apparatus.

Herrmann, O., Schœnbeck, Germany, for collection of Chemicals.

Haskell, Merrick, & Bull, New York City, U. S., for specimens of Powdered Drugs.

Husband, Thomas, J. Philadelphia, U. S., for Calcined Magnesia.

Holmes, Joseph E., U. S., for 129 specimens of American Woods.

Judd, Samuel & Sons, New York City, U. S., for specimens of Spermaceti and Patent Candles.

Kent, James H., Bury St. Edmonds, Gt. Britain, for Dried Preparations of British Plants, Fluid Extracts, &c.

Kohnstamm, Joseph, N. Y. City, U. S., for specimens of Ultramarine for Calico Printing, and other colors for Painting, Printing, &c.

Kohnstamm, Widow, Niederweren, Germany, for specimens of Ultramarine, with special approbation.

Loebbecker & Co., Breslau, Germany, for specimens of Zinc White.

Litchfield & Co., New York City, U. S., for specimens of Spermaceti, Sperm Candles, Oils, &c.

Menier & Co., Paris, France, for various Drugs and Extracts.

Martin, Abbess, M. C., Cologne, for Cologne Water and Carmelite Spirit of Melissa.

Nix, Arthur, McComb's Dam, N. Y. City. U. S., for specimens of fine Sun-Bleached Wax, from the Ordinary American Yellow Wax.

Nailer, Jefferson, Warren, & Co., Jefferson Co., Mississippi, U. S., for specimen of Cotton of superior color and handling.

Oomen, A. M., Genneken, Netherlands, for Oil Seed Cakes, Glues, Oils. &c.

Prins & Co., Wormerveer, Holland, for Urling's Patent Starch.

Payson, Ira F., Stapleton, New York, U. S., for specimens of a new and patent variety of Soap.

Perselaer & Son, Maestricht, Netherlands, for Odoriferous Soaps, Candles, &c.

Powers & Weightman, Philadelphia, U. S., for a fine assortment of Chemicals.

Pfizer, Charles & Co., N. Y. City, U. S., for Refined Camphor, Kreosote, &c.

Rosengarten & Davis, Philadelphia, U. S., for Sulphate of Quinine, Veratrine, &c.

Smith, Thomas & Henry, Edinburgh, Great Britain, for specimens of Aloine and Caffeine.

Schols, Frederick, N. Y. City, for specimens of Mass and Roll Brimstone.

Spear, Burke, & Co., Boston, U. S., for Starch from Potatoes.

Steinbach, James, Jr., Petit Quevilly, France, for Starch, Fecula, and Gums.

Tilden & Co., N. Y. City, U. S., for Medicinal Extracts, prepared in vacuo.

Taylor & Son, Chelsea, England, for Soaps and Perfumery.

Taylor, H. P. & W. C., Phila., U. S., for Transparent and Fancy Soaps.

Watherspoon, Robt., Maxwilton, Scotland, for Starch, from East India Sago.

Wood, Thomas, Smithfield, New York, U. S., for specimen of Wool.

Not in Catalogue.

Sweden and Norway, Commercial Nickel, entirely free from arsenic, from the Klapka mines, certified by Berzelius.

Class. 2.—No name. For a good assortment of Zinc paints.

Honorable Mention.

Alter & Gillespie, Freeport, Pa., U. S., for Bromine.

Ashard, Bros., N. Y. City, U. S., for patent perfumed Oriental Crystals.

Albani, Bros., Turin, Sardinia, for a variety of Chemical Productions.

Arnavon, Honore, Marseilles, France, for various kinds of Soaps.

Adam, J. N. Renwieg, Bavaria, Ultramarine.

Blanchard H., Paris, France, specimens of unalterable Pills of Iodide of Iron.

Benzel, Bros., Haubordin, France, samples of Ultramarine and Azure Blue.

Brewster, Samuel C., Geddes, U. S., for specimens of Solar Coarse Salt.

Burckhart & Co., Cincinnati, U. S., for Superior Lard Oil.

Blake, William, N. Y. City, U. S., for patent Fire and Weather-proof Paint, and Artificial Slates manufactured from the same.

Benda, George, Furth, Bavaria, for Bronze Colors and Powders.

Brandies. J., Jr,, Furth, Bavaria, for Bronze Colors and Powders.

Bo, Augustus, Turin, Sardinia, for samples of Chrome Yellow and other Colors.

Bully, Jean Vincent, Paris, for specimens of Aromatic Vinegar.

Brasseur, Eugene, Ghent, Belgium, for samples of Ultramarine Blues and White Lead.

Claude, Louis, Brussels, Belgium, for Rape Oil, purified for burning.

Cerceuil, France, for Colors for Paper Hangings.

Cookson, W. J. & Co., London, Gt. Britain, for specimens of Antimony, Red Lead, &c.

Christani, Richard S., Philadelphia, U. S., for specimens of Perfumery.

Dachonel, Heinrich, Quaritz, Lower Silesia, for Toilet Soaps in fancy designs.

Dixon, J. & Co., Jersey City, U. S., for Black Lead Crucibles, Furnaces, &c.

Delluc & Co., N. Y. City, U. S., for Flavoring Extracts.

Dupuy, E., New York City, U. S., for Concentrated Extract of Lemon and Vanilla.

Electoral Hesse Smalt Works, Schwarzenfeldt, for Collection of Colors.

Ellis, Charles & Co., Philadelphia, U. S., for an assortment of Medicinal Preparations.

Electoral Hesse Smalt Works, Schwarzenfeldt, Ultramarine.

Fabre, Repetto Pietto, Porto Maurizio, Sardinia, for Fine Bar Soap.

Farina, J. Maria, opposite George Platz, for Cologne Water.

Farina, J. Maria, opposite New Market Platz, for Cologne Water.

Farina, J. Maria, opposite Martin's Platz, for Cologne Water.

Farina, J. Maria, opposite Julich's Platz, for Cologne Water.

Farina, J. Maria, opposite Joseph's Place, Cologne, for Cologne Water.

Farina, J. M., Old Market Place, Cologne, for Cologne Water.

Farina, Johann Maria, 2 Julich's Place, Cologne, for Cologne Water.

Farina, Johann Carl, Cologne, for Cologne Water.

Farina, J. Maria, 4 Julich's Platz, Cologne, for Cologne Water.

Fabian, E. G., Breslau, Germany, for Samples of Fine Oil.

Faure & Escoffier, Avignon, France, for samples of Madder Root and Prepared Powder.

Fruchet, Paris, France, for samples of Aromatic Vinegar, Toilet Cream, and Essences.

Frank, F., Cincinnati, U. S., for specimens of Lard Oil.

Frutler, Counsellor, Leuterm, Silesia, for specimens of Wool.

Gerterayen, Van J. C., Hamme, East Flanders, for specimens of Starch.

Grass, Margaretta, Cologne, for Cologne Water.

Gehe & Co., Dresden, Saxony, for Chemical Apparatus.

Hjirta & Michaelson, Stockholm, Sweden, for specimens of Sulphuric Acid of 66 B.

Herbert, Franz Paul, Klagenfurt, Germany, for samples of White Lead.

Hotchkiss, H. G. & L. B., Lyons, Wayne Co., N. Y., U. S., for Oils of Peppermint, Spearmint, and Wintergreen.

Howards & Kent, Strafford, England, for fine collection of Chemical Preparations.

Hanle, Leo, Munich, Bavaria, for specimens of Bronze Colors.

Herring, Charles F., Brooklyn, U. S., for specimens of Blacking.

Jager, Evert De, Zandyk, Netherlands, for samples of Starch.

Jolly, F., Mer, Loire and Cher, France, for Purified Oil for Watches, &c.

Jennings, Thomas Cook, Ireland, for Calcined Magnesia and Carbonate of Magnesia.

Jones, Stephen U., for Pyramid of Fancy Soap.

Johnson, Jonathan F., N. Y. City, U. S., for specimens of Soap, plain and fancy, fine Perfumery and Extracts.

Knosp, Robert, Stuttgart, for Indigo, Carmine, &c.

Kinzelberger & Co., Prague, Bohemia, for Ultramarine and 180 samples of various colors.

Lindmark, John, N. Y. City, U. S., for fine Cologne Water.

Lyon, Emanuel, N. Y. City, U. S., for Magnetic Powder, for destruction of insects, vermin, &c., without poison.

Laumar & Pauris, Paris, France, for specimens of Perfumery, &c.

Luhme, J. F. & Co., Berlin, Prussia, for Chemical Apparatus.

Leistner, G. L., Paris, France, for Water of Paris and other Perfumery.

Lansa, Brothers & Co., Turin, Sardinia, for Stearine Candles and Stearine.

Le Fevre, B., Paris, France, for various kinds of Varnish (with special approbation.

Lill, William & Co., Chicago, U. S., for Cologne Water and Pure Spirits.

Le Fevre, Senr., Nantes, France, for specimens of Oxyd of Zinc.

Michel, France, for Extracts for Dying and Printing.

Mixer & Gilbert, Boston, U. S., for patent Starch and Spermaceti Candles.

Mitchell, R. S. & Co., N. Y. City, U. S., for Stearine Figures and Candles.

McFarline, Arch., Montreal, Canada, for samples of Glue, prepared from common stock, called Farmers' pieces.

Miller & Co., A., Newbern, North Carolina, U. S., for Resin Oil.

Marquart, Dr. L. C., Bonn, Prussia, for collection of Chemical Productions.

Mason, James & Co., Philadelphia, U. S., for specimens of Blacking.

Michael, Louis, N. Y. City, U. S., for specimens of Wool.

McFadden, John, Hanson County, Ohio, U. S., for specimens of Wool.

Mitchell, General J. D. Charleston, South Carolina, U. S., for a stalk of Pomegranate Cotton.

McClintock, W. & C., Demerara, for Birds' Nests.

Poimmier, P., Paris, Carriage Varnish.

Pitancier, G., Odessa, Russia, for fine Stearine Candles.

Parker, David (Trustee), Shaker's Village, U. S., for specimens of essential Oils, Medicinal Extracts, &c.

Poel, W. J., Zaandam, Netherlands, for specimens of Gelatine and Glue.

Pucchio, Antonio, Genoa, Sardinia, for specimens of Sulphate of Quinine.

Parola, Luigi, Cuneo, Sardinia, for specimens of Ergotine.

Paoli, Christian, Springfield, Ohio, U. S., for pure Alcohol and Deodorized Cologne, spirit 98 per cent., for Medical and Chemical purposes, &c.

Russell, Stiles, & Hubbard, Yonkers, U. S., for Extract of Logwood.

Roemer, Carl, Bruhl, Baden, for refined Oils, capable of bearing intense cold.

Rushton & Myers, Philadelphia, U. S., for specimens of Blacking.

Rice & Smith, N. Y. City, U. S., for specimens of Perfumery, and Fancy Articles.

Santo, A., Matanzas, Cuba, for specimens of Quinine and other Medicinal Preparations.

Setzer, T., Weitenek on the Danube, for various shades of Ultramarine, Madder, &c.

Siegle, Henry, Stuttgard, Germany, for various Colors.

Soehner, Bros., Paris, France, for various kinds of Varnish (with special approbation).

Sanger, Augustus H., Danvers, U. S., for samples of Glue.

Sheppard, Samuel C., Philadelphia, U. S., for Citrate of Magnesia.

Schramm, L. F., Dessau, Baden, for specimens of fine Vegetable Oils for watches.

Spahn & Schimmel, Leipsic, Saxony, for Essential Oils.

Stuurman, Jr., J., Zandyk, Netherlands, for samples of Starch.

Seabrook, William, Charleston, U. S., for sample of Sea Island Cotton.

Schiller, Caroline, Montreal, Canada, for Bark Box, with Moose Hair, &c.

Vanduura & Veusterven, Rotterdam, Holland, for samples of Oils and Colors.

Vandenbusch, J. J., Wilhelminadorp, W. Goes, Holland, for specimens of Madder, manufactured by steam.

Voute, W. H. & Co., Amsterdam, Holland, for assortment of Madder, Indigo, &c.

Violet, Paris, for collection of choice Perfumes.

Van Deventer, John, New York City, U. S., for Oil, Paste, Blacking, and Waterproof Composition for Leather.

Viard, Louis, Paris, France, for a variety of Colors.

Van Geetrugen, J. & Co., Hamme, East Flanders, for specimens of Starch.

Whitely, N., N. Y City, U. S., for patent perfumed Oriental Crystal.

Warteburg, Count, York, Silesia, for specimen of Wool.

Wright, W. P., N. Y., U. S., for a Cotton Plant, with opening pods.

Zinsser & Marx, N. Y. City, U. S., for bleached Shellac and French Varnishes (with special approbation).

Zuber & Co., Rixheim, Haut Rhin, for samples of Artificial Ultramarine Green, &c.

Zanoli, Carl A., High street, Cologne, for Cologne Water.

Zanole, Carl Anton, 92 High street, Cologne, for Cologne Water.

ON THE NATURAL ACIDITY OF THE URINE.

Much obscurity long prevailed as to the cause of the acid reäction of the normal urine, which was originally referred to lactic and even to acetic acid; but this subject has at length been set at rest by Liebig, who has shown that the acidity of normal urine can alone depend upon acid phosphate of soda, thus, for instance, when ordinary phosphate of soda, (which, as is well known, yields an alkaline reäction, is dissolved in water, and the solution is gradually treated with uric acid, which exerts no reäction on vegetable colors, a fluid is obtained, which on heating reddens litmus paper, and on being cooled deposits a white crystalline powder, which exhibits under the microscope the most beautiful groups of prismatic crystals of urate of soda. Since so extremely weak an acid as uric acid can abstract from the phosphate of soda a portion of its base, we can hardly deny that stronger acids, such as hippuric, lactic acid, and sulphuric acid, may immediately, after their formation by the metamorphoses of animal matter, convert the neutral phosphate of soda into an acid salt, in which form it then passes into the urine, together with the already formed sulphate, lactate and hippurate of soda. If this mode of explanation be applied to the acidity of every species of urine, freshly discharged urine would not saturate a larger amount of base than would correspond with the quantity of phosphate of soda which it contained.—*Lehmann.*

ON THE CONNEXION BETWEEN ATOMIC CONSTITUTION AND BOILING POINTS.

Favre and Silberman have deduced from their researches a very interesting law relative to the heat of combustion of rhe carburets of hydrogen of the formula $(C_2 H_2)_n$; and this law may be thus expressed: For every time that the elements of the carburet $(C^2 H^2)$ enter once more into the constitution of a new polymeric carburet, the heat of combustion diminishes 67·5 units of heat.

Liebig in his new letters on chemistry has pointed out the existence of a similar law with regard to the boiling points of certain chemical compounds which differ in composition only in the number of times that the carbo-hydrogen $C^2 H^2$ enters into their constitution.

Wood spirit, (methylic alcohol) boils at 138·2°—the spirit of wine, (ethylic or ordinary alcohol at 172·4° and the oil of potato spirit (amlyic alcohol) at 275° if we compare together these three points of ebullition, we shall find that ordinary alcohol boils at 34·2° (138·2° + 34·2° = 172·4°), and the oil of potato spirit at 4 times 34·2° (138·2° + 4 × 34 2° = 275.°) above the boiling point of wood spirit.

It will be seen from the following table in which the formula of these three alcohols are given that each fixation of this carbo-hydrogen $C^2 H^2$ correspond to an elevation of 34·2° in the temperature of ebullition:

Wood Spirit........	$C^2 H^4 O^2$
Spirit of Wine.......	$C^4 H^6 O^2 = C^2 H^4 O^2 + 1 (C^2 H^2)$
Oil of Potato Spirit..	$C^{10} H^{12} O^2 = C^2 H^4 O^2 + 4 (C^2 H^2)$

Boiling Point.............	138.2° wood spirit.
Spirit of Wine............	172.4° = 138.2°1×3+4.2°
Oil of Potato Spirit........	275. = 138.2°4×3+4.2°

Each of these alcoholic liquids placed in the same conditions gives by oxidation a particular acid; wood spirit is converted into formic acid; the spirit of wine into acetic acid; and the oil of potato spirit into valerianic acid. In their turn these three acids have each a constant point of ebullition, formic acid boils at 178.2° F., acetic acid at 212.4°, and valerianic acid at 315°. If we compare together these three degrees it will immediately be perceived that they present the same relation in their boiling points of the liquids from which they are derived. In fact acetic acid boils at 34.2°, and valerianic acid at four times 34.2° above the boiling point of formic acid. The following table in which are given the formulæ of the three acids with their corresponding points of ebullition, shows that with respect to them also each fixation of the carbo-hydrogen $C_2 H^2$ corresponds to an elevation of 34.2° in the temperature of the ebullition.

1. Formic Acid....	$C^2 H^2 O^4$
2. Acetic Acid.....	$C^4 H^4 O^4 = C^2 H^2 O^4 + 1 (C^2 H^2)$
3. Valerianic Acid..	$C^{10} H^{10} O^4 = C^2 H^2 O^4 + 4 (C^2 H^2)$

1. Boiling Point........	200.2°
2. "	244.2° = 210.2° + 1 × 34.2°
3. "	347° = 210.2° + 4 × 34.2°

Lardner's Nat. Phil.

Varieties.

In connection with the statements of Chatin, lately published, relative to the presence of iodine in air and water, (referred to at p. 368 of Vol. 2) and the hygienic importance of that fact, we may add that, about seven years ago, Mr. C. Percival, stationed with the British Artillery in Canada, stated that out of sixty horses quartered at Montreal, thirty are affected with bronchocele or goitre, without suffering, however, the slightest inconvenience from it. The general prevalence of the disease is ascribed, usually, to the snow and iced water. As, however, a serious objection has been raised to the value of his results, inasmuch as nitric acid almost always contains iodine, it is desirable that his experiments be repeated.

On a New Thermostat for Regulating Temperature and Ventilation.—By W. Sykes Ward.--This apparatus consists of a series of flat, hollow circular cases, about one foot in diameter, and an inch deep, attached together in their centres. Each case contains a small quantity of sulphuric acid, which is readily affected by change of temperature. The cases, comprising about six, are suspended one under the other, and to the lowest one is attached a weight by a cord, that passes over an eccentric pulley. On an increase of temperature, the ether expands, and the weight falls down, and it is drawn up again by the pressure of the atmosphere on the external disks of the cases when the air is cooled. By connecting the weight with the ventilators of a conservatory, or other building, the temperature can be thus regulated to any required degree by a previous adjustment of the apparatus.—Proceedings of the British Association, from the *Athenæum*, September, 1853.

Artificial Production of Diamond Powder.—M. Despretz has made two communications to the *Academie des Sciences* (Paris) upon carbon. In these he states that placing upon the inferior pole of a voltaic battery a cylinder of pure charcoal, purity being secured beforehand by preparing it from white crystallized sugar candy, and at the superior pole a bundle of fine platinum wires, so arranged that the charcoal was in the red portion of the electric arc, and the platinum in the violet, he found the carbon volatilized, and collected on the platinum wires in a changed state. In these experiments, the current has been continued during a month in activity, and the powder collected on the wires has been found to be sufficiently hard to polish rubies with great rapidity, and when burned it left no residue. M. Despretz asks himself—have I obtained crystals of carbon which I can separate or weigh, in which I can determine the index of refraction and the angle of polarization without doubt? No. I have simply produced, by the electric arc and by weak voltaic currents, carbon crystallized in black octohedrons, in colorless and translucent octohedrons, in plates also colorless and translucent, which possess the hardness of the powder of the diamond, and which disappear in combustion without any sensible residue. A similar result has been obtained by decomposing a mixture of chloride of carbon and alcohol by weak galvanic currents.—*Athenæum.*

Red Fire.--Three parts of powdered celestine, two of sulphur, and three of chlorate of potash.

URINARY DEPOSITS.

Table for Determining the Nature of the Saline Deposits in the Urine by the Microscope:

1.	Deposit white - - -		2
	" colored - - -		5
2.	" amorphous powder - -	Insoluble by heat, Phosphate of lime. Soluble by heat, Urate of ammonia.	
	" in defined crystals - -		3
3.	" in prismatic crystals -	Triple phosphate.	
	" in octohedral, or tabular crystals - - -		4
4.	" in octohedra - -	Oxalate of lime.	
	" in simple or compd. tables -	Cystine.	
5.	" in transparent crystals -	Uric acid.	
	" Amorphous, or in spherical masses - - -	Urates of ammonia or soda.	

—*Dr. Bird.*

Table for Discovering the Nature of Saline Deposits in the Urine by Chemical Reagents:

1.	Deposit white - - - -		2
	Deposit colored - - - -		5
2.	Dissolves by heat - - - -	Urate of ammonia.	
	Insoluble by heat - - - -		3
3.	Soluble in liquor ammonia - - -	Cystine.	
	Insoluble in ditto. - - - -		4
4.	Soluble in acetic acid - - -	Earthy phosphates.	
	Insoluble do. - - - -	Oxalate of lime.	
5.	Visibly crystalline - - - -	Uric acid.	
	Amorphous - - - -		6
6.	Readily soluble by heat - - -	Urates.	
	Slowly dissolves by heat, stained by purpurim,	do.	

—*Dr. G. Bird.*

Oil a Test for Copper.—The best mode of determining the presence of a copper salt in spirits is to drop a few drops of olive oil, and agitate it for a while, in the liquor. If any copper be present, the oil will assume a green tint.

Caustic Baryta from Carbonate.—The artificial carbonate of baryta, previously reduced to powder, is thoroughly mixed with twenty to twenty-five per cent. of powdered charcoal, and then put in a reverberatory furnace, made of good fire brick. At a yellow heat the reduction commences, and the aspect of the mass shows when it is complete. A single furnace will reduce a ton of carbonate of baryta. When finished, the baryta is collected in sheet iron boxes, in which it is cooled. It is not so easy to reduce the native carbonate.

EDITORIAL.

GRATULATORY.

In the closing number of our second volume it was notified that this journal, "as published by the authority of the College of Pharmacy of the City of New York," ceased. That severance is now an "accomplished fact;" and the present number commences alike the third volume of the *Journal of Pharmacy* and the first of individual existence. No longer tied down by rivaling interests, or restricted by any ties other than what should regulate all journals, namely, the interest of subscribers, it starts upon its career with whatever amount of good will it obtained in its collegiate pupilage. In entering the lists for public favor again, it presents higher claims, and, while it preserves the name of its predecessor, like a fair specimen of isomorphism, it has changed its internal composition until little of the original is left. Under the care of an individual publishing head, it has been deemed expedient to augment its monthly size to 48 pages, thus enlarging it to the standard size of our respected rival publications, and giving room for the addition of a large amount of extra matter; the size of the page of type is also increased, and a superior paper employed: this, with regularity in the future appearance and delivery, will form some of its leading novelties.

Delay in the appearance of the present number has unavoidably occurred, owing to delay in the selection of an editor. Of ourselves it is unbecoming to speak, and we shall leave the journal to speak for the propriety of the selection; and, having but a few days' notice to prepare this number, we pray a little indulgence for our desire to get out the number within its month. In our care, we shall endeavor to make it a journal worthy of this great city and the large number of its citizens devoted to pharmacy. While counting on the valued communications of our former contributors, we may state that we have been kindly favored with promises of occasional articles from Professors Torrey, Dr. Charles Enderlin, and Mr. Kent, whose names are sufficient warranty for the value of their labors. It is the chief aim of the journal to publish as much original matter as possible. With this aim, and with a careful selection of the most recent information abroad and at home, we can say of its future as of its past, that it shall be kept wholly free from personal matters or private interest; and, as we thus propose to keep the journal free for all, we hope to reap the support of all who have at heart the interest of pharmacy and the credit of our city, as capable of supporting a literary want. Among the novelties in our columns will be found a monthly list of the drugs imported into this city, and an account of the condition of the drug market, revised by one fully competent to the office; these additions will be of great advantage to many of our readers.

We desire to open a department for correspondence in matters connected with chemistry and pharmacy, where those at a distance, or not situated favorably to obtain the information they desire, may have any difficulties removed: we solicit, therefore, notes and queries from our friends for this purpose.

Our home exchanges have come to hand very imperfectly of late in many cases, and in a few, not at all. As we purpose to be regular ourselves in forwarding to our friends, we expect a similar favor from them.

American Pharmaceutical Association.—The Committee who were appointed, in reference to pharmaceutical education, at the last meeting of the Association (W. Procter, Jr., and Edward Parrish, of Philadelphia, John Meakim, of New York, and David Stewart, M. D., of Baltimore), in pursuance of the duty assigned them, would solicit from their brethren in all parts of the Union answers as full as possible to the following queries, viz.:

1. What is the usual mode of engaging apprentices to the drug and apothecary business, as to length of service, recompense, etc., in your district, city, or neighborhood?

2. Is it usual to give attention to the preliminary education and training of applicants, in taking apprentices?

3. Is any personal instruction extended to apprentices beyond the practical details of the shop, as regards chemistry, materia medica, and botany?

4. What books are usually provided for apprentices, from which they may derive scientific information bearing on their business?

5. Having been informed that the tenure of apprenticeship is very slight in the Southern and Western States, and that pharmaceutists have chiefly to depend on their salaried assistants, the Committee wish to learn to what extent they have been correctly informed.

6. Do you know of any instances of the apprentices or assistants of pharmaceutists attending lectures at medical schools; and how many?

The answers may be directed to the chairman, W. Procter, Junr., 166 South Ninth street, Philadelphia, or to either member of the Committee.

Local Formulæ.—The Executive Committee of the American Pharmaceutical Association (W. Procter, Jr., T. B. Merrick, and J. Laidley), wish to call the attention of their brethren to the following resolution of the Association:

"Resolved, that the letter of Mr. Meakim, in reference to securing uniformity in the preparation of unofficinal compounds, be referred to the Executive Committee, with instructions to request the forwarding to them of such local formulæ as pharmaceutists may wish to communicate."

In explanation of this resolution, the Committee will state that it has reference more particularly to recipes of unofficinal preparations prescribed by physicians, and for which there are no generally recognized formulæ—as, for instance, Dewee's Carminative, Syrup of Morphia, Tincture of Arnica; and that it ts the intention of the Association (should their request be attended to), to publish them in a compiled form, for the benefit of all.

Any pharmacentists who may feel disposed to respond to this call are requested to direct their communication to either member of the committee they may prefer to address.

Columbia College.—Dr. Renwick, having tendered his resignation of the Chair of Chemistry and Physics in Columbia College, a vacancy has occurred which has not yet been filled up. Dr. Gibbs, at present professor in the Free Academy, is a candidate, and from his attainments in science, is eminently qualified to fill it. The two branches of knowledge, physics and chemistry, have within the present century become so much enlarged, and each separating farther away from the other, it would subserve the interests of science and the college to split this professorship into two. It would be exceedingly difficult at the present day to obtain a teacher eminent in both departments; and the institution which places both under one head hardly merits the name of *alma mater.*

We have to offer an apology for the non-appearance of the article on the state of the drug market for the past month, which we had promised in our prospectus and editorial should appear, our arrangement for this month having been unavoidably delayed.

BOOKS.

Ellis's Medical Formulary; being a collection of Prescriptions, &c. New edition, revised to 1854. Edited by Professor R. P. Thomas, of the Philadelphia College of Pharmacy. This popular work has been just received. It will be noticed in the February number.

The American Medical Monthly. A new journal, devoted to medical topics, conducted under the auspices of the New York Medical College (13th street). It is brought out in Putnam's usual style of excellence, and under the editorship of Dr. E. H. Parker. In his initiatory, he seems to labor under the idea, that some apology is necessary for its appearance, and to have a comparatively inferior estimate of the state of medical science in this country, from both of which we dissent. In the department devoted to *materia medica* and pharmacy, there is nothing of novelty, and the two latter items are decidedly *antique*. As a good medical journal has been a desideratum, we rejoice in its appearance, and wish it all the success which it merits, and which is implied in its motto, "*Non progredi est regredi.*"

PATENT.

To J. C. Booth, Philadelphia, for manufacturing Chromate and Bichromate of Potash from Chrome Iron Ore.

This invention consists in reducing the oxide of iron in chrome ore either wholly or in part, by means of carbon, in any of its several forms, or by means of any of its compounds used as fuel, such as carbonic acid or carburetted hydrogen; this operation constitutes the first stage. The second operation consists in the removal of the iron, by means of sulphuric acid; and the remainder of the process is conducted in the usual way. The ore is ground and calcined with one-fifth its weight of charcoal. When removed from the furnace, it is thrown into vats, containing dilute sulphuric acid. The liquid is afterward drawn off, and crystallized (copperas), and the residuum (oxide of chrome), collected, dried, and heated with nitre or carbonate of potash, in the usual way.—*Newton's London Journal.*

TABLE OF IMPORTED DRUGS.

The subjoined List of Imported Drugs, extracted from the *New York Journal of Commerce*, January 7, we present to our readers, as we believe there are many Druggists and Apothecaries to whom an account of the amount of the importation of the various Drugs of Commerce and Pharmacy would be of special interest. The quantity for the years 1852 and 1853 are given, by which the increase of last year may be estimated. The quantity is given in packages when not specified.

	1852.		1853.	
	Quantity.	*Value.*	*Quantity.*	*Value.*
Drugs (not specified)........	282	8,959	1,014	27,714
Aconite........	1	100		
Acetate of lime........			7	570
Acetic Acid........	233	2,958	226	4,445
Acids (not specified)........	14	427	1	217
Alkali........	50	762	703	16,408
Alkanet root........			31	588
Aloes........	92	460	95	661
Albumen........	2	363		
Alum........	3,172	5.949		
Althea root........	7	254		
Ammonia........	42	1,626	148	5,780
Anise, green........	5	97		
Anise seed........	294	3,976	365	6,172
Annato........	1,098	10,209	339	2,453
Antimony........	38	2,359	151	10,663
Archil........	11	513	6	1,402
Argols........	866	53,860	1,586	131,135
Arrac........			12	723
Arrow root........	1,292	8,779	1,479	11,995
Arsenic........	2,580	14,952	737	4,947
Assafœtida........	121	4,873	58	2,372
Asphaltum........	7	123	422	3,823
Balsam copaivi........	860	12,321	2,465	39,983
Do. Peru........	3	412	28	2,430
Do. Tolu........	278	3,240	458	6,789
Bark (not specified)........			102	1,384
Barilla........	29,012	24.084	43,107	40,710
Barytes........	1,193	7,939	2,245	14,971
Bicarb. soda........	26,594	109,123	73,527	284,836
Bicarb. potash........	80	6,942	283	28,271
Bichr. potash........	172	16,457		
Bismuth........	14	2,201	20	3,295
Bitters........			50	167
Black lead........	1,125	5,458	1,767	11,274
Bleaching powders........	8,473	105,305	9,503	122,699
Blue gall........			9	940
Blue guimet........	150	20,471	188	15,501
Blue smalt........	10	80		
Blue vitriol........	162	6,854	164	13,469
Borax........	4,664	94,251	3,336	88,343
Brimstone........	50,233	106,652	42,316	89,073
Bromine........	4	397		

	1852.		1853.	
	Quantity.	*Value.*	*Quantity.*	*Value.*
Bronze powders	64	16,703	67	21,046
Buchu leaves	6	161	35	369
Burgundy pitch	55	284		
Calamus	15	164		
Calomel	33	2,539	38	2,243
Camphor	983	14,339	2,833	45,298
Cantharides	103	8,367	55	11,959
Capsules of balsam	1	65	1	78
Carb. of ammonia	393	16,618	579	24,014
Carb. of soda	618	2,335		
Cardamons	104	8,026	42	3,269
Carmine	5	2,156	24	1,476
Cassia buds	29	574	195	6,425
Castor oil	806	14,369	745	11,913
Chamomile flowers	76	1,079	134	3,303
Chapapote			25	195
Chemicals			1	552
Chicory	680	3,870	2,579	28,723
Chicory flour	39	328		
Chinqua bark			1,618	82,264
Chlorite of potash	98	3,050	132	6,353
Citric acid	33	10,529	43	16,727
Cobalt	127	1,012	35	389
Cochineal	1,975	296,548	1,414	322,827
Coculus Indicus	94	208	26	100
Cowhage	2	190		
Colcothar	20	110	30	200
Colocynth	171	4,495	25	371
Colombo root	225	1,010	306	1,620
Colsor oil	4	136		
Corvie gum	55	1,500		
Copperas	156	434	100	220
Cremser weiss	10	246		
Cream tartar	1,366	193,941	2,286	377,672
Crocus	20	89		
Crude	37	1,793	107	2,254
Croton oil	9	410	5	499
Cubebs	629	8,381	318	3,297
Cudbear	186	6,201	190	5,400
Cutch	2,480	4,638	1,616	8,995
Divi divi	3,445	2,207	1,351	3,102
Dragon's blood	1	85	15	783
Epsom salts	635	2,152	1,176	4,468
Ergot of rye	2	89	22	856
Essences (not specified)	190	11,492	275	22,520
Essence of bergamot	197	15,610	159	10,169
Do. lemon	243	14,431	298	16,203
Do. orange	6	591	56	2,153
Essential oils (not specified)	336	20,703	566	38,155
Ether			1	920
Extracts (not specified)	46	7,206	49	5,881
Extract of bark	2	206		
Do. indigo	20	815		
Do. logwood	125	335		
Do. safflower	3	477		
Flour of sulphur			210	2,221
Gallic acid	1	140		

	1852.		1853.	
	Quantity.	*Value.*	*Quantity.*	*Value.*
Galls			91	5,779
Gambier	2,525	11,052	3,843	24,960
Garracine			5	2,199
Gamboge	5	240	131	3,160
Gelatine	70	4,839	39	3,500
Gentian root	252	1,631	30	176
Glue	320	18,475	391	12,415
Grafit	21	347		
Grauilla	42	2,902	1,124	1,876
Gum (not specified)	41	422	124	3,627
Do. ammoniac	24	315		
Do. arabic	2,024	91,628	3,227	185,836
Do. benzoin	28	913	39	2,047
Do. copal	6,881	66,378	6,369	97,346
Do. corine	25	1,100		
Do. damar	897	17,813	258	6,438
Do. garrac	38	612		
Do. jedda			194	3,257
Do. kino	14	335		
Do. myrrh	53	2,633	48	2,849
Do. olibenum	11	150		
Do. sacharine	6	300		
Do. sandiac	5	331	118	4,481
Do. senegal	35	1,139	561	19,475
Do. storax	5	62		
Do. substitute	157	80,214	24	2,165
Do. suc	3	336		
Do. tragacanth	104	8,002	180	14,513
Harlem oil	54	283	309	1,160
Herbs	10	129		
Homeopathic med	2	367		
Hyd. of potash	123	15,178	236	65,440
Ipecac	230	15,610	131	16,991
Iodide of potash	42	9,006	21	7,741
Iodine	26	5,683	18	6,938
Irish moss			5	237
Isinglass			22	1,516
Jalap	278	17,831	236	17,031
Juniper berries	200	200	120	267
Kreosote	26	2,443	8	687
Lac dye	1,093	45,326	718	22,466
Lavender flowers	17	80		
Lemon peel			9	445
Licorice	11,320	265,922	13,631	413,440
Do. root	3,456	7,554	7,406	21,076
Do. juice	6	159	5	149
Loxa bark	22	430		
Macassar oil	1	285		
Madder	4,228	573,017	5,916	966,714
Magnesia	1,427	21,773	958	17,615
Manna	38	1,508	491	48,525
Maracho bark	187	1,170		
Med. extracts	2	174		
Do. preparations	135	27,903	1,691	85,534
Do. root	26	160	33	1,690
Mercury	129	5,352		
Mineral blue	71	2,605		

	1852.		1853.	
	Quantity.	*Value.*	*Quantity.*	*Value.*
Morphine	1	108	3	272
Muriate of potash			165	2,191
Musk	3	1,079		
New Grenada bark			100	2,824
Nitrate of potash			100	746
Nitrate of soda	4,494	30,113	1,205	8,565
Nutgalls	30	1,919	33	2,907
Nux vomica	459	517	79	101
Ochre	12,237	5,748	50	202
Oil of almonds	15	1,268	33	1,646
Do. amber	4	100		
Do. anisseed	326	18,422	226	20,079
Do. bergamot	103	8,021	120	10.904
Do. cajeput	4	140	23	766
Do. carraway	10	563	4	193
Do. cassia	111	10,942	141	19,977
Do. citronella	2	310	3	232
Do. cocoa	153	733	40	1,500
Do. cloves	42	2,327	14	800
Do. geranium	1	109		
Do. juniper	22	634		
Do. lavender	24	1,336	7	582
Do. lemon	222	12,463	97	6,938
Do. mace			3	94
Do. orange	31	2,000		
Do. poppy	7	817	7	717
Do. rhodium	4	443	1	90
Do. rose	4	2,352	1	528
Do. rosemary			23	569
Do. sassafras			7	525
Do. valerian	2	147		
Do. vitriol	2	44	7	109
Ointments	1	251	5	801
Opium	509	212.998	410	170,299
Orange lead	94	1,918		
Orange mineral	21	865		
Orange water	199	1,649		
Orchil	119	400		
Origanum	33	671		
Orris root	10	396	3	192
Ottar rose			6	2,416
Oxalic acid	87	5,284	199	13,666
Oxide of mercury	3	556		
Oxide of zinc			912	14,129
Paris white	51	193		
Patent medicines	2	502		
Peruvian bark	4,518	407,266	1,174	123,453
Persian berries	85	4,545	192	11,705
Phosphate of soda	12	286		
Phosphorus	323	18,835	187	10,592
Plantain bark	17,164	265,504	19,067	292,914
Potash			55	6,170
Prussian blue	7	1,268	20	911
Prus. of potash	515	58,508	250	31,936
Pumice stone	509	1,611		
Quicksilver	1,091	46.552	22	793
Quinas	52	258	277	1,187

	1852.		1853.	
	Quantity.	*Value.*	*Quantity.*	*Value.*
Quinine	344	72,216	1,051	251,827
Ratsbane			3,220	1,468
Red lake	42	1,175	32	642
Red lead	40	1,059	100	2,767
Reina algarabo			4	460
Reg. of antimony	370	25,246	622	42,184
Rhubarb	650	15,633	172	24,396
Rose leaves	40	972	7	692
Rotten stone	4	234		
Safflower	25	1,062	4	300
Saffron	19	2,247	15	1,718
Sal acetosella	17	1.585	16	1,831
Sal ammoniac	250	18,021	256	13,098
Salts	1,628	5,591		
Sal soda	8,715	46,489	3,792	17,922
Sarsaparilla	1,636	39,718	2,419	39.018
Scammony	8	1,842	7	437
Seltzer water	50	115		
Sem. bark	5	147		
Senna	272	7,247	150	3,691
Sesame oil	2	88	10	445
Shellac	1,059	14,086	1,446	2,414
Soda	8,077	39,402	8,443	44,129
Soda ash	11,820	254.446	16,838	384,914
Soda crystals	445	2,588		
Squills	3	80		
Succory	140	2,640	658	11,564
Sugar of lead	292	11,205	514	30,901
Sugar of milk	9	558	29	1,498
Sulphate ammonia	31	1,085	425	10,751
Do. antimony	2	138		
Do. copper	9	741	30	2,821
Do. lime			70	341
Do. morphine			2	356
Do. soda	16	200		
Do. zinc	133	773	265	768
Sulphur	1,139	11,925	1,443	29,962
Sumac	25,329	95,707	32,526	128,290
Tartaric acid	251	24,224	143	20,364
Terra alba	50	404	50	411
Do. japonica			125	665
Do. sienna	4	100		
Do. umber	987	336		
Tinct. iodine	1	218		
Tonqua beans	412	24,361	95	7,888
Ultra marine			180	9,893
Umber	150	891		
Valerian	61	1,281	25	1,130
Vanilla beans	71	14,706	11	2,029
Vermillion	496	36,047	370	29,521
Verdigris	179	31,907	186	35,212
Yellow bark	126	15,232	115	8,063
Yellow berries	273	6,715	388	22,781
Yellow ochre	686	3,349		

NEW YORK

JOURNAL OF PHARMACY.

FEBRUARY, 1854.

NOTICE OF THE "CALIFORNIA NUTMEG."

BY PROFESSOR J. TORREY, M. D.

About a year ago, I received from the late Mr. Shelton, who had just returned from San Francisco, a specimen of what was called the *California Nutmeg.* I immediately considered it a species of Arnott's genus Torreya, belonging to the order Taxineæ of the great natural family of Coniferæ. It had been discovered but a year or two before Mr. Shelton left the country, and had already attracted considerable attention, not only from the beauty of the tree, but from the singular character of the fruit and kernel, the latter strongly resembling the common nutmeg. Indeed, it has been frequently stated in letters from California that the nutmeg is a native of that country. The foliage has the form and deep rich green of the Florida species, or *T. taxifolia,* as well as of the yew; but the leaves are much larger, being from an inch and a half to two and a quarter inches long. They spread out on two sides, and are tipped with a sharp rigid point. The fruit, as it may be popularly called, is about the size and form of a green gage plum, and in the dried state has a pale olive color, but this may not be its natural tint. The outer covering is a thick, fleshy, nearly closed urceole, or dish, which completely invests the seed, and closely adheres to it, except near the summit. It is smooth and even, and soft to the touch. The seed is usually oblong, and greatly resembles a large pecane nut, but frequently it is more ovate. The shell is smooth, thin, and fragile. On each side, near the submit and just below the non-adhering portion of the dish, is a perforation, communicating with an interior canal, similar to what I described in *T.taxifolia*, and the use of which is still unknown. The kernel is conformed to the shell, and has the external and internal appearance of the nutmeg. When cut transversely the resemblance is perfect. The seed, however, is wholly destitute of the delicate aromatic odor of the oriental spice, for it has the strong terebinthine character of the Coniferæ. Neither is the fleshy covering of any known use. It is more probable that, like the fleshy cup-a-berry of the yew, it is of a poisonous nature. Still the discovery of this tree is interesting to the botanist and to the horticulturist. But two other species are known besides. One of them (*T. nucifera Sieb. and Zucc.*) is a native of Japan, and the other has only been found hitherto in Middle Florida, in very confined stations. The latter is erroneously stated by Zuccarini* to have a seed as large as a walnut, by which he undoubtedly means the *Juglans regia*, or Madeira-nut, as it is called in the United States.

As an ornamental tree, the California Nutmeg deserves to be extensively cultivated. It must be hardy, as it grows on the mountains, where the winter is very severe.

The enterprising Messrs. Parsons and Co., of Flushing, sent out a person to California for the express purpose of collecting the ornamental and useful plants of that country, and among other varieties, he obtained, last year, some ripe and fresh seeds of the Californian Nutmeg. These germinated freely, and, when I saw the young plants last October, they had a healthy

* In Endlich. Syn. Conif., p. 241

appearance, and had attained a good size. I have lately heard, also, that Mr. Lobb, an English collector, who has been exploring California for several years past, has sent seeds of this tree to England.

I close this notice with a short technical description of the new Torreya, which may be called T. Californica.

T. foliis distichis, brevissime petiolatis, cuspidatis pungentibus subconcoloribus ; floribus foemineis solitariis sessilibus; seminibus oblongis, disco carnoso clauso.

Hab. Upper part of the Yuba and Feather Rivers, on the western slope of the Sierra Nevada of California.

Differs from *T. taxifolia* in the leaves being much larger, and not glaucous underneath, as well as being furnished with a sharper and more rigid point. The seed is longer, and the fleshy covering much thicker.

96 St. Mark's Place,
February 3d, 1854.

ON THE INTRODUCTION OF AMYGDALINE INTO PHARMACY AS A MEANS OF PRODUCING PRUSSIC ACID.

BY THE EDITOR.

There are few articles in the list of the materia medica about which so much uncertainty prevails, both in the minds of physician and apothecary, as prussic acid. The former is often uncertain that the acid ordered will be dispensed, and the latter, in even dispensing the *nominal* article, is not certain he is fulfilling the spirit of the prescription. Leaving out of question the different strength of different hydrocyanic acids, even the article of Scheele's strength often contains 4 and 5 per cent. of real acid, and occasionally contains none at all. Its instability of composition, even with the addition of a mineral acid, renders it uncertain, and its variable strength renders it unsafe as a medicine. It is a desideratum in pharmacy to supply its place by an article yielding the same acid with certainty, and of a definite strength. Such an article is *amygdaline:* it is crystalline, solid, unalterable in air, and easily dispensed.

The beautiful researches of Liebig and Wöhler upon this substance have shown the connection between it and hydrocyanic acid, and leave little or nothing to be desired further on that head; and the large amount of waste cake left after the expression of the *fixed oil of almonds* from the fresh seeds points it out as a material from which *amygdaline* could be obtained and furnished to any amount, and at a comparatively small price.

These considerations have led me to recommend it as an article worthy of introduction into dispensing practice, as having advantages over every pharmacopeial form of hydrocyanic acid. With this intention, the following notice of its properties and applications is subjoined.

Amygdaline was discovered by Robiquet and Boutron. It may be prepared by bruising almonds in a mortar, compressing them, to remove the fixed oil, and treating the resulting paste or cake with boiling alcohol, of the strength of 94° The alcoholic solution should then be evaporated, and submitted to fermentation, to destroy the sugar. The liquor is then evaporated, and the amygdaline crystallises in silky plates out of the alcohol. As thus prepared, it is sparingly soluble in cold alcohol, but readily soluble in the boiling liquid. It may be purified by taking advantage of this property. It also dissolves in water, and retains a quantity of water of hydration, which amounts to about 10.50 per cent. (Pelouze). Heated to 120° Cent., it parts with this water, and becomes anhydrous. Alkalies decompose it, by eliminating ammonia, and producing a non-azotised acid, *amygdalic* acid.

Oxidating agents act differently with it, such as binoxyde of manganese, bichromate potassa, and nitric acid, decomposing it into ammonia, essence of bitter almonds, benzoic and formic acids. Concentrated sulphuric acid dissolves it forming a deep red liquid. Metallic salts have no action on amygdaline. From the indirect analysis of Liebig and Wöhler, it appears to have this formula:

$$C_{40}H_{27}NO_{22}.$$

The whole of the amygdaline does not crystallize out from its alcoholic solution, a considerable portion remaining dissolved. A pure article is not obtained crystalline by further evaporation of the alcohol; and a better mode is to add some ether to the alcoholic liquid, which, uniting with the alcohol, immediately displaces the amygdaline as a precipitate. This is usually mixed with some fatty matter, and requires frequent washings with ether; it is then to be pressed between folds of paper. When treated thus, it appears in the form of pearly white scales.

The change produced in amygdaline by the oxidating agents mentioned is also effected in the seed itself by fermentation, as in the cake, after the oil has been expressed. This fermentation is first commenced in another constituent of the paste *synaptase*, which, exposed to the air, decomposes readily, and in its alteration communicates molecular action to the amygdaline, re-arranging its particles into hydrocyanic acid, essence of bitter almonds, and the other bodies mentioned. In the fresh seed this does not occur, the presence of the oil protecting the amygdaline from the action of the synaptase, probably by the oily covering of its particles.

Amygdaline, when preserved in bottles, well stopped, and when prepared anhydrous, is not liable to change; it does not form hydrocyanic acid until brought into contact with fermenting synaptase, when the change immediately commences. In amygdaline we have thus a substance possessing many valuable properties which recommend it as a substitute for hydrocyanic acid, or the distilled waters containing this acid. It is a substance not liable to change, forms hydrocyanic acid just when it is wanted, and the amount of acid derived can always be *certainly* dispensed. The mode of dispensing it is by rubbing it up with almond emulsion in the way indicated further on: as it is the *synaptase* of the almond emulsion which developes the acid, of course it is hardly necessary to remark that the emulsion must be made with the *seeds*, and not with the *oil*.

As the amygdaline is produced from the cake *after* the oil is removed, the following directions about the manner of expressing the oil will be suitably introduced here.

Bitter almonds, when pressed between hot plates, lose their faculty of yielding their hydrocyanic acid, and oil of bitter almonds upon their subsequent distillation with water. Synaptase undergoes a modification by heat, which puts a stop to its action upon amygdaline. It is therefore invariably necessary to express the fat oil *cold*. It is for the same reason that the almonds freed from their fat oil by cold pressure, must not be drenched with hot water, else they will not yield any oil of bitter almonds; and it is also for this reason (and likewise due to the absence of water), that oil of bitter almonds cannot be obtained by boiling with absolute alcohol. There is also another matter which demands attention in producing oil of bitter almonds, *i. e.*, the amount of water in which the amygdaline and synaptase are dissolved. If we take less water than is needed from the solution of oil of bitter almonds that may be formed, a more or less considerable amount of amygdaline will escape decomposition, since no more oil of bitter almonds will be formed than is capable of being dissolved in the water present. The largest proportion of the oil of bitter almonds is obtained by keeping the bruised bitter almonds for some days in contact with the necessary amount of water in a close vessel. The distilled water of bitter almonds and cherry laurel water have been used by many European physicians with success, being in fact often esteemed the most appropriate form of hydrocyanic acid, generally preferring the laurel water, not from any difference in the properties of both waters, the experiments of Wöhler and Liebig having proved their absolute identity, but because there is a great difficulty in the distillation of the paste, much more than in that of the leather-like leaves of the *lauro cerasus;* and besides, the distillation of the water of bitter almonds is always attended with the loss of a large amount of the hydrocyanic acid formed. Some European pharmacopeias direct, to prepare these distilled waters certain quantities of bitter almonds or of lauro cerasus; but when it is recollected that it is by no means certain the leaves have the same composition through the whole year, or that bitter almonds are so often mixed with the sweet, and again that the quantity of prussic acid in the distilled waters of both is constantly diminishing, owing to molecular changes in the fluids, and to which this acid is liable, we cannot avoid coming to the conclusion, that the composition of these waters is subject to many vicissitudes.

It is advisable, therefore, to remove these waters from all pharmaceutical prescriptions, and to substitute for them a definite amount of amygdaline dissolved in water, and mixing it with emulsion of sweet almonds, since, if this remedy be prepared fresh each time it is wanted, it will invariably present the same constitution. Liebig states that 17 grains of amygdaline yield one grain of anhydrous prussic acid. If, then 34 grains of amygdaline be mixed with 66 grains of emulsion of sweet almonds, there is in the 100 grains a fluid corresponding to the medicinal hydrocyanic acid of Scheele's strength (2 per cent.) One third of a grain of amygdaline corresponds to one grain of medicinal acid. The solution of 1 grain of amygdaline in 3 ounces of emulsion of sweet almonds contains consequently one grain of medicinal acid for every ounce of the mixture (Liebig).

The foregoing appears to be so simple a mode of preparing hydrocyanic acid extemporaneously, and administering it with certainty, that it is now submitted for the approval of physicians and pharmaceutists.

ON VERATRIA.

BY JAMES BEATSON,

Manufacturing Chemist, U. S. Naval Laboratory, N. Y.

The formula of the United States and British Pharmacopœias for obtaining this article has always appeared to me more complicated and troublesome than necessary, which has induced me to adopt a modification of the process recommended by Christison, the last time I had occasion to prepare it. The manipulation is so simple, and the result so satisfactory, that I feel confident, when generally known, it will be universally adopted, wherever this article is required to be made, either upon the large or small scale.

Seventy-three pounds (avoirdupois) of sabadilla were rubbed upon a coarse wire sieve, which separated the seed from the capsules, reduced to a coarse powder, in Swift's drug mill. Finding that a portion of the veratria was still retained with the membraneous follicle, I passed the capsules likewise through the mill, which, from their elasticity, were but coarsely comminuted; the finer portions I separated with a coarse sieve, and mixed with the ground seeds, moistened with alcohol, and allowed them to stand for twelve hours. I then introduced them into a displacement apparatus, and exhausted them thoroughly, with rectified alcohol, in the following manner: Into the displacement apparatus I introduced thirty gallons of rectified alcohol, and, when a quantity had percolated sufficient to fill my still, I commenced distillation—returning the recovered alcohol into the displacement apparatus, and continuing the percolation and distillation, until the seeds were thoroughly exhausted—collected all the alcohol I could from the exhausted seeds, and continued the distillation until the tincture, in the bottom of the still, was of a syrupy consistence; poured this while hot into eight times its volume of cold water, threw the whole upon a calico filter, and washed with cold water, until the washings ceased to indicate the presence of veratria; mixed the washings with what passed first through the filter, and added liquor ammoniæ in excess, (about four pounds) which precipitated the veratria with a little of the coloring matter. Washed the precipitate with cold water, which removed the greater portion of the coloring matter. Dried with a very gentle heat; and, when the moisture was completely expelled, weighed eleven and a quarter ounces of pure veratria, with but a faint shade of coloring matter.

U. S. Naval Hospital, New York Station,
October 19th, 1853.

ON PRACTICAL PHARMACY.

BY JUSTUS LIEBIG, M. D.

[We publish the following articles on Practical Pharmacy from the pen of the illustrious German chemist as they first appeared in English in the London Annals of Pharmacy; they are interesting as showing to some extent the condition of pharmacy in Germany, and while they are not in some points applicable to the art in this country, they may serve as commentaries for the better understanding the Prussian and other pharmacopeial medicines in demand in our large cities. We shall complete the series in the first six numbers of the Journal.—Ed.]

No. 1.

The arrangements of a Pharmacy.

The name of Pharmacy is given to the building in which medicines are prepared, kept, and dispensed; it consists of three compartments, viz., the laboratory, the store-rooms, and the shop. The laboratory is the place in which medicines are made or prepared. It must be well lighted, airy, spacious and fire-proof. Therein are placed different stoves, among which, one for drying, and the different utensils necessary for all pharmaceutical operations. A drying-room may also be distinct from the laboratory. The stoves must be placed properly so as to occupy the least possible room, and to be easy of access. The implements must be in sufficent quantity, and of the best make; those which are not in daily use, and are likely to be spoiled by dust or effluvia, ought to be kept in a separate room.

In well arranged pharmacies there ought to be also a particular room for cutting, pounding, and sifting roots, herbs, and the like. This room ought to contain mortars, sieves, &c.

The store-room is the place in which are kept dry medicinal substances, either in their natural state or ready prepared. It is advantageous to choose for this purpose a dry room in the upper part of the house; medicines must be kept in well-closed drawers, boxes, and vessels of glass and china, all well arranged, and labelled alphabetically. Nothing is more injudicious than to indicate them by numbers, and to refer to a catalogue for their specification. In well arranged pharmacies there is a particular room for keeping herbs and roots. Aromatic and tender herbs and flowers, such as roses, lavender, arnica, ought to be kept in vessels of glass, or in well-closed boxes of blocked tin, well guarded against the changes of the weather.

Next to the store-room is the water-cellar, or aquarium. For this purpose we must select a cool place, exposed as little as possible to the rays of the sun, wherein distilled waters, ointments, syrups and tinctures are kept; indeed, it would be better to have also a separate room for tinctures. Every article in the water-cellar ought also to be alphabetically labelled, and properly arranged.

The shop is the place in which prescriptions are made up and dispensed; it ought to be spacious, light, and about twelve feet high, and, if possible, opening to the north, so as to be less exposed to the rays of the sun.

The medicines here must be kept in proper vessels; distilled waters, spirits, tinctures, oils, in bottles, with ground stoppers; ointments, extracts, and the like, in jars of china or earthenware. The shape of the vessels ought to be artistical, and adapted to the nature of their contents. Dry crude medicines are kept in drawers and wooden boxes; for substances which emit a strong effluvia, as musk, camphor, valerian, choose well-stopped china or glass vessels. No vessel ought to be used which might communicate to medicines the least deleterious quality; hence all vessels of copper or pewter must be banished from the shop.

These different vessels must be properly placed and labelled, in order to facilitate the dispensing of medicines, especially for new assistants. The medicines most in use ought to be nearest to the counter, placed all together on particular shelves; and real poisons ought to be kept in a closed compartment, together with the scales, measure-glass, and the like used in dispensing them. A large counter, easy to access, well lighted, and furnished with drawers for the different implements, and some ready-made medicines, ought to be placed in the most conspicuous place, according to the locality of the shop. Upon the counter are placed beams of scales of different sizes, but all must be as exact as possible. The best beams are of brass, they are not so easily subject to oxidation, and are less influenced by magnetism and electricity. They ought to be of equal length, and kept extremely clean, particularly the point of equilibrium. The scales may be of brass, glass, gilded silver, or platina.

Herbs and flowers were, and are still, sometimes prescribed according to the volume; a bundle, *fasciculus*, is equal to one ounce; a handful, *manipulus*, to half an ounce; a pinch, *pugillus*, one drachm. It is evident that this mode of prescribing is far from being scientific and exact.

Liquids are prescribed according to measure, for which graduated measure-glasses are used; but as the specific gravity of fluids varies, it would be useful, in some cases, to prescribe the fluid by weight.

The mortars most commonly employed are of glass, china, wedgwood, marble, iron, bell metal.

How to Procure and Preserve Medicines.

The pharmaceutist procures the medicines himself, or causes them to be collected by others, or purchases them from the wholesale druggist. By whatsoever means he procures them, his duty is to keep only the best drugs, and to destroy all those which have become injured by keeping.

Inorganic substances are, generally, got from the manufacturing chemist; in this case, the duty of the pharmaceutist is to see that they be pure and genuine; but, in procuring and preserving organic substances, great attention must be paid to the following rules:

Roots, herbs, and flowers must be collected at a proper time, and guarded against spoiling. Roots are collected in spring, before the leaves are perfectly formed, or in autumn, when the leaves have decayed; however, there are some plants, the roots of which may be also collected whilst they are in full vegetation. These, however, are but general rules, and it requires a thorough knowledge of medical botany to enable one to choose the best time for collecting the roots of different plants. The roots must be cleaned, the thick ones even sliced, and dried slowly at a gentle heat not exceeding 130° Fahr., and placed afterwards in well closed boxes, in a dry place. Barks (*cortices*), woods (*ligna*), and branches, (*stipites*) are gathered in spring, and even in autumn from young and healthy plants or trees. In spring, also, buds and spores (*gemmæ et oculi*) are collected. They are dried and kept in the same way as the roots.

Herbs (*herbæ*) and leaves (*foliæ*) are gathered when the plant is near flowering, on a fine dry morning. Narcotic plants form therein an exception, most of them being most pregnant with active principles when in full flower. Herbs thus collected are generally dried in the shade in a well ventilated room; however, if the season be wet, we must resort to artificial heat.

Flowers are gathered, when in full perfection, at noon on a fine dry day, and dried as quick as possible. Some flowers are freed from their calyx; others are gathered together with the tender stem, and are called summitates, as absinthum.

Fruits are generally collected when fully ripe; some, for instance oranges, when in an unripe state. Some are dried like roots, as momordica colocynthis; others used immediately, when fresh, to make extracts, like momordica elaterium, or made into confections.

Seeds are to be collected after their full maturity, and cleaned and shelled.

Mosses, lichens, and fungi, are gathered when arrived at perfect maturity, and dried by means of artificial heat.

Gums, balsams, and resins, being generally, with us, exotics, are procured from the wholesale druggists, and the only care of the pharmaceutist is to see that they be genuine, as many of them are adulterated, even by the natives.

Most of the medicines derived from the animal kingdom are imported from abroad, and require the same discrimination in purchasing them as the foreign drugs. Moreover, some of them are easily injured by age, and other casualties, and must be often renewed, and the sound ones kept in well-closed vessels, in cool, airy places.

What are strictly called chemicals, ought all to be prepared by the dispensing chemist himself; and though most of them are now got from manufacturers, it is the duty of every chemist not to dispense a single article procured from a manufacturer before having it submitted to a proper test to ascertain its purity.

No. 2.

Of Pharmaceutical Preparations in general.

Very few drugs can be exhibited for medicinal purposes without undergoing some preparation by which either their form or composition is altered; sometimes we are obliged to mix several bodies together, at other times we are compelled to separate mixed bodies into their different components. The operations required to attain this object are called pharmaceutical operations. Drugs which are intended to be exhibited as medicines are prepared in laboratories; the mixing up of medicines is performed in the chemist's shop.

The legal prescriptions contained in pharmacopœias or dispensatories are called official formulæ; the prescriptions of physicians for the exhibition of particular medicines are called magistral formulæ.

Pharmaceutical operations are divided into mechanical or galenic, and chemical. . The object of the first is a division of the homogeneous part of bodies, or a separation of their different components, separation of different visible parts, or a mixing up of different bodies. The object of chemical operations is the production of new compounds, or the analysis of compound bodies. It is, however, difficult to separate exactly the two operations, as, in some instances, different bodies cannot be mixed without forming new compounds; nevertheless, we shall be obliged to reckon among mechanical operations all those in which chemical combinations do not constitnte the principal object.

Of Mechanical Operations and the necessary Instruments. Separation of Bodies.

Cutting is a mechanical operation by which roots, herbs, flowers, are divided in more or less minute parts. To cut hard roots and woods, a root-knife is employed. A long straight knife, with a wooden handle, fastened at the end to a board by means of a ring; the roots are placed on the board under the knife. It acts both as a wedge and as a lever, and, if of a proper length, it will cut well. Several forms of this knife are described in French and German pharmaceutical journals. Herbs and roots of moderate hardness are cut with the rocking-knife, which is made of a semicircular-shaped blade, having a handle at each end. By rocking the knife on the herbs placed on a board, they are easily cut into small pieces. Some employ for the same purpose strong scissors.

In order to obtain particles of the same size, it is necessary to separate the coarser from the finer by means of sifting. For this purpose sieves are employed, made of iron or brass wire. The coarser particles are cut anew. The holes of these sieves are from one to three lines in diameter. Instead of the iron-wire sieves, the Spanish wooden may be employed, though less lasting. When all has been uniformly cut, the herbs are placed in a fine sieve to remove the dusty particles. Horns, bones, and hard woods and fruits, are reduced to a state of a coarse powder by rasping. The divided substances are called rasura.

Softer substances, fresh herbs and roots, are reduced to a pulpy mass (*conquassare*) by means of the pestle and mortar, or by a grater or sieve.

Pulverization, (*contusio*) trituration, (*trituratio*) are the means employed to reduce hard dry substances into powders of different degrees of fineness. The instruments required are the pestle and mortar, and the trituration board and muller.

The more dry the substances are, the easier they are reduced to powder. Bodies which attract easily moisture from the air, such as roots, herbs, and flowers, must be exposed to artificial heat before pounding them. Aromatic herbs and flowers require but moderate heat; and the operation must be performed quickly else they lose their aroma. On the other hand, nux vomica can only be pulverized after having been dried in an oven. Some substances are always soft at common temperature, and cannot be dried by heat without altering their properties, but become brittle when exposed to frost; for instance, assafœtida, galbanum, and ammoniacum. These substances ought to be pulverized in water. Other bodies, such as colocynthis, can only be reduced to powder after having been previously impregnated with some drying mucilage or gum; for which purpose they are bruised in a mortar with some mucilage, and afterwards dried. Substances thus prepared were called formerly trochisci, for example, trochisci alhandal, trochisci agarici. Some metals which are fire-proof, and insoluble in water, previous to their pulverization, are made red hot and cooled in water. Mortars are commonly of cast-iron or brass; the brass ones are only fit for less hard substances, and for such which do not easily attack the metal. Iron mortars are the best, both on account of their hardness and safety. In large pharmacies, the pestle is suspended by means of a cord to elastic beams, or several mortars are put at work at once by a steam-engine. To prevent the finer parts flying off during the process of pounding, the mortar is fitted with a wooden cover, perforated to admit the pestle; this object is still easier attained by tying round the mortar and the pestle a pliable piece of leather. Yet, notwithstanding these precautions, if euphorbium, veratrium, and similar substances are pounded, it is necessary for those employed in this operation to cover their faces with masks made of sponge, dipped in water, and tied behind the ears by a string. But woods, barks, and hard substances are better reduced to powder at proper drug-mills, such as exist in England.

To obtain powders of constant equal fineness, it is necessary to employ sieves made of different tissues, such as horsehair, gauze, silk, &c.

Sieves should have a cover and receiver, with a bottom of parchment or leather, so as to prevent any loss of the powder. For aromatic substances and poisons, separate sieves should be employed, as always some particles will adhere to them.

Substances which act or are acted upon by iron are safely pounded in stone mortars, in deep or flat mortars of Wedgwood ware, china, glass, and agate; flat mortars are most commonly employed for triturating small bodies.

Levigation is a process by which substances insoluble in water, chiefly metallic, are reduced to powder. The substance to be levigated is spread, coarsely pounded, and wetted with water, upon a flat table of porphyry or marble, and is there to be rubbed by a conical muller of the same material, till reduced to a paste, which is made into small cones and dried. However, he who possesses fine sieves of gauze, may, in many cases, avoid the process of levigation. Powders are distinguished according to the degrees of fineness, namely, coarse powder (*pulvis grossus*), which may contain particles of half a line dimension; common powder (*pulvis*), which must be fine and equal to the touch, yet the eye may discover the particles of which it is composed. Fine powder (*pulvis subtilissimus*) must be reduced to impalpable dust. The coarser particles which remain in the sieve after are called remanens. Of some substances remanens are still valuable, as the coarser particles can be pounded over again; but of herbs which have hard stocks, and woods with wooden fibres, the remanens must be thrown away. Powders of organic substances must be kept in close vessels; those which are aromatic must be pressed very closely, and they will keep longer and better than the substance from which they are derived.

Metals which cannot be pounded are reduced to powder by filing. These filings are of different degrees of fineness according to the files employed, and some, as that of iron, made by means of fine English files, and almost as well levigated as the finest powder, and is called limaturæ ferri. Some are beaten on an anvil to very thin foils. Metals which are easily fused are melted first, thrown afterwards in wooden boxes lined with pipe-clay, and shaken till by cooling they are transformed in small grains (*granulatæ*). Other metals, for instance tin, may be also pulverized, by throwing them melted in a hot iron mortar, and rubbing them briskly with the pestle. The powder is sifted through a sieve, and the remanens melted again, and triturated as before.

THE CLASSIFICATION OF MEDICINAL SUBSTANCES.

Dr. Alexander Fleming, Professor of Materia Medica, Queen's College, Cork, and Examiner in Materia Medica of the Queen's University, Ireland, has published, in one of the quarterly medical journals—"The Dublin Quarterly Journal of Medical Science"—an excellent and elaborate paper, bearing the title, "On the Classification of Medicines according to their Action on the Healthy Body," in which he says, "A scientific arrangement of drugs should be founded on the principle of placing those together whose properties present the greatest number of important points of resemblance, the relative importance of the properties being determined by their

5

value as guides in the application of the medicines to the treatment of disease." The properties of drugs are numerous, and of very different kinds, but a little reflection enables us easily to fix their relative importance in a system of classification.

"The physiological, chemical, and other properties of a medicine are examined not for their own sake, but to promote the discovery and explanation of its applications in the treatment of disease. *The discovery, therefore, of the therapeutic application, which is the grand object of the science, should be the presiding principle of its classification ;* and of the several kinds of properties which a drug possesses, namely, physiological, chemical, botanical, and sensible, it is beyond question, that the first are a long way before the others in their importance in guiding and suggesting its practical application. Indeed, our object in studying the other properties is to improve and give exactitude to our knowledge of the first. *The physiological action of drugs should form, consequently, the basis of their scientific arrangement.*" He then proceeds to describe the arrangement which he has adopted according to the principles thus laid down, and he divides the entire group of articles in the materia medica into two great divisions, which he terms, first, physiological, and, secondly, non-physiological, regarding all medicines whatsoever as falling within one or other of these two divisions; and he states that his classification relates exclusively to medicines or the drugs made use of in the relief or cure of disease.

The following list of drugs and medicinal preparations is arranged by Dr. Fleming according to the classification which he has proposed, confining himself to the officinal preparations, the directions for which are contained in the "Dublin Pharmacopœia":

CLASS 1.—TONICS.

(*a*) Cod-liver oil.

(*b*) Iron and its compounds.

(*c*) Vegetable bitter tonics. *Pure*—Quassia and simarouba; gentian and chiretta. *Stimulant*—Anthemis, taraxacum, and cascarilla. *Astringent*—Cinchona. *Emollient*—Calumba, pareira and cetraria.

(*d*) Acid tonics.—Sulphuric, nitric, and muriatic acids; lemon-juice.

CLASS 2.—ATONICS.

(*a*) Mercurials.—The metal and its mechanical forms, calomel and corrosive sublimate; green and red iodides.

(*b*) Arsenicals.—Arsenious acid and liquor arsenicalis.

(*c*) Iodides.—Iodine, and iodide of potassium.

(*d*) Alkalines.—Potassa, its carbonate, bicarbonate, nitrate, and chlorate; carbonate, bicarbonate, and borate of soda; lime and its carbonate; magnesia and its carbonate.

CLASS 3.—STIMULANTS.

(*a*) Alcoholic.—Spirits, wines, and malt liquors.

(*b*) Ethereal.—Sulphuric ether, spiritus æthereus oleosus, and spiritus æthereus nitrosus.

(*c*) Ammoniacal.—Liquor ammoniæ, aromatic and fetid spirits; sesquicarbonate, bicarbonate, acetate, and muriate of ammonia.

(*d*) Myrolic.—From the *Labiatæ*—peppermint, spearmint, and pennyroyal, lavender and rosemary. *Umbelliferæ*—anise, coriander, carraway, and fennel. *Myrtaceæ*—cajeput, cloves, and pimento. *Myristicaceæ*—nutmeg, lauraceæ, cinnamon and camphor. *Coniferæ*—oil of turpentine. *Valerianaceæ*—valerian, maliaceæ, canella. *Zingiberaceæ*—ginger and cardamoms. *Aristolochiaceæ*—serpentaria.

(*e*) Resinous.—*Oleo-resins*—copaiba, cubebs, matico; black and Cayenne peppers. *Gum-resins*—assafœtida, ammoniac, galbanum, myrrh.

(*f*) Animal excretions.—Musk and castor.

CLASS 4.—SEDATIVES.

(*a*) Pure.—Digitalis, aconite, hemlock, hydrocyanic acid, and cherry laurel; pyroxylic spirit.

(*b*) Atonic and irritant.—Tartar emetic, nitrate of potassa.

(*c*) Irritant.—Tobacco, lobelia, and colchicum.

(*d*) Mydraceous.—Belladonna, stramonium, and hyoscyamus.

CLASS 5.—TETANICS.

Nux vomica.

CLASS 6.—NARCOTICS.

Chloroform.—Opium and lactucarium; Indian hemp and hops.

CLASS 7.—PARTURIENTS.

Ergot of rye, Indian hemp, borax.

CLASS 8.—EVACUANTS.

(*a*) Emetics.—*Quick*—sulphates of zinc and copper; salt, mustard. *Slow*—tartar emetic, ipecacuanha.

(*b*) Cathartics.—*Laxatives*—sulphur, magnesia and its carbonate, manna, tamarinds, prunes, olive oil, and honey. *Saline Purgatives*—sulphate of magnesia, sulphate and phosphate of soda, tartrate of potassa and soda; sulphate, bisulphate, tartrate, and bitartrate of potassa. *Mercurial Purgatives*—calomel, mercurial pill, mercury with chalk, mercury with magnesia. *Vegetable Purgatives*—senna, castor oil, rhubarb, aloes, turpentine. *Drastic Purgatives*—jalap, scammony, colocynth and elaterium, gamboge and croton oil.

(*c*) Diuretics.—*Tonic*—muriate of iron; pareira, pyrola, taraxacum, broom. *Atonic*—mercurials, acetate, bitartrate, and nitrate of potassa, acetate of soda. *Stimulant*—spirit of nitric ether, turpentine, juniper, bucku, and cantharides. *Sedative*—digitalis, squill, colchicum and tobacco.

(*d*) Diaphoretics.—*Stimulant*—acetate of ammonia, guaicum, sassafras, and mezereon. *Sedative*—antimonials, opium and ipecacuanha, sarsaparilla and dulcamara.

(*e*) Expectorants.—*Stimulant*—balsam of tolu, benzoin and its acid, senega. *Nauseant Sedative*—tartar emetic, ipecacuanha, and squill. *Direct Irritant*—chlorine, iodine, tar, vinegar.

(*f*) Emmenagogues.—Savin, myrrh, (?) ergot, (?) aloes, and other cathartics.

CLASS 9.—ASTRINGENTS.

(*a*) Tannin, containing astringents.—Tannin; catechu, kino, krameria, galls, oak-bark, logwood, uvi ursi, and French roses.

(*b*) Acid astringents.—Sulphuric, acetic, and gallic acids.

(*c*) Metallic astringents—Astringent preparations of iron (tonic) lead, (atonic and sedative) zinc, bismuth, copper, silver, lime, alum.

CLASS 10.—IRRITANTS.

(*a*) Rubefacients.—*Mild*—Tar, resin, burgundypitch, elemi, creosote, ammoniac, camphor, oil of amber, iodine, yeast, the alkalies, their carbonates and chlorides, sulphur and its iodide, liver of sulphur, iodide, nitrate, and ammonio-chloride of mercury, &c.; nearly all the drugs applied in the form of ointment, plaster, liniment and wash, and which are neither astringent, sedative, emollient, nor strongly acrid, may be arranged under this head. *Strong*—cantharides, ammonia, mustard, turpentine, cayenne.

(*b*) Vesicants.—Cantharides, ammonia, nitrate of silver.

(*c*) Pustulants.—Tartar emetic, croton oil, ipecacuanha.

(*d*) Cauterants.—*Mild*—Acetic acid, nitrate of silver, subacetate of copper, red oxide of mercury, savin. *Strong*—nitric and sulphuric acids, arsenious acid, potassa, lime, chloride of zinc, terchloride of antimony, pernitrate of mercury.

CLASS 11.—EMOLLIENTS.

(*a*) Mucilaginous.—Gum arabic, tragacanth, hemidesmus, (mucilage and oil) linseed, sweet almonds.

(*b*) Amylaceous.—Wheat, starch, and flour, oatmeal, barley, carrot, Iceland moss, arrowroot, tous les mois, sago, tapioca.

(*c*) Saccharine.—Sugar, treacle, liquorice, figs, raisins, glycerine.

(*d*) Oily and waxy.—Lard, spermaceti, wax, oils of olive, almond and linseed.

(*e*) Albuminous.—Egg.

CLASS 12.—ANTHELMINTICS.

Pomegranate, oil of turpentine, quassia, cowhage, tin powder, male fern, kousso.

Dr. Fleming concludes by remarking, "No classification of medicines can pretend to freedom from errors and defects, which are unavoidable in the present imperfect state of the science of therapeutics. I hope simply to have founded the foregoing on true principles, of which a good proof will be its capability of assuming, without violence to its fabric, such corrections as are rendered necessary by the progress of knowledge."

In addition to this long catalogue of medicinal drugs, the several Pharmacopœias enumerate and describe other substances, such as the disinfectants and deodorizers, tests, and other chemical articles, perfumes, and coloring matter, which relate to hygiene and pharmacy, rather than to therapeutics. —*Annals of Pharmacy.*

CHEMICAL RELATIONS OF THE PLANTS OF THE ORDER ERICACEÆ.

BY F. ROCHLEDER.

All the plants examined of this order contain a tannic acid.

Arctostaphylos uva ursi, the gallic acid = $C^{14} H^{6} O^{10}$ in its basic lead salt.

Calluna vulgaris, the callutannic acid = $C^{14} H^{6} O^{8}$ in its salts dried at 212°.

Rhododendron ferrugineum, the rhodotannic acid = $C^{14} H^{6} O^{7}$ in its salts dried at 212°.

Ledum palustre, the leditannic acid = $C^{14} H^{6} O^{6}$ in its salts dried at 212°.

Erica herbacea contains quite an analogous acid, which is composed, according to a preliminary research, of $C^{14} H^{8} O^{7}$, and is thus isomeric with tanno-caffeic acid, and the tannic acid of *Portlandia grandiflora*, and which the author has named eritannic acid. All these acids are colored green with persalts of iron, with the exception of the gallic acid. In combination with alkalies they oxidize rapidly, and afford dark solutions. With sulphuric or muriatic acid, all give a yellow or red coloring matter under the loss of water, or its elements, which are separated as water. The gallic acid gives para-gallic acid; the callutannic acid, calluxanthin; the rhodotannic acid, rhodozanthin; the leditannic acid, ledizanthine; and the eritannic acid, erixanthin; the callutannic, rhodotannic, leditannic, and eritannic acids, give, with a solution of perchloride of tin, yellow precipitates. The basic lead salts of all these acids are as yellow as chromate of lead. With the exception of the gallic acid, all these acids color cloth, saturated with a tin salt, beautifully and permanently yellow, and also cloth impregnated with alum, if chloride of tin and muriatic acid are added.

Thus, as in the *Rubiaceæ* is contained a series of tannic acids of the form $C^{14} H^{8} On$, we have in the *Ericaceæ* a series of tannic acids of the form $C^{14} H^{6} On$. But they are not similarly constituted; their carbon is found distributed in two different ways or groups, as with the tannic acids of the *Rubiaceæ;* they lose only water, or its elements, by treatment with acids, while the acids of the *Rubiaceæ* undergo a disunion or splitting up.

Besides the above mentioned acids, all these plants contain an indifferent body, ericolin, the watery solution of which affords, when heated with acids, an ethereal oil amongst other products. The greatest quantity of this substance is contained in *Ledum palustre;* and nearest in this relation stands *Arctostaphylos uva ursi. Calluna vulgaris*, *Erica herbacea*, and *Rhododendron ferrugineum*, contain but very little of this body. An already-formed ethereal oil is contained in all these plants. *Calluna vulgaris*, *Erica herbacea*, and *uva ursi*, contain only a trace. *Ledum palustre* the most, and *Rhododendron ferrugineum* somewhat less.

Fat, in small quantities, chlorophyle, and a considerable quantity of wax, are contained in the leaves of all these plants.

In *Calluna vulgaris*, in *Erica herbacea*, and *Ledum palustre*, are contained matters which belong to the pectine series; but in *Rhododendron ferrugineum* and *uva ursi* none could be detected.

Citric acid can be recognized in *Ledum palustre*, and, in all probability, this acid is also present in the remaining plants in very small quantities.

We have, in the order *Rubiaceæ*, a series of bodies (tannic acids) with fourteen equivalents of carbon almost throughout, accompanied with substances with twelve equivalents of carbon, (citric and chinovic acids) and less frequently appearing a third series, whose members (alizarine, quinine and cinchonine) contain twenty equivalents of carbon. In the order *Ericaceæ*, likewise, we find one series of tannic acids with fourteen equivalents of carbon, and a second, whose members contain twenty equivalents.

The ethereal oils of *Ledum palustre* and *Rhododendron ferrugineum* contain C^{20}, and the oil which results from ericolin, contains likewise C^{20}. The arbutin of *Arctostaphylos uva ursi* is the sugar compound of arctuvin, which also contains C^{20}. (Arctuvin = $C^{20}\ H^{10}\ O^{7}$.) When five equivalents of oxygen in arctuvin are replaced by five equivalents of hydrogen, we have $C^{20}\ H^{15}\ O^{2}$, the composition of the oil which Willigk prepared from *Ledum* by means of sulphuric acid.

ON THE FORMATION AND CONSTITUTION OF RESINS.

BY DR. CHARLES LÖWIG.

Resins belong to the most widely-diffused compounds of the vegetable kingdom, and it is scarcely possible to find a plant in which a substance does not exist which can be considered as a resin. There are also many fossil bodies found in nature, whose origin may be traced back to the vegetation of ancient times, and which agree, in reference to their properties and composition, with the resins, and are termed fossil resins, as amber, berengelite, &c. Further, the so-called empyreumatic resin is obtained by the dry distillation of organic matter. In general, all compounds are considered as resins which are solid by ordinary temperatures, melt when heated, cannot be volatilized unchanged, by friction become negatively electric, insoluble in water, soluble in alcohol, partly soluble in ether and oil of turpentine, may be melted with fats, and are mostly inodorous, &c. Many bodies, however, which exhibit these relations, cannot be reckoned amongst the resins on account of their chemical characters; namely, a great number of coloring matters and some indifferent compounds: consequently, the notion of a resin is a very vague and undetermined one. Most resins are formed, without doubt, by the action of the air on volatile oil.

In many plants, thus in the whole family *Pinus*, in the different species *Copaifera*, a solution of resins in essential oils is found in such abundant quantity, that it flows out, partly from accidentally existing apertures and partly in great quantity from incisions made for that purpose. The mixtures are termed natural balsams. When they remain exposed for a long time to the air, the oil partly volatilizes and partly changes into resin; and when these balsams are distilled with water, the volatile oil passes over with the aqueous vapor, while the resin remains behind, and by continued boiling with water becomes freed from the still adhering oil. If the resin does not flow out freely, the plant or its parts in a dried condition are digested with alcohol. The spirituous solution, after the fat and waxy substances have separated, is mixed with water, the spirit then distilled from it, and the resin, which is insoluable in water, and is consequently precipitated, after being sufficiently washed with water, is freed from the adhering water by long exposure in a water-bath. The milky juices which exist in the peculiar vessels of many plants are mostly intimate mixtures of resin, gum, ethereal oil, and water. When these juices are dried the products are the so-called gum resins, as, galbanum, ammoniacum, assafœtida, sagapenum, &c. When these gum-resins are carefully triturated, emulsions are obtained. The resins of gum-resins can be extracted by means of alcohol.

As most of the resins are formed by the oxidation of volatile oils, and the latter, as they are obtained by the distillation of plants with water, consist generally of several oils, so must the resins which are formed from these oils be mixtures of different resins. Consequently, they can be separated into various resins by alternate treatment with alcohol, ether, petroleum, and oil of turpentine, &c. Many resins give with potash compounds soluble in alcohol; others, compounds insoluble in that menstruum; and a third class behave indifferently, and do not combine with potash.

Many resins crystallize out of their alcoholic solutions; on the contrary, others appear as transparent, mostly yellow-colored masses. In their pure state they are without odor, brittle, and easily pulverizable, but when they still contain oil, they appear soft and possess the odor of the oil. (Hard and soft resins.) Some resins are only soluble in boiling alcohol, and are precipitated entirely in the cold. (Sub resins.) Ether dissolves many, but not all resins. In hot water, resins soften, are then kneadable, and may be drawn into thin strings. Their specific gravity varies between .92 and 1.2. They are readily inflammable, and burn with a bright sooty flame.

Many resins possess distinctly acid properties. Their alcoholic solutions react acid and expel by boiling the carbonic acid from the alkaline carbonates. They agree in this view with the higher members of the fatty acids, and are to be regarded as true acids. From their capacity of saturation, the acid resins show that a great number of them contain forty atoms of carbon; thirty, twenty-eight, or twenty-seven atoms of hydrogen; and three, four, or more atoms of oxygen. It may be assumed that these acid resins altogether originate from the terebenes. The acid properties of the resins appear distinct in the proportion of the number of atoms of oxygen which they contain. The acid resins dissolve easily in alkaline ley, (resinous soaps) and their spirituous solutions are not precipitated on the addition of ammonia. However, there is also a class of resins which behave indifferently towards bases, and have chiefly only one atom of oxygen to forty atoms of carbon. These are insoluble in caustic alkalies. Nevertheless, sometimes they are soluble when they are treated with a concentrated solution of potash cotemporaneously with an acid resin, but are thrown down when the solution is diluted with water. The acid resins have been divided into strong acids, moderate acids, and weak acids. The latter are insoluble in ammonia and carbonate of potash, but dissolve in pure potash. The moderate acids dissolve in ammonia, but when the solution is boiled the ammonia is completely evolved, accompanied by the precipitation of the resin. Lastly, the strong acids can be boiled in their ammoniacal solutions without being precipitated, and upon evaporation remain as acid compounds.

ON CASTOR.

BY E. WEBER AND C. G. LEHMANN.

Accurate anatomical observations have induced E. Weber to draw the following important results concerning the nature and origin of Castor:

1. Castor is the accumulated exudation of the prepuce of the penis and clitoris, which prepuce has two sack-like dilatations, called castor-bags.
2. Castor is not derived from glands, but from the exudation of the skin of the prepuce, which is highly vascular.
3. Castor contains also the accumulated particles of the cel-

lules of the prepuce, which continually fall off, and are renewed in succession.

4. Its pungent smell is derived from small fatty globules, originally existing in the elementary cellules, of which the upper skin is formed, and sometimes penetrate through the envelopes of the dehiscent cellules of the upper skin, and form themselves into larger globules.

5. Since the prepuce, and its appendages, come in contact with urine, it is probable that those calcareous substances which I have found in the castor-bags of a recently-killed castor, are sediments of the urine.

5. Canadian-dried castor-bags, when moistened, present a formation similar to that of the Russian bag, and that of the castor found in Germany, but contain also a greater quantity of calcareous masses, which, when dry, are similar to resinous matter, the smell of which is not only weaker, but even different to that of the Russian castor.

Lehmann investigated, comparatively, castor and the exudation (*smegma*) of the præputium of horses and men, and found that castor was nothing else but an exudation of the prepuce, differing in odor from that of other animals, only on account of the difference of the peculiar food of the castor.

Lehmann examined, at first, fresh German castor, by means of the microscope, and observed, in its soft mass, three kinds of crystals, which appeared more clear in the residuum of the mass which was previously treated with ether and alcohol. The crystals, which occurred less frequent, were those of the twinform sulphate of lime; a fact proved also by the measurement of the angles, and by chemical analysis.

The numerous prismatic crystals appeared to be formed o f carbonate of lime, which proves that the carbonate of lime which is found in the ashes of castor, occurs ready formed in the same; a fact which explains the effervescence which takes place if castor is treated with acids; the third class of crystals, consisted of oxalite of lime, presenting square pyramids. No uric acid could be detected therein.

Lehmann afterwards took fresh German, Russian and Canadian castor, all three previously dried in vacuo, and treated them first with ether, afterwards with alcohol, water and diluted acetic acid, and obtained the following results:

		German.	Russian.	Canadian.	
Extract with Ether............		7.4	2.5	8.249	pr. c.
" Alcohol..........		67.7	64.3	41.340	"
" Water...........		2.6	1.9	4.795	"
" Diluted Acetic Acid,	carbonate of lime,	14.2	18.5	21.365	"
	albuminous substance,	2.6	3.4	5.841	"
Epithelium and pellicles........		5.7	9.4	18.510	"

Cholesterin, in rhomboid scales, was separated from the ethereal extract of German castor. This ethereal extract, treated with water, gave, with sulphuric acid and sugar, (Pettenkoffer's test for bile) a beautiful purple color; that of the Russian gave, also, a recation of bile; however, that of the Canadian afforded only a cherry color. This reaction could not be produced by treating the alcoholic extract with water; hence castor is similar to dry human fæces; mineral and organic acids produce in this extract considerable opacity. Neither in the Russian nor the Canadian castor could be observed those crystals, which were detected in the German; however, by chemical analysis, the presence of the same combinations of lime could be detected.

By adding muriatic acid to watery solutions of ethereal extracts of Canadian castor, crystals were deposited, which, under the microscope had all the appearance of phosphates of magnesia. Heated in a glass tube, they emitted a faint smell of hydrocyanic acid; in the cooler parts of which were deposited some drops of oily substance, and a white sublimate with an acid reaction, the nature of which could not be perfectly ascertained (perhaps hippuric or benzoic acid.)

The existence of albuminous matter in the solution of the acetic extract of the fresh German castor, was proved by ferrocyanuret of potash; and, in the Canadian, by concentrated nitric and muriatic acids. Carbolic acid, which Woehler discovered in the ethereal oil of castoreum, could not be detected, either by muriatic acid, (according to Runge,) or by nitric acid, (according to Laurent.)

This analysis harmonises with those which have been made before of the different kinds of castor. The reason why the German castor contains less particles of skin than the Russian and Canadian is, because only the interior soft mass of the German is employed, whilst the whole bag of the Russian and Canadian bag is subject to analysis. The difference in the organic elements depends not only on the age and season, but chiefly on the difference of food; the Canadian castors feed upon different kinds of pines, the Russian on birch, and the German on willows; this explains fully the difference in the less or greater amount of resins and salts found in the different kind of castor.

Lehmann afterwards subjected to experiments, the preputial exhudation of horses and men, dried in vacuo, with the following result:

SMEGMA PRÆPUTII.

	Horse.	Man.
Extract with Ether	49.9	52.8 pr. c.
" Alcohol	9.6	7.4 "
" Water	5.4	6.1 "
" Dil. Acet. Acid, salts	5.4	9.7 "
" Dil. Acet. Acid, albuminous substance,	2.9	5.6 "
Insoluble	26.8	18.5 "

The ethereal extracts were much similar, containing saponifiable fats, cholesterin, and a fat which was neither capable of saponification or crystallization; that of the man was sweetly pungent; none had the smell of castor. The aqueous solution of the ethereal extract gave the reactions of bile, which did not occur in the alcoholic extract. By adding an acid to the alcoholic solution of the smegma of the horse, a pulpy unctuous mass was obtained, composed of Benzoic acid and fats. The alcoholic solution of human smegma, reacted acid; and, by addition of an acid, deposited only a few flocculi, consisting probably of phosphoric acid salts. In the watery extract, and in the residuum, were found the same salts which were observed in castor, except that in human smegma some uric acid was detected. Acetic acid detected also, in both, the same albuminous substance which is found in castor; however, pure albumen or casein could not be detected.

The analysis of both smegmas, and their comparison with those of the different species of castor, offer a great analogy, particularly in the following points:

1. They all observe, in their solutions, the reactions peculiar to most of the constituents of bile. 2. They contain a saponifiable fat. 3. An unsaponifiable fat, soluble; or, at least, easily divisible in water (castorin.) 4. A fatty acid, or resinous acids combined with alkali, the acids of which are replaced by stronger ones. 5. Albuminous matter derived from the envelopes of the globules of fat dissolved by acetic acid. 6. Some elements which are only found in excreta; hippuric, benzoic, and uric acids, oxalate, carbonate, and phosphate of lime and magnesia. 7. Fragments of epithelium, which are always found in the glands of the upper skin.

The food peculiar to the castor, namely, the resinous barks of the pine tree and birch, accounts for its smegma containing more resinous elements, and that of the horse and man more fatty matters; and the occurrence of carbolic acid is owing to the decomposition of resins, of salicylic acid, and the salicylate of ammonia. By dry distillation, carbonate and oxalate of lime are more abundant in the excreta of herbivorous animals; on the other hand, the smegma of man contains more earthy phosphates. The difference in the nourishment accounts, likewise for the occurrence of hippuric and uric acids.

[The strongly marked resemblance between the odor of castor and that of carbolic acid has been lately noticed; and it has been suggested to determine the fact by chemical analysis as well as by the use of carbolic acid internally as a substitute for castor; it would be an interesting matter to find an acid the usual result of destructive distillation a natural product of the living organism; an analogous resemblance in odors has also often forced itself upon us, namely, between the odor of the human semen and hypoclorite of lime (bleaching powder), the existence of this acid has not been as yet looked for in that fluid; and the resemblance is not even noticed by Lehmann.]—Ed.

ON A QUICK APPROXIMITIVE METHOD OF ESTIMATING MINUTE QUANTITIES OF IODINE.

BY THORNTON J. HERAPATH.

The estimation of minute quantities of Iodine is not always accomplished without difficulty. I have, however, recently discovered a simple means of effecting this object, which I think is worthy of being generally known. The method in question is based on the mode of analysing silver coin proposed by Gay Lussac, and on that employed by Mr. Horsford for the determination of lead in potable waters; modifications of which processes have been successfully applied to the quantitative estimation of many other substances. It is the method of graduated solutions. The reagent I use is a salt of palladium, which, as is well known, produces in solution of iodine and the soluble iodides a brown or brownish-black precipitate of iodide of palladium. When, however, the quantity of iodine is small, the iodide instead of being immediately precipitated, remains suspended in the solution, to which it communicates a brownish tinge, more or less deep, according to the proportion of iodide present. Consequently, then, by by ascertaining the depth of tint of such a solution by comparing it with that of standard solutions properly prepared with known quantities of iodine, the proportion of the latter substance that is contained in the matters tested may be ascertained with the greatest exactness.

In an investigation of this kind, therefore, the first thing to be done is to prepare certain standard solutions. 1.309 grain of perfectly pure iodide of potassium—which is equivalent to one grain of iodine—is accordingly dissolved in 10,000 grains of water. This constitutes solution No. 1, and contains a little less than 0.1 gr. per cent. of iodine. By diluting this with water, other solutions—Nos. 2, 3, 4, 5, 6, &c.—are formed. The iodine in the substance to be tested having been converted into hydriodic acid or a soluble iodide, the latter is introduced into a colorimeter and diluted with water to the necessary degree,—that is to say, until it occupies exactly 100, 500, 1000, 10,000, or more water grain measures; the precaution being taken to first add the palladium solution drop by drop until no deepening of color ensues. The tint is then compared with that of the standard solutions before mentioned, contained in tubes or vials of similar diameter, in which certain known quantities of iodine are contained in the same bulk of water. Though it might be rarely possible to identify it with either one of two solutions in the scale, there can be no difficulty in deciding between which two it should fall, or nearest to which one of two it should be placed.

These standard solutions, it should be observed, may be sealed up in glass tubes, and thus rendered available in future investigations; the only precaution necessary to be taken in such cases being to well agitate the contents of the tubes, so as to again get the precipitated iodide of palladium in suspension in the fluid. Operating in this way it is possible to estimate the 1–20,000th of a grain of iodine with the greatest readiness. It is sometimes preferable to employ but one standard solution. The proportion of iodine in the liquid analysed is then determined by measuring the volume of water that is required to lighten the tint, so as to render it identical with that of the normal solution or *vice versa.*—*Edin. Phil. Mag.*

ON THE COMPOSITION OF ESSENCE OF THYME.

BY M. A. LALLEMAND.

The separation of the proximate principles of essences presents difficulties which ordinarily arise from the want of clearness of their reactions. We are obliged to have recourse to fractioned distillation, and to turn to account their various degrees of volatility. This process, which gives good results when the mixed substances have very different boiling points, isolates them only very imperfectly in the contrary case. The essence of thyme presents an example of this : it deposits in time a small quantity of stearoptene, which constitutes half of its composition, and whose presence in such large proportion has nevertheless hitherto escaped observation.

This stearoptene, or, in brief, thymol, presents very distinct composition and properties. It is easily obtained in the crystallized state by evaporating its alcoholic solution. It occurs, in this case, under the form of transparent rhomboïdal tables. Thymol is deposited sometimes from the essence in oblique prisms with a rhombic base, with supplementary facettes on the lateral angles, corresponding to the obtuse dihedral angles. The measure of the angles indicates that the crystalline form of this body is derived from an oblique prism with a rectangular base, and belongs, consequently, to the fifth crystalline system. Thymol has a sweet odor of thyme, and a very pungent and peppery taste. It enters into fusion at 108° F., and distils without alteration at the temperature of 446° F. It may remain liquid for a very long time at the ordinary temperature ; but its solidification is again determined by throwing into it small solid fragments of the same substance. This phenomenon of superfusion is one of the causes which have prevented the presence of thymol from being recognized in the products of the distillation of essence of thyme. It is very soluble in alcohol and ether, and very sparingly so in water, which, moreover, does not precipitate it from its alcoholic solution. It does not possess any rotatory power ; but in the solid state it acts on polarised light in the manner of birefringent media, which is a consequence of its crystalline form in this state. Its chemical formula, deduced from five concordant analysis and referred to four volumes of vapor, is $C^{20} H^{14} O^2$. It differs from that of the camphor of the *Laurinaceæ* only by two equivalents of hydrogen less.

Considered in a chemical point of view, thymol is neutral to litmus paper; it, however, combines with caustic soda and potassa. It dissolves at a moderate temperature in concentrated sulphuric acid. By cooling, the mixture assumes the form of a crystalline mass, very soluble in water. The solution, saturated with carbonate of lead or baryta, gives, by evaporation, saline crusts, which crystallize in absolute alcohol. By means of one of these two salts, we easily obtain all the other sulphothymates, and sulphothymic acid itself. They have the formula $C^{20} (H^{13} S^2 O^5) O^2$, MO; that is to say, that sulphothymic acid, like all the analogous vinic acids, results from the combination of one equivalent of thymol, with two equivalents of anhydrous sulphuric acid.

Chlorine powerfully attacks thymol in diffused light. Hydrochloric acid is abundantly disengaged, and when the reaction is over, a yellowish viscid liquid, of a very persistant camphory odor, which is represented by $C^{20} H^8 Cl^6 O^2$, is obtained.

Nitric acid also exerts a very vivid action on thymol, and resinifies it. By prolonging the oxidation until the resinous matter has almost completely disappeared, an abundant deposit of crystallized oxalic acid is formed.

The property which this stearoptene possesses of combining with caustic soda and potassa, enables us to detect its presence in essence of thyme, and to isolate it from the other principles of which it is composed. M. Doveri has ascertained that this essence furnishes, by distillation, two liquids, one of which enters into ebullition between 347° and 356° F., and the other between 437° and 455° F. The latter is almost entirely composed of thymol. It is sufficient, indeed, to throw into it a few solid pieces of this substance for the liquid to form a mass in a few days. The portion of the essence which distils between 365° and 437° F., contains more than a third of its weight of it. It is extracted by agitating the product with a concentrated solution of caustic soda. The stearoptene is dissolved, and, after having decanted the supernatant oil, the combination is diluted with water, and saturated with hydrochloric acid ; the liquid thymol which is separated soon congeals.

The most volatile portion of the essence contains also a considerable proportion of thymol, which is extracted from it in the same manner. However, the purification is complete only after it has been distilled several times over caustic potassa. A colorless hydrocarbon is collected of an agreeable odor of thyme, which enters into ebullition at 329° F.

Thymene is an isomer of essence of turpentine. It has the same vapor-density, and combines with hydrochloric acid, giving rise to a liquid camphor which possesses a composition identical with that of solid hydrochlorate of camphene. Thymene, as well as its combination, does not possess the rotatory power, at least after purification.

It may, therefore, be concluded from the researches which I have just described, that essence of thyme is in great part formed of two principles; thymene, a hydrocarburet isomeric with essence of turpentine, and thymol, which may be supposed to be derived by substitution from the former. Admitting, indeed, that thymene fixes four equivalents of oxygen, and that two equivalents of water are eliminated, we have:

$$C^{20} H^{16} + O^{4} = C^{20} H^{14} O^{2} + 2HO.$$

Whence we comprehend in the same molecular type the following bodies:

$C^{20} H^{16}$, thymene;
$C^{20} (H^{14} O^{2})$, thymol;
$C^{20} (H^{8} Cl^{6} O^{2})$, chloruretted thymol;
$C^{20} [H^{13} (S^{2} O^{5}) O^{2}]$. anhydrous sulpho-thymic acid.

The formula of the liquid oxygenous principle of essence of carraway, corrected by M. Gerhardt, is identical with that of thymol. The latter would, therefore, be an isomer of carvacrol.—*Comptes Rendus*, September 26th, 1853.

PREPARATION OF URIC ACID FROM THE EXCREMENTS OF PIGEONS.

BY A. E. ARPPE.

In a capacious copper boiler, 10 ounces of borax were dissolved in 70 pounds of water. Into this solution two linen bags, each containing 3½ pounds of the dried excrements of pigeons, were introduced, and boiled one hour, and stirred; after which, the bags were removed and allowed to drain In the boiling borax solution half a pound of sal-ammoniac was dissolved, the vessel then removed from the fire, and allowed to cool. After twelve hours, a considerable greyish white precipitate of urate of ammonia was deposited at the bottom of the vessel. The above clear, strongly brown colored fluid was removed with a syphon, fresh water poured on, and this operation repeated until the liquid had become quite colorless. The precipitate was then again boiled with a weak solution of borax, by which a large quantity of a slimy mass remained undissolved. The solution, which can now be filtered through paper and is colored slightly brown, is warmed and poured into a warm mixture, consisting of half an ounce of sulphuric acid, with one ounce of water. After cooling, the uric acid separates in the crystalline form. It is colored light brown, and is purified by solution in potash, evaporation of the liquid, and a repetition of this operation, and, lastly, by decomposition with sulphuric acid. I have in this way obtained ⅛ per cent. of quite snow white uric acid from the excrements of pigeons, and believe the modifications here described in the mode of the preparation of this important acid to be practically valuable, as opportunity is very seldom afforded to procure it from the more abundant excrements of serpents.—*Liebig's Annalen.*

CAMPHOR FROM SASSAFRAS OIL.

BY FALTIN.

In some experiments which were instituted, to observe the action of chlorine on sassafras oil, the author found that under the formation of hydrochloric acid this oil was thereby converted into a thick tenacious mass, which, after being neutralized with milk of lime, afforded, by distillation, a small quantity of camphor, identical in properties and composition with the ordinary camphor. He could not obtain it from the oil without the action of chlorine. It probably results from a non-oxygenated oil contained in the sassafras oil. This observation possesses some interest, because the sassafras tree belongs to the lauraceæ, and to the same family as the camphor tree.—*Liebig's Annalen.*

THE PREPARATION OF VALERIANIC ACID.

H. Gruneberg has tried the various methods proposed for making valerianic acid from fusel oil, and has found that when the ingredients are employed in the proportions indicated by him, a larger quantity of this acid is obtained than by any of the formulæ already published. He pours $4\frac{1}{2}$ lbs. of hot water on $2\frac{3}{4}$ lbs. of chromate of potash, in a retort, then adds in a thin stream a cold mixture, consisting of 1 lb. of fusel oil, 4 lbs. of sulphuric acid, and 2 lbs. of water. He distils the whole once gently, and obtains 9 ounces of oleaginous valerianic acid.—*Journal fur Prakticke Chemie.*

Varieties.

VARIETY IN THE MILK OF VARIOUS ANIMALS.

Woman's Milk is, in general, of a more bluish white color than that of the cow or any other animal, and is likewise sweeter in flavor. It has a strongly alkaline reaction, and turns acid less readily than other kinds of milk. Its specific gravity varies between 1.030 and 1.034, and it contains from 11 to 13 $\frac{0}{0}$ of solid constituents, amongst which there is on an average 3.5 of casein, and 4 to 6 of sugar o milk. The casein in woman's milk is less readily and completely precipitated by acids and by reunits, according to the concurring testimony of Simon and Clemm. The coagulum is also, in general, somewhat gelatinous, and not so dense or solid as that of cow's milk, and, therefore, more easily digested by the child's stomach. The butter of woman's milk is supposed to be richer in olein than that of cow's milk.

Cow's Milk is, in general, of a pure or somewhat yellowish white color; its specific gravity varies, according to Simon, between 1.030 and 1.035, and, according to Schurer, between 1.026 and 1.032, and contains, on an average, 14. of solid constituents, varying between 12.9 and 16.5; it contains more casein than woman's milk, and somewhat more butter, but less sugar of milk, and far more salts, although this increase principally affects the insoluble salts belonging to the casein, with whose augmentation they are likewise increased.

Mare's Milk is white, tolerably thick, with a specific gravity varying from 1.034 to 1.045 (according to Clemm it is 1.0203); it contains 16.2 of solid residue, a small portion of casein (.1.7), but a large amount of fat (6.95), and a considerable quantity of sugar of milk (8.75).

Asses' Milk, which is of a white color, and sweeter than cow's milk, has a specific gravity which fluctuates between 1.023 and 1.035; it contains from 9.16 to 9.53 of solid matters, of which from 1.6 to 1.9 is casein, from 12.1 to 12.9 butter, and from 6.8 to 6.29 of sugar of milk. It is, therefore, far poorer in casein and butter than cow's milk, but richer in sugar of milk. This milk, likewise, very readily becomes acid, and easily passes into vinous fermentation.

Goat's Milk is white, of a faintly sweetish taste, and a peculiar odor; its specific gravity is generally about 1.036; it contains from 13.2 to 14.5 of solid constituents, of which from 4.02 to 6.03 are casein, from 33.2 to 42.5 butter, and from 4.0 to 5.3 sugar of milk. It is, therefore, poorer in casein than cow's milk. It contains nearly the same, or, perhaps, a somewhat larger quantity of fat, and much more sugar of milk. When coagulated, the casein forms a dense mass.

Sheep's Milk is thickish, white, and of an agreeable odor and taste; its specific gravity varies between 1.035 and 1.041; it contains 14.38, amongst which 4.02 are casein, 4.20 butter, 5.0 sugar of milk, and 0.68 salts. It appears from the single analysis instituted by Chevalier and Henry to contain somewhat less casein and butter, and more sugar of milk, than cow's milk.—***Lehman*, *Physiol. Chem.***

Hot-Air Vessel.—The Ericsson vessel is again afloat. According to newspaper accounts, "the old cylinders have been removed with the pistons, furnaces, and regenerators which accompanied them. In place of the former—which were four in number, and of great size, placed perpendicular to the axis of the vessel—two other cylinders of less size are substituted in the direction of the keel, making with it an angle of forty deg., and more inclined toward each other; four auxiliary cylinders are placed at the sides of the principal cylinders, two on each side. The actual apparatus thus consists of six cylinders, in two of which the pistons will work, and the four auxiliary. The motor cylinders have each a width of six feet; eight feet to travel; these two cylinders, having a double action, are considered as being capable of doing as much work as the four large single acting cylinders of the former apparatus, as they will work at high pressure. Besides, in the new apparatus, the same air will be employed indefinitely, and will be condensed previously. Small cylinders and condensed air constitute the difference in the machinery of this vessel from that used in its former trials. The regenerator is also new—only in form—being intended to act similarly to the original one. This part of the apparatus, which Mr. E. thinks most about, is just that which the best engineers deem as useless. We are destined again to behold another trip of seventy-one hours to Norfolk, and to have the city press declare that the age of steam has passed away, and that of hot-air reigns. We perceive the French papers express regret at hearing of Mr. E.'s death before his machine was put in successful operation. We hope his life will be spared, though not to the extent wished by his Gallic friends, as it is unpleasant to outlive one's own offspring.

Etherizing Congress.—We see it stated in some of our cotemporaries that Dr. Morton, of Boston, is now in Washington, hard at work to get friends and favor among the members of Congress, in order that he may obtain an appropriation from Congress for the discovery of etherization in surgical operations.

On the 19th of February, 1853, Mr. Walker, Chairman of a Select Committee appointed by the Senate, to whom were referred certain memorials in regard to the discovery of the means for rendering the human body insensible to pain during surgical operations, reported in favor of granting $100,000 to Dr. Morton. A Select Committee of the House of Representatives, of which Dr. Bissell, of Ill., was Chairman, presented a majority report in favor of Dr. Morton's claims, while an able minority report, by Edward Stanley, of North Carolina, and Alexander Evans, of Maryland, awarded the credit of the discovery to Dr. Jackson, of Boston.

In reviewing the claims of both applicants, we took occasion to express our views upon the injustice done to Dr. Wells, of Connecticut, now deceased, who had performed a surgical operation upon one person at least, when under the influence of ether, two years before Dr. Morton obtained a patent. Congress did not grant any appropriation for etherization, because the claims of the applicants were altogether too conflicting. We hope that no appropriation will ever be made for any such purpose until the whole matter is sifted to the very foundation.

In the reports of the Committees of both Senate and House of Representatives, evidence is presented which proves that neither Dr. Jackson, Dr. Morton, nor Dr. Wells were the discoverers of "etherization"—that is, neither of these gentlemen originated the suggestion of rendering persons insensible to pain during surgical operations, by a gas or drug--or even the first to employ such means in surgical operations. On the sixth page of Senator Walker's report, it is stated that the Chinese surgeons used a preparation of hemp (haschisch) centuries ago, for rendering their patients insensible to pain during severe operations. On the eighth page it is also stated that in the thirteenth century, a liquid made by boiling opium, unripe mulberry, hemlock, mandragora, wood ivy, lettuce, and burdock, in water, was used by some surgeons for rendering patients insensible to pain, by applying it to the nostrils with a sponge, as chloroform is now applied. In 1832 experiments, which were but a revival of the old plans, were made in France, and M. Dauriol specifies five cases in which he performed painless operations. Sir Humphrey Davy employed nitrous oxyd gas to relieve pain, and suggested its use in surgery. On pages four, five, six, and seven of the report of Dr. Bissel, of the House Committee, a number of cases are cited of the employment of anesthetic agents in olden and modern times, before Drs. Jackson and Morton applied for a patent. These facts show that etherization was not a new idea, but the use of a particular agent—*sulphuric ether*--as a superior anodyne, perhaps was. The whole claims, therefore, of either Drs. Jackson or Morton must rest upon the agent first employed by them, namely, sulphuric ether. The use of chloroform, therefore, is a different discovery, and the person who first applied it to surgical purposes has as good claims to be considered a public benefactor as the first person who used sulphuric ether.—*Scientific American.*

ACCLIMATION OF THE DEODAR.—In England they are trying an experiment on a large scale worthy of notice. At the instigation of the Government, the East India Company have brought home one ton of the Seeds of the Deodar, which were gathered on the Himalaya Mountains, and which are intended to plant on the hills and ground of the unproductive land of Great Britain. The deodar is the cedar of the Himalaya's. The horticulturists are well acquainted with it, but up to the present time it has been used as an ornament of the garden merely. The rare elegance of this noble tree is appreciated by every one; it attains a height of sixty-five yards, to two or three yards in diameter. The wood is very hard, and almost incorruptible, as the monuments of traditionally many ages old have not been in the least degree injured by time; it resists the action of water to an almost indefinite time. When the English shall have replenished their ancient forests with this magnificent tree, she will have gained immense assistance to her maritime interests. It is supposed that the seeds brought by the East India Company will germinate and produce six million trees.

ARTIFICIAL WOOD.—MM. Barthe and Potin, of Paris, have invented a new process for making artificial wood, by the aid of which products are obtained whose beauty is superior and so like the natural substances as to deceive many. The many varieties of native woods which these inventors make are all composed of gelatine and sawdust, which are worked together and solidified by means of a peculiar process of tanning. This product being brought into a pasty mass can receive all kinds of stamp and variety of form. These stamped articles are on view in Paris, and the eye can scarcely distinguish them from fine specimens of carving in wood.

Cotton Tree.—A writer in the *Flag of our Union*, Jackson, Miss., gives the following account of the cotton tree growing in Navigator's Island, and of the island in general:

" The tree was about thirty feet high, its body about a foot in diameter, and the breadth of spreading of the limbs making a very bushy top of, perhaps, thirty feet in diameter; the bolls before bursting are very much the shape of the cotton bolls raised in the United States, but probably near the size of a goose egg. In *each* boll there are *three* of the pieces I here enclose. When the cotton is in bloom, my friend informs me, it presents a most magnificent appearance, and seems as if it was a mammoth *snow-ball tree*, seen in the gardens in the United States. The staple of fibre of the cotton seems to be a good length; whether it is of that silky fineness desirable in such an article, I cannot pretend to judge. It occurs to me that it might by possibility be of some use to the people of the South to have some of the seed with the cotton attached. The tree on the island grows wild and luxuriantly. There will be not only a constant but increasing trade between this port and Australia, and the Navigator's Island is almost on the direct route, and, if not already, will soon be made a general calling-place between the two places. From here to the Sandwich Islands—nearly a direct calling-place--is one-third, and the Navigator is another third of the distance between here and Australia. These islands, nine or ten in number, of pretty good size, and many smaller, are exceedingly valuable, and lie in about 14 deg. south latitude, and longitude about 171 deg. west of Greenwich, and belong to no nation--have a sort of patriarchal government by chiefs of different grades, mostly maintaining separate organizations, and are often at war. They are not *cannibals*.

These islands are going to be of great importance, as they lie on the route between the two great gold continents, and it does seem that they ought not to fall into the hands of any European nation. They probably contain 100,000 inhabitants; and yet if one or two hundred discreet, just men were there, and join in, in some of their wars, with the better sort or class, a government might be easily established there, after the fashion of the Sandwich Islands. These islands have some good harbors, and at present furnish a pecuniary prospect for a few energetic capitalists, that would pay enormously. The inhabitants live almost entirely on the fruits and vegetables that grow wild and spontaneously. The climate is not colder than 75 deg., nor hotter than 81 or 82 deg.; and as to health, no country on earth more so."

Fertility of Nile Mud.--The celebrated microscopic philosopher, Ehrenberg, has examined this mud, and finds its great fertility to be owing, not so much to any peculiar mineral contribution, or to the presence of vegetable matter, as it is to the vast accumulation of extremely minute forms of microscopic animals, which, by their decomposition, enrich the soil.

This may be true so far, but to a parched soil the addition of so much *moist* earth must be a great cause of its fertility.

M. Berthelot presented to the *Academy of Sciences*, in December, 1853, some remarks upon ethers formed from acids and ordinary ether. A curious result of these researches is, that it is possible at once to transform alcohol into an ether of a given character, and reproduce alcohol from any given ether.

At a December meeting of the London Society of Arts, &c., before the reading of the papers, the Secretary called attention to a number of specimens which had been received from the Imperial Printing Office at Vienna, produced by the process known in Germany as "Naturselbstdruck," and in this country as Phytoglyphy, or the art of printing from nature. These specimens included every variety--botanical, geological, entomological, fossil and fabrics. In 1851, Dr. Ferguson Branson communicated to the Society, "An Account of a Method of Engraving Plates from Natural Objects," which was read on the 26th of March in that year. Dr. Branson only contemplated the application of the process to fern leaves, seaweeds, and other flat plants. The method he adopted was to impress the object itself into gutta percha, or other soft material, and then to obtain an electrotype from the mould. The novelty in the present process consisted in the use of lead for receiving the impression, in place of gutta percha; and also for applying to the polished surfaces of minerals a weak acid, which acted with different degrees of intensity on the materials of which the mineral was composed, and so caused a greater or less indentation. The moulds from the fossils were taken in liquid gutta percha. Specimens were also exhibited by Messrs. Bradbury and Evans, who are working the process in this country. Samples were exhibited from Dr. Forbes Royle of cultivated Rhea fibre from Assam, produced by ***Boehmeria Hivea***, which was the plant which yields the Chinese grass, of which the fine grass cloth is made; also of the wild Rhea fibre. The Anglo-Franco-Algerian Vegetable Fibre Company also exhibited some samples of jute, palm, and ditz fibres in various stages of manufacture, prepared by Claussen's process.

French Prizes.—M. Briant left by will, dated August, 1849, several sums, which the Academy have been legalized to receive. Amongst these is 100,000f. to be given to the inventor of a specific remedy for cholera. The testator believes it arises from putrid miasms. As it may be long before the invention appear, the Academy is authorized to apply the interest (4,500f. to 5,000f.) for the best original researches on cholera. If such a remedial or preventive agent cannot be found, the principal is to be appropriated to a similar object, in respect to the disease known as *dartre*.

The import of sperm and whale oil into the United States, during 1853, was 103,077 barrels, and for 1852, 79,950 barrels. Of whale oil, the import in 1853 was 260,114 barrels, and in 1852, 83,775--showing aggregate increase in the import of sperm and whale oil, for the past year, of 119,466 barrels, or more than the entire import of 1852.

In order to promote the culture of tobacco in Connecticut, a company has been formed in Hartford, with a capital of $25,000, for the purpose of opening a tobacco inspection warehouse in that city, to be governed by a large board of directors, president, &c., representing the various tobacco growing districts. The capital invested is to be used to buy or advance on crops in growth, and the company is to provide suitable warehouses in which to pack, import, and store the crops that may be consigned to them, to keep the same insured, and hold till fully cured; then to sell, and pay over the nett receipts to the owners.—*Scientific American.*

M. Schesing presented researches upon the presence and quantity of nitric acid in plants, and especially in tobacco. The watery and alcoholic extracts of the plants are treated with a mixture of hydrochloric acid and protochloride of iron. Binoxide of azote is disengaged, which is collected over mercury. This binoxide is changed into nitric acid, and then determined by the method of M. Peligot. This process of analysis permits us to discover traces of acid which had escaped chemical research until now. It is found that the *nerves* of leafs are very rich in nitrates, much more than cellular tissue. The leaf gathered in the Department du Nord furnished 0.015 of nitric acid, and the nerves, 0.05. Tobacco of Algiers yielded 0.01; tobacco from the colonies, 0.06; Maryland tobacco, 0.05 of combined nitric acid. It is very easy to explain the deflagration of the ribs of the tobacco leaves so rich in nitrates. Other plants contain also a considerable amount of nitrates. M. Dubrunfaut has found them in the beet-root, and they have long since been remarked in the borage and parsnip plants.

M. Bertsch exhibited to the French Society for Encouragement, in October, 1853, photo-microscopic views, very beautiful and highly magnified, of the filaments of wool, cotton, and flax-cotton. These views are of value, inasmuch as they show that flax and hemp present their proper texture even after being Claussenized. The wool and cotton fibres can also be as readily distinguished as well after as before the process.

M. Jacquelain read a communication to the same society on the economic manufacture of bichromate of potass, for which he has obtained a patent. The processes of manufacture are:

1. To carry to a red heat the chrome mineral, and then quench it in cold water. This process to be repeated until the ore is in fragments.

2. Then to stamp the fragments with cast-iron rollers, or in a mill, and, finally with mill stones under water.

3. To make this powder into a suitable paste with forty-four per cent. of carbonate of potash in an iron boiler, to mix in ninety per cent. of chalk, and dry the mixture thoroughly.

4. Introduce this first into earthen retorts, having on their belly an iron head, with openings to admit heated air to oxidize the chrome ore, the beak of the retort being in connection with a draught or chimney, so as to regulate the current and throw it upon the surface of the pit, so as to evaporate the water.

5. After this roasting, to bruise the mass and treat it with five successive additions of boiling water, to extract all the chromate of potass. If the liquor contains chromate of lime, this salt may be decomposed by the addition of a little carbonate of potass.

6. Concentrate the solution of chromate, and treat it with sulphuric acid in the usual way to manufacture bichromate. By this process, Jacquelain estimates tha 1,000 lbs. of bichromate may be manufactured every day.

REVIEW OF THE NEW YORK DRUG MARKET.

COMPILED FROM BROKERS' SALES.

Business with the trade has been rather dull, even for this season of the year.

The following report comprises sales from the 15th January to the 10th February. In the subsequent issues they will be made up to the 15th of each month.

Manna, 150 cases; 20 bales Nutgalls; 10 rolls Ceylon, and 15 ditto Java Cinnamon, expt.; 10 casks Flor Sulphur; 100 ditto Virgin Scammony; 15 bales Levant Wormseed; 100 tins Tolu; 10 bales Mex. Sarza, expt.; 500 flasks Quicksilver; 25 pgs. Resin Guaiac; 15 casks Eng. B. Lead; 200 bbls. Am. Castor Oil; 25 cases East India ditto; 10 bales Jalap; Am. Quinine, as wanted, at manufacturing prices.

Large speculative sales of Quinine, to the amount of 10,000 oz., have been made, and held at higher prices, we think, without good reason, as foreign advices are not very favorable and large stocks being in the market. Notwithstanding, Barks are very firm and advancing.

10 casks Cream Tartar; 2 or 3 cases Turkey Rhubarb; 50 qr. casks Olive Oil; 500 ditto here and to arrive; 60 tons Sal Soda; 200 cases Crude Camphor; 8,000 ditto German Yellow Prus. Potash; 2,000 Red ditto; 10 cases Oil Anise; 10 ditto Cassia; 20 cans Oil Lemon; 20 cans Bergamot; 3 cases Dragon's Blood; 10 casks Cham. Flor.; 20 cases Cantharides; 15 casks Refined Argols; 250 Cerrons Bark; 20 Cerrons Ipecac, now held higher; Bal. Copaiva mostly for expt.; 700 Demg. Angostura; 9,000 ditto. Maracaibo; 12,000 ditto. Para, and 23,000 ditto. Maranhum; none now in market except 6 or 8,000 ditto Para, and 6,000 ditto Angostura; 20 cases Opium; 2,000 boxes Castile Soap, from the ship; 200 ditto old; 22 cases Nutmegs; Cochoniel, 50 bags London sifted; Hond., 25 ditto; 100 bales Liq. Root; 45 cases Hotchkiss Oil Peppermint, in glass; 130 bales Mex. and 30 ditto Hond. Sarza, for expt.; 10 ditto Loxa Bark; 230 tins Tolu, in bond; 5 cases Large Manna; 5 ditto Small; 100 cases Calab. Liquorice; 100 bags Cubebs, beingall in market, now held higher; 12,000 ditto Tartaric Acid, crystalized; 1,000 ditto Cardamoms; 10,000 ditto Anise Seed, for expt.; 10 bags Eng. Wh. Mustard Seed; 200 cases prime East India Rhubarb, a late arrival, now held higher, with a firm market, and a prospect of an advance, all foreign ports being quite bare: 94 Cer rons Carraccas Indigo.

EDITORIAL.

M. Gandillot, *ancien eleve* of the Ecole Polytechnique, has addressed a letter to various French journals to the following purport:

"A letter lately published by the Minister of Agriculture and Commerce, to the Prefects, forbids, in breweries and retail liquor stores, the use of lead, copper or zinc pipes. Experience has shown us, the circular says, that beer may, in consequence of its contact with lead, become contaminated with an appreciable quantity of this metal, and acquire poisonous properties. It cites the example of a whole family who were poisoned by using, during only a short time, a pump fed with lead pipes, by which the wine used for ordinary consumption was drawn. This does only confirm, by one among a thousand examples, the frequent poisonings arising from fermented drinks placed in contact with lead. If, besides this, there were noticed the experiments which I havo made and communicated in the journals, in February last, upon the poisoning of water by the same means, the accident at Claremont, by which the Orleans family have suffered,—and the statements and authority of the learned chemist, Chevalier,—we must believe that *any drink* flowing through leaden pipes exposed, in a marked degree, the public health to the gravest dangers.

"To obviate this, the circular of the Minister will only allow for such usages *tin pipes* which do not contain more than sixteen per cent. of lead, or *pipes of any other inoffensive matter*. But having a consideration for the public, rather than expose them to the least danger from lead by alloying the tin with it, would it not be better to get rid of lead totally, and to employ as the conduits for liquids, materials *wholly inoffensive* as that circular hints? Now, iron, which is perfectly impermeable, added to the advantage of never communicating to liquids other than wholesome properties, ought necessarily be placed at the head of all inoffensive materials, and be adopted as piping material, not only for beer but for all drinks."

The circular of the Minister and recommendations of Gaudillot have led to the extended use of iron in Paris for this purpose. The letters published last year in the *New York Tribune*, by Dr. W. H. Ellet, on the effect of Croton water in lead pipes, and his recommendation to use tin pipes, also must be fresh in the recollection of many of our readers. While the use of lead piping certainly does lead to the introduction of lead, in a soluble form, into the water, there is no doubt that it should be discontinued, as poisoning may occasionally arise from that cause. Everywhere in New England that lead has been used to convey spring water to houses, and that the water has been examined, it has been darkened by sulphuretted hydrogen. We have repeatedly been asked to examine water in such circumstances, and always found lead, but we have never found it in quantity nearly as abundant as it exists in *soda water*, and those ærated waters which are made in leaden vessels. This we believe to be, in cities during summer, a much more frequent mode of introducing lead into the system. We are not of the opinion of Gandillot, that iron pipes are the desideratum, for they will rust inside, and the smaller pipes will clog from that source alone, especially if there be but a very slight bend so as to allow lodgment. Neither do we think with Dr. Ellett, that tin pipes are the proper substitute, for tin always bears a higher price, and in our winters, unless made very strongly, will not resist frost, and cannot be mended at all as readily as lead after rupture. All organic materials, such as caoutchouc and gutta percha, are, from their nature, inadmissible, and there is not any material at present cheaply attainable which contains all the properties required in a conduit pipe of *an inch diameter* and downwards. Glass and earthenware are objectionable, as being too brittle and containing lead, and yet we are inclined to believe that it is from the class of silicates, either baked or fused, that the future piping should be obtained. In fact, we have not that material yet presented to us; and where public health is endangered by water remaining for even a short time in a pipe, it is high time that such material should be supplied.

We have seen reported in the *London Lancet* some cases of chronic poisoning with lead treated with Iodide of Potassium. The patients recovered, or, at least, were discharged almost perfectly free from colic or paralysis. The urine was examined frequently, and while the iodine was detected in each experiment, there were not found any traces of lead. In these cases, then, it is evident either that lead is not deposited in the tissues, and is not the nidus of the chronic ailment, or that Melsens' explanation of the action of the iodide is erroneous—namely, that iodide of lead is first formed, and this dissolves in an excess of the iodide of potassium, forming a soluble double iodide, which is removed by the kidneys.

While noticing the subject of poisons, we perceive that a bill, regulating the sale of poisonous drugs in this State, has been introduced before the Legislature at Albany.

M. Elie de Beaumont, the celebrated Geologist, has been installed as perpetual Secretary to the *Academie des Sciences*, in the place of the deceased Arago.

We have again to fall back upon the kindness of our subscribers in not bringing out this number in time. It shall, however, be the last delay—the March issue will be in good time.

REVIEWS.

The Medical Formulary. By Benjamin Ellis, M. D., 10th edition, by Robert P. Thomas, M. D. Philadelphia, 1854, pp. 296.

The appearance of a new edition of this work, which, although, as its title imports, and its contents corroborate, is intended rather for the young medical practitioner than the pharmaceutist, is nevertheless often required to be referred to by the latter, demands from us some notice, which shall be, however, in a general sense, rather than with regard to the comparative merits of this particular edition, which, as the title-page states, is "revised and enlarged to 1854,"—enlarged by some 20 or 30 pages, the additions being generally of a more useful and important character than the older formulæ, and the revisions, or rather alterations, in the main judicious; yet as the book now stands, are there to be discerned, not a few defects, inconsistencies, or absurdities. Many of the *formulæ*, so called, are not formulæ at all, but simply the technical name of a medicine, with the dose attached, to which is added some therapeutical observations altogether superfluous, if it may be presumed that the study of the *materia medica* occupies any of the leisure of a medical student. Thé sign R instead of the usual H attached to these *singular* formulæ would scarcely be expected in a work professing to be a medical grammar as well as formulary. "R Magnesia ʒ i," and such formulæ, and they are numerous, would be more appropriate if addressed to the patient to take this quantity than to the apothecary to dispense it. They had much better have been placed in the Posological Table—I beg pardon—the "Table of Doses." A little matter of bad taste which very much "stinks i' the nostril" are the new spellings introduced by the present editor Dr.Thomas. We know no right which the author of those innovations has to spell the word *drachm* d r a m, more than we have to spell his name "Tomas;" nor do I know what authority he has for changing the y in syrup into i, except that of the French, but they have it *sirop;* he writes it *sirup.* In the department of suppositories, the formulary is particularly *behind:* the directions for preparation are complex, the excipients improper, and *the size a dozen times too large.* Nearly all the medicinal agents which may be required to be applied "per anum," may be readily formed into suppositiories with cocoa butter, by means of simple trituration, and they should never exceed twenty grains in weight. The formulary directs them to be made of the size of half an ounce. The editor must have supposed them to be intended to act mechanically as a plug or wedge, which they do not, but are merely vehicles of astringent and other remedies. It would be tedious, and perhaps unprofitable, to note the whole, or even the quarter part of those —not exactly "spots on the sun," which catch the eye of the practical pharmaceutist, for criticisms like the above are out of place, nay, almost ungenerous, applied to a work, arising, as this did, in a semi barbarous state of scientific cultivation, when the raw student, after a very brief course of monotonous lectures, found himself vested with the authority to practice the healing art, a humble idea of the theory of which he had *perhaps* acquired in the lecture-room, but of the practical part of which he was quite innocent of any knowledge. Under such circumstances, some "Receipt Book," to teach young Æsculapius to prescribe, or rather to supply him with a prescription to suit his case as near as might be, in the absence of his ability to compose one, was neeessary; and it was also necessary to make such a book as plain as possible, *so as to be intelligent to the humblest capacity,* a rule which is very much "cracked up," even in the present advanced state of knowledge; but when it begins to be *presumed* that the physician has, or, at least, it is admitted that he ought to have some pretension to scholarship and practical professional training, and that useful animal, the apothecary becomes every day more abundant and more competent, such a work as this will either cease to be required, or one of a higher tone and more comprehensive design will become necessary, which will be not so much a mere model, as it will be of a cyclopedic character, not furnishing only a few rude specimens to guide the negligent student, but being a collection, complete as possible, of the most valuable formulæ of the most universally renowned physicians, to serve as a "*dernier resort*" for the sometimes puzzled but educated practitioner. "So much for Buckingham!" Let us make a suggestion. There is no work scarcely which would have a wider circulation, especially among apothecaries, than an "Annual Formulary," giving a yearly account of the various remedies, "good, bad, and indifferent," which the vanity of the little or the condescension of the big may have discovered to the world. There is no such work in our language, but we hope soon to see such an one. Let some one do it.

NEW YORK

JOURNAL OF PHARMACY.

MARCH, 1854.

ON SOME OF THE ERUPTIVE PHENOMENA OF ICELAND.

BY DR. JOHN TYNDALL, F. R. S.*

The lecturer adverted to the Geisers, and proposed, as his time was limited, to confine his attention to the Great Geiser. We have here a tube ten feet wide and seventy feet deep; it expands at its summit into a basin, which from north to south measures fifty-two feet across, and in the perpendicular direction sixty feet. The interior of the tube and basin is coated with a beautiful smooth plaster, so hard as to resist the blows of a hammer. The first question that presents itself is, how was this wonderful tube constructed? How was this perfect plaster laid on? A glance at the constitution of the Geiser water will, perhaps, furnish the first surmise. In 1,000 parts of the water the following constituents are found:

Silica - - - -	0.5097
Carbonate of soda - - -	0.1939

* From the London, Edinburgh, and Dublin Philos. Magazine, August, 1853.

Carbonate of ammonia - -	0.0083
Sulphate of soda - - -	0.1070
Sulphate of potash - -	0.0475
Sulphate of magnesia - -	0.0042
Chloride of sodium - -	0.2521
Sulphate of sodium - -	0.0088
Carbonic acid - - -	0.0557

The lining of the tube is silica, evidently derived from the water, and hence the conjecture may arise that the water deposited the substance against the sides of the tube and basin. But the water deposits no sediment, even when cooled down to the freezing point. It may be bottled up and kept for years as clear as crystal, and without the slightest precipitate. A specimen brought from Iceland and analyzed in this Institution was found perfectly free from sediment. Further, an attempt to answer the question in this way would imply that we took it for granted that the shaft was made by some foreign agency, and that the spring merely lined it. A painting of the Geiser, the property of Sir Henry Holland, himself an eye-witness of these wonderful phenomena, was exhibited. The painting, from a sketch taken on the spot, might be relied on. We find here that the basin rests upon the summit of a mound; this mound is about forty feet in height, and a glance at it is sufficient to show that it has been deposited by the Geiser. But in building the mound, the spring must also have formed the tube which perforates the mound; and thus we learn that the Geiser is the architect of its own tube. If we place a quantity of the Geiser water in an evaporating basin, the following takes place: in the centre the fluid deposits nothing; but at the edges, where it is drawn up the sides of the basin by capillary attraction, and thus subjected to a quick evaporation, we find silica deposited; round the edges we find a ring of silica thus laid on, and not until the evaporation is continued for a considerable time do we find the slightest turbidity in the central portions of the water. The experiment is the microscopic representant, if the term be permitted, of nature's operations in Iceland. Imagine the case of a simple thermal spring whose waters trickle over its side down a gentle incline; the water thus exposed evaporates speedily, and silica is deposited. This deposit gradually elevates the side over which the water passes until finally the latter has to choose another course; the same takes place here, the ground becomes elevated by the deposit as before, and the spring has to go forward—thus it is compelled to travel round and round, discharging its silica and deepening the shaft in which it dwells, until, finally, in the course of centuries, the simple spring has produced that wonderful apparatus which has so long puzzled and astonished both the traveller and the philosopher.

Before an eruption, the water fills both the tube and basin, detonations are heard at intervals, and after the detonation a violent ebullition in the basin is observed; the column of water in the pipe appears to be lifted up, thus forming a conical eminence in the centre of the basin, and causing the water to flow over its rim. The detonations are evidently due to the production of steam in the subterranean depths, which rising into the cooler water of the tube, becomes condensed, and produces explosions similar to those produced on a small scale when a flask of water is heated to boiling. Between the interval of two eruptions, the temperature of the water in the tube towards the centre and bottom gradually increases. Bunsen succeeded in determining its temperature a few minutes before a great eruption took place; and these observations furnished to his clear intellect the key of the entire enigma. A little below the centre the water was within two degrees of its boiling point, that is, within two degrees of the point at which water boils under a pressure equal to that of an atmosphere, *plus the pressure of the superincumbent column of water.* The actual temperature at thirty feet above the bottom was 122° Centigrade; its boiling point here is 124°. We have just alluded to the detonations and the lifting of the Geiser column by the entrance of steam from beneath. These detonations and the accompanying elevation of the column are, as before stated, heard and observed at various intervals before an eruption. During these intervals the temperature of the water is gradually rising; let us see what *must* take place when its temperature is near the boiling point. Imagine the section of water at thirty feet above the bottom to be raised six feet by the generation of a mass of vapor below. The liquid spreads out in the basin, overflows its rim, and thus the elevated section has six feet less of water pressure upon it; its boiling point under this diminished pressure is 121°; hence in its new position, its actual temperature (122°) is a degree above the boiling point. This excess is at once applied to the generation of steam; the column is lifted higher, and its pressure further lessened; more steam is developed underneath; and thus, after a few convulsive efforts, the water is ejected with immense velocity, and we have the Geiser eruption in all its grandeur. By its contact with the atmosphere the water is cooled, falls back into the basin, sinks into the tube, through which it gradually rises again, and finally fills the basin. The detonations are heard at intervals, and ebullitions observed; but not until the temperature of the water in the tube has once more nearly attained its boiling point is the lifting of the column able to produce an eruption.

In the regularly formed tube the water nowhere quite attains the boiling point. In the canals which feed the tube the steam which causes the detonation and lifting of the column must therefore be formed. These canals are in fact nothing more than the irregular continuation of the tube itself. The tube is, therefore, the sole and sufficient cause of the eruptions. Its sufficiency was experimentally shown during the lecture. A tube of galvanized iron, six feet long, was surmounted by a basin; a fire was placed underneath, and one near its centre to imitate the lateral heating of the Geiser tube. At intervals of five or six minutes, throughout the lecture, eruptions took place; the water was discharged into the atmosphere, fell back into the basin, filled the tube, became heated again, and was discharged as before.

Sir George Mackenzie, it is well known, was the first to introduce the idea of a subterranean cavern to account for the phenomena of the Geiser. His hypothesis met with general acceptance, and was even adopted undoubtingly by some of those who accompanied Bunsen to Iceland. It is unnecessary to introduce the solid objections which might be urged against this hypothesis, for the tube being proved sufficient, the hypothetical cavern disappears with the necessity which gave it birth.

From the central portions of the Geiser tube downwards, the water has stored up an amount of heat capable, when liberated, of exerting an immense mechanical force. By an easy calculation it might be shown that the heat thus stored up could generate, under ordinary atmospheric pressure, a column of steam having a section equal to that of the tube and a height of nearly *thirteen hundred yards.* This enormous force is brought into action by the lifting of the column and the lessening of the pressure described above.

A moment's reflection will suggest to us that there must be a limit to the operations of the Geiser. When the tube has reached such an altitude that the water in the depths below, owing to the increased pressure, cannot attain its boiling point, the eruptions of necessity cease. The spring, however, continues to deposite its silica, and forms a *laug* or cistern. Some of these in Iceland are of a depth of thirty or forty feet. Their beauty is indescribable: over the surface a light vapor curls; in the depths the water is of the purest azure, and tints with its own hue the fantastic incrustations on the cistern walls, while at the bottom is observed the mouth of the once mighty Geiser. There are in Iceland traces of vast, but now extinct, Geiser operations. Mounds are observed whose shafts are filled with rubbish, the water having forced a way underneath and retired to other scenes of action. We have in fact the Geiser in its youth, manhood, old age, and death, here presented to us—in its youth, as a simple thermal spring; in its manhood, as the eruptive spring; in its old age, as the tranquil *laug*; while its death is recorded by the ruined shaft and mound which testify the fact of its once active existence.

Next to the Great Geiser the Stokkur is the most famous eruptive spring of Iceland. The depth of its tube is forty-four feet. It is not, however, cylindrical, like that of the Geiser, but funnel shaped. At the mouth it is eight feet in diameter, but it diminishes gradually, until, near the centre, the diameter is only ten inches. By casting stones and peat into the tube, and thus stopping it, eruptions can be forced which, in point of height, often exceed those of the Great Geiser. Its action was illustrated experimentally in the lecture, by stopping the galvanized iron tube, before alluded to, loosely with a cork. After some time the cork was forced up, and the pent-up heat, converting itself suddenly into steam, the water was ejected to a considerable height, thus demonstrating that in this case the tube alone is the sufficient cause of the phenomenon.

ANALYSIS OF TIN PYRITES.

BY DR. J. W. MALLET.

This rather rare mineral is one of which the chemical composition has appeared somewhat doubtful, owing to the considerable discrepancy between the three or four analysis which have been made of it, and to the fact that it almost invariably occurs massive and so intimately mixed with copper pyrites and other minerals as to render it difficult to select a fair specimen for examination. The locality from which most of the specimens in cabinets have been derived is Wheal Rock, near St. Agnes, Cornwall; but the mineral has also been observed in two or three other Cornish localities, and at Zinnwald, in Bohemia. I have recently received a specimen (name unknown) from a friend in England, which he states to have been found on St. Michael's Mount, Cornwall, and which, on examination, proves to be tin pyrites, and apparently in a purer state than any hitherto analyzed.

This specimen occurs in quartz which has obviously been

taken from a vein in granate. The structure appears to be crystalline, although no distinct planes could be observed. The color is not steel-gray, as in that of the mineral from Wheal Rock, but iron-black, with slight superficial blue and red tarnish in some places. Streak black, lustre sub-metallic, fracture uneven. Hardness = 4. Sp. gr. = 4.522. Heated before the blowpipe, on charcoal, sulphurous acid is given off, oxyd of tin deposited in large quantity upon the charcoal, and a black globule obtained, from which copper and tin may be reduced on the addition of soda.

A carefully conducted quantitative analysis, in which chlorine was used to decompose the mineral, gave the following results:

			Equivalents.	
Sulphur	29.46		1.841	8.092
Tin	26.85		.455	2.
Copper	29.18		.920	4.044
Iron	6.73	.240	.464	2.040
Zinc	7.26	.224		
Gangue	.16			
	99.64			

Thus the relative number of atoms of sulphur, tin, copper, and iron and zinc, as given in the second and third columns above, are almost exactly as 8 : 2 : 4 : 2 ; whence we have the formula first assigned by Kudernatsch (Pogg. Ann., xxxix., 146), viz., 2 (FeS+ZnS), SnS^2+2Cu^2S, SnS^2. The present analysis agrees so closely with this formula, from which the results of Kudersnatsch, and even those of Rammelsberg (Handw. d. Chem. Theils d. Mineral. 2d Suppl., 179), sensibly differ, that it seems fairly to be considered as representing the composition of the mineral in the pure state. The analysis also possesses some interest in showing the presence of zinc in considerable quantity, therein agreeing with Rammelsberg's analysis above referred to of the mineral from Zinnwald. It is to be observed that in both cases the iron and zinc occur in very nearly atomic proportions, so that, *perhaps*, the formula should be written 2FeS, SnS^2+2Zns, $SnS^2+2(2Cu^2S, SnS^2)$, though this does not seem very probable, since Kudersnatsch found 12.44 p. ct. of iron to but 1.77 of zinc, while Johnston gives 10.113 p. ct. of the latter to 4.791 of the former, as contained in tin pyrites (from the same locality as the specimen submitted to the present analysis, St. Michael's Mount). The presence of this large quantity of zinc is, however, of importance, chiefly as proving that the tin must enter into the composition of the mineral as bi-sulphuret, since the other formula which has been proposed, namely, $2SnS, FeS^2+2Cu^2S, FeS^2$, would require us to admit the presence of ZnS^2, whereas no such compound is yet known either occurring in nature or formed by artificial means. It is remarkable that Fahlerz, the only other compound sulphuret in which zinc occurs in notable quantity, is the mineral whose composition ($7[RS], SbS^3$) seems to approach most nearly to that of tin pyrites, the latter containing two instead of four atoms of the sulphur bases to one of sulphur acid, and this electro-negative sulphuret being bi-sulphuret of tin, instead of ter-sulphuret of antimony. Indeed, some real connection between these two minerals seems to be further indicated by their occurrence in the same crystalline system, and their close resemblance to each other in hardness, specific gravity, and general physical characters.

Platinizing Copper Vessels (a new mode).—One hundred parts of platinum are converted into well dried chloride of platinum, which is dissolved in water, and one hundred parts of caustic potass added to the solution. The resulting precipitate is heated with a solution of several hundred parts of oxalic acid. This solution is filtered, and three hundred parts of a solution of caustic potass is added to it. The liquid now serves us for galvano-platinizing in the usual way.—*Jewrimoff.*

ON THE CONDENSATION OF GASES AT THE SURFACE OF SOLID BODIES.

BY MM. J. JAMIN AND A. BERTRAND.*

In the various experiments intended to establish the physical theory of gases, it is implicitly supposed that their state of equilibrium is not influenced by the walls of the vessels in which they are contained; it is supposed that no attractive or repulsive force exists between solid and gaseous molecules. Nevertheless, the general principles of molecular physics do not justify our thinking that this can be the case; we have no reason to suppose that gases are deprived of a property so energetically manifested by liquids; and if it were so, we could not explain many phenomena which only require to be generalized in order to demonstrate the existence of this property.

Porous bodies present, in a very small space, a considerable amount of internal surface; the gases which penetrate into these substances lose their repulsive force, and accumulate in them as though by the influence of an extremely energetic attractive force. The phenomenon of porous bodies may be compared to that of capillarity; and just as the elevation of water in a tube may serve to show the existence of attractions between liquids and glass, the absorption of gazes by charcoal is a proof of the attraction which a solid isolated, and continuous surface may exert upon gases.

After ascertaining and measuring the absorption of gases by various porous bodies, De Saussure called the attention of chemists to an important fact, namely, that he had proved the gases condensed in charcoal produced abnormal chemical actions. Since that time Döbereiner discovered spongy platinum; these combinations, anticipated by De Saussure, became more evident; but it was seen that they were preceded by a condensation of the gases, and, in fact, were the consequence of this. They, consequently, serve to prove it.

As soon as the discovery of Döbereiner was announced, Thenard and Dulong repeated his experiments with some va-

* From the Lond., Edinb., and Dublin Philosoph. Magazine, August, 1853

riations. They ascertained that the properties of spongy platinum were possessed by porous bodies; they found them to exist in thin leaves of all the metals, and even in pounded glass or porcelain. Now, if these combinations be the consequence of condensation, it must be admitted that this condensation takes place upon the metallic leaves and on the fragments of glass.

To these various experiments we must add the leading fact announced by M. Pouillet—the absorption of oxygen in a platinum thermometer, and the condensation of the vapor of water by glass.

Moreover, this general idea, admitted by geometricians, has often constituted the study of physicists, who, not hoping to prove it directly, have sought to verify it by indirect but very precise experiments. M. Arago proposed to cause the interference of two rays of light passing through the air, the one at a certain distance from, the other in contact with, a solid surface; he has recently returned to the same question, making use of the oscillations of a magnetized needle.

There exist, therefore, indirect proofs, which, however, to us, appear conclusive, of the condensation of gases by solid surfaces; thus it was with nearly a certainty of success that we undertook the following experiments.

We filled glass vessels, which had been carefully measured, with pulverized solid substances; we ascertained the densities of the powders and the quantities contained in the vessels, and we had all the elements necessary for calculating the space left free.

Thus arranged, the vessels were connected with a good air pump, and with a manometer with two branches; one of the two branches was open to the air; it allowed the pressures to be ascertained; the other was closed, and communicated with the vessel by a tube and stop-cock; it served to measure a constant volume of gas, which was then driven into the vessel by causing the mercury to rise. At each introduction of gas the pressure increased by a quantity which was measured, and which could be calculated by Mariott's law; the results of the experiment and of calculation were compared.

In this manner we have operated upon very various substances—Fontainbleau sand, pounded glass, of different degrees of fineness, and metallic filings and oxides. We have always found that the pressure observed was less than that calculated. We have, therefore, concluded that the gases were absorbed by the solid substances.

These absorptions present great analogy with those manifested by porous bodies; they are not produced instantaneously, but continue during several hours, only attaining their limit after a period which may be prolonged at pleasure; they vary in intensity according to the nature of the gas employed, being weak with hydrogen, stronger with atmospheric air, and very considerable with carbonic acid. We shall give their measure by the following results, obtained with pounded glass, washed and dried; the free space was 590 cubic centimetres, in which a vacuum was produced, and the gas was then allowed to fill it under the atmospheric pressure. It absorbed:

Carbonic Acid.	Air.	Hydrogen.
645	602	595

We are convinced, moreover, that the preceding results are too low, and that it is impossible to measure exactly the quantities of gas contained in such spaces. When a vacuum is produced in them, the equilibrium of pressure is evidently re-established very slowly; the air-pump must be worked several hours to obtain a vacuum within 1 millimetre; and besides this, pressure does not remain constant, it gradually increases, and the action of the machine must be recommenced without ever being able to attain the maximum vacuum which it is capable of producing. The condensation obtained is the more energetic according to the goodness of the vacuum produced; but it is necessary to remember that its exact measure is never obtained.

Carbonic acid manifests these properties very energetically; when the powder with which the glass vessel is filled, whatever may be its nature, is exposed to this gas for the first time, it absorbs it rapidly, but on a second operation it has partially lost this property. The vessel already mentioned received, after evacuation, successive equal charges of this gas; the increase of pressure which they produced were measured, and by calculating the volume of the vessel by Mariott's law, there were found:

721 cub. cent. 636 cub. cent. 629 cub. cent. 627 cub. cent. 622 cub. cent.

After these experiments a vacuum of the same degree was again produced, and the same successive introductions of gas being effected, gave:

644 cub. cent. 630 cub. cent. 621 cub. cent. 620 cub. cent. 616 cub. cent.

From these results we must conclude—1. That the absorption takes place with the more energy in proportion as the original pressure is weaker. 2. That, after having once absorbed a gas, the solid substance retains a considerable portion of it, of which it cannot be deprived, and which causes a proportionable diminution in its power of condensation.

These experiments require particular care, and can only be reproduced with very accurate apparatus; we will, however, describe one which any one may repeat without difficulty, and which will exhibit our results in a conclusive manner.

A fine powder (pounded glass or oxide of zinc) is mixed in a mortar with water which has been deprived of air, so as to form a clear paste without any bubbles of gas; this is poured into a flask with a long neck until it fills two-thirds of the bulb. After a short time, the solid substance is deposited, with a layer of water above it. A vacuum is then produced in the flask; at the first stroke of the piston the water rises, increases in volume so as to fill the flask, but no bubble of air makes its appearance; and if the cock of the air-pump be suddenly opened, the pressure is reproduced, and the fluid returns to its original volume with a rapidity which shakes the flask, and a sound like that of the water hammer. If the experiment be prolonged, and the vacuum completely formed, noticeable quantities of bubbles are produced.—*Comptes Rendus*, June 6, 1853, p. 994.

ON THE TOXICOLOGY OF BICHROMATE OF POTASSA.

BY M. JAILLARD.

To many pharmaceutists and medical men this subject may probably appear of but little scientific value, because they may think that bichromate of potassa is a poison of small energy, a medicament but little used, a substance little known, and a manufacturing product but seldom formed.

We find in the "*Archives générales de Médicine*" (1834), a memoir by Ducatel, in which he tells us that a workman having attempted to poison a comrade with bichromate of potassa, was acquitted in consequence of the report of the scientific men, who pronounced that this salt had no poisonous properties. This error still continues among us; and, with the exception of a few individuals, the medical men and pharmaceutists of the present day continue of the same opinion as those mentioned by Ducatel.

To remove this opinion, and to arouse the attention of scientific men and of the authorities, we have determined on making this investigation, and thus to prove that this salt, which is daily employed by dyers and paper-stainers, very often used in medicine as a substitute for mercurial salts in the secondary stage of syphilis, and sold without hesitation to all comers by colormen, druggists, and even pharmaceutists, possesses, even in very small doses, a poisonous action, which has hitherto been but little suspected.

The study of this poison has been consequently neglected; in works on toxicology we find it but slightly mentioned. M. Orfila himself gives only a few lines to its action on the animal economy, and even those are merely a quotation of what was published by Ducatel in the "*Archives*" of 1834. Nothing is given anywhere on the symptoms of the poisoning, the anatomical lesions, the means of discovering the poison either before or after death. The toxicological history of bichromate of potassa was still to be made; we have undertaken the sketch, and shall be satisfied if we can be, if only of little use to science, of some use to humanity.

In therapeutics, bichromate of potassa is known in external use as a resolutive, and as a caustic when in concentrated solution. Cumming, in the "*Edinburgh Journal*" (1827), says that he has used it with succes for warts and syphilitic growths. Internally it is administered as an emetic in the dose of 0.04 to 0.05 gr.

It may be used in disease of the chest, and in certain spasmodic affections. Lately, it has been given in the place of mercurial salts, for the secondary symptoms of syphilis.

This antisyphilitic property was first mentioned by M. Robin, in the "*Gazette des Hôpitaux*," of the 8th November, 1850; he there explains the action of this medicament on the venereal virus. It acts, he says, exactly like the mercurial salts, combining with the virus, and forming with it an inert compound, but it has a great advantage over them in not producing salivation and the other mischievous consequences of mercurial medication.

Its principal employment is in the manufactory of printed fabrics at Rouen, Mulhausen, and Roubaix. Dyers use it to obtain colors by double decomposition, and it has of late been employed as an oxidiser in the preparation of certain vegetable colors. Finally, a great quantity is used in the manufacture of chrome yellow (chromate of lead), which is very generally in use in painting.

To determine the dose necessary to cause death, M. Jaillard tried many experiments on animals, preferably on dogs and rabbits, varying the circumstances, causing the product to act sometimes in the stomach, sometimes in the sub-cutaneous cellular tissue, and sometimes in the circulating current.

From these experiments, M. Jaillard concludes that 0.25 gr. of bichromate of potassa, introduced into the stomach of a moderate sized dog, or deposited in its cellular tissue, or injected into one of its veins, will produce death in from two to six days.

The symptoms manifested after the administration of bichromate of potassa are the following.

This salt, administered in small doses, for instance in the dose of 0.05 or 0.10 gr., is an immediate irritant to the alimentary canal. It produces vomiting, sometimes diarrhœa, loss of appetite, and diminishes the rapidity of the circulation. This last phenomenon was always observed in the individuals subjected to the above-mentioned treatment by M. Robin. When the dose is larger, all the phenomena of severe gastritis are manifested; great thirst and spontaneous vomiting, accompanied with great retching, the introduction into the stomach of even the softest drink sufficing to produce it. The matters vomited consist of mucous, bilious matters, yellowish, and sometimes sanguineous. At the same time the extremities become cold, there is dyspnœa, great anxiety, loss of appetite, numerous vomitings, then the respiration becomes stertorous, and the patient sinks into death in the most complete state of prostration.

There have been attributed to it inflammation of the conjunctiva, the formation in the bronchial system of a coagulated mucus, colored with blood, exanthematous affections, convulsions and paralysis of the limbs—phenomena which M. Jaillard has not observed.

It may be observed that bichromate of potassa always has an action on the alimentary canal, causes softening of the mucous membrane, produces redness, ecchymoses, and sometimes ulceration followed by partial gangrene on the gastro-intestinal walls. The lungs are often the seat of mischief; sometimes they exhibit splenisation and hepatisation in some parts. The blood appears to have undergone some modifications; it is black, diffluent, and but sparingly coagulated. In the nervous cerebro-rachidian system, no lesions have been found; on one occasion a slight injection of the pia-mater could be distinguished.

Bichromate of potassa is essentially an emetic, and for this reason it is an antidote for itself.

But it may happen that there are no vomitings; what then must the medical man do? Should he endeavor by every means to cause the expulsion of the matters contained in the stomach? M. Jaillard does not think so, for the bichromate of potassa introduced into the stomach, acting as a caustic from its excess of acid, should be at once neutralized, and, consequently the first step should consist in the administration of alkaline salts, so as to transform this acid salt into a neutral chromate. Then the patient should be induced to vomit, by tickling the uvula, or throat, or by administering large quantities of oil or tepid water.

It may be objected that the neutral chromate of potassa is in itself a poison; the numerous experiments which Gmelin published in the *Journal de Chimie Médicale* (1825), on the poisonous action of this salt, permit no doubt on this point; but it results also from these same experiments that the yellow chromate has a much less energetic action than the red chromate, for 0.30 gr., 0.60 and 1.50 of the first salt might be given to a dog without any consequence but retching and vomiting. Twelve grains administered to a rabbit produced no effect.

On comparing these results with those observed by M. Jaillard, it becomes evident that the bichromate of potassa is a much more powerful poison than the neutral chromate, whence the direction given above to neutralize the chromic acid in excess by an alkali or alkaline carbonate.

Bicarbonate of soda must, therefore, be prescribed, and then vomiting should be produced by the means which have been already mentioned.

In cases where bicarbonate of soda is not at hand, magnesia, or even a solution of soap, may be administered.

Study of the Processes to be Employed to prove its Presence either before or after Death.

FIRST CASE.—The individual is living, we can act on the remains of the poison.

If the substance examined in the solid state is of an orange yellow color; if, by putting a small quantity on a piece of boracic acid, and exposing it to the flame of the blow-pipe, a green color is obtained; if, dissolved in distilled water, and treated by the salts of barium, a straw-colored precipitate is produced; by the salts of bismuth, a canary yellow precipitate; by those of lead, a yellow precipitate; by the proto-salts of mercury, a brick red precipitate; by the salts of silver, a precipitate the color of venous blood; if, finally, dissolved in the presence of an alcoholized mineral acid, and treated by the alkalies or alkaline carbonates, a dirty green precipitate is obtained, we may with certainty conclude that bichromate of potassa is present.

It is supposed that the substance was unmixed; it is possible that it may be mixed with mineral acids, or with organic matters.

In the first case, it would be easy to determine the presence of chrome by following the ordinary processes of qualitative analysis; it would take too long to pass in review the manual operations which would lead to a positive result under all possible circumstances.

In the second case, the poison must be discovered by following the process which we shall give in the fourth case.

SECOND CASE.—The individual is living; all the poison has been swallowed; the matters vomited can be acted upon.

Of all poisonous substances none colors the matters vomited in so striking a manner as bichromate of potassa.

Nevertheless, the characters furnished by the coloration should not be considered as of the first value in recognizing the presence of this salt, for simple vomitings of bile might have the same aspect, and thus cause error unless we are on our guard.

If the matters vomited are both solid and liquid, they must be strained through a fine sieve, and the filtered portion must be treated as follows: it is only the liquid portion which must be thus treated.

It must be treated first by the mineral salts which give such very distinct precipitates.

But when the quantity of bichromate is small, the reactions are hidden, and this direct means only gives uncertain results.

We must, then, seek only for the chrome, which is easily done by the process which we shall give in the fourth case.

THIRD CASE.—The individual is living; all the poison has

been swallowed, and the matters vomited cannot be procured.

Chemistry can in no way aid in this difficult and embarrassing case.

Fourth Case.—The individual is dead.

All the matters found in the digestive tube are carefully removed; the physical characters are observed; their action on colored reagents is determined; then they are filtered through a fine sieve; the solid part left on the cloth is washed, and the liquid obtained is tested with the salts of lead, bismuth, silver and mercury; it is then evaporated to dryness; the residue is mixed with an excess of nitrate of potassa; the mixture is thrown in separate portions into a platinum crucible, heated to redness; the organic substance is likewise burnt, and a mass of inorganic salts remains.

The product thus obtained is taken up again with distilled water, which holds in solution alkaline salts, carbonate, nitrite, nitrate, chromate and sulphate. By adding alcoholized hydrochloric acid, by degrees, so as to avoid a too considerable disengagement of carbonic acid and nitrous acid, and by operating at a temperature of 122 to 140° F., this liquor, which at first was yellowish, from the presence of chromate of potassa, becomes of a light green color; if treated with ammonia, a dirty green precipitate is produced, the formation of which will be assisted by boiling.

We have now to ascertain whether this precipitate is really the oxide of chrome of which we are in search. For this purpose it is thrown on a filter, carefully washed and dried in a stove, then it is tried with the blow-pipe on fused boracic acid, which it likewise colors green; then it is dissolved in hydrochloric acid; a solution of sesquichloride of chrome is thus obtained, which, when treated with the alkalies and the alkaline carbonates, gives a dirty green precipitate (Cr^2O^3), soluble in an excess of reagent; with phosphate of soda, a green precipitate soluble in an excess of reagent; with hydrosulphate of ammonia, a precipitate of hydrate of sesquioxide of chrome.

Conclusions.—If the matters present a yellow coloration; if, after filtration, the liquid obtained gives a yellow precipitate with the salts of lead and bismuth, red with the salts of silver, brick red with the protosalts of mercury; if, finally, the dirty green precipitate obtained with ammonia gives a green pearl with boracic acid, and if dissolved in hydrochloric acid it causes the same reactions as the salts of sesquioxide of chrome, the certain conclusion is, that among the vomited matters there existed a salt of chromic acid.

If it is desired to find the poison in the viscera, in the liver for instance, it must be cut into thin slices; it is dried and mixed with an excess of nitrate of potassa; the organic matter must be burnt as in the preceding case; the saline residue must be taken up by distilled water, and the whole operation must be exactly the same as has been described for the vomited matters.

By following this process, M. Jaillard has been able, in the vomited matters of the first and second case, to prove the presence of a salt of chromic acid; and, in the liver of the dog of the seventh experiment, to discover traces of chrome.

M. Jaillard has procured from M. Ricord, at the *Hôpital du Midi*, urine from venereal patients under treatment with bichromate of potassa; and, in all the experiments which he made, by following this process he made manifest the presence of chrome, even when the patients were only taking 0.02 gr. to 0.05 gr. of bichromate of potassa per day, and he only operated on 800 gr. of urine, about half of that which was passed in the twenty hours.

M. Jaillard, therefore, concludes that the bichromate of potassa being a very energetic poison, producing the death of a moderate sized dog in the dose of 0.25 gr. in from two to six days; it should not be sold to all comers without any caution, but that the sale should be under the same restrictions as that of the arsenical and mercurial salts, which is far from being the case, since very considerable quantities of this poison may be procured without any difficulty from colormen, druggists, and even from pharmaceutists.—*Journal de Pharmacie et de Chimie.*

REMARKS ON THE STRUCTURAL CONDITIONS OF IRON.

BY T. R. V. FUCHS.*

The difference in phyiscal characters presented by the several kinds of iron is generally attributed to the presence of a variety of substances, among which carbon is considered the most important. It is contained in all kinds of iron, almost always accompanied by silicon, which perhaps exercises the same influence. Raw iron contains the largest quantity of carbon, bar iron the least, and steel is in some sort intermediate between the two; but the quantity of carbon does not in any case bear a constant proportion to the iron, nor are these three kinds of iron separated from each other by any definite limits. These two facts are sufficient to show that the carbon cannot be in a state of very intimate combination with the iron, and there are no sufficient grounds for assuming that the different conditions of this metal are determined solely by the quantities of carbon contained in it. The numerous, and in many respects valuable, analyses of iron have served only to prove the truth of the above remark. Upon the gratuitous assumption that the varying percentage of carbon is the cause of the differences in the character of iron, attention has been too exclusively devoted to this point, while another, and perhaps more essential one, the crystalline structure, has been overlooked.

Fuchs expresses his conviction that iron is a dimorphous substance; that there are, in fact, two species (varieties) of iron,—the tesseral and the rhombohedral. He considers it as proved that malleable iron belongs to the tesseral system; and if any doubt still exists, it may be inferred from analogy that such is the case, inasmuch as all other malleable metals, possess crystalline forms belonging to this system.

The crystalline form of raw iron has not been ascertained with so much certainty, but Fuchs considers it highly probable that it belongs to the rhombohedral system, because it comes within the class of perfectly brittle metals, the crystalline forms

* From the London Repertory of Patent Inventions, Nov. 1853.

of which, as far as we are acquainted with them, are rhombohedral.

But the difference between malleable and cast iron does not consist merely in the crystalline structure, which may be open to doubt, but likewise in their physical characters, and to some extent in their chemical behavior; for instance, the cohesion, hardness, resistance to fracture, fusibility, oxidizability, solubility in acids, &c. He is of opinion that these circumstances alone would justify the inference that there is a specific differ ence between malleable and cast iron, which he compares with those presented by the modifications of sulphur, phosphorus, arsenious acid, by glass and Reaumur's porcelain.

Finally, with regard to steel, Fuchs is of opinion that it is an alloy of tesseral and rhombohedral iron. The per centage of carbon which it contains varies from 0.625 (Gay-Lussac) to 1.9 (Karsten.) It cannot therefore be regarded as a definite and constant compound. It differs from other alloys in the circumstance that its characters may suffer considerable alteration without an accompanying addition or loss of substance, as in the hardening or softening of steel, changes which Fuchs supposes to be the result of an internal and alternating metamorphosis, by which the relative position of the two species of iron is altered. Thus, according to his views, in hardened steel the rhombohedral preponderates over the tesseral iron, and the reverse in soft steel. Very hard steel would, therefore, from the very small proportion of tesseral iron, approximate closely to cast iron; and this conjecture is favored by the low specific gravity of hardened steel. By the process of tempering, the proportion of tesseral iron in steel would increase with the temperature. The two kinds of iron in steel may be regarded as in a state of constant mutual tension, which may perhaps be the reason why steel retains permanently communicated magnetism, while malleable iron does not.

An experiment of Schafhäutl's* would appear to favor the above views. He submitted a piece of a razor-blade to the action of tolerably strong hydrochloric acid for several days,

* Prechtl's *Technologischer Eneyclopedie*, *Abhandlung uber den Stahl*, vol. xv., p. 377.

at the end of which time it was found to have been very unequally attacked. When washed, dried, and broken in a mortar, it furnished fragments, some of which could be powdered, while others were malleable.

With regard to the important and much-discussed question of the alteration of malleable iron when exposed to continuous vibration, concussion, or torsion, in consequence of which it requires a granular fracture, Fuchs admits that such an alteration takes place even in the best worked metal, but does not altogether agree with the explanation usually offered for it, viz., the gradual assumption of a crystalline texture; and is of opinion that it consists in the passage of the iron from a fibrous crystalline state to a granular crystalline state, a change in the aggregation, not an essential metamorphosis. When iron passes from the fibrous into the granular texture, the cohesion of the molecules is lessened; and by their aggregation into rounded groups a heap of distinct particles is produced, which may be compared with what mineralogists call granular minerals. The continuity of the mass is thus to some extent destroyed, inasmuch as these granular particles only adhere together more or less, and consequently the greater the size and number of these particles the greater is the diminution in tenacity. According to the statement of Kohn, the original condition of iron thus altered cannot be restored by heating to redness and forging, but only by exposure to a welding heat; and Fuchs considers this a sufficient proof that this alteration of iron consists in a breaking up of the continuity of the mass. The restoration of this continuity requires that the granular iron should, by exposure to a welding heat, be rendered amorphous, when the cohesive force again becomes active, a condition which in the case of most other bodies obtains only when they are liquid.—*Schweizerisches Gewerbeblatt*, *September*, 1852.

ON A NEW METHOD OF DETERMINING THE QUANTITY OF UREA IN THE URINE.

BY JOHN W. DRAPER, M.D.,

Professor of Chemistry and Physiology in the University of New-York.

Much attention has of late been paid to the methods of determining the composition of the urine, it being very generally acknowledged, that if we possessed the means of a quick and accurate analysis of it, we should be able to settle many contested questions, both in physiology and pathology.

Among the constituents of the urine, the nitrogenized bodies, urea and uric acid, are perhaps of the greatest interest, for they represent the waste which has taken place in the soft tissues generally. Accordingly from time to time new processes have been published for the estimation of these bodies, and more particularly of the first—urea. The methods recommended in the works on annual chemistry and organic analysis are, however, very far from satisfactory. Thus Simon, in his *Chemistry of Man*, effects the determination of the quantity of urea by forming the sparingly soluble nitrate; and Bowman, in his medical chemistry, resorts to the acetate, but both of these are very tedious and very disagreeable operations, and, what is worse, uncertain in their results. Liebig has recently recommended the ternitrate of mercury, but the preparation of the test liquids is troublesome, and since the estimate eventually depends on the production of a particular tint or shade of a yellow color, it cannot be exact.

There are, however, some simple methods which will give absolutely accurate results. These all depend on the principle, that urea and uric acid, when brought in contact with nitrous acid, undergo immediate decomposition with a brisk effervescence, owing to the escape of carbonic acid and nitrogen gas.

The quantity of these nitrogenized principles in the urine

may be ascertained by determining the quantity of carbonic acid or of nitrogen thus set free, during the destructive decomposition of urea and uric acid by nitrous acid. Forty-four parts of carbonic acid, or twenty-eight of nitrogen, answer to sixty of urea.

One of these methods, which is extremely exact, I have recently described in the *London and Edinburgh Philosophical Magazine.* It is to conduct the disengaged carbonic acid into water of barytes, and weigh the resulting carbonate of barytes.

I have also, in examinations which I am constantly making of the urine, frequently resorted to the other plan of estimating the urea, from the quantity of nitrogen set free; and this I have done in two different ways: 1st, by determining the quantity of nitrogen by weight; or, 2d, by volume. The following is a more particular description of each of these.

A liquid suitable for the decomposition of urea is easily and economically prepared by taking a single cell of Grove's voltaic battery, and placing strong nitric acid in the porous cup, and otherwise charging the cell in the usual way. After a few minutes the nitric acid turns green, becoming charged with nitrous acid. It is then to be decanted for use. If this liquid be poured into urine, filtered from its mucus, or into a solution of urea, a brisk effervesence sets in, and if a sufficient quantity of acid is used, so that red fumes are disengaged, the urea is totally decomposed, corbonic acid and nitrogen gases escaping.

In the first of the preceding methods, viz: That of determining the urea from the weight of the nitrogen, a known weight of urine (two grammes), filtered from mucus, is placed in a bottle containing a tube filled with the nitroso-nitric acid above discribed; from the bottle a bent tube conducts the escaping gases through potash water, and then through a chloride of calcium tube. The operation is conducted in the manner well known in laboratories for the analysis of a carbonate; the loss of weight of the whole apparatus gives the quantity of nitrogen which has been set free. This operation requires about half an hour, and is quite exact.

In the second method, viz.: That of determining the urea from the volume of the resulting nitrogen, the operation is essentially the same, only instead of letting the nitrogen escape into the air, it is received into a gasometer, and its quantity ascertained. As conducted in my laboratory, the amount of urea in a sample of urine may thus be determined in from ten to twelve minutes, and with certainty, one thousandth part of the weight of the urine; a degree of exactness far beyond that of the old processes, and an expedition which at once recommends this method to the physiologist and pathologist.—*Virginia Medical and Surgical Journal.*

ON THE VENOM OF SERPENTS.

BY J. GILMAM, A.M., M.D., LLD.

There is much in the history and habits of the reptile tribes, however repulsive they may be in appearance, that is very interesting. During a sojourn of two or three months in the interior of Arkansas, which appears to me to be the paradise of reptiles, I paid some attention to that branch of natural history called ophiology: I found four distinct varieties of rattle-snakes (*Crotalus*), of which the Crotalus Horridus and Crotalus Kirtlandii are by far the most numerous. The former is the largest serpent in North America. The family of moccasin snakes (Colluber) is also quite numerous, there being not less than ten varieties, most of which are quite as venomous as the rattlesnake. By dissecting great numbers of different species I learned that the anatomical structure of the poisoning apparatus is similar in all the different varieties of venomous serpents. It consists of a strong frame-work of bone, with its appropriate muscles in the upper part of the head, resembling and being in fact a pair of jaws, but externally to the jaws proper, and much stronger. To these is attached by a ginglymoid articulation, one or more moveable fangs on each side, just at the verge of the mouth, capable of being erected at pleasure. These fangs are very hard and sharp and crooked, like the claws of a cat, and hooking backwards, with a hollow from the base to near the point. I have occasionally seen a thin slit of bone divide this hollow, making two. At their base is found a small sac, containing two or three drops of venom which resembles thin honey. The sac is so connected with the cavity of the fang during its erection, that a slight upward pressure forces the venum into the fang at its base, and it makes its exit at a small slit or opening near the point, with considerable force; thus it is carried to the bottom of any wound made by the fang.—Unless the fangs are erected for battle they lie concealed in the upper part of the mouth, sunk between the external and internal jaw bones, somewhat like a pen-knife blade shut up in its handle, where they are covered by a fold of membrane which encloses them like a sheath; this is the *vagina dentis.* There can be no doubt but these fangs are frequently broken off or shed, as the head grows broader, to make room for new ones nearer the verge of the mouth; for, within the vagina dentis of a very large crotalus horridus, I found no less than five fangs on each side—in all stages of formation—the smallest in a half pulpy or cartilaginous state, the next something harder, the third still more perfect, and so on to the main, well-set, perfect fang. Each of these teeth had a well defined cavity like the main one. Three fangs on each side were frequently found in copper-heads, vipers, and others.

The process of robbing serpents of their venom is easily accomplished by the aid of chloroform, a few drops of which stupifies them. If, while they are under this influence, they are carefully seized by the neck, and the vagina dentis held out of the way by an assistant, with a pair of forceps, and the fang be erected and gently pressed upwards, the venom will be seen issuing from the fang and dropping from its point. It may then be absorbed by a bit of sponge, or caught in a vial, or on the point of a lancet. After robbing several serpents in this manner, they were found after two days to be as highly charged as ever with venom of equal intensity with that first taken.

During the process of robbing several species of serpents, I inoculated several small but vigorous and perfectly healthy vegetables, with the point of a lancet well charged with venom. The next day they were withered and dead, looking as though they had been scathed with lightning. In attempting to preserve a few drops of venom, for future experiments, in a small vial with two or three parts of alcohol, it was found in a short time to have lost its venomous properties. But after mixing the venom with aqua ammonia, or spirits turpentine, or oil of peppermint, or of cinnamon, or of cloves, or with nitric or sulphuric acid, it still seemed to act with undiminished energy. It is best preserved, however, for future use by trituration with refined sugar or sugar of milk.

A very fine large cotton-mouth snake, being captured by putting a shoe-string around him, became excessively ferocious, striking at even the crack of a small riding-whip. Finding himself a prisoner, without hope of escape, he turned his deadly weapons on his own body, striking repeatedly his well-charged fangs deeply into his flesh. Notwithstanding this, he was put in a small basket and carried forward. In one hour after he was found dead, and no amount of irritation could excite the least indication of life. Four hours after, while removing the skin for preservation, the blood oozed slowly from the vessels in a dissolved state. No violence was done to his snakeship, except what he did to himself.

Another moccasin, shot by a pistol about two inches back of the head, and skinned immediately, gave decided evidence of vitality four hours after being flayed, by wreathing the body whenever it was irritated by a scalpel.

A large rattle-snake beheaded instantly, with a hoe, would, an hour and a half after, strike at any thing that pinched its tail. Of several persons who were testing their firmness of nerve, by trying to hold the hand steady while the serpent struck at it, not one could be found whose hand would not recoil in spite of his resolution, and one man, a great bulley, by-the-by, was struck on the naked throat with considerable violence by the headless trunk of the serpent, and staggered back, fainted, and fell from terror. Mr. Stewart, of Miss., tells me he witnessed a similar scene once. An old hunter shot a rattle-snake's head off, and after reloading his gun and standing sometime, he stooped to pull off the rattles, and the bloody but headless trunk of the snake struck him in the temple and he fainted and fell down with terror.

Seven venomous serpents belonging to five different species were made to fraternize and dwell amicably in one den. A beautiful pair of long bodied speckled snakes, known as king-snakes, and found to be fangless, and consequently without venom, were duly installed as members of the family. Some uneasiness was perceivable among the older members, but no attempt was made to destroy the intruders, though they might have been killed instanter. The next morning four of the venomous serpents were found to have been destroyed by the king-snakes, and one was still within their coil, and the two remaining ones would make no effort at self-defence. A large rattle-snake seemed stupid and indifferent to his fate. He could not be made to threaten or give warning even with his rattles. The smallest king-snake was afterwards inoculated with the poison of one of the serpents he had destroyed, and died immediately after—thus evincing that they must have exercised some power besides physical force to overcome their fellow-creatures.

In short, the results, of a great number of experiments performed with the venom of a great variety of serpents, seem to lead to the following conclusions:

1st. That the venom of all serpents acts as a poison in a similar manner.

2d. That the venom of some varieties is far more active than that of others.

3d. That a variety of the colluber, known as the cotton-mouth. is the most venomous serpent in Arkansas.

4th. That the venom of serpents destroys all forms of organized life, vegetable as well as animal.

5th. That alcohol, if brought in contact with the venom is, to a certain extent, an antidote.

6th. That serpents do possess the power of fascinating small animals, and that this power is identical with mesmerism.

7th. That the blood of small animals, destroyed by the venom of serpents, bears a close resemblance to that of animals destroyed by lightning or hydrocyanic acid; it loses its power of coagulation and cannot be long kept from putrefaction.

ON PRACTICAL PHARMACY.

BY JUSTUS LIEBIG,

Professor of Chemistry at the University of Giessen.

NO. III.

Of Mechanical Separation of Heterogeneous parts.

The mechanical separation of heterogeneous parts is mostly very simple; for example, the plucking of leaves and flowers from the stems, the cleaning of roots from their filaments, or the stripping them from their bark, and the separation of seeds from their husks.

The object of decantation (*elutriatio*) is to separate, by means of water, finely divided solid bodies from coarser particles, or those which are of a less specific gravity, from those which are of a greater specific gravity. When the substances are reduced to powder, they are first mixed with a sufficient quantity of water, so as to form a thin mixture, and afterwards poured out gently from one vessel to the other. The coarser particles settle first to the bottom, and are kept back in the decanting vessel, the more minute and lighter particles deposit themselves slower. This mode of operation is of great use in many analyses.

Solid bodies are separated from the fluids by means of causing the liquor in which the solid particles are suspended, to pass through a porous body. If the body thus employed has pores large enough to allow some of the less coarser parts to run away with the fluid, it is called straining. When, on the other hand, the body employed is such as to prevent the most minute solid parts from escaping with the liquid, it is called filtration.

The instruments employed for the object of straining, are the colatorium, which is a piece of flannel or linen, fixed by tacks on a square wooden frame (*tenaculum*); if the material is made of a conical form, the instrument is called a filtering bag (manica Hippocrates). Sometimes sieves, or colanders of tin are also employed; and for fatty and resinous substances for salves and ointments, wire baskets are used, covered with hemp. Strong acids are percolated in funnels filled with coarsely powdered glass. Filtration is performed by means of unsized paper made into a cone, placed in a funnel so arranged as to keep up some space between the cone and the funnel, in order to facilitate the operation. This object is obtained by small pieces of wood or glass arranged round the inside, or when the funnel is ribbed, or the filtering papers made to assume several folds, or by using a filtering basket made of small rods, in the shape of a funnel. Bishof and Gmelin have suggested an ingenious contrivance for obtaining, by means of small filters, a great quantity of fluid, without being continually obliged to pour fresh liquid in the filter. It consists in turning a large bottle, filled with fluid, in the filter, so as to plunge its neck half an inch in the filter filled with fluid. The bottle is fixed to a board. By these means the operation goes on without interruption. As soon as the liquid in the filter is sunk below the neck of the bottle, the liquor in the bottle begins to fill it anew, and ceases to flow as soon as the orifice is covered. However, it being possible for some parts of the solid materials, when the air strikes upon the fluid, to be driven into the bottle, which in some cases is detrimental, Berzelius has suggested to stop the bottle with a perforated cork, containing a small glass tube open on both ends, the lower part ending in a small point, bent a little upwards. The glass tube has a lateral opening half an inch above the point, formed with a smaller tube turned upwards. When the fluid in the funnel runs off to a certain point, the air penetrates through the lateral opening in the bottle, and causes the liquid to flow. According to Scheefer, the same object can be accomplished by means of a cork having two holes, one fitted with a small straight tube, the other with one bent upwards in an acute angle. Several more contrivances may be found in Poggendorf. The instrument recommended by Gay Lussac for filtering, consists in a Woulfe's bottle, with two openings, in the one of which is adapted a glass syphon, the one branch of which reaches almost to the bottom of the flask, and the other an exterior one, which is the longest. A straight glass tube is fixed in the second opening, with its lower end placed higher than the external end of the syphon. The vessel is filled almost to the brim with the liquid which is to be filtered, and stopped with perforated corks. The filter is placed under the external end of the syphon. In order to operate, you blow through the straight tube, and once the fluid is in motion, the air always filling the vacuum, will keep up the action. This action itself can be accelerated or retarded by shifting the position of the straight tube. Common blotting paper is often impregnated with metallic impurities, which are dissolved, as often as the fluid contains some acids ; hence it is better to use paper, such as is manufactured for printers, before it is sized.

When a great quantity of liquid is to be filtered, the paper is spread on a bag of linen, or felt, made in the shape of a cone Several other filters have been suggested, founded on the application of hydrostatic laws; the simplest of them is that invented by Schindler. It consists of a bottle with the bottom cut off, this gap is closed with filtering paper and a coarse cloth, bound around the flask with a string. The bottle is filled with the fluid which is to be submitted to filtration, and placed in a large fixed funnel. Stop the bottle with a cork, on which is fixed a funnel with a long tube. Fill the funnel also with the fluid, and keep it always replenished. The filtering goes on most admirably.

Despumation is the operation by which the solid parts are separated from the fluids by means of a gentle heat or ebullition. By these means the impurities thrown off as a scum to the surface are removed with a perforated spoon or ladle. The reason is, that heat coagulates the albumen of such fluids, which combines with the solid parts, and ascends to the surface.

If the liquid does not contain sufficient albumen, the white of egg is added to facilitate the operation. Heat, however, must be applied gently and gradually, else the foam, instead of floating on the surface, mixes again with the liquid, and renders it turbid. Syrups are allowed but to boil up a few instants, and are filtered whilst yet warm. Care also must be taken not to be too particular in clearing medicinal extracts, else some of their more active principles will be lost. Spirituous and acidulous fluids are clarified without the assistance of heat, by adding isinglass, the white of eggs, or bullock's blood, and decanting them after a few days' infusion.

Expression (*expressio*) is often employed to separate solid parts from the liquid by mechanical pressure. If only small quantities are to be worked upon, and little strength is required, the mass is put in a coarse cloth, and the liquid is wrung out by the hand. In order to avoid this troublesome manipulation, Beindorf invented a decoction press. It consists in a solid piston, moved like a root knife by a lever, which enters a cylinder of tin enclosed in a wooden box, having a tin sieve at the bottom. By this contrivance, decoctions are more easily extracted. But if considerable strength is required, presses are employed, particularly presses with screws.

There are two kinds of presses in use—the dish press and the plate press.

The first has but one perpendicular screw, which works up and down through an horizontal beam, supported by two columns, containing the nut. The objects to be pressed, enclosed in a bag of linen, are put in a metal dish with a beak, which is fixed under the press. It is useful to have a second dish with holes, fitting in the first. The dish has a metal perforated cover upon which the screw plays, which is moved by a handle of iron, which fits exactly in the upper end of the screw, which has four holes.

The plate press has two parallel screws, placed perpendicularly at a proper distance, and fixed to a strong board. A second board with two holes, corresponding to the screws, is placed on the screws, and the nuts attached afterwards. Two plates of iron, brass, or tin, are placed between the boards, and the object to be pressed, enclosed in a bag, is put between the plates, and the nuts closed by the key.

The goodness of a press depends on the goodness of the screw and nut. Both ought to be made of hard but pliable iron. If the screw is of brass, there is little friction. The worms must be strong, uniform, and well fitting; the less they rise, the more acute is the angel which they form with the horizontal basis, the stronger is the action of the screw. All other parts of the press, the dishes, covers, boards, plates, &c., must be equally strong to afford necessary resistance to pressure, and to prevent breaking down. The key acts as a one-sided lever; hence, the longer it is, the stronger it acts. Sometimes the keys have holes in the centre, in which case they act as double-sided levers. It is requisite to be slow and uniform in pressing. Hydraulic and other complicated presses are not much used in pharmacy. Presses are chiefly used in preparing fresh vegetable extracts, oils, &c., to separate the solid parts from the liquid. To make vegetable extracts (*succi expressi*), the herbs are first divided in small parts by cutting and bruising, then enclosed in a bag, and put under the press. If the herbs are not very juicy, it is useful to wet them with a small quantity of cold water.

Expressed oils (*olea expressa*) are prepared in a similar way. Seeds, after being bruised, are exposed to the gentle heat of a water-bath or of steam, and pressed between warm plates or dishes. Some oil-seeds, however, are more advantageously pressed without heat, and it makes a great difference if some are drawn cold, or hot pressed, as for instance, the oil of bitter almonds and castor oil.

Some solid fats (for instance, cocoa butter, which is not fluid at ordinary temperature,) must be hot pressed. The cocoa beans, after having been deprived of their husks and roasted, are spread on a hair sieve, and after being put in a bag, are placed over a pan of boiling water, and pressed as soon as they are warmed through between two heated metal plates; or they are rubbed into a pulpy mass in a warm pan, or after bruising them in a warm pan, adding some hot water (two ounces of water to twelve ounces of cocoa); the mass is thus rendered a little moist, and it is pressed easily between warm plates. It is necessary at the beginning to press very slightly, but at the end of the operation, you may press with all possible strength. The residuum contains still some oil, which can be obtained by pulverizing it, and wetting it again with water. Some seeds, when old, (for instance, henbane seeds) require after being powdered, the addition of water, else they yield but very little oil. The castor seeds, after being deprived of their husks and powdered, required to be moistened by spirits of wine (one-fourth of their weight.) The oil, after being pressed, is exposed to a water-bath to expel the alcohol. Fresh drawn oils are turbid; they require to be left to settle for a few days, after which they are decanted. The residuum is removed by filtering.

Decantation (*decantatio*) is a simple process, by which are separated two different fluids of different specific gravity, or solids and fluids. This can be effected by inclination of the vessel. To facilitate this operation, decanting cylindrical vessels of earthenware or china are constructed, having openings at different places or heights, by which the fluid can be poured out without much shaking. This object can also be better obtained by syphons, the best of which are those which at one end have the tube bent upwards; thus, the shorter branch of the syphon is placed in the liquid, and one draws the air from the longer one without filling his mouth with the liquor. Or you may fill the syphon with fluid, and put your finger to the longer end, and plunge the other in the fluid; when you remove your finger the fluid will flow. If minute quantities are to be decanted, the capillary attraction of cotton or blotting paper may be employed instead of a syphon. Fluids may also be decanted by means of a syringe. Two fluids are also separated by the virgin's funnel, *vulgo* separatory funnel. Pipettes are more handy than syringes. These are tubes of glass, with a round globe blown in the middle, having one end drawn to a fine point. The separatory funnel differs from a common funnel from it assuming a convex shape after its enlargement, and having a mouth closed by a stopper. It ends in a fine point.

ACTION OF CARBONIC ACID ON QUININE AND CINCHONINE—FORMATION OF CRYSTALLIZED CARBONATE OF QUININE.

BY M. LANGLOIS.

We passed a current of carbonic acid gas into water, containing recently precipitated quinine and cinchonine. The prolonged action of carbonic acid gas determines the solution of quinine and cinchonine; but the former is more readily dissolved than the latter. Both solutions, exposed to the air, lose a portion of their carbonic acid, and furnish the first crystals of carbonate of quinine, the other cinchonine only. We shall see, as we proceed, to what this difference is owing.

Crystallized carbonate of quinine may easily be obtained by following the directions which we shall give.

Ten grains of sulphate of quinine must be dissolved in distilled water, with the addition of a few drops of sulphuric acid. Ammonia is added in order to precipitate the quinine; the latter is collected on a filter and washed; it is afterwards diffused while moist, in a quart of water. The liquid, which has a milky appearance, is put into a test-glass with a foot, into which is passed a stream of well-washed carbonic acid, procured by the decomposition of marble, by means of hydrochloric acid. In less than an hour, the quinine is almost entirely dissolved. The liquor, although super-saturated with carbonic acid, always retains an alkaline reaction.

The quinine combines directly with the carbonic acid without dissolving, when it is not diffused in a large quantity of water. By operating, on the contrary, in the way which we have directed, we obtain a complete and very limpid solution, from which are obtained, after exposure to the air, crystals of carbonate of quinine, which increase in size during from twenty to twenty-four hours. After this time no more is deposited, although the liquor still contains some. Spontaneous evaporation furnishes only quinine; the latter is instantly precipitated by ammonia, potassa and soda, which saturate the carbonic acid. Lime-water acts in the same way, forming, moreover, a deposit of carbonate of lime.

The solution of this carbonate of quinine furnishes, at first, as is evident, crystals, represented by the saline combination; and afterwards, this combination is destroyed, giving rise to carbonic acid and quinine. There is, therefore, a perfect analogy between these phenomena and those produced by a solution of carbonate of cinchonine. This latter never gives crystals, because the salt exists in small quantity in it; which is owing, doubtless, to the solubility of cinchonine in water, increasing very little by the intervention of carbonic acid.

Carbonate of quinine is under the form of transparent, acicular crystals; these crystals promptly effloresce in contact with the air; they are soluble in alcohol, insoluble in ether, and they restore the blue color of reddened litmus paper. In the presence of the acids, they cause a brisk effervescence.

At the temperature of 230° F. they are decomposed; the carbonic acid is disengaged, and the quinine remains without undergoing any alteration. It melts only when the heat reaches 338° F.

We found in the decomposition of carbonate of quinine, at a moderate temperature, an easy means of analysing it. The experiments were repeated several times; but we shall content ourselves with detailing only one.

We took the weight of a glass tube twelve to fifteen centimetres long, and closed at one end. We introduced into it 0.399 of carbonate of quinine. It was then put into communication by means of a cork covered with caoutchouc, with a bent tube, which is passed under a graduated bell glass, placed over mercury contained in a test-glass, with a stand. The extremity of this tube went beyond the surface of the metal, and reached into the empty part of the bell glass, into which the carbonic acid gas was received. The sealed tube containing the salt was heated in an oil-bath, into which dipped the bulb of a thermometer. As soon as the temperature of the oil-bath attained 230° F., the carbonate of quinine was decomposed, disengaging carbonic acid, and without undergoing perceptible changes in its physical characters.

I obtained from the 399 milligrammes of salt employed for the experiment, 21.36 of carbonic acid gas at the temperature of 32° F., and at the pressure of 76 centimetres. This volume of gas weighed 0.0422 gr. Carbonic acid ceased to be disengaged a long time before the oil-bath had attained the temperature of 338° F., which is that at which quinine enters into fusion, and at which it is entirely freed from the water which it contains. By means of a few pieces of blotting-paper, the moisture which remained adhering to the sides of the tube was easily removed. The weight of this empty tube being known, I obtained, by weighing it again, that of the quinine contained in it. The weight of the latter was 321 milligrammes. We have thus, on one hand, in this analysis, the proportion of the carbonic acid, and on the other, that of the quinine. The water was estimated by the difference. 0.399 gr. of carbonate of quinine furnished:

	Grammes.
Quinine	0.3210
Carbonic acid . . .	0.0422
Water	0.0358

These numbers lead us to represent the composition of this salt by the following formula:

$$(C^{20}H^{12}NO^{2},HO)\ CO^{2},\ HO.$$

In fact, we have in hundreths:

	Theory.	Experiment.
Quinine . .	80.21 . .	80.45
Carbonic acid .	10.88 . .	10.58
Water . .	8.91 . .	8.97
	100.00	100.00

Six successive experiments on various quantities of carbonate of quinine gave similar results.

As it must be regarded as neutral, in establishing its composition, we shall also have fixed the cypher of the equivalent of quinine, which corresponds with that admitted by Liebig.

The decomposition of carbonate of quinine at a moderate temperature has enabled us to prove again the non-formation of this salt by double decomposition, that is to say, by treating a saline solution of quinine with carbonate of potassa or soda, the precipitate which is formed contains only quinine, retaining always, notwithstanding repeated washings, a greater or less quantity of the carbonate employed. It is to the presence of the latter, that the precipitate owes the property of effervescing with the acids; but when it is fused in a glass tube, not the smallest trace of carbonic acid is evolved. That which I here say of quinine, applies also to cinchonine, and, perhaps, even to all the other vegetable bases. We had already given this idea in a note inserted, some years ago, in Vol. xxxii. of the "*Annalen der Chimie*," but then our opinion was founded solely on the results of some reactions which were not of the value of those which we now obtain, by the employment of heat.—*Comptes Rendus*, Nov. 7, 1853.

MEDICINES HOLDING GUM-RESINS SUSPENDED.—Myrrh, ammoniacum, assafœtida, and other gums, may be successfully suspended in menstrua by adding 6 or 8 drops of almond oil to a very small quantity of the gum-resin employed. A mass is made by trituration, and, when both are incorporated, the result is a smooth paste, to which the vehicle in which it is intended the gum-resin shall be administered is to be added very gradually—an emulsion may be speedily prepared in this, and this mixture may be heated, if necessary, without causing the least coagulation; whereas emulsions prepared with yolk of egg will not allow of heat being applied without coagulation.

THE FORMATION OF WHITE LEAD.

Barreswil gives the following explanation of the Dutch method of manufacturing white lead:

It can be proved by experiments, that the neutral anhydrous carbonate of lead, in contact with basic acetate of lead, is converted into the hydrated basic carbonate of lead. In the manufacture of white lead, all the lead is oxidised under the influence of the air and acetic acid, and is converted into basic acetate of lead, which is decomposed by the carbonic acid into neutral acetate of lead, and into carbonate of lead, which, by the presence of an excess of acetate of lead, is transformed into a basic salt (white lead.) When, therefore, the basic acetate of lead is absent, which sometimes happens, and when the white lead remains longer in the process of manufacture than is necessary for the complete disappearance of the lead, the basic salt is gradually converted into a neutral carbonate, changing the constitution of the white lead. These differences in the composition correspond to the varieties in the quality of the white lead.—*Journal de Pharmacie.*

Lac Varnish to Prevent Iron and Steel from Rusting.—For this object, 5 parts of shellac varnish, made by dissolving shellac in linseed oil, are mixed with 4 parts of oil of turpentine. Mathematical and surgical instruments, and all kinds of iron and steel implements, may be varnished with this liquid, which prevents rusting.—*A. Wolf.*

Varieties.

Mode of Determining the Optical Power of a Microscope.—By Professor Harting (Quart. J. Mic. Sci., July, 1853, 292.)—I conclude by noticing another method of testing the optical power of the instrument, which, although rather troublesome, appears to me among the best, permitting us, as it does, to ascertain with a great degree of accuracy and certainty, the utmost limits of penetrating and separating power possessed by a microscope, and hence easily to express numerically its optical qualities in the most varied circumstances.

This method consists simply in subjecting to observation under the microscope the dioptric images of certain minute objects instead of the objects themselves. These images can be diminished at pleasure by withdrawing to a distance from the lens the object which forms them; and hence we have it in our power to measure the extreme limits at which the object continues to be visible.

For the formation of the dioptric images achromatic object-glasses might be used; but even where those of the shortest focal length are employed, the object whose image it is required to form must be placed at a great distance. This would cause various difficulties, and only be practicable with a microscope placed horizontally—unless, indeed, the object selected were very minute, in which case the accurate determination of its diameter (from which that of its image must be afterwards deduced) would be rendered difficult.

Small air-bells, in a fluid, are, for this purpose, far better. I employ, by preference, a watery solution of powdered gum arabic, which always contains numbers of such air-bells, originating in the air entangled among the particles of the powder. The water employed should have stood for a considerable time freely exposed to the air, or been shaken up with the air for some time; for, when we use water which is not saturated with air, the bubbles in the fluid gradually become smaller, and images formed in them decreasing in magnitude, cause errors in the subsequent measurements, as we shall actually find to be the case.

A drop of the fluid must then be placed on a clean glass object-slide, and covered with a good clear mica plate, a ring-shaped piece being interposed, in order to prevent the flattening of the air-bells by pressure. The object-slide is then placed under the object-glass upon the stage of the microscope, and an air-bell, of suitable size for the formation of the images, is sought for. All do not give images of the same degree of sharpness; a peculiarity dependent on the fact that some air-bells are in contact with the covering-plate, and consequently have their spherical form disturbed to some extent, or on the presence of small molecules in the fluid above or beneath the air bell, or even in its interior, causing some haziness of the image, just as defective polish of a glass lens would do. It will, however, be always easy to find some which will form images of the utmost distinctness and purity.* This may be ascer-

* The following example will demonstrate this. I brought a printed page of a book to such a distance from an air-bell that the length of the image of the whole page was 1-7th millimetre = about 1-180th of an inch, and that of the image of each letter about 1-480th millim. = 1-12,000 of an inch. In spite of their minuteness, these images, formed by reflective light, possessed such clearness and sharpness that, under a magnifying power of 154 diameters, the whole page was without difficulty legible.

tained in the first instance by holding between the mirror and stage some easily recognized object, *e. g.*, a piece of paper or the like. The image is always formed on the under surface of the air-bell, which must consequently be brought nearer to the object-glass than when it is desired to bring its margins into focus.

The object whose image is to be the subject of examination should be placed upon an apparatus which can be moved upward and downward in the space between the mirror and stage. In some microscopes this can hardly be done, either from the space being too limited or in consequence of the drum-like form of the foot of the microscope, which quite envelopes the space. If such microscopes, in place of a mirror, be provided with a reflecting prism, the object may be placed opposite the side external to the microscope. The instruments best adapted for the manipulation which we are describing are, however, those whose illuminating apparatus consists of a mirror and converging lens, which can be shifted up or down. The lens being removed from the ring which supports it, the object is substituted in its place. The relative magnitudes of object and air-bell must be such that the image shall be exceedingly minute when the object is tolerably near to the stage. On afterwards increasing the distance between the object and air-bell, it is not difficult to find the limit at which the image (under a given magnifying power) is barely visible.

Of course it is impossible to measure *directly* the dimensions of this most minute visible image, for our best micrometric methods will here be found of no avail. Yet their size may be estimated with extreme accuracy in the following manner. At the same distance from the air-bell, and in place of the object used, substitute another body, such as a piece of card, of 4 to 5 centimetres = 1 3-5ths to 2 inches diameter, which has been exactly measured. Let this be now again measured (by some of the micrometric methods elsewhere alluded to*), just as if it were a real object. By dividing the real diameter by the apparent diameter, the amount of diminution is found ; and this is the same for all objects at a like distance from the air-bell. We have, consequently, nothing to do, in order to find the amount of diminution of the image of the more minute object, but to divide its *true* diameter by the figure expressing the diminishing power.

For example, let the true diameter of the greater object be 5 centimetres = to 1-969 English inches, and the diameter of its image = 32-2 micromillimetres,† = .00127 English inches, then the figure expressing the amount of diminution will be 1.969-.00127 = 1553 very nearly. If now the smaller object have a diameter of 175 micromillimetres = .00689 English inches, then must its image at the limit of vision be in diameter = .00689-1553 = 0000044, or about 1-225,000th of an English inch. When exact metrometric methods are employed, it is easy in this way to estimate the diameter of an image even to millionth parts of a millimetre, *i. e.*, to 25,400,000th parts of an inch.

As for the object suitable for these investigations, it is plain that we have an extensive choice. To find the limit of vision for bodies of a round or long thread-like form, grains of pearl sago, or vegetable bodies, such as mustard-seed, or the pollen-

* See translation from *Het Mikroskoop* in *Monthly Journal of Medical Science*, June, 1852, p. 453, *et seq.*

† The micromillimetre is equal 1-1000th millimetres = .0000394 English inches. See *Monthly Journal*, June, 1852, p. 456.

granules of many plants, hairs of animals, metallic wires, &c., may be employed. Small round openings and chinks may serve for the determination of the visibility of positive images of light. In the last case, care must of course be taken, by means of suitable screens, to shut off all light except what passes through the aperture. To determine the defining power, metallic wire gauze is a suitable object, or two holes placed near each other in a black metallic plate. The images of such objects resemble exactly a double star viewed through a telescope (kijker). The bodies may likewise be placed in different circumstances in order to ascertain the influence of these upon the limits of vision. Thus we may use as an object a very thin glass capillary-tube placed in water, and compare it with tender organic tubes and vessels, which may also be seen in water, but whose limit of visibility is of course far more circumscribed than that of absolutely opaque objects.

In fact, this method admits of innumerable variations, and is, consequently, of most extensive application. Besides, when proper precautions are taken, it gives results perfectly sure and comparable. Especial care is, however, requisite in the mode of illumination. For it is certain, that when the field has a clear white ground, the contrast causes minute opaque bodies (*i. e.*, objects which are dark by transmitted light) to continue visible, which against a grayish or light-blue background could not be seen. Hence it is by no means indifferent to receive on the mirror light from a white cloud, from a dull overcast, or clear blue sky. Artificial light cannot be used in these experiments, for the image of the flame becomes diminished like the object, and hence a clear field of view is not to be obtained. The observations must, consequently be made by daylight; and whenever comparable results are sought for, the mirror should always be directed to the clear, blue, cloudless sky—this being a distinct atmospheric condition to which others in similar circumstances may refer in conducting the same experiment. The mode of ascertaining the limit of vision, with a given amount of illumination, may be gathered from different examples in the body of this work. It will likewise be found that for all such observations, even when the highest magnifying powers are employed, the *flat* mirror is perfectly sufficient, since in the image in the field in view formed by the air-bell, all the rays proceeding from the mirror are united, and constitute an object of considerable luminous intensity.

Oleo Resin of Male Fern.—Some months since, Professor Christison drew the attention of the profession to the efficacy of the oleo-resinous extract, obtained by ether from the root of the male shield fern, in the treatment of tape worm. Subsequently to the appearance of his remarks the remedy had been tried by himself and others in upwards of twenty cases; and in no case did it fail, after a single dose, to discharge the worm, and commonly in one mass. The operation of the medicine was not, for the most part, attended by pain or other uneasiness, and the certainty with which it brought away the worm is more remarkable than that of any other remedy.

At first, Professor C. gave eighteen grains for a dose, but afterwards to insure greater certainty, the dose was increased to twenty-four grains. The worm, he thinks, is more speedily killed by the latter dose.—*Monthly Journal.*

On the Waters of the Great Salt Lake, Rocky Mountains.—By Dr. L. D. Gale (Stansbury's Expedition to the Great Salt Lake, Philadelphia, 1852.)—Amount of solid contents, 22.422 per cent. Specific gravity, 1.170. Composition:

Chloride of sodium	20.196
Sulphate of soda	1.834
Chloride of magnesium	0.252
Chloride of calcium	*trace.*

On the Waters of the Warm and Hot Springs of Salt Lake City.—By Dr. L. D. Gale (ibid.).—The mineral water of the warm spring has a strong smell of sulphuretted hydrogen. Specific gravity, 1.0112. Solid matter afforded on evaporation 1.08200 p. c. Analysis afforded:

Sulphuretted hydrogen uncombined . . .	0.037454
" " combined . . .	0.000728
Carbonate of lime, precipitated by boiling . .	0.075000
" magnesia	0.022770
Chloride of calcium	0.005700
Sulphate of soda	0.064835
Chloride of sodium	0.816600
	1.023087

The Hot Spring has the specific gravity 1.0130, and yielded 1.1454 per cent. solid contents. Composition in 100 parts:

Chloride of sodium .	0.8052	Chloride of magnesium .	0.0288
Chloride of calcium .	0.1096	Sulphate of lime .	0.0806
Carbonate of lime .	0.0180	Silica . . .	0.0180 =1.0602

Manufacture of Sal-Ammoniac from the Residues of Gas Works.—The Industrial Society of Mulhaussen offers annually a number of prizes for inventions and improvements made during the year; and it also offers a prize to those who introduce a new branch of industry into the department of the Haut-Rhin. This last prize was taken by M.M. Moerhlin and Stoll, who manufacture sal-ammoniac from the ammoniacal liquid of gas-works. The main difficulty in the operation consists in separating the tar-like material which it contains. The following is the process adopted.

The ammoniacal liquid is mixed with slaked lime; then submitted to distillation in a boiler, heated by steam; the parts volatilized pass into a worm, in which the larger part of the tar is deposited; the ammonia passes on into a Wolff's apparatus, where it leaves the foreign substances present, and finally is carried into cold water, where it is condensed. In this state it is nearly free from its impurities; it is neutralized with chlorohydric acid and evaporated in a lead boiler. As it deposits it is withdrawn by means of a wooden rake; it is allowed to drain, and then introduced into a brick mould and subjected to strong pressure. Blocks of sal-ammoniac are thus obtained, which are dried in an oven, heated by part of the heat furnished by the evaporating furnace.

Preparation for the Destruction of Vermin.—In 1846, when the sale of uncombined arsenic was prohibited by the Government of France, the School of Pharmacy in Paris recommended the following formula for the destruction of animals:

Melted fat	1,000 parts.
Fine wheat flour . . .	1,000 "
Arsenic	100 "
Lampblack	10 "
Essential oil of aniseed . .	1 "

A preparation containing phosphorus has been recommended by Mr. Simon, of Berlin, for the same purpose. This is as follows:

Rye flour	180 parts.
Melted butter . . .	180 "
Sugar	125 "
Phosphorus	8 "
Tepid water . . .	180 "

Another formula containing phosphorus, and even more simple than the above, is this:

Phosphorus	6 parts.
Fine wheat flour . . .	300 "
Boiling water . . .	1,000 "

M. Duboys, who appears to have given considerable attention to this subject, gives the preference to this formula:

Melted fat	400 parts.
Nut oil	200 "
Fine wheat flour . . .	400 "
Powdered sugar . . .	250 "
Boiling water . . .	400 "
Phosphorus . . .	20 "

He recommends the phosphorus to be placed in a stone or porcelain mortar, and to be liquified by the boiling water; the flour is then to be quickly, yet gradually, added, the mixture being stirred with a wooden pestle. When this mixture has become almost cold, the fat, already melted and gently warm, is to be added to it; the nut oil is next to be added, and lastly the powdered sugar; and the whole composition is then to be well stirred till it becomes cold. The compound or paste should be kept in vessels, so as to be preserved from the action of the air and light. When employed for the destruction of animals, it is to be very thinly spread on slices of bread, or bread and butter, and most probably it will be eaten by them with the greatest eagerness.

Preparation of Pure Quinine.—When so many salts of quinine are as at present employed for medical purposes, which require pure quinine in an uncombined state for their preparation, it is important to know the best means by which this alkaloid can be separated from the disulphate pure, and with as little loss as possible.

The following method is founded on a well ascertained fact—that while quinine is soluble in caustic potash and ammonia, it is insoluble in caustic soda. Take any quantity of disulphate of quinine, and dissolve it in twenty times its weight of distilled water, with the aid of a few drops of diluted sulphuric acid. Drop this solution, until it has a slight alkaline reaction, as much solution of caustic soda as is necessary, and until a portion of the fluid filtered from the precipitate gives no turbidity upon the addition of a few drops of the soda solution. The precipitate is collected on a filter when it has settled, washed with distilled water, and then dried in a gentle heat. Ten parts of the disulphate of quinine yield seven parts of quinine, consisting of $C^{20} H^{12} N O^{2} + 3 H O$.

The quinine thus prepared is a snow-white, fine crystalline powder, without odor, and very bitter. It browns moistened turmeric paper. In the heat it melts and loses its water of crystallization, and upon cooling becomes a resinous transparent mass. It is very slightly soluble in water, but easily soluble in alcohol. Ether dissolves 1-60th part of quinine. When rubbed with chlorine water, and afterwards, upon the addition of caustic ammonia, a dark green flocculent precipitate ensues, which is very characteristic of quinine.

Ether Impregnated with Quinine in the Treatment of Intermittent Fever.—By M. A. Pignacca.—A limpid fluid, of peculiar and not pleasant odor, is obtained by the distillation of quinate of lime, alcohol, and sulphuric acid; its exact chemical nature has not been yet ascertained. M. Manetti, a young student in medicine, deserves the honor of first suggesting the administration of quinine, in this form, by inhalations. He was struck with the death of a patient, who sank under a severe attack of fever, from the impossibility of giving him, in a short time, the medicine in sufficient quantity; and he set about discovering some preparation by which it could be absorbed through the air passages. A scruple, poured on a handkerchief, must be held alternately to the nostrils; first ensues lachrymation; then a little heat of throat and coughing; sometimes singing in the ears. M. Pignacca has known severe cephalalgia disappear, in some patients, during the inhalation. It is recommended in tertian fevers; in neuralgia, especially of the branches of the fifth pair; in marsh fevers, some of which cases are often accompanied by uticaria and symptoms of gastro-enteritis, &c. In some cases the fever was permanently arrested by four inhalations in the intervals of the attacks.—*Gazetta Medica Lombarda*, from *St. Louis Med. and Sur. Journal.*

Separation of Bromine from Iodine.—Balard's process, as carried on by M. H. de Luca, gives a method of recognizing traces of iodine, and at the same time of separating it from bromine, with which it is so often associated. It is based partly on the greater affinity of bromine for the metals, and partly on the violet color which iodine communicates to sulphuret of carbon. An impure bromine is treated by potash (of carbonate of potash, which may be more easily obtained pure and free from chlorine); it is evaporated and calcined, to transform the bromate into bromid; it is then neutralized by means of an acid; the liquid is put into a test tube, and a drop of sulphuret of carbon is introduced, after which a drop or two of bromine dissolved in distilled water is added; it is then agitated, and if there is iodine present, the sulphuret of cobalt is colored violet. It is colored yellow by bromine. It is important to avoid an excess of bromine, lest it form a bromid of iodine, which does not act. I have tried the process, and found it exact nearly to a tenth of a milligram of iodine.

ARTIFICIAL SILIFICATION OF LIMESTONES.—It is some years since M. Kuhlmann, of Lille, proposed to preserve pieces of sculpture, etc., by impregnating them with a solution of silicate of potash. $SiO^3 KO + CO^2 CaO = SiO^3 CaO + CO^2 KO$. This process has been used on a grand scale in certain parts of the Cathedral Notre Dame. The architect of the cathedral reports as follows: 1. That the infiltration of silica made "sur les terrasses et contre-fort du choeur," in October, 1852, have preserved the stone from the green moss that covers stones in moist places. 2. That the gutters and flagging of limestones subjected to this process present surfaces perfectly dry, covered with a silicious crust. 3. That upon the stones so prepared, dust and spider webs are less common than upon the stone in the ordinary state. The report also states that tender stones have been rendered hard; they have lost part of their porosity, and after being washed, they dry more rapidly than stones not silified. The process has succeeded completely on all calcareous blocks, whether isolated or forming part of the structure, new and old.

It is not yet known how this process will act on mortars; but if successful, the silicification of an entire monument may be accomplished, and its restoration when old. The whole exterior might be thus covered with a thick bed of artificial silicate of lime, and a whole edifice be protected by this means from all atmospheric causes of destruction.

NEW VARNISH FOR HELIOGRAPHIC ENGRAVING ON STEEL.—By M. Niepce de Saint Victor.—This varnish has the fluidity of albumen, and spreads and dries as easily as collodion, which enables us to operate ten minutes after the steel plate has been covered. The following is its composition:

Benzine	100 grammes.
Pure Bitumin from India . . .	5 "
Pure yellow wax*	1 "

I have also modified the solvent† in the following manner:

Oil of naphtha	5 "
Benzine	1 "

I may also mention, that I have been enabled to render my varnish sufficiently sensible to light to be able to operate in ten minutes, or a quarter of an hour, at most, in the *camera obscura*, and a few minutes suffice when we operate by contact of the solar rays.

The varnish is rendered sensitive by pouring on the plate anhydrous sulphuric ether, containing a few drops of essence of lavender.

After the plate is dry, it is exposed to the light.

The heliographic operations being completed, the steel plate is engraved by the processes described by M. Lemaitre (Sitting of May 23, 1853.)

---

* When the substances are dissolved, the varnish is strained through a cloth with pressure, and is then allowed to settle, and decanted; if the varnish becomes too thick, benzine may be added.

† See *Comptes Rendus*, May 23d, 1853.

PHOTOGRAPHIC ENGRAVINGS ON GLASS.—M. Niepce de Saint Victor has commenced to apply his new varnish upon plates of glass, and to operate with them similarly as with steel. When the plate has received the image, it is submitted to the vapors of hydrofluoric acid, or a little of the liquid acid is applied.

DETECTION OF PICRIC ACID IN BEER.—By J. L. Lassaigne.—The very powerful bitterness of picric acid, which resembles that which characterizes the principle extracted from hops, and which has led to its use as a partial substitute for hops, in certain localities, cannot be distinguished in beer which contains it by the taste alone, as we have proved by direct experiments; but the employment of some very simple chemical reactions enabled us to determine its presence.

In studying the properties of picric acid, we remarked that this acid, which communicates to water its color and bitterness, when dissolved in beer, is not precipitated by subacetate of lead, whilst the bitter and coloring principles of the hop are almost entirely precipitated by this basic salt. We have likewise proved that ordinary animal charcoal, as that which has been purified by the acids, absorbs, precipitates, and combines with, the coloring principle of the beer, whilst the picric acid remains in solution with its natural tint, and does not combine with the charcoal.

The means which I employ for detecting small quantities of picric acid added to beer is founded on the application of these two properties.

In the experiments which I have made on this subject, I acted comparatively on pure beer, of good manufacture, and on a certain quantity of the same beer to which I had added 1-12000th, and even only 1-18000th of picric acid.

By pouring into these beers an excess of tribasic acetate of lead, or agitating them with an excess of powdered animal charcoal, I proved that pure beer was very nearly, if not completely, decolored, whilst beer containing picric acid, in the abovementioned proportions, remained of a citron-yellow color owing to the non-precipitation of this acid.

I do not think that this process will enable us immediately to detect in beer a smaller quantity of picric acid than I have mentioned; in such cases, it will be necessary to concentrate the liquids by evaporation.—*Journal de Chimie Medicale.*

THE ERICSSON.—The caloric ship, yesterday, made a private trip down the Bay as far as the Quarantine. In consequence of the leaking of the cylinders, but little power was got up, and no effort at speed was made. The other portions of the machinery worked well, and as soon as the cylinders are properly tightened we may expect another public trial [and another public failure.—ED.]—*N. Y. Tribune*, Feb., 18.

BRITISH ASSOCIATION OF CHEMISTS AND DRUGGISTS.—An association under this head has been formed, with the view of establishing a "College of Pharmacy," and a Board of Examiners to grant certificates to persons properly educated and fully qualified to dispense medicines, whereby chemists and druggists will secure to themselves a professional status.—*London Lancet.*

The Chiropodist and the Tiger.—The magnificent tiger in the Hull Zoological Gardens, England, had, for some time past, experienced great torture by the growth of its claws into the fleshy part of its foot. It was determined to make an attempt to cut them, by stupefying the animal with chloroform. Mr. Taylor, veterinary surgeon, was the operator, and several medical gentlemen were present to advise and assist in the operation. Sponges, well saturated with chloroform, were fastened to the end of long staffs, and held to the tiger's nose. He broke several of these, and seemed disposed in this unceremonious way to disappoint all expectations of success. For some time no opportunity was afforded of performing the operation, but when 2lb 8oz. of chloroform had been used, the animal was so far stupefied as to induce Mr. Taylor to commence. Ropes were got round the animal's neck, his head was drawn close to the bars of the den, and his body kept close down, so as to prevent the struggles which he was expected to make. Smaller ropes were slipped over each of the tiger's paws, which not only rendered him helpless, but were of use in pulling each paw, as wanted, under the bars, to have the claws drawn, which was speedily done by the aid of a pair of forceps. Since the operation he has continued well.

Extraordinary Malaria Visitation.—A few days ago, the Race Ball, in connection with the Cowbridge Hunt, was celebrated at the Bear Hotel, Cowbridge, and attended by the *elite* of Glanmorganshire. Soon after the ball, about forty ladies and gentlemen, who took part in the festival, were seized with a frightful fever similar to the "Croyden malady," produced by the sudden falling of an old drain that had not been opened for twenty years, and which emitted a most overpowering malaria. The servatns and other inmates of the hotel have also been attacked by the fever.—*Lancet.*

French Academy of Medicine.—Among the prizes offered for 1854, is one of $200 for the best essay on cod-liver oil as a therapeutic agent.

Faculty of Medicine of Paris.—The chair of Medical Chemistry in this Faculty rendered vacant by the death of M. Orfila, has, by an imperial decree of the 10th of December last, been abolished, and in its place a chair of pharmacy has been instituted, which has been filled by the appointment of M. Soubeiran.

NEW YORK

JOURNAL OF PHARMACY.

APRIL, 1854.

ON THE PHARMACY OF CIMICIFUGA.

BY WM. PROCTER, JR.

Cimicifuga, or black snake root, belongs to the natural family Ranunculaceæ, with black hellebore, aconite, hydrastis, and coptis. Although a prevailing character of the plants of this family is acrimony, exceptions exist, as in hydrastis and coptis, which are simple bitters. The cimicifuga appears to hold an intermediate position. Like the coptis it is exceedingly bitter, but in addition to its tonic power it possesses some acrimony, and exerts considerable influence over the nervous system with tendency to the brain. In its merely chemical relations it is more analogous to Helleborus niger than to any of its congeners. Like that root it contains a large quantity of bitter resin, readily separable; and also a volatile principle, which diminishes by keeping, and appears to be concerned in giving medicinal activity to the root. Unlike Helleborus, however, it is not drastic, yet it exercises some influence over the uterus. It is probable that the discrepancies in the testimony regarding its medical powers are due in part to the variable quality of the drug, as well as to the imperfect pharmaceutic treatment which it has undergone preparatory to use.

It has been administered in powder, decoction and tincture, but most frequently in decoction, and this prepared at the house of the patient. Too often the root is dispensed imperfectly bruised, or perhaps not at all, and thus treated by ebullition "to get all the strength out," until the resulting decoction is deteriorated. No one thinks of decocting black hellebore, and the old process for the extract with water has been wisely abandoned, the tincture and hydro-alcoholic extract being chiefly relied on. The tincture of cimicifuga is a good preparation, but is too alcoholic when its use is to be long continued. In view of this, the following recipes for a solid and a fluid extract are offered, as affording to the practitioner the most eligible means of prescribing this drug either in pills or mixture.

Fluid Extract of Cimicifuga.—Select sixteen ounces (troy) of recently dried black snake root, reduce it to coarse powder, introduce it properly into a displacer for volatile liquids, and pour on gradually a mixture of one pint of alcohol and half a pint of ether. When the liquid commences to pass, close the orifice so that its passage shall be by drops; and when the menstruum disappears above, immediately add diluted alcohol until the filtered tincture measures a pint and a half. Set this aside in a capsule, in a warm place, until it is reduced to half a pint, and has lost its ethereal odor. Meanwhile continue the percolation with diluted alcohol until two pints more tincture are obtained. Evaporate this in a water bath to eight fluid ounces, and mix it gradually with the first product so as to avoid as much as possible the precipitation of the resin from the latter. After standing a few hours the fluid extract should be filtered, and if it does not measure a pint add a sufficient quantity of alcohol to make that measure.

If the amount of resin precipitated is considerable, it may be separated by a cloth strainer, redissolved in a little alcohol, and added to the solution, which should then be filtered.

As thus prepared, fluid extract of cimicifuga has a dark reddish brown color, like laudanum, is transparent, and possesses the bitter disagreeable taste of the root in a marked degree.

Extract of Cimicifuga.—In making this preparation proceed in the same manner as above described to exhaust the root, and continue the evaporation of the solutions separately until they have a syrupy consistence, mix them, and finish the evaporation with care over a water bath with constant stirring. Eight grains of this extract represent a drachm of the root.

Macroytin or Cimicifuga Resin.—The eclectic practitioners attribute the powers of the cimicifuga to this substance. Some have regarded it as having a more decided effect on the cerebral nerves than the root at large. As it is readily obtainable, and can easily be prepared,* by pouring the concentrated alcoholic tincture into water, its medicinal value should be tried by some of our medical men.—*Amer. Jour. of Pharmacy*, March, 1854.

ON THE MEANS FOR DETECTING FRAUDULENT ALTERATIONS IN DOCUMENTS.

BY MM. CHEVALLIER AND LASSAIGNE.

The numerous experiments which have already been tried at various times, have made known the processes which may frequently be put in practice for causing the reappearance of traces of writing effaced by chemical reactions, and for throwing light on the work of the guilty person. But there are cases in which all the means proposed for this purpose fail, and then the criminal may escape justice from the want of conclusive material proofs.

The study which we have made of many questions connected with this subject has led us to undertake various experiments, some of which have given results too important for us to defer their publication.

If, as has already been proved, it is not always possible to cause the reappearance of the effaced writing, for which other written words have, with a fraudulent intention, been substi-

* See E. Parrish's artiele, Vol xxiii., p. 329, *Amer. Jour. Pharm.*

tuted, at least, as our experiments demonstrate, we may recognise by some effects which are manifested on the surface of the altered paper, the places where the criminal act has been performed, circumscribe them by a simple chemical reaction visible to the least practiced eye, and even measure their extent. In a word, the invisible alterations produced on a deed are susceptible, owing to the partial modifications which the surface of the paper has undergone, of being differently affected by certain chemical actions, and of being rendered visible.

The experiments to which we devoted ourselves, on the occasion of a judicial investigation of great importance, committed to us by one of the judges of the *Tribunal de Première Instance* of the Department of the Seine, have led us to the knowledge of the facts which we now publish.

1. The surface of paper, sized in the ordinary way, or letter paper, no longer presents, with certain reactions, the same uniformity when it has been either accidently moistened in several places by various liquids, or left in contact, for a certain time, with agents capable of removing or destroying the characters which have been traced on it with ink.

2. The application of a thin layer of gum, of starch or farina, of gelatine or fish glue, with the view of sizing certain parts of the paper, or of causing certain bodies to adhere to it momentarily, is detected by an action similar to that which shows paper to have lately been blotted by the contact of liquids.

3. The heterogeneousness of the pulp of the papers, and the kind of size with which they are impregnated, lead to differences in the results which are observed with the same chemical reagents.

We shall now, with the details into which we think we ought to enter, examine each of these propositions, and describe the means which we have employed in endeavoring to solve questions of so high a degree of interest.

1. The homogeneousness of the surface of sized paper, not partially altered by the contact of liquids (water, alcohol, salt-water, vinegar, saliva, tears, urine, acid-salts, and alkaline-salts), is demonstrated by the uniform coloration which this

surface takes on being exposed, if not wholly, at least in various parts, to the action of the vapor of iodine disengaged at the ordinary temperature from a flask containing a portion of that metalloïd.

In order to study the effect of this iodous vapor on the surface of a paper, we used with advantage a bottle with a wide mouth; this mouth was kept closed with a round plate of ground glass. Twenty or thirty grammes of iodine crystallized in plates, as it occurs in commerce, were placed at the bottom of the bottle. The portion of the paper on which we wished to make the vapor of iodine act, was placed in connection with the mouth of the bottle, and was kept there by covering it with the ground glass lid, on which a weight was added so as to exert a slight pressure, thus closing it more perfectly.

The surface of the dry paper was thus left to the action of this vapor for three or four minutes only, in a room, the temperature of which was about 60° F., and, after the expiration of that time, the paper was withdrawn and attentively examined.

The employment of a small square vessel of glass or porcelain covered with a plate of glass, enabled us to expose a greater surface of the sheet of paper to the action of the vapor of iodine; we also made use of a wooden box closed with a lid sliding in a groove, such as is used for iodising the silvered plates in the daguerreotype.

When the surface of the paper has not been stained by any of the above-mentioned liquids, an uniform yellowish, or light brownish yellow coloration is noticed on the whole extent exposed to the vapor of iodine; in the contrary case, the surface which has been moistened, and afterwards dried in the open air, is perfectly distinguished by a different and well circumscribed tint.

On the papers into whose paste starch and resin have been introduced, as glazed letter paper and common papers prepared mechanically, the stains present such delicate reactions that we may sometimes distinguish by their color the portion of paper which has been moistened with alcohol from that which has been moistened with water. The stain produced by alcohol takes a bistre-yellow tint; that formed by water is colored of a more or less deep violet blue, the dessiccation having been effected at the ordinary temperature.

For the stains occasioned on these same papers by other aqueous liquids, the tint, apart from its intensity, resembles that of the stains of pure water. The feeble or dilute acids act like water on the surface of the same paper containing starch in its paste, but the concentrated mineral acids, by altering, more or less, the substances which enter into the composition of the latter, give rise to stains which present differences.

These reactions are not the same with regard to the papers employed in the manufacture of stamped paper. However, as we have established by numerous proofs, we may always recognise by the action of the vapor of iodine the parts of the paper which have been put in contact with chemical agents, the energy of which has been arrested by washing with cold water. We were able, on several ancient deeds, written on stamped paper, and a few words of which had been removed by us with chemical agents, to recognise the places where their action was exerted, to see and to measure the extent which they occupied on the surface of the paper.

The testing of a paper with the vapor of iodine will present this double advantage over the methods hitherto practised for detecting falsifications in writings, that it points out at once the place in the paper in which any alteration may be suspected, and that, on the other hand, it enables us to act afterwards with the reagents proper for causing the reappearance of traces of ink, when that is possible. If the means which we now propose cannot always make the former writing appear, they demonstrate the places where the alterations must have been made, when, however, the want of uniformity presented by the surface of the paper is not explained by any circumstance. This proof becomes, therefore, a weapon which the guilty person cannot avoid. But might not the presence of a stain or several stains developed by the vapor of iodine, in different parts of a public or private deed, give rise to suspicion when these stains have, perhaps, been occasioned by the spilling of some liquid on the surface of the paper, and would it not be rash and unjust to raise an accusation from such a fact?

There would, indeed, be great temerity in drawing such a conclusion from a fortuitous circumstance, but the inferences which may be drawn from the place occupied by these stains on the surface of the paper, from the more or less significant words found in those places, would not permit an accusation to be so lightly brought, when simple reasoning would be sufficient to destroy its basis. Besides, the subsequent reactions which would be made would certainly never revive words formerly written and effaced, whilst the latter effects may often be produced, more or less visibly, on those parts of the paper on which falsification has been practised, figures or words being substituted for other figures or words.

The more uniform pulp of stamped papers, the different way in which they are sized, renders these papers more or less susceptible of being stained with water, alcohol, saline solutions, and the weak acids, and then the stains which are demonstrated in them by means of the vapor of iodine are due to liquids, the energy of which has affected the fibres of the pulp, or the size which holds them together. In all these respects, the stamped paper, the preparation and sale of which are superintended by the government, will always present greater guarantees against falsification than the ordinary papers made of a pulp to which starch and resin have been added.

The forger cannot allege in his defence that the want of homogeneousness of the surface of the paper is due to the presumed action of water, saliva, tears, or other liquids which may have fallen on it accidentally, and may have modified that part of the surface of the paper with which they may have remained in contact for any length of time.

2. The applications made to the surface of a sheet of paper, with the view of covering it again at certain parts with a fine layer of gum, gelatine, starch or flour paste, or in other places to cause other sheets of paper to adhere, may be recognized not only by the reflection of light falling on the paper inclined at a certain degree of obliquity, and by the transmission of

light through the paper, but also by the varying action which the vapor of iodine exerts on this surface which is not homogeneous. Papers containing starch and resin are more powerfully acted on by this vapor than stamped papers of a less complex composition. Both, in the parts covered with starch or flour paste, are colored, in a few minutes, of a violet blue, but, with starched papers alone, a more intense coloration is manifested on the places covered again with a thin layer of gum arabic, fish-size or gelatine, whilst the same substances spread on some portions of the surface of stamped papers are not colored more perceptibly than the parts which are not covered. By looking, then, at the surface of the paper, held somewhat obliquely to incidental light, we distinguish clearly, by their different aspect, the parts on which these various substances have been applied.

The vapor of iodine, in condensing at the ordinary temperature on the surface of the papers to which any kind of size has been applied in various places, produces differences which are most commonly well recognized by the greater or less transparence of the paste of the paper.

3. The heterogeneousness of the pulp of the various papers of commerce, and the nature of the size with which they are penetrated cause differences, either in the coloration which the surface of these papers takes when exposed to the vapor of iodine, or in the tint which is manifested in the portions of size deposited in certain portions of that surface; thus, papers with starched pulp generally turn brown or blue, according to the amount of water which remains in their interstices; papers, like those of the Imperial stamp, turn yellow only under the influence of the vapor of iodine, and the parts which have received superficially a layer of another agglutinative body, resist this action for a certain time, and are distinguished from the parts of the paper which are not covered with it.

The means mentioned in the course of this memoir were successfully applied by us, on the occasion of a cause tried this year before the Court of Assize of l'Hérault.—*Journal de Chimie Médicale*, November, 1853, in the *Chemist.*

AMORPHOUS PHOSPHORUS.

BY A. PUTTFARCKEN.

The author has examined some amorphous phosphorus obtained from England. He received it in the form of a brownish red, shining, coherent powder, the peculiar odor of which powerfully affected the eyes.

By long washing with pure water, the phosphorus lost 13 per cent. in weight. The wash-water contained phosphorus and phosphoric acids, and a small quantity of phosphate of lime. The powder, when exhausted by water, was put, when dry and neutral, into well-stopped vessels; it had, however, again become acid in a very short time.

15 grms. of the so-called amorphous phosphorus were oxidized with nitric acid; this was readily effected without the assistance of heat, merely by the gradual addition of the phosphorus to the nitric acid. 135 grms. of fluid phosphoric acid, of spec. grav. 1.13, were obtained. Sulphuretted hydrogen, however, threw down so much sulphuret of arsenic from the phosphoric acid, that the quantity of that metal in the phosphorus must have been equal to one-half per cent.

For the sake of comparison, 15 grms. of common phosphorus were converted into phosphoric acid of the same specific gravity. The quantity of acid was 160 grms.

Exposure to a temperature of 392°—437° F. for three days left the amorphous phosphorus unchanged, so that even the microscope could detect no globules of ordinary phosphorus. When heated in a glass tube drawn out to a capillary point, it became black, with evolution of a strong odor of phosphuretted hydrogen, which probably arose from the decomposition of the moist phosphorous acid. It did not fuse during the operation, and on cooling reacquired its original color. After the tip of the glass tube had been sealed up, the tube was inserted into another a little wider, and then strongly heated for a considerable time with the blowpipe. No sublimate was produced, nor had the substance undergone any change by its exposure to a red heat. Boiled with solution of caustic potash, the substance evolved no phosphuretted hydrogen. Oil of turpentine dissolved much less of it than of ordinary phosphorus.

From this the author concludes that the so-called amorphous phosphorus does not deserve this name. It is rather a low oxide of phosphorus.—*Chem. Gaz.*, Dec. 1, 1853, from *Archiv der Pharm.*, lxxv. p. 136.

BENZOIC ACID, AND TESTS FOR ITS PURITY.

Dr. Mohr's process for obtaining benzoic acid which is adopted by the Prussian Pharmacopœia, unquestionably has the reputation of being the best. According to this process, coarsely powdered gum benzoin, is to be strewed on the flat bottom of a round iron pot which has a diameter of nine inches, and a height of about two inches. On the surface of the pot is spread a piece of filtering paper, which is fastened to its rim by starch paste. A cylinder of very thick paper is attached by means of a string to the top of the iron pot. Heat is then applied by placing the pot on a plate covered with sand, over the mouth of a furnace. It must remain exposed to a gentle fire from four to six hours. Mohr usually obtains about an ounce and a half of benzoic acid from twelve ounces of gum benzoin by the first sublimation. As the gum is not exhausted by the first operation, it may be bruised when cold and again submitted to the action of the heat, when a fresh portion of benzoic acid will sublime from it. This acid thus obtained, is not perfectly pure and white, and Mohr states that it is a question, in a medicinal point of view, whether it is so valuable when perfectly pure, as when it contains a small portion of a fragrant volatile oil, which rises with it from the gum in the process of sublimation.

The London Pharmacopœia directs that it shall be prepared

by sublimation, and does not prescribe that it shall be free from this oil, to which it principally owes its agreeable odor.

By the second sublimation the whole of the benzoic acid is not volatilized. What remains in the resin may be separated by boiling it with caustic lime, and precipitating the acid from the resulting benzoate of lime with hydrochloric acid. Benzoic acid can be obtained also in the wet way, and the resin yields a greater product in this process than in the former; yet it has a less pharmaceutical value, because it is free from the volatile oil which, as above stated, gives it its peculiar odor. The old method devised by Scheele is still the best, which is as follows: —Make one ounce of freshly burnt lime into a milk with from four to six ounces of hot water. To the milk of lime, four ounces of powdered benzoin and thirty ounces of water are to be added, and the mixture boiled for half an hour, and stirred during this operation, and afterwards strained through linen. The residue must be a second time boiled with twenty ounces of water and strained, and a third time with ten ounces; the fluid products must be mixed and evaporated to one-fourth of their volume, and sufficient hydrochloric added to render them slightly acid. When quite cold, the crystals are to be separated from the fluid by means of a linen strainer, upon which they are to be washed with cold water, and pressed, and then dissolved in hot distilled water, from which the crystals separate on cooling. When hydrochloric acid is added to a cold concentrated solution of the salts of benzoic acid, it is precipitated as a white powder. If the solution of the salts of this acid is too dilute and warm, none or only a portion of the benzoic acid will be separated. However, the weaker the solution is and the more slowly it is cooled, the larger will be the crystals of this acid. In the preparation of this acid in the wet way, lime is to be preferred to every other base, because it forms insoluble combinations with the resinous constituents of the benzoin, and because it prevents the gum resin from conglomerating into an adhesive mass, and also because an excess of this base is but slightly soluble. Stoltze has recommended a method by which all the acid can be removed from the benzoin:—The resin is to be dissolved in spirit, to which is to be added a watery solution of carbonate of soda, decomposed previously by alcohol. The spirit is to be removed by distillation, and the remaining watery solution, from which the resin has been separated by filtration, treated with dilute sulphuric acid, to precipitate the benzoic acid. This method gives the greatest quantity of acid, but is attended, with a sacrifice of time and alcohol, which renders it in an economical point of view inferior to the above process of Scheele. It is so far valuable, that the total acid contents of the resin can be determined by it.

Dr. Gregory considers the following process for obtaining benzoic acid the most productive*. Dissolve benzoin in strong alcohol, by the aid of heat, and add to the solution, whilst hot, hydrochloric acid, in sufficient quantity to precipitate the resin. When the mixture is distilled, the benzoic acid passes over in the form of benzoic ether. Distillation must be continued as long as any ether passes over. Water added towards the end of the operation, will facilitate the expulsion of the ether from the retort. When the ether ceases to pass over, the hot water in the retort is filtered, which deposits benzoic acid on cooling. The benzoic ether and all the distilled liquids are now treated with caustic potash until the ether is decomposed, and the solution is heated to boiling, and supersaturated with hydrochloric acid, which afterwards, on cooling, deposits in crystals, benzoic acid.

Benzoic acid, as it exists in the resin, is the natural production of the plant from which the resin is derived. It may also be produced artificially. Abel found that when cumole ($C^{18} H^{12}$) was treated with nitric acid, so dilute that no red vapors were evolved, for several days, this hydrocarbon was converted into benzoic acid. Guckelberger has, by the oxidation of casein with peroxide of manganese and sulphuric acid, obtained as one of the products benzoic acid. Albumen, fibrin, and gelatin yielded similar results when treated as above.—Wöhler has detected benzoic acid in Canadian castor, along with salicin. It is also formed by the oxidation of the volatile oil of bitter almonds. Benzoate of potash results when chloride

* "Handbook of Organic Chemistry."

animal economy is converted into hippuric acid, which may, by the action of acids, be reconverted into benzoic acid.

Benzoic acid should be completely volatile, without leaving any ash or being carbonized when heated. When dissolved in warm water, to which a little nitric acid has been added, nitrate of silver and chloride of barium should produce no precipitates. Oxalate of potash should give no turbidity to an ammoniacal solution of this acid. When heated with an excess of caustic potash it should evolve no smell of ammonia, otherwise, it has been adulterated with sal ammoniac. In spirit, benzoic acid is easily soluble, and requires 200 parts of cold and 20 parts of boiling water to dissolve one part of it. It forms two beautiful salts with ammonia which are frequently used in medicine, which, although not occupying a place in the Pharmacopœia, are yet readily prepared by direct combination of the acid with ammonia. With lime, it forms a salt soluble in water; which circumstance, together with its own comparative insolubility in that menstruum, distinguish it from all the organic acids of the Pharmacopœia.—*Annals of Pharmacy.*

ON THE COMPOSITION OF BUTTER.

BY PROF. HEINTZ.

Since Chevreul's investigation of butter, that substance has been regarded as a mixture of several fats containing glycerine, for when saponified it furnishes various fatty acids, whilst glycerine is separated from all of them. These fatty acids are partly volatile and partly not volatile with watery vapor; partly fluid and partly solid at ordinary temperatures. The former, according to Chevreul, are butyric, caproic and capric acids; the latter, stearic and margaric acids. He considered the fluid acid to be oleic acid.

Lerch has since shown that a fourth acid, caprylic acid, was to be added to the first group; and Bromeis states that the fluid non-volatile acid of butter is a peculiar acid, distinct from oleic acid, and that its solid acid contains no stearic acid, but consists entirely of margaric acid.

As Heintz regards margaric acid as a mixture of stearic and palmitic acids, he was of course led to suppose that stearine and palmitine are contained in butter. This he ascertained with certainty in consequence of Bromeis having sent him a small quantity of the margaric acid prepared by him from butter. He succeeded by partial precipitation with acetate of magnesia in obtaining therefrom pure stearic and margaric acids.

The examination of a considerable quantity of butter has led the author to the following results.

The fluid non-volatile portion of the fatty acids produced by the saponification of butter is not a peculiar acid, butyroleic acid, distinct from oleic acid, as stated by Bromeis, but is completely identical with ordinary oleic acid. It is, however, very difficult to obtain compounds of this acid in a perfectly pure state directly from the butter. The baryta salt first prepared by the author contained exactly the quantity of baryta attributed by Bromeis to the butyroleate of baryta. By minute separative methods, however, he at length succeeded in obtaining pure oleate of baryta, the composition of which agreed exactly with the formula $C^{36}H^{33}O^{3}$, BaO.

From the solid portion of the acids obtained from the butter, the author procured a remarkably large quantity of pure palmitic acid, by the process already described by him for the separation of mixtures of fatty acids. He had, however, to contend with greater difficulties in preparing the stearic acid, which had been shown by previous experiments to exist in butter. These difficulties arose, to a considerable extent, from the small quantity of stearic acid existing in butter, but more especially from the circumstance that that substance contains another acid, which is richer in carbon, more difficult of solution in alcohol, and more readily precipitated by acetate of magnesia. This the author was unable to separate in a state of purity, in consequence of the small quantity of it present; he ascertained, however, that it must contain more than 38 atoms of carbon. From his investigations it appears very probable that its composition is to be expressed by the formula $C^{40}H^{40}O^{4}$. For this new acid the author proposes the name *butic acid.* The solid portion of butter consequently contains *butine* and stearine in addition to palmitine.

Lastly, the author succeeded in procuring from the fatty acids of butter a small quantity of an acid which fuses between 118° and 172° F., and which, although it was not obtained perfectly pure, agrees so exactly in its properties and composition with myristic acid, that no doubt can be entertained that this acid also is contained in butter. Butter, consequently contains myristine.

According to the investigations of Lerch, butter contains compounds of glycerine with—

Butyric acid,	formula	$C^{8}H^{8}O^{4}$
Caproic acid,	"	$C^{12}H^{12}O^{4}$
Caprylic acid,	"	$C^{16}H^{16}O^{4}$
Capric acid,	"	$C^{20}H^{20}O^{4}$

The author found in addition compounds of glycerine with—

Myristic acid,	formula,	$C^{28}H^{28}O^{4}$
Palmitic acid,	"	$C^{32}H^{32}O^{4}$
Stearic acid,	"	$C^{36}H^{36}O^{4}$
Butic acid,	"	$C^{40}H^{40}O^{4}$

We thus arrive at the conclusion, that the entire series of the fats of the fatty acids, from butyric acid to butic acid, the composition of which may be expressed by the general formula $C^{4}nH^{4}nO^{4}$, is contained in butter, with the single exception of pichurmeic acid ($C^{24}H^{24}O^{4}$), and that all those members of the series in which the number of equivalents of carbon are not divisible by 4, but only by 2, do not occur in it; a conclusion already arrived at by Görgey for cocoa-nut oil.

Butter consequently consists of a mixture of oleine with butyrine, caproine, capryline, caprine, myristine, palmitine, stearine and butine.—*Chem. Gazette*, Dec. 1, 1853, from *Berichtder Akad. der Wiss. zu Berlin*, Aug., 1853.

SACCHARINE CARBONATE OF IRON AND MAN GANESE.

BY T. S. SPEER, M. D., OF CHELTENHAM.

The introduction of the metal manganese into the domain of therapeutics, due, I believe, in the first instance, to the Belgian physician, M. Hannon, has within the last two years been followed by a careful investigation of its medicinal properties on the part of several French physicians.

From them it would appear that this metal when given in combination with iron is capable of rendering signal services in those diseases where iron alone has been hitherto prescribed, and at the present moment, the ferro-manganic preparations hold a prominent place in continental practice. As I am not, however, aware that they have yet undergone a trial in this country, or at least one, the results of which have been made public, I venture to state shortly, what a limited experience of two years enables me to say upon this subject ; inasmuch as during that period I have embraced every legitimate opportunity of prescribing the combination mentioned at the head of the present communication.

In a paper published in the *Revue Medico-Chirurgicale* for June, 1849, M. Hannon first suggested the following preparations or manganese, viz., the carbonate, the tartrate, the phosphate, the neutral malate, and the iodide. With none of these was a similar salt of iron associated.

M. Petrequin, of Lyons, however, having taken up the subject of manganic preparations, published in the *Bulletin General de Therapeutique* for March the 15th and 30th, 1852, two papers containing the results of his experience relative to the utility of the metal in question when administered in conjunction with iron.

The preparations employed by him consisted chiefly of the iodide and lactate of iron and manganese in the form of syrup, and of the carbonate of the two metals in the form of pill.

Being desirous of trying the effects of such a combination in some of the numerous cases where iron is usually indicated, I endeavored to associate the two metals in the shape of a carbonate of the protoxide, and to retain them in this condition through the medium of sugar, as is done in the case of the saccharine carbonate of iron, very recently introduced into the London Pharmacopœia—a chalybeate perhaps superior to every other, and possessing an advantage which few practitioners will not recognise in these days of tasteless globules, namely a complete freedom from the nauseous inky flavor which the preparations of iron usually impart to the palate.

The following is the formula I suggested, and according to which the preparation in question is made—

Saccharine Carbonate of Iron and Manganese.

Take of finely powdered sulphate of iron	℥ iij. ʒ j.
Carbonate of soda	℥ v.
Sulphate of manganese	ʒ j. ℈ j.
White sugar	℥ iiss.

Dissolve each of the three first mentioned ingredients in a pint and a half of water, add the solutions, and mix them well; collect the precipitate on a cloth filter, and immediately wash it with cold water; squeeze out as much of the water as possible, and, without delay, triturate the pulp with the sugar, previously reduced to a fine powder. Dry it at a temperature of about 120° Fah.

The compound thus prepared is a powder of a reddish-brown color, and devoid of all taste, save that imparted by the sugar, with which the salts of the two metals are conjoined. The dose is five grains, gradually increased up to ℈ j., three times a day; it should be given with the meals, or at least immediately after.

In the papers alluded to above, Mr. Petrequin asserts, that cases of anæmia, which had resisted the administration of iron alone, yielded rapidly to a combination of this metal with manganese. In confirmation of this statement, I may say, that in two cases which lately came under my notice, the one of chlorotic anæmia, with amenorrhœa, the other of uncomplicated traumatic anæmia, both of long standing, the saccharine carbonate of iron and manganese succeeded entirely, after iron alone had failed. In each of these cases, its effect upon the composition of the blood, and through this, upon the general health, were extremely rapid, thus affording a contrast to the effects of the simple preparations of iron, which, even when eventually successful, are usually slow in their operation.—*Pharm. Journ.* from *Medical Times and Gaz.*

ON PRACTICAL PHARMACY.

BY JUSTUS LIEBIG,

*Professor of Chemistry at the University of Giessen.**

NO. IV.

The Mixing of different Bodies.

The mixing of different medical ingredients is, in many cases, a very simple operation; some cases, however, require more attention, as in mixing there often occurs some chemical combination; and consequently, such cases ought most properly to be treated under the head of chemical operations.—However, we are obliged to mention here all operations in which the mixing forms the principal object, and the chemical combination the secondary one.

Species are a mixture of different organic substances previously cut, or coarsely pounded, such as roots, herbs, flowers, barks, woods, fruits, seeds. The mixing is effected by the hand. The larger quantities are mixed first, afterwards the smaller ones.

---

* We have preferred to retain the title of the University to which he was attached at the time these papers were written rather than to alter it to Munich, where the illustrious chemist now resides.—ED.

The ingredients must be mixed as uniformly as possible. If camphor or ethereal oils are to be added, they ought to be previously dissolved in spirits of wine.

Species for tea consist in coarsely cut roots and herbs; and all dust and fine powder must be removed from them.

Species, for fomentation, must be cut finer, and species for cataplasms must be in a coarse powder.

The compound powders (*pulveres compositi*), are made by rubbing the different ingredients together in a mortar; they must be mixed very evenly. Fine powders must be rubbed long enough, so as to present to the naked eye an uniform mass. First, rub the less quantities, and add afterwards, by degrees, the larger ones. If extracts or adhesive substances form part of the compound, mix them previously with the dry substances, or with a little sugar, and add afterwards the other ingredients.

It is not always proper to dry the extracts previous to mixing them with powders. Some aromatic substances—for example, musk—do not admit of drying. The physician ought to know well the proportions in which certain substances mixed together will admit to be dispensed as powders, or else he will find his powder to be wet, or even formed into a mass fit for making pills rather than a powder. Deliquescent substances, such as tartarus boraxatus, potassæ acetas, ought never to be prescribed as powders. Powders must be equally divided, and dispensed in separate papers.

Formerly, some compound powders were called species, such as species diatragacanthæ, species diaireos; those which are still in use, are classed now under the head of pulveres compositi.

The eleosacchara are sugar. imbibed with ethereal oils; since these oils are either volatilized, or undergo many changes through mixing, they ought never to be dispensed otherwise than according to magistral formulæ, the physician prescribing always exactly the quantity of oil and sugar to be employed.

Eleosacchara of lemon and orange are generally prepared by rubbing the sugar against the fresh rind of the fruit.

Conservæ.—Preserves are mixtures of sugar and fresh herbs or flowers. The fresh parts of vegetables are reduced to pulp by pounding them in a stone mortar, and adding to them a prescribed quantity of sugar.

Electuaria.—Electuaries are mixtures of powders and sugar, or syrups and honey, to form masses of moderate consistence. The consistence varies according to the intention of the physician; it is called *tenue*, when it flows easily from the spatula; the common electuaries are firmer, and do not run from the spatula if kept in the air transversely.

The preparation of them is very simple. First, the powders are mixed, afterwards the syrup added. If extracts are to form part of the electuary, they are first mixed with the syrup. The proportion of syrup to the powders varies according to the specific nature of the last. Powders of fibrous vegetable substances, roots, barks, &c., require three-fourth parts of syrup. Powders which attract much moisture, and are very light, require often six parts of syrup; on the other hand, gums, and other substances which are soluble in syrup, require much less. Earthy and heavy metallic substances require less than one-half of syrup. However, the last substances ought never to be administered in electuaries, because they fall to the bottom, even in one of firm consistency, and form thus an unequal mixture. Electuaries containing fibrous substances ought to be made softer as they are apt to become hardened by keeping.

Most electuaries are subject to a fermentation, which, however, is not injurious if the electuaries are properly made. They ought to be kept in cool places, and at first not closed up too tightly. As all electuaries are liable in a short time to spoil, it is better not to make them in large quantities.

At present, electuaries are only made after magistral prescriptions. Opiates, confections, and marmalades belong to the class of electuaria.

Boli.—Boluses differ from electuaries only on account of their shape and consistence. Powders mixed with honey or syrup are made into a stiff mass, and dispensed in the shape and size of bullets.

Pilulæ.—Pills are small globules from the size of a peppercorn to that of a pea. They are prepared of all sorts of substances, reduced to a fine powder, and mixed by means of an extract into a stiff paste, difficult to be kneaded, called pill mass. The mass is made by a pill machine into cylinders, and cut into pills. The sticking of the pills is prevented by causing them to roll in a powder. If no specific powder is prescribed for this purpose, pulvis lycopodii (powder of the club moss) ought to be used.

Great care must be taken in making pills, since substances are often prescribed for making them, which by all care will not hold together. Physicians often omit a good binding medium, or prescribe too much or too little of it; so that, by following their prescription, instead of massaæ pilularum, you have a wet powder, or an electuary. In such cases, the chemist is obliged to make up the deficiency according to his own knowledge, and as this may be different in different subjects, the patient is exposed to have, instead of the intended remedy, products of the most different nature.

To prescribe a new formula for pills requires great practical pharmaceutical knowledge, particularly a knowledge of the form and nature of the ingredients prescribed. Since all sorts of things are prescribed to be made up in pills, it is difficult to give general rules upon this subject. However, it may be safely taken as a rule, that whenever oils, resins, or any other substance which does not easily combine into a mass, be prescribed for making pills, that it is necessary to add to it a corresponding quantity of binding medium. Vegetable extracts are more useful for that purpose that syrups or honey. If the powders of which pills are to be made are full of vegetable fibres, the best mode is to bind them with a thick extract. In this case it would be better for the physician to prescribe rather less than the required quantity of extract, which could be rendered more ductile by the addition of water. If the powders consist of earthy or metallic substances, or salts, very little extract is required. If the powders contain much mucilage, a few drops of water will suffice; if they contain much resin, spirit of wine or a spirituous tincture will be sufficient. It this case, the physician abandons this point to the discretion of the chemist, and sometimes does the same with regard to the extract. This discretional power has both its good and its bad side. If the physician knows how much you may take or not of the extract or fluid, it is all right; but if he does not know it, and the chemist is obliged to add much more or much less than the prescriber fancies, in this case the patient has a dose quite different from that intended by the physician, an occurrence of the greatest consequence with strong remedies. Hence, in such cases, it would be better if the prescriber would prescribe only the number of pills to be made from a certain prescribed compound, and allow the chemist to bind up the mass at his discretion. If the physician has not entirely overshot the mark, so that by making as many pills as he prescribed, the chemist is not obliged to compound boluses or to dispense homœopathic globules, the patient is safe. It must be well understood that this is to be allowed where the powders are made of the most active principles, and the binding extract of a neutral or indifferent one. The contrary must take place if the extract prescribed is the most powerful drug, as copaiba, turpentine, or even a narcotic. In these cases, the dose of the extract must be carefully marked down by the prescriber, and discretion to add more or less of the powder to be granted to the chemist.

The goodness of a pill mass depends, first, on the uniform mixture of its ingredients; heterogeneous particles ought not to be traced in it either by the eye or by the touch; secondly, that it be strong, but at the same time ductile and plastic; the more worked upon the better it is; a mass which is too moist, gives pills which soon stick together. The mass for pills is worked up in mortars, of metal or iron; with caution, even stone and composition mortars may be used. Brass mortars are of little use, because of their becoming soon worn, and being easily corroded by various substances, particularly by sulphur and quicksilver, which ought never to be worked up in them. Substances easily deliquescent in the air ought never to be made into pills; but should pills containing these substances be prescribed, they must be kept in well closed glass vessels.

Pills to be perfect must be of firm consistence, perfectly round, and of equal size. Instead of using powder, sometimes pills are gilded or silvered. The operation of gilding is performed by means of a spherical box, divided into two hemispherical halves. A few leaves of gold or silver are placed in one hemispherical half, twelve to twenty pills yet moist are placed over the leaves, and covered afterwards with the same quantity of leaves, and the box closed with its other half. The box is then moved quickly with a rotatory action, and after working them a little in this manner they will be found perfectly gilded or silvered.

Wax Sponge.—Sponge cerate is prepared by immerging sponges cleansed from all impurities, into melted wax, and pressing them afterwards between two heated metal plates. Prepared sponges are preferable to wax sponges, to obtain which, fine, not too thick, and rather long sponges are chosen, which are immersed in a thin solution of gum arabic, and afterwards bound closely with string all their length, so as to press them into fine cylinders, which are left to dry.

Some salves and common plaisters belong to this class, but since in most of them chemical changes occur, we shall treat of them among the chemical operations. Chemists ought to understand how to tin their own utensils. The inner surface of copper kettles and pans is covered with a coating of tin. For this purpose, pure melted tin is poured into the vesssl, previously cleaned and dried, a little quantity of powdered muriate of ammonia is added to it, and the mass spread evenly by means of a ball of tow. This operation requires great care in regulating the heat and spreading uniformly the metal.

Salting.—To preserve fresh flowers and aromatic herbs, they are placed in layers in tubs, barrels, or jars, sprinkling each layer with salt, and pressed.

The cutting of labels, labelling, packing, forming bags, lining and covering boxes, making filters, &c., belong to the mechanical operations, which can be better learned by practice, than by any, even the most graphic description.

NO. V.

Of Chemical Operations, and of the necessary Apparatus.

The objects of chemical operations are mixtures and separations; they are much more difficult and complicated than mechanical operations, and require not only manual skill, but a thorough knowledge of chemistry. We give here only a general outline of them, as we suppose the reader acquainted with the principles of natural philosophy and chemistry. Chemical combinations are divided into solution, mixtures of the first degree, and chemical definite combinations, mixtures of the second degree, or real chemical mixtures. The operations are arranged in a similar way. We begin with those which effect slight solutions, proceed afterwards with those which effect slight combinations, and finally describe those operations which effect more complete solutions and chemical compounds. This division, however, is not altogether correct, as in many cases there is a natural transition of one operation into the other.

Heat must be regarded as one of the first agencies in chemical operations, because we know, from the principles of chemical affinity, that on heat principally all chemical activity depends. Hence we begin with the means employed for producing and regulating heat. The fuel employed chiefly is coal and charcoal, very seldom anthracite or peat. Furnaces are the apparatus employed for producing and regulating heat. There are different kinds of furnaces employed in the laboratory.

The furnaces employed in pharmacy have generally four compartments :—the ash-pit, at the basement, into which the ashes fall, and through which fresh air is admitted to the burning fuel ; it has usually a small iron door ;—the body or fireplace, for holding the fuel, which contains a grate that separates it from the ash-pit ; the chimney, by which the heated air and smoke escape ; and a superstructure above the fireplace to hold the vessels employed in the operation.

The different furnaces are, the wind furnace, the reverberating furnace, the Cupel furnace, and the blast furnace.

The wind furnace is either portable or fixed. The portable one consists usually in a cylinder made of a sheet of iron, one and a half or two feet high and one foot in diameter, closed at the bottom and open at the top, resting on feet. Above the ash-pit, which has a small opening closed with a door, is placed the grate, above which is built the fire-place, which is made either of a coating of bricks, 1½ inches thick, or by inserting a hollow cylinder of burnt clay. The cylinder is sometimes provided with a second door, for introducing the fuel; otherwise it is introduced from above. In this kind of furnaces, the fireplace and the place for introducing the retorts or stills are one and the same.

If an arched Cupel with a long tube is adapted over this furnace, it is transformed into a smelting furnace, which is much the same as a reverberating furnace. Furnaces are also made of burnt clay, with different superstructures, and holes to introduce retorts and the like; they are very useful for small operations. Fixed furnaces are usually made of bricks, and in all respects according to the same rules as the portable ones, with the exception that the interior may be square instead of cylindrical. By building over the fireplace a kind of chimney, 8 feet to 10 feet high, proportionally enlarging towards its summit, allowing a large opening closed with an iron door, for the introduction of the fuel, we obtain a powerful smelting furnace, the power of which may be increased by bellows, which however, is not necessary for pharmaceutical operations.

Furnaces in which Cupels are fixed deeply with brickwork are in some way different from the former. The ash pit is built on the light side, 8 inches or 6 inches high, with bricks, and provided with an iron door, well fitted. The grate, from 8 inches to 9 inches long and of equal breadth, is made of thick square, 6-inch iron bars, at a distance of one-fifth of an inch apart, placed flat, not on their corners. It is placed not quite in the centre, but 1 or 2 inches nearer the place where the fuel is introduced, according to the size of the vessel which is going to be fixed, and placed so that the bars lie lengthway towards the firing place. The grate is enclosed by four bricks laid flat, so as to produce a space 1½ inches high between the grate and the bricks; the opening for introducing the fuel ought also to be provided with an iron door. From this square encasement the fireplace is made immediately to assume a spherical form, which by degrees ends in a cylindrical opening. There remains a vacant space of 1⅓ inches between the upper enclosure and the kettle, the keystone being from 1½ inches to 2 inches thick. The height of the fireplace, from the grate to the bottom of the kettle, is about 8 inches to 10 inches. Where the draught is carried out, it is advisable to cause a brick from 4 inches to 6 inches broad to project above the bottom of the kettle, to cause the fire to rebound upon the same be fore escaping by the draught. The opening of the fireplace must be of equal dimensions as the grate, and its height must stand parallel with the kettle. The draught is carried off by means of iron tubes, or by bricked chimneys; they must neither be too low nor too narrow; they must be about five or six feet high and five or six inches in diameter, provided with valves or registers. The draught can be carried through the drying room.

This furnace is used for sand Cupels, stills, &c. of 2 feet in diameter. If larger vessels be employed, the grate must be made larger, but not considerably. This furnace is very powerful and requires but little fuel, and by means of registers the heat can be regulated at pleasure. A circular fire is also useful for bricked up kettles and water-baths. For this purpose the vessel is so bricked up that a keystone is made to run almost parallel with its bottom, and another brick is made to project 4 inches or 6 inches around the vessel; so that commencing from opposite the opening of the fireplace, a space is formed 4 inches or 6 inches high and 1½ inches wide, around the vessel, which space ends in the chimney, which causes the fire not only to centre upon the bottom of the vessel, but to move around it before it escapes through the chimney. Care must be taken to cause the draught to play around the lower part of the vessel, or else it acts too violently upon the upper part, and injures the vessel if not always full of water. The usual fault of furnaces is that the grate and fireplace are too large. If the bars lie too far asunder, the waste of fuel is too great. Sometimes the fireplace is too high or too low; in the first case, the fire does not act with full effect, being too far from the vessel; in the second, the heat escapes too quickly by the draught. Moreover, the fire never burns briskly in a narrow space; the flame must have room to develope itself; this is also the case with charcoal. Even the close conduct with a strong conductor somewhat hinders quick combustion. Proper draughts are sometimes neglected or improperly arranged. Grates and ash-pits must be kept particularly clean. The fuel must be placed upon the grate only, not on the enclosing brickwork; hence the wood must be properly cut for this purpose, 8 inches in length. The door of the fireplace must be kept always closed, and the heat regulated by registers.

Galley ovens or furnaces which contain sundry Cupels, heated by a common fireplace; the necks of the retorts project from both sides of the furnace. They are not employed in the laboratory but in chemical manufactures. There are other kinds of furnaces, even such in which the fire may be applied in different directions. However, the utility of such complicated apparatus does not always answer our expectations. Simplicity and ingenuity are better than all artifices.

The lamp furnace is used merely for small operations; a lamp constructed upon the principle of Argand, particularly one with a double concentric wick, and a metal stand with rings, is all that is requisite for this purpose. Spirit of wine is the best fuel.

The most useful instrument for producing intense heat with little trouble is the blow-pipe or blow-lamp. The last is chiefly used in bending glass tubes. To this end, atmospheric air is blown by bellows through a blow-pipe, which is applied to an oil or spirit lamp, and the flame thus driven to the glass which is held on the other side, and by this heat the glass is made to become ductile, and to assume any cast that is required. The use of the blow-pipe is invaluable for experiments on a small scale.

Vessels intended to be exposed to heat, are not always put into immediate contact with the fire, but immerged in something else in order that the heat may penetrate gradually, or be longer retained in the bodies which are contained therein. This is attained by vessels called baths. There are sand-baths, water-baths and steam-baths.

Cupels are generally used in sand-baths; these are kettles of iron, with a reverted broad brim, having on the upper part, on one side, a semicircular cut. They are built in the furnace above described, and filled with sand. They are used chiefly for distillation by means of retorts.

Since water under usual atmospheric pressure can only be heated to 212° Fahr., and the watery fluids contained in closed vessels, are slowly volatilized in a water-bath, and on the other hand, a high temperature destroys organic bodies, it would be useful to find a bath which should be only a few degrees higher in temperature, so as to cause the fluids contained in the closed vessel to boil, without being destroyed. Solutions of some salts will answer this purpose, for instance, of common salt. I found also, by experience, that a solution of muriate of lime, which is often a waste product in chemical operations, answer exceedingly well. The distillation of water is brisk ; even acetic acid, obtained from sulphate of potash and acetate of tin, was perfectly distilled without any empyreumatic smell. The solution reached from 212° to 220° Fahr. To maintain uniform heat, it is necessary to replace the evaporated fluid by a small addition of fresh water.

BROMINE AND IODINE IN CHILI NITRE.

From the daily increasing consumption of Chili nitre, it is advisable that some attention should be paid to the small quantities of iodine and bromine present in it. These substances would be accumulated in the mother-liquors of the refining operations, and their quantity would render them worth extraction.

Rebling states, that in the liquors from the purification of twenty-five lbs. of Chili nitre, amounting to a few pounds, he obtained, by the addition of a solution of sulphate of copper in sulphurous acid water, a precipitate equivalent to 4.5 grs. iodide of sodium.

The purification was effected in the following manner:—The salt, broken into pieces about the size of peas, was briskly agitated with cold water for a few seconds, and the liquid poured quickly off before the suspended matter was deposited. This operation was repeated a few times until the salt was colorless, when it was drained upon a funnel and washed with pure water until no further reaction with silver salt was given.

Grüneberg has examined the liquid which flowed spontaneously from 50 tons of raw Chili nitre, that had been stored in a damp place, and the mother-liquors obtained from the subsequent purification of this nitre.

He first proceeded by removing from these liquors as much as possible of the crystallizable salts, chloride of sodium and nitrate of soda. During the evaporation for this purpose a remarkable circumstance presented itself. As the concentration increased, the liquid became more turbid and brown, evolving a sensible odor of iodine, and when treated with starch gave a deep blue color.

It subsequently appeared that this was owing to a decomposition of iodide of magnesium. The addition of caustic soda prevented this inconvenience.

When the liquids had been concentrated as much as possible they weighed ninety pounds. The iodine was separated by heating with iron filings, and adding gradually sulphate of copper, as long as there remained any iodine or iodic acid in solution. During the precipitation the liquid again became brown from the liberation of iodine. By this action of sulphate of copper upon iodide of sodium $= 2\,(I\,Na) + 2\,(Cu\,O\,SO^3)$ there were produced $2\,(Na\,O\,SO^3) + Cu^2\,I + I$. The brown color was, however, removed by the gradual action of iron filings, for from $I + 2\,Fe + 2\,(Cu\,O,\,SO^3)$ there were produced $2\,(Fe\,O\,SO^3) + Cu^2\,I$, so that all the iodine of the iodide of sodium was ultimately converted into iodide of copper, while the iodine of the iodates was contained in the precipitate as proto-iodate of iron and iodate of copper.

This precipitate washed, dried, and mixed with broken glass, to render it more porous, was treated with sulphuric acid and oxide of manganese. On distillation the action was at first violent, and a large quantity of iodine mixed with chloride of iodine passed over. The water into which the product of distillation passed became brown from the solution of chloride of iodine, which after a time began to decompose and deposit iodine, generating at the same time oxygen and hydrochloric acid. Grüneberg obtained in this manner 18 ozs. of iodine. In order to obtain the bromine, the liquid from which the iodide of copper had been precipitated was filtered, evaporated to the consistence of a syrup, mixed with oxide of manganese and sulphuric acid, distilled, and the products of distillation led into a solution of caustic potass. The bromine obtained amounted to more than half an ounce.

According to these results the Chili nitre would contain:

Iodine - - - -	0.000010
Bromine - - - -	0.000005

—*London Pharm. Journ.*, Jan. 1854.

ON THE SULPHURETS DECOMPOSABLE BY WATER.

BY E. FREMY.

The sulphurets can be divided, by the action of water on them, into three classes. The first includes the sulphurets of the alkaline metals and the metals of the alkaline earths, which dissolve in water. The second, the insoluble sulphurets; and the third, the sulphurets of boron, silicum, magnesium, and alumina, which are decomposed by water. These last are but little known, because their preparation until now was attended with great difficulties.

The study of these bodies promises much interest, because the action of water on them will explain the phenomena which accompany the formation of sulphur springs.

It is known that sulphur exercises no action on silicic acid, boracic acid, magnesia, or alumina. I hold it, however, possible to replace the oxygen of these bodies by sulphur when I allow a second affinity to co-operate, as that of charcoal to oxygen. This decomposition by action of two affinities frequently happens. In my yet unpublished researches on the compounds of fluorine, I have observed already the complete decomposition of fluoride of calcium mixed with silicic acid, by sulphuret of carbon, into sulphuret of calcium. I must, therefore, conjecture that the sulphuret of carbon separates the oxygen by its carbon, and at the same time a sulphuret becomes formed because it acts by its two elements on the above oxide. Experience confirms this statement.

I have obtained by this action sulphur compounds of boron, silicium, magnesium, and alumina, when I submitted boracic acid, silicic acid, magnesia and alumina to the action of sulphuret of carbon, at elevated temperatures. To effect this reaction readily, and to withdraw these sulphurets from the decomposing influence of the alkalies contained in the porcelain retort, it is always advantageous to mix the oxide to be reduced with the charcoal, and to form small balls of this mixture, which should be treated in a manner resembling the preparation of silicium.

I have convinced myself, by analysis, that these sulphurets correspond to the oxides employed in their preparation. Sulphuret of silicium has been already obtained by Berzelius, through the action of sulphur on silicium, in small quantities, and by Pierre, through the decomposition of chloride of silicium, by sulphuretted hydrogen.

I have prepared with great care this body, when the vapor of sulphuret of carbon was conducted over small balls of charcoal and gelatinous silica, which were heated in a porcelain retort to a strong red heat. The sulphuret of silicium condenses in the tube, and appears in fine, white, silky needles, which are slightly volatile, but are by steam easily carried away.

To show the entire interest which is attached to the study of these bodies, it is sufficient to mention two reactions. When sulphuret of silicium is heated in a moist stream of air, it is decomposed under the formation of silky crystals of anhydrous silicic acid. It is evident that, with the aid of this research, the natural formation of feather-like crystals of silicic acid can be explained.

In the presence of water sulphuret of silicium gives, as is known, a vivid evolution of sulphuretted hydrogen an l silicic acid, which remains dissolved in water, and which is only deposited when the solution is evaporated. It is impossible not to compare this remarkable peculiarity of sulphuret of silicium with the natural conditions under which certain mineral waters and siliceous incrustations are formed.

As sulphuret of silicium is probably formed in all cases where silicic acid is exposed to the double action of a binary compound, which supplies sulphur to it and takes up its oxygen, so this occurs more frequently than is believed at present. If we assume its presence in districts where sulphur springs exist, the contemporaneous existence of silicic and sulphuretted hydrogen in the most important sulphuretted waters is explained.

This hypothesis has found some support in the interesting observations of Descloiscaux, which show that the siliceous waters of the Geiser contain a considerable quantity of sulphuretted hydrogen.

This explanation is only an extensionof Dumas' ingenious theory on the origin of boracic acid.

The sulphur compounds of boron and aluminum are produced as the sulphuret of silicium, and are decomposed in the same way by water. Sulphuret is obtained when sulphuret of carbon is conducted over magnesia; in this case, the presence of charcoal appears to be not advantageous. It is crystallizable and soluble in cold water. When its solution is kept by ordinary temperatures, it evolves only slowly sulphuretted hydrogen; but when it is boiled, a rapid evolution of sulphuretted hydrogen ensues under the precipitation of magnesia.—*Comptes Rendus*, in *Ann. Pharm.*

NON-EXISTENCE OF ARIDIUM.—Bahr has rëexamined the chrome iron stone in which Ulgrev supposed he had discovered the new metal aridiron, and has arrived at the conclusion, after a careful investigation, that the new metal is nothing more than iron with phosphoric acid.

ON IRON ALUM.

The Curator, Mr. Greaves, drew the attention of the meeting to a specimen of *Iron Alum* which had been sent by Mr. Lindsey Blyth, of St. Mary's Hospital, accompanied by a note, which was read. The object of Mr. Blyth's communication was to describe the composition of this salt, which has recently been prescribed by some of the medical officers attached to St. Mary's Hospital, under the name of *Iron Alum*, to explain the circumstances under which it was first brought under their notice, and the process which had been adopted at the hospital for making it. The salt first used at St. Mary's Hospital was part of a sample obtained by Mr. Davenport as a bye-product in the preparation of some ferruginous compounds. It was found by Dr. Tyler Smith to be a more powerful astringent than common alum, and not liable to produce the stimulating effects of other salts of iron. The salt obtained from Mr. Davenport consisted of sulphate of peroxide of iron and sulphate of ammonia, having the constitution and crystalline form of common alum. Some of the salt had been prepared by Messrs. Hopkin and Williams, and it had subsequently been made at the hospital, both with potash and ammonia. It was well known that the name Alum had for some time past been applied by chemists, as a generic designation, to a long series of salts which coincided with common alum in constitution and form. Thus, common alum, which is usually viewed as a double salt, consisting of sulphate of alumina and sulphate of potash, being taken as the type, iron alum is formed by substituting peroxide of iron for the alumina. And as, in common alum, the potash may be replaced by ammonia or soda, as well as by many other protoxides, so a similar replacement may be effected in iron alum without altering the type. Mr. Blyth directed the attention of those who had not particularly studied this subject to a table representing the composition of some of the salts which have been described under the generic name of alum.

Series of Alums described by different Authors.

General formula	$M^2 O^3, 3 SO^3 + MO, SO^3 + 24$ Aq.

COMMON ALUM.

With Potash	$Al^2 O^3, 3 SO^3 + KO, SO^3 + 24$ Aq.
" Soda	$Al^2 O^3, 3 SO^3 + NaO, SO^3 + 24$ Aq.
" Ammonia	$Al^2 O^3, 3 SO^3 + NH^4O, SO^3 + 24$ Aq.
" Magnesia	$Al^2 O^3, 3 SO^3 + Mg O, SO^3 + 24$ Aq.
" Lithia	$Al^2 O^3, 3 SO^3 + Li O, SO^3 + 24$ Aq.
" Manganese	$Al^2 O^3, 3 SO^3 + Mn O, SO^3 + 24$ Aq.
" Iron	$Al^2 O^3, 3 SO^3 + Fe O, SO^3 + 24$ Aq.

IRON ALUM.

With Potash	$Fe^2 O^3, 3 SO^3 + KO, SO^3 + 24$ Aq.
" Soda	$Fe^2 O^3, 3 SO^3 + NaO, SO^3 + 24$ Aq.
" Ammonia	$Fe^2 O^3, 3 SO^3 + NH^4O, SO^3 + 24$ Aq.

CHROME ALUM.

With Potash	$Cr^2 O^3, 3 SO^3 + KO, SO^3 + 24$ Aq.
" Soda	$Cr^2 O^3, 3 SO^3 + NaO, SO^3 + 24$ Aq.
" Ammonia	$Cr^2 O^3, 3 SO^3 + NH^4O, SO^3 + 24$ Aq.

MANGANESE ALUM.

With Potash	$Mn^2 O^3, 3 SO^3 + KO, SO^3 + 24$ Aq.
" Soda	$Mn^2 O^3, 3 SO^2 + NaO, SO^3 + 24$ Aq.
" Ammonia	$Mn^2 O^3, 3 SO^3 + NH^4O, SO^3 + 24$ Aq.

It would be seen from this table that many of the salts to which the term *alum*, in its most comprehensive sense, was applied, and including the iron alum in question, contain no alumina. He had been principally induced to bring the subject under the notice of the meeting in consequence of some doubt and misapprehension having existed among pharmaceutists to whom prescriptions ordering iron alum had been taken, as to the salt intended to be indicated by that term. As already stated, the salt now used at St. Mary's Hospital is the double sulphate of peroxide of iron and potash. It is prepared either by dissolving peroxide of iron in sulphuric acid, or by peroxidizing protosulphate of iron with nitric acid, and adding an equivalent of sulphate of potash. If the salt with ammonia be required, sulphate of ammonia is added instead of sulphate of potash. The solution, with excess of sulphuric acid, is to be evaporated until crystals are formed on cooling.—*Pharm. Journ.*, Jan., 1854.

ON THE PRODUCTS OF THE DISTILLATION OF BITUMINOUS SHALE.

BY THE EDITOR.

My attention having been lately directed to the product of the distillation of bituminous shales, and especially to one liquid hydrocarbon derived therefrom, I have been led to think that a new compound of that class has been so formed. The bituminous shale is from the province of New Brunswick, in proximity to (though not in contact with) the vein of mineral which has been described by Dr. Charles Wetherell, of Philadelphia, as melan-asphalte.* It (shale) is a silicious limestone, of a dull black color, like Indian ink, fracture uneven, dry surface, marked with polished wavy lines, streak brown, powder light umber brown. Incinerated it blackens, and gives off a bituminous odor, and leaves a greyish ash, which effervesces. It has the sp. gr. of 1.77. The powder treated with boiling alcohol is not dissolved, and the digestion in its own hydrocarbon liquid, or in turpentine, is also without the solution of any appreciable amount of the bituminous matter.

The ash examined after ignition afforded no traces of organized structure.

To determine the amount of volatile matters, four several

---

* Transactions of the Academy of Nat. Sciences, Phil.

experiments were made, yielding the following per centage results—

	I.	II.	III.	IV.
Ash - -	72.26	78	88.23	56.34
Bitumen -	27.74	22	11.77	43.66
	100.	100.	100.	100.

Their varied results would give an average of—

Ash - - - - - - -	73.70
Bitumen - - - - - -	26.29

When the shale is placed in a coal-gas retort, and subjected to a temperature of a dull red heat, it yields a thin tarry liquid, having an acid reaction, smelling strongly of creosote, and gives off a large quantity of inflammable gas. The proportion of gas and liquid of course vary with the temperature exhibited. At the point just below a red heat of retort, a ton of rock yields (by repeated experiments) about sixty gallons of liquid, and about 500 cubic feet of a gaseous mixture, containing hydrogen, carbonic oxide, and olefiant gas. The coke which is left behind is ashy, and generally weighs two-thirds the weight of the shale used.

If this tarry liquid be treated with five or six per cent. of concentrated sulphuric acid, and allowed to lie for twelve hours, a semi-solid tar settles down. Creosote (or carbolic acid) and paraffine are present in the tar. By pouring off the supernatant liquid, and distilling it at a low temperature—not above 212°—or by driving steam of that temperature through it, a volatile liquid is obtained, which has a strong naptha odor, and still contains traces of carbolic acid. By agitation with strong alcohol the latter is removed; by decanting the liquid and again distilling it, in glass vessels, at a temperature not above 200° F., a liquid is obtained in the receiver possessing the following properties:

Colorless, translucent, of a faint naptha odor.

Sp. gr. at 60° = .735.

In a glass retort, with thermometer inserted, it commences to boil at 180°, and the temperature during ebullition rises to 184° F.

Subjected to artificial cold it does not freeze at 12° below zero.

It is not effected by concentrated sulphuric acid, nor by nitric acid, in the cold. The latter, when warmed, oxidizes it. It is sparingly soluble in alcohol, and dissolves caoutchouc, gutta percha, lac and resin, and burns with a white flame, yielding much smoke.

Having obtained this liquid free from every trace of carbolic acid, by washing with alcohol and subsequent distillation, and from water by the use of phosphoric acid, I submitted it to an ultimate analysis with the following results:

Liquid examined	- - - -		5.66 gr.
Obtained—Water	- - - -		6.50 gr.
Carbonic acid	- - -		18.66 gr.
Equal to—			
Hydrogen	- .722	or in 100 parts.	12.79
Carbon	- - 4.925		87.01

This would probably yield the empirical formula of—

C^{73} H^{64} or perhaps C^{7} H^{6}

The color of the liquid, its approximate boiling point, and the odor first impressed me with the idea that the liquid was benzole, but the specific gravity and the lesser quantity of carbon yielded on analysis by this liquid forbids the supposition.

Saint Evre describes, in the *Comptes Rendus* (xxiv. 339, Inst. 1849, 306) a series of liquids obtained from the oil of schist, which, after being treated with potass and anhydrous phosphoric acid, gave the following results:

C^{72} H^{68}	boils at	275°—280°
C^{56} H^{52}	"	255°—260°
C^{52} H^{48}	"	215°—220°
C^{36} H^{32}	"	132°—135°

There does not appear to be any steady relation in the foregoing series between the composition and the boiling point of these four liquids. In the case of the liquid under consideration, whose composition is apparently so close to the first on the series of Saint Evre, but whose boiling point is so much less, I am at present unable to fix the precise figure to the elements, the boiling point affording no certain guide, and I have not as yet taken the gravity of the vapor.

Reserving this for a future determination, I think sufficient has been adduced to show that it is not benzole nor any of the liquids hitherto obtained from bituminous or tarry matters by distillation. The complete history of these bodies is but in embryo, and I am inclined to the opinion that more than one liquid having different gravities, boiling and congealing points, is described as benzole. Certainly much of the benzole in the market does not solidify at the temperature which Mansfield assigns to it. Possibly the number of these liquids is legion, depending on the varying temperature at which they are produced; and I am only desirous of placing it in that list as one not previously described.

Dr. Gesner, who first separated this liquid, by repeated fractional distillations from the tarry liquid, has given it the very objectionable name of Kerosene, and has made it the basis of a patent which he has obtained, applying it to the purposes of illumination, similarly as benzole is used.

When the tarry liquid from which this volatile hydrocarbon is obtained is submitted to another distillation, at a temperature above 400° F., another liquid is obtained, which is also colorless and transparent, of a slightly fragrant odor, and boiling at 400°—410° F. It has a sp. gr. of .790, and does not solidify at 10° below O. It burns with a white light and less smoky flame than the first liquid, is more soluble in alcohol, and exerts a less solvent power on the resins and elastic juices. The ultimate composition of this liquid I have not yet determined. It contains no oxygen however.

By subjecting the liquid remaining after this second liquid has been obtained, to another distillation, a liquid heavy oil is obtained, and a mass of semi-solid tar with paraffine remains behind in the still or retort. The proportion of these substances in the first distillate of sixty gallons to the ton may be averaged as follows:

Water and pyrogenous acids - -	12 gallons.
Hydrocarbon, boiling at 180° - -	13½ "
Hydrocarbon, " " 400° - -	20 "
Heavy Oil - - - -	5 "
Tarry matters separated by Oil of Vitriol, and remaining as the final residue - - -	10 "
	60 gallons.

Purity of Balsam Copaiba.—If 4 parts of sulphuric acid be added to 30 parts of balsam copaiba, and then well triturated together in a mortar, a solid mass is produced, provided the balsam be pure and unadulterated; whereas, if it should have been adulterated with castor oil, as it is very frequently reported to be, the solid defœcation does not take place. This mixture of balsam copaiba and sulphuric acid constitutes a good solid mass, by means of which this nauseous medicine may be administered in the form of pills, covered with starch or sugar.—*Guibourt.*

Varieties.

DEVILLE'S NEW LAMP-FORGE.

This furnace which produces temperatures capable of melting hydraulic limestone and refractory cement is of a simple construction. A tubulated flask used as a constant level liquid reservoir communicates with a double copper cylinder, and is kept full of fuel, which may be hydrocarbonaceous or of spirits of turpentine. The inner cylindrical envelop is pierced with holes, through which the inflammable vapor escapes, and at the centre of the apparatus is placed the orifice of the blast-pipe. In the annular space comprised between the two cylinders, and at the upper part, two copper tubes are placed; these, after having left the apparatus, unite into one tube, to which a stop-cock is attached. A two-necked flask keeps up the draught between the blast-pipe and the tube with the stop-cock. The apparatus is completed on the exterior by a channel, which receives the water to prevent the different parts of the lamp from getting too hot, and on the upper part by a copper dome, pierced by an opening and a chimney, which moderate and retain the flame. At the outset, the spirits of turpentine in the cylinder is heated until the water in the trough commences to boil, when the draught is let on, and the jet of vapor formed is lighted. The heat disengaged during the operation suffices for the evaporation of the combustible.

M. Deville remarks that those hydrocarbons whose vapor have the highest specific gravity and whose boiling point is lowest, give the maximum of heat. This has been verified by employing different kinds of oil of shale and tar.

Magnetism of Volcanic Rocks.—M. Melloni has transmitted to the Academy of Sciences a letter upon this subject. Lava and almost all rocks which attract either pole of a magnet are themselves magnetic, and consequently possess North and South magnetic polarity. This magnetic polarity has, up to now, passed unperceived, because the repulsive action being very feeble, it was necessary to bring the rock very close to the needle or bar magnet, which then developed by *reaction* attractive forces in the particles next to the magnet, which reactive attractive forces were much greater than the natural repulsive power.

To show this feeble natural repulsive power in minerals recourse must be had to a magnetoscope, or astatic needles, which are much longer and farther apart than in galvanometer, and whose great sensibility permits the mineral to be kept at a reasonable distance from the superior needle, and thus avoid the development of attractive forces.

Many rocks which in their natural state have no apparent action either upon the magnetoscope nor on the dipping needle, attract both extremities of a bar magnet of considerable size when the latter is suspended freely from its centre, and acquire at the same time a sensible permanent magnetization.

From this phenomenon, and from the more or less intense forces exerted by every mineral species upon bar magnets of different dimensions, it follows that that force is variable.

These facts, and the well marked magnetic character of Pyritiferous rocks, show that the method, adopted of late, of submitting powdered minerals to the action of a very powerful magnet, so as to strike an average of the magnetic power of these rocks, and the disturbance they exert upon instruments exhibiting terrestrial magnetism, is quite erroneous.

For equal forces, the perturbative action due to the magnetic reaction of the rocks is much inferior to the magnetic force. It does not spread indefinitely in space as the direct attractive and repulsive forces, and is destroyed completely at a force dependent on the power of the instruments employed.

Steel and Pyritiferous rocks may be magnetized, so as to produce at the same pole attractive and repulsive phenomena, upon similar poles of magnets of different sizes, whence it appears that the force residing in bodies susceptible of being magnetized is not a simple one, as now supposed, but two forces, one a *magneto-resistant* action and the other a *magneto-persistent* action.—*Cosmos*, December, 1853.

Alcohol from Beet Root.—With the present price of alcohol in France, distillers are commencing to manufacture alcohol from beet root juice rather than to produce sugar from it. At Lille, Tilloy Casteleyn carries on an extensive distillery, and Dumas exhibited to the Society of Encouragement a specimen of beet alcohol which for purity left nothing to be wished for. Other distillers, near Douay, in place of directly treating the juice, filter and concentrate it to 35 deg. before converting it into alcohol. Tilloy doubts if this plan be as advantageous as his own.

The French beet contains about 11 per cent. of sugar. By the actual processes, not more than 5 or 6 per cent. of crystallizable sugar is obtained, while in the transformation into alcohol the whole 11 are used up. The cost price of this alcohol is 80 francs the hectolitre (22 Imperial gallons); 100 litres of absolute alcohol sells at from 180 to 200 francs; and Basset has shown that there are numerous vegetable juices which contain notable quantities of sugar, from which alcohol might be obtained, and thus again leave the beet solely for the manufacture of sugar.

Twenty-one sugar manufactories have been turned into distilleries, and it was calculated would manufacture from beet 50,000 hectolitres of alcohol. Seventy thousand hectolitres are annually made there from molasses, but it is never so pure as that made from beet juice.

Telegraph Insulators.—At a stated monthly meeting of the Franklin Institute, February 24th, Dr. Turnbull called the attention of the meeting to the very great importance of proper insulation of the metallic wires of the electro-magnetic telegraph. He exhibited two new forms of insulators. The first was a modification of the form designed by J. M. Batchelder, Esq., of Boston, but omitting the use of iron, and being composed of flint, quartz, and feldspar, very compact, thoroughly vitrified on the surface, was equal to the best forms of glass insulators and much stronger; it is in the form of a cap, with a ridge for the purpose of fastening the wire, and an inverted edge, so as to divert the rain downward and prevent it from entering the inside of the cap. He remarked that even this form of insulator is defective, and the moisture settles upon it, and this acts as a carrier of the electricity to the ground. A still further modification of this apparatus is desirable, so as to give the surface of the insulator a downy covering, to cause the moisture to remain in isolated dress upon it; this Mr. Batchelder is endeavoring to accomplish. He has also produced a change by heat, &c., in the best electric substances known, namely, caoutchouc, so as to render it impervious to moisture, heat and rapid decomposition, and fit it for insulating caps for the tops of posts.

The composition is of a dark color, and in the form exhibited, has a ringing noise when struck. Subjected to water at 212 deg. it did not soften; strong sulphuric acid had no action upon it; even pure nitric acid did not destroy its elasticity, while it completely altered a piece of pure caoutchouc, converting it into a mass of brown color, which, when pressed between the finger, falls to powder. The only change noticed was its color, which was yellow instead of black. When placed in the flame of gas it burned with freedom, giving off scintillations as if combined with metallic oxide, and leaves a polished surface, while ordinary caoutchouc liquid, when burned, produced a pyro-oil, which stains the fingers, so that it has all the qualifications of a good insulating substance, being an electric not affected by a heat of 212 deg., nor altered by acids, and not liable to decomposition.—*Journal Franklin Institute.*

Photography.—The Abbé Laborde, writing of the fixing liquid, says:—It is desirable to avoid in positive proofs those chocolate tints, more or less deep, so common in photographic copies, especially in those made by those not expert. Blanquart some time showed how to prevent these defects, by adding acetic acid to the solution of hyposulphite. The change of tints is more rapid and surer in proportion as the acid is stronger, but the solution cannot be used long as it gets turbid and decomposed. The sulphur floats in a state of fine division in the liquid, and, if the proof be immersed long in it, it acquires earthy yellow tints, which spoil it. All these difficulties may be avoided, and no advantage lost, by adding to the hyposulphite solution, before it is acidified, some salt whose base will form with the sulphur a soluble compound. Thus, by neutralizing 25 grammes of ammonia by acetic acid, and 500 grammes of water, a solution which does not undergo any change is obtained. When this is to be used, 100 grammes of it are poured upon 8 grammes of hyposulphite. When many proofs have been washed with this solution, a little sulphuret of silver is formed in the liquid which lines the sides of the vessel, and does not obstruct the further use of the liquid.—*Cosmos.*

When sulphate of iron with excess of sulphuric acid is used to produce negative proofs, it is well to add a little ammonia to the hyposulphite to fix it, for the sulphuric acid in excess penetrates the tissue of the collodion, and is very difficult of removal. This excess renders the hyposulphite solution turbid and precipitates the sulphur which forms a thin veil over the proof. This is avoided by adding a little ammonia beforehand to the hyposulphite bath.—*Ibid.*

Effect of Intense Cold.—The following account of an Arctic climate upon food is drawn from Dr. Kane's account of the Grinnell Exploring Expedition, lately published.

Such latitudes seem eminently adapted for experiments upon the condensation of gases. We should think that oxygen itself, after a few night's exposure with Dr. Kane, and then treated to solid carbonic and ether, would be found melting into tears, and suspect that this would be the legitimate use of a North-west passage:

"All our eatables became laughably consolidated, and after different fashions, requiring no small experience before we learned to manage the peculiarities of their changed condition. Thus, dried apples became one solid breccial mass of impacted angularities, a conglomerate of sliced chalcedony. Dried peaches the same. To get these out of the barrel, or the barrel out of them, was a matter impossible. We found, after many trials, that the shortest and best plan was to cut up both fruit and barrel by repeated blows with a heavy ax, taking the lumps below to thaw. A crow-bar, with chiselled edge, extracted the *laminæ* badly; but it was, perhaps, the best thing we could resort to.

Sugar formed a very funny compound. Take *q. s.* of cork raspings and incorporate therewith another *q. s.* of liquid gutta percha or caoutchouc, and allow to harden; this extemporaneous formula will give you the brown sugar of our winter cruise. Extract with the saw; nothing but the saw will suit. Butter and lard, less changed, require a heavy cold chisel and mallet. Their fracture is conchoidal, with hæmatitic (iron ore pimpled) surface. Flour undergoes little change, and molasses can, at --28 deg., be half scooped, half cut, by a stiff iron ladle.

Pork and beef are rare specimens of Florentine mosaic, emulating the lost art of petrified visceral monstrosities seen at the medical schools of Bologna and Milan: crow-bar and handspike! for at --30 deg. the ax can hardly chip it. A barrel sawed in half, and kept for two days in the caboose house at +76 deg., was still as refractory as flint a few inches below the surface. A similar bulk of lamp oil, denuded of the staves, stood like a yellow sand-stone roller for a gravel walk.

Ices for the dessert come of course unbidden, in all imaginable and unimaginable variety. I have tried my inventive powers on some of them. A Roman punch, a good deal stronger than the noblest Roman ever tasted, forms readily at --20 deg. Some sugared cranberries, with a little butter and scalding water, and you have an impromptu strawberry ice. Many a time at those funny little jams, that we call in Philadelphia "parties," where the lady-hostess glides with such nicely regulated indifference through the complex machinery she had brought together, I have thought I noticed her stolen glance of anxiety at the cooing doves, whose icy bosoms were melting into one upon the supper-table before their time. We order these things better in the Arctic. Such is the "composition and fierce quality" of our ices, that they are brought in served on the shaft of a hickory broom; a transfixing rod, which we use as a stirrer first and a fork afterward. So hard is this terminating cylinder of ice that it might serve as a truncheon to knock down an ox. The only difficulty is in the processes that follow. It is the work of time and energy to impress it with the carving knife, and you must handle your spoon deftly, or it fastens to your tongue. One of our mess was tempted the other day by the crystal transparency of an icicle to break it in his mouth. One piece froze to his tongue, and two others to his lips, and each carried off the skin; the thermometer was at --28 deg."

Purity of Milk.—Attempts have been made to invent instruments and methods for determining with promptness the goodness of the milk, in order to detect some of the numerous modes of adulterating cow's milk, usually practised in large towns. These instruments, which are termed *galactoscopes* and *galactometers*, are designed to furnish an average determination of the quantity of the fat contained in the milk, since the goodness of this fluid for ordinary purposes is estimated according to the amount of fat which it contains. The best known of these instruments is the galactoscope, invented by Donne, which consists of two tubes that may be pushed into one another by means of a fine screw, each tube being closed at the opposite extremities by a plane of glass. The determination is made by ascertaining the thickness of the milk stratum, through which the light of a taper may be detected, the opacity of the milk being usually regarded as a test of the quantity of fat contained in it. Areometric determinations, such as Jones, Chevalier and Henry, as well as Quevenne, have proposed for the determination of the density, and consequently of the goodness of the milk, frequently fail in their object, while Simon's suggestion of the employing a solution of tannic acid of known strength, which precipitates butter and casein from the milk, may in many cases be open to objections.

We may calculate with tolerable accuracy the quantity of milk secreted by milch cows. According to the experiences of agriculturists, which coincide pretty closely with the results which Boussingault obtained in his experiments on the effects of different kinds of food, a cow yields, on an average, 5½ litres, or about 6 kilogrammes (a kilogramme weighs 2 lbs. 3 oz. 5 dr. avoird.) of milk in twenty-four hours. Since on an average a cow weighs 580 kilogrammes, there are thus 10.4 grammes of milk secreted for each 1,000 grammes weight of the animal.—*Lehmann Phys. Chem.*

Determination of Iodine.—By M. de Luca.—The ioduretted liquid is introduced into a tube, closed at one end, along with a few drops of sulphuret of carbon or chloroform. A very weak aqueous solution of bromine is added, and the mixture agitated. The iodine, being displaced by the bromine, dissolves in the sulphuret of carbon, which becomes of a violet color, or rose colored when the quantity of iodine is very small. In this way, the iodine contained in one-hundreth of a millogramme of iodide potassium is readily detected, and with some precautions this delicacy may be pushed as far as the one-thousandth of a milligramme. By using an aqueous test solution of bromine, of known strength, the quantity of iodine present can be determined. The quantity of bromine liquor employed, substracted from that which produces no violet or rose color in the sulphuret of carbon, indicates by a simple calculation the amount of iodine liberated.

By the same process, De Luca determines in a given liquid the amount of chlorine, bromine and iodine present, all by a single experiment.

Thus, by an estimated solution of silver the quantity of silver necessary to precipitate the three metalloids is found. Then by means of bromine the iodine is determined, and lastly by the chlorine estimation, the bromine and iodine is determined together, and thus all the elements of the calculation are obtained.

In all the operations care must be taken to avoid using an excess of bromine, which would color the sulphuret of carbon yellow, and also to avoid alcalinity in the liquor, as the bromine would be dissolved.—*Cosmos.*

M. Martin, of Marseilles, has made some observations on the constitution of rain water, gathered during a storm on the 27th of May, 1853, in that city. Iodine, chlorine, ammonia, and nitric acid were the substances looked for The following results were obtained--*Iodine*, not a trace; chlorine, 4 milligrammes per kilogramme, or per litre of water, chiefly in the form of chloride of calcium (this excess of chlorine is accounted for by the fact of the wind which accompanied or produced the storm coming from the south, or off the sea); *ammonia*, 3 milligrammes per kilogramme, or per litre of water; *nitric acid*, not a trace. The absence of iodine is at variance with the determinations of Chatin. The absence of nitric acid is still more extraordinary, as many chemists, Liebig particularly, affirm that it is always found in the water of rain storms.--*Ibid.*

NEW MODE OF DETECTING STRYCHNIA AND ITS SALTS.—Dr. Edmund W. Davy, a lecturer on chemistry in one of the Dublin Medical Schools, has communicated to the *Dublin Quarterly Journal* a paper on the above subject, which we here abridge. In order to detect the alkaloid he adds to the strychnia, in powder, or small crystals, a drop of strong sulphuric acid, so as to moisten it then a little of the ferridcyanide of potassium (red prussiate), in powder, or a drop of a strong aqueous solution, and mix all well together, when a fine deep violet color is immediately produced. This test is so delicate, that, less than the one-thousandth of a grain will give the violet color, which can be extended over a large surface. He dissolved the fiftieth of a grain of strychnia in one thousand grains of distilled water. One drop of this, weighing a grain, on being evaporated on a surface of glass, and treated as above, yielded a faint though characteristic violet tint—that is, detected the fifty-thousandth of a grain. Mr. Davy thinks his test equal to Lefort's in delicacy, and superior in practice. Lefort's mode of detection consists in moistening the alkaloid with concentrated sulphuric acid and then adding a little bichromate of potass when a violet color is produced. Davy affirms that the violet produced by his test is more permanent, changes into a brick red, which holds for several hours, that it is not affected by organic matters, by alcohol, ether or sugar, all which produce a green tint in Lefort's, and that his test is less affected by ale or beer. Mr. D. recommends the removal of the strychnia from the organic matter previously. If the sulphuric acid be weaker than the sp. gr. of 1.488, the violet color will not appear.

INDIGO IN THE ANIMAL ECONOMY.—Dr. Harral has shown, in a paper read before the Royal Society, England, that blue indigo is frequently formed in the urine of man in variable quantity, sometimes only tinging it light green, in other cases forming a pellicle of a deep blue color floating on the top. To form it, it is necessary the urine should be exposed to the air for some days, when, from the absorption of oxygen, the blue color is produced. In summer it is developed quicker than in winter, and when the color is so produced, by excluding further air from the urine, the indigo is deoxidized and the color destroyed. From some of the cases recorded it would appear that this indigo circulated in the system, and not merely produced in the urine after the latter was voided. A brown extractive usually accompanies the indigo in the urine, which matter yields a farther supply of indigo, and resembles hæmatin in its composition and chemical reactions.

Dr. H. believes the indigo to be formed from hæmatin, altered or modified, and sometimes from an urine pigment, itself derived from hæmatin.

The indigo usually occurs in urine of a pale straw color, which readily becomes turbid, alkaline, and of low specific gravity. This rule does not always hold good. Indigo, Dr. H. thinks, is always the result of disease, and its presence to be looked on as pathological phenomenon, and he thinks there is some connection between its presence and the existence of Bright's disease.

Improvement in Sticking Plaster.—It appears from a recent number of the *London Lancet* that Mr. Nickels has invented an elastic adhesive plaster. The adhesive material is spread on an elastic fabric, expressly manufactured. It possesses great elasticity, allows a free play of the muscles, and does not impede the circulation. No external bandaging is needed. It seems particularly applicable to wounds and ulcers on the face and hands, as it may be moulded to, or laid on, any prominence or cavity.

Medical Use of Strychnia.—Dr. F. E. Wilkinson details cases of neuralgia, ague, and dyspepsia, treated with minute doses of strychnia, dissolved in phosphoric acid. He was led to try this form by the success of Dr. M. Hall's use of strychnia dissolved in acetic acid. Dr. W. dissolves two grains of the alkaloid in one ounce of phosphoric acid of the London Phármacopœia, which he finds a speedy and certain solvent, and administers five minims three or four times daily, and finds in many cases relief to have followed when the twenty-fifth of a grain has been taken in these doses.—Abridged from *London Lancet.*

Valerianic Acid from Fusel Oil.—Gruneberg recommends the following proportions as the most advantageous—2¾ lbs. of bichromate of potass are to be introduced into a retort, and 4½ lbs. of hot water poured on the salt. A cooled mixture of 1 lb. of fusel oil and 4 lbs. of sulphuric acid, diluted with 2 lbs. of water, is to be allowed to flow very slowly, in a thin stream, into the liquid in the retort, and the whole is then to be distilled. The distillation goes on quietly, and 9 ounces of oily valerianic acid are obtained.—Journal of Practical Chemistry, in *Silliman's Journal.*

Preparation of Ferrocyanhydric Acid.—Liebig gives the following simple method of preparing this acid. When a cold saturated solution of ferrocyanate of potass is mixed with its own volume of fuming muriatic acid, added in small portions at a time, a snow white precipitate of pure ferrocyanhydric acid is thrown down. These are to be washed with muriatic acid, dried upon a brick, and dissolved in alcohol; from the alcoholic solution the acid may be obtained in beautiful crystals.—*Ibid.*

Vessels for Preserving Fluohydric Acid.—Stadeler found that vulcanized caoutchouc and gutta percha resist the action of this acid almost completely. The concentrated fuming acid, after remaining some time in a gutta percha bottle, was found colorless, and the only alteration which the gutta underwent was a little whitening on the inside. Dr. Gibbs (in *Silliman's Journal*) suggests the coating glass vessels with a solution of the gutta in chloroform. The only difficulty would be the formation of flaws and pores in the epidermis so formed.

Dolomite.—M. J. Durocher has obtained dolomite artificially through the action of magnesia vapors. He put in a gun-barrel some anhydrous chloride of magnesium and porous carbonate of lime, the latter being so placed that it could be reached only by vapors from the former. The gun-barrel was closed, and then kept at a low red heat for three hours. The limestone, when taken out, was partly scoriaceous externally, and covered with a mixture of chloride of calcium and chloride of magnesium. Within it was altered mostly to a dolomite, as ascertained by analysis.—*Silliman's Journal.*

M. Bussy communicated to the Academy of Sciences, Paris, some important observations made by M. Cassagnol, at Point-a-Pitre, upon the urine and blood of persons who had died of yellow fever. The results obtained were:

1st. That the urine contained very little urea, and that the uric acid had almost entirely disappeared.

2d. That the blood, on the contrary, contains a relatively large amount of urea, one-fiftieth. So that in sixty grammes of blood there is found three decigrammes of urea.

EDITORIAL.

The American Pharmaceutical Association will hold their next meeting at Cincinnati, Ohio, on Tuesday, the 25th July, 1854, at eleven o'clock, A.M.

Edward Parish, Secretary.

August Laurent, whose name is so connected with the progress of organic chemistry, at his death left his wife and two children extremely poor. Indeed, his whole life was one struggle against poverty. A few days after his death, the entire chemical section of the Academy of Sciences, Paris, with the dean (Biot) at their head, waited upon the Minister of Public Instruction in behalf of his family. The Minister received the deputation graciously, and promised attention. In October last, the son of Laurent was examined, approved, and entered in the Imperial Lyceum, Rheims, at the public expense; and, in December last, Mdme. Laurent was placed on the public pension list—1,000f. yearly.

The article in the March number on "Tin Pyrites," by Mallet, should have been credited to *Silliman's Journal*, whence it was extracted. In the February number the article on "Veratria," should have been accredited to the *American Journal of Pharmacy*. When we borrow, we purpose to honestly acknowledge, as we have no desire to appear in borrowed plumes and parade them as our own. The neglect arose from inattentive reading.

We have published in the present number Puttfarcken's experiments on the "Amorphous Phosphorus," in which he comes to the conclusion that it is not the simple substance but the oxide. About a year since, Professor R. Schrotter communicated to the Academy of Sciences, Vienna, some experiments upon the same substance, and upon the substance regarded as oxide of phosphorus, having the formula P^2O, in which he comes to the conclusion that both substances have a similar constitution, are not oxides, but merely phosphorus in a finely divided state. It would be desirable to have Puttfarken's experiments repeated and verified.

The February number (1853) of the *Comptes Rendus* contains an account of some experiments of Blandet in preserving dead bodies by injection. He poured blood into solutions of hyposulphate of soda and chloride of zinc. The former rendered the blood fluid and black, and the latter precipitated it. He then tried chloride of barium, and found that this salt prevented putrefaction, and preserved the blood in a fluid state. Having made some experiments with this salt in conjunction with Dr. Moore, of Rochester, N. Y., we found it the only one which preserved the blood without alteration. At the end of twelve months, lying together, the blood corpuscles were quite distinct and normal, and no trace of putrefaction had set in. Nitrate of potass destroyed the color after a time, and sulphate of soda dissolved the globules, and with both salts putrefaction was not arrested. It would appear, therefore, that chloride of barium is the best salt to be used in injections where color is desirable to be retained, and preparations set up in a solution of this salt will retain their life-like appearances longer than in most other solutions.

Prof. Ezra Carr, since his appointment to the Albany Medical College, has induced the trustees to open a department entitled the "Working Laboratory," where the students of medicine may learn practical chemistry. The charge is $5 for each student, being the same fee as the dissecting ticket. The faculty recommend the students to take one course of laboratory practice, at least, during the term of study. This is a move in the right direction—the medical student ought to learn practical as well as theoretical chemistry. All the graduating institutions of Great Britain require it from physicians, surgeons and apothecaries, and all the medical schools there teach it. The colleges of this country should add it to their curriculum, and until it is made *compulsory* very few students will avail themselves of the advantage. We think the fee charged by Mr. Carr too low. We are of opinion that the College of Pharmacy of this city ought to require of, or to recommend to, the aspirants for its certificate the attendance in the laboratory of an analytical chemist. A good knowledge of manipulation is of essential service to a druggist.

NEW YORK

JOURNAL OF PHARMACY.

MAY, 1854.

ADDRESS

DELIVERED TO THE GRADUATES OF THE COLLEGE OF PHARMACY OF THE CITY OF NEW YORK, BY THE PRESIDENT, GEORGE D. COGGESHALL, AT THE STATED MEETING, HELD MARCH 16TH, 1854.

[At the close of his address, on motion, the President was requested to furnish the Secretary with copies, to be offered for publication in the *New York* and *American Journals of Pharmacy*.

By order,

F. A. HEGEMAN,

Secretary to N. Y. College of Pharmacy.]

GENTLEMEN, GRADUATES OF THIS COLLEGE:

It is a pleasure to congratulate you upon the successful issue of your term of study, and we have invited you to meet with us this evening that we may present you with the diploma, according to prescribed form. Your connection with the college as students closes with this ceremony, and the full responsibility of accredited professional standing, from this time, devolves upon you. We trust that this diploma will be so regarded by you, and that it may never suffer reproach through neglect or dereliction from duty on your part.

It is an appropriate custom on occasions like the present, to unite with our congratulations on past success some considerations upon the duties of future professional life. And it is not only an appropriate but a wholesome custom, for such is the relaxing influence of habit upon the mind, that it is good for us all, at successive points of our progress, to improve occasions which most naturally arrest our serious attention, and claim an earnest reconsideration of our duties in the community. Surely this, if rightly estimated, is to us a proper time for reflection, when we are giving our official sanction to practice as pharmaceutists to young men whose relation to us as students is thus closed; whose praiseworthy application to the early study of their profession gives fair promise, as we hope, of honorable distinction in the future practice of it.

The business of an apothecary, which you are hereafter to pursue, is of a two-fold character. It is not only that of a shopkeeper, in the ordinary sense, and in which you are bound by the ordinary rules of fair dealing with your customers; it comprises also the cares, the duties, the full accountability and the prerogatives of a most important profession. "To buy and sell, and get gain," to practice your art for emolument, is certainly and justly the ultimate object of your pursuit; let it not be, as it too often is, the first and only controlling object. Far higher considerations of duty are incumbent upon you than upon a mere tradesman. You are to assume the great trust of preparing medicines for the sick, upon which are placed their hopes of arresting disease, of restoring health, of saving life itself, or at least of alleviating, so much as human remedies can, hopeless, fatal suffering. If it be true that "all that a man hath will he give for his life," so far as the safety of any one of your fellow-men may be intrusted to your care, it must be held sacred, first of all considerations for the time, in the discharge of your professional duties. If emolument ensue it is well, and honestly earned; but first of all, and paramount to all the mercenary impulses of trade, should be your duty, your professional honor. Your calling is an arduous and comparatively ill-requited one. It demands continuous study, if you would keep up with the constantly accelerating progress of science, constant watchfulness against frauds and adulterations in drugs, careful examination of the qualities of those you select for dispensing, and against their having suffered depreciation at the time you use them, that your combinations are accurately made, with accurate weights and measures. In all these particulars you must be vigilant and faithful. The immediate responsibility of the medicines required by the sick rests upon you as the dependence of last resort, upon whose skill and integrity all hopes of restoration may be placed, and from whose incapacity, unfaithfulness, or error, there often may be no appeal—it may be too late for a "correction of errors." Far removed from the sick chamber are the counting-house of the importer and the warehouse of the wholesale dealer, where medicines are merchandise, the Price Current outweighs the Dispensatory; and the anxious fear, the trembling hope with which the ultimate destination of their "goods" may be watched by sleepless eyes and aching hearts, are matters too remote to interrupt the current of trade, yet these are the commercial sources, whence you derive the crude materials, upon which your art is to be employed for the immediate use of the sick. The direct responsibility, therefore, rests upon you, and neither in manner nor in part can you evade or transfer it.

Amongst the prominent objects of interest continually presented to you, continually forced upon your attention, as practitioners of pharmacy, is one that is at once the reproach of medicine and the bane of society—Quackery. It is ever present and ever ready with its temptations, in opposition to the common understanding of right-minded men connected with the regular professions of medicine and pharmacy, that discoveries of any means calculated to alleviate human suffering should be made generally known; that all whose province it is to prepare or apply remedies may have the knowledge requisite for their proper manipulation and use, be enabled to suggest improvements, and to combine or separate, so as to adapt them to particular cases, and that to keep secret any useful discovery in medicine, for the selfish purpose of gain, is unworthy of, and below the honorable standard of character that every physician and pharmaceutist should scrupulously maintain, while the tampering with medicine, by ignorant persons, and the manufacture of worthless trash under its name, are grades of depravity with which no compromise should ever be made.

The monstrous growth of quackery in modern times has, at least, kept pace with the advancement of the age in arts and sciences designed to benefit, or when State policy requires, more expertly to destroy the human race. It protrudes itself with the most business-like assurance into all classes and circles of society; it is ever present at the corners of the streets and in our dwellings; mixes with our daily news, buying up the easily purchasable public press, which subsists in a great measure upon it, (the only honorable exception, so far as we know, being *Arthur's Home Gazette*, an excellent weekly, published in Philadelphia); and it promptly makes up all deficiency of fact with brazen falsehood. History, ancient and modern, is ransacked, or even made when it is needed; current events and discussions of general interest, political, social, moral and religious, all are used as materials for introductory paragraphs to the most preposterous eulogies of quack medicines. Many of these literary productions are by a class of scribblers of prose and verse (such as it is), who, not esteemed in any other, and probably incapable of any better employment of their talents, hire themselves to write puffs of nostrums they know nothing about. Great names are dragged into base connection with pills, mixtures, lotions, plasters, etc., to give them currency, and fictitious ones are often substituted as more likely to be popular, or perhaps less objectionable, than those of the real actors and recipients of the profits. Names, too, of all countries and people are appropriated whenever they can be made available. "The poor Indian" and the self-inflated Chinese are made involuntary sponsors for things as little known to them as their language or methods of treating disease are to the nostrum-makers from whom they receive such unexpected distinction. Frightful maladies, which are providentially of rare occurrence except in these advertisements, are multiplied to suit the market, detailed with revolting minuteness, and the text illustrated with literally horrible cuts. Certificates of cures that never occurred are signed by persons that cannot be found, though their story is "told with a circumstance" of street and number, and sworn to before the Mayor, or some other prominent functionary, before whom, by the way, anything may be sworn, as he never reads it, because it matters nothing to him, yet the appendage of his name helps to pluck the great public goose. In many cases, medicines in common use are dressed in some insignificant disguise, when, "presto!" what had been only simple matter of fact becomes astonishing, and worth a great deal more in cash; whereupon it is put up in set form, with printed envelopes, showing that to bring this great discovery to the point of projection required besides a vast expenditure of money, the whole depth of knowledge, all the skill, and through many years the self-sacrificing devotion of the wondrous genius that has finally brought it forth, "without whose signature none can be genuine"—said signature being engraved or stereotyped. New remedial agents, discovered or developed by the researches of the best minds engaged in medical science, are at once seized upon by quacks as the bases of names for new nostrums, they, forsooth, covering with the slime of their "*Compound*" the brilliant results of learning, which, from inception to promulgation, would have been as far beyond the reach of their intellect as above the level of their morals. With parasite meanness they attach themselves to the productions of men whose names will be cherished with honor and gratitude, when the whole pack of charlatans are

"Forgotten as fools or remembered as worse."

As the wares of these men are got up to entice customers, every popular prejudice must be turned to account; the most petted being one that really exists to some extent, though greatly exaggerated, against minerals and in favor of vegetables. Accordingly we find this string especially harped upon, a large proportion of quack medicines being named and strenuously declared to be "vegetable." There are favorite vegetables also, of which the popular estimation is duly encouraged, and of all these, Sarsaparilla may be considered the "best abused" root in the Pharmacopœia. Other popular notions are treated with respect in proportion to the demand they create;

and from time to time new and marvelous theories are broached as there appears to be vacancy in the public mind for their reception. It is propounded by the pill or purging school of quacks that there is but one disease, all that are called by different names being but different forms of it, for which "Universal Pills" are obviously the very remedy. The universal school, however, comprises more than this class, whose chief mission appears to be to open men's purses by opening their bowels. There are some who do not regard the pill machine as the only instrument of human relief, there being various lights in which the one disease may be considered according to the nostrum that is made for it: with one it is heat, with another cold, with a third both. Again, it is in the stomach, the skin, the nerves or the blood. Some "Universal Vegetable Renovators" (their very name is nonsense) are applied internally, others upon the surface, but each is declared to be the only medicine that should ever be bought, that no family is safe without it, or with any other, that all others are "base and dangerous impositions," the work of ignorant rogues. This latter opinion appears to be cordially reciprocated by most of the fraternity, and is, perhaps, the nearest truth of any they express. Other quacks denounce the universal system as unprincipled quackery, and declare that none but a simpleton or imposter ever denies the existence of many diseases; they, therefore, condense their wisdom upon certain specialities, making, however, as extravagant stories as any of universal pretensions. In short, the whole system, based as it is upon the ignorance, the fears and the credulity of mankind, in reference to all matters affecting health and disease, is yet so monstrous, so impudent in falsehood, that it would be ludicrous if it were not so mischievous. If its continued presence from the dark ages had not rendered it familiar, if habit had not blunted our sense of its depravity, if it could now be presented in all its deformity before a civilized community for the first time, it would be regarded with wonder at its audacity, with execration at its reckless tampering with the best temporal interests of humanity.

We hope better things of our graduates, (though we must

confess we are sometimes disappointed,) than that they should degrade their profession and deprave themselves by such prostitution of their talents and position. It is pitch that you cannot touch without being defiled. Its temptations are often great it is true; its success in one sense, and one only, sometimes astonishing, yet it often, probably in a large majority of cases, fails to secure even pecuniary success, always unsatisfying at best when gained at the cost of honor, self-respect, and the respect of the intelligent part of society, perhaps coupled with some nick-name of derision; and poor indeed is he who, having staked all of principle and good repute upon such a cast, has not won even that.

Gentlemen, in the honest and honorable pursuit of your profession, you will find, with many cares and much tedious labor, many sources of interest that will improve and elevate your minds; the frequent association with the learned and intelligent, the respect and confidence of those who require your professional services, and the unfailing reward of duty well done. Your path will not be one of roses altogether—do not hope for it. Act faithfully and honorably as you may, your best motives will be misconstrued, your best efforts underrated, by the weak-minded and unworthy, but the respect and confidence of the better part of those who know you will overbalance such annoyances; and in proportion to the consciousness of doing right is the comfort of self-approval. In the practice of your profession you will find scope enough for the exercise of all the cardinal virtues if you have them, and need enough for the cultivation of those in which you may be deficient. You must not only be scrupulously honest in what you do, you must be equally conscientious in making sure that nothing is left undone which ought to be done. You are required to be careful as much as you are to be honest in the dispensing of medicine. You have no right to indulge in absence of mind when the safety of a fellow-creature depends upon your undivided attention, and you may be roused from such abstraction by consequences of your criminal inadvertence alike frightful and irretrievable. Your profession demands from you constant, unremitting devotion to duty, duty in little things which are unknown save to yourself, and in this consists your true virtue. It is easy enough to be great upon occasion, when public applause and silver plate are the showy rewards in prospect—men of base and selfish minds might even court opportunity for such display—but the true gold of a man's character is proved by his devotion to duty for the sake of duty, the performance of duties unknown to others, that are often tedious and burdensome, the full and faithful discharge of all his duties, not because in so doing he is seen or praised, or will ever be appreciated or rewarded, but from his own sense of right.

In your practice as pharmaceutists nothing can be wholly unimportant. Your course cannot be a matter of indifference to the community around you. If you are anything in your profession, if you move at all in it, you must exert some influence, more or less, good or evil. Be ever watchful that it is good. Be great if you can, but be faithful whether or not; and if your name be not famous, it will be honorable, if not spoken all over the earth, it will be a pleasant sound to your neighbors, reminding them of a trusty friend in seasons of anxiety and suffering, and synonymous in their estimation with all that designates the upright and useful man.

ON THE MANUFACTURE OF SPERMACETI AND WHALE OILS.

BY GEORGE THOMPSON, OF NEW YORK.

There are certain marine animals, particularly those of the whale tribe, or the *Cetaceæ*, which yield a fluid or oil, named according to the fish from whence it is extracted. The principle kinds are sperm oil and whale oil.

The sperm oil is obtained from the white whale, or *Physeter macrocephalus*, the blubber of which yields what is known in commerce as head-matter, or oil, and body-oil—the proportion being one-third of the former to two-thirds of the latter. The former is found in the cavities of the head, which constitutes one-third of the length or size of the animal; these are filled with a kind of oily matter, which, on being removed from the body of the dead animal, soon begins to deposite small crystalline *laminæ*. This is crude sperm oil, and it has the sp. gr. 875 at 60° F.

When this oil comes into the hands of the manufacturer it is generally tried or boiled over, and allowed to crystallize. After becoming sufficiently cool, it is put in canvas bags, which are placed between iron plates, and by pressure, in an ordinary screw-press, the greater part of the fluid, fat, or oil flows out. This is generally of a yellow color, and has a weak but not altogether disagreeable smell, and is known as natural or unbleached sperm oil. It is the best of all oils for purposes of illumination or lubrication.

The oil is sometimes bleached with an alkali, which attacks the coloring matter, and deposites a substance called *oil soap*, which is extensively used by woollen manufacturers.

The residue, or *sperm foots*, remaining in the bags is melted and crystallized by slow cooling, cut up, put in square pieces of bagging, placed between iron plates, and subjected to the pressure of a powerful hydraulic press. Next it is refined with a moderately strong alkali, at a temperature reaching from 235° to 250° F., which attacks the spermaceti with difficulty. After being repeatedly washed in water it is run into blocks, and forms the spermaceti of commerce. This has the sp. gr. of .943 at 60° F., and is ready for druggists' use, or for being made into ordinary sperm candles. Even now, however, it is still contaminated with more or less oil, which it retains with great tenacity, and by which its melting point is greatly lowered. When it is intended for "patent spermaceti candles," it is again cut up, and put into cloth bags, which are inclosed in hair mats, covered with leather, and placed between iron slabs or plates (which up to the moment of being used are shut up in cases heated by steam), and pressed in a horizontal hydraulic hot-press incased with steam.

The residue is again refined as before, and, on cooling, presents a cake or block, of a brilliant white color, with the lustre of mother of pearl, semitranslucent, with a lamellar crystalline texture, and presents a beautiful appearance. Its melting point is now raised to 121° F.

The next step is the addition of a certain portion of wax, to prevent crystallization, when the material is ready to be made into patent spermaceti candles, which are moulded in the usual manner. They have a delicate semitransparent texture, and burn with a pure white flame. The wicks are of fine plaited, bleached cotton, and are so prepared as to require no snuffing. These candles are extensively used, and preferred to all others. They are often colored red, green, blue, and yellow, and are known as colored candles.

The different kinds of sperm oil are named according to the season in which they are manufactured, such as *summer* sperm oil, which contains a large portion of spermaceti, and hence readily congeals at a comparatively high temperature. *Spring* and *Fall* spermaceti are strained, and contain less spermaceti, and will remain limpid at 45° or 40°, while winter sperm oil is pressed as above, and, containing still less spermaceti, becomes specifically heavier or denser, and will remain limpid at 35° or 30° F.

It is a popular error that winter sperm oil will or ought to remain limpid during any weather, while the fact is that it cannot be pressed much below 30° F., and the oil thus made will rarely remain limpid at or below that point.

There is a difference in the specific gravity or density of sperm oil taken in the different oceans, a fact which has never been satisfactorily accounted for.

Whale oil is obtained from what is known as the Black or Right whale, *Balaena anstralis* and *Balaena mysticetus*, and is extracted and bleached by a process similar to that for procuring and bleaching sperm oil. The liquid oily portion separated by pressure from the crude oil is inferior (although of late extensively used for purposes of illumination) to sperm oil. The residue, or fatty matter, known as *whale oil foots*, or *pressings*, is mostly used by soap-makers. The specific gravity of whale oil is .927 at 60° F. In its manufactured state it is also known as Summer, Spring, Fall and Winter Whale Oil,

The latter, when properly pressed, will be found limpid as low as 20° F. Bleaching improves its burning qualities.

There is also a difference in the specific gravity or density of whale oil taken in the different oceans, that taken in the South Pacific, and known as South Sea oil, being 6° heavier than that taken on the North-west coast.

Whalebone is obtained from the mouth of the right whale, which yields about eight hundred pounds to every one hundred barrels of oil produced.

It is designated in market as South Sea, North-west coast, and Polar bone, and is too well known to require any description here.

Sea elephant oil is obtained from the sea elephant (*Phoca proboscidea* or *Cystophora proboscidea*). This animal is the largest of the seal tribe. It is amphibious, and is a native of the islands in the Southern and Antartic Oceans. One of them yields from three to five barrels of oil, which is specifically lighter than whale oil.

ON THE FATAL EFFECTS OF, AND IMPURITIES IN CHLOROFORM.

BY THE EDITOR.

The many and grave results which have ensued from the use of chloroform as an agent of inhalation has led of late to the conclusion in the minds of many medical practitioners that it is so uncertain in its effects as to be unsafe in the administration.

The results when fatal are in those cases (almost hitherto without exception) suddenly produced, and the symptoms are then, in some cases, referable to—

1. Paralysis of the respiratory function, or of the heart.

In others to—

2. Apoplectic symptoms.

Or, lastly—

3. Those of syncope.

The symptoms of the second class may be produced where some physical confirmation exists favorable to cerebral congestion.

Those of the third class might possibly arise from idiosyncracy in a few instances. Similar effects occasionally arise from the odors of flowers in rooms, as from the scents of the rose and the poppy, &c. But the symptoms of the first class are clearly referable to the drug and not to the individual.

When death arises from the effects of the *drug* alone, it may proceed from—

1. The improper administration of *pure* chloroform.

2. The administration of chloroform containing *foreign substances.*

3. The administration of chloroform once pure but having undergone decomposition.

(1.) When death arises out of the first mentioned circumstances it is from an overdose of the vapor, by which the patient is precluded from inhaling an oxygenated air, and the symptoms of venous blood traversing arterial vessels are evidenced. This is one mode of action of chloroform on the system. Another is the fact that air impregnated with the vapor of chloroform is of a specific gravity greater than that of common air, greater than that of oxygen. The specific gravity of chloroform vapor is =4.2, or 4¼ times heavier than air. Supposing that by the process of inhalation an atmosphere, containing 3 parts of pure air and 1 part of chloroform vapor, is inhaled, the specific gravity of such an atmosphere would be 1.800, or nearly twice as heavy as air. Suppose that even an atmosphere of six measures of air and one of vapor be inhaled, the density of such a mixture is still 1.45, almost equal to that of carbonic acid.

What would be the consequences of breathing such an atmosphere of this given density?

When it is recollected that the permeation of the oxygen of the air into the blood is effected by endosmore, and that the absorption of that oxygen occurs *because* it has a less specific gravity than the gas in the blood (free oxygen and carbonic acid)—that the favorable circumstances for healthy respiration must be a heavy gas in the blood vessels and a lighter in the pulmonary cells—we can understand what must occur when a chloroform atmosphere is inhaled.

Then the material circumstances are reversed—the heavy gas is (in the mixture first mentioned) in the lungs, and the lighter gas (oxygen and carbonic acid) is in the blood. Now, in this case, no air is inhaled into the lungs, the current on the contrary setting in now from the blood to the pulmonary cell, that is to say, both the free oxygen of the blood, in large quantity, and some of its carbonic acid, stream *from the blood* into the lung—and thus the blood is rendered impure, not merely by the absence of supply of free oxygen but by the *positive* removal of the free oxygen which had been inspired previous to this chloroform inhalation.

When a mixture of air and chloroform, in the proportions of six to one, are inhaled, the same reverse actions go on, but to a lesser degree than in the first case, inasmuch as the gravities of the two gases more readily correspond; they still bear the relation of air 1 and chloroform air 1.45, a difference quite sufficient to empty the blood-vessels of their free oxygen. In this instance the carbonic acid of the blood would not be removed; the physical fact being thus stated, that, when gases of densities nearly similar are separated by membrane they do not tend (save in a slight degree) to diffuse themselves through each other.

Thus the chloroform air acts in two ways—

1st. It does not allow the blood to be supplied with oxygen.

2d. It removes from the blood the free oxygen already existing there.

Both effects acting together must unite to produce the fatal symptoms rapidly.

When the chloroform is burned in contact with watery vapor, at low temperatures, hydrochloric and carbonic acids are formed, thus:

$$\text{Chloroform} = C^2\,H\,Cl^3 \text{ and 2 eq water} = 2\,H\,O.$$

With the oxygen in the air $= O^2$ produce:

$$3\,H\,Cl + 2\,C\,O^2.$$

When chloroform vapor is inhaled and permeates through the blood there it undergoes slow combustion (the Eremacausis of Liebig), producing those two acids in the blood. Now, as regards carbonic acid, the blood is already charged with it to its full extent, and the latter is held dissolved by the tribasic phosphate of soda therein. This additional carbonic acid will in all likelihood retain its gaseous form, and traverse the blood-vessels undissolved.

In the meantime, the hydrochloric acid thus formed in the blood would react upon the solution of phosphate of soda, neutralize it, destroy the power of dissolving carbonic acid which it once possessed, and thus some more carbonic acid would be thrown into the vessel in a gaseous form.

The effects of free bubbles of gas traversing the circulation is well known, from the fatal results of the admission of air into the veins, in surgical operations, an accident almost invariably followed by sudden death. In a few cases of death from inhalation of this vapor, the fatal result was equally rapid.

It is not meant by the foregoing to assert positively that sudden death by chloroform arises from the last mentioned occurrence. Nor is it meant to assert that the formation of these acids occur to any extent within the body. The *experimentum crucis*—the actual presence of these in the blood is wanted. But what is desired to be shown is this—that these results *do* occur out of the body, are likely to occur within it, and in the latter case will certainly produce the chemical and physiological results indicated.

Such are the accidents liable to occur with *pure* chloroform.

(2.) With regard to the second cause of death—that from chloroform containing *foreign substances*—we are in possession of more exact information than upon any other portion of the subject.

Dr. Charles J. Jackson has shown one impurity, as *fusel oil* derived from the alcohol used, which oil is not decomposed in the manufacture, and when breathed producing rapid death (in the lower animals). This evil is obviated by the use of pure alcohol.

H. Pemberton has shown the formation of two volatile ethers, of the amyle series, which are changed by oxidizing with bichromate of potass into valerianate of amyl-oxide, with the escape of chlorine or muriatic acid. These also arise from the oils in common brandy.

Souberain and Mialhe have detected compounds formed of oleaginous bodies united with chlorine. Pemberton believes he has detected in these bodies, formed where common brandy is used, paramyl and metamyl. These arise in the manufacture, independent of the alcohol; they are formed in large quantity when wood spirit is used instead of alcohol.

In this country this substitution is not to be feared, as alcohol is so cheap; but an impure alcohol is almost always used instead of a dilute *rectified* spirit, as ordered by the U. S. Pharmacopœia. Even in the latter case, *pure* alcohol distilled with hypochlorite of lime always produces chlorinated oils in the distillation. To obviate this, slaked lime is added, which prevents their formation to a great extent. To remove these wholly, purification is required. Gregory's process, which even still is much used, is wholly improper when the chloroform is destined for medical use, for, by the action of the sulphuric acid washing, some hydrochloric acid and chlorine with nitrous acid is liberated in the liquid, and these are not entirely removed by the subsequent manganese filtration. Indeed, some sulphate of manganese is formed in the chloroform by the last operation.

The proper mode of purifying this liquid appears to be, to mix it with two-thirds its weight of sulphuric acid, and let the mixture cool. When cold, the supernatant liquid is distilled along with carbonate of baryta and slaked lime, or the latter alone, and if the distillate have a specific gravity above 1.48 it should be distilled again over lime at a temperature of 160° F.

By this process both fusel and pyrogenous oils are removed and a pure chloroform obtained. Nine-tenths of the chloroform at present in use is not so purified. It is made in large quantity for commercial purposes, for which purification is unnecessary, and it is unfortunately too true that much of the chloroform on sale in this city is of the unpurified kind. Much of it is weakened by the presence of alcohol and ether. These, however, are harmless adulterations.

(3.) Chloroform properly prepared and purified may still, if kept long, produce death.

This liquid is by no means stable—the union of chlorine with formyle is constrained—when exposed to the light of the sun, perfectly neutral chloroform, in a few days, becomes acid, and precipitates nitrate of silver. Hydrochloric acid is produced, and perhaps also chloride of carbon; and the use of sulphuric acid to purify it tends, if any traces of acid remain, to develop the hydrochloric acid in a few hours. This takes place to a less extent when it has been twice purified over lime.

It might be advantageous to place a layer of fresh slaked lime at the bottom of the chloroform stock bottles in apothecaries' stores, and keep the bottles covered from the light. The lime would prevent or remove the first traces of hydrochloric acid when formed and put a stop to any further change.

With regard to the manufacture and preservation of pure chloroform, it appears that the following requisites are essential:

1. That rectified alcohol, and not any form of brandy or whiskey, be used.

2. That slaked lime be used along with the hypochlorite.

3. That a low temperature (170°) be used for distillation.

4. That, after purification with sulphuric acid, it be rectified once or twice over lime, at the foregoing temperature.

5. That it be preserved in vessels (filled) excluded from sunlight.

6. That a little lime (fresh slaked) be added to the store bottles.

CONTRIBUTIONS TO PHARMACY.

BY JOHN P. METAUER, M. D., LL.D., OF VIRGINIA,

Professor of the Principles and Practice of Medicine and Surgery in the Medical Department of Randolph Macon College.

It will not be denied that the operation of therapeutical agents is essentially influenced by the mode by which they are prepared.

This fact, so generally true, is particularly exemplified in the preparations of cinchona, cantharides, colchicum, guaiacum, and several other medicinal substances, of which I shall speak presently.

For more than twenty-five years my attention has been particularly directed to this subject, and, during this period, I have adopted several new methods of preparing some of the articles of the materia médica, and have satisfied myself, by repeated practical trials, that these preparations possessed superior efficacy to those generally employed.

Many years ago I prepared an acetous infusion of cantharides,* for blistering purposes. This infusion was first designed for vesicating the scalps of infants, without removing the hair, and its action was very satisfactory. It was applied simply by wetting the surface of the head, and the hair nearest its roots, and then carefully covering the parts with a cabbage leaf, or oiled silk, to prevent the too sudden evaporation of the blistering fluid. When other parts of the body were to be blistered, a thin compress of bibulous paper, or cloth saturated with the infusion, was applied to them, and carefully covered with oiled silk. To insure speedy and effective vesication, I usually re-applied the tincture two or three times, after intervals of half an hour. I found this agent equally as efficient and certain in its action with adults as with infants.

* ℞. Canth. contus., 2½ oz.; Acid acet., 2 pts. Digest for fourteen days, and filter.

14

It rendered the removal of the hair unnecessary, as it blistered every part of the surface, even when a very thick head of hair existed. This preparation has been used by many of my medical friends, and with entire satisfaction. Within the last ten years I was induced to prepare an œthereous solution of cantharides* as a vesicant, and have found it far more prompt and certain in its operation than the acetous infusion. It may be applied in the same manner as the latter. Frequently, merely wetting the skin with the solution, without covering the part, will blister; especially in infants. When adults are to be blistered, the preparation should generally be applied with a thin compress, and carefully covered, as already suggested—moistening the compress from time to time, until the skin is decidedly reddened. I have found this by far the most convenient and reliable means of blistering that I have ever employed. This œthereal tincture of cantharides is also an efficient internal remedy. As an emmenagogue and diuretic, it has greatly exceeded my expectation. The œthereous menstruum seems not only to promote the operation of the cantharidin upon the genito-urinary organs, but at the same time to guard against strangury. I now use this preparation of cantharides almost exclusively, both externally and internally, when the lytta is indicated, and have done so for seven or eight years.

The remarkable efficacy of the œthereous preparation of the Spanish Fly induced me, five years ago, to employ spirits of nitric œther as a menstruum for cubebs, colchicum, guaiacum, squill, ergot, gossypium, sanguinaria, ipecacuanha, digitalis, nux vomica, and some other articles of less importance. The œthereous tincture of cubebs† is a most valuable remedy in all the sub-acute inflammations of the bladder, of the urethra, of the uterine cavity, and of the mucous lining of the stomach and intestines. It should be administered in some mucilaginous vehicle.

---

* ℞. Canth. contus., 3 oz.; Spirit. œth. nitric, 2½ pts. Digest for eight days, and filter.

† ℞. Pip. cubeb. contus., 4 oz.; Spirit. œth. nitric, 2 pts. Digest for eight days and filter.

The tincture of colchicum* is applicable to the treatment of all of the cases demanding the use of the colchicum, and is decidedly preferable to the vinous seminal tincture now in use, by reason of its tendency to act on the urinary system. It is very well adapted to the treatment of sub-acute rheumatism, gout, œdema, and neuralgic rheumatism, especially if the urinary secretion is materially diminished in quantity. In the bloating occasionally connected with the dysmenorrhœa, a combination with this tincture with the œthereous tincture of cantharides, sanguinaria, and gum guaiacum, will be found a most valuable remedy. It should be taken three or four times daily, in an infusion of pine tops, in doses of ten to twenty drops each. The same combination will also be found valuable in the sub-acute stage of gout and rheumatism.

The œthereous tincture of guaiacum† is superior to the preparations of that article now in general use in the treatment of rheumatism, by reason of its tendency to act on the urinary system; and the same may be said of it as an emmenagogue when there is rheumatic irritation of the uterus as an associate cause of dysmenorrhœa.

The œthereous tincture of squill‡ is adapted to all cases in which squill is indicated, and is an elegant preparation. In dropsy, œdema of the mucus lining of the larynx, and of the lungs, in asthma, and as an expectorant and diuretic, it will be found a most convenient and valuable preparation. A combination of equal parts of this tincture and of the syrup of lobelia inflata, taken three or four times daily, in doses of ʒ ss. to ʒ j. each is the most efficient remedy I have ever used in asthma.

The œthereous tincture of ergot§ is best suited to cases of inaction or torpor of the uterus, connected with debility or

* ℞. Sem. colchic. contus, 4 oz.; Spirit. œth. nitric, 2 pts. Digest for ten days and filter.

† ℞. Guaiac. gum. resin, 4 oz; Spirit. œth. nitric, 2 pts. Digest eight days, and decant.

‡ ℞. Scill. maritim. contus, 4 oz.; Spirit. œth. nitric, 2 pts. Digest eight days, and filter.

§ ℞. Ergot. contus, 2 oz., Spirit. œth. nitric, 1 pt. Digest ten days, and filter.

exhaustion; it may be used either as an emmenagogue or as a parturient. In uterine hæmorrhage, or menorrhagia dependent on debility, or exhaustion of the uterus, it will be found a valuable remedy. Its action upon the uterus is greatly influenced by the œthereous menstruum. It is best to give it in some diuretic vehicle, such as pine tops tea, or flax seed or elm tea; and it may be taken in doses of ʒ ss. to ʒ ij., once in four or five hours.

The tincture of gossypium* is possessed of properties very similar to that of ergot, and may be employed in like doses with it, and in similar diseases.

The tincture of sanguinaria† is valuable when combined with the tinctures of cantharides, guaiacum, colchicum, cubebs, and indeed any other emmenagogue, in the treatment of dysmenorrhœa. It is also a valuable expectorant and diaphoretic in pneumonia, bronchitis, and œdema of the mucous lining of the air passages. It is administered in doses from ʒ ss. to ʒ ij., once in three or four hours. The tincture may also be employed alone as a diaphoretic and expectorant.

The œthereous tincture of ipecacuanha‡ is so closely assimilated to the tincture of the sanguinaria in its therapeutical properties, as to be applicable to the treatment of the same diseases. It is an elegant and most convenient preparation. In typhoid fever it will be found far superior to the ipecac pill as a diaphoretic, especially when the tongue is dry and the thirst urgent. It may be used also in typhus fever, or indeed in any febrile affections during the sub-acute stage. This valuable preparation acts both as a diaphoretic and diuretic in these cases, as well as an expectorant.

The œthereous tincture of digitalis§ is a far better prepara-

---

* ℞. Gossypii. herbac, 4 oz.; Spirit. œth. nitric, 2 pts. Digest for ten days. and filter.

† ℞. Sanguinar. canadens. contus, 4 oz.; Spirit. œth. nitric, 2 pts. Digest eight days, and filter.

‡ ℞. Cephæl. ipecac. rad. contus, 2 oz.; Spirit. œth. nitric, 2 pts. Digest eight days, and filter.

§ ℞. Digital. purp. fal., 1½ oz.; Spirit. œth. nitric, 2 pts. Digest ten days, and filter.

tion than the alcoholic, on account of its greater activity; and this it derives chiefly from the œthereous menstruum. In doses from ʒ ss. to ʒ j., in some diuretic infusion, taken three times daily, it will be found well adapted to all such cases as require the foxglove.

The œthereous tincture of nux vomica* is especially indicated in the treatment of seminal debility, or, to speak more properly, debility of the generative organs. In this, the gravest of human ills, after such a preliminary treatment as may be demanded for the correction of constipation and prostatic tenderness, this tincture will be found a most excellent means of restoring the erections. It is also valuable in exciting appetite for food, and in the invigoration of the digestive organs. This preparation is well adapted likewise to the treatment of paraplegia, especially when the bladder and rectum are implicated, as well as such other forms of paralysis as demand the nux vomica or its alkaloid. It may be given in doses from ʒ ss. to ʒ iss. three times daily, before or after meals, in some bitter infusion. The cold infusion of wild cherry bark I have generally preferred as the vehicle for it.

The œthereous solutions or tinctures are more readily prepared, requiring to be digested for a less time than the alcoholic, and keep without the least deterioration. They are also adapted to those conditions of the constitution in which alcoholic menstrua would be objectionable.

Hydrargyrum cum creta. This valuable preparation of mercury is usually formed by triturating ℥ iij. mercury with ℥ v. of prepared chalk, until the globules are extinguished. This is a tedious process, and the resulting powder is not of uniform strength, nor is the mercury completely rubbed down. Indeed, it is questionable whether the powder, when apparently well formed, always contains mercury, as a compound may be readily formed by uniting other coloring substances with chalk, to imitate the blue mercurial powder; and I think I have met with such imitations several times. The blue pow-

---

* ℞. Nucis vomicæ pulv., 2 oz.; Spirit. œth. nitric, 2 pts. Digest ten days, and filter.

der that I have procured from the shops has generally disappointed me; and for a number of years I have prepared it myself, according to the following method.

Take one part of pure starch; eight parts of prepared chalk, and sixteen parts of mercury. Reduce the starch to fine powder. The chalk may now be added, and after being well mixed, the mercury can be united. The powder must next be moistened with water, but not to the extent of wetting it; and the whole rubbed until nearly dry, when the mass should be again moistened and rubbed dry. In this manner the process must be repeated from time to time, as may be convenient, until the powder assumes a uniform bluish appearance. After the chalk seems to be saturated with the mercury, rub the mass perfectly dry, and then moisten it sufficiently to make it adhere to the surface of the mortar by pressing with the pestle. By carefully passing the pestle over the adhering mass, so as to render its surface smooth, the superfluous mercury will now escape from it in small globules and fall to the bottom of the mortar, and the separation may be facilitated by striking the bottom of the mortar against the table repeatedly, and by pouring the mercury over the surface of the mass where any globules appear. The mercury may now be removed from the mortar; and as soon as the mass becomes sufficiently dry, the trituration must be renewed and continued until the mass becomes a smooth, dry power. Prepared according to this method, I have used blue powder in my practice more than twenty-five years, and have uniformly found it far more certain in its operation than that obtained from the shops. I prescribe it in the ordinary doses, or nearly so, and yet I am satisfied it is stronger than that in general, use. I invariably direct it to be administered nearly dry united with brown sugar, and to be mixed in a cup by stirring the powder and sugar together with a straw or the point of a knife. The dose may then be taken into the mouth and swallowed, first with the saliva, and afterwards with a mouthful of water. The powder should never be mixed in a silver spoon, or any other utensil possessing an affinity for mercury, or the powder may be rendered entirely inert; and such an accident once befel a patient of mine, who nearly lost her life before the cause of failure of the medicine in producing its proper effects was discovered.—*Virginia Medical and Surgical Journal.*

ON ALEXANDER AND MORFIT'S PROCESS FOR ORGANIC ANALYSIS.

BY CHARLES M. WETHERILL, PH.D., M. D.

In the last number of the journal,* there is described an "improved" apparatus for Organic Analysis, by J. H. Alexander and Campbell Morfit. This process has been in use for some time in Germany, and was proposed by Hess, whose description may be found in *Poggendorff's Annalen* and in Erdmann and Marchand's *Journal fur Practische Chemie*, vol. xviii. pages 98 and 399, year 1839. It is also described in the last edition of *Rose's Chemistry*, and in the second supplement to *Poggendorff's Dictionary of Chemistry.* Erdmann and Marchand, as well as Wöhler, have employed it with modifications of their own; and since the method is an exceedingly neat and cleanly one, and since Alexander and Morfit have introduced modifications not, as I think, to its improvement, it may be worth while to occupy a short space in the journal with a description of the process, from the above sources, and which may be illustrated by the cut in the former number of the journal.

The combustion tube is about seventeen or eighteen inches in length, and instead of a stop-cock immediately before it, a rod of ten inches in length is fastened to the cock of the gasometer to enable one to regulate the flow of the oxygen with greater delicacy than can be effected in the ordinary way, and upon the proper regulation of which depends the accuracy of

---

* *Journal Franklin Institute*, February, 1854.

the process. The tube is heated by an alcohol lamp, which consists of a long and narrow trough, connected by means of a tube, with an alcohol reservoir similar to the oil lamp, with inverted cistern; wick holders of tin, of a rectangular section, are made of such size that they fit easily in the trough; these are added and lighted, one after another, as occasion requires. The contents of the combustion tube are arranged differently by different chemists; but in all cases a reagent, such as oxide of copper, is necessary. This cannot, in most instances, be omitted, as Alexander and Morfit have proposed, since the greater portion of substances subjected to analysis would give off liquid or volatile products of dry distillation, before the temperature is reached at which they would unite with the oxygen. Anthracite coal, or such bodies as would not yield volatile products at a low temperature, might, indeed, be subjected to this process. Perhaps experiment would show that a long portion of the tube filled with asbestus, placed beyond the substance and kept at a high temperature, could replace the oxide of copper.

Oxide of copper, therefore, or some similar reagent, must be used in the combustion tube. Some prefer to make the mixture as in Liebig's process. Erdmann and Marchand introduce the oxide of copper alone and for two-thirds its length, into the tube, which is closed at the further end with a dense plug of copper turnings, and heat the tube, passing slowly a current of dry air, (which requires a quarter of an hour,) and let cool. The organic substance is then introduced and mixed with the oxide of copper by means of a copper wire, fashioned at the extremity like a corkscrew, and the remaining space is filled with oxide, which has just been ignited over the lamp, in a platinum crucible. The pure oxide of copper, at either end of the tube, is first heated by adding the wicks, and finally the mixture itself, passing, at the same time, a slow current of dry oxygen. The corks are not dried, but evaporation and absorption are prevented by coating them with lead foil. This is effected by placing upon the cork a small disk of foil, of a couple of lines greater diameter, and with a pointed glass rod, which fits the hole, breaking through the foil and pressing it against the inside of the cavity; the Chloride of Calcium tube is then carefully introduced at the other end.

Hess (in his original memoir) and Wöhler, introduce the organic substance in a little boat of platinum or glass, which enables the residue, where there is any, to be further treated.

In combustions of salts of the alkalies or alkaline earths, where the boat contains resulting carbonates, the apparatus which I have described in the May number of the last year's Journal will be found convenient for determining this carbonic acid, as it is well calculated for small quantities of substance.

In all cases, the regulation of the oxygen stream is an important point, and should be such, that when the apparatus is filled with carbonic acid, almost no gas (in case of nitrogen free bodies) passes through the potash apparatus. Cases of carelessness in this respect, Hess says, may be detected by applying a light to the end of the potash apparatus, which causes slight detonations of the mixture of oxygen with the unconsumed inflammable gases of the substance. Erdmann and Marchand employ, in addition to the oxygen gasometer, one containing air, and milk of lime instead of water, which is used for heating the oxide of copper, and for cooling, at the close of the operation, in a current of air.

For those regardless of expense, and who are disgusted with the intolerable heat of a combustion in summer, and with the ashes of the charcoal, which fill the laboratory, Hess' process is a very acceptable one. He calculates the quantity of alcohol for one combustion to vary from a little less than a litre* to one litre and a half. Where gas may be had, it forms an advantageous substitute for alcohol. Apparatus for combustions by gas have been described by Kühn Liebig's *Annalen*, lxxiv., p. 115, by *Beale Pharm. Jour. Transactions*, x. 9, by Sonnerschein, Erdmann and Marchand's *Journal*, lv., p. 478, and by *Magnus*, idem., lx., p. 52.

I have been myself engaged in perfecting an apparatus for combustions with illuminating gas, a description of which, if it stands the test of experience, will appear in some future number of the Journal.

---

* Litre, two and one-tenth pints.

The other modification of the Hess process, proposed by Alexander and Morfit, consists of measuring the oxygen used for the combustion and examining the gaseous products of combustion, to serve as a control for the analysis. As they have not given the results of such controlling experiments, compared with the analysis itself, it was, probably, found not to answer their expectation. The father of organic analysis, Lavoisier, first employed the method of determining the elements of an organic substance, by comparing the oxygen used in combustion with the products of combustion, and determined the composition of coal, wax, alcohol and sugar. Saussure and Prout have both described processes of the same nature. To be of any avail as a check to the analysis, the controlling process should be of at least equal accuracy with the analysis itself; and it is difficult to see how an accurate determination of the oxygen used can be obtained by the method described by Alexander and Morfit. On the perfection of the modern process of organic analysis, all such methods were generally abandoned as being (with the same degree of care) much less accurate and much more difficult to carry on with proper results.—*Journal Franklin Institute*, March, 1854.

ELIMINATION OF LEAD BY IODIDE OF POTASSIUM.

BY J. OUTRAM, JR.

The value of iodide of potassium, as a therapeutical agent in cases of lead and mercurial poisoning, is now well known, many cases having been cured by this treatment alone in our hospitals. M. Melsens (the originator of this treatment) has given several cases of both lead and mercurial poisoning, which he had treated successfully by this means. He was of opinion that the metal was acted upon by the iodide of potassium converted into a soluble salt, and eliminated through the kidneys. To prove this to be the case, the metal must of course be found in the urine. This M. Melsens did not show, as he did not examine the urine chemically.

I have lately had an opportunity of examining the urine of several patients at the city hospital, who have been under the above treatment for lead disease, and the experiments have entirely corroborated M. Melsens' theory, viz.:

That the lead *is not* eliminated before treatment; and,

That it is eliminated in the urine after treatment.

The following is the process to which I subjected the urine. I evaporated it to dryness, and burned the residue until all the organic matter was driven off. This residue I boiled in diluted nitric acid, filtered, and then precipitated the lead by a stream of sulphuretted hydrogen gas. When the metal was present, it was thrown down as a black sulphuret.

I examined a number of samples of urine before the patients had been put on M. Melsens' treatment, and could not detect any trace of metal; while in those examined after treatment, the evidences of the metal were well marked. Sometimes, however, the lead could not be detected until the patient had been under treatment for some time. In most of the cases in which I detected the metal the patients had been under treatment for at least four days: but in one case, which I examined every second or third day, from the time of his admission into the hospital, it was about two weeks from the time of his being put on treatment till the time I first detected the metal in his urine. The dose of iodide of potassium that was given in those cases was ʒi daily, in divided doses.

There was one patient to whom iodide of potassium was given for another cause, lead not being suspected in his case. After a few days, the characteristic blue line appeared on the gums, and in a day or two afterwards I detected lead in his urine.

The quantity of urine examined each time was not less than six ounces. I have examined twelve cases from the hospital, and three or four from private practice, and all of them with highly satisfactory results.—*Stethoscope*, (Va.).

ON PRACTICAL PHARMACY.

BY JUSTUS LIEBIG,

Professor of Chemistry at the University of Giessen.

NO. VI.

Operations which involve Mixing and Separation of the first degree.

Solid bodies become frequently, through heat, fluid, and sometimes volatile. By these means all separation and mixing of the first and second degrees are effected. The solving power of menstrua is increased by heat. When a body is per fectly soluble in a fluid, the solving is termed total; and when only a portion of substance is soluble, it is termed partial.

The total solving is mostly a very simple process. When bodies are fluid, this is accomplished by shaking them together. When several fluids are to be mixed, the smallest quantities should be mixed first, and then the larger ones added. Many liquids, such as alcohol, or vitriol and water, evolve heat when mixed; consequently, the former should be added carefully to the latter. Solid bodies ought to be pulverized, except those which are easily soluble, such as sugar and some salts, before being added to the menstruum. Solution is facilitated by heat, and by shaking and stirring. When pure substances are used, the resulting solutions must be clear; and when foreign substances are present in an insoluble form, they should be removed by the filtration or straining of the solution. The solution of salts and alkalies in water requires no particular manipulation. It is only necessary to observe that the vessel employed shall not communicate any contamination by the action of its contents. On the small scale, vessels of earthenware, porcelain, glass, or serpentine, are employed; on the large scale, vessels of stoneware, tin, tinned copper, or tinned iron. Alkalies should be dissolved in iron vessels, because they act on tin and other metals. According to the greater or lesser solubility of salts, by the aid of heat or cold, must the use of these agents be determined.

Deliquescence involves solution, for it consists of the property which many solid bodies possess—of abstracting moisture from the air, in which moisture they become dissolved. To accomplish this, it was formerly the custom to place these substances in a damp cellar until they had absorbed sufficient water to dissolve them. They were called oils, as, for example, oil of tartar. Many salts, which contain much water of crystallization, become fluid when gently heated, which is one form of solution.

Mucilage is a thick, somewhat tenacious, watery solution of gum. Frequently it is prepared by rubbing powdered gum, with water gradually added, until the gum is dissolved. In the first instance, sufficient but not too much water must be added to prevent the formation of lumps, or the formation of mucilage will not be perfectly effected by trituration. Gum, according to its description, requires different quantities of water to form a thick mucilage; for example, gum arabic requires three parts, and tragacanth forty-eight parts of water, to form a fluid of equal consistence. The best course for the physician to pursue is to order the quantities of gum and water to be mixed, because the thickness of the mucilage required is often different.

Emulsions are not pure solutions, but partly intimate mixtures of oils and resins with mucilaginous or albuminous liquids, by which a turbid fluid is produced. They are prepared in various ways. Generally, equal parts of powdered gum and oil, or one of the former and two of the latter, are rubbed with a little water until the oily particles disappear; then the remainder of the water is gradually added with constant trituration, or sometimes the gum is formed into a thick mucilage of water, and the oil gradually rubbed in until it has disappeared, when the remainder of the water is, by degrees, added. To one part of oil, twelve parts of water are usually used. In the same manner are resins and balsams, with gum, sugar, and yolk of egg, made into emulsions. There are some gum resins, as ammoniacum, galbanum, and assafœtida, which produce, with water alone, emulsions when rubbed with it by the method described. The preparation of emulsion of almonds is a case of partial solution. The almonds are beaten with a little water into a thick paste, and then the rest of the water added in small portions at a time, until the milk is formed, which is to be strained. One part of almonds is necessary for twelve parts of water. Other oily seeds may in similar way be formed into emulsions. When a little gum arabic is added to the milk of almonds, it is called emulsio arabica sine oleo.

Syrups are watery solutions of sugar, of a thick consistence. Their preparation is very simple. Sugar, with half its weight of the juice of some fruit or watery extract, is gently heated until dissolved, and the mixture boiled for a few minutes and strained. Some syrups, as that of violets, must not be boiled, or they will be injured. With the exception of syrup of almonds, they must be clear. Syrup of almonds is prepared by beating in a mortar well dried blanched almonds, with half the weight (above described) of sugar, until a homogeneous mass is produced, then adding by degrees two-thirds of the quantity of water used for making ordinary syrups. The whole is then strained, and the residuum washed with the remaining third of water. To the resulting liquids is added the other half of the sugar, and the whole submitted to gentle heat, until the sugar is dissolved: this syrup throws nothing down. Syrups should be of a proper consistence, which is best determined by the hydrometer. They should not, when dropped hot on a cold plate, skin over; nor, from their disposition, flow but slowly away.

Mellita, or honeys, resemble syrup very much. Raw honey is purified by boiling it with water, removing the scum, and straining. A better process to purify honey is to dissolve it in two or three times its weight of water, and put the solution into a high pot, which has an opening from one to two inches from the bottom, which can be closed, for two or three days in a cool place; when the clear liquid is run out at the side opening, the thick residue is placed on a strainer to separate the remaining clear portion of the honey, both of which are then mixed and evaporated to the consistence of honey, in a water bath. Honey, thus purified, retains all its natural color, sweetness, and flavor, which is not the case when purified by the ordinary methods.

Spirituous solutions are called either spirits or tinctures, and consist of either solid or liquid substances, dissolved in alcohol, more or less diluted. They are generally prepared in closed glass vessels. When made from solid bodies, these are first reduced to a state of minute division, and then macerated with frequent agitation in the spirituous liquid, until it has extracted their virtue, when the clear portion is removed by filtration.

Mixtures are either solutions of solid substances, or mixtures of fluid ones, or both, and frequently contain finely-divided particles of insoluble substances, and sometimes partake of all these characters. They are seldom officinal preparations, being prepared generally from the magistral formulæ of the physician. Liquors are sometimes alcoholic or ethereal solutions, but generally watery solutions of saline bodies, of a clear and seldom colored nature. Fatty solutions, and resinous compounds with fats, are sometimes fluid; for example, camphor oil, which is prepared by triturating camphor with oil until it dissolves. Heat may be applied with advantage in this operation.

Salves are compounds of fat oils, with solid fats, wax, and resins, and often contain other solid bodies in a pulverent form. They should possess the consistence of lard.

Plaisters are distinguished from salves by having a more solid and hard consistence, and being of a more adhesive nature. They become soft by being gently heated, without becoming quite fluid, and are then very adhesive.

Partial solution has for its object not only mixing, but also separation. When a solid is partially dissolved in a fluid, and the dissolved portion thrown away as useless, and the insoluble portion retained, the operation is called edulcoration. When the portion dissolved in the fluid is retained, and the insoluble part rejected as valueless, it is called elixivation; or when, from a seeming homogeneous body, some portion is dissolved out by a menstruum, it is called extraction—a process generally applied to organic bodies, to remove their active principles. According to the way in which extraction is accomplished, it receives its name.

Maceration is that description of extraction which takes place when a body is left for some time in contact with a menstruum, without the application of heat for the purpose of dissolving out its soluble portions. The products are cold infusions, and are called either spirituous, or vinous, or watery, after the vehicle used.

Digestion is a kind of extraction, which is brought about by the aid of a gentle heat, that is from 80° to 100° F. Most tinctures, medicated wines, essences, and medicated vinegars were formerly prepared in this way, but are now made by maceration. Tinctures should be clear fluids, and have the smell and taste strongly of the substances from which they are prepared. The proportion of the menstruum employed should be, in general, about six times as much as the solid substances to be extracted. The same remarks apply to medicated wines and vinegars. When the menstruum is poured boiling hot on the substance to be extracted, and allowed to remain until it is cold, the operation is called hot infusion, which is very suitable for many substances; however, there are others, such as herbs, which contain essential oils, where it is detrimental, as these oils are driven off in the process. The best remedy for this evil is to conduct the operation in vessels which admit of being closed air-tight. The products are called decoctions when the menstruum is boiled for a long time with the body to be extracted. This process is applicable to substances such as roots, barks, and woods, which possess a tough, hard texture, when it is difficult for the fluid to penetrate them readily, and when their active principles are not volatile by a boiling heat. Decoctions should be made in tinned copper or silver vessels. When substances contain anything which would act upon these metals, it is imperative that glass or porcelain should be employed for this purpose. It is a bad plan to direct that the reduction from a larger quantity to a smaller one shall determine the time during which the boiling is to take place, as the fluid must evaporate according to the strength of the heat to which it is exposed; consequently, by this test, the decoction will boil three times as long in some cases as in others. Far better it is to boil decoctions for a specified time, depending upon the nature of the materials to be extracted, and taking care to adjust the quantity of the product by a subsequent addition of the menstruum if necessary.

Infused and boiled oils are prepared in a similar way. Either dried vegetable substances are digested for a time with a fat oil, or fresh ones are boiled with the oil until their moisture is expelled, and then the oil is pressed out. Care must be taken to ascertain when the moisture is expelled; because, if this be not done, the oil, which possesses very little capacity for latent heat, soon becomes very hot, and when the moisture is volatilized, becomes empyreumatic. The best method to prevent this result is to conduct the operation in a chloride of calcium bath.

In recent times the method of extracting organic substances has been very much improved. For hot extraction the water-bath is very much to be recommended, in which a box, with a well-closed cover, containing the substance to be extracted and the menstruum, is placed. By constant agitation of this box the operation is quickly performed. The water in the bath must be kept at a boiling heat, but it is not necessary that it should be kept constantly full, as the steam arising therefrom keeps up the temperature of the contents of the box as readily as the water. The only precaution to be observed is, to take care that the water does not entirely evaporate from the boiler.

Also by high-pressure steam alone is the process of hot extraction performed. The steam is conducted from a closed boiler, through tubes, into the vessel wherein the substance to be extracted is placed with water. The steam, by passing into the liquid form, evolves so much heat that the water is speedily heated to the boiling point, by which means extraction is rapidly and completely effected.

Extraction has for its object, as a rule, the separation of

active from inactive principles. The extracted portion ought to be of the same quality in the extract as it is in the substance from which it is obtained. The application of heat for extraction has for its aim a complete exhaustion of the substance to be extracted, by the softening of its fibres, &c. Sometimes the extracted constituents are themselves changed, as well as their medical properties, by heat. To obtain these in the greatest degree unchanged, cold extraction is the most suitable means. Alone, maceration produces very incomplete extraction, and besides employing much time with the necessary quantity of fluid, the watery extract is frequently spoiled. It consequently follows that those substances should alone be extracted in this manner which require a limited time for the completion of the process, if a good extract be desired. The best means to facilitate the progress of this operation are the Real and Romershausen presses. In the first, this object is accomplished by the pressure of a high column of fluid acting on the substance to be extracted, which should be in a finely divided condition, and pressed into a cylinder of much larger diameter than the column of fluid. This cylinder should possess a small aperture at the bottom to allow the fluid to escape, and be collected as it filters through the substance to be extracted. Care must be taken to keep the column of pressure constantly full with fluid, which is generally the same liquid as that which is used as the menstruum for extraction. The second is very similar in its character, except that atmospheric air is the agent employed for pressure, by means of a vacuum pump.

NO. VII.

Operations which involve Mixing and Separation of the first degree continued.

Substances, which through solution have been combined, are frequently separated by cooling or volatilization; when by volatilization the fluid portion is distributed in the air, and the fixed portion which remains is the useful one, the operation is called evaporation. Often evaporation and cooling are applied for the precipitation of bodies. When a solid body is thus precipitated from a fluid in regular geometrical forms, the operation is called crystallization. Crystallization is the means by which solid bodies, mostly salts, are separated from their solutions. It has for its object either the separation of solid bodies in regular forms, or their purification by crystallization from foreign substances; or when several salts are dissolved in one menstruum, a separation of them, in consequence of the property which different salts possess of separating from their solutions in different times, according to their solubility; and, moreover, many salts in a crystallized form can thus be partly separated by mechanical means. To perform the operation of crystallization, the body to be crystallized is dissolved in a menstruum, or by other chemical powers a crystallizable solution is formed, which is evaporated to the point at which crystallization commences. The solution is then placed in the cold; or, when the salt is almost equally soluble in both warm and cold solution, the fluid is exposed to a slow but continued evaporation.

The vessels in which solution and evaporation are performed must not communicate any foreign substances. Salts are thus made on the large scale in tin, and tinned copper or iron vessels, and on the small scale in glass, porcelain, or earthenware vessels. For alkalies, an iron utensil is the most suitable. When the entire solution is not clear, it should be filtered before it is evaporated. When colorless crystals are desired, and the solution is strongly colored by organic matter, it should be treated with fresh animal or vegetable charcoal, and then filtered. The point at which crystallization commences may be known either by a pellicle forming on the surface of the hot liquid, or when a drop of it is placed on a cold plate, by cooling, it contains crystals. It is only with salts which are with difficulty soluble that evaporation must be continued until scales of crystals are formed. With easily soluble salts, particularly such as are more readily soluble in the heat than in the cold, the first test must not be applied, but only the second. Even the formation of crystals on a cold plate proceeds with difficulty with very soluble salts, particularly when the temperature of the plate is not low enough, then the best test is the specific gravity of the solution. The crystallization of such salts proceeds more easily in winter than in summer. The more slowly solutions to be crystallized are cooled, the larger and more regular are the crystals produced, and, moreover, shaking or stirring solutions interferes with this result. Crystals form, by the cooling of the solution, on the surface, at the sides of the vessel, and particularly around any particles of solid bodies which may be present in it. When strings or wires are suspended in the liquid, fine crystals form on them. Salts which are equally soluble in hot or cold liquids, crystallize by slow evaporation, and the more slowly this is conducted, the more regular is the form of the crystals. The largest crystals are produced by the spontaneous evaporation of their solutions in the air.

The resulting crystals are, when necessary, washed with water and dried, either in a gentle heat, or by the ordinary temperature of the air, according to their nature. The mother liquor from the crystals still contains crystallizable matter, to obtain which it must be treated as above described, and this operation repeated with the liquor separated from every crop of crystals as often as it continues to produce them.

Crystallization can also be effected when to a solution a fluid is added, which has affinity for the menstruum, but not for the salt; for example, by the addition of alcohol to the watery solutions of salts; in this case both fluids combine, and the salt is separated. By this means regular crystals can be obtained, when their separation is slowly performed, which can be accomplished by carefully pouring alcohol on the surface of saline solutions, so that the combinations of their water and the alcohol proceed very slowly.

Freezing is, under all circumstances, nothing but crystallization. It is sometimes employed in pharmacy to separate water from acids, as in the case of acetic acid; in this instance the portion which remains fluid is the valuable one. Also, by melting and slowly cooling substances is crystallization effected, as in the preparation of cyanide of potassium.

In crystallization many remarkable anomalies are to be observed. To the smooth side of glass vessels crystals will attach themselves; but when the sides are covered with grease, crystals are repelled from so doing. In vessels of stoneware or wood, the crystallization of salts proceeds readily. Many very soluble salts crystallize with difficulty in glass: as, for example, a hot saturated solution of acetate of soda frequently does not crystallize at all when it is cooled in tall glass cylinders. Even agitation prevents crystallization in solutions when they are so concentrated, that, even when warmed, they deposit saline crusts. Crystallization is best conducted by placing in solutions of salts pointed or angular bodies, metallic wires, or a crystal. It then proceeds rapidly, with the development of heat, which sometimes is so great as to re-dissolve a portion of the substance which has crystallized from the fluid. A solution of Glauber's salts saturated at a temperature of 95° F., does not crystallize when cooled in closed and full bottles. When blown upon, it crystallizes. It may be kept unchanged in the air when covered with a film of oil of turpentine, and also without this film when the vessel is lightly covered with paper, and kept free from motion. Acetic acid can be kept without crystallizing in a closed vessel, at a temperature of 9° F., and besides can be strongly agitated without producing this result; but, when the vessel is opened, even at from 46° to 50° F., crystallization ensues immediately, whether the air which enters be warmer or colder than the solution.

Bodies do not always, by their separation from a menstruum, receive a regular or crystalline form. Organic compounds, especially when many are dissolved in one common menstruum, and are separated by evaporation, form an uncrystallizable mass. To this class belong extracts, resins, and other substances. When the juice of a plant, or its extract, is freed by evaporation from the greater portion of its fluid, an inspissated extract is obtained in the widest sense of the term. This operation has for its aim the separation of the active principles from the greatest portion of their watery menstruum, so as to concentrate them into a small space, by which they may be preserved for a long time, because, when combined with water, extracts are readily spoiled by fermentation.

The preparations of extracts requires much care. The evaporation must be conducted quickly, yet with a very gentle heat. In no case should the heat reach the boiling point of water. A variety of vessels are employed for their evaporation, such as pans, iron and porcelain vessels, and those previously described for crystallization. Care must be taken not to use metallic vessels which could communicate any injurious matter to the extracts.

Extracts possess various names. Succi inspissati are extracts prepared from the fresh expressed juices of vegetables. The plants must be collected at the proper time, when they are most effective, their juices strained when cold, and evaporated in a gentle manner, either in a water bath or by being placed on plates in dry air or sunlight. The scum, which consists of albumen, &c., should be removed during this process, and mixed with the extract at the termination of the evaporation. Inspissated juices should possess the consistence of a pill mass, or else they are readily spoiled by the albumen contained in them. Their color is generally green, arising from the green fecula which they contain. They give with water a turbid solution. Inspissated juices are generally made from narcotic plants, and can be prepared from recently dried plants, by pulverizing them, by extraction of the powder with cold water, and subsequent evaporation, observing the above precaution with reference to the albumen. These inspissated juices should be kept in a dry place to preserve them.

Very powerful narcotic extracts are obtained when these inspissated juices are digested with alcohol, the spirituous solution filtered, then the alcohol distilled therefrom, and the residue evaporated to the proper consistence. In this way those ingredients which are ineffective, and have only a tendency to spoil the extract, may be removed; and, moreover, these ingredients are always present in extracts in variable quantities, which renders the strength of such extracts uncertain. In Pharmacopœias, therefore, proper directions should be given for the preparation of these alcoholic extracts ; but as long as this is not the case the pharmaceutist must not on any account deviate from the old methods of making extracts by the instructions laid down in the Pharmacopœias, as dangerous results might arise from such deviation, unless by the express direction of the prescriber.

When the juices of fruits are evaporated to the consistence of honey, in the same manner previously described, they are also inspissated juices, although generally known under the name of *rob*, and are much used in France.

Pulps are distinguished from the last preparation by consisting of the soft solid portions of fruits as well as the liquid parts. To produce pulps, fresh juicy fruits, with or without previous expression, are gently boiled with water; if necessary, rubbed through a fine hair sieve; and the resulting mass evaporated to the consistence of a soft extract. When dried fruits are employed, they must for some time be boiled in water before they are rubbed through a sieve. Many fruits, such as the tamarind, contain much free acid, consequently they must not be heated in iron or copper vessels, but in pure tin or earthenware vessels. Generally a portion of sugar is added to pulps for their preservation.

In the narrow sense of the word, all substances obtained by decocting roots, flowers, barks, and other vegetable matter, and evaporating the decoctions thus obtained, to deprive them of their fluid portions, are called extracts, which are divided into watery, spirituous, ethereal, hot and cold, and simple and compound extracts.

Cold aqueous extracts were formerly prepared by macerating finely powdered substances in sixteen times their weight of cold water, from one to two days, with frequent agitation. The expressed and filtered liquid was evaporated in a water bath; again filtered, if rendered turbid by this process, and at last evaporated by a gentle heat to dryness. At present, watery extracts are made by exhausting substances with cold water in Real's press. With many bodies it is a matter of indifference whether these extracts are manufactured by cold infusion or decoction; but with some—as, for example, extract of bark—it is more than probable that the extract from the decoction is the most potent.

Spirituous extracts are prepared by the same process; except for economical reasons, the spirit should be evaporated in a distillatory apparatus to recover it.

Evaporation should be conducted in a moderate heat, and the fluid kept in continual motion in a current of air, by which means the operation is much quickened.

The consistence to which extracts should be evaporated is various. Most extracts from dry roots, barks, and herbs, should be evaporated to the thickness of common turpentine. In consequence of extracts being thinner when hot than when cold, it is necessary, from time to time, during their evaporation, to place a small portion on a piece of cold metal to ascertain if the desired consistence has been arrived at. When extracts are only evaporated to the consistence of a syrup, they are denominated fluid extracts. These extracts are generally prepared from fresh roots and herbs, but may also with advantage be made from dry materials, and require about one-eighth of their bulk of alcohol to preserve them.

Extracts belong to the most important class of pharmaceutical preparations, because they contain in the smallest bulk the active parts of plants. But as those active principles are liable to be injured during the process of evaporation, the greatest care is required to prevent this result. Different modifications in the processes for making extracts depend upon the nature of the active principles which the plants contain, and with which it is necessary to be well acquainted to carry out the necessary modifications. A well prepared extract should possess in the highest degree the odor, and particularly the taste, of the plant from which it was made. It should be without empyreumatic odor or taste. It must be homogeneous, and have the proper consistence. When dissolved in water, it should not be turbid from woody fibre or anything else, except from the presence of chlorophyll, albumen, and resinous matter, which have been dissolved in the process of extraction. Injurious metallic contaminations are detected by burning the extract and examining its ash with the usual reagents.

Resinous extracts are prepared in a similar manner, except

that alcohol is always applied as the extracting medium. Sometimes it is advisable to macerate the substance first with water, then to dry and pulverize it, by which means it is more readily acted upon by the alcohol. These resinous extracts, or pure resins, should be entirely soluble in alcohol, but quite insoluble in water.

IRON ORE IN THE CARBONIFEROUS LIMESTONE AND COAL MEASURE OF IOWA.

Not far from Dam No. 26, and near the line between Sections 11 and 11, Township 77 North, Range 22 West, there are, probably, one or more beds of coal. Within three or four feet of the top of the shale, *i.e.*, at a height of forty or forty five feet from the Des Moines River, there is, at this locality, a band of ironstone having a specific gravity of 3.45, associated with some sulphuret of zinc, the joints being coated. with a crust of silicate of alumina.

The following analysis, by the humid method, gives as follows:

Bituminous or carbonaceous matter	01·0
Insoluble earthy matter	07·6
Carbonate of the protoxide of iron	65·0
Carbonate of lime	07·2
Carbonate of magnesia	10·0
Alumina	01·8
Peroxide of iron	04.8
Phosphate of iron	02·6
	100·0

After pounding and sifting the raw ore, a quantity weighing 1,225 was roasted and exposed to a red heat in a shallow vessel; after roasting it weighed 865 grains; loss by roasting 360 grains, being equal to 29·4 per cent.

The color, after roasting, was a purple-brown. An assay was then made, in a black lead crucible, at a high temperature, with the following ingredients in the proportion of—

Roasted ore - - - - - -	865	grains.
Bottle glass - - - - - -	865	"
Chalk - - - - - - -	865	"
Charcoal - - - - - -	134	"

There resulted therefrom a button of light gray iron, weighing 377 grains, equal to 43·5 per cent. of the roasted ore, and 31 per cent of the raw ore, differing only 2.5 per cent. from the per centage of metallic iron by the humid method. It appears from the above analysis that this ironstone is very analogous in its composition to the ore known in Scotland as "Mushet's Black Band," the chief difference being a smaller per centage of carbonaceous matter, and the substitution of phosphorus for sulphur. It is more than probable that a repetition of the analysis of the "Scotch Black Band" would give also a small per centage of phosphorus, since Dr. Owen only succeeded in detecting and estimating this element in the Des Moines ore by methods which have been introduced into analytical chemistry within the last few years.

The existence of phosphorus in this ore is not a matter of merely scientific interest, but of practical importance also. Collier and Rinman assert that the "cold-short" property of iron (that is, its liability to become brittle when cold) is due to the presence of the phosphuret; while Mushet, whose knowledge of iron and its properties is, probably, superior to that of any other writer, doubts the assertion.

It has, he says, been matter of common remark, that iron of the most perfect quality, as the Swedish, gives out, in working, a strong phosphoric smell; and he adds, that any iron can be made cold-short by introducing into the blast-furnace, through the medium of the flues or otherwise, silica in excess.

In support of this view, he remarks, in his work on iron and steel—"The flue cinder of the balling furnace, which on an average contains thirty per cent. of silica, and the flue furnace cinder of the puddling furnace contains forty per cent., while sand bottoms were in use, furnished striking illustrations of that fact. At first, when these cinders, containing from forty to fifty-two per cent. of iron, were returned to be smelted for the production of forge pigs, the brittleness of the iron was so much increased that fears were entertained as to the practicability of their use, and maintaining a marketable quality of iron. The change of system which took place, from puddling on sand to puddling on iron bottoms, by introducing a less quantity of silica into the blast-furnace, had a great tendency to reduce this evil, and restore fibre to the bar-iron."

And he concludes by saying—"From this fact being so clearly ascertained, we obtain a clue to explain the probable cause of cold-short in iron generally, by attributing it to a predominant quantity of silica in the ore, rather than to the existence of phosphorus."

Here is a marked difference between the opinion of so experienced a man as Mushet and the statement of Renman, made in the summer of 1849, to the British Association, at their annual meeting: the statement, namely, that in every instance in which Swedish iron has proved cold-short he had been able to detect the presence of phosphorus. To this important subject Dr. Owen invites the attention of American chemists and iron masters. It is only by careful chemical analysis, conducted after the most approved method, that this moot point can be finally determined. Should phosphorus invariably be found in cold-short iron, while it should prove to be uniformly absent in iron free from that defect, the inference will be a fair once, that phosphorus is the producing cause.—*Journ. Franklin Institute*, condensed from Dr. Owen's Survey.

Varieties.

External Use of Ipecacuanha.—M. Delioux speaks highly of the external employment of ipecac in the form of an ointment, as having the same virtues as the tartar emetic ointment, without any of its inconveniences. Soon after its application an eruption appears of small elevated papules, of a bright red color, often confluent; afterwards they become true pustules, of small size and umbilicated, but attended with little pain, and quickly drying up without leaving a cicatrix. Unguent, ipecac, should be preferred to that of tart. emetic, in diseases of children, as it causes less pain, in diseases of females, and upon exposed surfaces where we wish to avoid scars. The following is M. Delioux's formula. ℞ Pulv. ipecac, one part; olive oil, one part; lard oil, two parts. Or the powdered ipecac may be sprinkled upon a pitch plaster, and this applied.—*Bulletin de Therapeutique.*

Value of Phosphate of Lime.—M. Mouries has announced to the French Academy the following propositions as capable of proof:

Ist. Phosphate of lime plays a more important part in the animal economy than has been thought hitherto; besides its influence in the growth of bone, this salt acts by keeping up that irritability without which neither assimilation nor of course nutrition can go on. Thus a well marked deficiency produces death with all the symptoms of inanition, while an absence less marked produces a train of diseases of the lymphatic system.

2d. The alimentation of towns is defective in this salt. The milk of women has consequently the same defect, and both fœtus and child suffer from the absence of this salt, so indispensable to their life and growth. Thence the excess of death in new-born infants and the mortality of infants in towns.

3d. The addition of this salt united to animal matter renders the nourishment complete and delays diseases and death, which always arise from the absence or deficiency of phosphate of lime.

New Hæmostatic Agent.—M. J. Ruspini, a distinguished Italian chemist, has substituted with success the acetate of sesquioxide of iron in place of the perchloride of this metal, in the treatment of hæmorrhages. The experiments of Dr. Pravur upon the employment of chloride of iron for the cure of aneurisms is well known. It appears, after several trials of a similar kind by Ruspini, that the acetate of the sesquioxide is far superior to the perchloride as a hæmostatic, and the former salt has the additional advantage of containing an organic acid whose action on the animal economy never produces any unpleasant consequences.

Deleteriousness of London Gas.—Dr. Letheby, in detailing before the Court of Sewers some of the results arrived at by him in his analytical researches on the gas supply of London, said: "In the course of the investigations which I have been making during the last two years, I find that some of the companies are supplying gas in this metropolis which, in the course of a few years, will tend to damage very much the atmosphere and the property in it, for it is so highly charged with sulphuret, that I am able to obtain twenty-one grains of oil of vitriol from one hundred cubic feet of gas, which is getting into the atmosphere. Then, again, there is a a quantity of ammonia, which holds in solution a large quantity of tar, and whenever there is a leakage in the streets, it oozes out. During the last fifty years, when it has got into the public roads, it has rendered the soil near to it so offensive that you can hardly move the pavement without doing a great deal of harm. What it may be in twenty years hence I cannot say, but I think it will be almost unsafe that you should then disturb the pavements at all. There is not a library in the metropolis the books on the upper shelves of which are not tumbling to pieces from this cause; and there is no controlling power over the different companies, because the public are not aware of the presence of these impurities. I think nothing is so important as that the chemical qualities of the gas should, from time to time, be tested. Testing gas at the works is all nonsense, because after traveling two or three miles it undergoes such a change that there is no comparison between the quality of the gas supplied to the public and at the works. Whatever is destructive to inert matter must necessarily be more injurious to living matter."—*Dublin Medical Press.*

A case of poisoning by arsenious acid and chromate of lead is recorded in the *London Lancet*, by T. R. H. Thomson, M. D. The patient recovered after four day's illness. She had taken about thirty grains of oxide of arsenic and the same quantity of chrome yellow by mistake. Eighty-three of light magnesia, diffused in water, gruel, and emolients was the treatment during the four day's illness. The arsenic was detected in the urine by Reinsch's test, as well as by the ordinary tests. The chromate of lead could not be detected in that fluid.

Iodine in Natural Waters.—By Chatin.--Iodine has been found in rain spring and river water from Guiana and Gaudaloupe, existing as mere traces; more lately also in tobacco from Havana and Frankreich. Martin mentions the occurrence of iodine in the rain water of South Frankreich.—*Comp. Rend.*, T. 37, p. 958.

Medical Statistics of France.--Ronbaud, in a work with the foregoing title, gives the number of physicians in the empire as 11,217; officers of health, 7,221; pharmaciens, 5,175.

Purple-Red Ink for Marking Linen.—The place where the linen is to be marked is first wetted with a solution, consisting of three drachms of carbonate of soda and three drachms of gum arabic, dissolved in an ounce and a half of water, then dried and smoothed. The place is now to be written on with a solution composed of one drachm of chloride of platinum, dissolved in two ounces of distilled water, then allowed to dry. When quite dry, the writing is to be painted over with a goose feather, moistened with a liquid consisting of one drachm of protochloride of tin, dissolved in two ounces of distilled water.—*Annals of Pharm.*, from *Bottger's Polyt. Notizblatt.*

REVIEWS.

Douze Lecons de Photographie.—Par M. le Docteur Fau. Twelve Lessons on Photography, by Dr. Fau. Paris, 1854.

This small work has no pretentions to novelties, or to recommend new processes instead of the old—on the contrary, it is rather to present an easy and satisfactory mode of operating. The author's own words explain his object, " Here is a simple process given, easy to execute, which will obtain for you fine proofs; learn it first, and when you have mastered it thoroughly, you may boldly attempt modifications of it, or new process of more or less value, and, perhaps, at the end of you experiments, you will return to your A, B, C, glad to rest after fatiguing and unsuccessful wanderings." Good advice quaintly told—in other words, it is to study one process at a time, and not to take up another until complete master of the first.

Each lesson is a step in the whole operation, and generally contains the newest information on the art. We subjoin the heads of each lesson.

1. Of negatives on dry paper, choice of paper, varnishing and removing varnish: The operator is to prefer Canson's paper, select sheet by sheet, and prepare it himself.

2. Iodizing: Iodizing bath contains, distilled water, 9 ounces; iodide of ammonium, 150 grains; clarified honey, a teaspoonful.

3. Sensitive coating—exposure in camera: The sensitive bath contains, nitrate of silver, 278 grains in 4½ ounces of distilled water; dissolve 140 grains of nitrate of zinc in 4½ ounces of distilled water. Mix the two solutions, and add 140 grains of *glacial* acetic acid.

4. Development of the image—fixation of the proof: The developing bath is formed of a solution of 46 grains of gallic acid in 30 ounces of distilled water. The fixing bath is made of 230 grains of hyposulphite of soda dissolved in 3½ ounces of water. The image must not be developed too rapidly, as the proofs are then crusted over and destitute of transparency.

5th. Negatives on moist and unprepared paper—iodizing and sensitiving: Iodizing bath—distilled water, 9 ounces; iodide of ammonium, 154 grains; honey, three teaspoonfuls. Sensitive bath—distilled water, 9 ounces; nitrate of silver, 278 grains; nitrate of zinc, 140 grains; acetic acid (glacial), 140 grains.

6. Developing, fixing, and waxing: Developing bath—water, 30 ounces; gallic acid, 15 grains. Fixing bath—distilled water, 3½ ounces; hyposulphite of soda, 150 grains. The proof is waxed by passing a cake of white wax on the surface of a hot iron, which is then carried back and forward over the back of the proof. It is laid first between two folds of blotting paper, and afterwards tissue paper.

7. Gun cotton and collodion: The gun cotton is prepared by Martin's process; the collodion by dissolving 30 grains, or nearly so, of gun cotton in 5 ounces (by weight) of pure sulphuric acid, and then adding 17 drachms of alcohol. For preparing collodion with iodide of ammonium, dissolve 30 grains of iodide in 6 drachms, and add 6 ounces of collodion.

8. Cleaning glass plates—spreading collodion, &c.: The sensitive bath to make the collodion receive the image consists of, distilled water, 5 ounces; nitrate of silver, 150 grains.

9. Exposure in camera, development, and bringing out of the proof: It is developed by treating it with this solution, distilled water, 10 ounces; protosulphate of iron, 14 drachms; sulphuric acid, 10 drops; alcohol, 2 drachms. To bring out the proof, it is dipped in a second bath of 150 grains of nitrate of silver, dissolved in 7 ounces of distilled water, and adding nitric acid 6 drops, alcohol 1½ drachms.

10. Fixation, varnishing, positive images: Fixing bath—water, 3½ ounces; hyposulphite, 220 grains. The varnish for negatives is a fine "table varnish"—for positives, "asphalte solution."

11. Positive proofs, choice and preparation of paper, albuminizing, process for cloudy days and for lamplight: For positives, "saxe" paper, small size, prepared by immersion, in turn, in two baths, viz., distilled water, 10 ounces; common salt, 1 ounce; and, distilled water, 3½ ounces; nitrate silver, 220 grains.

12. Removal, fixation, process of obtaining good and varied tones in the proof.

The whole is a neat little volume, and a welcome addition to our photographic artists. These are at present in this country but a small number, but we are of opinion that for all landscape and architectural copies, photographic pictures are very superior to daguerreotypes. We think a translation of this work would advance the art in the States.

JOURNALS RECEIVED.

Boston Medical and Surgical Journal; Medical News and Library, Philadelphia; American Medical Monthly, for March, N. Y.; American Journal of Insanity; People's Gazette, Abbeville, S. C.; Eclectic Medical Journal, Cincinnati; Western Medico-Chirurgical Journal, Keokuk; Medical Chronicle, Montreal; Medical Examiner, Phil.; N. Hampshire Journal of Medicine; Southern Journal of the Medical and Physical Sciences, Nashville; Charleston Medical Journal and Review; American Journal of Pharmacy, March, 1854; Journal of the Franklin Institute; Abstract of Med. Sciences, (Rankin,) Jan. to July, 1853; Cosmos, Feb. and March.

EDITORIAL.

MASSACHUSETTS COLLEGE OF PHARMACY.—The Massachusetts College of Pharmacy held its annual meeting in Boston, on the 6th of March, at the College in Phillip's Place. Daniel Henchman presided. The attendance was large, and the proceedings were of interest.

The following officers were elected for the ensuing year:

Daniel Henchman, president. Samuel M. Colcord, first vice-president. Joseph T. Brown, second vice-president. Joseph Burnett, corresponding secretary; Henry W. Lincoln, recording secretary; Ashel Boyden, treasurer; Thomas Farrington, auditor; Thomas Hollis, Samuel N. Brewer, Charles H. Atwood, Andrew Geyer, Atherton T. Brown, Thomas Restieaux, Samuel H. Woods, Henry D. Fowle, trustees.

Many subjects of importance were discussed by the members. In consequence of an unusually large amount of business it was found necessary, at a late hour, to adjourn to meet again three weeks from date.

COLUMBIA COLLEGE.—At the stated monthly meeting of the Board of Trustees, April 3, Professor Richard M'Culloch, of the College of New Jersey, was elected to fill the vacancy in the Chair of Natural and Experimental Philosophy and Chemistry, occasioned by the resignation of Professor Renwick. The ballot (there was only one) was—For Professor M'Culloch, 11; Professor O. W. Gibbs, 9; Professor A. D. Bache, 1. Professor Bache was not a candidate. There was also an election for a trustee to supply the resignation of Beverly Robinson, Esq., when Mr. George F. Allen, an alumnui of 1829, was chosen. This is, we believe, the fourth ballot, which has taken place to fill the vacant chair. In all the previous ones, Professor Gibbs stood at the head of the list; and as the college heads resolved not to elect him, they felt themselves compelled to advertise for additional candidates, and to continue ballotting until a contra majority was obtained. Time will show whether the college have lost or gained in losing Professor Gibbs. His present position in the Free Academy is, we believe, of more emolument than the chair in the college, but the college have lost in public estimation by the manner of conducting this ballot. Professor M'Culloch is well quallified to fill the chair.

In the present number we have printed Mr. Outram's remarks upon the appearance of Lead in the Urine of patients ill with Lead Diseases and under treatment with Iodide of Potassium. Mr. Outram's mode of determining lead, if it terminated with what he described in his article, is very unsatisfactory, for sulphuretted hydrogen in acid urine will often throw down a black precipitate of sulphur and extractive even when no lead is present. It is to be regretted that he did not push his results to quantitative determination. We are of opinion that lead has not yet been proved to have been eliminated by Melsen's treatment. Iodide of potassium will not dissolve iodide of lead out of the body until the liquid is heated up to 180 deg. F. Why is it assumed that it does dissolve it in the body at a less temperature?

NEW YORK

JOURNAL OF PHARMACY.

JUNE, 1854.

ON THE COMMERCIAL TEST OF SODA ASH.

BY EDWARD N. KENT, NEW YORK.

Many processes have been devised by chemists for testing the soda ash of commerce, for the purpose of ascertaining its value by a speedy and expeditious process, and with sufficient accuracy for commercial purposes. The processes which have hitherto been most generally used are those accomplished by the use of the graduated alkalimeter or French burette, neither of which is, in my opinion, so accurate as that which I am about to describe, and which I have been accustomed to use for several years.

With the graduated alkalimeter, or burette, great variations or inaccuracies are likely to occur, from variations of temperature in the normal test acid, as this increases or decreases in *volume* according to the temperature. If, for example, the test acid is prepared at the temperature of 60° F., it will not give a correct test by *volume* at 70° or 80° F., unless the difference of temperature be ascertained by the thermometer and a correction made, or the test acid be brought to the original temperature by artificial means, neither of which I believe, is ever done in practice, and if it were, this would involve too much labor and time to render the process sufficiently simple for the purpose intended.

A still greater cause of error in the process by *volume* is that produced from the inability of any person to measure so accurately as he can weigh. The normal test acid can be weighed as often as required without the slightest error, provided a good balance be used. But no one can measure so accurately as this. To illustrate this, let a graduated alkalimeter be filled with dilute acid, or water, to a certain mark, and weigh it carefully. Let it be emptied, and again filled with another portion of the same liquid, to the same mark as before, as carefully as the eye will allow, and again weigh it. By deducting the difference in the weights of the two trials it will show the amount of inaccuracy, and prove that it is impossible to measure twice exactly alike, and consequently the same person cannot make two tests from the same sample of soda ash which will agree with each other, when the process by volume is used.

The process by *weight*, which I am accustomed to use, is free from the above objections, is simple and easy of execution, and two or more tests of the same sample of soda ash may be readily made by it, which will agree with each other within a very small fraction, and this is all that can be desired in a process designed for commercial purposes or use in the arts.

In the preparation of the normal test acid it is necessary that pure anhydrous carbonate of soda should be first obtained, to be used for determining the strength of the acid. Much depends upon the purity of this carbonate. It may be easily prepared, by putting a quantity of bicarbonate of soda into a funnel or displacement apparatus, and washing it with separate portions of cold water till the washings no longer give a precipitate with nitrate of silver or chloride of barium, after being previously neutralized with pure nitric acid. The washed bicarbonate is then to be dissolved in distilled water, boiled with a little carbonate of ammonia, filtered, evaporated to dryness, and heated to redness in a silver or platinum crucible.

A quantity of dilute sulphuric acid is then prepared, by diluting commercial oil of vitriol with five or six parts of water. After being well mixed, it should be left till next day to cool, then decanted or filtered, if necessary, into a clean bottle with a tight glass stopper.

One hundred grains of the pure anhydrous carbonate of soda is now to be carefully weighed, and introduced into an 8 oz. flask. Two fluid ounces of water are to be added, and heat applied till the carbonate is dissolved. The lamp is then removed. A portion of the dilute acid is to be put into a small, flat-bottomed flask, of about two ounces capacity, having a short pipette attached to it upon one side, to serve as a dropping tube for the acid. This vessel with contents is to be weighed, and the weight marked down. The acid is then gradually and carefully added to the solution of pure carbonate until the evolution of carbonic acid is no longer very brisk; a slip of blue litmus paper is to be introduced into the flask, and the addition of acid continued, drop by drop, until the litmus paper is slightly reddened after agitation. As this may be caused by carbonic acid now held in solution, heat is again to be applied, and the liquid boiled a few minutes until it is expelled, and if the red color has been caused by this, the paper will again become blue. In this case a little more acid is very carefully added until the solution is fully and exactly neutralized, and the litmus paper remains permanently of a slight red color after continued boiling. The vessel and acid remaining in it are to be again weighed, and this deducted from the first gives the weight of the test acid required to neutralize one hundred grains of pure anhydrous carbonate of soda. This weight should be verified by repeating the process, and if the two experiments agree, the larger quantity of test acid first prepared is to be labelled, the above weight marked upon it, and preserved for use.

In testing commercial soda ash, with the above acid, it is evident that the quantity required to neutralize it will be in exact proportion to the per centage of pure carbonate of soda which it contains, or, in other words, that one hundred grains of the commercial ash will require less acid in proportion to the quantity of impurity or water contained in it. To find this proportion, or per centage of pure carbonate in a sample of commercial soda ash, one hundred grains of the sample to be tested is to be put into a clean flask, dissolved in water, and neutralized with the test acid in the same manner, and with the same care as described above. The quantity of acid required for this purpose, is obtained by weighing the vessel before and after using, and the per centage of pure carbonate of soda is then calculated by the simple rule of proportion.

Suppose, for example, that 558·6 grains of the test acid is required to neutralize 100 grains of pure anhydrous carbonate of soda, and that only 455.9 grains of the same acid is required to neutralize 100 grains of a sample of commercial soda ash:

$$548{\cdot}6 : 100 :: 455{\cdot}9 : 83{\cdot}12.$$

The sample under examination, therefore, contains 83.12 per cent. carbonate of soda.

The foreign ash imported into this country always contains moisture, which is doubtless derived by absorption during its transportation, and consequently the English and American tests seldom agree with each other. The casks of ash also increase in weight, in proportion to this absorption of water. Purchasers in this country, therefore, generally prefer to buy the ash by the English weight and American test, rather than vice versa. The cause of this is obvious, and some controversy has been occasioned by it. To prevent this, as far as practicable, and avoid the discrepancies which have heretofore existed between the English and American tests, I have suggested the propriety of drying the ash before testing it in this country, so as to bring it as nearly as possible to the state in which it is represented by the English weight marked upon the cask, and in practice I have found this to give results satisfactory to all parties interested, and nearly corresponding to the English test.

116 *John street*, May, 1854.

POISONING BY ACONITE—THE HENDRICKSON TRIAL.

The evidence given in the case of the trial of John Hendrickson, Jr., for the murder of his wife is of so extraordinary a character both as to want of correctness and completeness, and as it has led to the conviction and execution of the prisoner, who made positive protestations of his innocence the moment before death, it may not be amiss to point out some remarkable portions which led the jury to find the prisoner guilty.

The portions selected are passages from the testimony of Drs. Swinburne and Salisbury, whose statements being given very positively carried much weight with the jury.

The death of the young woman occurred suddenly on the 6th of March, 1853, at Bethlehem, Albany County, N. Y., and the trial of J. Hendrickson, Jr., for the murder, took place in June and July, 1853.

From the District Attorney's opening of the case it appears that the prisoner was married in January, 1851 ; his conduct previously "rowdyish." In December, 1851, a child, six week's old, was found dead in the bed in a very singular manner—H. occupying the middle, the wife the back, and the child the front part of the bed.

On account of several improprieties he was obliged to leave his wife's father's home, where the couple had resided, he going to his father's, at Corning, his wife remaining at her father's, in Clarksville. He visited Clarksville occasionally, and she also came over to his father's at times. During January, 1853, she visited at his father's three times that month, and returned home to her parents for a week. The prisoner, with his sister, came for her again, and she returned with them, about the middle of February, and was not seen again by her family until the 7th of March, when she was returned a corpse.

From the evidence it appears that Maria H. returned from church, on Sunday evening, between nine and ten o'clock, and shortly after ten retired to her room with her husband. About 2 o'clock, H—'s voice was heard hallowing. On the inmates of the house going up to the room, Maria was found dead. She had been ill all the day previous, with a dreadful pain in the top of her head and in her back.

The post-mortem examination of the body did not reveal the actual presence of any poison. Such was inferred from the appearances of the stomach and alimentary canal—such as "extreme emptiness," "congestion of the mucous surface," "contraction and corrugation of the tissue," "emptiness of the gall bladder," &c.

Those who are acquainted with pathological appearances can easily estimate how little value is to be placed upon such symptoms as these, and others of a similar character adduced by Dr. Swinburne, as proofs of excessive vomiting, and *a priori* proof of the presence of an acrid poison.

The Doctor, in his examination, after detailing the post-mortem appearances, in reply to the question put, "What was the cause of Mrs. H.'s death?" replied—

"*Acrid* poison; I base it on this; I find entire emptiness of the stomach and small intestines so far as the fœcal matter is concerned; also contraction and corrugation of the same to a great extent; I find in place of that a reddish *viscid* mucus adhering to the coat of the stomach and intestines; the emptied condition of the gall bladder, the appearance of the tongue, which was very much furred and slightly swollen; I inferred from these that vomiting had taken place, and that, too, induced by some acrid matter, which would not only expel the contents of the stomach but of the small intestines, and the presence of which acrid matter would induce the vomiting.

"I believe the act of vomiting is accompanied by more or less contraction of the stomach; when that act is induced by the presence of acrid matter the contraction will be proportional to the material used, be it more or less irritating; I would state in reference to this corrugation, or any corrugation, that it would depend in part on that contraction of the muscles and in part owing to the irritating matter which is applied to the mucus surface."

What is the strength of your opinion that she died of poison?

"*I have no doubt of it;* I have no doubt she vomited; one of my reasons for thinking she died of poison was her having vomited, and also the absence of congestion."

The chemical portion of the evidence is even more dogmatic and more incorrect than the pathological, and it is difficult to conceive how a "State Chemist" could be guilty of such inaccuracies and general ignorance, and at the same time be so confident in the truth and value of his results. The following portions of his evidence will satisfy the chemical reader how wholly fallacious his proofs of the presence of aconitine were.

Dr. G. H. Salisbury, on the 8th March, received from the coroner the stomach and a small portion of the small intestines; on the 13th, the remainder of the small intestines, the large intestines, portions of the liver and of the lungs, pancreas, and a portion of the blood—the latter was in a six ounce phial.

"With the portions of the stomach submitted to me I proceeded to make my tests for poisons; in this case my chemicals were all pure and my implements and vessels clean.

"First, I took a small portion of the stomach, its mucus surface and a small portion of the duodenum; tested first for prussic acid: did not detect its presence; then tested for some of the mineral poisons, first for arsenic then for corrosive sublimate, the antimonial compounds, the mineral acids, such as muriatic, nitric, and sulphuric acids, also tested for oxalic acid—did not detect the presence of any of these; next tested for morphine, strychnine, stramonium; also for other poisons—none of which I discovered.

"I then tested for *aconite.* The tests indicated aconitine, the poisonous principle of aconite; took a small portion of stomach and duodenum, digested it with alcohol over a water bath, then filtered, evaporated the filtrate partially—the oily matter rose to the surface, this I separated by decantation, and then absorbed it from the surface by bibulous paper, then mixed the solution with purified animal charcoal, agitating it for some little time after mixing, filtered, and to the solution I applied my tests as follows.

"I boiled a small portion of this solution with sulphuric acid, the solution was turned a deep port wine color; I then boiled a small portion of the solution with hydrochloric acid: this turned the solution to a light port wine color; then boiled a small quantity of the solution with nitric acid: the solution remained clear, with no change of color; from these tests I inferred the presence of aconitine; I repeated these tests several times, with the same results; the stomach and duodenum were what I made my preliminary tests with; these tests are what are laid down for aconitine by the best authors; I had made these tests previously, and had also made aconitine my special study; my tests produced the same result; I have applied them since with similar results; for two years previous to this I had paid much attention to vegetable alkaloids, and among them especially aconitine, the poisonous principle of aconite.

"On the 15th of March, commenced the process of analysis, for the purpose of separating aconitine, if present in sufficient quantity; I divided a portion of the remaining portions of the stomach and duodenum, and their contents, the small intestines, a portion of the liver, and a portion of the blood into two equal parts; one of these parts or portions I digested in alcohol, for several hours, over a water-bath; then filtered, partially evaporated, separated the oily matter by decantation and absorption; evaporated nearly to dryness; mixed with the alcoholic extracts pure caustic potassa, distilled; treated the distilled matter with dilute sulphuric acid, sufficient to neutralize it; evaporated this over a water-bath; treated it with pure alcohol, between 75 and 80 per cent.; filtered it, evaporated it nearly to dryness; treated the residue with pure caustic potassa, and again distilled; evaporated this slightly, and set it aside for future use.

"The other and the second portion was digested in alcohol

over a water-bath for several hours; filtered, evaporated partially; separated oily matter by decantation and absorption; evaporated nearly to dryness; treated the alcoholic extract with pure distilled water, and filtered; evaporated the filtrate to near dryness; treated the water extract with dilute sulphuric acid and distilled water filtered; I then evaporated it partially; treated the solution with ammonia to a slight excess; a precipitate was formed; this was carefully washed by a small quantity of water; this precipitate was re-dissolved in dilute sulphuric acid and distilled water; added to this solution a small quantity of purified animal charcoal, agitating for some minutes, and then filtered it; evaporated the filtrate slightly at a low temperature; added ammonia in slight excess; a precipitate was formed; this I carefully washed with a small quantity of distilled water; this result I mixed with the result obtained by the other process; in all there was about two-thirds of a tea-spoonful; I was from the 15th to the 19th of March in getting through this process; it was going on day and night.

"In testing for this matter I placed it on my tongue; it had a bitter taste, a sparkling sensation at first, which in three or five minutes turned to numbness, producing a stiffness of the surface; the sensation produced was very much like that in the foot when it is said to be asleep; this matter, which I separated by the process just mentioned, I gave to a cat; gave it in small pieces of beefsteak; in about half an hour she exhibited a choking sensation and swallowing; this was followed by slight contraction of the muscles, twitchings which moved the limbs slightly, and this by a tendency to vomit; these spasms lasted from one to two minutes; considerable stupor succeeded; she lay down upon her side, and breathed heavily, as though she was under the influence of some narcotic; this lasted for some time; it gradually passed off, and in about three hours she was quite natural again."

Dr. S. is quite confident that Mrs. H. died from aconitine; poisoned several cats with Tr. Aconite, and examined one; the post-mortem appearances resembles those in the case of Mrs. H.; and by a like plan of analysis he obtained like results.

It is not certain that Dr. Salisbury obtained any portion of aconitine at all in any of his processes. His first process (described in the first half of page 248) would not eliminate it; his second process is objectionable from the use of caustic potassa, which would, by its solvent property on protein compounds, be likely to introduce them; and the third, which is the best process to adopt, is liable to an objection with the other two, the omission of the use of ether to separate fatty matter, which must be unavoidably present. The objection to the use of animal charcoal will be alluded to presently.

Aconitine may be obtained in various ways; that of Morson and the London Pharmacopœia is by boiling the bruised root with alcohol, in repeated quantities, and distilling over; press out the root, and mix all the liquors; evaporate to an extract, and dissolve the extract in water; evaporate this to a syrup, and add dilute sulphuric acid to dissolve the aconitine; then drop in solution of ammonia, and re-dissolve the alkaloid in dilute acid, so as to purify it; add some purified animal charcoal, and agitate for a quarter of an hour; strain and add ammonia, to precipitate the alkaloid, which may finally be washed and dried.

Geiger and Hesse obtained it by adding lime to the alcoholic extract, removing it from the clear solution by sulphuric acid, and precipitating the aconitine from the sulphate by carbonate of potassa. It crystallizes in whitish grains, inodorous, of a bitter taste; dilates the pupil, reacts alkaline, unchangable in air, fuses without volatilization. Morson's, as prepared by the process already indicated, has the properties described by Pereira when obtained pure. The following are the properties of pure aconitine as given by Pereira: "It is a white, odorless solid, either dull or amorphous, or somewhat sparkling and apparently crystalline. As it is usually described as being crystallizable, I have carefully examined a supposed crystalline mass with the microscope, but I could not detect distinct crystals. The fragments appeared like thin plates of chloride of potassa, and though they varied greatly in shape the triangular form seemed predominant. Heated in a tube, aconita readily fuses, and forms a pale amber colored liquid;

and at a higher temperature decomposes. It is not volatile. Heated on platinum, or over a spirit lamp, it is speedily and entirely dissipated. It is soluble in ether, alcohol and the acids. From its acid solution it is precipitated by ammonia. A minute portion of it mixed with lard, and applied to the eye, causes contraction of the pupil. One-fiftieth of a grain has endangered the life of an individual. It is the most virulent poison known, not excepting hydrocyanic acid."

Geiger and Hesse found it in A nap. and A ferex. Perhaps, that is an altered product, for it has different properties from that which Turnbull and others obtained—it dilates while Turnbull's contracts the pupil.

The salts of aconitine are not crystallizable, and are soluble in alcohol and water. The addition of an alkali to their solution precipitates aconitine. The latter has not been subjected to ultimate analysis, and its equivalent is unknown.

Dr. S. does not rely upon the chemical tests alone to prove there was aconite; "I did swear, before Cole, that in my judgment I obtained not far from a twenty-fifth part of a grain of aconite; I have not altered my judgment since; after all I have seen in my search for aconitine, and of the effect produced, I will swear that I have detected aconitine."

Mr. D. A. Wells, of Boston, impressed with the inadequacy of the testimony, and the danger that would accrue from the conviction of persons charged with crime upon such loose statements and processes, addressed a letter, on the 12th of April, to the Editor of the *Albany Evening Journal*, enclosing the opinion of a number of physicians and chemists, all of whom agreed in condemning the mistaken views and misstatements of the witnesses for the prosecution, especially those of Dr. Salisbury.

Dr A. A. Hayes, in his letter, condemned in a general way the plans of Dr. S., and remarked strongly upon the absence of any experiments made upon *tincture* of *aconite* itself (the substance asserted to have been the poison used).

Dr. Emmons objected to the conclusions drawn from the colors produced by acids, asserting that such coloration was produced by the presence of fatty matter, and not by aconitine in any shape; that it was not produced by solution of aconitine, nor by the tincture of aconite, but was immediately produced by the contact of oleaginous matter, and hence that Dr. S. had not taken due precaution to have his precipitate free from fatty matters.

With regard to these colorations, it may be mentioned here that when a protein compound is boiled with concentrated hydrochloric or dilute sulphuric acids, *leucine* and *tyrosine* are formed, the liquid assuming a purple tint, which, on exposure, passes into brown. The tyrosine (the formation of which produces this change of color) is identical with that obtained by Warrington, from cochineal, and by Warren de la Rue, who calls it *carminic acid*, which, when treated with nitric acid, loses its purple color and forms a yellow solution.

The reactions of acids upon a protein compound are thus precisely similar to those which Dr. Salisbury obtained, and upon which he grounds his belief of the presence of aconitine.

Dr. Emmons, in a communication to the Governor of this State, lays much stress upon the worthlessness of these tests where animal matter is present, and dwells upon the fact that *fatty* matters will produce like colorations with acids.

Thus, either protein or fatty matters may have been the aconitine of Dr. Salisbury. Again, as Dr. Emmons justly remarks, great objection may be laid against the use of animal charcoal as a filter. The doctor quotes Stass as an authority against its use, and he might have added those of Scheerer and R. Warrington. The experiments of the latter are interesting. He filtered some London ale through animal charcoal, hoping to convert it into a "pale ale," but, while he deprived it of its color, he also deprived it of its bitterness—the lupuline being retained on the filter. He then tried solutions of strychnine, and other alkaloids, with a like result, the greater portion of the principle being retained. This is a property which this exerts in common with all porous varieties of charcoal which have the power of separating oxygen and haloid metallic salts out of plain water.

Indeed, Dr. Salisbury, at the same time that he is confident he obtained aconitine from the stomach of the deceased, is by no means certain of either the physical or chemical properties of it; he is apparently in doubt whether it is a substance which is volatile or fixed. Geiger and Hesse, in a paper in the twentieth volume of the *Journal de Pharmacie*, describe it as a white powder, of a bitter taste, fusible, *not volatile*, alkaloidal soluble in ether and alcohol, and sparingly so in water. Dr. S. obtains about the one-twenty-fifth of a grain of a precipitate; he does not preserve it for the court, he expends it in unsuccessful attempts upon a cat. The animal does not die in the experiment; it is doubtful whether it suffered any more than oppression from eating too much beefsteak. He takes the officinal tincture of aconite and kills animals with it; but does not apply his tests to it—does not show that its reactions are similar. In fine, he obtains half a tea-spoonful of something which has not the physical properties of aconite, the chemical properties of which he does not examine; its effects on other animals cannot be said to be poisonous. And, after all this, he comes into court, and swears that such substance is aconitine.

Can language find utterance strong enough to condemn the introduction of such evidence into a court of justice when the life of a man is at stake? or to condemn the conduct of the man who in the face of such imperfect experiments and negative results hesitates not to swear that that which he has obtained by processes not likely to yield aconitine, and which does not possess its properties, is nevertheless that substance? Were this the only error committed by the State Chemist in his short chemical career, one might hesitate to express an opinion injurious to the reputation of a young man; but where public errors are repeated and boldness is added to ignorance, forbearance ceases to be a virtue, and it becomes a duty to warn the public against the blunders and the follies of the State Chemist.

ON PRACTICAL PHARMACY.

BY JUSTUS LIEBIG,

Professor of Chemistry at the University of Giessen.

NO. VIII.

Operations which involve Mixing and Separation of the first degree.

When, by volatilization, the volatile parts are collected in a proper apparatus, and are fluid at ordinary temperatures, this operation is called distillation. When the volatile parts are solid at such temperatures, it is called sublimation. The objects of this process are manifold. Sometimes it is employed to separate volatile bodies from non-volatile ones, or more volatile substances from less volatile ones, or to combine several volatile bodies together. These processes are used for mixing or separating in the first or second degree. The character of the apparatus required, as well as the temperature, depends upon the nature and quality of the material which is to be operated upon. Fluids are generally distilled in retorts or metallic vessels called stills, and solid bodies are volatilized in subliming apparatus of various forms and materials.

The preparation of distilled water is a separation of pure water from its saline contents by distillation. The water of springs and rivers always contains more or less saline and other substances dissolved in it, from which it must be purified before it can be applied to pharmaceutical purposes. This operation is generally performed in a still, and seldom in a retort. The water passes by heat into steam, which is again condensed in the cooling apparatus, whilst the saline contents remain in the still, being non-volatile. Three parts of the water are usually collected.

The separation of alcohol from the water, with which it is usually mixed, is also performed by distillation. Alcohol distils at a lower temperature than water, by which means it can be, for the most part, separated from it. The separation of alcohol from fluids which have undergone various fermentations, is conducted on the large scale in distilleries, by means of large stills. To obtain the spirit sufficiently strong, it is customary to re-distil the fluid which results from the first operation. It is also further rectified by a third distillation, slowly performed, either with or without the addition to the contents of the retort of saline substances, such as chloride of calcium, which has a great affinity for water.

The natural ethereal oils are volatile aromatic fluids, to the presence of which plants are indebted for their peculiar odor. They are nearly all obtained by distillation, except a few, as oils of lemon and bergamot, which are prepared by expression. The substances from which the oils are to be obtained are either heated with water in a still, or a stream of hot steam is passed through them to separate their volatile oils. They are generally treated with eight or ten times their weight of water, and reduced into small fragments when necessary. The still should not be full by about one-sixth of its capacity, or the contents would jump over by ebullition. Distillation should be proceeded with as long as the water comes over laden with oily particles. However, care should be taken that it is not continued until the water in the still becomes so low that the vegetable substances are in danger of being burnt. The cooler the condensing apparatus is kept, the greater will be the product.

Heavy volatile oils, which sink in water, should be distilled more rapidly than those which are lighter, because they are less volatile, and not so readily separated from the substance which contains them. It is oftentimes necessary, in these cases, to repeat the distillation with a part of the water which has previously passed over, to separate all the oil, and even to repeat this operation as long as the water comes over surcharged with oil.

The oil is separated from the water by means of a separatory funnel. The addition of common salt to the water facilitates this result. Ethereal oils should be preserved in a dark, cool place, in vessels well closed and quite full.

Distilled waters are solutions of ethereal oils in water, with or without a small portion of alcohol. They are prepared in the same manner as ethereal oils, and often prepared simultaneously with them, that is to say, the water, from which the chief part of the essential has been separated, still contains the ethereal oil in a state of saturation, and is, therefore, an aromatic distilled water. When the distilled water is re-distilled from a substance to impregnate it with more oil, the operation is called cohobition, and the product cohobited water.

The quality of distilled water depends upon their being colorless, bright, and very fluid. They should possess in the highest degree the odors and tastes of the aromatic substances from which they were prepared, and not be empyreumatic. In the first instance, when prepared in the ordinary way, they have a disagreeable odor, which they lose when placed in a dark, cool place, and are only slightly covered. Those which are prepared by steam or in a water-bath, as a rule, acquire the best odor. Many waters, when kept some time, spoil and become slimy, particularly under the influence of light, heat, and air. Waters often remain longer unimpaired when they are re-distilled.

Aromatic waters can also be prepared by simply mixing ethereal oils with distilled waters, and possess, when thus prepared, the advantage of being more uniform in their characters. They can further be prepared by distilling water, with a slight admixture of alcohol, from aromatic plants, as long as the fluid comes over free from turbidity. These alcoholic solutions are to be mixed with the necessary quantity of simple distilled water, before being employed for medical purposes, and constitute what are termed concentrated waters. With some substances, whose volatile oils distil only at high temperatures, it is necessary to increase the boiling point of the water in the still by the addition of some saline body, as a common salt, so that the water may acquire the temperature at which those oils become readily volatilized with the aqueous vapor.

When aromatic substances are distilled with spirit, or a mixture of spirit and water, in which the former predominates, the products are called aromatic spirits. The method of their preparation is the same as with distilled waters, with the difference only, that less heat is required. When, from the large quantity of solid substances in the still, there is danger of these being burnt, it is advisable to add some water to the contents of the still, which may be left behind, as the spirit passes over first. These aromatic spirits can be readily made by mixing alcohol with the volatile oils. Aromatic spirits should be clear, and have the odor and taste of the substances from which they were prepared, and also possess a proper specific gravity, which should be ascertained by the hydrometer. They will retain their virtues a long time in well stoppered bottles.

Operations which involve Mixing and Separation of the second degree.

The processes whereby mixture and separation of the second degree (chemical mixture and decomposition), are accomplished, presuppose in particular, a special knowledge of chemistry. Many of these processes we have already partially treated upon, as well as the implements required for them. It only remains to discuss their general characters. Solution in the wet way takes place frequently in the formation of salts, when two or more bodies with opposite properties (as acids and bases) combine, whereby their opposite properties become neutralized; this operation is simple as ordinary solution. The bodies penetrate one another by contact, either at ordinary temperatures, as by alkalies and acids; or they require heat for their solution, as by difficultly soluble earths; decomposition mostly ensues by solution. Either the dissolved body must take up a constituent of the compound menstruum, to be able to enter into combination with it, or the menstruum separates a constituent of the dissolved body. When the separated body is gaseous it is evolved in bubbles, and escapes from the fluid, which is said to effervesce. It should be remarked that the menstruum should be sufficiently dilute, and the solid body added to it in a comminuted state, and in small quantities at a time, to prevent the fluid, by effervescing, rising over the sides of the vessel in which the mixture takes place.

Sublimation is most applied in pharmacy for the purpose of obtaining mixture and separation of the second degree. It is employed either for the separation of volatile from non-volatile substances, or for the combination of several volatile bodies by heat, and sometimes for both purposes. The volatile solid products or educts are termed sublimates. Those which are of a flocculent nature were formerly called flowers, as, for example, flowers of sulphur.

The sublimation of very volatile substances, or of such as pass over with fluid bodies, should be conducted in a retort with a receiver, as in the case of distillation. The retort should be placed deep in a sand-bath and be bound air-tight to the receiver, which should be large, as well as the neck of the retort. To remove partly the atmosphere in the retort, a small tube can be introduced at the joint, through which the air will pass when heat is applied to the retort. The receiver, when the substance is very volatile, must be surrounded by cold water or ice, to keep it as cool as possible. When it is necessary to allow moisture to escape, and the body to be sublimed is not very volatile, the receiver need not be luted to the retort.

A few volatile substances which evolve no moisture may be sublimed in an alembic or any similar vessel. The heat should be applied gently at first, and gradually increased until sublimation is effected. The alembic should be placed in sand up to its mouth, and the sand partially removed when sublimation commences, so that the sublimate may attach itself to the upper part of the vessel. Vessels with narrow openings must be watched from time to time, to see that the openings are not stopped up with the sublimate, which should be carefully removed when such is the case. The sand-bath may be raised at last to a red heat, if anything remains to be sublimed. To separate the sublimate from the glass vessel, the latter, whilst hot, should be struck with a wet cloth in that part where the sublimate is, which causes the glass to break into pieces, and to be easily separated from the sublimate.

PULVIS FERRI—IRON BY HYDROGEN.

BY WILLIAM PROCTER, JR.

There has recently been considerable discussions in the London Pharmaceutical Journals, as to the composition of the substance sold as Quevenne's metallic iron, and as manufactured by Mr. Morson and Mr. Heathfield, both of London. Having for several years been a manufacturer of this preparation, although not now so engaged, it may be appropriate to say a few words in relation to the subject at issue.* It appears (*Pharm Jour.*, page 333, January, 1854,) that iron reduced by hydrogen, made by both the gentlemen named, was on sale in Edinburg by different pharmaceutists. Messrs. Duncan, Flockhart and Co, who sold the preparation of Mr. Morson, were complained to, that their iron was not *black* like that of Mr. Robinson made by Mr. Heathfield. Messrs. D. F. and Co. then forwarded to Mr. Morson a sample of the black iron, and he pronounced it magnetic oxide of iron, and not metallic iron. On this, Mr. Robinson placed samples of both kinds in the hands of Dr. George Wilson, of Edinburg, who pronounced both to be impure, that is, contained oxygen, but that Heathfield's was seven per cent. purer than Morson's. On this being published in the *Chemist*, Mr. Morson obtained a specimen of Heathfield's iron, as sold in Edinburg, and had it analysed by Dr. Gregory, Dr. Stenhouse, Professor Williamson and Dr. Garrod, all of whom pronounced it to be magnetic oxide of iron, and published the whole affair in the *Pharmaceutical Journal* of January. In the next number, Mr. Heathfield pursues the subject by bringing forward microscopical evidence, and vindicates the *black* iron from the charge of impurity, attributing its color to minuteness of division, rather than to magnetic oxide, and endeavors to throw doubt on the correctness of the four analysis obtained by Mr. Mor-

* See a paper by the Author, *Amer. Jour. Pharm.*, vol. xix., p. 11.

son. And, finally, Dr. George Wilson appears in the March number, reasserts the correctness of his analysis, and claims for specimens of the preparation of Mr. Heathfield, since examined, the strength of 91 and 98½ per cent. of metallic iron.

By one who is practically familiar with what takes place in the process of reducing iron by hydrogen, the causes of the controversy above noticed are easily explained. The reduction tube, when ready for the operation, is nearly filled with red oxide of iron, obtained by calcining the sub-carbonate of iron of the Pharmacopœia, to free it from its water of hydration. After the current of hydrogen is established and the fire is kindled, the operator is made aware of the commencement of the reduction by the appearance of aqueous vapors at the exit pipe; and when it is continued for a length of time and stopped, the contents of the tube will vary considerably in appearance. Near the point of ingress of the gaseous current, if the heat has been sufficient, the red powder will have assumed an iron gray color, whilst further along the color will be blacker, and finally perfectly black. If the tube and contents have not been heated to a dull red, the reddish color of the oxide will be retained at such point, and it sometimes happens in the same operation, that the unreduced oxide and all the grades of reduction to the perfect metallic state may be observed. It nevers happens in practice that all the oxide is reduced, as the fire would have to be continued too long, to the injury of the reduced portion, and it is usual to employ the partially reduced oxide of one operation for the next. The line of complete reduction is distinctly marked, so that the chemist can by means of a spatula separate readily the perfectly reduced iron; yet between this and the black oxide there is a portion consisting of metallic iron and oxide in variable proportion. Hence there is no reason why imperfectly reduced iron should be sold except either through ignorance of the process, carelessness or fraud. Mr. Heathfield, therefore, in alleging the action of hydrogen in a hot tube as a reason for purity, is only conditionally correct.

It sometimes happens in operating in a four inch tube, that

the interior particles in a part of the oxide are black, and the exterior iron gray. Now, in reference to color, it may be said that no metallic iron is *perfectly* black; but when the oxide is reduced at the lowest heat possible, so that its particles do not contract or weld together by excess of heat, after reduction, it is of a dark iron gray hue, and will dissolve with rapid effervescence of hydrogen in dilute sulphuric, acid like a carbonate; when, however, the heat has been allowed to become cherry red, after the reduction, the particles contract more and more, until, if the heat has been continued long enough, a metallic mass is obtained, difficult to powder, and requiring the avoidance of blows of the pestle to prevent its condensation into solid shining pebble-like masses. The color of overheated iron is light iron gray, with a peculiar lustrous appearance, derived from the trituration necessary to pulverize it.

Now, when the operator opens his tube and finds that he has but a partial product, and that the interior part of the oxide is not thoroughly reduced, he is tempted to overlook the presence of the latter, and convert all to powder. This may be occasional and accidental, or habitual, according to the conscientiousness or knowledge of the manufacturer, and, whilst this is the case, iron by hydrogen will constantly vary in composition. We see by the analysis of Dr. Wilson, admitted by Mr. Heathfield, that his own preparation varies from 2 to 22 per cent. of foreign matter.

Undoubtedly, the best condition of this preparation, when removed from the tube, is that of a light spongy mass, like light carbonate of magnesia, yet more compressible, and of a dull, rather dark iron gray color. When a fragment is struck on a bright anvil with a smooth hammer, a thin brilliant lamina of metal is obtained, and when the powder is strongly pressed with a bright spatula, with traction, the compressed surface exhibits a metallic lustre.

It may be well to say a word in reference to the sulphur found in reduced iron: it may arise from two sources. First, from the presence of sulphuretted hydrogen in the hydrogen used, when the sulphuret present is that of iron; or it may be due to the deoxidation of sulphate of soda in the oxide of iron, when sulphuret of sodium is the sulphuretted body, as may be proved by washing the iron. It is almost impossible, on a manufacturing scale, to wash all the sulphate of soda from the hydrated carbonate of iron in the process of making the sub-carbonate, hence it is necessary to thoroughly wash the dried sub-carbonate after it is pulverized, till the washings are free from sulphate. The success of this operation is known by testing the reduced iron with dilute sulphuric acid, when, if any sulphuret is present, the odor of hydrosulphuric acid is perceptible.

In my experience in operating with a wrought-iron tube, forty inches long and four inches diameter, the charge of oxide is six to eight pounds, and the hydrogen is furnished by the solution of twelve pounds of zinc in dilute SO^3. The current is kept up rapidly for eight hours, during which time the tube is kept at as near a dull red heat as possible; and after the removal of the fire and the cooling of the walls of the furnace with water, the evolution of gas is moderated to a slow bubbling at the exit end, until the tube is *perfectly cold*. The yield of reduced iron, on the average, is between two and four ponnds to an operation. The black pulverulent oxide in the other end of the tube is used for part of the next charge. The most difficult point in the process is the regulation of the heat; the next, the management of the gas, which should be carefully purified by passing it twice through a solution of subacetate of lead.

RESEARCHES UPON THE NEW COMBINATIONS OF SALICYL.

BY CHARLES GERHARDT.

It is known to chemists that the salicylic ethers, for the knowledge of which we are indebted to M. Cahours, present a singular anomaly in the history of their combinations. These ethers, in fact, while they correspond to neutral salicates, have the property of combining with bases, and produce well marked metallic salts. Thus the salicylate of methyle (oil of gualteria) presents a composition similar to that of salicylate of silver:

$$\left.\begin{matrix} C^7 H^5 O^2 \\ C H^3 \end{matrix}\right\} O = \text{Salicylate of Methyle.} \qquad \left.\begin{matrix} C^7 H^5 O^2 \\ Ag \end{matrix}\right\} O = \text{Salicylate of Silver.}$$

And yet the salicylate of methyle combines with potassa soda, baryta, &c. It is the same with the salicylate of ethyle. These two ethers comport themselves then as veritable acids.

Again, there is another anomaly, when an ordinary ether is treated by chlorine and bromine, the first effect of these agents consists always in producing substitutions in the ethylic or methylic elements so as to give chlorine or bromine products, which the alkalies do not transform into alcohol or wood spirit, but which they may convert, as Malagutti has shown, into acetic or formic acids. The salicylic ethers behave quite differently; in acting on these, chlorine and bromine commence by attacking the salicylic elements, and thus give ethers of chloro-salicylic and bromo-salicylic acids, &c.

This difference of behavior, arising evidently from a difference in molecular constitution, I have been led, by applying my last theories to salicylic ethers, to consider them, not as a molecule of water whose two atoms of hydrogen were replaced, one by salicyl and the other by methyle or ethyle, but as a molecule of water of which an atom of hydrogen alone was replaced by the methyl-salicyl or ethyl-salicyl group, that is to say, by the salicyl containing in itself some methyle or ethyle substituted for the hydrogen:

$$\left.\begin{matrix} C^7 H^4 (CH^3) O^2 \\ H \end{matrix}\right\} O = \text{Hydrate of Methyl-Salicyl.}$$

$$\left.\begin{matrix} C^7 H^4 (C^2 H^5) O^2 \\ H \end{matrix}\right\} O = \text{Hydrate of Ethyl-Salicyl.}$$

The salicylate of methyle becomes thus a hydrate of methyl-salicyl, or oxide of hydrogen and of methyl-salicyl; the salicylate of ethyle becomes hydrate of ethyl-salicyl, or oxide of hydrogen and of ethyl-salicyl.

Whence it follows naturally that the combination of salicylate of methyle with potassa represents oxide of potassium and of methyl-salicyl:

$$\left.\begin{matrix} C^7 H^4 (CH^3) O^2 \\ K \end{matrix}\right\} O H \qquad \text{Oxide of Potassium and of Methyl-Salicyl.}$$

Now, since it is demonstrated by my experiments upon the anhydrous acids, that the basic hydrogen of these acids or the metal of the salts of the oxygenated groups, the benzoiles, cumyles, acetyles, &c, I ought to be able to effect a like change in the salicylic ethers if my view of the constitution of bodies were correct.

Experiment has justified my view. Nothing is easier, in fact, than to etherify the salicylic ethers as one etherifies alcohol or wood spirit. If, for example, we put alcohol or wood spirit in contact with chloride of benzoile, or chloride of succinyle, hydrochloric acid is disengaged, as well as benzoate of ethyle, succinate of methyle, &c. When the salicylic ethers are treated by the same chlorides, the reaction is still the same, and there is formed the benzoate of ethyl-salicyl, succinate of methyl-salicyl, &c.. In fact, with a salicylic ether and a chloride of any acid, we may produce as many compounds as can be produced from alcohol and a similar chloride. All the compounds which I have thus prepared are perfectly crystalline.

The benzoate of methyl-salicyl is obtained by acting with heat upon oil of gualteria and chloride of benzoil, and crystallizes in fine rhomboidal prisms, containing—

$$\left.\begin{matrix} C^7 H^4 (C^2 H^3) O^2 \\ C^7 H^5 O \end{matrix}\right\} O = \qquad \text{Benzoate of Methyl-Salicyl, or Oxide of Benzoil and of Methyl-Salicyl.}$$

The benzoate of ethyl-salicyl is prepared by the same process, using salicylic-ether:

$$\left.\begin{array}{r} C^7 H^4 (C^2 H^5) O^2 \\ C^7 H^5 O \end{array}\right\} O = \text{Benzoate of Ethyl-Salicyl, or Oxide of Benzoil and of Ethyl-Salicyl.}$$

The cuminate of methyl-salicyl crystallizes from boiling alcohol, in brilliant rhombic scales:

$$\left.\begin{array}{r} C^7 H^4 (C H^3) O^2 \\ C^{10} H^{11} O \end{array}\right\} O = \text{Cuminate of Methyl-Salicyl, or Oxide of Cumyl and of Methyl-Salicyl.}$$

The succinate of methyl-salicyl is obtained by means of chloride of succinyl, which M. Chiozza and myself have lately formed. It is deposited from the alcoholic solution, on cooling, in the form of large rectangular lamellæ, composed of fibres, laid alongside each other, and which are readily separated. It takes two molecules of water, like succinic acid, which is well known to be bi-basic:

$$\left.\begin{array}{r} \left.\begin{array}{r} C^7 H^4 (C H^3) O^2 \\ C^7 H^4 (C H^3) O^2 \end{array}\right\} O = \\ C^4 H^4 O^2 \ \} O = \end{array}\right\} \text{Succinate of Methyl-Salicyl, or Oxide of Succinyl and of Methyl-Salicyl.}$$

These examples might be easily multiplied.

I have also tried, with the object of producing the chloride of methyl-salicyl, to submit the oil of gualteria to the action of perchloride of phosphorus, but in the very energetic reaction of these two bodies the methyl-salicyl group is broken, and there is obtained chloride of methyl as well as a new chloride, the chloride of salicyl:

$$\left.\begin{array}{r} C^7 H^5 O^2 \\ Cl \end{array}\right\} \text{Chloride of Salicyl.}$$

This compound should not be confounded with that to which M. Piria has given the same name, and which, in my opinion, represents the hydruret of chloro-salicyl. The chloride which I obtained is a fuming liquid, decomposed by water, like the chlorides of silicon, phosphorus, and acetyl, into hydrochloric acid and salicylic acid. It reacts in a violent manner upon alcohol and wood, transforming them into salicylic ethers. It is the same with the chloride of salicyl when the salicylate of ethyle is prepared more readily from a mixture of salicylic acid, alcohol, and sulphuric acid. M. Drion, who carries out the study of these combinations that I have described, has also, with the new chloride of salicyl, obtained the salicylate of amyle (hydrate of amyl-salicyl), which many chemists had vainly sought to prepare by the previously known processes.

The preceding results appear to confirm the views which I laid before the Academy of Sciences in my last communications.—*Cosmos*, February, 1854.

THE NEW METAL—"ALUMINIUM."

At a meeting of the Academy of Sciences, Paris, February 6, M. Dumas asked leave to bring forward some new researches made by one of the most distinguished chemists of the rising generation, M. Sainte-claire Deville, *maitre de conferences* in the Normal School, and then read the following notes of M. Deville on the abundant and economical production of aluminium:

"It is known that M. Wöhler obtained aluminium, in a pulverulent form, by treating the chloride with potassium. By a suitable modification of his process, the decomposition of the chloride of aluminium may be regulated to produce a sufficient incandescence so that the particles of this metal may be seen to agglomerate and run into globules. If a mass, composed of metal and chloride of sodium (it would be better to employ sodium) be taken and heated to strong redness in a porcelain crucible, the excess of chloride of aluminium is set free, and there remains a saline substance with an acid reaction, in the midst of which is found globules, more or less large, of aluminium.

This metal is white, like silver, malleable and ductile to the highest degree, yet, when it is worked, it presents considerable resistance; and it may be presumed, therefore, that its tenacity is greater than that of silver. The melting point is nearly the same as that of silver, its density is 2.56; is a good conductor of heat, and may be melted and cooled in the air without sensible oxidation.

It is completely unalterable in the air, whether dry or humid, does not tarnish on exposure, remaining brilliant after zinc and tin, freshly cut, have lost their lustre, is not altered by the presence of hydro-sulphuric acid, cold water has no action on it, and boiling water does not tarnish it. Nitric acid, concentrated or dilute, and sulphuric acid, have no action on it in the cold. Its true solvent is hydrochloric acid, disengaging hydrogen and forming sesqui-chloride of aluminium. When the metal is heated to redness in hydrochloric acid gas it also forms the sesqui-chloride, which is anhydrous and volatile.

It is easy to comprehend a metal which is as white and inalterable as silver, which does not tarnish in the air, which is fusible, malleable, ductile, and tenacious, and which has the singular property of being lighter than glass, and how serviceable such a metal would be were it possible to obtain it with ease. When it is considered also that the metal is very abundant in nature, that its *mineral* is clay, its easy procurement is desirable. I have every hope that it will be so, for the chloride of aluminum is decomposed with remarkable facility, at a high temperature, by the common metals; and a reaction of this kind, upon which I am engaged, so as to obtain it on a larger scale than a mere laboratory experiment, will solve the question in a practical point of view.

M. Debray, a young *agregé*, and an able chemist, attached to the laboratory of the Normal School, who has prepared, some time back, a complete account of glucinum, is still occupied with its properties. M. de Senarmont has been good enough to endeavor to procure me for the study, a sufficiency of the Zircon of Expailly, and I shall extend to Zirconium, and I hope will be soon able to submit to the Academy, the general results obtained from the separation of these metals of the earths and the order of their chemical combinations among the list of metallic bodies."

The metal was exhibited at the meeting, and during the reading of the paper by Dumas, Chevreul, Payen, Regnault, Leverrier, and other members, examined the plates and fibres of the metal, which, while lying under water, weak nitric and sulphuric acids, still preserved its lustre.

Some remarks being made after the reading of the paper, M. Thenard rose to ask the Academy, in view of such beautiful results, to place at the disposal of M. Sainte-claire Deville a sufficient sum to enable him to proceed with his experiments at once on a large scale. This proposition, warmly supported by many members of the chemical section, was passed by a unanimous vote, and it was determined that at the next meeting the committee would fix the precise sum that could be granted.—*Ibid.*

WHEAT FLOUR DEFICIENT IN GLUTEN.

In January last M. Millon communicated a note to the Academy of Sciences, Paris, on the gluten of wheat. In 1848 and 1849, the analysis of many samples of wheat harvested in the Arrondissemont of Lille enabled this chemist to detect a very variable amount of glutin furnished by the meal. He met with some wheat (English red) pretty rich in azote, and yielding six parts of it in one hundred of gluten. Called to Algiers, in his capacity of military pharmacien, he received from M. Roy, colonial inspector, a very tender corn, long in the grain, harvested at Guyotville, in 1852, and singular enough, in operating with every precaution, he could not extract any gluten from its meal. In its place was a friable gray substance, representing, when dry, 4.8 per cent. of the weight of meal; yet the proportion of azote contained in the wheat was very large, and corresponded to 11.5 per cent. of gluten, or rather of albuminous principle. The harvest of 1853 gave the same result as that of 1852. Again, on examining this wheat closer, Millon found it composed of two distinct varieties, the one composed of grains glazed on the surface, and with a fracture hard and horny, which yielded an amount of gluten equal to 11.8 per cent. of weight of the meal, the other variety had a whiter ear and a more feculent interior, but the meal did not yield the least trace of gluten. An attentive examination of other tender wheats from Algiers or Provence has developed the important fact, that wheat beautiful in appearance may yet be destitute of gluten. It may also happen that the freshest and finest flour contains very frequently less than seven per cent. of gluten. In cases of law trials, *this* is an important discovery. Millon had been already engaged upon a case of a seizure of corn upon the suspicion of fraud and adulteration. A minute attention to it led him to believe that the small deficiency of gluten, as ascertained by the examiners, was to be charged to the nature of the wheat itself and not to the holder, who was liable to confiscation of the flour and imprisonment for his alledged offence. In times of scarcity, attempts at adulteration of corn are likely to occur, and it is just at this time when exports ought to redouble their vigilance and that their conclusions should bear in view the most recent results of science and experiment. This distinction of corns, rich or poor in gluten, is advantageous in this respect, that the flour of wheat rich in gluten better admits of the addition of Indian corn meal, of potato starch, and probably also of all fœculent substances. Panification occurs readily with the admixture of these substances, when the wheat flour is rich in gluten; and the hard variety wheat, in which all the azote is contained as gluten, is very superior to all tender grained wheat. Millon remarks, however, that gluten is not indispensable to panification; the dough is in this case short and the fermentation slow.—*Ibid.*

ANALYSIS OF MINERAL WATERS AND ORES IN TENNESSEE.

BY R. O. CURREY, M. D.

MACON RED SULPHUR SPRINGS, MACON COUNTY, TENN.

Sp. Gr. 1.004.

Gaseous contents—

Sulphuretted hydrogen,
Carbonic acid.

Solid contents in a fluid pint—

Sulphate of magnesia	15 grs.
" lime	8
Carbonate of lime	6
" magnesia	3
Chloride of sodium	26
Protoxide of iron	1
Silica	1.5
Loss	1.5
	62 grs.

MACON CHALYBEATE SPRING, MACON COUNTY, TENN.

(Same locality.)

Carbonic acid,
Carbonate of iron,
" lime.

WAYLAND'S SPRING, NEAR FLORENCE, ALABAMA.

Specific Gravity 1.002.

In each gallon:

Gaseous contents—

Carbonic acid gas, 346 cubic inches.

Solid contents—

Carbonate of magnesia - - -	4 grs.
" soda - - -	1.2
Chloride of sodium - - -	3.7
Protoxide of iron - - -	3
Potash—a trace.	
Iodine - - - - - - -	1.8
Bromine—a trace.	
	13.7 grs.

Properties.—*Alterative, tonic, and diuretic*—Useful in glandular and cutaneous diseases; in enfeebled states of the system, and in affections of the digestive organs.

LEAD ORE, MARION COUNTY, TENNESSEE.

Sulphur - - - -	22
Lead - - - - -	78
Silver—a trace.	
	100

The locality from which this specimen was obtained is said to be very interesting. The vein of lead ore is said to be cropping out for more than a mile on the side of a creek, and is of considerable thickness. Large masses are said to be lying detached on the ground. From these representations, and from the purity of the ore, I would unhesitatingly pronounce it a valuable mine. The ore is of the granular variety.

BLACK OXIDE OF COPPER—POLK COUNTY, TENNESSEE.

Copper - - - - -	68
Oxygen - - - -	32
	100

Other varieties of copper ore are found in same locality, as red oxide, green carbonate, sulphuret, and native copper.

CARBONATE OF ZINC—CLAIBORNE COUNTY, TENNESSEE.

Oxide of zinc - - -	63
Carbonic acid - - -	37
	100

The oxide of zinc, in this analysis, yielded nearly fifty per cent. of pure metal.—*Southern Journal of the Medical and Physical Sciences.*

ON SOAP AS A MEANS OF ART.*

BY FERGUSON BRANSON, M.D., SHEFFIELD.†

Several years ago I was endeavoring to find an easy substitute for wood engraving, or rather to find out a substance more readily cut than wood, and yet sufficiently firm to allow of a cast being taken from the surface when the design was finished, to be re-produced in type-metal or by the electrotype process. After trying various substances, I at last hit upon one which at first promised success, viz., the very common substance called soap, but I found that much more skill than I possessed was required to cut the fine lines for surface printing. A very little experience with the material convinced me that, though it might not supply the place of wood for surface printing, it contained within itself the capability of being extensively applied to various useful and artistic processes in a man-

---

* Dr. Branson has also employed beeswax, white wax, sealing wax, lacs, as well as other plastic bodies ; and in some of these cases a heated steel knitting-needle, or point, was substituted for the ivory knitting-needle.—Ed. *Journal of the Franklin Institute.*

† From the *London Artizan*, February, 1854.

ner hitherto unknown. Die-sinking is a tedious process, and no method of die-sinking, that I am aware of, admits of freedom of handling. A drawing may be executed with a hard point on a smooth piece of soap almost as readily, as freely, and in as short a time as an ordinary drawing with a lead pencil. Every touch thus produced is clear, sharp, and well defined. When the drawing is finished, a cast may be taken from the surface in plaster, or, better still, by pressing the soap firmly into heated gutta percha. In gutta percha several impressions may be taken without injuring the soap, so as to admit of "proofs" being taken and corrections made—a very valuable and practical good quality in soap. It will even bear being pressed into melted sealing wax without injury. I have never tried a sulphur mould, but I imagine an impression from the soap could easily be taken by that method. The accompanying specimens will show, that from the gutta percha or plaster cast, thus obtained, a cast in brass, with the impression either sunk or in relief, can at once be taken. If sunk, a die is obtained capable of embossing paper or leather; if in relief, an *artistic* drawing in metal. This suggests a valuable application. The manufacturer may thus employ the most skilful artist to make the drawing on the soap, and a fac-simile of the actual touches of the artist can be reproduced in metal, paper, leather, gutta percha, or any other material capable of receiving an impression. By this means even high art can be applied in various ways—not a translation of the artist's work by another hand, as in die-sinking, but the veritable production of the artist himself. One of the specimens sent is a copy of Sir E. Landseer's "Highland Piper," a rude one, I must confess, though its rudeness does not militate against the principle involved in its production. Suppose the drawing had been made by Sir E. Landseer himself, that accomplished artist's actual drawing might have been embossed on various materials in common use, and disseminated amongst thousands, thus familiarizing the eyes of the public with high art, and giving a value to the embossed transcript which no translation of the die-sinker, however skilful, could give it. The raised gutta percha impression of this specimen is from the soap itself; the sunk impression is cast in gutta percha from gutta percha. The works in metal, during the fourteenth, fifteenth, and sixteenth centuries, owe their excellence, in a great degree, to the combination in the same individual of artist and artizan. The metal was finished by the artist himself, who left the stamp of his genius unmistakably upon it. By the plan just explained, something like a return to this combination might be effected, and the artist would, at least, have the satisfaction of finding his own work accurately rendered, and not enfeebled, in the translation; for the art of casting in metal has of late been so much improved that little difference can be detected between the impression on the cast and the mould which produced it. I wish to lay particular stress upon the fact that *drawing touches* can be thus rendered, and an effect *rapidly* produced, unattainable by modeling. The larger plaster casts were taken from drawings freely made—as the appearance of the touches will prove—in common brown soap. The finer kind of soap is, of coarse, better fitted for fine work; but should the process now described be adopted by the manufacturer—and I trust it may never become the subject of any patent—soap better suited to the purpose than any now made will doubtless be specially manufactured. In proof that fine lines can be drawn upon the soap as well as broad vigorous touches, I can state that one of Rembrandt's etchings has been copied on soap, the soap pressed into gutta percha, and an electrotype taken from the gutta percha cast, from which a print has been obtained very little inferior in delicacy to the original etching. Doubtless, persons engaged in manufactures will see applications of the process which I have not contemplated, and I leave it to their ingenuity to discover them. I would particularly call the attention of ornamental leather and paper manufacturers, bookbinders, and, possibly, manufacturers of china, to the process; for it must be remembered that soap, when made, can be run into moulds of any form, so as to obtain curved as well as flat surfaces for the artist to draw upon. It has also occurred to me that it would prove a very ready and expeditious method of forming raised maps, pictures, and diagrams for the use of the blind. The manipulation is very simple. A lead pencil drawing, if required, can readily be transferred to the smoothed surface of the soap, by placing the face of the drawing on the soap and rubbing the back of the paper; every line of the drawing is then distinctly visible on the soap. The implements used are equally simple; all the specimens sent were drawn with ivory knitting-needles, and small ivory netting-meshes for scooping out larger and deeper touches. The only caution necessary is to avoid under-cutting. Having felt the greatest interest in the establishment of schools of design, so well calculated to re-connect fine art with manufactures, it will afford me sincere gratification if the simple process now pointed out—and I trust its simplicity will be no bar to its being carefully tested—shall be the smallest degree instrumental in accomplishing the re-union.

Sheffield, Dec. 31, 1853.

P.S.—The date 1850 is on some of the illustrative specimens.—*Jour. So. of Arts*, in *Jour. Franklin Institute.*

CONDENSATION OF THE GASES BY POROUS BODIES.

BY MM. FAVRE AND SILBERMANN.

(*Ann. de Chem. et de Phys.*, April, 1853, p. 471.)

M. Mitscherlich sought to determine, by calculation, the state in which carbonic acid must exist in the charcoal, after the absorption of the gas; and he arrived at the conclusion, that at least one-third of the condensed carbonic acid must be in a liquid state on the surface of the cells, and that this liquid layer was not thicker than 54 thousands of a millimetre, distributed over the whole absorbing surface. The layer would be thicker for other gases more easily absorbable and liquefiable.

It was interesting to know the heat disengaged by this condensation; we might hope to obtain some data or some suitable hints upon the numbers which express the latent heat of liquefaction of some gases which it would be difficult to determine directly.

MM. Favre and Silbermann have found that one gramme of gas, condensed by charcoal, disengages—

Chlorhydric acid,	232·5	Units of heat.
Sulphurous acid,	139·9	
Carbonic acid,	129·6	

One gramme of charcoal absorbs of—

Chlorhydric acid,	69.2	cubic centimetres.
Sulphurous acid,	83·2	"
Carbonic acid,	45·2	"

On comparing the heat disengaged by the condensation of sulphurous acid with its heat of vaporization, we find that the first surpasses the second by 45·34 units.

This difference is so great that it may include the latent heat of solidification of the sulphurous acid, so that it is not impossible that the gas may be fixed in the same state as the coloring matters or certain salts which carbon has the property of removing from water.

If we admit that the liquid sulphurous acid wets the pores of the charcoal, the experiment leads us to allow a part of the heat disengaged as due to the affinity of the charcoal for the liquefied product.

These experiments show no ratio between the power of condensation of charcoal and the solubility of the gases in water. —*Archives des Sciences Phys. et Nat.*, vol. xxiii., p. 386, in *Jour. Franklin Institute.*

Sthamer has pointed out that the crystals of sugar occurring in the flowers of *Rhododendron ponticum* consist of pure cane sugar.

RESEARCHES ON EVAPORATION.

BY PROFESSOR MARCET, OF GENEVA.*

The following experiments were instituted with the view of throwing some light on the tendency of certain circumstances to promote or diminish the evaporation of liquids. Water and alcohol were the liquids chiefly used. The results obtained by the author may be recapitulated as follows.

1. The temperature of a liquid, allowed to evaporate freely in an open vessel, is always inferior to that of the surrounding atmosphere. The higher the temperature of the atmosphere, the greater is the difference between its temperature and that of the liquid exposed to evaporation. Between 40° and 50° centigrade the difference was found to vary from 5° to 7°; between 20° to 25° it varied from 1½° to 1¼°; at 12° it was 0.8° only, and between 3° and zero about 0.2°. The explanation of this result is obvious. The evaporation of a liquid diminishing with the external temperature, the cold which is the consequence of this evaporation, must diminish in the same proportion; and if it were possible to prevent evaporation altogether, the author presumes there would be no difference whatever between the temperature of a liquid and that of the surrounding medium.

2. The temperature of liquids, such as water and alcohol, as well as the rapidity with which they evaporate, varies, all other circumstances remaining the same, according to the nature of the vessel in which these liquids are contained. For instance, the temperature of the surrounding atmosphere being from 15° to 20°, water is, on the average, 0.3° warmer in an open metallic vessel than in a similar one of polished porcelain, and 0.2° warmer than in a similar one of glass. It is the same with alcohol. Again, both water and alcohol evaporate more rapidly from a porcelain vessel than from a metallic or

---

* From the London Repertory of Patent Inventions, Jan., 1854.

glass vessel of precisely the same size. For example—three similar vessels, one of metal, the second of porcelain, and the third of glass, containing each 600 grains of water, having been exposed to evaporation during seven days, the temperature of the surrounding atmosphere varying from 20° to 25°, it was found, that at the end of that time, the porcelain vessel had lost 303 grains of its previous weight, the metallic one 277, and the glass vessel 275.5 grains only. The author enters into considerable detail as to the precautions he took to make sure that these differences could not be attributed to any difference in the radiating or conducting powers of the vessels employed.

The difference observed in the temperature of liquids, according to the nature of the vessels in which they are contained, depends, no doubt, on the property with which these vessels appear to be endowed, of accelerating or delaying evaporation. It is evident that, in each case the quantity of sensible heat subtracted from the liquid, or, in other words, the diminution of its temperature, must be in proportion to the quantity of vapor formed. For instance, the fact that water and alcohol are constantly colder in a porcelain vessel than in a similar vessel of metal or glass, is the natural result of the more rapid evaporation of these liquids from the former of these vessels than from the two latter. The reason why a porcelain vessel evaporates more freely than a metallic or glass one is far less evident. The author has proved, by placing a hermetically-closed bottle of porcelain, containing water, under the vacuum of the air-pump, that it cannot be owing to any perviousness of the sides of the vessel, as he was at first inclined to suspect.

3. The influence of the mass or depth of a liquid was next examined. The author's experiments appears to lead to the curious fact, that the rapidity with which any given liquor evaporates depends not only on the extent of its surface, but also, within certain limits, on its depth. He found, for instance, that with two similar cylindrical porcelain vessels, containing, the first a layer of water of one-twelfth of an inch in depth, and the second a layer of half an inch, the evaporation

from the latter exceeded that of the former in the proportion of nearly 4 to 3. A similar result was obtained with alcohol. If thin glass vessels were used, the same increase of depth accelerated the evaporation in the proportion of 6 to 5. As the author himself observes, this apparent influence of the depth of a liquid on evaporation may, very possibly, be merely owing to the greater facility with which the different layers are conveyed, one after the other, to the surface, when the liquid is of a certain depth than when it is quite shallow.

4. Water containing a solution of salt in about the same proportion of sea water, evaporates less rapidly, and, consequently, produces less cold than the same quantity of distilled water. The higher the temperature of the surrounding atmosphere, the greater the difference between the quantities of salt and fresh water evaporated in a given time, under similar circumstances.

5. A given quantity of water, mixed with certain pulverulent substances, such as a siliceous sand, for the particles of which it has but a slight adhesion, evaporates more rapidly than the same quantity of distilled water *alone*. The fact was ascertained in the following manner. The author, having procured two small porcelain vessels, exactly of the same size, introduced into one of them three hundred grains of distilled water, and into the other a small quantity of siliceous sand, over which three hundred grains of water were poured, so as not only to saturate the sand, but also to leave a layer of water of about one-tenth of an inch in thickness over and above its surface. At the end of five days, it was observed that the water standing alone had lost 184 grains of its previous weight, while the water mixed with the sand had lost no less than 196 grains. The average difference, resulting from a series of experiments, was 7½ per cent. in favor of the more rapid evaporation of water mixed with sand compared with that of water standing alone. If the experiment be made with glass or metallic vessels, the difference is only about 4½ per cent.

6. The last result which we shall mention, and which may be regarded as a direct consequence of the preceding one, is

the following. Water mixed with sand remains habitually at a slightly lower temperature than an equal surface of water standing alone. The difference varies to a certain extent, according to the nature of the vessels in which the experiment is performed, never, however, exceeding half a degree centigrade. It is greater when the comparison is made between water and wet sand placed in two similar metallic vessels, than when they are placed in porcelain or glass vessels. In the latter case it seldom exceeds 0.1° to 0.2°.

The author concludes by remarking, that the foregoing result tends to confirm an opinion expressed some time since by Professor De la Rive, in a letter to M. Arago, published in the *Comptes Rendus de l'Académie des Sciences* for October, 1851. In this letter, M. De la Rive attributes the sudden appearance of vast glaciers in divers parts of Europe to a temporary refrigeration produced at the period of the elevation of the most recent European strata, by the evaporation of the water with which they were recently covered. If, as the author's experiments tend to show, evaporation takes places more rapidly from water mixed with sand, earth, or any similar substance than from the surface of clear water, it becomes natural to conclude, that the cold produced by evaporation from the recently elevated and still humid strata, must have been greater than that resulting from the evaporation of the sea or freshwater lake which covered them previously to a great depth.—*Bibliothèque Universelle*, April, 1853, in *Jour. Franklin Institute.*

Souberain has shown that bees' honey contains three varieties of sugar, viz., grape sugar, another sugar which diminished in quantity as the honey was kept, rotated the plane of polarization to the right, and was altered by acids, and an uncrystallizable sugar which rotated the plane to the left.

THE NATURE OF THE LAVA FROM THE ERUPTION OF ETNA IN 1852.

BY C. HAUER.

The author has analyzed the lava from the most recent eruption in 1852. As far as the mass is crystalline, which with the greatest part is the case, it consists, according to the mineralogical investigation by Dr. Kenngott, of labrador and augite, sprinkled with grains of olivine. The presence of magnetic iron enables it to exhibit a very slight action on the needle, as Abich has shown with former specimens of lava. Its specific gravity is 2.86, while Abich found that of the lava of 1838 to be 2.94.

The analysis of the lava, as a whole, afforded, in one hundred parts:

	I.	II.	MEAN.
Silica	49.41	49.85	49.63
Alumina	22.55	22.40	22.47
Protoxide of iron	10.84	10.76	10.80
Protoxide of manganese	.52	.75	.63
Lime	9.27	8.83	9.05
Magnesia	2.54	2.82	2.68
Soda	3.00	3.15	3.07
Potash	.99	.97	.98
	99.12	99.53	99.31

If we consider this analysis, except the relative proportions of alumina to protoxide of iron, the composition is almost the same as Löwe found for the lava of the eruption of 1669.—*Central-Blatt.*

Varieties.

TABLE OF PRODUCE AND GRAVITY OF VOLATILE OILS.

Van Hees gives the following table of the produce of ethereal oils and their specific gravities. The oils heavier than water were prepared by surrounding the still with high pressure steam; those which were lighter, by passing steam through the plants:

		Ozs.	Sp. Grv.
Oleum Anisi, 20 lbs. gave		5¼	0.977
——— Anisi Stellati, 20 lbs. gave		8	0.976
——— Calamus Arom. (old oil)		–	0.984
——— ——	55 lbs. Calamus, of a previous year	12	0.956
——— ——	85 lbs. New Calamus, partly dry	10	0.950
——— Carui	12½ lbs., last year's seeds	8	0.923
——— ——	25 lbs., fresh seeds	17	0.913
——— ——	⅛ cwt., Saxony seeds	6	0.926
——— Caryophylli	10 lbs., Amboyna Cloves, by six distillations	31	1.040
	8 lbs., Bourbon Cloves	21	1.035
	25 lbs., Dutch Cloves, by eight distillations	74	1.033
——— ——	¼ Cwt., Clove Stems	16	1.049
——— Cass. Cinnam	⅛ Cwt., Bruised Bark	2⅝	1.035
——— — Flor	12½ lbs.	3⅛	1.023
——— Fœniculi	10 lbs.	5	0.968
——— Juniperi Bac	44 lbs., Berries, ripe, dried	2¼	0.870
	96 lbs., fresh	7⅛	0.862
	53 lbs., unripe	3	0.864
——— Lavandulæ	⅛ Cwt., Dry Flowers	3	0.892

Red Indigo.—Haeffely has successfully applied the red sulphate of indigo (phenicine) to dyeing worsted and silk. This compound is produced by allowing sulphuric acid to act upon indigo for a few minutes, and then throwing the mixture into a large excess of water. A red precipitate is thus formed, which, when well washed on a filter, differs entirely from the blue sulphate of indigo in composition, property and tinctorial power. It produces shades superior in every respect to those yielded by the ordinary indigo extract, and also purples resembling those produced by logwood and cudbear. The dye is not applicable to cotton.

IMPROVED METHOD OF MANUFACTURING LIQUID CEMENTS, PIGMENTS, AND PAINTS.—By Mr. George Bell.—To produce a liquid cement suitable for outside walls and other like situations, Mr. Bell mixes together the following ingredients in the proportion of six bushels of lime, one pound of sulphate of iron or zinc, one quarter of a pound of sal ammoniac; these are ground together with a little water, and to the mixture is added about six pounds of ochre, and about six pounds of amber, to give the required tint. If the mixture, when ground, is not sufficiently fluid for use, it may be rendered so by the addition of water to the extent desired.

To produce a liquid cement or color having a more adhesive character, and suitable for inside walls and other situations, six pounds weight of gum Arabic, and one-and-a-half pound of beeswax, are dissolved and mixed with the above.

To produce a paint for common purposes, two pounds of slaked lime, two pounds of sulphuric acid diluted with one gallon of water, and ten gallons of gas tar, are mixed well together in any suitable stirring or mixing apparatus.

An elastic paint especially suitable for damp walls, but applicable for other purposes, is made by combining one cwt. of oxichloride of lead or oxide of zinc, 28 lbs. of slaked lime (dry), and one gallon of solution of India-rubber diluted with one part of linseed oil, and two parts of spirit of turpentine. The oxide of zinc, or the oxichloride of lead, is to be first ground up with the linseed oil, and the other matters added. An oil suitable for thinning this elastic paint may be obtained by combining one gallon of spirit of turpentine, half a gallon of turpentine varnish, one pint of linseed oil, and one pint of resin oil.

IMPROVED PROCESS FOR BLEACHING BEESWAX AND THE FATTY ACIDS.—By Mr. G. F. Wilson.—This improved process consists of two parts—1st. The application of highly heated steam to heat the fatty matters under treatment, by which means the requisite heat for melting these substances is obtained, and at the same time the atmosphere is thereby excluded; the heated steam, so applied, in its passage off, carries with it the offensive smells given off by the fatty matters, and being made to traverse a pipe or passage, up or along which gaseous chlorine is allowed to flow, a complete disinfection of the offensive products is thereby effected. 2d. The treating of beeswax in a mixture of hard acid fat and beeswax, with compounds of chlorine and oxygen, preferring to employ that disengaged from chlorate of potash by treating it with sulphuric acid. For this purpose, Mr. Wilson takes at the rate, say, of a ton of yellow beeswax, and melts and boils it up with free steam for about half an hour. It is then allowed to stand a short time, and is then decanted into another vessel provided with a steam-pipe to emit free steam; about 20 lbs. of chlorate of potash is added, and the steam turned on; 80 lbs. of sulphuric acid, diluted with a like weight of water, is then gradually added. The matters are allowed to stand for a short time, and are then decanted into another vessel, and again boiled up with free steam, and treated with a like quantity of diluted sulphuric acid. The beeswax is then decanted into a receiver, and is ready for use. The beeswax may, before undergoing these processes, be combined and boiled up with a hard fatty acid; and then treated as above described.

IMPROVED METHOD OF MANUFACTURING EPSOM SALTS.—By Dr. Richardson, F.C.S.—A large quantity of sulphate of magnesia is made from the "rough Epsoms," obtained as a residuary product in the manufacture of alum. At present, in some manufactories, this impure sulphate of magnesia is calcined at a high temperature, in order to convert the iron and manganese, with which it is contaminated, into insoluble oxides. This operation is attended with considerable loss of sulphate of magnesia, even with the addition of magnesia to the impure Epsoms previous to calcination. To obviate this loss, Dr. Richardson employs one part of the fluor spar for every four parts of the sulphates of iron or manganese present in the impure Epsoms, together with the ordinary quantity of magnesia, and calcines this mixture at a very low temperature. A double decomposition ensues between the metallic sulphates and the fluor spar, while the metals are rapidly peroxidized and rendered insoluble. The calcined materials are lixiviated and treated in the usual way for obtaining pure Epsom salts, while the metallic oxides may be employed as a coloring material.—*Ann. Pharm.*

NEW VARIETY OF COPAIVA BALSAM.—The known varieties of copaiva yield, when mixed in proper proportions with potassa or ammonia, a more or less perfect and clear solution. From the ammonia solution are deposited, after some time, crystals of copaivate of ammonia. Posselt has investigated a variety of this balsam, which, although unadulterated, does not exhibit this reaction. It smells and tastes like the ordinary kinds of copaiva, but is thinner, of a brighter yellow color, and sp. gr. 0.94. It forms with potassa or ammonia, in all proportions, an opaque mixture, from which the balsam again speedily separates. It dissolves but imperfectly in alcohol, and contains 82 per cent. of oil and 18 per cent. of resin. The oil distilled with water, rectified, and dried over chloride of calcium, is colorless and of a thick consistence, is readily soluble in ether, but only slightly soluble in absolute alcohol. It has a strong and pure copaiva odor, and burning taste, and a sp. gr. of 0.91. It boils at 222° with decomposition and rise of the boiling point. Its composition is $C^{10} H^{8}$. It explodes with concentrated nitric acid, and with the dilute it forms a resin.—*Liebig and Kopp's Ann. Rep., Vol. 3.*

CRYSTALLINE HYDRATE OF OXIDE OF IRON.—The officinal hydrated oxide becomes crystalline under certain circumstances, and, therefore, less efficacious as an antidote for arsenic. Limberger finds this to be produced not only by time but also when the preparation is subjected to a temperature below the freezing point of water—it is effected at 21° F. It is then a much paler substance, and but slightly soluble in acetic acid of gravity 1.030, but readily dissolves when the acid has the gravity 1.0759. If eight volumes of water be added to this solution, a portion of the iron separates in a few days as a reddish yellow deposit. Wittstein examined this crystalline hydrate, and found it to contain—Oxide of iron, 10.46; water, 3.60—representing $Fe^2 O^3 3 HO$. This hydrate is less soluble in organic acids than the amorphous variety, and of the two varieties of crystalline hydrate, that obtained by long keeping is more insoluble than that obtained by freezing.

A Delicate Reagent for the Detection of Reducing Bodies.—By J. Lowenthal.—This reagent is a freshly-prepared diluted solution of red prussiate of potash, mixed with a few drops of a solution of perchloride of iron, free from protoxide of iron.

When this reagent is introduced into a liquid containing protochlorine of tin, sulphurous acid, sulphuretted hydrogen, or alkaline sulphurets, a blue precipitate or a blue coloration immediately results. With alkaline sulphurets and salts of sulphurous acid an addition of muriatic acid is naturally necessary. The same effect is immediately produced when the quantity of the reducing body is so small that it cannot be detected by any of the tests already known, as the nitro-prussiate of soda, gold solution, &c. Arsenious acid, protochloride of antimony, protonitrate of mercury, do not exhibit this behavior.

In a similar way, peroxide of iron can be detected in a fluid wherein sulpho-cyanide of potassium no longer produces a reaction, if the fluid is mixed with a little of the solution of the red prussiate of potash, and then a very dilute solution of protochloride of tin added when the blue coloration immediately appears. This test is, of course, only applicable in those cases where it is previously known that only one or the other of any of these reducing bodies are present, which very often happens, such as that of protochloride of tin in perchloride of tin, sulphurous acid in wine.—*Journal fur Practische Chemie.*

Test for Quinine.—A. Vogel gives the following as his improved test for quinine. Dissolve sulphate of quinine in a test tube, leaving, however, an excess of the salt undissolved in the bottom of the tube; shake so as to keep the salt suspended; pour a few drops into a watch glass, and add a sufficient quantity of chlorine water until a clear fluid of a yellow color is obtained. To this chlorinated solution, finely powdered ferrocyanide of potassium is added until it acquires a pale rose red color. This soon passes to deep red, and with great rapidity if a little more powdered ferrocyanide be added.—*Jour. Am. Pharm.*

Preservation of Leeches.—It was stated in the "Allgemeinen Polytechischen Zeitung," that metallic iron is an excellent means to prevent water becoming foul. With reference to this statement, Wittstein observes that he has remarked the efficiency of this remedy in water where leeches are kept, and that these can be preserved for a whole year in the same water, if that which is lost by evaporation be from time to time replaced, and if several iron nails be placed therein, without the water becoming foul. The slime which leeches throw off combines with the rust of the iron, and thus prevents the water becoming putrid, and destroying the leeches.

EDITORIAL.

Not a little fuss has been made in England and France by the alleged improvements of Messrs. Morlin, Martin, and Journel in the art of baking, by which the same quantity of flour delivers out of the oven a larger number of loaves than by the present processes, the increase being such that 360 lbs. of flour forms 520 lbs. of bread. That this should be heralded as any improvement only shows the popular ignorance on matters of diet, the additional weight being only water, which the flour is made to absorb by the addition of some hygrometric substance. The process has been introduced into the Marylebone Poorhouse, we suppose, for the purpose of trying how far a poor man may be contented with less victuals, giving him a Barmecide feast of *water*.

A similar attempt was made in 1847, in Ireland, during the famine there, when the English Government sent over Soyer, the cook of the Reform Club, to make *soup* to feed laboring men three times a day with, and that soup not containing one-fourth of the protein compounds required.

An adult loses about 240 grains of nitrogen *daily* by the waste of his muscles, which has to be supplied by protein compounds. 16 ozs. of meat (dry) accomplishes this: 33 ozs. of wheat flour answers the same purpose, or 50 ozs. of bread. Now, this fifty ounces of ordinary bread is the minimum quantity when it is used alone as food; and to give bread which contains more water entails the necessity of consuming a larger quantity, and distending the stomach unnecessarily, overtaxing that organ, and producing dyspepsia, the universal result of a potato diet, where 16 lbs. is required to be taken daily to supply the same nourishment as is in the 50 ozs. of bread.

Columbia College.—Since the election recorded in our last, the Senate of the State has taken the matter up, and Mr. Brooks has succeeded in getting a committee of inquiry appointed.

The prompting for this investigation is found in the charge that the trustees have lately been guilty of requiring that a candidate for a professorship should subscribe to a particular religious creed. It was asserted by several Senators that these charges had been really made to them on the occasion of their late visit to New York. Upon the impression made by these assertions the following resolution was passed:

"*Resolved*—That a select committee of three be appointed, whose duty it shall be, during the recess of the Legislature, and at as early a day as practicable, to inquire whether Columbia College or any of its trustees have violated any provision of law or of its charter, and particularly whether said college or any of its trustees have in any way required any, and, if any, what religious qualifications or test from any candidate, as a condition of appointment to any professorship in said college. And further, to inquire into the means and resources of said college and the administration of its affairs at large—and that such committee have power to send for persons and papers."

Mr. Spencer made an attempt to induce Senators not to vote for the resolution, alleging that he was satisfied the charges made were groundless. Failing in this, he endeavored to engraft upon the original resolve an amendment providing for an inquiry into all the colleges in the State. This was refused, and the resolution adopted.

The committee appointed were Judge Mason and Messrs. Mason, Jay, Nicoll, Cornell.

It appears, further, that the mode of conducting the election has rendered the appointment of Mr. McCulloch null and void, inasmuch as the charter requires that trustees shall not hold any office in the college, and also that they shall be residents of this State; whereas, in the last election, Mr. Wm. Betts, a trustee, who voted, is also professor of law to the college, and Thomas L. Wells, also a trustee, and who voted, is a resident of New Jersey.

The trustees held a meeting to consider this matter, but postponed any action until June, by which time probably the committee will have released them from any further action, by furnishing their report.

The "Société Medico-Pratique de Paris" offers a prize, in the form of a gold medal, worth three hundred francs, for the best dissertation on the mode of action of the principal purgatives used in medicine, with the special indications for their use. The memoirs to be written in French or Latin, and sent before the 31st of December, 1854, to "M. Martin, de la Société, á l'Hotel de Ville."

The curious effects attributed to the extract and various other preparations of the Cannabis Indica, as used in Egypt, has induced the above society to offer a prize of one thousand francs for the best analysis of the *cannabis*. The applicants for the prize are expected to send specimens of the principles obtained, with a written memoir, descriptive of the processes, &c., which must be written either in the French or Italian languages, and addressed to "M. Soubeiran, Secrétaire General de la Société de Pharmacie de Paris, Rue de l'Arbalete, 21," before the 1st of July, 1854.

The sale of poisons in this city has arrived to that pitch that it is absolutely necessary the law should interfere. Two cases of death have been published lately where arsenic was the poison used, and which was purchased readily at a drug store. One was the case of Rose Williams, poisoned by her husband; and the second that of a widow, Lancaster, tired of life, who took *one ounce* of arsenic, which her son had procured at a drug store, in Avenue C, owned by Dr. Barry. The store attendant, in his evidence before the coroner, stated that "he knew nothing of pharmacy; that the boy asked him for four ounces of arsenic; he gave him *only two*, as the boy had not sufficient money." This attendant had the entire charge of the store and of the disposing of drugs. We are satisfied that the regulations with regard to the sale of poisons are duly observed by the majority of pharmaceutists in this city. In such instances as that given above a strong penalty should be enforced.

The following constitution of Diabetic Urine was determined lately by us. It is remarkable as occurring in extreme youth, and while under a diet *wholly* made up of flesh.

The patient was a boy, aged nine years, suffering from the disease about five months, restricted at present to meat diet *solely*, under which he is getting strong and fleshy ; passed about forty ounces of urine daily, specific gravity, 1,010 at 48° F., pale, of a hay odor, faintly to litmus.

In one thousand parts there were—

Water	976
Solid matters	24
	1,000

Solid matters—

Sugar	13·73
Urea	2·27
Uric acid, Urate of ammonia, Extractive, Triple Phosphate, Confervæ	8·00
	24

The presence of urate, phosphate, and confervæ was determined by the microscope ; the urea by separation by oxalic acid ; the glucose by alcohol. One drachm of this urine gives a well marked reaction when an alkaline solution of the double tartrate of potash and copper is used, which test is the most delicate of the copper salts for this purpose.

NEW YORK

JOURNAL OF PHARMACY.

JULY, 1854.

ON CREOSOTE AND ITS PRODUCTS OF DECOMPOSITION.

BY M. VON GORUP-BESANEZ.

In his introduction the author proves that creosote is not to be regarded, as has been done more and more of late, as identical with hydrate of phenyle. This observation refers especially to Gmelin's mode of treating this subject in his 'Manual." At the same time the author shows that mistakes and uncertainties with regard to creosote are especially caused by the circumstance, that the substance sold as creosote consists sometimes of certain products of the distillation of coal-tar, and then of course contains hydrate of phenyle, and sometimes of products obtained from wood-tar, which are quite different from the preceding.

The creosote employed by the author in the following experiments was obtained from Batka of Prague. According to Professor Lerch it is manufactured at Dobriss in Bohemia, and Blansko in Moravia, from beech-wood tar, in accordance with the directions of its discoverer, Reichenbach.

This creosote is an oily, strongly-refractive fluid, of a pale yellowish color, and a peculiar, penetrating, disagreeable, smoky odor, quite different from that of phenylic acid. It had a sharp burning taste, produced a white spot on the mucous membrane of the tongue, and completely stopped bleeding by coagulating the albumen of the blood. It was completely soluble in alcohol and æther, but sparingly in water. Nevertheless, water shaken with it acquired the taste, smell, and even the reactions of creosote. It entirely dissolved in sulphuret of carbon, but only partially in acetic acid, even after long boiling. It was also soluble in watery ammonia, acquiring some color; but all the ammonia was driven off on the water-bath. Muriatic acid produced no change in it; in concentrated sulphuric acid, on the contrary, it was entirely dissolved, and acquired a violet-purple color. A chip of deal, moistened with muriatic acid and dipped into it, did not exhibit the least trace of a blue or violet color; nor did the addition of chloride of iron, free of acid, produce any trace of that blue-violet color which is caused by this reagent even in very dilute solutions of phenylic acid. It could not be obtained crystallized, although the author repeatedly exposed the perfectly anhydrous substance to very low temperatures. The specific gravity of the crude product varied between 1.046 and 1.049.

Boiling soon showed that this creosote is a mixture of different substances. It began to boil at 194° F., and the boiling point then rose to 421° F.

The author now separated, by fractional distillation, from the substance purchased as creosote, the body, the boiling point of which lay between 398° and 406° F. This body constitutes the greater portion of the crude creosote, and the thermometer remains stationary for some time between these points.

For this substance the author retains the name of creosote. It is a colorless, oily, strongly refractive fluid, of a peculiar, penetrating, smoky odor, and a pungent burning taste; its specific gravity is 1.040 at 52°.7 F.; it is not crystallizable, but remains fluid at very low temperatures; it is but sparingly soluble in water, but dissolves in alcohol and æther in all proportions. In ordinary acetic acid it is only partially dissolved; it dissolves sulphur and coagulates albumen. In a dose of from 5 to 10 drops, it destroys animals in a few minutes, producing convulsions. It preserves flesh and animal substances generally. Ammonia dissolves creosote, even in the cold. If the ammoniacal solution be evaporated on the water-bath, all the ammonia is driven off. If ammoniacal gas be passed into an alcoholic solution of creosote until saturation, and then followed by sulphurous acid gas, a substance is thrown down in white shining crystals, which retains creosote obstinately, although only mechanically; it is bisulphite of ammonia, with 16 equivs. of water; if sulphuretted hydrogen gas be passed into the ammoniacal solution, bihydrosulphate of ammonia is thrown down; if creosote saturated with ammonia be mixed with alcohol, and sulphuretted hydrogen be then added, yellow crystals are soon formed in the fluid, which from their properties appear to be carbosulphide of ammonium. Creosote is also dissolved by hydrate of potash; the solution, after standing for some time, becomes brownish; when heated with a watery solution of potash, all the creosote is driven off, apparently unchanged. But if creosote be distilled with an alcoholic solution of potash, partial decomposition takes place, and an aromatic oil goes over with the alcohol. Fusing caustic potash decomposes creosote; caustic lime also produces decomposition.

Perchloride of iron produces no change when added to creosote. Nitrate of silver, when heated with it, is reduced, with formation of a beautiful mirror of silver. When creosote is dropped upon freshly precipitated oxide of silver, it produces sufficient heat to cause ignition and explosion. In this case, together with reduced silver, oxalate of silver is produced. Salts of gold, platinum, peroxide of mercury, as well as permanganates, are also reduced by creosote. Concentrated sulphuric acid mixes with creosote, producing a slight heating of the fluid, which acquires a fine purple-violet color. If this be neutralized with carbonate of baryta, heated to boiling, and filtered, a baryta compound is dissolved in the filtrate, which, however, becomes decomposed during evaporation on the water-bath, or even at a temperature of 86°–104° F.

Nitric acid, whether concentrated or diluted, resinifies creosote, and brown, uncrystallizable products are obtained. Nitrosulphuric acid acts upon it very violently, and a small quantity of a yellowish-white explosive compound is obtained. Chlorine gas acts upon it, with formation of muriatic acid; the substance first acquires a brown, and afterwards a purple-red color. It is readily decomposed by chlorine; but the author could not obtain a crystallizable chlorinated compound.

Iodine is dissolved by creosote, forming a brown fluid; bromine is also dissolved in considerable quantity. Muriatic acid and chlorate of potash furnish crystallized products of decomposition containing chlorine.

Peroxide of manganese and sulphuric acid, and also chromate of potash and sulphuric acid, produce resinization, with formation of small quantities of a light aromatic oil, and, perhaps, of formic acid. Peroxide of lead does not act perceptibly upon the acetic acid solution of creosote, nor does it produce any more effect when added to creosote by itself. A chip of deal or fir-wood, moistened with muriatic acid, then dried and passed through creosote, does not acquire the least violet or blue color. The analyses of the creosote with the boiling point above given are as follows:

	I.	II.	III.	IV.	V.	VI.	VII.	VIII.
C..	75·32	75·72	75·54	74·76	75·82	75·02	74·78	74·68
H..	7·84	7·94	7·85	7·95	7.98	7·95	7.98	7.84
O..	16·84	16·34	16·61	17·29	16·30	17·03	17·24	17·48

From the preceding the author concludes—1st. That the creosote under investigation is not identical with hydrate of phenyle. 2d. That it is not a chemically-definite compound. Combinations with lead and oxide of silver led to no fixed formula.

The author obtained more favorable results by treating creosote with muriatic acid and chlorate of potash. By this treatment the creosote undergoes a change, first becoming brown, then thick and tough, and of a red color, and settling to the bottom. After it has been exposed to this treatment for several days, a mass is obtained, which, on cooling, is plaster-like, and filled with yellow scaly crystals. This mass is repeatedly treated with cold alcohol until the latter no longer acquires a color; in this manner the yellow scales are left behind, and these are purified by re-crystallization from boiling alcohol. To this substance the author gives the name of—

Hexachloroxylone.—Its composition is $C^{26} H^{6} Cl^{6} O^{6}$. It appears in beautiful golden-yellow scales, forming rhombic tables with acute angles of about 21°–25° ; it is idioelectrical, and may be triturated into a pale yellow powder, of a slightly aromatic odor. If the crystals be heated to 248° F., they begin to sublime, during which the phenomenon of iridescence may be witnessed in great beauty. Sublimation takes place best between 356° and 374° F.; a very small carbonaceous residue is left. When it is too rapidly and strongly heated, decomposition takes place; the compound becomes brown, and needles and scales of a copper-red color are sublimed. In water the substance is insoluble, or nearly so. When it is boiled for a considerable time in water, the latter acquires, after standing, a pale cobalt-red color; but on evaporation a mere trace of a carbonaceous residue is left. It is also very sparingly soluble in cold alcohol, but dissolves in boiling alcohol of sp. grav. 0·857, forming a yellow solution; it is again deposited, however, on the cooling of the solution. One part of it requires about 171 parts of boiling alcohol for its solution. It is readily soluble in æther. It is dissolved by acetic acid with the assistance of heat, but is again precipitated on the cooling of the solution. It is not attacked by muriatic acid; but concentrated sulphuric acid decomposes it even in the cold, and still more rapidly when aided by heat. Hot nitric acid dissolves it without change, but it separates on cooling. Solution of potash dissolves the crystals with a reddish-brown color; no crystals separate from the solution even after long standing; after evaporation in a gentle heat, chloride of potassium and an amorphous resinous body remain. If any acid be added to the alkaline solution, an amorphous brownish precipitate is thrown down. Ammonia behaves exactly in the same manner. On analyses it gave numbers which agree in some degree with the composition of a mixture of equal equivalents of chloranile and of Städeler's bichloroquinone; but the crystals appeared homogeneous under the microscope; and the author also concludes, from the properties of the substance, that it is a definite compound. Analyses:—

Carbon........	36·78	36·65	36·78	36·69	26	=156	36·88
Hydrogen......	1·59	1·54	1·51	1·53	6	6	1·42
Chlorine......	——	——	50·62	50·53	6	213	50·35
Oxygen......	——	——	——	——	6	48	11·35

When hexachloroxylone is treated to saturation with sulphurous acid gas, and left standing for twenty-four hours in a closed vessel, it is converted into a brownish-white substance, which forms four-sided prisms. These are separated by filtration and washed. The filtered fluids also contain a body, which remains after evaporation in an amorphous state, and of a fine violet color. This substance dissolves in a mixture of alcohol and æther, forming a fluid of a pale yellowish color, which soon becomes darker and brownish-yellow; on the sides of the vessel, needle-like crystals, of an inch in length, are then formed, which appear dark violet by transmitted, blackish-green by reflected light; from the mother-liquor brownish-white needles afterwards crystallize. These consist of a substance which is produced from the preceding compound by the accession of four equivs. of hydrogen; the author, therefore, calls it—

Hexachlorhydroxylone.—Its composition is C^{26} H^{10} Cl^6 O^6. The brownish-white crystals of this compound are soluble in cold strong alcohol and in æther; they dissolve in dilute alcohol by boiling, but are again deposited from it on cooling; in water they are but sparingly soluble; water boiled with them acquires a dingy violet color in time. If the crystals be dissolved in strong alcohol and æther, a portion of them is apparently converted into another violet compound. If hexachlorhydroxylone be boiled for a considerable time with constantly renewed water, the water takes up a small quantity of it, but lets it fall again even during filtration at a boiling heat; during this, the fluid, which is at first only of a pale yellow color, acquires a distinct cobalt-red, and afterwards a dingy violet color; after some time acicular crystals are formed on the surface, which are blackish-green by reflected, dark violet by transmitted light. They probably consist of the compound to be mentioned hereafter. Acetic acid also dissolves hexachlorhydroxylone with the aid of heat, and that deposited on cooling contains numerous intermixed blackish-red needles; if the treatment with acetic acid be repeated, a portion is always changed in this manner. The compound may be almost completely precipitated from its cold alcoholic solution by means of water. At 356° F. it sublimes without previous fusion, forming acicular crystals of from 1 to 1½ line in length, and leaving a very small carbonaceous residue.

Dilute solutions of potash and ammonia give a chrome-green color to the crystals; then they dissolve into a dingy green fluid, which soon passes to brownish-red. From the solution in potash muriatic acid throws down a brownish yellow, resinous, amorphous body. Concentrated sulphuric acid does not act upon hexachlorhydroxylone in the cold; but with the assistance of heat this reagent produces a rapid decomposition, with a dark brown color. Concentrated nitric acid, after acting upon it for a considerable time, converts it into golden-yellow rhombic laminæ. A neutral solution of perchloride of iron also converts it into yellow scales and laminæ. If an alcoholic solution of hexachlorhydroxylone be treated with nitrate of silver, a mirror of metallic silver is formed; and the filtrate, when evaporated, furnishes dark violet crystals. Hypochlorite of soda converts it into yellow laminæ. Analysis:—

Carbon	36·86	36·92	37·02	26	=156	36·53
Hydrogen	2·23	2·39	2·38	10	10	2·34
Chlorine	——	——	——	6	213	49·88
Oxygen	——	——	——	6	48	11·25

Violet Compound, probably of the same composition. Even

in solution in a mixture of alcohol and æther, and still more when boiled, the preceding substance becomes converted into a violet compound. The same thing takes place when it is treated with nitrate of silver and acetic acid.

This compound forms prismatic crystals of a dark red or nearly black color, which appear dark violet under the microscope, and by reflected light of a blackish-green; they are inodorous, and have a caustic taste; they are insoluble in cold water, and dissolve very sparingly in boiling water, to which they give a yellow color; they dissolve in alcohol and æther, but during solution a portion of the compound is always converted into yellow rhombic tables; hot acetic acid also dissolves them, but they crystallize from this solution on cooling, and are partially converted into brownish white needles. Potash and ammonia dissolve the violet compound with the assistance of heat, forming a reddish-brown solution; the crystals first become dingy green, then pale green, and finally pale yellow; acids generally produce amorphous precipitates in these solutions. Concentrated sulphuric acid dissolves them with a brownish-red color when heated; if the solution in sulphuric acid be diluted with much water, a powder of a violet-red color falls to the bottom; this appears amorphous under the microscope. The violet compound is only dissolved with difficulty by boiling concentrated nitric acid; muriatic acid does not touch it. Nitrate of silver produces a white flocculent precipitate in its alcoholic solution. Hypochlorite of soda produces no change. If a small quantity of strong alcohol be poured over the crystals, they become converted into yellow rhombic prisms during the spontaneous evaporation of the spirit.

From these properties the author concludes that the violet hexachlorhydroxylone corresponds with Städeler's violet bichlorhydroquinone. It would then be possible that the yellow compound into which the violet crystals are converted by alcohol may represent Städeler's yellow bichlorhydroquinone, if it be not hexachlorhydroxylone again.

From these analogies the author then comes to the conclusion, that just as when kinic acid is treated with chlorine, quinone, $C^{12} H^4 O^4$, becomes converted into chloroquinones with

1-3 atoms of chlorine instead of hydrogen, there are also several chloroxylones; so that he supposes hypothetically that there is a xylone, $C^{26} H^{12} O^{6}$, in which the hydrogen may be replaced by chlorine. It appeared, in fact, that several compounds were still contained in the fluid filtered from the yellow scales.

This fluid, after standing some hours, deposits a sediment, in which the microscope shows resinous flakes, crystalline scales, needles and oleaginous drops. Strong alcohol dissolves all except the scales, which were not in sufficient quantity for analysis. The solution obtained by the treatment of the mass of crystals with very dilute boiling alcohol also deposited, on cooling, a flocculent granular sediment, in which the microscope likewise showed oleaginous drops, resin, transparent tabular scales, and laminæ resembling cholesterine. This was repeatedly washed on the filter with cold strong alcohol, and then repeatedly recrystallized from boiling dilute alcohol. This compound now formed tolerably large, beautiful, glassy, four-sided rhombic tables, of a pale golden-yellow color, which were distinguished from hexachloroxylone by their general appearance. For analysis this substance was sublimed; it was thus obtained in beautiful, extremely thin, flexible laminæ, which appeared iridescent by transmitted light. This compound is—

Pentachloroxylone, $C^{26} H^{7} Cl^{5} O^{6}$.—It is insoluble in water, but soluble in boiling dilute alcohol, from which it may be completely precipitated by water. A portion of it is separated even during cooling. It is soluble in æther in all proportions. It is also soluble in boiling acetic acid, although apparently with more difficulty than hexachloroxylone.—Nitric acid dissolves it only after long boiling; it dissolves in sulphuric acid with a brownish-red color.

Cold ammonia slightly attacks the crystals; when heated, it dissolves them with a violet color; potash also acts upon them with difficulty when cold, but dissolves them when heated, forming a blackish-brown solution. Nothing is separated from the solution in potash after standing a considerable time.—The crystals sublime at from 329° to 356° F. without fusing.

Analysis gave—

Carbon..........	39·79	26=	156·0	40·15
Hydrogen........	1·91	7	7·0	1·80
Chlorine.........	——	5	177·5	45·68
Oxygen.........	——	6	48·0	12·37

Oxide of Silver and Creosote.—When creosote is dropped upon oxide of silver, a very violent action takes place, with production of heat, ignition, and explosion. On the other hand, when oxide of silver is added to an excess of creosote, a mass, which is constantly becoming thicker, is obtained, which finally acquires a purple-red color, and a thick syrup-like consistence. The silver lies at the bottom, partly in the metallic form and partly as oxalate.

These products are not pure or definable bodies. Amongst them the author distinguishes *a*- and *b* resin. The mass, except the silver and oxalate of silver, is soluble in strong boiling alcohol; this deposits one resin on cooling, but retains the other in solution.

a-Resin is that which is soluble in cold alcohol. It is a brown mass (liver-colored when powdered), strongly idioelectrical, with an aromatic, and by no means unpleasant odor. It fuses between 131° and 141° F., and is insoluble in water, but readily soluble in alcohol and æther. It is insoluble in ammonia and alkaline carbonates, but soluble in caustic potash; during solution the fluid first acquires a dingy green color, then becomes dark violet, and lastly brownish-green. When the alkaline solution is supersaturated with acids, the fluid first of all acquires a pale vermillion color, and then deposits the resin. The separation of the resin from its alcoholic solution by means of water is greatly assisted by the addition of a small quantity of chloride of sodium or sulphate of magnesia. The alcoholic solution of the resin has a weak acid reaction. When heated, it becomes inflated, takes fire, and burns without residue. When heated, it becomes inflated, takes fire, and burns without residue. Lastly, its alcoholic solution is precipitated by acetate of lead, without the addition of ammonia.

Its analysis gave—

Carbon	72·49	24=144		72·72
Hydrogen	6·93	14	14	7·07
Oxygen	20·58	5	40	20·21

The lead compound of this *a*-resin is of a silvery color, and insoluble in water and æther. Its analysis gave—

Carbon	48·28	——	——	24=144		46·45
Hydrogen	4·36	——	——	14	14	4·51
Oxygen	——	——	——	5	40	12·91
Oxide of lead	——	37·00	36·37	1	112	36·13

The b Resin is that which is insoluble in cold alcohol. Its analysis gave—

	I.	II.
Carbon	75·52	76·23
Hydrogen	7·09	6·65
Oxygen	17·39	17·12

which nearly corresponds to the formula C^{24} H^{13} O^{4}.

On distillation of creosote with strong bases, compounds are obtained, some of which may be isolated, and appear to have a constant composition. If lime be employed for this purpose, the fluid, when heated above 204° F., begins to boil; at 212° a milky fluid goes over. The thermometer then rises, and at 356°–374° F. a fluid of an aromatic odor and lighter than water passes rapidly over; but when the thermometer has risen to 397° F., there passes an oil, which distils in æther-like bands, and is heavier than water. Almost the whole of this goes over between 397° and 406°. It was deprived of water over chloride of calcium, and then distilled, when a small quantity of a light oil passed over at 342° F., which possessed the properties of capnomor.

The oil which passed over between 397° and 406° F., when rectified, gave, on analysis—

	I.	II.
Carbon	78·74	78·55
Hydrogen	8·54	8·61
Oxygen	11·72	12·84

This is almost the same composition as that of the oil obtained by Völckel in the dry distillation of wood at 221°–230° F.

To determine whether a sample of commercial creosote is, or contains, carbolic acid, the boiling-point, according to the author's experience, is generally sufficient. It is also safe to test the product with perchloride of iron and acetic acid. When carbolic acid is present, perchloride of iron always produces a violet-blue color, and afterwards a whitish turbidity; acetic acid completely dissolves carbolic acid with the assistance of a gentle heat. Creosote prepared from beech-wood tar is not altered by perchloride of iron, and is only partially dissolved by hot acetic acid of ordinary concentration. In conclusion, the author shows that it still remains to be ascertained whether phenylic acid occurs generally in wood-tar.—*Ann. der Chem. und Pharm.*, lxxxvi. p. 257, in *Chem. Gaz.*

ON THE DEODORIZING AND DISINFECTING PROPERTIES OF CHARCOAL, WITH THE DESCRIPTION OF A CHARCOAL RESPIRATOR FOR PURIFYING THE AIR BY FILTRATION.

BY JOHN STENHOUSE, LL.D., F.R.S.

The powerful effects of freshly-burned wood-charcoal, especially when coarsely powdered, in absorbing gases and vapors, have been long known. Hence the limited extent to which charcoal has been occasionally employed to sweeten fœtid water and animal substances in the incipient stages of putrefaction. Sufficient attention has not, I think, however, been hitherto bestowed on a second and still more important effect which charcoal exerts upon those complex products of decomposition, viz., that of rapidly oxidizing them and resolving them into the simplest combinations they are capable of forming.

When coals or wood are burned with an inadequate supply of air, a variable amount of intermediate or secondary products is generated, constituting what are called soot and smoke; when, on the other hand, the combustion of the fuel is conducted with an adequate supply of oxygen and a sufficiently high temperature, carbonic acid, water, ammonia, with perhaps a little nitric acid, are almost the sole products.

The putrefaction of animal and vegetable substances is likewise, in general, a process of imperfect oxidation. Hence, under ordinary circumstances, when this is the case, a variety of more or less complex secondary products is formed, which usually possess very disagreeable odors, and exert exceedingly injurious effects upon the animal economy. To these substances the general name of *miasmata* has been given. Not much is known of their nature, but they are believed to be heavy, complex, nitrogenated vapors, which are decomposed by oxygen, chlorine, sulphurous acid, nitric acid, and other disinfecting agents.

My attention was particularly drawn to the importance of charcoal as a disinfecting agent by my friend, John Turnbull, Esq., of Glasgow, the well-known extensive chemical manufacturer. Mr. Turnbull, about nine months ago, placed the bodies of two dogs in a wooden box, on a layer of charcoal powder, of a few inches in depth, and covered them over with a quantity of the same material. Though the box was quite open, and kept in his laboratory, no effluvium was ever perceptible; and, on examining the bodies of the animals at the end of six months, scarcely anything remained of them except their bones. Mr. Turnbull sent me a portion of the charcoal powder which had been most closely in contact with the bodies of the dogs. I submitted it for examination to one of my pupils, Mr. Turner, who found it contained comparatively little ammonia, not a trace of sulphuretted hydrogen, but very appreciable quantities of nitric and sulphuric acids, with acid phosphate of lime.

Mr. Turner, subsequently, about three months ago, buried two rats in about two inches of charcoal powder, and a few days afterwards the body of a full grown cat was similarly treated. Though the bodies of these animals are now in a highly putrid state, not the slightest odor is perceptible in the laboratory.

From this short statement of facts, the utility of charcoal powder, as a means of preventing noxious effluvia from churchyards and from dead bodies in other situations, such as on board ship, is sufficiently evident. Covering a churchyard to the depth of from two to three inches with coarsely powdered charcoal, would effectually prevent any putrid exhalations ever finding their way into the atmosphere. Charcoal powder also greatly favors the rapid decomposition of the dead bodies with which it is in contact, so that in the course of six or eight months little is left except the bones.

In all the modern systems of chemistry, such, for instance, as the last edition of Turner's "Elements," charcoal is described as possessing antiseptic properties, while the very reverse is the fact. Common salt, nitre, corrosive sublimate, arsenious acid, alcohol, camphor, creosote, and most essential oils are certainly antiseptic substances, and, therefore, retard the decay of animal and vegetable matters. Charcoal, on the contrary, as we have just seen, greatly facilitates the oxidization, and consequently the decomposition, of any organic substances with which it is in contact. It is, therefore, the very opposite of an antiseptic.

The object of the present paper, however, is chiefly an application of the absorbent and oxidizing properties of charcoal, which, so far as I am aware, has never yet been proposed, viz., to employ a new species of respirator, filled with powdered animal charcoal, to absorb and destroy any miasmata or infectious particles present in the air in the case of fever and cholera hospitals, and of districts infected by ague, yellow fever, and similar diseases. I have got such a respirator made by Ferguson and Sons, Smithfield, instrument-makers to St. Bartholomew's Hospital. It fits closely to the lower portion of the face, extending from the chin to within half an inch of the eyes, and projects about an inch on either side of the mouth. It, therefore, includes the nostrils as well as the mouth. The frame of the respirator is made of thin sheet copper, but the edges are formed of lead, and are padded and lined with velvet, so that it can be easily made to fit tightly to the face. The powdered charcoal is kept in its place by means of two sheets of fine wire gauze, from a quarter to an eight of an inch apart. As the body of the apparatus is metallic, it has been electro-plated with silver. Electro-plating the respirator with platinum or gold would certainly be an improvement. There is a small opening, closed with a wire gauze-screw, by means of which the respirator can be filled with charcoal or emptied at pleasure. The respirator is kept in its place by an elastic band passing round the back part of the head. I have employed *animal* charcoal as the more porous substance, but I should think wood charcoal would answer perfectly well.* The object in view is, by filtering the air through such a porous substance as animal charcoal, to intercept the miasmata which may have got mixed with it. These, I think, cannot fail to be absorbed by the pores of the charcoal, where they will be rapidly oxidated and destroyed by the condensed oxygen with which they will be brought into the most intimate contact. The probability of this expectation being realized is greatly strengthened by the results of repeated trials with the respirator on certain noxious and offensive gases, such as ammonia, sulphuretted hydrogen, hydrosulphate of ammonia and chlorine. I have found that air strongly impregnated with these gases, and which could not be respired for any length of time under ordinary circumstances, may be breathed with impunity when the charcoal respirator is worn, the odor of these gases being rendered almost, if not

* Since the above was written, I have ascertained by experiment that common wood charcoal is even more efficacious than animal charcoal.—J. S.

altogether, imperceptible. Any other highly porous substance, such, for instance, as sponge platinum, or pounded pumice-stone, might probably be found to answer perfectly well for filling the respirator; but I have selected charcoal as the cheapest and most easily available material.

While the filtration of water through charcoal powder and other porous substances has been advantageously practised for many centuries, the object in view being to deprive the water of numerous impurities diffused through it, which produce injurious effects on the animal economy, it is certainly somewhat remarkable that the very obvious application of a similar proceeding to the lighter fluid in which we live, viz., air, which not unfrequently contains even more noxious impurities floating in it than are usually present in water, should have, up to the present time, been so unaccountably overlooked.

In addition to the precaution of wearing such a respirator as that just described, persons necessitated to live in especially pestiferous districts might have their houses made as air-tight as possible, with the exception of such openings as are necessary to maintain a proper amount of ventillation. By means of these openings the air could be freely admitted through gauze, into which the requisite quantity of charcoal had been quilted. The doors of such houses could also be made double, and be constructed of coarse cloth, likewise containing a thin layer of charcoal powder. As an additional precaution, if it were thought desirable, the walls, floors, and ceilings of houses in very unhealthy districts could be easily lined with mattrasses filled with a couple of inches of charcoal powder. Were these and similar precautions adopted, I confidently anticipate that Europeans will be enabled to reside with comparative impunity in some of the hitherto most pestilential districts of the world.—*Journal of the Society of Arts*, Feb. 24, 1854, in *Chemical Gazette.*

ON PRACTICAL PHARMACY.

BY JUSTUS LIEBIG,

Professor of Chemistry at the University of Giessen.

NO. IX.
(CONCLUSION.)

Operations which have for their objects Mixing and Separation of the second degree.

Precipitation is the name applied to the process which takes place when a solid body, in the form of a powder, and mostly without a crystalline structure, is thrown down immediately, or after a short time, from a fluid, by cooling, by the action of the air, or by the addition of another fluid, or even a solid substance. The body which causes the precipitation is named the precipitant, whilst that which is precipitated is called the precipitate or magisterium, and when it swims on the fluid it is termed a cream; the precipitate is either a product or an educt. It is termed the former when the precipitant, or a portion of it, combines in a solid form with a portion of the substances to be precipitated, as by mixing a solution of acetate of lead with sulphuric acid, or a solution of sulphate of magnesia with carbonate of soda. It is an educt when the precipitant combines to form a fluid with one portion of the compound to be precipitated, whilst another portion is thrown down, as by adding caustic potass to a solution of sulphate of magnesia. Many substances fall from their solutions when exposed to the atmosphere; then either the menstruum escapes, or the precipitant is absorbed from the air, as in the cases of carbonate of lime dissolved in water by means of carbonic acid, and lime water when exposed to the air.

In ordinary cases of precipitation, the following rules must be observed. The fluid to be treated, as well as the precipitant solution, must be quite clear, and if not, they must be filtered. The vessel in which precipitation is to take place should be cylindrical, of greater height than breadth, and so large that the mixture only three parts fills it. Precipitants, and solutions to be precipitated, should be somewhat dilute, so that the precipitate may fall in a finely divided condition and flocculent, and also that the salts contained in the solutions may not crystallize out of them. But care must be taken not to dilute the solutions too much, as some precipitates are slightly soluble, and a portion of them would in consequence be lost.

The precipitant should be added by degrees in small quantities to the solution, with constant stirring or shaking, to increase the points of contact, and to prevent, in some cases, the liquid running over by effervescence. The liquid should be tested from time to time, to ascertain if enough of the precipitant has been added, which is to be accomplished by filtering a portion of the liquid, or by removing a clear portion of it, and adding thereto some of the precipitant. If nothing now falls therefrom, enough of the precipitant has been employed.

When the whole of the precipitate has been collected and washed it should be dried in the air, or according to its nature in a gentle heat. Many precipitates coagulate when they are long diffused in the fluid, and soon partake more or less of a crystalline texture. In a medicinal point of view, this change is often detrimental, therefore, they should be removed as quickly as possible from the fluid. Precipitates can be dried rapidly between folds of blotting paper, which paper must be renewed as soon as it becomes wet; or they can be dried by being placed on porous tiles, which rapidly absorb their moisture. By this latter means, very flocculent precipitates may be obtained in a dry state.

Metallic precipitation is distinguished from the former by the metallic body adhering frequently into masses when precipitated. This process is conducted both in the dry and wet way. In the former way, precipitation happens when a metallic mixture, as a metallic sulphuret, is melted with a body, which will combine with the substance with which the metal is mixed, whereby it becomes separated. In the latter way, precipitation results when the solution of a metallic salt is brought in contact with another metal, which becomes oxidized and dissolved; whilst the metal of the salt is precipitated in various forms, sometimes as a powder, and sometimes in the form of a tree. Coagulation is also a kind of precipitation, which takes place either by heat alone, as in albuminous solutions, or by the addition of another body, as in the case of milk, when the curd is separated.

Efflorescence is a name applied to the breaking up of solid coherent bodies, as salts into powders, by the action of dry warm air. This happens with sulphate and carbonate of soda placed in a dry atmosphere, whereby they lose their water of crystallization, and fall into powders.

When salts which contain much water of crystallization, and retain it at ordinary temperatures, are to be deprived of their water, they must be heated. This process is called calcination. Salts are heated in a gradually increasing temperature until they cease to lose water. In the beginning they melt in their water of crystallization and then become dry again, when they frequently swell and form a porous mass, as in the case of burnt alum. Sometimes, when the heat is too long continued, the salt is decomposed.

When, by heat, a salt jumps with a crackling noise, because water is enclosed in its interstices, and which is converted into steam by the heat, the phenomenon is called decrepitation.

Incandescence, or heating bodies to redness, is applied to separate volatile substances from non-volatile ones, as carbonic acid from lime or magnesia. This operation is also called calcination, and is further employed for combining volatile substances with non-volatile bodies, as for example, sulphur with lime or iron, and to render hard, non-volatile substances brittle, as flints, so that they can be powdered. When red hot, they are thrown into cold water for this purpose.

One of the most important chemical operations is oxidation, that is, the combining of oxygen with other bodies, which was in former times called calcination. This process is effected in many ways and requires a special knowledge of chemistry, and, therefore, cannot be treated of here at length. When accomplished in the wet way, it involves solution, as when phosphorus is oxidized by nitric acid. Frequently oxidation is accomplished by the aid of heat, and is also attended with the evolution of heat, it is then termed combustion, which combustion, when extremely rapid and accompanied with a loud noise, is further called detonation.

For the same reason, as with reference to oxidation, reduction cannot be here entered upon in general. It consists in the separation of oxygen from other bodies. Metals are reduced in the wet way by precipitation with other metals, as previously explained. In the dry way, they are generally reduced by mixture with charcoal or bodies containing carbon, and exposure to a red heat.

Fermentation is a remarkable chemical process, which organic bodies, in combination with water, undergo, when subjected to certain temperatures, partly under the influence of the air. It is divided into vinous, acetic, and putrefactive fermentations, which are seldom employed by the pharmaceutist.

Carbonization of non-volatile organic bodies is an operation which requires a strong and continued heat. The body to be carbonized is placed in a vessel which, for the greater part, excludes the action of the air on it, and heated strongly until it ceases to evolve gaseous matters; the residue is carbon. When the volatile bodies are collected by means of a receiver, this operation is called dry distillation.

Incineration is the complete combustion of an organic body in the presence of the air, when a non-volatile and incombustible substance remains, which is termed an ash. This process was formerly much employed by pharmaceutists to obtain potash and soda, by burning various plants rich in these substances.

There are many other operations performed by the pharmaceutist besides those previously described, but as they belong especially to chemistry, they may, in this treatise, be omitted.

On Lutes.—In chemical operations, lutes are frequently necessary, which are of different kinds, according to the description of vessel to which they are to be applied, the nature of the substance to be treated, and the heat to which they are to be exposed. The knowledge of these particulars is important for the pharmaceutist.

Starch jelly, thickly prepared in the ordinary manner, serves as a lute for many kinds of distillation. It is applicable with strips of paper to the joints of the apparatus. Pieces of bladder are useful to fasten retorts to receivers. They should be firmly bound to the joints with string. Strips of sheet Indian rubber form a most valuable lute to connect tubing together, or tubes with flasks, or any kind of pneumatic apparatus. The Indian rubber should be placed in hot water, after being cut of the size necessary. When this has been done it should be immediately bound round the tubing, and the recently cut edges brought into apposition, when they will unite and form a tube impervious, when united, to gases. Almond powder, flour, and linseed meal are serviceable as lutes. They may be mixed into a paste with water, or with the white of eggs. Clay is frequently employed as a lute, especially for operations on a large scale. Chalk and linseed oil or putty forms a lute which resists the action of moisture. A lute which dries rapidly and adheres firmly can be made by mixing white of egg with freshly burnt lime in a state of powder. Lutes to resist the action of intense heat are made by mixing clay and sand with hair and iron filings. A lute to resist the action of water is prepared by melting three parts of pitch and one part of wax, and mixing with them four parts of brick dust. It is applied by saturating pieces of canvas or linen with it whilst hot, and applying them in this condition to the joints of any apparatus to be secured. There are many other kinds of lutes to be found in works on practical chemistry.

ON THE EMPLOYMENT OF MOLYBDATE OF AMMONIA FOR DETECTING ARSENIC.

BY H. STRUVE.

Some time ago, the author, in conjunction with Professor Svanberg, suggested the use of molybdate of ammonia for the detection of phosphoric acid; subsequently, H. Rose showed that it formed a similar compound with arsenic acid.

The author now proposes to make use of this property of molybdate of ammonia, to show in medico-legal analyses that the spot obtained by Marsh's apparatus is produced by arsenic, and when arsenic is present in any substance, to separate it in such a compound as may be afterwards tested in Marsh's apparatus.

The phænomena of this reaction depend upon the peculiar behavior of a solution of arsenic acid towards a great excess of a solution of molybdate of ammonia in nitric acid under the influence of heat. In this case, as with phosphoric acid, a yellow precipitate, in well-formed but microscopic dodecahedra, is separated; this precipitate is insoluble in acids and in many saline solutions. Concentrated sulphuric acid at ordinary temperatures has no action upon this compound but when heated, dissolves it completely, forming a colorless solution, from which no precipitate is producd on dilution with water. The precipitate consists of pentamolybdate of ammonia, in which about seven per cent. of arsenic is present.

If this salt, after drying, be heated in a thin glass tube closed at the bottom, it is decomposed with evolution of water and ammonia, whilst arsenious acid sublimes and oxide of molybdenum remains behind. If the compound has been previously mixed with a little charcoal, metallic arsenic is sublimed, by which means the presence of arsenic in this substance may be readily shown.

If the yellow salt be put with zinc, sulphuric acid, and water into a gas-bottle, arseniuretted hydrogen gas is not evolved until after some time, partly because the insolubility of the compound in dilute acids causes it to elude the action of the zinc, and partly because the molybdic acid must first be reduced to oxide. In one experiment, traces of arseniuretted hydrogen gas only made their appearance a quarter of an hour after the addition of the yellow compound; up to that time nothing but pure hydrogen was evolved.

To cause the instantaneous formation and evolution of arseniuretted hydrogen gas with this compound, all that is necessary is to break up the combination of the arsenio-molybdate of ammonia. This may be effected by any alkali (ammonia is the best), or by boiling with concentrated sulphuric acid.

The mode of employing this test for arsenic is as follows:—Suppose that by means of Marsh's apparatus the well-known spot has been produced in a glass tube or on a porcelain slab, and that it is desired to determine whether it does or does not arise from arsenic.

For this purpose the spot is to be dissolved by heat in a small quantity of concentrated nitric acid; the solution is put with a few drops of water into a test-glass; a great excess of the solution of molybdate of ammonia in nitric acid is then added, and the whole heated to boiling. If the spot were produced by arsenic, a yellow precipitate is formed, either immediately, or, if the spot to be tested were very small, after standing some time; this is a most unequivocal indication of the presence of arsenic. The appearance of the reaction is considerably hastened when the test-tube with its contents is exposed for some time to the heat of the sand-bath, as in this case the same effect is produced by the continued action of heat, as in other cases is done by time. This method of ascertaining the presence of arsenic after its oxidation into arsenic acid is so sensitive, that a perfectly distinct precipitate may be obtained after a little time from solutions which do not contain more than 1-30,000dth of arsenic acid. The reaction is no longer produced in solutions containing only 1-60,000dth of arsenic acid.

When other metals are to be tested for arsenic, in which the reaction with the blowpipe cannot be employed, the molybdate of ammonia may be used with advantage. This is especially the case when antimony or tin are to be tested for arsenical impurities. In these cases all that is necessary is to oxidize a small quantity of the metal to be examined by concentrated nitric acid, to collect the oxide formed upon a filter, and test the filtrate. The presence of other metals does not prevent the reaction, as they are all soluble in nitric acid.

The above behavior of arsenic acid is also employed by the author for the separation of the arsenic from any compound, in such a form that it may be treated in Marsh's apparatus without the necessity of a subsequent examination of the arsenical spots. The operations required for this purpose are the following.

The substance to be tested for arsenic is treated in a glass flask with chlorate of potash and muriatic acid, until the greater portion of the organic substances is destroyed, and the solution has acquired a pale brown color. The contents of the flask are then evaporated to dryness in a porcelain cup, in order to expel the excess of acid; it is then dissolved in water and filtered. The clear solution is evaporated to a small volume, and after cooling, a solution of molybdate of ammonia in nitric acid is added to it in excess, when a yellow precipitate is instantaneously thrown down. If nothing further is separated on the addition of more of the precipitant, the precipitate is collected on a filter, washed with water containing nitric acid, and characterized by the letter A. The filtrate is placed with the wash-water upon the sand-bath until the solution is brought to a boiling heat, at which it is kept for some time. The action of heat causes the separation of a fresh precipitate, which is collected when it no longer appears to increase, and characterized by the letter B.

The precipitate A, separated at the usual temperature, consists of phospho-molybdate of ammonia; and if all heating of the solution has been avoided during the addition of the precipitant, it contains no trace of arsenio-molybdate of ammonia. The phosphoric acid required for the formation of this precipitate is derived from the organic matter, in which phosphorus is present, partly as phosphoric acid, and partly in protein compounds containing phosphorus. If it be not certain that all heating of the fluid was avoided during the addition of the precipitant, it is possible that small portions of arsenic acid may be in this precipitate A, and in that case a testing of this salt by Marsh's apparatus is always necessary.

The precipitate B, which is produced by heat, consists partly of small portions of phospho-molybdate of ammonia, as this compound does not separate completely until the solution is gently heated; but if arsenic be present in the substance under examination, principally of arsenio-molybdate of ammonia, a portion of the precipitate is consequently tested in Marsh's apparatus after it has been dissolved in ammonia. If the substance contained arsenic, it is certain to be found in the precipitate B, and may be recognized by the spot furnished by Marsh's apparatus, which can then be due to nothing else. —*Bull. de St. Pétersb.*; *Journ. für Prackt. Chem.*, lviii. p. 493, in *Chem. Gaz.*, April 15.

ON THE FLUORIDES.

BY M. FREMY.

Some years since, M. Louyet communicated to the Academy several important facts relative to fluorine, hydrofluoric acid and the fluorides. According to M. Louyet, fluoride of mercury, heated in tubes of fluoride of calcium, was decomposed by dry chlorine, furnishing fluorine; anhydrous hydrofluoric acid, prepared by a method of M. Louyet, did not act upon glass, and the equivalent of fluorine fixed by Berzelius must be replaced by a new number. The author having assisted in some experiments made by M. Louyet, and not being satisfied with them, has endeavored to verify his facts.

Pure anhydrous hydrofluoric acid is prepared according to the author's method, by submitting hydrofluate of fluoride of potassium to distillation in a platinum retort. Thus obtained, it is gaseous at ordinary temperatures, but may be condensed by a freezing mixture of ice and salt; it then forms a very fluid liquid, which volatilizes as soon as it is taken out of the freezing mixture, acts upon water with the greatest energy, and diffuses in the air white fumes, which may be compared in intensity to those of fluoride of boron. Contrary to the assertion of M. Louyet, anhydrous hydrofluoric acid attacks glass with rapidity.

This acid may also be obtained by decomposing fluoride of lead by dry hydrogen; the action was carried on in a platinum tube, the fluoride being placed in a charcoal cup to avoid the action of the lead upon the platinum.

To avoid the errors of his predecessors caused by the employment of impure fluorides, the author has always made use of an acid prepared from crystallized and perfectly pure hydrofluate of fluoride of potassium. He has obtained some new fluorides and others presenting characters not given by Berzelius. The fluorides of zinc, iron, and lead were obtained in the crystalline form; protofluoride of tin was produced in very distinct and large prisms, and bifluoride of mercury in well-formed crystals. Fluoride of silver, which has been considered as uncrystallizable, deposits crystals of very regular form from its concentrated solution.

All the fluorides analysed by the author were obtained directly by the action of the pure acid upon the anhydrous or hydrated metallic oxides. Hydrofluoric acid does not act upon all the oxides which are attacked by muriatic acid; it would not combine with peroxide of gold or with peroxide of platinum. From this similarity in its action to an oxyacid, the author endeavored to ascertain whether it really contained oxygen; but all his researches served only to confirm the views of its constitution generally admitted by chemists. From these researches it appears that fluorides are to be divided into three classes.

The first class includes the acid fluorides or hydrofluates of fluorides; these compounds are formed with great facility; they are decomposed by heat, furnishing, when anhydrous, neutral fluorides and pure hydrofluoric acid. By means of the potash salt, the author prepared the hydrofluoric æther of ordinary alcohol, by submitting to distillation a mixture of this salt with sulphovinate. This æther is gaseous, and resembles in its properties the corresponding compound of wood-spirit, discovered by MM. Dumas and Peligot.

The second class is composed of the hydrated neutral fluorides, characterized by the facility with which they are decomposed into hydrofluoric acid and oxides when we attempt to remove the water which enters into their composition; they appear to be true hydrofluates. Thus crystallized fluoride of silver, belonging to this class, evolves hydrofluoric acid, and produces oxide of silver when it is dried even *in vacuo;* when it is heated, it also evolves hydrofluoric acid and oxygen, and leaves a residue of very pure silver; it acts, therefore, as a hydrofluate of oxide of silver. Fluoride of mercury, when heated, acts in exactly the same manner.

The third class includes the anhydrous fluorides. These salts are not decomposable by heat, and may be decomposed, according to the metal they contain, by oxygen, hydrogen, chlorine, sulphuret of carbon and vapor of water.

The author attaches great importance to this classification of the fluorides, and thinks that it is from their having neglected it that his predecessors have fallen into such grave errors. Thus M. Louyet thought he isolated fluorine by decomposing fluoride of mercury by heat and chlorine; as fluoride of mercury belongs to the second or hydrated class, it behaves like a hydrofluate, and the gas obtained by M. Louyet was a simple mixture of hydrofluoric acid and oxygen. The author's analyses of fluorides for the determination of the equivalent of fluorine do not agree with those of M. Louyet, but confirm those of Berzelius.

With the view of obtaining fluorine, the author first turned his attention to the less oxidizable metals. But of these, the oxides gold and platinum do not combine with hydrofluoric acid; the fluoride of mercury is hydrated, and the fluoride of silver, when anhydrous, is undecomposable.

He, therefore, availed himself of a fact, ascertained in some experiments just made by him with Mr. E. Becquerel, from which it appeared that chloride of calcium in fusion is decomposed by the pile with great rapidity. By submitting the anhydrous fluorides of potassium, lead, and calcium to this process, the decomposition was readily effected, and a gas was liberated at the positive pole which quickly acted upon platinum. He was, however, unable to collect this gas, or to make any examination of it.

Sulphur, aided by heat, acts upon some anhydrous fluorides, displacing the fluorine; but compounds of fluorine and sulphur are then formed.

The action of dry chlorine on fluoride of calcium at a red heat decomposes the latter very slowly, disengaging a gas which attacks glass and platinum, and which appears to be fluorine. The experiments were carried on in platinum tubes, which are not acted upon by chlorine; and the latter gas was dried by being passed through several tubes containing anhydrous phosphoric acid, to avoid all chance of watery vapor.

Oxygen passing over fluoride of calcium at a red heat decomposes it still more rapidly than chlorine, and also produces a gas which acts upon glass.—*Comptes Rendus*, Feb. 27, 1854, p. 393.

ON THE DETERMINATION OF IODINE.

BY R. KERSTING.

The author has instituted some experiments upon the estimation of iodine, especially with a view to finding a method for the more exact determination of this substance in the urine. Having found that the cyanide of potassium, formed by incineration with potash, prevented the precipitation by chloride of palladium, as both free hydrocyanic acid and cyanides dissolve iodide of palladium, he distilled the urine with sulphuric acid. Solutions of iodine, as well as urine containing iodine, when they have been distilled to the concentration of the sulphuric acid, part with their iodine. According to the author, determination of iodine may be completed within two hours by the following process.

If the fluids be very poor in iodine, potash is to be added

to them; 200-250 cub. centims. are then to be distilled down to 20-40 cub. centims.; the distillate is free of iodine. The residue is mixed without shaking with 20 cub. centims. of sulphuric acid. The distillation contains iodine, hydriodic acid, sulphurous acid, sulphuric acid, carbonic acid, and the volatile acids of the contents of the retort.

It is necessary to convert the sulphurous acid into sulphuric acid. For this purpose three fluids are to be prepared, viz., first, a saturated solution of chloride of lime; second, the solution of sulphurous acid or bisulphite of soda; third, a solution of one part of starch in 1-10th of sulphuric acid and twenty-four parts of water. One or two drops of the solution of starch are first added to the fluid; this is followed by the solution of chloride of lime, which is added until the production of a blue color; the solution of sulphurous acid is then added until this color just disappears. In this manner the fluid is rendered fit for determination by means of chloride of palladium.

In determinations of iodine it is necessary to concentrate the fluids. If they be too much diluted, all the iodine does not pass over. In this remark the author wishes to correct a statement of Osann, according to whom, when dilute fluids are distilled with sulphuric acid, all the iodine is obtained; and to prove its correctness, he has instituted special experiments. These show that dilution does not prevent the formation of hydriodic acid, which, as it is not readily volatilized, remains in part in the retort. Nor does the addition of oxidizing substances, such as nitrosulphuric acid, chlorate of potash, or hypochlorite of lime with muriatic acid, and solution of chlorine or bromine give the whole of the iodine. When from one-half to one-eighth of the fluid has distilled over, the fluid in the retort still contains iodic acid.

Direct precipitation of the iodine by protochloride of palladium may also, under some circumstances, take place very imperfectly. The addition of protochloride of palladium to urine containing iodine produces a precipitate, which contains protiodide of palladium, an organic salt of palladium and reduced metal. One part of the protiodide of palladium always.

remains dissolved in the urine. This solution, when starch and solution of chlorine or bromine are added to it, gives no reaction of iodine ; if it be evaporated to dryness with potash and ignited, then dissolved in water and the solution tested, iodine, which was not precipitated by the protochloride of palladium, will always be detected. Protiodide of copper behaves in the same manner.

The extraction of the iodine by chloroform, according to Rabourdin's method, is so far valuable that the chloroform always takes up some iodine, with which it settles to the bottom of watery fluids ; but it cannot be recommended for quantitative determinations, as the quantities which it extracts from a fluid are very unequal.

Volumetric Determination of Iodide by Protochloride of Palladium.—If an excess of chloride of palladium and muriatic acid be added to a solution of a metallic iodide, and the whole heated to 140°–212° F., and shaken, the iodide of palladium separates in black flakes, which are of a gaseous consistence, like chloride of silver. But if iodine be present in excess, the precipitate is only deposited with difficulty. A millionth of iodine in a solution will still be indicated by the fluid acquiring a brown color. Iodine may consequently be determined volumetrically by means of protochloride of palladium. For this purpose three fluids are employed.

1. *Pure Solution of Iodide of Potassium*, containing exactly 1-1000dth of iodine.

2. *Acid Solution of Protochloride of Palladium*, containing 1-2370dth of palladium. This is prepared from the metal, by dissolving one part of it by heat in nitromuriatic acid, evaporating the salt to dryness at 212° F., adding to this fifty parts of concentrated muriatic acid and 2,000 parts of water, and leaving the solution to become clear by standing. The exact determination of the strength is effected by the solution of iodide of potassium.

3. *The Solution of Iodine to be Tested.*—If the iodine compound be dry and in a suitable form, it is to be dissolved in a small quantity of water ; an approximate determination of the amount of iodine is then made by the method described be-

low; the remainder of the solution is diluted to contain about 1-1000dth of iodine, and then again determined exactly. When urine containing iodine is to be analysed, the acid distillate, obtained as above directed, is employed.

These fluids are employed in the following manner—10 cub. centims. of the solution of protochloride of palladium are poured into a white bottle capable of containing 100-200 cub. centims.; the bottle is then lightly corked, and placed in a pot with hot water (140°-212° F.). The solution of iodine is now added from a burette, and the whole is shaken and heated for some seconds. As soon as the fluid is clear, some of it is to be poured into two colorless test-glasses, so as to fill about two inches of both. If a few drops of solution of iodine be added now to one glass, it may be seen by comparison with the other whether any brown tinge is produced. The necessary quantity of iodine, as nearly as can be judged, is then added, the contents of the test-glasses are returned into the first vessel, which is heated, shaken, left standing, and again tested in the test-glass; this is continued until a fresh addition of iodine no longer produces any coloration. Lastly, a filtered sample is to be tested; and if neither the addition of solution of iodine nor of solution of palladium produce any brown color in this, it can scarcely contain a millionth part of either of these substances. No perceptible error occurred in testing the distillate of urine, although this fluid of itself communicates a slight color to solution of palladium. Such a determination as this may be effected with properly-prepared solution of iodine in 10-15 minutes. If it be required to determine the palladium for the more exact dilution of the crude solution No. 2, 10 cub. centims. of this are precipitated with the solution of iodine No. 1. Each cubic centimetre of the latter represents 0·42 milligrm. of palladium. The amount of iodine in the solution No. 3 is determined with the standard solution of palladium No. 2, each cubic centimetre of which represents 1 milligrm. of iodine.

The author then ascertained, by a series of experiments, what bodies had no effect upon the reaction on which the method of volumetric analysis depends. These are—dilute muriatic acid, sulphuric acid, phosphoric acid, nitric acid, and acetic acid; as also the neutral potash, soda and ammoniacal salts of these acids; chloride of calcium, chloride of zinc, acetate of lead, sugar, uric acid, the distillate of urine with sulphuric acid, alcohol, æther, oil of lemons, starch-paste and bromide of sodium; the latter, however, only when no free mineral acid is present at the same time; the presence of acetic acid is not disadvantageous. The following, on the contrary, have a preventive action—free alkalies, which precipitate protoxide of palladium; free chlorine, bromine and iodine, cyanogen, much nitric acid when heated, and sulphurous acid. The preventive agents can generally be got rid of. The alkalies are saturated with sulphuric acid. Free chlorine, bromine, and iodine are converted by watery sulphurous acid, in the presence of one or two drops of starch-paste, into hydracids, and these neutralized by potash. Sulphurous acid is oxidized by solution of chloride of lime and muriatic acid, so as to form sulphuric acid. In this operation starch-paste indicates the exact point of saturation; the commencement of blue coloration shows an excess of chlorine; its disappearance on the addition of sulphurous acid indicates the saturation of the chlorine.

Volumetric Determination of Iodine by Bichloride of Mercury.—Blue iodide of starch is discolored by bichloride of mercury, with formation of iodide of mercury and chlorine. If we use a mixture of iodide of starch and hydriodates, the salts are first decomposed, and then the iodide of starch. A solution, so diluted as to contain only 1-10,000dth of iodine, retains the iodide of mercury formed in solution, so that the discoloration of the iodide of starch is produced very distinctly. For these determinations the following fluids are prepared.

1. Pure solution of iodide of potassium, containing 1-10,000dth of iodine, 1·308 grm. of calcined iodide of potassium are dissolved in water to form 100 cub. centims. of fluid. 10 cub. centims. of this, mixed with water sufficient to form 1,000 cub. centims., give a solution containing 1-10,000dth of iodine.

2. *Solution of Bromine.*—Water shaken up with an excess of bromine contains about 1-32 bromine; this, when diluted with 49 vols. of water, gives a solution of 1-1600dth of bromine.

3. *Starch-paste*, prepared by boiling 1 part of starch with 1-10th of sulphuric acid and 24 parts of water.

4. *Solution of Bichloride of Mercury* with 1-1000dth HgCl.—1 grm. of the salt is dissolved in 1,000 grms. of water by heat. It is valued by means of the iodide of potassium solution No. 1.

The fluid containing an iodine compound to which this method is applicable must be so far diluted as to contain about 1-10,000dth of iodine, and then tested exactly for this substance. With this view the quantity of solution of bichloride of mercury required to saturate one part by weight of iodine is first ascertained. 100 cub. centims. of the solution of iodine No. 1, (containing 0·010 grm. of iodine,) are poured into a white beaker capable of holding 1–2 litres, and 10 drops of starch-paste and 10 drops of solution of bromine are added to them. The fluid appears deep blue. The solution of bichloride of mercury is now poured in from the burette, the solution of iodine being kept constantly shaken until the blue color has completely disappeared. The number of cubic centimetres employed represents a quantity of 0.010 grm. of iodine, and is marked upon the vessel in which the mercurial solution is kept. According to the experiments, 10 cub. centims. of this solution were required, and, therefore, 1·1 cub. centim. to 1 milligrm. of iodine. When the unknown solution of iodine, No. 5, is treated in the same manner, the volume of the standard mercurial solution gives the amount of iodine.

The reaction upon which this method depends is not prevented by the presence of neutral sulphate, phosphate, or nitrate of soda, sulphate of ammonia, acetate of lead, concentrated acetic acid or sugar. On the other hand, the following have a preventive action: free mineral acids, and also acetic acid and its salts when the quantity of the latter is about 20 times that of the iodine. The most important thing is, that muriatic and hydrobromic acids are also preventives. All these substances necessitate the employment of a larger quantity of solution of bichloride of mercury for the complete decolorization of the iodide of starch. Free alkalies, on the contrary, strongly deoxidizing bodies, (such as sulphurous acid,) and various organic compounds, (even urine,) also destroy the action, because they decolorize the iodide of starch directly.—*Ann. der Chem. und Pharm.*, lxxxvii., p. 19, in *Chem. Gaz.*, April 15.

THE MEDICINAL PLANTS OF AUSTRALIA.

BY P. L. SIMMONDS, ESQ.

Scientific research and investigation is opening up much valuable information in various quarters of the world. The officers of the East India Company's territories are from time to time contributing many useful papers to the periodicals of the day. The medical officers of the navy and army in our own service and that of the United States are more alive than formerly to the importance of accumulating useful facts respecting indigenous plants of various localities, and their reputed properties as remedial agents. The valley of the great Amazon River, the Parana, Paraguay, Magdalena, and other tributary streams of the various South American Republics are now opened up by steam navigation, and much new information may be anticipated as to the products of those comparatively unknown regions of the interior.

Even in another quarter, in our southern possessions at the Antipodes, where little information relating to the pharmaceutical products was to be anticipated, in the present exciting thirst for gold, some valuable facts have recently come to hand. Dr. Ferdinand Mueller, who was not long ago appointed Government botanist at Melbourne, has already explored the colony of Victoria, under his charge, in various journeys made into the interior from February to June, and has submitted a general report of his researches and discoveries to the Colonial Governor, under date September 5, 1853. This report is exceedingly interesting in a botanical point of view, but it is only that portion bearing upon the peculiar feature to which your Journal is devoted that I shall proceed to give an abstract of.

The inestimable truth, that we may safely deduce the closest affinities of the medicinal properties of plants from their natural alliances—a truth which achieved the most complete triumph of the natural system over all artificial classifications—will generally guide us in tracing out which plants might be administered in medicine. By this guidance Dr. Mueller observed that the Australian Thymeleæ were pervaded by that acridity for which the bark of *Daphne Mezereum* is employed ; that the *Polygala veronicea*, the only described Australian species of a large genus, and in close relation to one lately discovered in the Chinese empire, not only agrees, like some kinds of *Comesperma*, with the Austrian *Polygala amara* in those qualities for which that plant has been administered in consumption, but also participated in the medicinal virtue of *Polygala Senega* from North America. *Gratiola latifolia*, and *Gratiola pubescens*, *Convolvulus erubescens*, and the various kinds of *Mentha*, are not inferior to similar European species. The bark of *Tasmannia aromatica* appears to possess the medicinal properties of the Winter's bark gathered from a similar tree in Terra del Fuego; and its fruit is allied to that of the North American Magnolia, used in cases of rheumatism and intermittent fever. The whole natural order of Goodeniaceæ, with the exception, perhaps, of a few species, contains a tonic bitterness never recognized before, and discernible in many plants in so high a degree, that Dr. Mueller was induced, for this reason, to bestow upon a new genus from the interior the name of *Picrophyta*. This property, which indicates a certain alliance to Gentianeæ, deserves the more consideration, as the true Gentianeæ are so sparingly distributed through Australia, while the Goodeniaceæ form everywhere a prominent feature in the vegetation. "Our alps, however, (remarks the Doctor,) enrich us also with a thick-rooted Gentian, (*G. Diemensis*,) certainly as valuable as the officinal *Gentiana lutea*, and in the spring, *Sabœ evata*, *Sabœ abidiflora*, and *Erythrœa Australis* might also be collected on account of their bitterness. The bark of the Australian Sassafras (*Atherosperma moschata*) has obtained some celebrity as a substitute for tea; administered in a greater concentration it is diaphoretic as well as diuretic, and has for this reason already been practically introduced into medicine by an eminent colonial physician.

Isotoma axillaris surpasses all other indigenous Lobeliaceæ in its intense acridity, and can be, therefore, only cautiously used instead of *Lobelia inflata.* The root of *Malva Bebriana* scarcely differs from that of *Althæa officinalis*, and Salap might be collected from many Orchideæ. Few may be aware that the Cajeput oil of India is obtained from trees very similar to the common *Melaleuca* of Australia; that even from the leaves of the *Eucalypti* an oil can be procured of equal utility. The Sandarac exuding from the Callitris or Pine tree; the balsamic resin of the grass trees, and, moreover, the *Eucalyptus* gum, which could be gathered in boundless quantities, and which for its astringent qualities might, locally at least, supersede the use of kino or catechu, will probably at a future period form articles of export.

Several Acaciæ are of essential service, either for their durable wood or for the abundance of tannin in their bark, which has rendered them already useful, or for their gum, but the latter is even excelled in clearness and solubility by that obtained from *Pittosporum acacioides.* This species, as well as many other plants of the same order, is distinguished by a surprising yet apparently harmless bitterness, a quality that warrants our expecting considerable medicinal power, and which deserves so much more attention, as till now we knew nothing of the usefulness of the *Pittosporæ*, although the order extends over a great part of the eastern hemisphere. The Australian manna consists in a saccharine secretion condensed chiefly by the cicades from a few specimens of Eucalypti, but it is chemically very differently constituted to the Ornus manna, and much less aperient.

The orange-yellow gum, or acaroid resin, secreted by the grass tree, (*Xanthorrhœa hastile*,) resembles very much in appearance, though not in quality, gamboge; externally it has a dull, yellow appearance, but breaks with a bright yellow fracture, and is often streaked internally with red. In its natural state it has no fragrant smell, but by the action of fire it diffuses an agreeable odor, resembling frankincense.

It exudes spontaneously from the trunk in very small globules, and is found in very thin layers about the base of the petioles of the leaves, but may be melted into larger masses.

The resin (more commonly known as the gum acaroides) is slightly bitter, pungent, and astringent, and has been used in dyspeptic, dysenteric, and other cases ; but not with such success as to cause it to be admitted into our *Materia Medica.*

"Black-boy gum," as it is locally termed, is obtained from another species (*X. arborea*) ; it is a red brittle resin. These valuable resins may be obtained in the various Australian settlements, in large quantities and at a low price. They are gradually coming into use in the manufacture of varnish, and for other purposes, being in some respects quite as good as, if not superior to, shell-lac.

All the splendid Diosmeæ of Australia—a real ornament to the country—approach more or less in their medicinal effect (diuretic) to the leaves of the South African Buchu bushes (*Barosma Crenulata*).

Bæckia utilis, from Mount Aberdeen, Victoria, might serve travellers in those desolate localities as tea, for the volatile oil of its leaves resembles greatly in taste and odor that of lemons, not without a pleasant peculiar aroma.

Trigonella suavissima proved valuable as an antiscorbutic spinach in Sir Thomas Mitchell's inland expedition ; and the *Tetragonella implexicona*, the various *Cardamines*, *Nasturtium terrestre*, or *Lawrencia spicata*, may likewise be used for the same purpose.

It would be out of place here to touch upon the culinary plants ; but I may incidentally notice that Dr. Mueller suggests that the root of *Scorzonera Lawrencii*, a favorite food of the Australian aborigines, would form, if enlarged by culture, an agreeable substitute for *Scorzonera hispanica*, or asparagus ; and *Aristome glacialis*, a large-rooted umbelliferous plant from the snowy top of Mount Barker, will probably be added hereafter to the culinary vegetables of the colder climates.—*London Pharm. Journ.*, May, 1854.

ESSENCE FOR PRESTON SALTS (MOUNSEY'S).

℞ Ol. Caryoph. Ver., ʒj.
Ol. Lavendula, Ang., ʒij.
Ess. Bergamot, ʒv.
Liq. Ammon. Fortiss, s. gr. 880, Oj.
M. ft. Essentia.

The bottles to be half filled with rough carbonate of ammonia, and filled up with carbonate of ammonia in fine powder, and then as much of the essence as the ammonia will absorb added.—*Lond. Pharm. Journ.*

Separation of Copper from Silver.—This can be effected when a filed alloy of those metals is digested with a solution of chloride of zinc, by which means the copper is completely dissolved and the silver remains behind pure. A solution of chloride of zinc can also be employed to restore sheets of plated copper, which have been rendered unsightly by soldering, to their former condition.—*Polyt. Central-Blatt.*

Dr. W. H. Edwards, of Surry, Va., recommends the use of the mucilage of the slippery elm bark in order to mask the bitter taste of quinine.

Varieties.

HOW FAMILIES ARE POISONED.--SCHEELE'S GREEN IN BAKERS' SHOPS.

To the Editor of the Pharmaceutical Journal.

Sir—The fact which I am about to mention shows in what an insidious manner arsenic may be introduced into articles of food supplied to a family. Cases now and then occur to a medical practitioner in which certain symptoms, strongly indicative of irritant poisoning, appear simultaneously in several members of a family. No source of poisoning can be discovered, no motive may exist for its administration; and persons affected recover, and the matter is forgotten. In another, and more serious class of cases, several members of a family die suddenly, one after another. Poison is suspected to have been the cause of death, and traces of it may be actually found in the body; but it will be impossible to discover how or when it entered the body. In a case which I was required to investigate in January last, the father mother, and three children were carried off within the short period of about ten days, as it was supposed, by disease. The body of the mother was exhumed a month after interment, and arsenic was found in the liver. This created a strong suspicion that all had died from poison; but the most minute inquiry has failed to show how or in what way the arsenic could have entered the body of the mother Nevertheless, it was quite clear that she must have taken it during life, as it had been absorbed, and was found deposited in the liver.

On the 17th of the present month, when about to cut the loaf on my table for breakfast, I observed some green patches and streaks over the partially burnt under-crust. The appearance was something like that caused by green mould; but, on examining the slices of toast in the toast-rack, I found similar green spots in the depressed portions of the crust of the toast. I then examined the green spots with a lens, and subsequently a portion was scraped off, and examined under a microscope of low power. The colored particles then resolved themselves into a mineral powder, having all the appearances of Scheele's green, or arsenite of copper. I scraped from the bottom of one loaf from one and a half to two grains of this powder; and, on applying Reinsch's process, I separated a quantity of metallic arsenic sufficient to coat two square inches of copper. The metallic arsenic was converted to crystallized white arsenic, and examined under a high magnifying power, when the arsenious acid was plainly perceptible. The green substance adhering to the crust of the bread and toast, was, therefore, proved to be Scheele's green, a pigment which contains about fifty per cent. of white arsenic.

On inquiring of the servants, I found that five loaves had, the day before, been taken from the baker, a respectable tradesman, with whom I have dealt for twelve years. On examining these loaves, three of them were stained in the under-crust with closely adherent patches of the green arsenite of copper. It appeared clear from the circumstances, that there had been no intentional admixture of poison, or this would have been found inside and not on the outside of the bread. It was quite certain that the loaves must have been delivered with the poison adhering to them, because there is no green paint in the house.

Thinking that some accident might occur in other families, I immediately went to the baker, and showed him the Scheele's green and metallic arsenic extracted from it. On entering his shop, I at once saw the cause of the poisoning of the bread. He had had his shop newly decorated, and there were eight long shelves (holding some hundreds of loaves) painted of a bright glass green color, top, front, and sides. They had been evidently very substantially coated with the green paint. The warm loaves, placed on the recently painted shelves, had imbibed a quantity of the poisonous pigment, which had dried in the under crust. He took down five or six loaves in succession, and all were found stained with the arsenite of copper. The baker assured me that he had not the least idea there was arsenic in the green paint; but the painter, who was summoned, took the matter more coolly and professionately, remarking that it was impossible to get a good green without arsenic, that he had used it for many years, and had never heard of any one being killed by it. Although he knew the shelves were for the purpose of storing loaves of bread, he was evidently waiting for some fatal cases in his own experience before he could make up his mind to lay aside the practice of using this paint.

The baker, at my strong request, had the whole of the loaves rasped, and, without loss of time, the tops of the shelves were planed off, so that the loaves should rest upon nothing but plain and unpainted deal. There was enough on the crust of one of the loaves to have killed an infant; and I can suppose a case in which a nursemaid, about to quit a service for misconduct, might be seriously implicated by such an occurrence as this, unless the cause were at once traced.

In foreign countries there are strong restrictions placed on the sale and use of this noxious pigment. In England, however, green sweetmeats are actually colored with it; and lemon, acid, and other drops, are sometimes sold, wrapped in paper coarsely tinged or dyed green with this dangerous compound of arsenic.

I am, &c.,

ALFRED S. TAYLOR, M.D., F.R.S.,

Lecturer on Medical Jurisprudence and Chemistry in Guy's Hospital.

15 *St. James's Terrace, Regent's Park,*

March 29, 1854.

—*London Pharmaceutical Journal.*

DETECTION OF BLOOD-STAINS ON A KNIFE COVERED WITH RUST.—M. Daubrawa was requested to ascertain the existence of blood-stains on a knife which was suspected to have been used in the commission of a murder. The knife, having lain a long time in a damp place, was rusted; but certain bright rust-free spots could be distinguished amidst the rust. On heating the point of the blade, these spots scaled off while the rust remained adherent; on the other hand, on immersing the knife in dilute hydrochloric acid, the bright spots remained untouched, although the rust was readily dissolved. It was probable that these bright spots were blood-stains;

but as some non-nitrogenous organic acids will produce similar marks, some of the detached scales were heated in a test tube, and by the disengagement of ammonia from the hæmatine of the blood, caused a blue color on reddened litmus paper. The whole blade was then macerated for a long time in distilled water, which acquired a reddish discoloration; and by the aid of a lens, fibrine could be seen adhering to the blade in the situation of the bright spots. Ammonia added to the solution caused no precipitate; nitric acid gave a white precipitate; it became turbid from heat; solution of chlorine at first produced a green tint, this color then disappeared, and white flocculi were deposited. These different fluids having been evaporated to dryness and burnt, and the residue dissolved in hydrochloric acid, demonstrated the presence of iron by its appropriate reagents.—*Jour. de Chimie Medicale.*

Adulteration of Sulphate of Quinine.—The School or College of Pharmacy in Paris, and a special committee appointed for the purpose of examining into the subject of the adulteration of sulphate of quinine, agree, that the presence of three per cent. of foreign matters, in any given sulphate of quinine, may be allowed; but if such foreign substances be found in greater quantity than that, the law for the suppression of frauds or adulteration of articles of commerce should be put in force. A late number of the *Journal de Chemie Medicale* contains a long report or circular in reference to suspected sulphate of quinine, from the Director-General of Agriculture and Commerce, the chief particulars of which we proceed to submit to our readers.

Sulphate of quinine, in a proper state for medical purposes, is white, crystallized in delicate, detached needles, and has a very bitter taste. For its solution, it requires something more than seven hundred parts of cold water, and about thirty parts of boiling water. It is constituted of two equivalents of quinine, one equivalent of sulphuric acid, and eight equivalents of water, thus representing in one hundred parts of sulphate of quinine, 74.31 quinine, 9.17 sulphuric acid, and 16.51 water.

Sulphate of quinine has a very feeble alkaline reaction upon reddened litmus paper, and this alkaline reaction is weakened, and may even become acid, in cases in which the salt contains a stronger proportion of acid.

At a temperature of 100° (centigrade thermometer) sulphate of quinine loses seven equivalents of water, or 14.55 parts in one hundred parts. It effloresces, although only partially, in a dry atmosphere, and at the ordinary temperature. Ignited in the air, on a plate of platinum, it is consumed without leaving any appreciable residue. It is not perceptibly colored when submitted to the action of cold concentrated sulphuric acid. The substances that have been most commonly employed in the adulteration of sulphate of quinine are, sulphate of lime, salicine, sugar in powder, sulphate of cinchonine, and certain fatty bodies, such as stearic and margaric acids.

Sulphate of Lime may be recognized in the same manner as mineral bodies in general, by means of incineration. For this purpose, one gramme of the sulphate of quinine is to be burnt in a small capsule of platinum, until all traces of carbon shall have disappeared; the residue left after incineration represents the weight of sulphate of lime which had been present in the sulphate of quinine.

Another method consists in treating the suspected sulphate of quinine with alcohol, which, when heated, dissolves the sulphate of quinine, leaving as a residue the sulphate of lime. This method is recommended in case of operating upon large quantities of any suspected sulphate of quinine, as it does not involve the loss of the sulphate of quinine that may be the subject of experiment.

Salicine may be recognized, if, on the addition of concentrated sulphuric acid in small quantity to the suspected sulphate of quinine, it assumes a deep red color. This colored reaction is perceptible if the proportion of salicine does not exceed one-hundred of the adulterated salt. It is, however, necessary to observe that salicine is by no means the only organic substance which possesses the property of being reddened by the action of concentrated sulphuric acid; to be convinced of the presence of salicine, subsequent manipulations become necessary, yet, in all cases, a red color caused by the addition of concentrated sulphuric acid would indicate some kind of adulteration of the suspected sulphate of quinine, for if this be pure, it should not assume a red color.

Sugar may be recognized (for this has been used in the adulteration of sulphate of quinine) by burning the suspected sulphate of quinine in the air, when, if it be present, the peculiar odor of caramel is given off, which is not the case on burning pure sulphate of quinine. Besides, the sugar may be separated from the mixture in its natural state, in this manner: the suspected salt is to be dissolved in water, baryta is to be added thereto in excess, so as to precipitate all the sulphuric acid and all the quinine; a stream of carbonic acid is then to be passed through the liquid, so as to separate entirely the excess of baryta; the liquid is then to be heated, filtered, and evaporated, when it will be found to contain only sugar.

Fatty acids, or any other substance insoluble in water, and in weak acids, may be recognized by treating the mixture with water acidulated with sulphuric acid, which separates the sulphate of quinine from insoluble fatty substances.

Sulphate of Cinchonine is more frequently employed than any other substance for the purpose of adulterating sulphate of quinine. A mixture of sulphate of cinchonine and sulphate of quinine may be the result of designed fraud, but it may also be the result of imperfect purification of the latter salt. The presence of sulphate of cinchonine, however, in such a mixture, may be recognized in the following manner: one gramme of the suspected sulphate, or, as nearly as possible, fifteen grains of apothecaries' weight (English) are to be introduced into a long, narrow flask, with a small orifice; upon this sulphate, ten cubic centimetres of sulphuric ether, entirely freed from alcohol, are to be poured; the mixture is to be well shaken, and subsequently two cubic centimetres of liquid ammonia are to be added thereto. If the suspected sulphate be pure, it will entirely dissolve, without leaving any residue, in the mixture of ammonia and ether; whereas, if it contain any cinchonine, this latter alkaloid remains insoluble, forming a white deposition between the two liquids, ammonia and ether. On decanting the liquids, the cinchonine may be collected, and its weight determined; however, when it is desired not only to determine the presence of cinchonine in any suspected specimen, but also to ascertain its proportion, it is better to operate on some considerable quantity at once.

Other alkaloids have been pointed out as being sometimes mixed with sulphate of quinine, particularly quinidine, a base which appears to be present in notable quantity in certain varieties of cinchona bark. Quinidine may be recognized by employing the same process as that just indicated for the detection of cinchonine. Like this latter base, quinidine remains undissolved in ether, in the form of a white precipitate; still, quinidine is not so insoluble in ether as is cinchonine, which requires at least twelve hundred parts of ether for its solution; whereas quinidine is perceptibly soluble in ether; and this comparative solubility of these two bases in that fluid will suffice for practical purposes to distinguish the one from the other in any adulterated sulphate of quinine. In cases where the suspected sulphate may contain both cinchonine and quinidine at the same time, the comparative solubility of the precipitate obtained will determine the proportion of cinchonine and quinidine present in the adulterated specimen.

Sulphate of quinine, however, must not invariably be considered as adulterated if it contain traces merely either of sulphate of lime or of cinchonine. A certain allowance must be accorded to the necessary process of its manufacture; our judgments must depend upon the quantity present, which, however, should not exceed three parts of either of these substances in one hundred parts of sulphate of quinine.

Specific and Latent Eefects of Vapors.—By MM. Favre and Silbermann.—(*Ann. de Chem. et de Phys.*, April, 1853, p. 461.)—MM. Favre and Silbermann have, by means of their Mercurial Calorimeter, found the following values:

Name of the Substance.	Specific Heat.	Latent Heat.
Bicarburet of Hydrogen (from Amylic Alcohol. Boiling point, 200°—210° Cent.)	0.489	59.91
Bicarburet of Hydrogen (from Amylic Alcohol. Boiling point, 240°—260° Cent.)	0.496	59.71
Wood Spirit	0.671	263.86
Wine Alcohol	0.644	208.92
Amylic Alcohol	0.587	121.37
Sulphuric Ether	0.503	91.11
Acetic Ether	0.483	105.80
Essence of Turpentine	0.467	68.73
Sulphurous Acid		94.56

—*Archives des Sciences Phys. et Nat.*, vol. xxiii., p. 385.

Oxidized Silver.—The high appreciation in which ornaments in oxidized silver are now held, render a notice of the process followed interesting. There are two distinct shades in use, one produced by chlorine, which has a brownish tint, and the other by sulphur, which has a bluish-black tint. To produce the former, it is only necessary to wash the article with a solution of sal ammoniac; a much more beautiful tint may, however, be obtained by employing a solution composed of equal parts of sulphate of copper and sal ammoniac in vinegar. The fine black tint may be produced by a slightly warm solution of sulphuret of potassium or sodium.—*Journ. Indus. Progress*, April, 1854.

On the Preparation of Copal Varnish.—By Professor Heeren.—There is no difficulty in dissolving copal in fatty and volatile oils when the resin has been previously fused; by this process, however, a more or less distinct coloration is produced, and the natural hardness of this fine resin is injured. It has, therefore, been often attempted to dissolve copal without previous fusion; but, as is well known to all who have occupied themselves with this question, great difficulties have been found in effecting the solution. Directions have been given to soak the pounded copal in æther or ammonia until it swells up into a gelatinous form, and then to dissolve it in strong alcohol; but this process never succeeded with the author, though he tried it repeatedly. Others recommend hanging the copal in a small bag in a retort, in which absolute alcohol is gently boiling. This method also failed, in the author's hands, in producing even a tolerably-concentrated varnish.

The best prescription appears to the author to be that given by Freudenvoll in his treatise on the preparation of varnishes. According to him, four ounces of West Indian copal are dissolved in a mixture of

4 ozs. oil of turpentine, and
6 ozs. alcohol of spec. grav. 0.813;

or a mixture of

4 ozs. sulphuric æther,
4 ozs. oil of turpentine, and
4 ozs. alcohol of spec. grav. 0·851.

When engaged in testing this process, which gave very good results, the author found a small variation, which he describes as follows, particularly efficacious:—

Two sorts of copal occur in commerce, the East and West Indian. The former is usually in small, irregular, rounded pieces, with a finely verrucose surface, the resemblance of which to the skin of a goose has obtained for it the name of "goose copal." It is of a somewhat yellow color, and is preferred for the manufacture of oily copal varnish, because it acquires less color by fusion than the West Indian. The latter does not possess a warty surface; it is very pale in color, often nearly colorless, and occurs in large irregular fragments, partly with a rounded surface and partly with a shelly fracture.

West Indian copal only can be employed in the following solution, the East Indian forming only gelatinous lumps, but never a solution. The solvent is a mixture of

60 parts by weight of alcohol of spec. grav. 0·813,
10 parts by weight of sulphuric æther,
40 parts by weight of oil of turpentine,

in which 60 parts of copal are to be dissolved for the production of a varnish of an oleaginous consistence. Solution takes place, even in the cold, without any previous gelatinous swelling of the copal; but it is effected much more rapidly with the assistance of a gentle heat. As, however, single pieces are often found in the West Indian copal, which instead of dissolving only swell up in the fluid, by which the rest of the solution is spoiled, it is advisable to select only the large and perfectly clear pieces for the purpose of varnish-making, and to test each first of all as to its solubility. This little trouble is richly repaid by the certainty of the result.

To test this quality, a small splinter of the copal is put into a small test tube; a little of the solvent fluid is then poured in, and the whole is heated. If the copal dissolves completely in a few minutes without becoming gelatinous, it is good.

When the desired quantity of good copal has been got together in this manner, it is to be pounded to a tolerably fine powder, which is to be put into a glass retort or flask, the necessary quantity of the solvent added, and the whole heated and shaken until solution is effected. To clear the varnish, which may appear somewhat dull, from dust or other impurities, it may be allowed to stand a long while until these settle; or if it be desired to effect this quickly, it may be filtered through blotting paper, placed as a filter in a glass funnel; the filter must not project above the edge of the funnel, so that the latter may be closed by a glass plate laid over it. The passage of the thick varnish is of course very slow, but the varnish is obtained perfectly clear in this manner; and if the copal employed were very clear, it is nearly colorless. It dries rapidly, but like all turpentine varnishes retains a slightly sticky surface for some days.—*Dingler's Polytech. Journ.*, cxxx. p. 424.—(On page 189 of the present volume we have described a much more delicate mode of detection.—Ed.)

On the Detection of Strychnine in Saccharine Powders.—By A. Vogel, Jun.—Otto has recommended bichromate of potash as a test for strychnine. The substance to be tested is mixed with the finely-powdered salt, and then moistened with sulphuric acid; a dark-violet color is produced. Brieger states that strychnine mixed with sugar cannot be discovered in this way. The author says that in this case the substance to be tested must first be moistened with sulphuric acid, and the salt afterwards added to it. By adopting this plan, moreover, the reaction is not prevented either by quinine, cinchonine, starch or dextrine.—*Buchner's Neues Repert.*, ii., p. 560.

On the Estimation of Tin.—By Peter Hart, Manchester.—In the last number of the Chemical Society's Journal (April, 1854) there is an article by Dr. Penny on the bichromate method, in which he recommends the addition of a protosalt of iron and sulphocyanide of potassium to the test, with a view to render distinct the point at which sufficient bichromate solution has been added; I must confess that in my hands, some months back, before the appearance of his paper, this was not very successful, but the contrary, so much so that I gave it up as having a tendency to render the operation more difficult than it otherwise would be.

I found that on each addition of the bichromate solution a quantity of sulphcoyanide of iron was formed, which, while there was comparatively a large amount of protochloride of tin present, was easily reduced, but towards the close of the operation, when there was but a small quantity of protochloride present, required some time. I often found, after placing the flask on one side, supposing it finished, that in a few minutes the red color had disappeared, and the solution remained of the ordinary green color; on the addition of more bichromate solution it again became red, only to disappear again in a short time; and this would, perhaps, be repeated three or four times.

The process I propose, is to add to the dilute solution of protochloride of tin in the flask a small quantity of iodide of potassium solution and a little thin starch-paste; with this addition it will be found that one drop of the bichromate solution in excess will cause the contents of the flask to assume a strong blue color, the chromic acid setting free a quantity of iodine, which combining with the starch present produces the blue iodide of starch.

This improvement, by means of which the veriest tyro, with common precautions, can estimate tin with as much exactness as the most practised person can by the bichromate process, will, I think, prove an acquisition to the student, and any one who may only occasionally have to test a solution of tin; for whatever may be said to the contrary, it is certain that considerable practice is requisite before precision can be attained by using the bichromate solution simply.

It must be borne in mind that this process does not remove the difficulty pointed out by M. Leishing, but that his objection to the simple bichromate test still holds good after the addition I propose; in short there must not be more than a trace of iron present, or the result is vitiated in a corresponding degree.

Detection of Blood-stains on Garments.—M. Morin has related a series of experiments to illustrate the mode of detecting blood-stains from which the coloring matter has been removed by boiling water. Some human blood was received on a cloth as it escaped from an open vein. The stains were, after some hours, washed in water, at a temperature above that required for the coagulation of albumen; they were then immersed in boiling soap and water, and afterwards in cold water, until the water presented no longer any opoline tint. When dried, the spots were firmer in consistence than the surrounding tissue. These portions having been cut out, and macerated in distilled water for a considerable time, the fluid acquired no discoloration, nor did the application of heat give any indication of a trace of dissolved albumen. Macerated in a solution of potash, the addition of nitric acid occasioned a white precipitate.

Blood-stains on garments that have been washed, do not, by this alkaline treatment, lose what color they may have retained. The tests for iron will detect the presence of this metal as the cause of their color.

The coexistence of iron and a protein element in suspected stains, furnishes an important element of the proof of culpability.—*Journal de Chimie Medicale.*

Cast-Iron for Artificial Magnets.—M. Crahay found, several years ago, that cast iron may acquire, by tempering, a coercitive force sufficiently great to allow it to be strongly and permanently magnetized. The grey iron is the best for this purpose. The pot metal is too brittle, and the first quality of cast iron gives but moderate results.

The permanence of the magnetism depends on the temper. A bar tempered at a dull red heat, may be powerfully magnetized, but loses its force in twenty-four hours.

If the tempering is done at a red heat, the bars not only will take a powerful magnetism but keep it indefinitely. Experiment has shown that the following is the best mode of tempering large bars. They are to be heated to redness in a wind furnace, then withdrawn, one by one, the two faces of the bar are sprinkled for three-fourths of their length with yellow prussiate of potassa, and immediately plunged into a great mass of cold water, stirring it about violently.

A little more thickness should be given to bars of cast iron than to steel.—*Pros. R. Acad. Belgium*, July 29, 1853, in *Jour. Frank. Institute.*

Saltpetre.—Professor W. H. Ellet informs the *N. Y. Tribune* that there has been discovered, in Bradford County, Pennsylvania, a regular vein of nitre, believed to be unique in its character. He describes it as a narrow vein occurring in sandstone rock, the salt itself being of a remarkable degree of purity.

EDITORIAL.

AMERICAN PHARMACEUTICAL ASSOCIATION.

The annual meeting of the American Pharmaceutical Association will be holden in the city of Cincinnati on the last Tuesday (25th) of July next, at eleven o'clock, a.m.

The object of the Association being the advancement of pharmacy in the United States, it is desirable that a general interest in its favor should be created among the pharmaceutists and druggists. According to the requirement of the constitution the following conditions of membership are published, and an invitation is hereby extended to all who are eligible to membership, and who feel an interest in the association, to attend the ensuing meeting.

WM. A. BREWER, President.

Extract from the Constitution of the American Pharmaceutical Association, Sec. ii., Art. i.

All pharmaceutists and druggists who shall have attained the age of twenty-one years, whose character, morally and professionally, is fair, and who, after duly considering the obligations of the constitution and code of ethics of this Association, are willing to subscribe to them, shall be eligible for membership.

Sec. ii., Art. ii. The members shall consist of delegates from regularly constituted Colleges of Pharmacy and Pharmaceutical Societies, who shall present properly authorized credentials, and of other reputable pharmaceutists feeling an interest in the objects of the association, who may not be so delegated, the latter being required to present a certificate signed by a majority of the delegates from the place whence they come. If no such delegates are present at the Association, they may, on obtaining the certificates of any three members of the Association, be admitted, provided they be introduced by the committee on credentials.

Section ii., Art. 5. Every local Pharmaceutical Association shall be entitled to five delegates.

Copied from the official announcement of the President by

EDWARD PARRISH, Recording Secretary.

Philadelphia, May 24, 1854.

COLUMBIA COLLEGE.—We perceive by the daily papers that the Senate Committee of Investigation (Hopkins, Brooks, and Danforth) are at work in the examination of the college. The Board of Trustees issued an invitation to the committee to visit, which was accepted on the 3d, when President King conducted them through the several class rooms. The entire sophomore class were expelled the same day, owing to some disrespectful occurrences enacted in the presence of the President.

Dr. D. M. Reese, in the *N. Y. Medical Gazette* for June, has an item on the Hendrickson trial, in which he judges harshly of the motives of Professor Wells and those who interested themselves in endeavoring to delay the execution of Hendrickson. Dr. R. remarks of it:

"We honor his (Governor Seymour's) judgment and firmness in this case, for had he let loose this Hendrickson upon society, he would have merited the public censure as widely and justly as it has been hurled at the court and jury in Kentucky, who have set at liberty that other murderer, Ward. Even if the medical testimony were erroneous, this could not vitiate the other evidence before the jury, else a blundering doctor could be used to secure the acquittal of any murderer. Nor should any number of physicians, or others known to be *opposed to capital punishment*, be allowed to cajole or intimidate the authorities into conformity to their creed, which makes a virtue of preventing any murderer from being hanged."

The last paragraph is unfair. Neither Professor Wells nor any chemist or physician who objected ever expressed any objection to the death of the prisoner, if the testimony were to the point, but they did object to the life of any one, guilty or innocent, being taken away upon such slight grounds as the defective and erroneous testimony given by Drs. Salisbury and Swinburne. We cannot agree with Dr. Reese that defective medical and chemical evidence on a trial for poisoning ought not to vitiate the other evidence, for as the prisoner is convicted upon the whole evidence and one part be faulty, which defect cannot be supplied by the other evidence, it is clear the whole evidence is faulty, and the prisoner, therefore, should not have been convicted.

As for letting loose Hendrickson upon society, that is beside the question and an *ad captandum* appeal of Dr. R. The whole question is, was Hendrickson convicted rightly upon the evidence? We still think not.

NEW YORK

JOURNAL OF PHARMACY.

AUGUST, 1854.

ON THE PURITY OF ALCOHOL.

BY EDWARD N. KENT.

In a recent investigation which required the use of alcohol perfectly free from fusel oil, I was led to suspect that nitrate of silver could not be depended upon as a test for this substance, and upon mixing pure fusel oil with pure alcohol, verified my suspicion. Nitrate of silver is not reduced by fusel oil, even by boiling, but it is true that alcohol frequently contains other organic substances by which nitrate of silver is reduced when mixed with it and exposed to heat and light. Most of these substances can be removed by simple distillation, but fusel oil cannot be removed in this manner, and consequently this substance constitutes the most usual and injurious impurity in all commercial alcohol. To detect its presence I find that pure sulphuric acid is the best and most convenient test, and as I am not aware that this acid has before been used for this purpose, I will proceed to describe the method of using it as a test for fusel oil.

It is well known that when concentrated sulphuric acid is mixed with fusel oil that a dark purple mixture is produced, with the formation of sulpho-amylic acid. This fact forms the basis of the new test for fusel oil. When pure sulphuric acid is added slowly to *pure* alcohol, the mixture remains perfectly colorless; but if it be added to alcohol containing the least trace of fusel oil, the mixture becomes colored in proportion to the amount of impurity.

The most convenient method of applying this test is to fill a small test tube to one-half its capacity with the spirit to be tested; the tube is then to be filled with pure concentrated sulphuric acid, which must be added very slowly, otherwise the heat produced will cause the spirit to boil and project the acid violently from the tube. If the spirit is impure, the mixture will immediately become colored, and if but slightly so, it is best to examine it by looking down through the open end of the tube. The color, if any, becomes deeper on standing some hours, but generally a few minutes will suffice to determine as to the purity of the spirit under consideration.

I have tried the above test on spirits of different strength, from absolute alcohol to proof spirit, and find that the water in the latter does not perceptibly affect the test, when the quantity of sulphuric acid used is equal to that of the spirit to which it is added.

ON CONCENTRATED INFUSIONS AND DECOCTIONS.

BY ISAIAH DECK, M.D., CHEMIST.

The advantages possessed by having infusions and decoctions concentrated to an extent that will ensure their keeping an indefinite period, combined with the certainty of their uniform strength, must be obvious to dispensers and apothecaries, who frequently may not have time to prepare them fresh as soon as the patient requires it, while a temperature above 65° is inimical to their keeping more than twenty-four hours if prepared in readiness.

The accompanying formulæ may fully be depended on in supplying all the desiderata of economy, convenience and uniformity of strength, in themselves and the Pharmacopœias, and have been introduced by the author many years and successfully used and testified to in hospitals and public dispensaries.

In preparing these infusions, where the ingredients contain much starch or glucose, add the *water only* for three or four hours, until the root or bark has absorbed a large quantity, then pour the liquor off and drain, add the spirit to the liquor, and then return the ingredients, and macerate the specified time, at a temperature between 75° and 85°,—frequently shaking.

The weights and measures are apothecaries—the water used distilled or rain, and cold or at the above temperature.

A small quantity of sugar coloring must be added to nearly all the infusions when poured off, to bring them to the required tinge ; and, instead of filtering it, is better to let them stand until they deposit, after pouring and straining off the dregs.

Care must be taken to keep them well corked and in a cool place:

Infus. aurant. comp., 1 part to 7 of water,
Cort. aurant., ℥ iv., cort. limonis, ℥ i., caryophill, ℥ i.,
Aqua, ℥ xxv., S V Rect., ℥ iij., stand three days.
The cloves are not to be bruised.

Infus. Colombœ, 1 part to 7 of water,
Rad. Colombœ, (whole,) ℥ v., aqua, ℥ xxiii.,
S V Rect., ℥ iv., stand four days—strain off 20 oz.

Infus. Caryophil., 1 to 7
Caryophil., (whole,) ℥ iij., aqua, ℥ xxiii.,
S V Rect., ℥ iij., stand six days—strain off 20 oz.

Infus. Cascarillæ, 1 to 7,
Cortex Cascarilla, ℥ xij., aqua, ℥ xxx.,
S V Rect., ℥ v., stand twelve days.
Strain and press, ℥ xx.

Infus. Gentian, comp., 1 to 7,

Rad. Gentian, ℥ ij., cort. aurantii, ℥ ij.,
Cort. Limonis, ℥ ij., aqua, ℥ xxx.,
S V Rect., ℥ iv., stand four days, strain ℥ xx.

Infus. Lupuli, (Humuli,) 1 to 7,
Ext. Lupuli, ℥ i., tinct. lupuli, ℥ vi.,
Aqua, ℥ xiv., dissolve and filter.

Infus. Quassiæ, 1 to 7,
Rasa Quassiæ, ℥ i., aqua, ℥ xviii.,
S V Rect., 2 oz., stand four days.

Infus. Rhæi, 1 to 7,

Steam ℥ iij. Rad. Rhæi for five minutes, cut into thin slices, then add—

Aqua, ℥ xxi., S V Rect., ℥ v., stand four days,
Strain, 20 oz.—do not press.

Infus. Rosæ, comp., 1 to 7,
Fol. Rosæ rub, ℥ iij.,

Macerate in 18 oz. of Aq. Rosæ for three days, strain gently in a cloth, without much pressure, filter, and add—

2 oz. Acid Sulph. Dil., and q. s. Syrup Papaver Rubri, or Syrup Mori, to make 22 oz.

Infus. Sennæ, comp., 1 part to 3 water,
Fol. Sennæ, parv., 6 oz., sliced ginger, ℥ ss.,
Aquæ, ℥ xiij., S V Rect., ℥ iii.,
Liquor. Potassæ, ʒ ss., stand four days—
Press strongly and stand till clear.

Infus. Chirayetta, 1 to 7,
Chirayettæ herba, 8 oz.,
Aqua, 26 oz.,
S V Rect., ℥ iij.
Let stand four days.

ON THE RAMÈE, A NEW FIBRE ADAPTED FOR TEXTILE MANUFACTURES.

It is well known that the common nettle (*urtica dioica*) yields an excellent fibre of great strength and considerable fineness, but from the smallness of the plant, and still more from the small proportion in which the fibre exists in the stem, no practical application has been made of it, although ladies have sometimes exhibited their perseverance and skill by the manufacture of polka jackets and other similar articles from it. Some time since specimens of a curious kind of cloth were brought to England from China, under the very absurd name of *grass cloth*—there, in Mandarin Chinese, it is called *Nia-pou*, (summer cloth,) and *ma-pou* or *ma-cloth*, the word *ma* being apparently applied to all fibre-yielding plants. According to the most accurate information which we possess, this cloth is made from the fibres of many plants, but the finest and most superior qualities are said to be produced from a kind of nettle, the *urtica nivea*, which grows to the height of five or six feet; supposed specimens of this fibre were exhibited at the Great Exhibition of 1851, as well as of another called *Callooee Kalmoi* or *Rami*, from Assam and other parts of Eastern India, which is said to be the produce of a distinct species of Urtica, the *Urtica* or *Boehmeria tenacissima* of Roxburgh. Professor Blume, of Leyden, who was formerly in the service of the Dutch East Indian Company, has brought under the notice of the public a new fibre, under the name of Ramée, the produce of the Islands of the Indian Archipelago, which he considers to be obtained from the *Boehmeria* (*urtica*) *utilis* (Blume). Whether this may not be the *Urtica tenacissima*, and the fibre the same as that already exhibited at London, is uncertain, but this is a point of secondary importance at present, as it would appear that the fibres of all the different species are, commercially speaking, nearly identical.

Two or three years since, by the advice of Dr. Blume, the Dutch Government attempted the cultivation of this plant in the Island of Java, but with very little success, in consequence of having planted it in rice fields; the Urtica being a genus of plants which require shade as well as moisture. Lately, however, the importance of this fibre has begun to be appreciated, and several trials have been made in order to bring it into use, especially in Germany, to the whole western parts of which, Holland is the great market for tropical products. These facts, and the great probability which exists of a great deficiency of hemp occurring in a short time, has induced us to direct attention to the subject, and to give a brief statement of all the information we have been able to collect upon the subject. This is a matter of special importance to Ireland, which, as being the centre of the linen manufacture, must inevitably become that of every manufacture connected with allied fibres.

The plant which yields the Ramée fibre is, like the nettle, a perennial plant, and like it can be propagated by dividing the roots. Its culture is very simple, and in this respect well suited for tropical countries; the roots are only torn or cut asunder, and the pieces planted at about three to four feet apart, the soil around being previously hoed a little. If planted under suitable conditions as to shade, &c., the roots rapidly throw out their stalks, to the height of from five to seven feet. As soon as the external rind has become thoroughly brown, it is cut down for the preparation of the fibre; experience has shown that it may be cut at least four times in the year, and that the first cutting yields four stems, the second six to eight, the third, ten to twelve, and the fourth sixteen to twenty; during succeeding years the produce is still greater, provided it be cut as close to the root as possible. The first cutting is usually rejected, but may be employed if cut a little earlier than the browning of the stem.

The preparation of the fibre is attended with some difficulty in consequence of the resistance of the woody part of the stem, and of a cork-like epidermis. The process followed in Borneo and Sumatra is very rude, and consists in steeping the plant in water for five or six days, and then stripping off the fibrous bark, which is dried, and afterwards exposed for several days to the action of the dew, and is then subjected to a very rude hackling. This imperfect process accounts for the very course and inferior fibre which is usually prepared in the East Indies, and there can be no doubt that if a perfect system of steeping and a suitable hackling machine were employed, that a very beautiful fibre might be produced. It is necessary, however, to remark, that the separation of the fibre would not require the long and tedious process required for flax. When well prepared the fibre is remarkably strong, and may be bleached of a perfect white, and in this state has a remarkably beautiful silk-like lustre. It was formerly much used in the Indian Archipelago to manufacture a kind of cloth, which was remarkable for its extraordinary durability as an article of clothing; this has, however, been entirely superseded by the cheap cottons of Manchester and Glasgow. Fishing nets are still made of it, and for this purpose it would be invaluable, as it appears to resist the action of water far better than common hemp, or indeed most other fibres. So far as the experiments made in Holland and Germany upon this material go, the following facts appear to be satisfactorily established: 1, that the Ramée fibre is fifty per cent. stronger than flax; 2, that it is stronger than the best European hemp, and less injured by wet; 3, that it gives less refuse than hemp; 4, that it can be spun finer than hemp, and at least as fine as the common low numbers of flax; and 5, that the Ramée, being a perennial plant, produces more fibre than any other known fibre-producing plant. Should further experience confirm these statements great benefits will be conferred upon industry by its immediate introduction as an article of commerce.

With the exception of parts of Spain, Naples, Sicily, and parts of Greece, it is not probable that the Ramée plant could be successfully cultivated in Europe; but there can be no doubt that it might be grown in every tropical country. There is one region which, after its native country, the East Indies, we believe to be more fitted than any other to produce it, and that is British Guiana. If it were introduced into that colony, which would be a very easy matter, it might become a great source of wealth to it, at the same time that it would afford us an excellent substitute for hemp, and its refuse an excellent material for the manufacture of paper.

[Since writing the above, we have seen a notice of a lecture delivered by Dr. Forbes Royle on "Indian Fibres fit for Textile Fabrics, or for Rope and Paper Making," at one of the last meetings of the Society of Arts. As he is, perhaps, the best living authority upon such subjects, any remarks of his are of great importance. According to him, we have boundless resources of material, not only for paper making but for cordage, in the white-fibred plants of India; such as the bow-string hemp, the aloe, the pita-fibre, the pine-apple, and, above all, the plantain, which would rival Manilla hemp or the American aloe, which bridged over broad rivers. The oakum of these plants might be converted into paper, and the fibres into fabrics of different qualities; and though they might not be fitted for making knots, they would answer for many kinds of ropes, which would be capable of bearing considerable strains. But it was important to find a substitute for Russian and Polish hemp, which we possessed not only in the hemp of the Himalaya, but in the various nettles which clothed the foot of these mountains, from Assam to the Sutlej. One of the latter, the Rheea fibre, (in all probability the same as the Ramée,) would not only undersell every other fibre, but in point of strength would take a position second to none of all the fibres at present imported. Some of these fibres had been made into a five inch rope, and had been tried at Messrs. Huddart's rope manufactory, when it was found that each square inch made from the wild rheea bore, in the first experiment, 844 lbs.; in the second, 894 lbs.; and that from the rheea fibre, 910 lbs.; while the average strength of rope make with the best hemp, and after numerous experiments, from the year 1803 to 1808, was 815 lbs. per square inch. In December last some experiments were made at the East India Company's military stores with fibres in equal weights and of equal lengths. The following are the results obtained—St. Petersburg hemp broke with a weight of 160 lbs.; Jubbulpore hemp, 190 lbs.; Wuckoonar fibre, 175 lbs.; Mudar or Yercum fibre, (common over all India,) 190 lbs.; China grass, 250 lbs.; *rheea fibre*, 320 lbs.; wild *rheeea* from Assam, 343 lbs.; the Rote Kangra hemp, no breakage at 400 lbs. This is the fibre of the plant known as the *Cannabis Sativa*, or Indian hemp, so well known for the remarkable narcotic action of its seeds and leaves, for which purpose it is extensively cultivated in every part of India. From the statement of Dr. Royle, it appears that the East India Company had ordered twenty tons of the rheea fibres, as well as of the Himalayan hemp, to be annually sent from India for the purpose of having them tried. Some of the rheea fibres lately sent by the Court of Directors to the Manchester Commercial Association have been valued by the Messrs. Marshall, of Leeds, at from £48 to £50 per ton.—***Dublin Jour. Indus. Progress.***]

ON QUININE.

BY DR. NEVINS.

Dr. Nevins delivered a lecture on "The Characteristics of Quinine and Quinidine." He said, in bringing this subject before the meeting, he regretted he should not be able to present any very striking facts, or to communicate any tests of such decisive and easy application, as to enable the members to ascertain with readiness and certainty even that quinidine is present, much less could he state any unexceptionable method by which its amount might be readily ascertained. He regretted also that much time would be occupied in pointing out the inaccuracies, real or apparent, in various tests which had been proposed for ascertaining the purity of quinine; but in doing this he did it with the hope that the defects in these tests might be shown to be apparent rather than real, and to arise from the omission in the description of some small matter of detail or point of manipulation, rather than from inherent defect, as every chemist must be aware how often a really good test fails, from the omission of some little matter of detail in the description, which has appeared self-evident to the proposer of it, and so has escaped mention. He did not propose to occupy the attention of the meeting with such adulterations as were fraudulent in every sense, both medicinally and commercially, such as starch, sugar, sulphate of lime, &c., but rather with those admixtures, viz., salicine, cinchonine, and especially quinidine, which possess medicinal properties similar to those of quinine, but are still frauds, because their price and value are inferior to those of the pure alkaloid. The first test he should mention was that proposed by Mr. Barry, in the fifth volume of the *Pharmaceutical Journal.* It is based upon the assumption, which was true at the time he proposed it, that all the probable adulterants were readily soluble in cold water, and it is so simple and elegant that a feeling of regret naturally arises to find it open to considerable error. Mr.

Barry says, "Take 12 grains of pure sulphate of quinine, and dissolve them by the aid of heat in 3500 grains of water. When the solution has become perfectly cold only a few feathery crystals will remain at the bottom of the bottle undissolved. Then take the same weight of the suspected salt, and dissolve it in the same quantity of water; if it remains *perfectly* dissolved it shows that the sample has been too soluble, therefore add another grain, and if it leaves about the same amount undissolved as the pure sample did, it will show that there have been 12 grains of sulphate of quinine in 13 grains of the adulterated compound. If, however, the 13 grains are perfectly soluble, add another grain, and so on." This test depends upon the pure sulphate of quinine being soluble in 291 parts of water, but Dr. Nevins took six grains of Howard's sulphate, and showed that they were not *perfectly* dissolved in 3500 grains of cold water, instead of that quantity of water being sufficient for 12 grains, as assumed in the test.

As a test for quinidine, it answered for 14 per cent., but failed when the proportion of quinidine amounted to 20 per cent., and beyond this it fails completely. In making this statement, however, the original error of taking 12 grains instead of 6, for 3500 grains of water, must be corrected. It must not be forgotten, that quinidine was unknown when the test was first proposed.

The next test mentioned was Schweitzer's ether test for cinchonine, which is very simple and correct. It depends upon the solubility of quinine in ether, but the insolubility of cinchonine in that liquid. On putting some sulphate of quinine, purposely mixed with sulphate of cinchonine, into a test tube, dissolving it in water by the addition of the smallest quantity of dilute sulphuric acid, and adding equal parts of liquor ammoniæ and ether mixed together, both the alkaloids are precipitated, but on shaking them up, the quinine is dissolved at once but the cinchonine remains perfectly insoluble at the line of separation of the two fluids. Now, a very similar test has been proposed by Mr. Robert Howard for the detection of quinidine, an account of which may be found in vol. xii. of the *Pharmaceutical Journal;* but Dr. Nevins stated that in his hands it had always failed, perhaps from some error of manipulation; and on performing this experiment before the meeting with quinine, purposely mixed with 10 per cent. of quinidine, the whole was redissolved, as if pure sulphate of quinine had been employed. In connection with this test, the lecturer observed he had found quinidine much more soluble in ether than it was usually represented to be. Pereira states that it requires "about 142 parts of ether at 62° F.," *Mat. Med.*, 3d. edit., p. 1656; and Van Heijningen that it requires about 90 parts, *Ph. Jour.*, 1849—50, p. 325. But Dr. Nevins took the washed precipitate from 15 grains of Herring's sulphate of quinidine, which amounted to nearly eleven grains of the alkaloid, and it was almost perfectly dissolved by f ʒ ij. of rectified ether, which is less than 10 parts, instead of 90 or 142. In reference also to the statement that it readily crystallizes from its ethereal solution, some of the solution was evaporated upon a watch-glass, but the alkaloid remained in a perfectly amorphous state, and in some which had been prepared in the same way several days previously, no crystalline form was perceptible.

As a means of detecting any considerable admixture of quinidine, the lecturer referred to Zimmer's test, *Ph. Jour.*, vol. xi., p. 393, as the best and easiest of application that he was acquainted with; but he showed that even with that test it was difficult to pronounce with any certainty upon the presence of five or six per cent. of quinidine, beyond what is met with in the purest commercial sulphate of quinine. All the experiments were performed with Howard's sulphate of quinine, and Howard's and Herring's sulphate of quinidine.

Dr. Nevins next alluded to a test proposed by Mr. Robert Howard, *Ph. Jour.*, vol. xi., p. 393, in which he says that 100 grains of sulphate of quinine are dissolved by f ʒ vij. of boiling water, whilst *eight* hundred grains of sulphate of quinidine are soluble in the same amount of water. This the lecturer thought must be a misprint, 800 having been printed instead of 300; for the first quantity was not dissolved, whilst he found that the latter was.

Dr. Nevins concluded by referring to several other tests,

none of which he regretted to say were positive in accurately distinguishing between quinine and quinidine. He also referred to the formation and peculiar properties of Herapathite, or the iodo-sulphate of quinine, several specimens of which, as well as samples of pure and adulterated quinine, he showed under the microscope.

With regard to the employment of salicine as an adulterant of quinine, it was very readily detected by the addition of a few drops of concentrated sulphuric acid to the suspected sample, when, if salicine were present, a blood-red color was produced, two other substances only, viz., veratria and piperin, producing the same reaction; but the presence of salicine might be corroborated by adding to the salt a small portion of bichromate of potassa and sulphuric acid, and heating, when, if salicine was present, the peculiar odor of hydruet of salicyl, or oil of meadow sweet, was distinctly perceptible.

The interest of the lecture was considerably increased by its being illustrated with a large number of experiments. A vote of thanks was unanimously passed to Dr. Nevins, and a very interesting discussion on several of the tests referred to was joined in by most of the members present.

Mr. Abraham then brought before the meeting the subject of the decimal currency, and proposed that a petition, signed by members of the Association, be presented to parliament in its favor.

The motion was seconded by Mr. Sumner, and carried.

It was announced that the next lecture would be delivered by Dr. Brett, on some original and important reactions of the vegetable alkaloids.—*Meeting Liverpool Chem. Ass.*, in *Pharm. Journ.*, June, 1854.

SYMPATHETIC INK.—Dissolve 1 oz. of oxide cobalt at a gentle heat, with 4 oz. of nitro muriatic acid, till no more is dissolved, then add 1 oz. of common salt and 16 ozs. of water.—*Beasley.*

ON LUPULINE.

BY J. PERSONNE.

Lupuline is the yellow powder so readily obtained by rubbing the catkins of hops. To this powder the peculiar properties of the hops, their bitterness and aroma, are due. It has been investigated by D. Ivey, of New York, and by Payen and Chevalier. (Also by Dr. Rudolph Wagner.*)

Lupuline furnishes both volatile and non-volatile bodies to boiling water. When distilled with water, an acid and an essential oil pass over as volatile constituents. The non-volatile substances are an organic acid and nitrogenous bitter matter, both of which are soluble in water. The author has not investigated these any further.

The *volatile acid*, determined by the analysis of the salts of silver, baryta and copper, is valerianic acid, of which lupuline contains about one per cent.

The *volatile oil* is lighter than water, becomes resinified in the air, and acquires acid properties. The boiling point rises from 284° to 572° F. By fractional distillation, the author separated it into two different oils. One boils between 302°–320° F., the other at 572° F. Both have the constitution $C^{22} H^{18} O^{2}$; they turn the plane of polarization to the right, and do not solidify at 0° F. Concentrated sulphuric acid dissolves them with a red color; they are again separated by water, and the sulphuric acid then furnishes with baryta a salt of a conjugate sulpho-acid; nitric acid converts them partly into resin and partly into valerianic acid. If let fall in drops upon hydrate of potash, they are converted into a hydrocarbon of the formula $C^{10} H^{8}$, with formation of carbonic and valerianic acids. If this hydrocarbon be deducted from the oil, $C^{22} H^{18} O^{2} — C^{10} H^{8} = C^{12} H^{10} O^{2}$, the latter expresses the valerole which Gerhardt prepared from valerianic acid. The hydrocarbon of

* See *Chem. Gaz.*, vol. xi., p. 272.

the oil of hops, however, furnishes no Borneo camphor, and it has also a smell more like that of thymene.

The large quantity of resin contained in lupuline renders it difficult to obtain valerole from it. The solid resinous mass left after exhaustion with water consequently still contains much of this substance. If it be distilled with lime, taking care that it is not carbonized, Chancel's aldehyde of valerianic acid goes over; its composition is $C^{10} H^{10} O^{2}$. It boils at 194° F., and is rendered brown and resinous by potash, and very readily reduces salts of silver. Its specific gravity was 0·8009 at 68° F.—*Comptes Rendus*, March 20, 1854.

DETECTION OF POPPY OR NUT OIL IN OLIVE OIL.

BY E. MARCHAND.

In consequence of the frequent adulteration of olive oil, the author had occasion to examine the various methods of detecting it, and has found that the use of sulphuric acid gave satisfactory results.

He describes the process thus—When four drops of olive, poppy, or nut oil are placed separately upon a slab of porcelain, and two drops of pure concentrated sulphuric acid added, and mixed with the oils by inclining the slab to one side and the other, the following phænomena are observed.

Olive Oil acquires, at the points of contact with the acid, a yellow color passing into orange; the liquid portion surrounding the magma rapidly becomes dirty gray, and then brownish-black, while the yellow color first produced by the acid gradually passes into bright chesnut-brown. There is never any appearance of blue or lilac tints.

Poppy Oil acquires, immediately at the points of contact with the acid, a fine lemon-yellow color, which becomes rapidly darker at some parts. The liquid portion in contact with the colored portions never acquires the dirty gray color characteristic of olive oil. After the reaction has continued for ten or fifteen minutes, there is observed, at several points of the liquid portion which immediately borders upon the colored part, a rose color, passing rapidly into bright lilac, and gradually increasing in intensity. After half or three-quarters of an hour, the lilac color passes into a violet blue, while the original yellow gradually becomes dull brown.

Nut Oil behaves almost exactly the same as olive oil, except that the yellow substance is more abundant, more rapidly formed, and becomes brown more rapidly, so that within less than ten minutes it acquires a chestnut color. Sulphuric acid is far more easily miscible with this oil than with olive or poppy oil. The gray border, which is characteristic of olive oil, is produced with nut oil as well; but in this case, instead of gradually becoming black, it passes rapidly into olive green. This oil never produces a tint of lilac.

Mixtures of Olive and Poppy Oils may be tested by means of the above reactions. After a certain time, the colors characteristic of poppy oil, pink, lilac, violet, blue, present themselves successively, with an intensity proportionate to the quantity of poppy oil present. Marchand states, that, with practice, one-tenth poppy oil in olive oil may be detected with certainty by this method.

Mixtures of Olive and Nut Oils.—When the nut oil amounts to one-fourth of the whole, sulphuric acid produces a bright orange-yellow color, with a gray border, the innermost parts of which pass into olive green. A mixture of equal parts of both oils gives an orange yellow color, with a very distinct gray border, which soon becomes greenish and brown at the outer edge. When the mixture contains three-fourths nut oil, a reddish-yellow color is produced, surrounded by an olive-green bordrr, paler than that produced with pure nut oil.

Mixtures of Poppy and Nut Oils acquire with sulphuric acid a yellow color, and at the borders a grayish tint, gradually diffusing itself over the liquid part. When the mixture contains one-fourth nut oil, an intense lilac is subsequently produced, while the yellow color passes into chestnut brown. When the mixture contains three-fourths nut oil, an orange yellow is produced, with gray borders, passing at certain points into olive green. Subsequently the yellow becomes bright chestnut-brown.—*Jour. de Pharm.*, October, 1853, and *Pharmaceutical Journal.*

UREA IN ITS RELATIONS TO THE GENERAL PHENOMENA OF ANIMAL PHYSIOLOGY.

BY TH. BISCHOFF.

There is no longer any doubt that accurate knowledge of the phenomena of animal organisms can only be acquired by the aid of a more intimate acquaintance with the unceasing chemical metamorphoses which take place in them. These changes must be understood, not only qualitatively but quantitatively, before our views on the subject can possess any scientific precision.

Towards the attainment of this object much has already been achieved, but indefinitely more remains to be done. This is particularly the case with regard to the metamorphoses of the nitrogenous constituents of the organism which are justly considered to be of such predominant importance in its actual activity. The history of the nitrogenous elements of food is at the present time incomparably more extended and minute than formerly. So likewise the study of the nitrogenous excretions, particularly urea, has been abundantly and productively cultivated. No doubt is entertained that it is derived from the nitrogenous elements of food, but with regard to quantitative and even qualitative relations which obtain between them there is the greatest uncertainty and diversity of opinion.

While some regard urea as the ultimate product of a series of metamorphoses of the nitrogenous elements of food which can be developed only in the living organism and by the action of the organs, others entertain the opinion that the albumen of the blood is converted directly into urea, even in the blood.

According to the former view, urea, independently of some other less important nitrogenous excretions, might be regarded as a quantitative measure of metamorphoses in the nitrogenous organs, a circumstance which would be of incalculable value with reference to the functions and agency of these organs. Such a proceeding is, however, inconsistent with the latter view, which represents the quantity of urea as dependent upon the accidental quantity of albumen in the blood.

An unprejudiced consideration of the researches which have hitherto been instituted for the purpose of deciding these questions, will at once show that they are altogether unsatisfactory. For on the one hand the chemical methods adopted for the quantitative estimation of urea were either liable to inaccuracy, or involved troublesome and tedious operations, which were applicable only in a few particular instances. On the other hand, it was certain that the constitution of urine and the quantitative relation of its several constituents are variably influenced by so many circumstances, that a correct insight into its qualitative importance and quantitative excretion could only be attained from a very great number of observations, and when the conditions under which they were made were exceedingly varied, and at the same time well known and definite.

If, therefore, the relation of urea to the general functions of life are to be more exactly investigated, and if the quantity in which it is excreted is to be recognized as the measure of metamorphosis of nitrogenous constituents of the organism, a method must be found for its quantitative estimation which will be at once certain, facile, and rapid in its execution.

Such a method has been contrived by Professor Liebig, which, with a little practice, admits of an estimation of urea being made in a quarter of an hour. I have in this manner instituted a large number of experiments with human urine and that of dogs and rabbits. The quantity of urea that the dog formed under the most diverse conditions of feeding was daily estimated during a whole year. The same was done for a period of five months with a rabbit.

For the human organism I have only endeavered to ascertain the quantitative relations of urea under the normal circumstances of life, during long periods, and for individuals of different sex and age. The results which have thus been obtained present very considerable discrepancies with the statements previously made.*

In the case of the animals mentioned, however, I have more especially convinced myself that the determining conditions for the formation and excretion of urea are far more variable and multiform than has hitherto been supposed, and that they are influenced by circumstances so numerous and changeable that there is still a necessity for a much larger accumulation of accurate observations before the laws of this excretion and its correlative phenomena can be definitely evolved.

Although at present we can only consider the first step as having been taken, I believe that I have obtained some results which, while they remove previous doubt and present the subject under new aspects, may perhaps serve as the basis of further research.

Among these results are the following:

1. Urea is unquestionably under all circumstances the measure of the metamorphosis of nitrogenous constituents of the organism. It never originates from a direct metamorphosis of the albumen of the blood and vascular system. It is formed in the blood only from gelatin, and this perhaps never enters the blood unaltered in the normal conditions of life. The urea in this case is not a product of the metamorphosis of solid portions of the organism.

2. But, although urea always originates in this manner from the metamorphosis in the organs, still the quantity and quality of the food exercise a far greater influence upon the production of urea and the general metamorphosis than could hitherto have been supposed. It is, indeed, true that urea is formed and excreted under a total deprivation of food; but the per centage of nitrogen in the food exercises so great an influence upon the quantity, that when, for example, the dog on which I made my observations consumed in twenty-four hours 4,000 grms. of cow flesh, without fat or bone, he ex-

creted in the same time 190 grms. of urea, while with 500 grms. of potato, and 250 grms. of fat, the quantity excreted was only six to eight grms.

Food destitute of nitrogen, such as fat, under all circumstances produces a limitation of the metamorphosis of the nitrogenous portions of the organism. At the same time there is, in most instances, *cæteris paribus*, a diminution in the quantity of urea excreted, but not always. When the food consists solely of fat both consequences obtain; the excretion of urea as well as the metamorphosis is diminished. The same is the case with a very full flesh diet. With a flesh diet merely sufficient for maintaining the weight of the body, fat limits the metamorphosis, but the quantity of urea excreted is not necessarily diminished at the same time; it may indeed become greater than that excreted when the same quantity of flesh is consumed without fat, in accordance with a law stated subsequently.

3. It has moreover been found that the quantity of nitrogen in the food or portions of the organism metamorphosed within a certain period, never appears entirely as urea, but that a certain, and under some circumstances considerable, part must be excreted in another form. This is likewise true in the case of dogs, although their urine does not contain uric acid, and scarcely a trace of other nitrogenous organic substances. Only very small quantities of nitrogen are excreted in the fæces, and as this is also true with regard to the lungs and skin, according to admirable researches of Regnault and Reiset, it is difficult to form a correct opinion as to the form in which that part of the nitrogen of metamorphosed portions of the organism that is not found in the urine is excreted. It is most probable that this deficiency is owing to a partial conversion of urea in the blood, or perhaps even in the bladder, into carbonate of ammonia, which is excreted, either by the skin and lungs or in the urine. However worthy of confidence the observations of Regnault and Reiset may be, I am still of opinion, that it has not hitherto been possible to continue them for a sufficiently long period, and under the necessary alterations of diet for determining, with absolute certainty, whether

or not carbonate of ammonia is excreted by the skin and lungs. The presence of carbonate of ammonia in the urine would be very probable, at least when, even with an exclusively flesh diet, or under a deprivation of food, it was alkaline while quite fresh and effervesced on the addition of an acid.

The quantity of nitrogen of the metamorphosed portions of the organism, which does not make its appearance as urea, is upon the whole tolerably constant under very diverse circumstances of diet and metamorphosis. It was found greatest, both relatively and absolutely, under a deficient supply of nitrogenous food (250 grms. of flesh). It might in this case amount to more than two-thirds of the total nitrogen of the metamorphosed tissues. With a supply of nitrogenous food adequate for maintaining the body (500 grms of flesh) it amounted to one-third. Under a very full and excessive flesh diet it was smaller absolutely than in the above cases, and was consequently so much reduced, relatively, as to be almost insignificant. I regard these facts as the strongest evidence that the original product of metamorphosis of nitrogenous tissues is solely urea, of which a certain portion experiences a further change—into carbonate of ammonia—proportionately greater when the quantity of urea is large than when it is small. The presence of fat in the food appears, under certain circumstances, to prevent or limit this further alteration of urea. It is owing to this influence that, although fat, as already remarked, limits the metamorphosis, and consequently the formation of urea upon the whole, still, under a diet consisting of flesh and fat, the quantity of urea excreted may become greater than when the same quantity of flesh is taken without fat, because the nitrogen of the metamorphosed tissues remains in the form of urea. I am of opinion that fat exerts this influence by virtue of its connexion with the process of respiration. Lastly, water exercises an influence upon the deficiency of nitrogen appearing as urea. Thus, for instance :

4. The quantities of water and urea always bear a very constant relation to each other. No other constituent of the urine has so decided an influence upon its density as urea. Dense urine always contains much urea; specifically light

urine is always poor in urea. Nevertheless, the quantity of urea excreted upon the whole, within a given period, is related in the most intimate manner with the quantity of water, and *cæteris paribus* a large quantity of urine carries off more urea than a small quantity passed in the same time, although its specific gravity may fall considerably at the same time.

This influence of water may be owing to several circumstances—an increased facility in the solution and extraction of urea; perhaps also to an increased facility in the formation of urea. But it is moreover quite certain that water has an influence upon the quantity of urea in so far as the time and rapidity with which the urine is evacuated depend upon its greater or less quantity. In the presence of much water the urea formed is very rapidly separated from the blood and from the organism. There is not much time then for any further alteration of the urea, and consequently its quantity is greater, while the quantity of nitrogen not in the form of urea becomes less. Hence it is more particularly explicable why with different quantities of nitrogenous food (flesh); with little there is a comparatively and even absolutely great deficiency of nitrogen in the state of urea, and with much flesh, on the contrary, little deficit. For in the former case the quantity of urine passed is very small, often only a few cubic centimeters during several days; in the latter, on the contrary, very great, amounting to 1,200 or 1,500 cubic centimeters in twenty-four hours.

It follows from these facts, perhaps with certainty, that the quantity of urea excreted under certain circumstances, and within a certain time, cannot be taken as the direct measure of metamorphosis in the tissues, even when the urine does not contain any other nitrogenous constituent. Still it will always be the most important element for ascertaining its amount, and it will only be necessary to study more closely the influences exerted upon its formation and excretion, towards the elimination of which I hope to have furnished some contribution.—*Annalen der Chemie und Pharmacie*, October, 1853.

ON THE USE OF HYDROGEN AS A CALORIFIC AGENT.

BY DR. HENRY HARTSHORNE.

Dr. Henry Hartshorne made the following remarks on the use of hydrogen as a calorific agent: The practicability and convenience of cooking and warming rooms or houses by gas has been proved by numerous and sufficient trials. Its advantages over the ordinary employment of anthracite are obviously immense, except in the one item of *expense*. Those interested in the subject have, therefore, been waiting in anticipation of a possible reduction in the price of gas. According to a calculation based upon statements made by Mr. Mayer, who has devised and put in use an excellent gas-cooking apparatus, it would require the reduction of gas to *one-half* its present cost to the consumer, in order to make its use in ranges and stoves as economical as that of coal. If gas were but $1 per thousand feet, the end would be gained.

But, instead of reduction, a proposition has been recently made in the City Councils to *increase* the price of gas, on account of the greater present expense of the materials from which it is made. In view of this fact, and of the very high price of the coal used for domestic purposes, two questions are very naturally suggested: 1. Can a *cheaper* quality of the ordinary luminous gas be made, containing less carbon, and therefore unfit for light, but well adapted to calorific use? 2. If that be impracticable, cannot some *other* gas be substituted for this purpose, as, for instance, hydrogen?

If either of these inquiries may be answered in the affirmative, it will have an important bearing on the interests of all householders. For, if light is an object of consequence, heat is still more indispensable; if light ever has been and must be expensive, heat for cooking and warming our domicils must ever require a still greater expenditure. The contrast between the old-fashioned, dull, and disagreeable glimmering of oil lamps and the delightful convenience of gas is not by any means so great as would be the change from the time-reconciled use of coal-bins, coal-scuttles, shovels, and ash-barrels, to the clean and comfortable substitute of simple gas-burners arranged in Mr. Mayer's stoves.

Putting aside, for the present, the question as to the possibility of making a cheap hydro-carbonous gas for heating purposes, let us consider the subject of hydrogen, as this gas is known to produce more heat in burning than any other substance.

There are at least three ways of manufacturing hydrogen gas.

1. By decomposing water through the means of the voltaic battery.

2. By the action of dilute sulphuric acid upon zinc or iron filings.

3. By passing the vapor of water over iron filings, heated to an intense redness, or over coke.

The first of these methods has, perhaps, the greatest scientific beauty. Take, for example, a Bunsen's battery of a large number of cells; immerse the wires in water, the vessels containing which is divided by a septum into two parts; at the one pole will be given off hydrogen—at the other, oxygen gas, in the proportion of two volumes to one. The gases may be collected in separate reservoirs, and rejoined in a jet at the desired place, on the plan of Dr. Hare's compound blow-pipe. The most intense heat can thus be generated.

Unless, however, as Professor Frazer has suggested, some improvement in the adaptation of the battery be obtained, so as to make the residue of the process available in some way, this plan of producing heat appears to be outside the pale of *economy.*

With regard to the second method, the same objection would probably apply; a considerable amount of zinc or iron, as well as of sulphuric acid, being consumed in the process, and the resulting compound having but little value.

As to the third method, Dr. Kennedy informs us that in some parts of New England, hydrogen gas is manufactured by passing steam over heated iron filings, in order to *dilute* a luminous gas made from resin. The substitution of coke for the iron filings has been devised by M. Gaillard, of Paris, who constructed a burner in which a jet of hydrogen made luminous a platinum wick; and the expense of this process, apart from the platinum, Dr. Rand believes to have been but thirty cents per thousand feet. The experiment has been repeated, in part at least, at the gas-works in this city. Now, if the cost of hydrogen used as a calorific gas be but thirty cents per thousand feet at the gas-holder, it will be an interesting inquiry easily solved by those familiar with gas manufacture, at what cost the same gas can be furnished, through main, pipes, and metres, *to the consumer?*

This, therefore, is the question intended to be suggested by these remarks; and, with a view of eliciting important information with regard to it, I make the following distinct proposition:

I propose, as the most convenient and desirable mode of supplying heat for cooking and warming purposes, the use of *hydrogen gas*, manufactured by passing the vapor of water over coke at a sufficient temperature, distributed through apparatus similar to that now in use for luminous gas, and applied by means of stoves, heaters, and ranges of such construction as shall prove, upon trial, to be the best.

I submit that if this can be done at a cost to the consumer of not more than $1 per thousand cubic feet, it will be equal in economy to the ordinary use of anthracite, and vastly superior in comfort, cleanliness, and convenience. One very great advantage, affecting even the health, is, that hydrogen produces *only water* in burning. The objection apparent at first sight in regard to the necessity, were such a plan approved, of creating new works, pipes, metres, &c., for the calorific gas, in addition to those already laid for the luminous carbo-hydrogen, is really null. The whole matter turns upon the question of expense. If it *pays*, it should be done, precisely as all who can afford it have pipes with warm water to supply their bath rooms, with none the less readiness because they already have had cold water pipes in the same place.

The remarks gave rise to an interesting discussion, which was participated in by Professor Frazer, Dr. Rand, Dr. Hartshorne, Dr. Kennedy, and Mr. Williams. At the request of Dr. Hartshorne, the subject was referred to the Committee on Science and the Arts for investigation.—*Extracted from the Proceedings, in Journal Franklin Institute.*

ON PREPARED CITRATE OF MAGNESIA.

BY CHARLES ELLIS.

The article which is the subject of this notice is called *Prepared Citrate of Magnesia*, to distinguish it from soluble citrate, an account of which will be found im the *American Journal of Pharmacy*, vol. xxiv., page 115, by Edward Parrish.

Citrate of magnesia has within a comparatively short period of time been introduced into very general use. It is so destitute of bitterness or unpleasant taste that its preference as an aperient medicine over the nauseous potion of epsom salts is readily accounted for.

The liquid citrate which is so favorite a remedy with physicians, whenever a saline cathartic is indicated, is one of the most eligible preparations of its kind yet introduced to the notice of the faculty. It is in consequence of its popularity that enquiries have been made for an article of similar properties *in powder.*

To render the "soluble citrate" pleasant to the taste and capable of forming an effervescing solution when dissolved in water, it is necessary to combine with it sugar, and either bicarbonate of soda or potash, with the requisite quantity of citric or tartaric acid to decompose the latter.

If citric acid be used, care must be observed to dry it over a water-bath, so as to deprive it of water of crystallization, previous to its combination with the alkaline bicarbonates.

The *prepared citrate of magnesia* is not recommended as equal to the *solution*, because the citrate in powder, however carefully prepared, is only slowly soluble in cold water, and does not readily make a clear solution.

When such a preparation, however, is wanted, the following formula is submitted as having been found in practice to answer the desired purpose.

The *soluble citrate* used is that made by the formula published in a previous volume of this Journal, and referred to in the first part of this notice—

Take Magnesiæ citras,	℥ iv.
Sacchari pulv.,	℥ viij.
Acid citric, *vel* tartaric, pulv.,	℥ iiss.
Soda bicarb.,	℥ iij.
Ol. Limonis,	gtt. xx.

Combine the acid and sugar, and rub into a fine powder, (if citric acid is used dry all the water out over a water-bath,) add the magnesiæ citras and ol. limonis, and mix intimately; then the bicarb. of soda, and triturate the whole into a fine powder, which must be preserved in bottles properly excluded from the air. The dose for an adult is from one to three tablespoonfuls mixed in a tumbler of water, and drank in a state of effervescence.—*Am. Jour. of Pharmacy.*

ON THE MARSH LEECHES OF MONT SALUT (LANDES).

EXTRACT OF A REPORT TO THE ACADEMY OF MEDICINE FOR A COMMISSION.

A Mr. Rollet owning some real estate in the "Landes," (France,) which was almost worthless in point of productive capability, and having a number of cows who eked out a miserable support on rushes and brambles bethought himself that as the marshes on the land contained leeches, that the best mode of turning the property to some utility would be to tend leeches and feed them at the expense of the cows, but the number of cattle was too small for that purpose, so he bought more, and these manuring the ground made it more fertile, and thus the cows fattened, and made better provender for the leeches. He thus writes in a report to the Academy (Paris):

"I employ the following simple and natural method in my ponds. When the little leeches appear at the surface of the water, an animal, not an old broken-down horse, but a fat and well-fed cow, is introduced into the pond. The noise made by walking into the water, and the odor of the animal, attract a great number of these little creatures, who in a moment attach themselves to the limbs of the animal, and cast about to find under the hair the tenderest parts of the skin, where they attach themselves and become gorged with a rich blood, and then naturally tumble down into the water, having enlarged so considerably that they resemble very much little puddings before being cooked. This is a good feast!—such as will require many days, many weeks of digestion, but which pushes the leeches on from the state of youth to become much larger, and after a succession of similar feasts the leeches pass in the first year to the state of middle size, and at the end of 18 months attain the size of leeches fit for reproduction."

Mr. Rollet found it necessary to modify his ponds to divide the leeches from one another, so that the cows might be driven in at different points, and thus feed a larger number of leeches. He proceeds:

"I began then by emptying my natural marshes by means of trenches, and thanks to a natural slope I emptied them completely to the turf, except some places towards the side, which I left covered; here I placed the leeches which I could not feed heretofore. They emigrated almost wholly; a few only made their nests, but they placed them at four inches above the surface of the water, for, in spite of my drainage, the head water still rolled in to give that depth. This position of the nests gave me instantly the key to my plans. I carried some peaty earth to the middle of my marsh, and formed it into some islands of 1 metre (39 inches) wide and

40 centimetres above the surface of the water. Then gradually guided by experience, I made grass to grow on these islands as well as on the banks of the marsh, and fenced them round; but, as the soil was not solid, I carted on quantities of gravel, and thus obtained a firm footing for my cows. These latter did not stay long quiet here; the leeches in vain chased them, very few of them could get a bite. I then had the thought to fix up mangers in the interior of the islands, and to deposit the fodder there for the cows, so as to prevent them moving about. It happened, both by the disposal and by the number of cows placed together in the pond, that all the leeches left the earth, and were able to nourish themselves at the same time—an immense advantage.

"Just as a cow had been well bitten, it left the pond and freed itself from these leeches which had not fallen off in its passage. In this way the cow did not suffer from much loss of blood. This process was carried on only in fine weather, first once a week, then twice, for in the second week there only came those leeches which had digested their food or had been lazy the first time. The cows were left in one or even two hours, or a little over, in the pond at a time. Those cows, better fed than ordinary, fattened instead of thinned. The milk they gave was of good quality, as determined by repeated analysis, and of more than usual quantity."

Mr. R. constructed a second pond, of a larger size, after the same plan, and placed in it 12,000 leeches, fished up when fat out of the first basin. The leeches he bred were those indigenous to the Landes, and he says he carefully avoided purchasing leeches from Hungary. Those indigenous leeches he describes as large, healthy, bear transport well, require little care, and are in demand with the Pharmaciens of Bordeaux. Mr. R. keeps 60 cows for feeding the leeches inhabiting a basin the area of which was one-fourth of a hectory (a square of 310 yards each side).

Mr. R. believes it to be productive even in such narrow basins, which is interesting to hygiene. He counted as many as 300 nests in an island 1 metre long, which would give an average of 3,000 leeches in the same space, and, perhaps, thus to be able to supply the demand in Bordeaux, and thus lower the cost of these animals.

The conditions necessary for rearing leeches are:

1. A natural pond, divided into many compartments or islets covered with grass, with a southern exposure, and raised 40 to 50 centimetres above water, by 1 metre wide, surrounded by floors, and fitted with mangers, a few metres apart, the whole forming many distinct compartments.

2. To keep the water of the ponds at a constant level.

3. To breed only indigenous leeches, if possible.

4. To have a firm bottom to the pond.

5. To have a large number of well fed animals, so that no particular one may suffer from too much depletion, that they be driven in only twice a week, and then in fine weather, and so that all the leeches of each compartment may have the opportunity to bite on the same day.

6. To establish a reservoir for "disgorging," made of the earth of the marsh, so that the leeches may deposit their nests there and prevent their escape.

Mr. Coyard, who raises leeches in the marshes of Strasburg, feeds them with horses; and Mr. Guenard, at Courtenay, on the Loire, uses these animals also. The latter gentlemen has remarked that leeches have an unusual liking for the blood of sheep, which animal they immediately attack should one happen to stray into the pond.—Condensed Extract from *Journ. de Pharm.*, May, 1854.

ON IODIDE OF SODIUM.

BY WM. PROCTOR, JR.

Among the new remedies (or, perhaps, old remedies in new forms) is iodide of sodium, which has been called for by several physicians in this city.

It may be economically and easily made by the following recipe.

Take of Iodine, two ounces,
Iron filings, an ounce,
Carbonate of soda, in crystals, two and a half ounces.
Water, a sufficient quantity.

Mix the iodine with six fluid ounces of water in a flask, add the iron filings, and agitate them together till the reaction ceases and all the iodine is combined; throw the whole on a filter, and when the solution has passed, wash and filter with water till the whole measures a pint. Dissolve the carbonate of soda in half a pint of water, and add it to the solution of iodide of iron, till it ceases to produce a precipitate of carbonate of iron; then heat the mixture nearly to the boiling point, filter and wash the residue on the filter with half a pint of water, and add it to the filtered liquid. Lastly, evaporate this in a porcelain capsule, till a pellicle begins to form, and set it aside to crystallize by cooling. Pour off the mother liquid from the crystals when formed, and again evaporate and crystallize.

Iodide of sodium may also be made precisely as directed for iodide of potassium in the United States Pharmacopœia, substituting caustic soda for caustic potassa; but indepedent of the fact, that pure caustic soda is expensive, it is necessary in deoxidizing the iodate of soda to avoid contact of air, else there is a loss of iodine with the formation of carbonate of soda.

Iodide of sodium obtained as above, by the cooling of a hot solution, crystallizes in white anhydrous cubes. When formed by spontaneous evaporation it contains four equiv. of water of crystallization. The crystals are striated oblique rhombic prisms, melt when gently warmed, and on being heated lose their water, leaving dry iodide of sodium. The hydrated iodide is more stable when exposed to the air than the anhydrous salt, but is more deliquescent, and very soluble. (*Gmelin.*)—*Am. Journal of Pharmacy.*

UNGUENTUM HYDRARGYRI NITRATIS.

During the proceedings of the Chemical Discussion Society, London, Janury 26, 1854,

Mr. Greenish read a prescription for making an ointment composed of unguentum hydrargyri nitratis and creosote. It was very troublesome to mix in the first instance, but when, apparently a satisfactory result had been attained, slow decomposition ensued, resulting in a kind of fermentation, the lid of the pot being pushed off, and, after a lapse of twenty-four hours, no odor of creosote remaining.

Mr. Williams explained the cause of the decomposition, and stated that if creosote was dissolved in glacial acetic acid, and the solution added to strong nitric acid, and the mixture left for some days, a great number of crystals of oxalic acid were produced, while carbonic acid was evolved. This result could not be obtained by adding the creosote direct to the nitric acid, as the action was then so violent as to cause more complicated results. He imagined that the lard, &c., in the ointment acted in a similar manner to the glacial acetic acid in his experiments, namely, by diluting the active agent, and moderating the subsequent reactions. Thus he conceived the ultimate result of adding creosote to the ung. hyd. nitr. was the production of oxalate of mercury, and the carbonic acid formed at the same time caused the ointment to swell, and so become unfit for use. If no free acid had existed in the ointment, no such result would occur.

Mr. Collins suggested that the ungt. hyd. nitr. might contain free acid, which was often left in it in order to leave it soft and of a good color.

Mr. Greenish thought the ointment should be prepared at a low temperature, in order to prevent decomposition of the nitrate of mercury, and thus prevent the occurrence of free acid in the ointment. He thought it unwise to sacrifice the efficiency of the ointment to its color and consistence.

Mr. Hopkin begged to differ entirely from Mr. Greenish.

He thought the ointment could be prepared of a good color and soft consistence, perfectly free from the acid. The plan he adopts is to raise the temperature of the melted lard, &c., in a water bath, and add the solution of mercury in the nitric acid as soon as complete, which increases the temperature also very much ; a brisk effervescence ensues, and he keeps it constantly stirred until it no longer tastes acid, and he has always found the result satisfactory.

Mr. Spencer stated that in preparing this ointment a reaction took place between the nitric acid and the oleic acid which not only got rid of any nitric acid which might be present, but converted the oleic into elaïdic acid. If this process was conducted at a low temperature, the elaïdic acid formed would give rise to a solid product, but if the temperature were raised a further decomposition was effected. The free acid was decomposed, and the resulting ointment was of the color and consistence of butter, and kept good for a length of time.

The experience of several members present was certainly in favor of making the ointment at a raised temperature.

Mr. Greenish stated that he had found that after washing the ointment in distilled water, the creosote could be mixed with it without decomposition ; and he further observed that the ung. hyd. nitr. mixed with the ung. sulphuris of the old Pharmacopœia became speedily discolored; but, as in the new Pharmacopœia, the Ol. Bergamotte was omitted, this did not now take place, and might lead to some confusion if the cause was not distinctly pointed out.

Mr. Hopkin mentioned a somewhat similar circumstance, which had occurred in his own experience, except that instead of slow decomposition, rapid action and inflammation (?) had arisen from the dropping of creosote on to oxide of silver, ordered in a prescription. He warned members to be careful of an explosion if they should happen to have such materials to mix together.—*Chemist*, May, 1854.

Varieties.

DR. STENHOUSE'S CHARCOAL RESPIRATOR FOR PURIFYING THE AIR BY FILTRATION.

Of the London Pharmaceutical Society, March 1, 1854.

Mr. Allchin brought this subject under the notice of the meeting, and exhibited the apparatus and some of its effects. The respirator, which was made by Messrs. Ferguson and Sons, of Smithfield, under the direction of Dr. Stenhouse, consists of a wire-gauze case, made sufficiently large to cover the mouth and nose. The edges are formed of lead, and are padded and lined with velvet, so that it can be easily made to fit tightly to the face, to the exclusion of all air except that which passes through the instrument, which is filled with freshly burned charcoal. There is also a small opening closed with a wire-gauze screen, by means of which the charcoal can be removed and re-introduced at pleasure.

The following is Dr. Stenhouse's paper on the subject, which, with a slight modification, has already appeared in the *Journal of the Society of Arts:*

"The powerful effects of freshly burned wood charcoal, especially when coarsely powdered, in absorbing gases and vapors, have been long known. Hence the limited extent to which charcoal has been occasionally employed to sweeten fetid water, and animal substances in the incipient stages of putrefaction. Sufficient attention has not, I think, however, been hitherto bestowed upon a second and still more important effect which charcoal exerts upon those complex products of decomposition, viz., that of rapidly oxidizing them, and resolving them into the simplest combinations they are capable of forming.

"When coals or wood are burned with an inadequate supply of air, a variable amount of intermediate or secondary products is generated, constituting what are called soot and smoke; when, on the other hand, the combustion of the fuel is conducted with an adequate supply of oxygen and a sufficiently high temperature, carbonic acid, water, ammonia, with, perhaps, a little nitric acid, are almost the sole products.

"The putrefaction of animal and vegetable substances is likewise, in general, a process of imperfect oxidation. Hence, under ordinary circumstances, when this is the case, a variety of more or less complex secondary products is formed, which usually possess very disagreeable odors, and exert exceedingly injurious effects upon the animal economy. To these substances the general name of *miasmata* has been given. Not much is known of their nature, but they are believed to be heavy, complex, nitrogenated vapors, which are decomposed by oxygen, chlorine, sulphurous acid, nitric acid, and other disinfecting agents.

"My attention was particularly drawn to the importance of charcoal as a disinfecting agent by my friend, John Turnbull, Esq., of Glasgow, the well-known extensive chemical manufacturer. Mr. Turnbull, about nine months ago, placed the bodies of two dogs in a wooden box, on a layer of charcoal powder, of a few inches in depth, and covered them over with a quantity of the same material. Though the box was quite open, and kept in his laboratory, no effluvia was ever perceptible, and on examining the bodies of the animals at the end of six months, scarcely anything remained of them except the bones. Mr. Turnbull sent me a portion of the charcoal powder which had been most closely in contact with the bodies of the dogs. I submitted it for examination to one of my pupils, Mr. Turner, who found it contained comparatively little ammonia, not a trace of sulphuretted hydrogen, but very appreciable quantities of nitric and sulphuric acids, with acid phosphate of lime.

" Mr. Turner subsequently, about three months ago, buried two rats in about two inches of charcoal powder, and a few days afterwards the body of a full-grown cat was similarly treated. Though the bodies of these animals are now in a highly putrid state, not the slightest odor is perceptible in the laboratory.

" From this short statement of facts, the utility of charcoal powder, as a means of preventing noxious effluvia from churchyards and from dead bodies in other situations, such as on board ship, is sufficiently evident. Covering a churchyard to the depth of from two to three inches with coarsely powdered charcoal would effectually prevent any putrid exhalations ever finding their way into the atmosphere. Charcoal powder also greatly favors the rapid decomposition of the dead bodies with which it is in contact, so that in the course of six or eight months little is left except the bones.

" In the modern systems of chemistry, such, for instance, as the last edition of '*Turner's Elements*,' charcoal is described as possessing antiseptic properties, while the very reverse is the fact. Common salt, nitre, corrosive sublimate, arsenious acid, alcohol, camphor, creosote, and most essential oils, are certainly antiseptic substances, and, therefore, retard the decay of animal and vegetable matters. Charcoal, on the contrary, as we have just seen, greatly facilitates the oxidization—and, consequently, the decomposition—of any organic substances with which it is in contact. It is, therefore, the very opposite of an antiseptic."

I find, indeed, a recognition of the oxidizing action of charcoal in the fifth edition of *Brande's Manual of Chemistry*, at page 511, where the following paragraph occurs:

" According to Vogel, when recently ignited charcoal, which has been cooled under mercury, is put into a jar of atmospheric air, it absorbs the oxygen of the air to a much greater extent than the nitrogen.—*Schweigger's Jonrnal*, iv. A piece of well-burned charcoal, cooled under mercury, and then introduced into a mixture of oxygen and sulphuretted hydrogen gases, rapidly absorbed them, and then became ignited and caused explosion.—*A. Taylor.*"

" The object of the present paper, however, is chiefly an application of the absorbent and oxidizing properties of charcoal, which, so far as I am aware, has never yet been proposed; viz., to employ a new species of respirator filled with powdered animal charcoal, to absorb and destroy any miasmata or infectious particles present in the air in the case of fever and cholera hospitals, and of districts infected by ague, yellow fever, and similar diseases. I have got such a respirator made by Ferguson and Sons, Smithfield, instrument makers to St. Bartholomew's Hospital. It fits closely to the lower portion of the face, extending from the chin to within half an inch of the eyes, and projects about an inch on either side of the mouth. It, therefore, includes the nostrils as well as the mouth. The frame of the respirator is made of thin sheet-copper, but the edges are formed of lead, and are padded and lined with velvet, so that it can be easily made to fit tightly to the face. The powdered charcoal is kept in its place by means of two sheets of fine wire gauze, from a quarter to an eighth of an inch apart. As the body of the apparatus is metallic, it has been electro-plated with silver. Electro-plating the respirator with platinum or gold would certainly be an improvement. There is a small opening closed with a wire gauze screw, by means of which the respirator can be filled with charcoal or emptied at pleasure. The respirator is kept in its place by an elastic band passing round the back part of the head. I have employed *animal* charcoal as the more porous substance, but I* should think wood charcoal would answer perfectly well. The object in view is, by filtering the air through such a porous substance as animal charcoal, to intercept the miasmata which may have got mixed with it.

These, I think, cannot fail to be absorbed by the pores of the charcoal, where they will be rapidly oxidated and destroyed by the condensed oxygen, with which they will be brought into the most intimate contact. The probability of this expectation being realized is greatly strengthened by the results of repeated trials with the respirator on certain noxious and offensive gases, such as ammonia, sulphuretted hydrogen, hydrosulphate of ammonia, and chlorine. I have found that air, strongly impregnated with these gases, and which could not be respired for any length of time under ordinary circumstances, may be breathed with impunity when the charcoal respirator is worn, the odor of these gases being rendered almost, if not altogether, imperceptible. Any other highly porous substance, such for instance as spongy platinum, or pounded pumice-stone, might probably be found to answer perfectly well for filling the respirator, but I have selected charcoal as the cheapest and most easily available material.

"While the filtration of water through charcoal powder and other porous substances has been advantageously practised for many centuries, the object in view being to deprive the water of numerous impurities diffused through it, which produce injurious effects on the animal economy, it is certainly somewhat remarkable that the very obvious application of a similar proceeding to the lighter fluid in which we live, viz., air, which not unfrequently contains even more noxious impurities floating in it than are usually present in water, should have, up to the present time, been so unaccountably overlooked.

"In addition to the precaution of wearing such a respirator as that just described, persons necessitated to live in especially pestiferous districts might have their houses made as air-tight as possible, with the exception of such openings as are necessary to maintain a proper amount of ventilation. By means of these openings the air could be freely admitted through gauze into which the requisite quantity of charcoal had been quilted. The doors of such houses could also be made double, and be constructed of coarse cloth, likewise containing a thin layer of charcoal powder. As an additional precaution, if it were thought desirable, the walls, floors, and ceilings of houses in very unhealthy districts, could be easily lined with mattresses filled with a couple of inches of charcoal powder. Were these and similar precautions adopted, I confidently anticipate that Europeans would be enabled to reside with comparative impunity in some of the hitherto most pestilential districts in the world.',

* Since the above was written, I have ascertained that wood charcoal is even more efficacious than animal charcoal.--J. S.

[The tubs containing the animals, covered with about an inch of charcoal, were then shown to the meeting, but not a trace of unpleasant smell was perceptible.]

Mr. Whipple could bear testimony to the great power of the charcoal respirator, which Dr. Stenhouse had allowed him to try at St. Bartholomew's Hospital. He was so satisfied of its value for certain purposes, that he intended keeping one for use in the laboratory.

Mr. Jacob Bell alluded to the very important application which was made of charcoal, and especially of peat charcoal, in deodorizing excrementitious matter to be used as manure.

Mr. Allchin thought that in this application of charcoal it was important to bear in mind, that, according to Dr. Stenhouse, the charcoal not only deodorized, but at the same time oxidized and destroyed those substances, such as urea and ammonia, which were the most valuable constituents of manures.

Dr. Garrod thought that sufficient evidence had not been adduced by Dr. Stenhouse to prove that charcoal caused the oxidation of substances which were absorbed by it. Certainly such an effect was not quickly produced, for when the active principles of vegetables were absorbed by it and rendered inert, as he had proved by numerous experiments, they could afterwards be extracted in an unaltered state.

Mr. Porrett said, that from what had been recently advanced on the subject, it would appear that charcoal exerted a twofold action; namely, that of absorbing certain substances and condensing gases within its pores, which had long been known, and that of causing oxidation through the influence of condensed oxygen contained in its pores, which was a new idea. This second action was similar to that exerted by spongy platinum. He thought it was important to ascertain from experiment the extent to which each of these actions took effect in certain cases.

PREPARATION OF PARAFFIN AND PURE ACETIC ACID UPON A LARGE SCALE FROM THE DISTILLATION PRODUCTS OF WOOD.

BY REINHOLD V. REICHENBACH.

The author having had occasion to prepare a large quantity of pure paraffin, was desirous of adopting some less tedious process than that by which his father obtained this substance in the first instance. Under these circumstances he was induced to try the action of sulphuric acid at a high temperature, supposing that it would then be more efficacious in destroying the empyreumatic substance mixed with the paraffin. For this purpose he half filled a large glass retort with fuming sulphuric acid, and added one-third its weight of well pressed raw paraffin. The temperature was gradually raised in a sand bath until distillation began, and after a time he found that the whole of the paraffin had passed over and presented an appearance of perfect whiteness and purity.

From the success of this operation, he applied the method to the preparation of pure acetic acid. The substance employed was the ordinary raw acetate of soda. This salt, containing a large quantity of empyreumatic resin, yielded, when distilled with concentrated sulphuric acid, about half its quantity of very strong acetic acid, which was clear, perfectly colorless, and free from any empyreumatic odor. It was not until the temperature was raised, in order to continue the distillation, that the distillate began to present a brownish-yellow color, and at the same time a peculiar turbidity. Both these circumstances appeared to be owing to some other cause than the presence of empyreumatic admixtures, and they were found to result from a decomposition of sulphuric acid, by the carbonaceous matter in the retort, and a consequent distillation of sulphur with the acetic acid. The turbid and somewhat colored acid was rendered perfectly pure by redistillation.

The author then endeavored to conduct the distillation in such a manner as to prevent this inconvenience. The layer of acetate and sulphuric acid next to the heated wall of the retort would obviously become dry first, and acquire a temperature sufficient to set up a reaction between the sulphuric acid and carbonaceous substance. He, therefore, interrupted the distillation at this moment, and after well stirring the contents of the retort continued it again. By repeating this two or three times he succeeded in drawing over almost the whole of the acetic acid clear and colorless.

The product thus obtained, of course, contained sulphurous acid, and traces of sulphuric acid, carried over mechanically. This objectionable circumstance cannot be altogether avoided, even when pure acetate is used; but both substances may be easily separated by the addition of a little peroxide of manganese or lead together with a simple redistillation.

The form of apparatus afterwards employed by the author was a basin-shaped vessel of cast-iron, with a broad-flat rim, upon which fitted a flat lid, with a copper dome in the centre, capable of being cooled by a stream of water. The iron-lid may be removed at intervals, when the distillation is interrupted for the purpose of stirring the contents with shovels. He has thus been able to prepare about a hundred-weight of pure concentrated acetic acid daily.—*Jahrbuch der K. K. geologischen Reichsanstalt, Jahrg.* iii., No. 2, in ***Pharm. Journ.***

Responsibility of the Pharmaceutical Chemist.—When a serious accident occurs from the administration of an overdose of a strong medicine, the first inquiry which is made is, whether it was taken under medical advice? When this was not the case the next inquiry is, where was it procured—did the chemist give the needful directions? If the result was fatal, this leads to a searching investigation at the inquest, and unless the chemist can show that he used proper precautions, he may expect to receive a reprimand from the coroner, or a similar expression in a rider, appended to the verdict of the jury.

Sometimes the reflections cast upon the chemist on these occasions are unjust, and he is held to be responsible for the imprudence or carelessness of persons who either disregarded his instructions or gave him no opportunity of furnishing the requisite information. At a recent inquest on a lady, who died from taking lozenges containing calomel, the coroner and the jury imputed blame to the chemist for alleged negligence in this respect. We have reported several cases of fatal accidents to sheep from the use of a wash containing arsenic, and have had occasion to point out what appeared to us to be undue severity in the verdict against the vendor. In proportion to the progress of education among pharmaceutists more is expected of them, and a qualified man is more likely to be severely dealt with, in the event of an accident arising from drugs purchased of him, than a huckster or general dealer would have been under similar circumstances. The reason is obvious : in the former case the purchaser trusts to the experience of a person in whom he has confidence, in the latter he takes the responsibility on himself.

In the case of patent or secret medicines the responsibility rests chiefly with the purchaser. He sees an advertisement recommending a medicine in strong terms as a certain cure for a variety of disorders, and " to be had of all respectable chemists, grocers," &c. He applies to a chemist who is ignorant of the composition or properties of the medicine, and executes the order without pledging himself to the veracity of the advertisement or the printed envelope. If he were to recommend it, or express a favorable opinion as to its qualities, he would, to some extent, make himself responsible, and in the event of mischief arising from its use, he would be liable to censure. The maker of a proprietary medicine or nostrum would incur liability if it should prove deleterious or dangerous, while he recommends it as a safe remedy, and this is the case also where a medicine is administered casually across the counter. We have always maintained that the qualified pharmaceutical chemist is less likely to incur such risk, than one who is not acquainted with his business; first, because his knowledge enables him to guard against danger; secondly, because, having a character to lose, he has an additional inducement to be cautious. It is now generally admitted that *posology*, or a knowledge of the doses of medicines, forms a necessary part of the education of the pharmaceutist, and this is included among the subjects of examinasion at the Pharmaceutical Society. The possession of this knowledge does not imply any interference with the province of the medical practitioner, but it is requisite as a precaution against accidents, and for the convenience of the public in the use of domestic medicines in cases where medical advice is not necessary. It is also important that the dispenser should be able, from his knowledge of the ordinary doses, to prevent mischief in the event of a mistake occurring in a prescription. To what extent he would be responsible for failing to guard against the consequences of such an oversight, is a question which would depend on circumstances. If, for example, the mistake were an important one, resulting in loss of life, the chemist could scarcely exculpate himself, although sanctioned by medical authority; for it is well known that all men are occasionally liable to accidents, and it is one of the duties of the dispenser to exercise his sagacity and prudence when a " *lapsus pennæ*" comes under his observation.—*Ibid.*

Manufacture of Alum from the Residuum of the Distillation of Boghead Cannel Coal.—It has been found that some varieties of coal, more especially that kind known as Boghead cannel coal, after having been distilled and exposed to the action of steam in retorts, furnishes an ash which contains a considerable quantity of alumina, in a state in which it is readily dissolved by acids, and which is capable of being used in the manufacture of sulphate of alumina. For this purpose, in Barlow's process, (dated April 15th, 1851,) the ash is introduced into a pan or boiler, with a sufficient quantity of dilute sulphuric acid, and it is heated so as to dissolve the alumina and form a solution of sulphate of alumina. The boiler which is employed for this purpose has a vertical partition perforated with holes, which divides it into two compartments. The ash of the Boghead cannel coal is placed in one compartment, and heat is applied under the alumina from it, while the undissolved silica contained in the ash remains in the compartment which is not exposed to the direct heat of the fire. The sulphate of alumina thus obtained is mixed with solution of sulphate of potash or ammonia, and the alum is crystallized in the ordinary manner.

Instead of employing the ash resulting from the treatment by steam of the residue of Boghead cannel coal, this residue may be employed in the manufacture of alum without such treatment by steam, in which case the residue is first used as fuel to heat the pans, and the ashes obtained from its combustion are placed in the pans and heated with dilute sulphuric acid in the way above mentioned.

Mr. Laming's mode (dated August 12, 1852) of obtaining alum from Boghead, or other coal of a like nature, is as follows: The coke is burned in the open air to reduce it to a white ash, care being taken that the ignited coke never lies in heaps of more than a few inches thickness, and that its temperature never rises from any cause high enough to fuse together the alumina and the silica with which this kind of coke abounds. The white ash thus made or obtained in any other manner is lixiviated in leaden vessels, with repeated doses of hot sulphuric acid, (the strength may be about seventy or eighty per cent.,) until the ash is nearly exhausted of alumina. The solutions thus obtained are again heated and used for lixiviating one or more portions of fresh ash, each dose of the acid being withdrawn as it acquires its maximum quantity of alumina. The iron with which the solution of ammonia is contaminated may be removed by the ordinary means. The solution is then to be concentrated by evaporation, or the sulphate of alumina may be made into alum in the usual way. Sometimes, instead of first reducing the coke to a white ash, the coke itself is lixiviated in the manner described.—*Pharmaceutical Journal*, June, 1854.

On the Relative Values of the Different Kinds of Meat as Food.—By Marchal, of Calvi.—M. Marchal took twenty grammes of the muscles of the pig, ox, sheep, calf, and hen, which contained neither sinews or cellular tissue, or adhering fat, except what naturally exists between the muscular fibres, and dried them in a water-bath for several days, and thus ascertained the loss which each sustained by desication. The following are his results in 100 parts:

	First Experiment.		*Second Experiment.*	
	Solid Matter.	Water.	Solid Matter.	Water.
Pork	29·45	70·55	30·25	69·75
Beef	27·70	72·30	27·50	72·50
Wether Mutton	26·65	73·45	26·35	73·65
Chicken	26·35	73·65	26·30	73·70
Veal	26·00	74·00	25·55	74·45

According to these numbers we should arrange the meats in the following order of their relative nutritive powers—pork, beef, mutton, chicken, veal. This order is, however, not the true one, because the leanest meat contains a certain amount of fat, and because this substance is not so important an article of food as the pure muscles, it is necessary to ascertain how much a certain quantity of meats contain, before we can judge properly of its relative nutritive value. M. Marchal accordingly treated the dried flesh with ether, to dissolve out the fat, and obtained the following results :

	Fat soluble in ether.	Pure muscle insoluble in ether.
Beef	2·54	24·95
Chicken	1·40	24·87
Pork	5·97	24·27
Mutton	2 96	23·38
Veal	2·87	22·67

The last table shows that the true order should be, beef, chicken, pork, mutton, and veal, a result which experience confirms. (It may, however, be remarked that there is considerable difference between the same kind of meat derived from different animals, and that the same amount of two different kinds of beef-broth, both containing the same amount of water, may have very different nutritive values. Further investigations are required upon this point.)—*Comptes Rendus de l'Academie*, 1852. No. 16.

NON-SOLUBILITY OF MORPHIA IN CHLOROFORM.—M. Saint Lager having written a note to the Society of Pharmacy, (Paris,) stating that morphia could be dissolved by chloroform, Mr. Le Page, Pharmacien, on the contrary, asserts that morphine and its salts are quite insoluble in chloroform. He also states that the sulphate and hydrochlorate are but little soluble in fatty bodies when cold ; when they are heated the salts dissolve readily in these. The morphine salts do not dissolve in sweet oil or oil of almonds ; and Souberain remarks that the use of an oleaginous preparation of morphine are inadmissible, but that advantage might be taken of the use of glycerine as prepared by Cass. Thus a *glycerole* of morphia may be an useful sedative embrocation, and may be prepared thus—

Acetate of Morphia.............................. 1 gramme.
Glycerine.......................................100 grammes.

Solution may be accomplished by heat or cold.

Condensed from *Jour. de Pharm.*, April, 1854.

MODE OF USING BI-SULPHATE OF SODA AS A SUBSTITUTE FOR CREAM OF TARTAR AND ALUM.—The use of this substitute in the dyeing of woollen goods is becoming more general every day, in consequence of the saving of nearly one hundred per cent. effected by it. The colors in the preparations of which it has hitherto been employed are chrome-black, chrome-brown, grey, all fancy colors, green, carmine, blue. A decoction made in four pounds of the bi-sulphate has the same effect as four pounds of alum and two pounds of tartar; in the dyeing of some colors some alum is, however, still employed. For every fifty pounds of wool to be dyed of a chrome-black, one pound of chromate of potash and one-half pound of the substitute are required. The wool is to be introduced at a temperature of 190° F., then boiled for fifty minutes, and dyed in a fresh bath of brazil wood, containing, according to the shade, one-quarter to one-half pound of the dye-wood. To dye the same quantity of wool of a chrome-brown, one pound of chromate of potash, one and one-half pounds of substitute and half a pound of alum are employed. The wool is boiled for one hour, and then dyed in a bath of logwood; or for a yellowish brown and bronze shade, in a bath composed of fustic, Brazil wood and logwood in certain proportions. In the dyeing of green some add alum to the substitute, and throw the substitue, in the proportion of half a pound to ten pounds of wool, directly into the dye-bath, omitting altogether the previous boiling.—*Deutsche Musterzeitung*, No. 6, 1853.

Method of Communicating a Dull Black Color to Brass.—According to M. Leykauf, a dull black color, such as is frequently employed for optical instruments, may be given to brass, by first carefully rubbing the object with tripoli, then washing it with a very dilute solution of a mixture of one part of neutral nitrate of tin and two parts of chloride of gold, and then wiping off the excess of liquid, after the lapse of ten minutes, with a wet cloth. If there has been no excess of acid, the surface of the metal will have assumed a dark black color. The neutral nitrate of tin may be prepared by decomposing the perchloride with ammonia, and dissolving the precipitated oxide thus obtained in nitric acid.—*Le Technologiste.*

Syrup of Elderberries (Sambucus Canadensis) as a Substitute for the Compound Syrup of Sarsaparilla.—By W. H. Worthington, of West Chester, Pa. (*Med. Reporter.*)—There being much dissatisfaction attending the use of the compound syrup of sarsaparilla in the hands of some physicians, the syrup of elderberries was recommended to my notice by Dr. Benjamin H. Stratton, of Mount Holly, N. J., who for some years has been in the habit of using it in all cases of disease in which an alternative action upon the system was desired, and for which the sarsaparilla is usually employed. In the treatment of gout, chronic rheumatism, eruptive and syphilitic affections, he has used it combined with the iodide of potassium, with marked benefit. The formula used by him is the following:

℞ Juice of elderberries, Oxvj.
Sugar crystal, lbxvj.

Mix and boil to a syrup; after allowing it to cool, add to every pint of syrup one ounce of the best fourth proof French brandy, bottling and keeping in a cool place Dose, from a desert to a tablespoonful three times a day.

Flattering myself that an improvement could be made in the preparation of the above syrup without injury, I have prepared a compound syrup of elderberries, containing some, if not all, of the most active ingredients of the compound syrup of sarsaparilla (*Guaiaci lignum and Sennæ fol.*); by this means, as I think, increasing the alterative virtues of the syrup, giving it a more marked and active character in the treatment of gout, rheumatism, &c., than it possessed without them. To this syrup may be added the iodide of potassium to suit the views of those prescribing. The formula is as follows:

℞ Juice of elderberries, Oxvj.
Sugar crystal, lb.xvj.
Guaiacum wood, ℥ iv.
Senna leaves, ℥ iii.

Put the sennæ fol. and the guaiac lig. in three pints of water, boiling it down one-half, and strain. Put the juice and sugar in a kettle, place it on the fire, and when it comes to a boil add the decoction of guaiac. lig. and sennæ fol., allow it to boil to a syrup, when it must be taken off, strained, and let to cool. To every pint of syrup add one ounce of the best fourth proof French brandy, bottling, and keeping in a cool place.

Dose, the same as preceding.

The syrup of elderberries is given to the profession chiefly upon the recommendation of Dr. Stratton, whose skill and experience as a practitioner is entitled to the confidence of his medical brethren. If, as he believes, it possesses more certain and prompt remedial virtues as an alternative than sarsaparilla, it ought to be added to our catalogue of officinal articles. The difficulty of obtaining at all times good sarsaparilla, and especially in the country, increase the claims of this syrup upon our rural practitioners, who can command with facility, and in great abundance, the material for its preparation.—*Charleston Med. Journ.*

Employment of Glycerine in Diseases of the Skin.—(*Journ. de Med. et de Chir. Praetiques*, Feb.)—M. Cap read a notice on glycerine, which he asserted was serviceable in most affections of the skin. It penetrates easily into the pores, softens the surface, cicatrises fissures and openings. Its usage is indicated in all cutaneous diseases which fatty substances would irritate. Excellent effects have been observed from it in eczema, zona, acne, icthuosis, and it is much preferable to the oil of Cade or the lotions of (corrosive sublimate). Glycerine can be employed simply, or added to various medicaments. It unites in all proportions with water used for burns and other wounds, it preserves them from exposure to air, and keeps their edges in a supple and moist state. When it is added to cataplasms, it keeps them in a moist state, and, which is important, it prevents their borders adhering to the receiving surfaces.

Glycerine can be added to aqueous and alcoholic fluids, being also incorporated with lard, ointments, pomades, and soaps. It can serve as a basis for liniments and embrocations. It can be united to extracts, tinctures, medicated wines, and thus can serve in almost all medicinal compounds and those employed in surgery, adding to each substance its soothing, sedative, softening properties upon the tissues, and disposing them to the absorption of the medicinal substances to which it is united. This substance should, therefore, form the basis of a new class of remedies, to which we may give the name glycerole.—*Ibid.*

The Seeds of Asparagus a Substitute for Coffee.—Baron Liebig has discovered that the seeds of asparagus contain large portions of tannin analogous to that which is found in coffee, and, therefore, may be found a substitute for that delicious and universally-adopted beverage. They have been tested in England, and found to possess all the richness, flavor, and aroma of the best Mocha coffee. This will be interesting information to the consumers of coffee, as the imported article now commands an exorbitant price in our markets, while the asparagus is easily cultivated and prolific in its yield.—*Boston Med. and Surg. Journ.*

AMERICAN PHARMACEUTICAL ASSOCIATION.

The American Pharmaceutical Association met at the Mechanics' Institute, Cincinnati, July 25th, 1854, at eleven o'clock, a.m. In the absence of William A. Brewer, of Boston, President of the Association, the meeting was called to order by C. B. Guthrie, Vice-President, of Memphis, Tennessee. In the absence of the Recording Secretary, Edward Parrish, Esq., of Philadelphia, E. S. Wayne, of Cincinnati, was appointed Secretary, pro tem.

A Committee of Credentials, consisting of Wm. B. Chapman, M.D., of Cincinnati, Wm. Proctor, Jr., of Philadelphia, and C. Augustus Smith, of Kentucky, was appointed to the chair, who subsequently reported the following list of delegates and gentlemen who are properly recommended for membership, viz.:

From the Philadelphia College of Pharmacy: Henry C. Blair, Charles Ellis, John H. Ecky, Charles Bullock, Charles H. Dingee.

From the College of Pharmacy of the City of New York: Geo. D. Coggeshall, Benj. Canavan, Eugene Dupuy, John Meakim.

From the Massachusetts College of Pharmacy: William A. Brewer, Samuel M. Colcord, Daniel Henchman, Joseph Burnett, Henry W. Lincoln.

From the Cincinnati College of Pharmacy: A. M. Stevens, Theodore Marsh, William Coolidge, E. S. Wayne, W. M. M. Gordon.

The following persons were, on recommendation of the Committee on Credentials, elected members of the Association, and signed the Constitution and By-Laws, viz., Lewis Rehfuss, W. S. Merrill, W. C. Arons, and W. Adderly, of Cincinnati, and Hamilton Creighton, of Xenia.

The roll being called, the following members were found to be present:

Samuel M. Colcord, C. Augustus Smith, Wm. Proctor, Jr., C. B. Guthrie, W. B. Chapman, Henry T. Cummings, Wm. C. Arons, Wm. H. Adderly, Wm. S. Merrill, Hamilton Creighton, E. S. Wayne, W. H. Coolidge, A. M. Stevens, T. Marsh, W. J. M. Gordon, Lewis Rehfuss.

On motion, a committee was selected to nominate officers for the Association. The members of this committee were appointed by the respective delegates as follows:

Wm. Proctor, Jr., of Philadelphia, S. M. Colcord, of Boston, Wm. H. Coolidge, and C. A. Smith, Cin., Henry T. Cummings, of Portland, Maine, and H. Creighton, of Xenia.

The committee reported the following nominations:

For President—W. B. Chapman, M.D., Cincinnati, Ohio.

For Vice President—Henry T. Cummings, M.D., Portland, Me.; Joseph Laidley, of Va.; and John Meakim, of New York.

For Recording Secretary—E. S. Wayne, of Cincinnati, Ohio.

For Corresponding Secretary—Wm. Proctor, Jr., of Philadelphia.

For Treasurer—Samuel M. Colcord, of Boston.

For Executive Committee—Edward Parrish, of Philadelphia, A. M Stevens, of Cincinnati, and C. B. Guthrie, M.D., of Memphis, Tenn.

The report was accepted, and, on a ballot being taken, the nominations were unanimously confirmed by the Association.

Dr. Chapman, the President, was conducted to the chair, and returned thanks for the honor shown him.

The Association adjourned until three, p.m.

AFTERNOON SESSION.

Members generally present—Dr. W. B. Chapman, President, in the chair.

The annual report of the Treasurer was read and referred to A. M. Stevens and H. T. Cummings to be audited.

The report of the Executive Committee was read by Professor Proctor and accepted.

The report of the Committee on Certificates was read.

Professor Proctor read an interesting paper on Pharmaceutical education.

It took high grounds calculated to encourage the Pharmaceutists of the United States to give more attention to those under their care, and to induce young men to devote their leisure to a better purpose, and in time become prominent and useful members of the profession of pharmacy.

The Professor recommended an address which accompanied the report.

The Association ordered it to be printed and extensively circulated.

By an inquiry extended to all sections of the Union, the committee ascertained that a vital defect existed in the very budding process of pharmaceutical education—the apprenticeship. In all the pharmaceutical institutions of Europe, where degrees are granted to apothecaries, the preliminary service in the shop is a *sine qua non* to admissions to the examinations, it being generally four years, and in many of them the attendance on lectures follows this term of practical initiation into the duties of the shop and laboratory. In England, and some of the Atlantic cities, particularly in Philadelphia, a system of apprenticeship exists, yet it scarcely happens that a lad is legally indentured.

The causes assigned for the ill supply of competent clerks arises primarily from the want of a correct feeling of the dignity and responsibility of the calling of the apothecary, as a branch of the medical profession.

Many buy their preparations ready made, except the simple ones, and at the lowest price; and the business, thus *shorn* of its most interesting department, the application of chemistry to the conversion of crude drugs into medicines, becomes a mere store keeping, where the drug clerk is kept putting up and selling parcels and bottles of medicine, the preparations of which, and the beautiful reactions often concerned in their manufacture, he is a complete stranger to, as though they did not exist.

Making the officinal preparations is, therefore, an indispensable part of pharmacizitical education, and no apothecary, whose scheme of business does not include, at least, a considerable portion of them can efficiently educate those under his care.

The same gentleman, Chairman of the Committee, appointed last year, to whom the circular of instructions, issued by the Secretary of the Treasury, was committed, made an extended report, which was adopted.

The same gentleman, Chairman of the Committee to whom was referred the subject of the expediency of endeavoring to obtain such congress and action as will compel all special examiners of drugs and medicines to be either graduates of pharmacy or to receive certificates of qualification for such office from some college of pharmacy recognized by the Association, reported that application had been made by letter to a prominent member of Congress, but received no encouragement to proceed further. They believe, in view of the partizan character of political appointments, and the little dependence that can be placed on the judgment of the appointing power in cases like the one under consideration, it will be inexpedient to make any application to Congress until such time as the drug law itself may require a general change or re-enactment, when a clause might be inserted making it obligatory on the Secretary of the Treasury to appoint fully qualified pharmaceutists, or persons who have been educated as such.

The same gentleman, Chairman of the Committee to consider that part of the report of the Committee on the Inspection of Drugs, relating to the fixing of standards of quality for those drugs capable of it, together with the appropriate tests for detecting adulterations when practicable, made an able report, which was read and adopted.

A communication was read from Gustavus L. Simmons, of Sacramento City, correspondent of the Association, giving a report of the state of pharmacy in the State of California, for the past year. He states that there are 77 drug stores in that State.

Dr. Guthrie, from the Committee on the subject of "Home Adulterations," asked further time to report, which was granted. Many interesting facts were mentioned as to adulterations of drugs both in Eastern and Western cities. It was stated that for several years there is shipped from Cincinnati to the East tons of the outside bark of the Sycamore tree, which is an inert powder, and can only be intended to adulterate some compound.

Professor Proctor made a report on the subject of quack medicines, which closed with the following suggestions:

1st. That this desire for medicine can be gratified in a legitimate way by regular official preparations.

2d. That it is the duty as well as interest of the apothecaries and druggists to advocate the use of the official medicines in lieu of the quackery of the day.

3d. That it is the rightful interest of regular pharmaceutists to divert the thousands, which now annually flow into the coffers of quacks, into their own limited stores, where of right it belongs.

4th. This can only be done by a united and sustained action on the part of the pharmaceutists and druggists of the Union, by which they will *practically* refrain from the sale or advocation of secret medicines and substitute regular official compounds for them, correctly labelled with name and directions for use.

5th. This course should receive the sanction of physicians as the only one likely to remedy the evil, as the tendency to take medicine *ad libitum* is a feature of the Anglo-Saxon race, duly inherited by the American people, which, whatever may be its faults, is as much their nature as is the love of political and personal freedom.

With regard to the propriety and efficacy of Legislative action, we think that movements in that direction should originate in the several States, and be the joint action of the medical and pharmaceutical professions, and when applications are made to Legislatures they should be based on a real interest on the part of druggists and apothecaries generally, to abate the evil, and not on a partial or very local movement.

An evening session was held, the proceedings of which will be given to-morrow.

[The continuation of the proceedings of the Association, not having reached us in time, will be given in the September number.

It is much to be regretted that the entire delegation from New York has been prevented from attending, owing to the prevalence of cholera in this city. We perceive that other cities on our seaboard have also been poorly represented, owing to the epidemic visitation.]

EDITORIAL.

The London Pharmaceutical Society have had in progress of execution, by Mr. Wyon, a medal commemorative of the late Dr. Periera, which will shortly be completed, the cost to be defrayed by voluntary subscription, the amount of which has been already received. The same society have also established a "Council Medal" for prizes, which is intended as a substitute for books.

A Dr. Griseler has observed that a few drops of nitric (nitrous?) ether added to rancid oil destroys the disagreeable odor, and that the oil thus treated, when heated, loses its turbidity, and that a few drops of this ether added previously prevents vanudity being produced. This action is produced no doubt by oxidation, and has little advantage, that we can see, over bichumate of potass and sulphuric acid or nitric acid.

The number of patent medicine vendors in England, in 1852, was 8,379, and in Scotland, 604, and the number of chemists and druggists in both countries, 7,000. In Ireland, the number of apothecaries is a little under 600, of whom 129 are in Dublin and the vicinity. The number of those who sell medicine as druggists is about 400 additional, making in the British isles the total number about 17,000. The number of apothecaries in this city is about 400.

The American Pharmaceutical Association hold their annual meeting on the last Tuesday of July, in the city of Cincinnati. We are of course precluded from having a full notice of the proceedings in our columns this present number. The association has already been of great service, and is highly deserving of the support of the pharmaceutists of the United States. Formed as it is of the select men from each city and state it represents the intelligence of the profession better than any other body, and its proceedings are generally of benefit to the community as well as the profession.

At the seventh annual meeting of the American Medical Association, held at St. Louis, Mobile, in the first week of May, Dr. C. B. Guthrie offered the following resolutions, which were unanimously carried:

"Resolved—That in the Secretary of the Treasury's recommendation to Congress to abolish or materially modify the duty on such crude drugs not producible in this country, as are used in the laboratories of the country in the manufacture of chemicals, we recognise a wise provision for the further protection of the profession and the community at large, from impure and sophisticated medicines.

"Resolved—That a copy of this resolution be signed by the proper officers of this Association, and the same be transmitted to the Secretary of the Treasury and to the Committee on Ways and Means."

We agree with this resolution as far as it goes; we are inclined, however, to go farther. If it be desirable to admit drugs *free* which are intended for laboratory use, why not admit those for medicinal use generally for the same reason?

Professor Doremus states, in the *American Medical Monthly*, having examined several gallons of soda water lately in which he detected *copper* as carbonate held in solution by carbonic acid, the quantity found in one quart being equal to 1½ grains of metallic copper, and from the same liquid 0.65 of lead (metallic). He examined the soda water which was bottled, and found it to be devoid of either copper or lead. This is contrary to the experiments of Dr. Ellet, who found lead in all forms of soda water. He concludes by recommending condensers of stone, iron, or block tin, with conducting pipes of tin or gutta percha, the latter of which he thinks unexceptionable. Both of these materials for piping are objectionable, for the reasons stated in our February number, (page 94,) where we have already discussed this matter.

We believe that it is the *fewer* number of druggists who use tinned copper condensers. Cast-iron is the material most in use in this city, so that our soda water drinking friends need not be alarmed at the prospect of being poisoned by *two* metals at once, as Prof. D. would lead them to suppose.

Dr. Wolcott Gibbs has received a "call" from the Trustees of the Antioch College, Ohio, to fill the office of Professor of Chemistry in that institution.

Wöhler has been elected a foreign member of the Royal Society, London.

NEW YORK

JOURNAL OF PHARMACY.

SEPTEMBER, 1854.

PHARMACEUTICAL NOTES.

BY BENJAMIN CANAVAN.

ELATERIUM.—Having lately met with an article of Elaterium of the most villainous quality, which, as I have been informed, some thousands of ounces of it have been disposed, I take the opportunity to describe, so that all who may be in possession of any may purify their hands of it and be warned for the future not to take on trust so important an article the purity of which can be so easily ascertained.

It is put up in flint-glass phials about the size and shape of an ordinary, long, 2 oz. phial, tied over with leather, and without any seal or address of any kind, but bearing a label with the botannical name of the cucumber, and a description of its therapeutical and some other properties ; it is of a fine green color, much finer than usual, indeed too fine, and, no doubt, given to it for purposes of deception. It sinks *heavily* and *instantly* in *water* and *effervesces vividly* with acids, showing it to be composed of chalk, and that I suspect principally if not nearly altogether. It seems to answer the description of what is called Maltese Elaterium. I did intend, if I could have found time, to have made an exact analysis, but not having been able to do so, perhaps some of the many who may find themselves seized with it will confer a favor "on suffering humanity, and entitle themselves to the everlasting (?) gratitude of the world in general," by giving us a quantitative analysis to enable us to guess how near a person may have been to be—purged by it.

IODIDUM CINCHONIÆ.—Not having been aware of a formula for this preparation, the subjoined one was used by my brother on a late occasion, to prepare some of this salt for a prescription, in relation to which it may be allowable to say, "en passant," that the writer of the prescription, in which it was ordered with another article of a very elaborately technical nomenclature, who is a *celebrated* professor in some college, was so much *dissappointed* that the preparation had been obtained as it had never been prepared except by a formula of his suggesting and known only to him, and the patient to whom the same "prodigious" statement had been made being so much more *dissappointed*, that samples of the preparation were required to be sent to the worthy "savant," for his examination and authentication, both of which acts, it is hoped, were duly performed. It might be well in such cases that the discoverer of any "new discovery" would condescend to make some explanatory remark to enlighten the ignorance of the apothecary and enable him to meet his wishes without *dissappointment* if *desirable*, and also for the charitable purpose of saving that useful drudge some unnecessary exercise of the brain, an organ which I confidently believe the advance of knowledge in this enlightened age will one day show him to be possessed of in common with the lower animals, and thus dispel the doubts of some *very learned* men on that *head*. The process is very simple, viz., mix together equivalent proportions of sulphate of cinchonine and iodide of potassium in solution; let it stand for some hours, and evaporate to dryness; wash the residue with absolute alcohol to exhaustion, and evaporate spontaneously in open air. A semi-crystalline resinoid product, of a saffron color, is the result, which is iodide of cinchonine or hydriodate, or some other synonym, but, at any rate, containing iodine and cinchonine in saline combination.

TINCTURÆ QUINQUE.—This name has been adopted by some for the sake of brevity and easy remembrance for the following mixture, now frequently used, viz.

Tinct. Opii,
" Rhei,
" Camphoræ,
" Capsici,
" (Ess.) Menth Pip ana partes æquales.

ON LITHO-PHOTOGRAPHY.

Extract from the work of MM. Barreswil and Davanne entitled " Chemical Photography."

To obtain upon stone by photography an image which presents the same properties as the lithograph drawing it is necessary to employ a substance having the following conditions:

To form on the stone an uniform and regular layer.

To be sensible to light so that a final washing can develope all the white parts of the drawing and to disengage the demi-tints.

To preserve sufficient adherence to the stone to keep the latter from the action of the mordant.

Lastly, to present a susceptible layer to receive the ordinary lithographic ink.

The bitumen of Judea, originally employed by Nicephore Niepce, has still remained without further application to photography. It appears to us to unite in itself all the conditions, and we have used it in fact in processes which are common to us, with MM. Lemercier and Lerebour, to obtain a medium producing proofs of great fineness and of wonderful freshness. The work is accomplished thus: The different qualities of Syrian bitumen afforded by commerce is searched through for that which appears the most sensitive to length. It is sufficient for this trial to dissolve the bitumen in ether, to spread it in a thin layer upon any surface, for instance a leaf of grass, and to expose it to light. The best bitumen is that which, after exposure, resists best washing by ether. Of this bitumen a certain amount is taken, such as experience can dictate. Since the solubility of bitumens vary very much, it is powdered fine and then dissolved in ether; this ethereal solution ought to be made so that when spread upon stone it makes a fine layer, smooth, and not like a varnish, but what engravers call a "grain." On looking at the stone with a lens this layer ought to present över its whole surface a kind of even fracture, and furrows where the stone is exposed. The fineness of this "grain," which is obtained by a little practice, depends very much upon the dryness of the stone, upon the temperature, which ought to be sufficiently high to produce rapid volatilization, and, finally, upon the density of the liquor. We think that the formation of the grain may be facilitated by adding to the ether a small proportion of a solvent having less volatility than the latter.

The solution of bitumen, thus prepared, is taken and spread evenly over the surface of an ordinary lithographic stone, which is placed perfectly level, and brushed so as to remove the dust from its surface. The liquid may be previously filtered; the excess rolls off and falls on each side. To prevent the return of the liquid upon itself, which would form unequal thickness, rods of glass are placed at the edges to facilitate the rolling off.

The least agitation of the air, induced either by the breath or by too rapid movements of the body, which would produce undulations on the surface of the liquid, ought to be carefully avoided during these operations. The bitumen would in that case be of unequal thickness, and the operation ought to be gone over again.

When the bed is perfectly dry, there is applied to it a negative,* obtained by any process upon stone, upon albumenized glass, or by collodion, and it is exposed to a strong light during a period of time more or less as experience points out.

When the operation is thought finished, the negative is lifted off and the stone washed with ether everywhere the

* For lithography and plates in relief a negative is employed: for plates in intaglio, a positive is used.

light has operated; the bitumen has become insoluble, and remains upon the stone; and, on the other hand, where the bitumen has been protected by the negative, it is readily dissolved off by the ether.

If the time of exposure be too short, the image on the stone will be too faint, and does not yield any demitints; if it has been too long in, the image is obscure, and its fine parts are lost. Washing with ether ought to be used largely, without which stains form that cannot be removed.

The proof well produced and dried, receives then the same lithographic preparation as proofs made from Crayon. It is first acidulated with weak acid, to which gum is added, to preserve the whites, and to give more transparency to the drawing, then washed with plenty of water and a little spirits of turpentine, and, finally, inked with ordinary lithographic ink. A well prepared stone, properly acidulated, where the bitumen has not been *burned* by too long an exposure, ought to take the ink immediately when the latter is applied, and ought to give a sharp and fine "grain" *without being in the least degree touched up*. The printing off of these is conducted as with ordinary lithographic stones. The drawing is very much improved by the printing off—it becomes more transparent and brilliant. There can thus be obtained a like number of proofs as with the ordinary lithograph. As yet we have not seen a single stone which was overworked, and we have prepared a great number, and we had the occasion to print off a great number for the purpose of using them as specimens of litho-photography.—*Journal de Pharmacie*, April, 1854.

In digging for a well in the coal mines near the city of Prague, the workmen met, between the beds of gritstone, which forms the roof of the mine, and the first layer of coals, a bed of yellow amber, apparently of great extent. Pieces weighing from 2 to 3 lbs. were extracted.

ON THE ACIDITY, SWEETNESS, AND STRENGTH OF WINE, BEER AND SPIRITS.

BY H. BENCE JONES, M.D., F.R.S.

(1.) The acidity of the different liquids was determined by means of a standard solution of caustic soda. The quantity of liquid neutralized was always equal in bulk to 1000 grs. of water at 60° F.

The acidity in different—

Sherries varied from		1·95 grs. to		2·85 grs. of caustic soda.	
Madeira,	"	2·70	"	3·60	"
Port,	"	2·10	"	2·55	"
Claret,	"	2·55	"	3·45	"
Burgundy,	"	2·55	"	4·05	"
Champagne,	"	2·40	"	3·15	"
Rhine Wine,	"	3·15	"	3·60	"
Moselle,	"	2.85	"	4·50	"
Brandy,	"	0·15	"	0·60	"
Rum,	"	0·15	"	0·30	"
Geneva,	"	0·07			"
Whisky,	"	0·07			"
Bitter Ale,	"	0·90	"	1·65	"
Porter,	"	1·80	"	2·10	"
Stout,	"	1·35	"	2·25	"
Cider,	"	1·85	"	3·90	"

Hence the order in which these wines may be arranged, beginning with the least acid, is, Sherry, Port, Champagne, Claret, Madeira, Burgundy, Rhine, Moselle.

(2.) The sugar was determined by means of Soleil's saccharometer, which at least gives the lowest limit to the amount of sugar. The sweetness in different—

Sherries varied from		4 grs. to		18 grs. in the ounce.	
Madeira,	"	6	"	20	"

Champagne varied from		6 grs.	to	28 grs.	in the ounce.
Port,	"	16	"	34	"
Malmsy,	"	56	"	66	"
Tokay,	"	74			"
Samos,	"	88			"
Paxarette,	"	94			"

Claret, Burgundy, Rhine, and Moselle contained no sugar.

Hence the order in which these wines may be arranged, beginning with the driest, is—

Claret, Burgundy, Rhine, Moselle,
Sherry,
Madeira,
Champagne,
Port,
Malmsy,
Tokay,
Samos,
Paxarette.

In a dietetic view, assuming that the sugar becomes acid, then the mean results as to the acidity of the different fluids examined, beginning with the least acid, is—

Geneva, Whiskey,
Rum,
Brandy,
Claret,
Burgundy,
Rhine Wine,
Moselle,
Sherry,
Madeira,
Champagne,
Cider,
Port,
Porter,
Stout,

Malmsy, Madeira,
Ale,
Tokay.

(3.) The alcohol was determined by means of the alcoholometer of M. Geisler, of Bonn.

The strength of different samples of—

Port varied	from	20·7	per cent. to	23·2	per cent. by measure.	
Sherry,	"	15·4	"	24·7	"	
Madeira,	"	19·0	"	19·7	"	
Marsala,	"	19·9	"	21·1	"	
Claret,	"	9·1	"	11·1	"	
Burgundy,	"	10·1	"	13·2	"	
Rhine Wine,		9·5	"	13·0	"	
Moselle,	"	8·7	"	9·4	"	
Champagne,		14·1	"	14·8	"	
Brandy,	"	50·4	"	53·8	"	
Rum,	"	72·0	"	77·1	"	
Geneva,	"	49·4	"		"	
Whisky,	"	59·3			"	
Cider,	"	5·4	"	7·5	"	
Bitter Ale,	"	6·6	"	12·3	"	
Porter,	"	6·5	"	7·0	"	
Stout,	"	6·5	"	7·9	"	

The Burgundy and Claret have less alcohol than was found by Mr. Brande forty years ago in the wines he examined. The Sherry is now stronger, the Port is not so strong, the Marsala is weaker, the Rhine Wine is the same strength, the Brandy is as strong as formerly; the Rum is nearly half as strong again; the Porter is stronger, and the Stout rather stronger than formerly.

Lastly, the specific gravity of each liquid was taken. As this, however, chiefly depends on the amount of alcohol and sugar present, and, as these were directly determined, the specific gravity may be taken as a distant control on the amount of sugar present.

Thus, in those wines in which the amount of alcohol was

the same, the specific gravity was found to vary with the amount of sugar found by the saccharometer.

The results of the analysis of each sample of wine, &c., is given in a series of tables, which do not admit of any abstract.—*London Chemical Gazette.*

ON A SUBSTANCE PRESENTING THE CHEMICAL REACTION OF CELLULOSE, FOUND IN THE BRAIN AND SPINAL CORD OF MAN.

BY RUDOLPH VIRCHOW.

Virchow's Archiv. B. VI., H. 1, p. 135 (Sept. 4, 1853.)

It is well known that Carl Schmidt* was the first to discover in the Ascidians the presence of a principle previously known to exist only in plants, viz., *cellulose*, and to show that it was a constituent of the animal tissue. The researches of Kölliker and Löwig,† of Scacht,‡ and of Huxley,§ have established this important fact. The occurrence of this substance, however, was limited to a comparatively very low class of the invertebrata, and the further discovery made by Gottlieb, in *Euglena viridis*, viz., that this *infusorium* contains *paramylon*, a body isomerous with starch, also had reference only to a creature in the lowest class of the animal kingdom.‖ Nothing of the kind, on the other hand, has been known as existing in the vertebrata, and it is only since the discovery by C. Bernard—that the liver produces sugar—that we have

---

* "Zur Vergleichenden Anat d. Wirbellos." Thiere, 1845, p. 61.

† "Ann. d. Sci. Nat.," 1846, p. 193.

‡ "Mull. Archiv.," 1851, p. 176.

§ "Quart. Journ. Micr. S.," vol. i., p. 22, 1853.

‖ The pertinacity with which German naturalists cling to the animal nature of Euglena, we must confess, is very surprising to us, who are equally satisfied that it is as much a subject of the vegetable kingdom as the motile zoospores of any Alga, such as *Volvox*, *Hydrodictyon*, *Protococcus*, &c.

had reason to suppose that substances belonging to the *amylum* series may also have a representative.

From histological considerations, it had struck me that the umbilical cord of man presented a great resemblance in structure to the cellulose tissue of the Ascidians (Wurzb. Verh. 1851, Bd. II., p. 161, *note*,) and I was only the more confirmed in this notion by Scacht's observations, so that I have since directed my researches with care to the subject. But in many instances this was in vain, as, for instance, in the *ova* of amphibia and fishes, the remarkable vitelline plates of which I described (Zeitsch. f. wiss. Zoologie. 1852. Bd. IV., p. 240).

I was more fortunate when, a short time since, I directed my attention to the so-termed *corpora amylacea* of the brain, upon the precise nature of which, contrasted with the other kind of amyloid bodies in man, I had not previously arrived at any accurate notion. (Wurzb. Verh. 1851, Bd. II., p. 51.) It was now apparent that these bodies assumed a pale-blue tinge upon the application of iodine, and upon the subsequent addition of sulphuric acid, presented the beautiful violet-color which is known as belonging to *cellulose;* and which in the present instance appears the more intense from the contrast with the surrounding yellow or brown nitrogenous substance.

I have repeated this experiment so often, and with so many precautions, that I regard the result as quite certain. Not only have I instituted comparative researches in different human bodies, and in the most various localities, but I have also noticed the action of the reagents under all possible conditions. The experiment is best made in the mode adopted by Mulder and Harting, with regard to vegetable cellulose (*vide* Moleschott "Physiologie des Stoffwechsels," p. 103), viz., by causing the action of diluted sulphuric acid to follow that of a watery solution of iodine. The iodine solution should not be too strong, for the observation may then be impeded by its precipitation; and, on the other hand, care must be taken that the iodine exerts due action upon the substance. Owing to the volatility of the iodine, and its great affinity for animal substances, its action is usually very unequal, so that the border of the object and not the centre may be penetrated by it; or, perhaps, of spots in close contiguity, one will contain iodine and the other not. It is, consequently, always advisable to repeat the application of the iodine several times, but to avoid the addition of too much. Upon the subsequent addition of sulphuric acid, if the action have been too powerful, the result is perfectly opaque, red-brown color. The most certain results are obtained if the sulphuric acid be allowed to act very slowly. In fact, I have procured the most beautiful objects in allowing a preparation covered with the glass to remain undisturbed with a drop of sulphuric acid in contact with the edge of the covering-glass for twelve to twenty-four hours. Under these circumstances, the most beautiful light violet-blue was occasionally presented. Lastly, I would just intimate that accidental mixtures of starch or cellulose may readily happen, seeing that very light fibres or minute particles from the cloths with which the object and covering-glasses have been cleaned, may very easily be left upon them, which would afterwards exhibit the same reaction as the above.

Every precaution having been taken, the following results will be obtained:

1. The *corpora amylacea* (Purkinje) *are chemically different from the concentric-spherical corpuscles, of which the brain-sand is composed*, and with which they have hitherto usually been confounded. The organic matrix of the brain-sand granules is obviously nitrogenous; it is colored of a deep yellow by iodine and sulphuric acid. This is true not only of the sabulous matter in the pineal gland and choroid plexuses, but also of that of the Pacchionian granulations and of the *dura mater*, as well as of the dentate plates in the spinal arachnoid. In all these parts, I have, in general, nowhere obtained the blue reaction, except in a few spots in the pineal gland. It would, therefore, for the future, be convenient to restrict the name of "corpora amylacea" to the bodies containing cellulose.

2. These bodies exist, so far as I have at present found, only in the substance of the *ependyma ventriculorem* and its prolongations. In this I include especially the lining of the cerebral ventricles and the transparent substance in the spinal cord described by Kölliker as the *substantia grisia centralis* (Mik-

rosk. Anat. Bd. II.1, p. 413). With respect to the cerebral ventricles, I have already repeatedly stated that I find them to be lined throughout with a membrane belonging to the connective tissue class, upon which rests an epithelium. This membrane contains very fine cellular elements, and a matrix, sometimes of more dense, sometimes of softer, consistence, and is *continued on the internal aspect without any special boundary between the nervous elements.* In the deeper layers of this membrane, and in immediate contiguity with the nerve fibres, the cellulose corpuscles are found most abundantly, and they are also especially numerous where the *ependyma* is very thick. They are, consequently, very abundant on the *fornix, septum lucidum,* and in the *stria cornea* in the fourth ventricle. In the spinal cord, the substance corresponding to the *ependyma* lies in the middle, in the grey substance, in the situation where the spinal canal exists in the fœtus. It there forms evidently a rudiment of the obliterated canal, such as is presented in the obliteration of the posterior cornu of the lateral ventricle, which is so frequently met with. In a transverse section of the cord, it is easily recognised as a gelatinous, somewhat resistant substance, which may be readily isolated. Its cells are much larger and more perfect than those of the cerebral *ependyma.* This *ependyma spinale* forms a continuous gelatinous filament, which extends to the *filium terminale,* and might, therefore, perhaps, be most suitably described as the *central ependymal filament.* In it the cellulose granules are also found, though, as it would seem, more abundantly in the upper than in the lower portion. In other situations I have sought for these bodies in vain, and in particular I have been unable to find them in the external cortical layer of the cerebrum, or anywhere in the interior of the cerebral substance.

3. Since, from the experiment of Cl. Bernard, who produced saccharine urine by wounding the floor of the fourth ventricle in the rabbit, there appeared to be reason to conclude that the existence of cellulose was connected with that phenomenon, I sought for it also in rabbits, but in vain. I found in that situation, both in the fourth and the third, and

in the lateral ventricles, a very beautiful tessellated *epithelium* with very long vibratile cilia, but no cellulose.

4. The cellulose granules, therefore, appear to be everywhere connected with the existence of the *ependyma-substance* of a certain thickness, and might, perhaps, be regarded as a constituent of it. They occur of excessively minute size, so that the *nuclei* of the ependyma scarcely correspond with them. Can they be formed out of the latter? The larger they are the more distinctly laminated do they appear. But there is never any indication in them of a nitrogenous admixture, recognizable by a yellow color. The centre only is usually of a darker blue, and, consequently, perhaps, more dense than the cortical laminæ.

5. As to an introduction of these bodies from without, such a supposition is the less probable because a similar substance is nowhere else known. We are acquainted with a series of varieties of vegetable cellulose, but the substance now in question appears to be distinguished above all by its slight power of resistance to reagents, seeing that concentrated acids and alkalies attack it more powerfully than is usually the case with the cellulose of plants.

6. In the child I have as yet sought for it in vain; so that, like the "brain-sand," it appears to arise in a later stage of development, and probably may have a certain pathological import.

Since writing the above, Professor Virchow has repeated and confirmed his observations, and ascertained in addition that similar bodies also occur in the higher nerves of sense. He found them most abundantly in the soft gray interstitial substance of the olfactory nerve, less frequently in the acoustic, although the observations of Meissner (Zeitsch. f. rat. Med., N. F., Bd. III, pp. 358, 363) would indicate a proportionately great disposition to their formation in that situation. Rokitansky appears to have seen them in the optic nerve, and from an oral communication the author has learned that Kölliker has found them in the retina.

Having already stated that the *ependyma* is continued without special limitation among the nervous elements, the author goes on to observe that it is now apparent that there is a continuous extension of the same substance in the interior of the higher nerves of sense. From a series of pathological observations, he concludes that a soft matrix referrible mainly to connective-tissue substance, everywhere pervades and connects the nervous elements in the centres, and that the *ependyma* is only a free superficial expansion of it over the nervous elements. The opinion, that the epithelium of the cerebral ventricles rests immediately upon the nervous elements, appears to have arisen from a confusion of this interstitial substance with the true nerve-substance.

The isolation of the *corpora amylacea* in larger quantity, in order that they should be subjected to chemical analysis, the author has not yet succeeded in effecting. Nevertheless, it seems impossible to entertain any doubt as to their cellulose nature. No other substance is known which affords the same reaction; and although the author has examined the most various animal tissues, and has accurately investigated, particularly, the concentric corpuscles occurring elsewhere, as in the *thymus* in *tumours*, &c., nothing of the same kind has presented itself.—(Sept. 25, 1853.)—*U. Canada Journal*, July, 1854.

EXAMINATION OF THE GAS OF THE PHILADELPHIA GAS WORKS.

BY CHARLES M. WETHERILL, PH.D., M.D.

The following examination of the Philadelphia gas was made for the engineer of the works, Professor J. C. Cresson, in the beginning of the year 1852, but, unfortunately, was not completed in sufficient time to be inserted in detail in his report for that year. As the results of the examination of the gas at that time, by different operators, are at total variance, and since particular pains were taken in my examination to check its results, I have thought proper, with the permission of Professor Cresson, to offer them in full to the criticism of the scientific public. The analysis was performed with the apparatus of Bunsen, which I made and graduated with care, and following Bunsen's process and precautions, as detailed in the *Hand woerter-Book de Chimie*, vol. ii., p. 1050.* The course of analysis and calculation is as follows:

The gas was tested for carbonic acid and sulphuretted hydrogen by passing through lime water and solution of acetate of lead, (in one instance a direct examination for CO^2, by measurement, was made,) of which being found absent, it was dried in the small eudiometer by a chloride of calcium ball, and measured.

The olefiant gas and hydrocarbon vapors were absorbed by a coke ball saturated with a mixture of anhydrous and concentrated sulphuric acid, followed by a ball of oxide of manganese and one of caustic potassa.

Oxygen was absorbed by a phosphorus ball by aid of heat followed by a caustic potassa ball.

The residual gases, supposed to consist of nitrogen, light carburetted hydrogen, carbonic oxide, and hydrogen, were transferred to the large eudiometer mixed with a known quantity of oxygen, and the absorption noted after explosion. The resulting carbonic acid having been determined by a potassa ball, the unconsumed oxygen was ascertained by exploding with a known quantity of hydrogen, and the nitrogen obtained by subtracting this oxygen from the volume left as above, by the absorption of carbonic acid.

Calling x=hydrogen,
y=light carburetted hydrogen,
z=carbonic oxide,
A=the sum of combustible gases;
B=the oxygen used for their combustion,
C=the carbonic acid formed, we have, according to Bunsen's formulæ,

$$x = A - C,$$

$$y = \frac{2\,B - A}{3},$$

$$z = C - \frac{(2\,B - A)}{3}.$$

* I discovered a typographical error in one of the equations in this article: on page 1066, the equation $\frac{1}{2}x + \frac{1}{2}y + 2z - B$, should be $\frac{1}{2}x + 2y + \frac{1}{2}z - B$.

On measuring the above results, the temperature was ascertained by an accurate Centigrade thermometer by Greiner, which indicated half degrees. The mercury column in the eudiometer was subtracted from the barometric pressure, which was determined by an excellent Gay Lussac barometer, of Lerehours and Secretan, and the hydroscopic state of the gas also noted. The volumes were then reduced to 0° centigrade, and 1,000 millimetres pressure, *dry*, by the formula.

$\log r' = \log. r + \log. (B - b - T) - \log. [1000 + \log. (1 + d\, t^\circ)]$ in which

r = measured volume,

r' = corrected volume,

B = barometric pressure,

b = mercury column in eudiometer,

T = tension of aqueous vapors at temperature t°, and

d = 0·003665.

The volume per centage was the calculated

EXPERIMENT A.

Gas collected in a Scaled Tube, at my Laboratory, 206 *Cherry Street, Jan.* 26, 1852, 11¼ *A.M., letting Gas run for a quarter of an hour before Sealing.*

	r	t°	B m. m.	b mer. col. in eudiomer.	r' Vol. at 0°, and 1,000° m. m.
1. Original vol. (*moist*,)......	119·0	13°	758·8	67	77·32
2. After absorb. by potassa (*dry*,)	118·0	15°	759·6	68	77·35
3. Olefiant gas absorbed, "	109·2	14°	759·7	76	71·01
4. Oxygen absorbed by phos. "	110·4	19°	762·6	75	70·97

The rest of the analysis lost in the subsequent explosions.

January 27th.—Gas passed through a solution of acetate of lead for ten minutes ; no precipitate; absence of sulphuretted hydrogen.

Passed through lime water for half an hour, keeping a similar test tube with lime water alongside for comparison ; no carbonic acid could be detected.

B.—Gas collected for analysis, February 5th, at 1½ P.M., same locality. Passed, before collecting, through solution of acetate of lead and lime water for ten minutes ; no precipitate suffered to escape for ten minutes before sealing its tube.

	r	$t°$	B. m. m.	b	r' corrected volume.
1. Gas dried in eudiometer by Ca. Cl. ball [dry,]	95·4	17°	754·3	91·2	59·556
2. Olefiant gas absorbed [dry,]	87·0	18°	763·0	98·5	54·234
3. Oxygen absorbed [dry,]	86·0	16°	766·6	100·0	54·153
4. Transferred to large eudiometer [moist,]	130 8	13°	769·2	379·0	47·322
5. After admission of oxygen [moist,]	316·9	15°	768·0	189·0	170·110
6. Explosion [moist,]	210·5	16°	767·0	296·0	90·971
7. Carbonic acid absorbed [dry,]	165·5	16°	768·9	342·[illegible]	66·661
8. Hydrogen added [dry,]	456·6	16°	766·3	50·[illegible]	308.73
9. Explosion [moist,]	238·1	16°	765·8	268·[illegible]	108·82

Checks upon calculations.

1st. n + combustible gases = 47·332.

$$\begin{aligned} x &= 22·991 \\ y &= 21·665 \\ z &= 2·645 \\ n &= 0·031 \end{aligned}$$

47 332 same as above.

2d.—Let v = combustible gases = 47·301 } = 103.449
a = oxygen consumed = 56·148 }

m = the absorption 79·139 } = 103·449
n = the carb. acid found 24·310 }

$v + a = m + n$.

B.—*Second Analysis to Check First Analysis.*

	V	$t°$	B	b	r'
1. Dried ore, Ca. Cl.	101·8	16°	760 9	83·0	65·189
2. Olefiant gas, &c., absorbed.	94·5	16°	756·9	91·0	59·307
3. Oxygen absorbed	94·5	16°	754·5	91·0	59·229

The rest of the analysis lost in the explosion. The walls of the eudiometer were taken of thin glass of the size that Bunsen suggests, but being made of flint glass, and having once injured myself by a breakage of similar glass, I made the several explosions with great circumspection, endeavoring to increase the elasticity by not pressing the tube too hard upon the caoutchouc, by which, in the experiments lost, some of the gases were forced out of the eudiometer.

Feb. 11th, 20 minutes before 11. Same locality. Gas reacted alkaline to litmus paper. Passed for 10 minutes through a solution of nitrate of silver, the solution became yellowish, with a slight whitish precipitate, which, on applying heat to the test tube, became reduced to black silver, acquiring metallic lustre under the burnisher.

During the above analysis, the gas-meter at my laboratory

was filled with spirits on account of the cold weather; the gas, therefore, contained a small proportion of alcohol vapors.

The errors of observation and manipulation I believe to be within one-tenth of one per cent.

The following table shows the per centage volume of gases, according to my analysis:

Per Centage by Volume, Gases dry, at 0° Centigrade, and 1000 Millimetres Barometer.

	A	B 1	B 2
Carbonic acid	00·000		
Olefiant gas and hydrocarbon vapors	8·157	8·963	9·023
Oxygen	0·052	0·136	0·120
Hydrogen		44·168	
Light carburetted hydrogen		41·620	
Carbonic oxide		5·081	
Nitrogen		0·059	
		100·000	

With regard to the small amount of nitrogen, I would call attention to the fact that Bunsen and Playfair have shown the quantity of nitrogen in gas from coal to be exceedingly small in quantity; their results gave a per centage of 0·01 of this gas.

It was intended that I should have instituted comparative analyses of Philadelphia and New York gas, for which purpose there were given me three sealed tubes, one of Philadelphia gas, the other two from New York. On examining the sealed ends of these tubes with a microscope, very small holes were noticed in two of them, rendering an analysis useless, since diffusion must have taken place; the remaining tube was so thin at its closed end that the warmth of the hand in examining it exploded the tube.

The following are the results obtained by Professors Booth and Faber, Stewart and Alexander, of which the full details are not given. The first two chemists performed their analysis according to Bunsen's process, using an accurate German thermometer, and a French Aneroid barometer, indicating, according to a comparison with an ordinary mercurial barometer, 0·01 of an inch. Their report is dated Dec. 30th, 1851.

Professors Alexander and Stewart examined New York gas

(from the Manhattan Company,) collected in the New York Hotel, in the forenoon of Jan. 2d, 1852, and Philadelphia gas collected by Professor Booth from a burner in his laboratory, in the forenoon of Jan. 1st, 1852. The hydrocarbons were absorbed by chlorine water in the dark, and which, the analysts say, appear slightly in excess from the vapor of naphtha accompanying the potassium used as one of the reagents. The following table of direct measurements, corrected for thirty inches barometer, and 32° Fahr., is given in Professors Stewart and Alexander's report:

	Manhattan Gas.	Philadelphia Gas.
Carbonic Acid	0·0222	0·0087
Hydro Carbons	0·0928	0 0996
Olefiant Gas	0·0344	0·0204
Light Carburetted Hydrogen	8·7089	0·3227
Hydrogen		0·4049
Nitrogen	0·1231	0·1461
	8·9814	1·0024

The gas volumes of these different chemists are reduced to 32° Fahr., and barometric pressure 30 inches (about 762 millimetres).

Volume per Centage.

	Profs. Booth and Faber.		Profs. Alexander and Stewart.	
	N. York Gas.	Philada. Gas.	Manhattan Gas.	Philadelphia Gas.
Olefiant gas	8·32	6·38	3·50 } 12·95	2·04 } 11·17
Hydro-carbon			9 45 }	9·93 }
Marsh Gas	32·92	54·84	*32·04	32·20
Hydrogen	24·04	26·27	*40·20	40·39
Carbonic Oxide	11·60	4·42		
Carbonic Acid	2 10	0·97	2·27	0·87
Oxygen	0·19	0·04		
Nitrogen	20·83	7·08	12·54	14·57
	100 00	100·00	100·00	100.00

* Not separated experimentally, but their proportions calculated in the same ratio as in the Philadelphia gas.

As will be seen by a comparison of these results with each other, and with my own, their is no agreement at all between them. Perhaps a publication of the details of the abovementioned analyses would bring order out of apparent confusion. It is always well to publish details, for not only do they afford sometimes the only means of criticism, but are useful in preserving records of analyses from being lost, when from some newly observed fact a recalculation from the original data is necessary.—*Journal of the Franklin Institute*, July 10, 1854.

ON THE ADULTERATION OF OILS.

BY F. CRACE CALVERT, ESQ.

In consequence of the large quantity of oils used at the present day for machinery, woollens, &c., many varieties are introduced into the market, and thus much temptation exists to mix or adulterate the more expensive of them. Having been at various times called upon to examine samples of oil, I ascertained that the known processes for discovering adulteration were too general in their application to enable me to obtain satisfactory results; to this class belongs the delicate process recommended by Mr. F. Boudet, principally for the detection of drying oils in olive oil, by the action of hyponitric acid; or Mr. Rousseau's diagometer, which is based on the very inferior conducting power of olive oil, as compared with that of others.

For distinguishing one class of oils from another we may adopt Mr. Faure's method, which is founded on the brown or black tinge which fish oils exclusively assume, when a stream of chlorine gas is passed through them; or Mr. Maumené's, by which the drying oils may be distinguished from the non-drying ones, owing to the fact that the latter, when mixed with strong sulphuric acid, give rise to a much higher temperature, and, although Mr. Fehling has endeavored lately to give more precision to Mr. Maumené's process, yet it is still far from being satisfactory.

There are other processes, the results of which are not sufficiently distinct to be employed with any degree of certainty; such is Mr. Faure's, which consists in adding a given quantity of caustic ammonia to oils, and noticing after they have been mixed, the peculiar appearance which the thick white or yellow fluids present; the same may be said of the process proposed by Mr. Heidendreich, with mono-hydrated sulphuric acid, or that of Mr. Deisel, with concentrated nitric acid, for the chemical actions are so violent, that the characteristic colorations, which are at first produced, rapidly disappear in consequence of the destruction of the oils. These facts induced me to examine what would be the action on oils of the above acids when diluted, and the satisfactory results obtained are described in this paper. The marked colorations produced may be considered as derived from two distinct chemical actions. First, it appears due to certain foreign matters which are dissolved in the oils, and which existed in the substances from which they were extracted; secondly, the diluted acids have, probably, an action on the component parts of the oils themselves, for if caustic soda be added to oils so acted upon, a different result is obtained from that which would occur if no acid had been previously applied; this fact being clearly illustrated with French nut oil, as it gives a semi-saponified fluid mass when caustic soda of sp. gr. 1340 is alone mixed with it, and a fibrous mass when treated by diluted nitric acid previous to the addition of the alkali.

It may be interesting here to remark, that fish oils have presented distinct reactions from other animal or vegetable oils, consequently, in my opinion, not only has cod-liver oil a different composition to that of other oils, as shown by the researches of Mr. Winckler, but so also probably have sperm and seal oils.

The most difficult part of my researches has been to procure oils the purity of which I could depend on, and to arrive at this object, I was obliged, in many instances, to obtain samples from their sources of production on the continent, and even then I took the precaution of ascertaining their degree of purity, by applying to them the various tests which I shall describe further on.

The reason why I employed many reagents is, that the adulterations which occur in commerce are numerous, and that the reactions presented by organic substances, and especially oils, are exceedingly delicate. I would strongly recommend that samples of pure oil be tested comparatively with those suspected of being adulterated, and never to apply only one of the proposed tests, but all those which give characteristic reactions with the oil under examination.

I have great pleasure in acknowledging the intelligence, chemical knowledge, and industry exhibited in these tedious researches by my assistant, Mr. Charles Lowe.

As the reactions presented by the various oils depend upon the special strength and purity of the reagents, not only should great care be taken in their preparation, but also in the exact mode and time required for the chemical action to become apparent. These I have taken care to describe in the case of each reagent.

Solution of Caustic Soda, sp. gr. 1.340.

The reactions given in the following table are obtained by adding one volume of this test-liquor to five volumes of oil, well mixing them, and then heating the mixture to its point of ebullition.

DARK COLORATIONS.		LIGHT COLORATIONS.	
Fish Oils.	Vegetable Oils.	Animal Oils.	Vegetable Oils.
Sperm... Seal..... Cod-liver } Red	Hempseed { Thick brown yellow Linseed .. { Fluid yellow	Neat's-foot { Dirty yellowish white Lard........Pinkish white	Pale rapeseed... Poppy........... French nut...... Sesame .... } Dirty yellow white Castor.......... India nut (*thick*) } White Gallipoli........ } Yellow

Caustic soda, of sp. gr. 1.340 is principally useful to distinguish fish from other animal and vegetable oils, owing to the distinct red color which the former assumes, and which coloration is so distinct, that one per cent. of fish oil can be detected in any of the others.

This table should also be consulted when the object is not to discover other adulterations, but to distinguish some of the oils; for instance, hempseed oil acquires a brown-yellow color, and becomes so thick that the vessel which contains it may be inverted without losing any of its contents, whilst linseed oil assumes a much brighter yellow color, and remains fluid. India nut oil is characterized by giving a white mass, becoming solid in five minutes after the addition of the alkali, which is also the case with gallipoli and pale rape oils, while the other oils remain fluid.

Although it is probable that the reason why some of the oils acquire on the application of this reagent a mucilaginous appearance, whilst others become stringy or fibrous, is the greater or less facility with which they are saponified; still, I regret that I had not the time to examine this point carefully

ACTION OF DILUTED SULPHURIC ACID ON OILS.

As this acid, in different degrees of dilution, exerts distinct reactions on the oils that I had at my disposal, and as it may be employed to discover some known commercial adulterations, I shall discuss separately each series of reactions.

Sulphuric Acid of sp. gr. 1.475.

The mode of applying this acid consists in agitating one volume with five volumes of oil until complete admixture, and then allowing the whole to stand for fifteen minutes, when the appearance is taken as the test reaction.

NOT COLORED.		COLORED.		
Animal.	Vegetable.	Fish.	Animal.	Vegetable.
Lard..Dirty	India nut Pale rape-seed Poppy Castor	Sperm.. } Light red Seal.... } Cod-liver. Purple	Neat's-foot { Yellow tinge	Olive....... } Green tinge Gallipoli..... } Sesame..... } Linseed ......Green Hempseed .. } Intense green French nut...Brownish

The most striking reactions in this table are those presented by hempseed and linseed oils, for the green coloration which they acquire is such, that if they were used to adulterate any of the other oils to the amount of ten per cent., their presence would be indicated by the distinct green tinge they would communicate to the others.

The red color assumed by the fish oils with this test is also sufficiently marked to enable us to detect them in the proportion of one part in 100 of any other oil, and it is at the point of contact of the oil with the acid, on their being allowed to separate by standing, that the red color is principally to be noticed.

Sulphuric Acid of Sp. Gr. 1.530.

Having obtained, by the application of the preceding acid, a certain number of characteristic reactions, I was induced to try the influence of a stronger one, and therefore agitated one volume of it with five volumes of oil, and allowed the mixture to stand five minutes.

LIGHT COLORATIONS.		MARKED COLORATIONS.	
Animal.	Vegetable.	Fish.	Vegetable.
Lard........Dirty white Neat's-foot { Brownish dirty white	Olive...... { Greenish white Sesame.... { Greenish dirty white India nut.. } Poppy...... } Dirty white Castor..... } Pale rape-seed. } Pink	Sperm... } Red Seal..... } Cod-liver. Purple	Gallipoli .. } Intense grey French nut } Hempseed } Intense green Linseed.... } Dirty green

As hempseed, linseed, fish, gallipoli, and French nut oils are the only ones that assume with the above reagent a decided coloration, they can be discovered in any of the others.

Sulphuric Acid of sp. gr. 1.635.

This acid was used in a similar manner to those above, and the coloration noted after two minutes.

NOT COLORED.	DISTINCTLY COLORED.		
Vegetable.	Fish.	Animal.	Vegetable.
Poppy Sesame Castor	Sperm... } Intense Seal..... } brown Cod-liver }	Lard.....Light brown Neat's-foot... } Brown	Olive (light)........ } Green Hempseed (intense) } Green Linseed........... } Green Gallipoli .... } Brown Pale rapeseed...... } Brown French nut........ } Brown India nut (light)... } Brown

I wish to draw especial attention to this acid, as it gives distinct and widely differing reactions from those of the former acids. The colorations produced by sulphuric acid sp. gr. 1.635, are so marked, that they may be consulted with great advantage in many cases of adulteration; for example, I have been enabled to detect distinctly ten per cent. of rapeseed oil in olive oil, of lard oil in poppy oil, of French nut oil in olive oil, of fish oil in neat's-foot oil.

I was much struck with the increased coloration assumed by some of the oils when treated by sulphuric acid of different strengths; thus I found that gallipoli oil which was white with No. 1 sulphuric acid, becomes brown with No. 3; pale rape oil, which was white with No. 1 acid, gives a pink color with No. 2, and a brown with No. 3; whilst neat's-foot oil is of a light yellow with No. 1, but becomes brown with No. 3. These results, therefore, clearly show the decomposing action of sulphuric acid on oils, and that an acid of sp. gr. 1.635 is the maximum strength that can be used, for nearly all the oils then begin to carbonize, and their distinct coloration to be destroyed.

ACTION OF NITRIC ACID, OF DIFFERENT STRENGTHS, ON OILS.

For the reason given in the first part of this memoir, I employed diluted acid, and obtained a series of reactions, some of which will, I hope, prove useful in some special cases of adulteration, and interesting as showing the influence of gradual oxidation on oils.

Nitric Acid of sp. gr. 1.180.

One part of this acid, by measure, was agitated with five parts of oil, and the appearance, after standing five minutes, is described in this table.

NOT COLORED.			COLORED.		
Fish.	Animal.	Vegetable.	Fish.	Animal.	Vegetable.
Cod-liver	Lard	India nut Pale rapeseed Poppy Castor	Sperm { Slight yellow Seal ....Pink	Neat's-foot } Light yellow	Olive...... } Greenish Gallipoli... } Hempseed { Dirty green French nut } Sesame (*orange*) } Yellow Linseed.... }

This test is sufficiently delicate to detect distinctly 10 per cent. of hempseed oil in linseed oil, as the mixture assumes the greenish hue so characteristic of the former. Although olive acquires a green color, still its shade is such that it is easily distinguished from that of hempseed.

Nitric Acid of sp. gr. 1.220.

I employed this stronger acid with the view of increasing the coloration of certain oils, so as to render it sufficiently marked to ascertain the presence of these oils when mixed with others. The proportion of acid used and the time of contact were the same as above.

NOT COLORED.			COLORED.		
Fish.	Animal.	Vegetable.	Fish.	Animal.	Vegetable.
Cod-liver	Lard	India nut Pale rapeseed Castor	Sperm — Light yellow Seal.. — Light red	Neat's-foot — Light yellow	Poppy yellow....., French nut, Sesame ... — Red Olive. ...., Gallipoli... — greenish Hempseed — greenish dirty brown Linseed..... Yellow

The chief characters in the above table are those presented by hempseed, sesame, French nut, poppy, and seal oils, and they are such that they not only may be employed to distinguish them from each other, but are sufficiently delicate to detect their presence when mixed with other oils, in the proportion of ten per cent.

Nitric Acid of sp. gr. 1.330.

One part of this acid was mixed with five parts of oil, by measure, and remained in contact five minutes.

NOT COLORED.	COLORED.		
Vegetable.	Fish.	Animal.	Vegetable.
India nut Pale rapeseed Castor	Sperm..., Seal....., Cod-liver — Red	Neat's-foot — Light brown Lard.. — Very slight yellow	Poppy....., French nut (dark)..., Sesame (dark)... — Red Olive......, Gallipoli .. — Greenish Hempseed.. — Greenish dirty brown Linseed.... — Green, becoming brown

The colorations here described are very marked, and can be employed with advantage to discover several well-known cases of adulteration; for instance, if 10 per cent. of sesame or

French nut oil exists in olive oil; but the same proportion of poppy oil cannot be thus detected as the color produced is not so intense as in the other cases. But if any doubt remained in the mind of the operator, as to whether the adulterating oil was sesame, French nut, or poppy, he would be able to decide it by applying the test described in the next table, where he will find that French nut oil gives a fibrous semi-saponified mass, sesame a fluid one, with a red liquor beneath, and poppy also a fluid mass, but floating on a colorless liquor.

The successive application of nitric acid of sp. gr. 1.330, and of caustic soda of sp. gr, 1.340, can also be successfully applied to detect the following very frequent cases of adulteration; first that of gallipoli, with fish oils, as gallipoli oil assumes no distinct color with the acid, and gives with soda a mass of a fibrous consistency, whilst fish oils are colored red, and become mucilaginous with the alkali.

Secondly, that of castor oil with poppy oil, as the former acquires a reddish tinge, and the mass with the alkali loses much of its fibrous appearance.

Thirdly, rapeseed oil, with French nut oil, as nitric acid imparts to the former a more or less intense red tinge, which an addition of the alkali increases, and renders the semi-saponified mass more fibrous.

The colorations which divers oils assume, under the influence of the three test nitric acids, clearly illustrate the remarks made at the commencement of this paper, that the reason why the chemists who preceded me in these tedious researches had not arrived at satisfactory results in distinguishing oils in their various adulterations, was that the acids they employed were so concentrated that all the distinctive colorations were lost, the oils becoming yellow or orange; but there is no doubt that the above reagents will enhance the value of Mr. F. Boudet's process, as they afford very useful data to specify the special oils mixed with olive oil.

Caustic Soda of sp. gr. 1.340.

The following reactions were obtained on adding 10 volumes

of this test-liquor to the 5 volumes of oil which had just been acted upon by one part of nitric acid.

A FIBROUS MASS IS FORMED.		A FLUID MASS IS FORMED.		
Animal.	Vegetable.	Fish.	Animal.	Vegetable.
Neat's-foot..White	Gallipoli.. } White India nut. } White Castor.... } White French nut..Red Hempseed { Light brown	Sperm Seal Cod-liver	Lard	Olive............ } White Pale rapeseed... } White Linseed...........Yellowish Poppy (light)......Red Sesame { Brown liquor beneath } Amber

Having given in a previous paragraph some of the most useful reactions noted in this table, I shall simply call attention to the following mixtures: neat's-foot with rape, gallipoli with poppy, castor with poppy, hempseed with linseed, sperm with French nut, and gallipoli with French nut. It is also necessary here to mention that the brown liquor on which the semi-saponified mass of sesame oil swims, is a very delicate and characteristic reaction.

PHOSPHORIC ACID.

One part by measure of syrupy trihydrated phosphoric acid was agitated with five parts of oil, and gave the following results:—

NOT COLORED.		COLORED.	
Animal.	Vegetable.	Fish.	COLORED.
Lard Neat's-foot	India nut Pale rapeseed Poppy Sesame Castor	Sperm... } Dark red Seal..... } Dark red Cod-liver } Dark red	Olive (slight).......... } Green Gallipoli (slight)....... } Green Hempseed .... } Green Linseed (brown yellow) } Green French nut..............Brown yellow

The only reaction to be noticed is the dark red color rapidly becoming black, which phosphoric acid imparts exclusively to the fish oils, as it enables us to detect 1 part of these oils in 1000 parts of any other animal or vegetable oils, and even at this great degree of dilution a distinct coloration is communicated to the mixture.

MIXTURE OF SULPHURIC AND NITRIC ACID.

The results given in the following table are obtained on agitating 1 part by measure of a mixture of equal volumes of sulphuric acid of sp. gr. 1.845, and nitric acid of sp. gr. 1.330, with five parts of oil, and allowing the whole to stand two minutes.

Fish.		Animal.		Vegetable.	
Sperm...	Dark brown	Lard	Brown	Gallipoli....................	Dark brown
Seal		Neat's-foot (dark)		Pale rapeseed...............	
Cod-liver				French nut..................	
				Sesame (becoming intense red)	Green
				Hempseed (becoming black)...	
				Linseed (becoming black)......	
				Olive (orange, slight)	Yellow
				Poppy (slight)	
				India nut (orange, slight)	White

As three oils remain nearly colorless, viz., those of poppy, olive, and India nut, we are enabled to detect in them the presence of any of the others; and when olive or poppy oils are adulterated with sesame, the green color at first produced is much more persistent than with sesame alone, consequently it is necessary that the acid and the suspected oil should remain in contact for about ten minutes, in order to obtain the ultimate brownish-red color of the sesame; in fact, it is so intense that it may be usefully employed to detect this oil when mixed with others.

AQUA REGIA.

In consequence of the results obtained with nitric acid, I was induced to try the action of aqua regia, but I found that when it was made in the ordinary proportions of three volumes of hydrochloric and one of nitric acid, the reactions produced nearly coincided with the last-named acid. I therefore prepared several samples of aqua regia, in which I gradually increased the proportion of hydrochloric acid, and after having tested them, I adopted one composed of twenty-five volumes of hydrochloric acid of sp. gr. 1.155, and one volume of nitric acid of sp. gr. 1.330, and allowed them to stand about five hours; the reactions described in the following table are those which take place when a mixture of five volumes of oil with one of aqua regia is agitated and allowed to stand five minutes.

NOT COLORED.		COLORED.		
Animal.	Vegetable.	Fish.	Animal.	Vegetable.
Lard	Olive Gallipoli India nut Pale rape-seed Poppy Castor	Sperm (slight) } Yellow Seal...(slight) } Yellow Cod-liver..... } Yellow	Neat's-foot } Slight yellow	French nut } Yellow Sesame .... } Yellow Linseed (greenish) } Yellow Hempseed....Greenish

When the facts contained in this table are compared with the preceding ones, we are struck with their uniformity, and are led to infer that no marked action had taken place; but this conclusion is erroneous, as most of them assume a vivid and distinct coloration on the addition of solution of soda of sp. gr. 1.340, as seen in the following table :—

A FIBROUS MASS IS FORMED.		A FLUID MASS IS FORMED.		
Animal.	Vegetable.	Fish.	Animal.	Vegetable.
Neat's-foot } Brownish yellow	Gallipoli (yellowish) .... } White India nut.... } White Pale rapeseed (yellowish) } White Castor...... } Pale rose French nut ....Orange Hempseed.. } Light brown	Sperm } orange yellow Seal.. } orange yellow Cod-liver } orange yellow	Lard. Pink	Olive....White Poppy } Intense rose Sesame } Orange with brown liquor beneath Linseed. Orange

The effects described in this table are such that we can discover with facility ten per cent. of a given oil in many cases of adulteration; for example, poppy in rape, olive in gallipoli and India nut, as all of them assume a pale rose color; but when poppy is mixed with olive or castor oils, there is a decrease in the consistency of the semi-saponified matter.

By the aid of the above reagents we can also ascertain the presence of ten per cent. of French nut in olive or linseed oils, as the semi-saponified mass becomes the more fluid, and the presence of French nut in pale rape, gallipoli, or India nut oils, is recognized in consequence of their white mass acquiring an orange hue; linseed oil is detected in hempseed oil, as it renders the fibrous mass of the latter more mucilaginous.

Sesame oil also gives with this reagent the same reaction as with nitric acid and an alkali, and poppy oil is distinguished from all other oils, by giving, in this case, a semi-saponified mass of a beautiful rose color.

To give an idea how the above tables are to be used, I shall suppose a sample of rapeseed oil adulterated with one very difficult to discover. I first apply the caustic alkali test, which, on giving a white mass proves the absence of the fish oils, together with those of hempseed and linseed; and as no distinct reaction is produced by the sample of oil under examination, when mixed with the three sulphuric and nitric acids above mentioned, poppy and sesame oils are thrown out as they are reddened, neat's-foot, India nut, castor, olive, and lard oils resting only in the scale of probability. In order to discover which of these is mixed with the suspected oil, I agitate a portion of it first with nitric acid of sp. gr. 1.300, and then with caustic soda, and their mutual action excludes neat's-foot, India nut, and castor oils, as the sample of oil does not give a fluid semi-saponified mass. The absence of olive oil is proved by no green coloration being obtained on the application of syrupy phosphoric acid. As to the presence of lard oil, it is ascertained on caustic soda being added to the oil which has been previously acted on by aq. regia, as the latter gives a fibrous yellowish semi-saponified mass, whilst the former yields a pink fluid one.

In conclusion, I trust that the reagents described in this paper, and the new method of applying successively two of them to any particular oil, will prove useful not only to detect the numerous admixtures of oil we have noticed, but also to trace and determine in a given oil the presence of any other which we have examined, and I give a general table of the preceding reactions, in order to facilitate the detection of any adulteration.

GENERAL TABLE OF REACTIONS.

OILS.	Caustic Soda, Sp. gr. 1·340.	Sulphuric Acid, Sp. gr. 1·475.	Sulphuric Acid, Sp. gr. 1·530	Sulphuric Acid, Sp. gr. 1·635.	Nitric Acid, Sp. gr. 1·180.	Nitric Acid, Sp. gr. 1·220.	Nitric Acid, Sp. gr. 1·330. +	Caustic Soda, Sp. gr. 1·340.	Phosphoric Acid, Syrupy.	Sulphuric Acid, + Nitric Acid.	Aqua Regia. +	Caustic Soda Spec. grav., 1·340
OLIVE..................	Slight Yellow.	Green tinge.	Greenish white.	Light green.	Greenish.	Greenish.	Greenish.	Fluid white mass.	Slight green.	Orange Yellow.	....	Fluid white mass.
GALIPOLI...............	ditto.	ditto.	Grey	Brown.	ditto.	ditto.	ditto.	Fibrous ditto.	ditto.	Dark brown.	....	Fibrous yellowish white mass.
INDIA NUT.............	Thick and white.	....	Dirty white.	Light brown.	....	....	....	ditto.	....	Orange white.	....	Fibrous white mass.
PALE RAPESEED........	Dirty yellowish white.	....	Pink.	Brown.	....	....	....	Fluid ditto.	....	Dark brown.	....	Fibrous yellowish white mass.
POPPY..................	ditto.	....	Dirty white.	....	....	Orange Yellow.	Red.	Light Red fluid mass.	....	Slight Yellow.	....	Fluid intense rose colored mass.
FRENCH NUT...........	ditto.	Brownish.	Grey	Brown.	Yellow.	Red.	Dark Red.	Fibrous red mass.	Brown yellow.	Dark brown.	Yellow.	Fibrous orange mass.
SESAME.................	ditto.	Green tinge.	Greenish dirty white.	....	Orange yellow.	ditto.	ditto.	Fluid red mass with brown liquor beneath	....	Green, becoming intense red.	ditto.	Fluid orange mass with brown liquor beneath.
CASTOR.................	White.	....	Dirty white.	....	....	....	....	Fibrous white mass.	....	Brownish red.	....	Fibrous pale rose colored mass.
HEMPSEED.............	Thick brownish yellow.	Intense green.	Intense green.	Intense green.	Dirty green.	Greenish dirty brown.	Greenish dirty brown.	Fibrous light brown mass.	Green.	Green, becoming black.	Green.	Fibrous light brown mass.
LINSEED................	Fluid yellow.	Green.	Dirty green.	Green.	Yellow.	Yellow	Green, becoming brown.	Fluid yellow mass.	Brown yellow green.	ditto.	Greenish yellow.	Fluid orange mass.
LARD....................	Pinkish white.	Dirty white.	Dirty white.	Light Brown.	....	....	Very slight yellow.	Fluid mass.	....	Brown.	....	Fluid pink mass.
NEATSFOOT.............	Dirty yellowish white.	Yellow tinge.	Brownish dirty white.	Brown.	Light yellow.	Light yellow	Light brown	Fibrous white mass.	....	Dark brown.	Slight yellow.	Fibrous brownish yellow mass.
SPERM..................	Dark red.	Light red.	Red.	Intense brown.	Slight yellow.	ditto.	Red.	Fluid mass.	Dark red.	ditto.	ditto.	Fluid orange yellow mass.
SEAL.....................	ditto.	ditto.	ditto.	ditto.	Pink.	Light red.	ditto.	ditto.	ditto.	ditto.	ditto.	ditto.
COD LIVER OIL..........	ditto.	Purple.	Purple.	ditto.	....	....	ditto.	ditto.	ditto.	ditto.	Yellow.	ditto.

ON THE EMPLOYMENT OF CHLORINE IN ANALYSIS

BY MM. RIVOT, BEUDANT AND DAGUIN.

Report by M. Pelouze.

Chlorine has long been employed in the analysis of mineral substances. Sometimes these substances are exposed at an elevated temperature to the action of a stream of dry gaseous chlorine; sometimes the contact is effected in presence of water.

The former method is applicable to substances the chlorides of which are volatile, such as sulphur, arsenic, tin and antimony, to separate them from non-volatile chlorides, such as those of iron, copper, nickel, cobalt, &c. As however the latter chlorides are not absolutely non-volatile, the separation thus obtained in the dry way is never exact, and can never furnish a precise result, except to a very skilful operator, who has been much accustomed to experiments of this kind.

In the second method of analysis, the chlorine may become an oxidizing agent; it is thus that it peroxidizes iron and cobalt, and converts arsenious acid, dissolved in water acidulated with muriatic acid, into arsenic acid. It will be remembered that upon this property is founded the chlorometric method generally adopted in manufactories, which was invented by Gay-Lussac.

Chlorine then has long been employed in a certain number of analyses, both in the dry and humid way; but the present investigations will infallibly extend its employment.

The author's experiments all relate to the employment of chlorine in the humid way, sometimes in alkaline, sometimes in acid solutions.

In the former of these conditions, that is, in presence of a free alkali, the oxidizing action is extremely energetic, and generally causes the substance to attain its highest degree of oxidation: and it may be readily conceived that it may be especially useful in bringing metals or oxides, which furnish acids when combined with oxygen, to the state of soluble salts. These salts are thus separated from those oxides which are insoluble in alkalies.

In the second case, that is to say, in an acid medium, the oxidizing action of the chlorine is much less energetically exhibited: it is only exerted upon a very small number of metals, such as lead and manganese, which pass into the state of binoxides, and become insoluble in the acid.

The following are the principal results attained by the authors:—

I. *Action of Chlorine in Alkaline Solutions.*

Sulphuret of lead is converted into peroxide, which is completely insoluble, and into an alkaline sulphate. Thus the very difficult question of the complete separation of lead and sulphur is resolved, and the analysis of galena effected with equal rapidity and exactitude.

Oxide of lead, dissolved in potash, is converted by chlorine into peroxide, which remains dissolved, forming with the alkali a combination which is soluble in presence of an excess of potash. Thus, under different circumstances, which may be reproduced at pleasure, the peroxide of lead may be separated in a state of purity, and either become free, or remain in solution combined with the alkali.

Hydrated oxide of iron, natural or artificial, is rapidly converted into ferric acid, which, combining with the alkali, gives a solution of a very deep red color. This fact had already been pointed out by M. Fremy, at the time when he discovered ferric acid. The ferric acid is not formed when the temperature of the alkaline liquid is reduced below 32° F.; nor if the temperature be raised to 104° or 122° F. in presence of quartz and of some other substances which possess the singular faculty, which will shortly be referred to, of modifying the ordinary reactions of chlorine.

When chlorine in an alkaline solution reacts upon sulphuret of iron, the sulphur is dissolved in the state of sulphuric acid, whilst the iron remains insoluble in the state of sesquioxide; and it is only after the complete acidification of the sulphur that the oxide of iron becomes dissolved in its turn, passing into the state of ferric acid.

When an arsenical pyrites, well pounded, is treated in this manner, the sulphur and arsenic are readily obtained in solution in the form of alkaline sulphate and arseniate, and the iron as insoluble peroxide. This state is very easily attained by stopping the action of the chlorine as soon as the liquid begins to acquire color, and heating it for a few moments with a little pulverized quartz.

The oxides of manganese are pretty quickly converted into alkaline permanganate, if a tolerably concentrated alkaline solution be employed, and at a temperature of 104°–122° F. On the other hand, in operating at a temperature below 32° F., no manganic acid is produced by the action of chlorine. But if the solution be allowed to return to the ordinary temperature in contact with the oxide, the green manganate of potash is formed. Thus we may obtain at pleasure by the action of chlorine, binoxide of manganese, or an alkaline manganate or permanganate.

Oxide of copper has a great tendency to combine with the fixed alkalies; the compound is soluble, and stable even at the point of ebulition in presence of a great excess of alkali. In the determination of copper, precipitated in the form of oxide by potash, a certain quantity of this compound is always formed. Its presence may however be avoided, at least in great part, by effecting the precipitation in an ammoniacal liquid. It is still better avoided by passing the chlorine into the alkaline fluid, without ammonia, until the alkali is almost completely saturated.

The sulphurous copper minerals, well pulverized, may be easily analyzed by the action of chlorine in the presence of an alkaline fluid. The copper and other metals remain insoluble in the form of oxides; whilst the sulphur, arsenic, and antimony dissolve completely, forming alkaline salts. The presence of blende in these minerals is in general inimical to the precision of the reactions.

Oxides of cobalt and nickel, recently precipitated by potash and suspended in an alkaline fluid, pass rapidly to the state of sesquioxides under the influence of a stream of chlorine. In the analysis of minerals of nickel and cobalt, there is generally much difficulty in separating these metals exactly from arsenic and antimony; this difficulty may however be very easily got rid of by operating in the following manner:—

The mineral is dissolved in nitric acid, the solution diluted with water, and a great excess of potash added to it; it is then gently heated, and a stream of chlorine passed into it until the precipitate is quite black. The fluid then contains the arsenic and antimony in the form of alkaline salts; the insoluble portion contains the metals in the state of sesquioxide, and not retaining the least trace of arsenic or antimony.

Phosphoric acid may be separated, like arsenic and antimony, from those metals which form sesquioxides or deutoxides, such as iron, nickel, cobalt and lead.

The determination of free sulphur containing organic matters, such as is employed in such large quantities in the manufacture of sulphuric acid, present serious difficulties when it is attempted to peroxidize it with nitromuriatic acid, or with nitre in a state of fusion. The employment of chlorine as an oxidizing agent in a hot concentrated alkaline solution always succeeds well. If it be required to determine the sulphur contained in a sample of commercial sulphur, or in a precipitate of sulphuret of arsenic or antimony produced in an analysis, or in natural sulphurets, the sample is heated for some hours in a solution of potash, which dissolves the sulphur and the sulphurets of arsenic or antimony completely. Chlorine is then passed into the liquid, when in a very short time the three substances pass into the state of sulphuric, arsenic, and antimonic acids, which remain dissolved as alkaline salts. It is then only necessary to acidify the liquid by muriatic acid, to enable the sulphuric acid to be precipitated by chloride of barium, after the excess of chlorine has been driven off by heat.

The sulphate of baryta must be washed for a long time, calcined, and digested in muriatic acid and a little chloride of barium. It is only after a second washing and a second calcination, that the weight of the sulphate of baryta can be taken for the calculation of the quantity of sulphur. The necessity for these operations arises from the property possessed by sulphate of barium of carrying down with it a certain quantity of the salts contained in the solution, and only abandoning them by washing after calcination. They are indispensable in the determination of sulphur in the form of sulphate of baryta, whatever be the nature of the oxidizing agent employed.

The action of chlorine in a solution of potash serves for the determination of the sulphur in all metallic sulphurets. For this purpose the sulphuret must be perfectly pulverized, and digested for some hours in a solution of potash heated to 122°–140° F.; the chlorine is then passed in. The sulphur is rapidly oxidized, and dissolves in the form of sulphate of potash, whilst the metals are converted into oxides, and remain insoluble. The sulphuric acid is precipitated from the alkaline liquid when filtered and acidified with muriatic acid, by chloride of barium.

This method is advantageous, especially for the sulphurets which contain lead, because this metal remains insoluble in the state of peroxide. There is no reason to fear the numerous embarrassments usually caused by the slight solubility of sulphate of lead.

A great number of organic substances are directly soluble in potash, or become so by the oxidizing action of chlorine. In the solutions thus obtained, the reactions of mineral analytical chemistry can generally take place in the same manner as in the absence of organic matters. The action of chlorine and alkalies is particularly useful for the removal of the paper of filters, on which the sulphurets of zinc, lead, and some other more or less volatile metals have been collected. The getting rid of the paper by the action of chlorine in an alkaline solution is an advantageous substitute for burning, which almost always causes loss.

One of the substances which present the greatest difficulties is the vulcanized India-rubber, into which oxides of lead and zinc are often introduced. This substance is first of all submitted to the prolonged action of boiling nitric acid, which reduces it into a state of minute division; water and an excess of potash are then added to the turbid liquid, and a current of chlorine is passed into the mixture; the oxides of zinc and lead are deposited, together with a white resinous matter; the sulphur remains dissolved in the form of an alkaline sulphate, and is determined as sulphate of baryta. As to the insoluble portion, it is treated with acetic acid, which dissolves the oxides of zinc and lead, and these are afterwards precipitated as sulphurets by sulphuretted hydrogen.

By this means the exact determination of the mineral substances contained in the caoutchouc may be effected in very little time; and this is certainly an example of one of the most difficult analyses, in consequence of the presence of organic matter.

II. *Action of Chlorine in a Liquid containing Free Acetic Acid and a certain proportion of Alkaline Acetates.*

Under these circumstances chlorine has a much less energetic oxidizing action than in presence of caustic alkalies. Thus free sulphur and the sulphur of metallic sulphurets only become very slowly acidified; the metals, which do not form very permanent peroxides, remain dissolved, or dissolve as protoxides in the free acetic acid. On the other hand, those metals which are capable of forming stable peroxides, undecomposable by acetic acid, give rise to such peroxides, and in this manner may be exactly separated from the other metals.

Lead and manganese are those to which this action is the most readily applicable. They may be separated thus from the alkalies, magnesia, &c., and from several metals, especially zinc, copper, nickel, &c. The operation must be carried on in the following manner:—

An acetic solution of the oxides is prepared, to which a certain quantity of acetate of soda is added, and the whole heated to 122° or 140° F. A current of chlorine is then passed into it, and interrupted as soon as the peroxide is deposited, which soon takes place. This is washed by decantation, and filtered. The insoluble portion contains all the lead or manganese; the liquid, the other oxides.

This process cannot be employed for the separation of lead and manganese from iron and cobalt. In presence of these metals, the precipitation of the binoxide is effected with difficulty, and the precipitate always retains a noticeable proportion of oxides of iron and cobalt.

In concluding this report, we have yet to call the attention of all chemists to a fact mentioned in this memoir, namely, the very singular property possessed by many substances and certain powders otherwise inert, of inducing a rapid evolution of oxygen in alkaline solutions into which chlorine is being passed. This phenomenon resembles the remarkable decomposition of oxygenated water and that of chlorate of potash in contact with the oxides of copper and manganese. It may be produced with facility and certainty by directing a current of chlorine into a solution of potash previously brought to a temperature of 194° or 212° F., and holding in suspension some quartz in fine powder, iron pyrites, arsenical copper, or oxides of copper or oxides of copper, nickel and cobalt.

When this decomposition commences, it almost entirely resists the oxidizing action of the chlorine; but it may be prevented, in analytic operations, by reducing the mineral substances of which the composition is to be ascertained, to a very fine powder.

The evolution of oxygen just referred to is sometimes observed during the manufacture of chlorate of potash on a large scale, both when the chlorine passes into the milk of lime at a temperature above 140° E., and when the chlorate of lime is heated with the chloride of potassium.

The presence of silica in the lime is sufficient to explain this evolution of oxygen, and the diminution in the weight of the chlorate of potash which is caused by it.—*Comptes Rendus*, December 5, 1853, p. 835, in *Chem. Gaz.*, Feb. 1, 1854.

Debaugne has remarked that the addition of syrup of orange peel to water aids the solution of iodine, and that if two grains of tannin be added to six ounces of water it effects the solution of *ten* grains of iodine.

ANALYSIS OF THE MINERAL WATERS OF MONT DORE.

BY M. THENARD.

I evaporated in a large silver dish, which M. A. De Clermont placed at my disposal, $38\frac{1}{4}$ litres of the water of the source of the Madeleine, which is the water we drink. I reduced it to 765 cubic centilitres, and gathered the sediment deposited with great care. I then transferred the whole to the laboratory of my son at Talmay, where the experiments were carried on in the month of August. The deposit consisted of carbonic acid, lime, magnesia, silica, and a very minute quantity of oxide of iron; treated properly it yielded also small traces of arsenic.

As for the liquid portion, it only contained salts, with a soda base, carbonate sulphate and common salt; but by means of Marsh's apparatus, we could extract also as much arsenic as would coat over readily many porcelain capsules with the metallic film.

This experiment is made so easily to exhibit the arsenic in the waters of Mont Dore, that it is only necessary to take 2 litres and reduce them to 4 or 5 centilitres, and examine them in the ordinary way by zinc and sulphuric acid.

If it be inquired in what state the arsenic exists in these waters, it is easy to show that it is in the state of acid united with soda, since it is found in the liquor left by reducing the minera water to nearly 1·40 of its volume, and that this liquor only contains soda salts. Every thing leads me to believe that the salt is an arseniate and not an arsenite; perhaps formed by the action of carbonate of soda on arseniate of iron. What gives some probability to this is, that there is formed in the cisterns where the water has lain, a red deposit which contains an arseniated red oxide of iron. Still, how does this water contain arsenic, as an arseniate of soda?

To determine this the arsenic was converted into arseniuretted hydrogen, which was then decomposed completely by heat in a small glass tube; the tube was then dried and weighed accurately; then the arsenic removed by nitric acid, and finally washed, dried and weighed a second time. The difference between the two weights gives the quantity of arsenic.

Though the proceeding is well-known, yet it may not be useless to describe a careful experiment.

Into a small flask, with two tubules, water is put to fill the flask two-thirds, and some distilled and granulated zinc added. Into one opening, is passed a straight tube which is carried down to the bottom of the liquid, and the lower end of which is drawn out thin and turned up so as to prevent the entrance of bubbles. Into the other opening is fitted a tube bent at a right angle, the farther extremity is connected with a horizontal tube containing first a little cotton to retain the drops which may form there, and beyond this some fragments of chloride of calcium to dry the gas. This horizontal tube communicates with another tube also horizontal, long, straight, and as far as the first half of its length placed on a bar over a furnace, the other half being surrounded with ice and drawn to a point at its extremity. A leaf of tinfoil protected the heated portion from the intensity of the fire. The apparatus being thus disposed, the operation is commenced by pouring little by little the sulphuric acid into the two tubulures, by the straight tube, by means of a small movable funnel. When the vessels were full of hydrogen, the second horizontal tube was heated to redness, and care was taken that no deposit took incipient place in the cool part of the tube, and that in lighting the gas at the capillary extremity, no stain was produced upon a porcelain capsule (obvious precautions to ensure purity of the zinc and acid).

This done, the liquid to be analyzed was added very gradually into the tubulated flask, through the straight tube, surmounted by the little funnel, and by degrees the sulphuric acid was added to sustain the action.

The disengagement of the gas, which is the guide in this stage, ought never be too rapid, which may be known by lighting the hydrogen jet at the extremity of the tube. Should bubbles escape by the straight tube, even though drawn out and turned up, the upper opening may be closed with a small cork.

Presently, the arsenic may be seen deposited in the cooled part of the tube, where it forms a very brilliant metallic layer; no traces of it are carried beyond this, for when the hydrogen escaping is inflamed, it gives no stain upon porcelain.

The experiment was carried on for a long time to ensure the total removal of the arsenic.

When the reaction is terminated, (which is known by the absence of deposit of stain on the porcelain, nor is a weak solution of nitrate of silver rendered turbid by the gas) the apparatus is left to cool, and the portion of the tube containing the arsenic is separated with a file; the tube is then well dried within and without and weighed; the arsenic is next dissolved out by nitric acid, the tube washed with distilled water, dried and weighed a second time; the difference of weight gives the quantity of arsenic.

I have found thus, that 200 cubic centimetres arising from 765 centilitres, to which the 38·25 litres, of mineral water, reduced by evaporation, contained 4 milligrammes, 50 of arsenic Hence, the 765 centilitres, and of course the 38·25 litres, which furnished the foregoing, ought to contain 0.172 of a gramme.

Hence, also, one litre of the water of Mount Dore contains:

Gr. 0.00045 of arsenic.

Gr. 0.000689 of arsenious acid.

Gr. 0.001058 of neutral arseniate of soda,

Supposing that the arsenic acid is formed of 100 of metal and 53.139 of oxygen, and the neutral arseniate of soda of 100 of acid and 54.97 of baze.

It may be said then that these waters contain in a litre, at the temperature of their source, 1 milligramme, or more exactly, a little more than 1 milligramme of neutral arseniate of soda. It cannot be doubted that the powerful action of these waters on the economy is not due to this arseniate. Other waters in the vicinity of Mount Dore, and even some from a distance, contain probably arsenic also. Some experiments made on less than a pint of the waters of Saint Nectaire show that they also contain arsenic.—*Cosmos*, June 30, 1854.

Varieties.

OXIDE OF CARBON AS A POISON.

Some Experiments made upon Carbonic Oxide by M. ADRIEU CHERROT.

As carbonic acid gas plays only the part of an obturator, and that it is indecomposable at a low temperature, it is incapable of furnishing oxygen necessary for combustion or for supporting life, and it causes death by pure and simple asphyxia. It is quite otherwise with pure oxide of carbon. In fact, carbonic oxide in contact with our wonderful mechanism for combustion, produces the three following effects, by passing into the condition of carbonic acid:

1st. The subtraction of oxygen and its results.

2d. The combustion of this oxygen and its consequences.

3d. The formation of carbonic acid and its results.

These three effects are inseparable, and the last occasions immediate asphyxia, by stopping the action of the lungs and every act of movement; but, at the same time, the oxygen has been condensed, by which a compressing action and a tearing effect from the vacuum formed is produced; and, farther, the transformation of carbonic oxide into carbonic acid gives place to a disengagement of about 6,000 equivalents of heat for each litre (2 lbs. 2 ozs.) of oxygen burned up in the cellules which contained the oxygen going to enrich the blood. These 6,000 equivalents of heat, developed in contact with the cells and with the atoms or small spheres of oxygen, occasion inevitably a disorganization by cauterizing them, which produces the acute pain that accompanies the poisoning by carbonic oxide, so different from the effect of carbonic acid, which, as we have found occur in the mines of Pont Gibaud, produces an agreeable drunkenness, passing gradually into a mild lethargy, then into harassing sensations: consequently the study of the effect of carbonic oxide considered as a poison is a very complex question, and of which the study is of the highest interest in a toxicological point of view.

Contrary to what is usually stated, carbonic oxide produced by combustion is a very weak reducing agent, not being able to remove oxygen from the class of metals which embraces iron, so that theories based upon this action are erroneous. The carbonic oxide formed by combustion—that is to say, that containing four, five, or even six volumes of azote—is not a powerful reducer, while pure carbonic oxide is. A succession of poisonous inhalations of this gas produces a most distressing state of health. M. Cherrot made some experiments upon the inhalation of this gas at Stolberg, in Prussia, in 1846, while zinc ores were being smelted. M. Cherrot inhaled the carbonic oxide escaping through the chimney by means of a pipette, through which he sucked it, and expired the gas under a vessel of water. "While occupied with this operation, the engineer had occasion to speak with me, and struck me on the shoulder without my taking notice. I then made movements apparently as if swallowing the gas, and fell on my back as if struck by lightning. The note taken of my appearance then was as follows:

Externally—The eyes turned out backward, the limbs rigid, the skin discolored, the veins swollen and showing a deep black line under the skin.

Internally—The sensibility extreme, the life being so to say exalted, all the chief ideas, interests and dominant affections are presented to the perception as in an instantaneous mirage; severe pains in the thorax like an internal laceration, accompanied by a feeling as if the brain were strongly compressed; insensibility to the treatment applied, fresh air, lotions of vinegar and water, and ammonia, to the nostrils; in a quarter of an hour sensation returned, and with it the internal pains, passing into a sensation of suffocation, accompanied by chill and cold sweat over the head and body; lassitude continued for several days, and digestion was much impaired, and for many months the nervous system was much depressed, with dread of some impending shock, and terminating, in my case, in insensibility in the tops of the fingers, varying in degree with the state of the atmosphere."—*Repertoire de Pharmacie*, May, 1854.

NOTICE OF AN ATTEMPT TO POISON WITH STRYCHNIA.

BY H. F. FISH, OF WATERBURY, CONN.

On the 4th of March last, a gentleman of this city brought me a small basket containing his dinner, which, he said, he had been deterred from eating owing to the discovery of a very unpleasant bitter taste developed on biting a fried cake. The basket was wrapped loosely in a paper, and my attention was immediately called to some white grains lying near and under the bottom of the basket. On examining these, as well as the contents of the basket, with a magnifying glass, I was enabled to obtain and preserve nearly all the suspected substance, not actually absorbed by, or adhering to, the various articles of food. From the physical aspect and intense bitter taste of these small white grains, I was induced to think the suspected substance was *amorphous commercial strychnia*, combined, as that sort of strychnia generally is, with *brucia*, in just sufficient quantity to render it *chemically impure*. I employed the following means for identifying these substances.

1st. A portion of the suspected powder was boiled with water, but remained nearly, if not quite, insoluble, imparting to the water, on cooling, a slight opacity. The taste of this mixture was purely and intensely bitter, leaving upon the tongue, for many hours, a peculiar impression.

2d. A portion of the same powder was then submitted to the action of nitric acid of 44°. It was entirely dissolved, without any evolution of gas, and the mixture assumed a decided *brick red color*.

3d. A portion of the same substance, not more than one-tenth of a grain, was moistened with strong sulphuric acid; to this a minute quantity of red ferrocyanide of potassium was added, when a copious violet color, of remarkable beauty, was produced.

Again, some of the same powder was moistened with strong sulphuric acid, and a single drop of a strong solution of yellow chromate of potassa added. The usual violet color was decided and abundant, but not so striking in its effects as in the preceding experiment.

If it be asked, which, of all these results, was the most satisfactory, I reply, all of them were decided and characteristic; but I regard the last with red ferrocyanide of potassium, (next to the peculiar taste,) as the most decided and delicate. I should think that the violet color in this experiment could be produced by the presence of even so small a quantity as the one-thousandth part of a grain of the ordinary *commercial strychnia.*

The contents of the basket were bread and butter, dried beef, cheese, fried cakes, and a small fruit pie. The cakes and beef had retained a larger proportion of the strychnia than the other articles. On examining the upper crust of the pie, some minute particles of the strychnia were readily discerned adhering to it. The whole have been carefully sealed up and laid aside for future examination, if necessary. Judging from the quantity found in the basket and on the paper, I should think that at least ten grains of strychnia had been thrown into the basket.

The position of the basket during the forenoon of this day, the limited number of workmen who have access to the work-room, with some other attending circumstances, leave no doubt upon my mind, that an attempt at sure and fatal poisoning was made, and the individual suspected has since left the country.—*Amer. Journ. of Pharmacy*, July, 1854.

Syrupus Manganesiæ Phosphatis.—By Thomas S. Wiegand.—The attention of the medical profession having been called to manganese as a remedial agent, and many writers having recommended it as suitable to those cases in which the ferruginous salts were inapplicable by reason of their tendency to produce headache, it was thought that a phosphatic salt of manganese would be preferable to any other preparation, as the phosphates generally have been found advantageous in anemic conditions of the system. To be a satisfactory preparation, it should be in solution and unalterable by exposure to the air.

The following formula, combining these pre-requisites, is of such a strength that each fluid drachm contains five grains of phosphate of manganese:

℞. Sulphate of manganese (in crystals)	℥ jss. gr. xvii.
Phosphate of soda	℥ iiss. or q. s.
Chlorohydric acid	f. ʒ iv.
Water q. s. ft.	f. ℥ vii.
Sugar q. s. ft.	f. ℥ xiiss.

Dissolve the salts separately each in half a pint of water, and add the solution of phosphate of soda to the solution of sulphate of manganese as long as it produces a precipitate, which wash with cold water, and dissolve by means of the chlorohydric acid; dilute till it measures seven fluid ounces, then add sugar sufficient to make up the bulk of twelve and a half fluid ounces.—*Ibid.*

EDITORIAL.

The City Inspector (R. C. Downing) has, in his late public report, entered upon the pleasing office (to him no doubt) of enlightening the public upon a subject which he does not understand ; but it being the usual practice to run down distillery milk as injurious to health, especially that of children, he has placed side by side with an analysis of milk from Westchester, that of distillery milk also, and from the figures endeavors to prove the deficiencies of the latter. By condensing the figures of the analytic report they read thus :

	Water.	Butter.	Albumen and Cheese.	Sugar.	Phosphate lime, iron, and magnesia.	Chloride potassium and sodium.
Westchester Milk.......	87·7	30·5	65.	40·	4·3	2·2
Distillery Milk..........	891·5	6·55	46.	47·	5·75	8·

Now, without impugning the correctness of the analysis (which we think migh be done) we may state in the first place, that any argument derived from the foregoing to prove that distillery milk is injurious to health, or *inferior* to grass-fed milk, would go for nothing. To form a proper value of the two kinds of milk respectively, there should be exactness in the milk being obtained under similar circumstances, that is the variety or race of the cow, its own age, the age of the milk, and the time of day she was milked should be alike—not one of which in this case was noted—so that as *absolute* comparisons, the inspector's analyses go for nothing. As relative comparisons, they amount to little, and are in no way derogatory to the quality of distillery milk. If we contrast the quantity of solid matter yielded by both they stand thus in 1,000 parts of the milk :

	Westchester.	Distillery.
Butter...................... } Sugar...................... }	70·50	53·55
Phosphates and chlorides.....	6·50	8·75
Cheese.......................	65·	46·

The deficiencies here in the distillery milk are cheese and butter ; but butter and sugar nourish animals in the same way, and are equally appropriated in the stomach, and may, therefore, replace each other, and in this view their proportions are little below the average. The saline matter is *larger* in amount in the swill milk, and this is one reason why we do not think the analysis correct; but, were it also diminished, all that this report would prove, would be, that the distillery milk was more watery and *weak, but not, therefore, unhealthy*. It resembles very much *asses'* milk, so useful to the infantile and dyspeptic stomach, because it is a little less rich in cheese, and, therefore, easier of digestion. But even this "distillery milk" is not a bad sample of milk from a grass-fed cow. Professor Johnston, no mean authority in this matter, in his analysis of milk, gives a greater quantity of water as usually contained than is present in this *deleterious article.*

So much for the comparative analyses--they prove nothing—then as to the question they were meant to prove, namely, is swill milk deleterious? and to which the public voice shouts a responsive yes, and Inspector Downing in his report gives a Buncombe affirmative, we, on the contrary, boldly take the opposite ground, and assert that distillery milk is neither necessarily nor really weaker or worse than pasture fed milk. Why should it? The animal is in good health when it gives milk, and is placed in the circumstances to give good milk, and an abundance of it. Much is talked of sickly animals, filth of the place, diseased hoofs, &c. This is all nonsense. If the animals were in a state of disease they would not give milk, it would gradually diminish and ultimately dry up as the animal sickens. We know animals are badly cared in those places up town, where cows are kept until they sicken and die; but that does not make the milk unhealthy. If distillery milk were unhealthy, then would every one in the large cities of Great Britain be poisoned, for there the practice is universal in large cities to feed them on *wash* and *grains* from the distiller. In such establishments cows are fed on other food than swill, and by the sugar and small quantity of alcohol left in the swill they are *stimulated* to eat more hay than they would if pasture fed, and thence as well as from the greater rest enjoyed by the animal, more milk is given, the quality not deteriorated. It may be desirable to remove those places out of the city; they are nuisances no doubt, but they cannot nor should not be abolished. A large city demands them, and the police regulations of a city should control and improve them. But all these objections are of no value against the quality of the milk given when the animal is fed within doors and aided by the wash of the distillery. Mr. Downing's views on this point coincide with the public, but are, unfortunately for his point, wholly erroneous and similar to those which he has expressed upon the adulterations of city milk. In the trial which took place some time ago where a proprietor of a milk route sued the Irving House proprietor for the amount due for milk, the claim was denied on the ground that distillery milk was furnished instead of grass milk, as per contract. The papers of that date were loaded with details of those places and the quality of the milk, and analyses even were made, and these latter failed then as Mr. Downing's do now to show that the milk was *deleterious.* The plaintiff lost his case, no doubt not on the quality of the milk, but because he did not perform his contract.

Not having received a copy of the continuation of the proceedings of the American Pharmaceutical Association, at Cincinnati, in time for this number, we are obliged to hold it over till our next issue.

NEW YORK

JOURNAL OF PHARMACY.

OCTOBER, 1854.

AMERICAN PHARMACEUTICAL ASSOCIATION.

[In the August number we published an outline of the proceedings of the meeting during the first day. The Address, which was condensed into its recommendations, we reprint now in full, extracted from the *American Journal of Pharmacy*, from which as well as the local papers we have made up our report, and add the remainder of the proceedings of the Association.—Ed.]

ADDRESS TO THE PHARMACEUTISTS OF THE UNITED STATES.

The American Pharmaceutical Association, deeply impressed with the importance of adopting some measure by which the present and future apothecaries of this country may be improved in educational standing, viewed in reference to the practice of their profession, have determined to address their brethren everywhere in our widely extended country, believing that some good results may arise from the hints they will suggest.

By an inquiry extended to all sections of the Union, it has been ascertained that a vital defect exists in the very budding process of pharmaceutical education—the apprenticeship. In all the pharmaceutical institutions of Europe, where degrees are granted to apothecaries, the preliminary service in the shop is a *sine qua non* to admission to the examinations, it being generally four years, and in many of them the attendance on lectures follows this term of practical initiation into the duties of the shop and laboratory. In England, where as yet no degree-granting institution exists among pharmaceutists, the apprenticeship system is carried out by indenture, as in ordinary usage, so important is this preliminary training conceived to be to the education of a pharmaceutical chemist. In many stores in the Atlantic cities north of Virginia, and more especially in Philadelphia, a system of apprenticing exists, yet it rarely happens that a lad is legally indentured; the idea of such an instrument being exceedingly repulsive to most boys who aim at the apothecary business. In lieu of a legal indenture a feeling of honor-bound obligation should exist, equally binding on the part of apprentice and employer, capable of retaining the connection until the obligation is cancelled by termination of service and completion of education. For want of this tie between learners and employers, our country has been deluged with incompetent drug clerks, whose claim to the important position they hold or apply for is based on a year or two's service in the shop, perhaps under circumstances illy calculated to increase their knowledge. These clerks in turn become principals, and have the direction of others—alas! for the progeny that some of them bring forth, as ignorance multiplied by ignorance will produce neither knowledge nor skill.

When we investigate the causes of this state of things, it will be found to arise primarily in the want of a correct feeling of the dignity and responsibility of the calling of the apothecary as a branch of the medical profession. The larger number of those who deal in drugs and medicines do it solely to make money; they aim at making the most out of the least outlay of capital or trouble; to *sell* medicines is their vocation, and he is the best clerk who can sell the *most*, under whatever circumstances it is effected. To avoid the necessity of gaining the requisite knowledge of practical pharmacy, it is no uncommon habit to buy their preparations ready made, except the simpler ones, and at the lowest price, and the business, thus *shorn* of its most interesting department, the application of chemistry to the conversion of crude drugs into medicines, becomes a mere store keeping, where the drug clerk is kept putting up and selling parcels and bottles of medicines, the preparation of which, and the beautiful reactions often concerned in their manufacture, he is as complete a stranger to as though they did not exist. Is it any wonder, then, that, after one or two years service, the apprentice should fancy that he had learned the business as a *seller* of drugs and chemicals, and becoming uneasy at the prospect of a four years term, breaks the slender connection that binds him to his employer, and starts out as a fledged clerk? In these days of manufacturing pharmaceutists, when most of the nicer preparations, from Dover's powder to fluid extracts, are to be bought ready made, the temptation to purchase them is great, even to the qualified principal, who thus saves himself the responsibility and trouble attending their manufacture; but he is apt to forget the injustice thus done to his *protegés*, who are thus deprived of the important practical knowledge only to be gained by becoming familiar with the manipulations they involve. Having abandoned, to a large extent, the making of these preparations, such apothecaries are ready but too often to accept the agency of the numerous quackeries that abound to swell their sales, and from this are led into the origination of secret compounds, and become quacks themselves. Further, they are induced to trench on the business of the tobacconist and the variety storekeeper, by keeping their wares, and sometimes to a considerable amount.

So long as this abandonment of the legitimate duties of the pharmaceutist is permitted, it is hopeless to expect apprentices will feel that interest in the business they have embarked in that is excited when they are called upon to carry out the various chemical and pharmaceutical processes that properly belong to every well conducted apothecary's shop.

Familiarity with these processes, in which the phenomena of mechanical division, solution, extraction, distillation and other operations are practically studied, is the true basis upon which to build the knowledge required by a skilful extemporaneous pharmaceutist, or prescriptionist, whose vocation includes the highest department of the art of an apothecary. It is, indeed, the only basis upon which it should repose. *Making* the officinal preparations is, therefore, an indispensable part of pharmaceutical education, and no apothecary, whose scheme of business does not include at least a considerable portion of them, can efficiently educate those under his care.

It may be said that the preparation of the strictly pharmaceutical compounds by the manufacturer of character more surely supplies the dispenser with medicines of unexceptionable quality. This is only partially true, because the insttiution of such a branch of business by the qualified soon calls into its scope unquallified and careless men, who look at profit and not at therapeutic power in the purchase and treatment of drugs. Besides, the temptation to expand their business is a strong inducement, even to the skilful, to make quantities of fugitive and easily decomposable compounds, which are forced on distant markets, where they are to be dispensed, and where, too often, the dispenser deals them out in full assurance of their excellence. The gradual effect of this custom on the dispenser is to render him tributary to the druggist and manufacturing pharmaceutist for many preparations, the efficiency of which he is bound, by the highest calls of duty, to be personally assured of.

Before leaving this part of the subject we would urge a careful consideration of these hints by those of the brethren to whom they apply, that they may see whether their duty to themselves, to their apprentices and assistants, and to the medical profession does not require them to prepare all the officinal medicines that their shops will admit of (that are prone to deterioration, or are difficult to test). In this category certain of the extracts and of other classes of preparations are not included, where the use of steam or a vacuum pan, or some other peculiarity of the process may be required, not at the command of the apothecary. There are many chemicals that can be easily made in the smallest apothecary shop, from materials it must necessarily possess, and which will interest the apprentice, yet the safe guard which analysis offers to the apothecary, in protecting his stock of chemicals from adulteration, renders it less important to include these within the scope of his laboratory.

The correspondence with apothecaries before alluded to has placed the Association in possession of many facts bearing on the condition of pharmacy and pharmaceutical education within the United States. It appears that the tenure of apprenticeship resting on the simple agreement of the parties apprenticed has become so lax, especially in the Western States, that as a general rule very little dependence is placed upon it. Boys are taken at a venture by the year, the employer making the best bargain he can, feeling assured that the boy will leave or demand clerk's wages before he has been with him half a regular term. From this cause, it is stated, the number of half-educated assistants is quite large, and presents a serious difficulty in the prosecution of business in the way it should be conducted. As the result of this condition of things it has been found that there are three classes of individuals engaged in pharmaceutical pursuits who claim the interest of the Association, and to whom more particularly this address is directed, viz., *first*, those who are imperfectly acquainted with pharmacy and are in business for themselves;

secondly, those who have been but half educated as apprentices and who are now assistants receiving salaries, having the responsibility of business entrusted to them; and *thirdly*, those who are now apprentices or beginners under circumstances and with ideas unfavorable to the acquirement of a thorough knowledge of the drug and apothecary business. Of course all those instances, which happily are not a few, where individual ambition or natural talent for study or business has triumphed over the difficulties alluded to, are not included.

In thus addressing the individuals composing these three classes, the Association disclaims all disposition to arrogate to themselves *as a body* any superior claim to knowledge or skill. They have associated together to improve themselves, and to adopt measures to improve the profession of pharmacy at large. They know that these classes of individuals *exist;* they feel that a remedy is loudly called for, which, whatever it may be, can only be rendered efficacious by the consent and co-operation of the parties interested. It is, therefore, earnestly hoped that this address will be received in the kindly spirit in which it is offered, and its suggestions examined and weighed by all who may feel themselves to belong to the classes addressed.

After a young man has commenced business he rarely feels disposed, or thinks he has time for systematic study, and is apt to discard all attempts at it, depending on the occasional references to books rendered necessary by the absolute demands of business. This is a mistake. There is sufficient time if it is rightly applied. Let the young proprietor who feels his deficiency make it a rule, before making each preparation, as required, to read carefully the commentary in the Dispensatory, and afterwards note the correspondence or difference of his results with those laid down. This will cause him to detect errors, if they exist, or to correct his own, will soon give him a useful habit of observation of great practical value, and will gradually excite an interest in the collateral branches of science, chemistry and botany, that, if pursued, will place him on the high road to professional competency. The young proprietor should adopt at first an honorable scheme of conducting business; he should determine to sell *good* drugs and medicines, come what will, and in doing so he will have a right to the best prices, whether he gets them or not. He should cultivate a good feeling toward the medical practitioners of his neighborhood, should study the interest of the latter so far as the efficiency of medicines is concerned, and physicians will soon, from interest, incline towards him. He will aid his success by storing his memory with general information useful to his patrons, and render himself as necessary to the comfort as he is to the health of his neighborhood by his willingness to give it out.

These remarks apply to the dispenser of medicines rather than to one doing a mixed or wholesale business; on the former mainly depends the progress of pharmacy, and remembering his own imperfect opportunities, he should give to his apprentices or subordinates the best tuition he is capable of. It is a mistaken and short-sighted policy in the apothecary to withhold instruction beyond the merest calls of business, under the impression that it will react unfavorably to his interest. The man who has efficient assistants will have his reputation increased instead of diminished, and this will be a safeguard against ingratitude, when it occurs.

To this end he should improve and extend his pharmaceutical library by annual additions; he should encourage the periodical literature of pharmacy, to keep posted up with the improvements and discoveries of the day, and he should exhibit such an interest in his apprentices or assistants as will encourage them to adopt studious habits, which is the best safeguard against the temptations into which young men and boys are drawn, unless they have some regular object of pursuit.

The *second class*, or assistants but half educated, are a numerous and interesting portion of the pharmaceutical community. They are found everywhere, because the causes of their deficiencies exist everywhere, though not equally so. To induce these to do *now* what they should have done in their minority is the object of this appeal. The assistant, except in those instances where the pressure of business is continuous during business hours, has ample opportunities for study. He should not fail to embrace them on every occasion, whilst his mind is untrammelled by the troubles and responsibilities of the engagements peculiar to the proprietor. He should beware of the idea, that he "knows enough to conduct business." In offering himself as a pharmaceutical assistant, a young man tacitly declares that he is capable of conducting a dispensing establishment; that he is a fit adjunct to the physician in combatting disease. He assumes a responsible position, next only to that of his employer. In the eye of the law he *is* responsible, in the absence of his employer, for the conduct of business, and is actionable for the results of ignorance or carelessness. A proper sense of this should induce the assistant to qualify himself by study; to read regularly and understandingly, and assist his reading when necessary by experiment and observation. He should never let a false pride induce him to pass over an error uncorrected, and he should always keep in view that his destiny is to be a proprietor, and act as becomes a pharmaceutist. By pursuing these suggestions many third or fourth rate assistants might command the best situations and good salaries.

The *third class*—the beginners or apprentices—call forth the earnest sympathy of the Association. It depends much on the employer and his chief assistant whether the apprentice will make rapid or slow progress, or whether he will ever make a good apothecary: it very much also rests with himself. Some dispositions are so inimical to tuition that no amount of pains will fashion them into shape; yet it often happens that a promising youth will grow into irregularities from the want of a little candid training on the part of the employer. If there is any one fault in American boys more prominent than another, it is the inclination to act independently of authority. The "young America" spirit leads to various ill results, one of the chief of which is imperfect education, whether professional, mercantile or mechanical. It is one phase of this ill spirit that is now filling the ranks of pharmacy with half-educated clerks. Let the young apothecary do *well* what he attempts, and carry it out on al occasions, from the most menial service of the shop to the most accurate operation of the laboratory. Let him vie with his fellows in the graceful handling of the spatula and the pestle, in the neatness of folding a powder or bundle, in the accuracy of writing or attaching a label, and in the quick, quiet, and courteous mode of conducting business at the counter; these are all parts of the accomplishment of a perfect pharmaceutist. The beginner should early adopt the idea that his vocation consists of something besides a business for gaining a livelihood; it also partakes of the character of a liberal profession, and demands of its votaries that they uphold its ethics even at the sacrifice of gain, that they sell good medicines even if they get low prices, because it is wrong to dispense bad medicines when it is possible to get good. It would be well if every beginner could have a vision of the duties he has to perform before entering the precincts of the shop as an apprentice. The picture would discourage all but the earnest ones, who, seeing beyond present inconveniences and annoyances, aim at the highest qualification. To these the apothecary's store, with all its petty details and trials, its busy days and tedious evenings, affords a field rich in the produce it yields to the unremitting exertions of the earnest student; as with Scheele and Davy so with many an one in our day. World-renowned celebrity will cling to names unsuspected of greatness, the early efforts of whose possessors are now confined to the narrow limits of the shop.

It is a misfortune to many that an idea of the lucrativeness of the apothecary business has long since obtained popular credence; and often the fond parent, anxious that his boy should be started on the road to fortune, has unwittingly doomed him to an unhappy companionship with the pestle and mortar, when in the counting room of the merchant or the workshop of the machinest he might have attained to their desires.

The numerous instances of individuals in other callings who have commenced as apothecaries bear ample testimony to the truth of this statement, and are a speaking caution to all concerned, that the fitness of boys for pharmaceutical pursuits should be ascertained before placing them with apothecaries.

The difficulties in the way of sustaining schools of pharmacy will here, as in Europe, confine them to large cities, where the number of students and the accessories to study are numerous. Slow but regular currents will circulate between these and distant towns, and their graduates, in seeking spheres of action, will carry back with them the principles they imbibe, and thus act as examples to their less favored brethren, altogether advantageous to the public weal. The vast importance, therefore, of good schools of pharmacy, where the sciences pertaining to our art are regularly taught, is so evident, that this Association freely extends its countenance and encouragement to those already existing, and to all new efforts, claiming for them the patronage they deserve.

Such are some of the more prominent points at issue in the educational reform so greatly needed in the pharmaceutical body of the United States. If the incubus of quackery was removed, a general feeling of the necessity of better means of pharmaceutical education excited, and a strong chain of associations, linked together by fraternal feeling, established, the prospects of American pharmacy would be flattering indeed. The most sanguine believers in progress do not expect a sudden reformation; but there are many who look with strong faith and much interest to the silent influence of a better education in working a change among the individuals of the profession, and it is the earnest hope of this Association that the hints now offered in this address will not be lost, but that many a brother, in his distant unpretending scene of action, will be induced to raise his standing and usefulness by personal exertions, and become a light to his brethren and a boon to his neighborhood.

The fifth document accompanying the report, relative to the expediency of seeking Congressional action in reference to the appointment of drug examiners, was read and accepted. The committee observe that "in view of the partizan character of political appointments, and the little dependence that can be placed on the judgment of the appointing power in cases like the one under consideration, it will be inexpedient to make any application to Congress until such time as the drug law itself may require a general change or re-enactment, when a clause might be inserted making it *obligatory* on the Secretary of the Treasury to appoint fully qualified pharmaceutists," in lieu of abstract chemists, country physicians, and others, who are unfitted for the post.

The report on "The Circular of Instructions to the Special Examiners of Drugs, &c.," issued by Mr. Guthrie, Secretary of the Treasury, referred to the Committee on "Standards for the Inspection of Drugs," was now read and accepted.

The report of the Committee on "A System of Standards for the Government of the Special Examiners of Drugs, &c.," referred to Messrs. Proctor and Coggeshall, was now read by the Chairman of the Committee, was accepted, and laid on the table for future action.

A communication from Gustavus L. Simmons, of Sacramento, California, corresponding member of the Association, was now read, accepted, and laid on the table.

The report on the subject of "Home Adulterations" being called for, C. B. Guthrie, Chairman, stated that the committee had not been unmindful of the task assigned them, that in proceeding in their labors the subject had so increased in magnitude and importance that they did not feel ready to report this year, and thought that by the time of the next annual meeting they would be able to produce a report that would surprise the members of the Association. The committee was continued, and encouraged to proceed.

The consideration of the report on Statistics was postponed until to-morrow at the request of the committee.

The report on Quack Medicines, was now called for, read, and accepted. This report, after advising that no direct action should be taken by the Association, suggests in view of the strong popular feeling in favor of these medicines:

"1st. That this desire for medicine can be gratified in a legitimate way by regular officinal preparations.

"2d. That it is the duty as well as the interest of the apothecaries and druggists to advocate the use of the officinal medicines in lieu of the quackery of the day.

"3d. That it is the rightful interest of regular pharmaceutists to divert, in this manner, the thousands which now annually flow into the coffers of quacks, into their own limited stores, where of right it belongs.

"4th. That this can only be done by a united and sustained action on the part of the pharmaceutists and druggists of the Union, by which they will practically refrain from the sale or advocation of secret medicines, and substitute regular officinal compounds for them correctly labelled, with name and directions for use.

"5th. That this course should receive the sanction of physicians as the only one likely to remedy the evil aimed at, as the tendency to take medicine *ad libitum* is a feature of the Anglo-Saxon race, duly inherited by the American people, which, whatever may be its faults, is as much their nature as it is the love of political and personal freedom.

"With regard to the propriety and efficacy of legislative action, we think that movements in that direction should originate in the several States, and be the joint action of the medical and pharmaceutical professions, and when applications are made to Legislatures they should be based on a real interest on the part of druggists and apothecaries generally to abate the evil, and not on a partial or very local movement."

The Association then adjourned to eight o'clock, p.m.

EVENING SESSION.

At the appointed time the President called the meeting to order, and the afternoon minutes were read and adopted.

On motion, the Report on the Certificate of Membership was taken up for consideration. Some discussion ensued. The draft submitted by the Committee was objected to as not meeting the wants of the Association. The design of the artist was objected to as not being appropriate; and the suggested wording of the certificate was considered as being far too positive, making the instrument equal to a diploma, as it certified to the moral as well as professional character and qualifications of the holder.

Mr. Colcord observed that, unfortunately, none of the Committee were present, and he was unable to state their views.

On motion of C. A. Smith, the whole matter was laid on the table until next year, and the Committee continued.

On motion of C. B. Guthrie, the report of the Committee on Standards was directed to be printed in the proceedings.

The importance of the subject was dwelt upon, and it was resolved to continue the committee, (Messrs. Proctor and Coggeshall,) and increase it at the suggestion of its chairman, by the addition of Charles T. Carney, of Lowell, Massachusetts, and Edward S. Wayne, of Cincinnati.

The consideration of Mr. Simmons' report on the state of Pharmacy in California was now resumed, and the Executive Committee were directed to print it in the proceedings.

[We glean from this report, that California, with a population, permanent and floating, of 400,000 souls, has 77 regular druggists, of which San Francisco has 30, Sacramento, 19, Mary'sville, 5, Stockton, 4, Placerville, 3, Nevada, 2, Coloma, 2, Sonora, 2, Diamond Springs, 2, and eight smaller towns each one.

Throughout the mining settlements most of the storekeepers keep an assortment of drugs and patent medicines.

Mr. Simmons observes, "I am happy to record that some of the evils complained of in my last report are being remedied. This is more especially true of San Francisco, Sacramento, Mary'sville, and Stockton, where a great change in the habits of druggists, apothecaries and physicians has occurred. The members of each of these occupations appear to better understand their mutual relations, and, in a majority of cases, we find them adhering to their legitimate business. Most of the physicians who started in either branch of the drug business have found it impossible to go on smoothly and profitably with both professions; and those druggists and apothecaries who were addicted to the practice of prescribing at the counter, have found it to their interest to abandon the habit, observing that the well-educated physicians were adopting the system of separating the two departments of prescribing and compounding medicines."

Mr. Simmons further remarks on the increased attention to convenience and elegance in the pharmaceutical stores, and considers that a large proportion of them will compare favorably with those of the Atlantic States, and more attention is given to the qualifications of employees. Indeed, one of the San Francisco stores is arranged in the most costly and elegant manner. The dispensing spatulas are of gold and silver; attached to the store is a fine laboratory, and a suite of rooms apportioned into library, sitting and consulting apartments, for the special benefit of medical gentlemen, forming a kind of Exchange, where physicians may interchange their views, consult the best or latest authorities, or otherwise spend their time. The entire building is supplied with gas, and an Artesian well in the rear furnishes an abundance of water.

The excessive cost of advertising has proved a difficulty in the way of introducing new quackery, and it is only the older varieties, known at home to the people, that are much sought.—Ed. *Amer. Pharm. Journal.*]

On motion, it was resolved, that the unofficinal formulæ communicated by Messrs. Mathews, of Buffalo, Cummings, of Maine, and Meakim, of New York, be preserved by the Secretary, with a view to publication should future similar contributions accumulate sufficiently to justify it.

After the reading of a letter from the New York delegation to the late President, giving the reasons for their inability to be present, the meeting adjourned to eight o'clock to-morrow morning.

July 26th.—At eight o'clock, A.M., the Association met, and, on invitation, visited in a body the Cabinet of the Cincinnati College of Pharmacy, which has already attained a considerable variety and value, numbering over eight hundred specimens, carefully put up and arranged, the largest in the West, and is rapidly accumulating. It is located in the Museum room of the Miami Medical College, corner of Fifth street and Western row. There are in it seventy-five medicinal and botanical specimens from the East Indies, few of which are known to our Pharmacopœa, besides a large number of medicinal substances, new and not recognized by any of our works upon Materia Medica. The collection of cinchona barks is quite extensive, containing over forty specimens, among which there is a number of specimens of the Granada barks, a new variety which has been thrown into market through the monopoly of the Peruvian Government of the officinal barks. These barks contain a large per cent. of quinine, and the newly discovered alkaloid quinidine.

Before returning to the Hall, the members were gratified in visiting the new steam fire apparatus belonging to the city of Cincinnati, and the invention of one of her citizens.

At half-past ten o'clock, A.M., the President took the chair, and the minutes of the previous meeting were read and adopted.

Dr. Guthrie, as Chairman of the Committee "on the Collection and Arrangement of the Statistics of Pharmacy in the United States," read a sub-report by Joseph Laidley, of Richmond, Va., on the state of Pharmacy in the Southern, Atlantic and Gulf States, accompanied by tables containing much valuable information, which will prove very serviceable to future inquirers.

The sub-report of Dr. Cummings, on the state of Pharmacy in the New England States, was also read, detailing many deficiencies in the practice of pharmacy of that section, and attributing a portion of them to the illiberal course adopted by some physicians. He stated that there were in that part of the country, as by the census of 1850, 907 drug stores; that the condition of the profession was not looked upon as it ought to be; its character was that of a science instead of that of a trade. He alluded with some severity to the jealousy of some physicians to it. He remarked:

"That a great deal of blame attaches to a portion of the members of the medical profession, for the low character of many establishments of pharmacy. In some towns, large and abundantly able to support an apothecary, the physicians, actuated by a mean jealousy and a grasping avarice, covetous of the profits accruing from the sale of medicines, and, in some instances, fearful of displaying their own ignorance, frown down and oppose, by every means in their power, the establishment of a pharmacy by an educated and practical man, who, in his turn, in order that he may be able to keep body and soul together, until he can obtain a footing, is compelled to mingle with the sale of legitimate medicine, confectionary, fancy goods and quack medicines. In such cases, did physicians understand and consult their own interest, we should see them fraternizing with the apothecary, and instead of regarding his profession as merely subordinate and mechanical, recognizing it as nearly, if not equal, in importance and scientific value with their own, to the health and welfare of the community. One thing is certain, that the whole medical profession, with scarcely a single exception, by no means recognizes, as it ought, the importance, the respectability, and the real value of the pharmaceutical profession. Witness the muttering of some at an apothecary being allowed to introduce the Pharmaceutical Association to the medical profession of Maine, at the last meeting of the Maine Medical Association. Witness the National Medical Association excluding delegates from colleges of pharmacy or other pharmaceutical bodies. One grand duty we have to perform is to exalt our profession, to claim for it a place far above mere merchandise, and assert its dignity as a science, and not as a trade.

"A very small proportion of those who have taken up this profession, especially in towns and villages, are educated men, and a still more minute per centage have been educated expressly for it. This fact is the source of many and great evils and it is beginning to be recognized by the public. As a sample of what has just been remarked, let me quote from one of my correspondents in a large town in Maine: 'A few days since, several ounces of sulphuric acid were thrown into a man's face by a clerk in one of our drug stores, probaby under the mistaken idea that the effect would be but momentary. 'Tis a sad case, and will probably result in the loss of both eyes.' This ignorance is becoming known to the public, and there is scarcely a day that I am at home but I hear it rather publicly alluded to in terms indicating a constantly increasing disgust. This ignorance exhibits itself in various ways and on various occasions. A veteran pharmaceutist, from Vermont, writes me: 'On my return from Boston last August, I stopped at Troy, New York, a city of 40,000 souls. In conversation with three of its principle apothecaries, I found that they mistook the dispensatory of Wood and Bache for the Pharmacopœa and that not a single copy of that standard authority could be found in the city. In weight, also, none of the apothecaries used troy weights for weighing beyond two drachms, having no avoirdupois weight.' And in passing, I would remark that I do not believe that medical men themselves, in a larege majority of cases, know the difference between Pharmacopœa and Dispensatory, or can appreciate the difference in the strength of preparations compounded by troy and avoirdupoise weight. I say this on the authority of my own observation, as well as on that of the correspondent whom I have just quoted."

Dr. Guthrie continued the report for the Western States verbally, excused the physicians of that region from any unfriendliness to pharmaceutists, but gave ample evidence to the necessity of pushing measures of pharmaceutical reform in those States.

The Committee on Credentials brought forward the names of J. V. Whetstone and J. W. Hannaford, of Cincinnati, and

W. R. Smith, of Hillsborough, Ohio, who were duly elected members, and signed the constitution.

The report of the late Corresponding Secretary was read and accepted.

On motion of Dr. Guthrie, it was resolved that this Association recommend to the several Colleges of Pharmacy and Pharmaceutical Associations, the appointment of Committees of Correspondence from their own bodies, who shall address the apothecaries of their respective sections upon the objects of this Association, for the promotion of its designs.

The report of the Committee on Prizes was now read by its chairman, C. A. Smith, in which it is recommended, that in view of the limited finances of the Association, but two prizes be offered for the ensuing year. To make the award more honorable to the recipients, it was determined to make them in books rather than in money. The two following resolutions offered by the committee were then adopted.

Resolved, That a copy of twenty-three volumes of the *American Journal of Pharmacy* be (and hereby is) offered for the best essay which shall develope the commercial history of all drugs indigenous to the United States, as senega, spigelia, serpentaria, etc., as regards the manner and places of their collection and preparation for the supply of commerce, the amount annually collected, and the channels through which they enter general commerce.

Resolved, That a copy of the inorganic portion of Gmelin's Handbook of Chemistry, (as published by the Cavendish Society in six volumes,) is offered for the best essay on the question, "Do Hyoscyamus, Belladonna and Conium, grown in the United States, contain their active principles in the same proportions as the European grown plants."

To carry out the object of the resolutions in an efficient and impartial manner, it was

Resolved, That all essays, in answer to the above resolutions, be referred to a special committee of judges, who will report on their relative merit to the next annual meeting of the Association, this committee to consist of Daniel B. Smith, of

Philadelphia, Dr. David Stewart, of Baltimore, and John Meakim, of New York.

Resolved, That if, in the opinion of the judges, none of the essays received are worthy of the prizes, that they decline awarding them in their report; the contributors may then either withdraw their essays or leave them in possession of the Association.

Resolved, That all essays contributed for the prizes be delivered, free of charge, to Daniel B. Smith, of Philadelphia, on or before the second Tuesday of August, 1855, in order to give time for their examination.

On motion of C. A. Smith, it was resolved that when this Association adjourns, it adjourns to meet in the city of New York, on the second Tuesday in September, 1855, at three o'clock, P.M.

The President having announced that the members of the Association were invited by Mr. Lewis Rehfuss to visit his vineyard this afternoon, the invitation was accepted.

On motion of Dr. Guthrie, the names of A. J. Mathews, of Buffalo, and E. S. Wayne, of Cincinnati, were added to the Committee on "Home Adulterations."

The President announced the reception of a copy of an essay on "The Relation between the Atomic Weights of the Chemical Elements, by Josiah P. Cooke, Jr.," from Wm. A. Brewer, late President of the Association. When, on motion, the meeting adjourned to two o'clock this afternoon.

AFTERNOON SESSION.

The President called the meeting to order about the time agreed to, and the Secretary read the minutes.

On motion of C. A. Smith, it was resolved that a committee of three be appointed to draft a law regulating the sale of poisons, to be submitted to the Association at their next annual meeting, and if approved, to be presented to the Legislatures of the several States for their adoption.

The chair appointed Alfred B. Taylor, of Philadelphia,

Joseph Laidley, of Richmond, and Theodore Marsh, of Cincinnati, to this service.

On motion of C. A. Smith, it was resolved that a committee of three be appointed to inquire whether any and what amendments are required by the law regulating the importation of drugs and medicines, to render it more efficient, uniform, and advantageous to the public at large.

The chair appointed C. B. Guthrie, of Memphis, G. D. Coggeshall, L. W. Haskell, of New York, and A. M. Stevens, of Cincinnati, to this duty.

The following preamble and resolution, offered by William Proctor, Jr., were adopted:

This Association having learned with great interest that in the culture of the grape in the neighborhood of Cincinnati, attention has been turned to the production of wines and tartar, and that the success which has thus far attended this branch of industry leads to the belief that in a few years the crop of each will be extensive, it is therefore resolved, in view of the importance of these articles in medicine, that a committee of three be appointed to inquire into the adaptation of these wines for medicinal purposes, and the probable amount and quality of the tartar likely to be produced annually.

The chair committed this inquiry to Lewis Rehfuss, of Cincinnati, C. A. Smith, of Blue Licks, Ky., and C. B. Guthrie, of Memphis.

On motion of the same gentleman, it was

Resolved, Inasmuch as the Constitution of this Association was adopted at a time when the wants of this body were not so well known as at present, that the whole matter of its revision be referred to a suitable committee, to report such amendments as they may deem best to the next annual meeting.

To this important duty Edward Parrish, of Philadelphia, George D. Coggeshall, of New York, and Samuel M. Colcord, of Boston, were appointed.

It was further resolved, that the attention of the pharmaceutists of the United States be directed to the idea of universally adopting a single name to indicate the business of the apothecary, and that the subject be revived at the next annual meeting with a view to officially adopting it if approved.

On motion of S. M. Colcord, the following resolutions were adopted:

Resolved, That those members of the Association who are strangers in Cincinnati express their warmest gratitude for the kindness and attention they have received from the Cincinnati College of Pharmacy.

Resolved, That the thanks of the Association are tendered to the President and Secretary for the able manner in which they have discharged their duties.

Resolved, That we appreciate the efforts of the Cincinnati College of Pharmacy to improve the standing and qualifications of the drug dealers of the West, and that we recommend them to extend their sphere of action to meet those of other pharmaceutical societies, until such time as new organizations are made within their sphere.

The Association now adjourned to accept the invitation of Mr. Rehfuss to his hospitable mansion, situate a few miles west of Cincinnati, agreeing to meet on their return for final adjournment.

[Mr. R., one of the most skilful apothecaries of Cincinnati, is about relinquishing his business, and devoting his attentiun wholly to the grape culture and its consequents. Being a practical chemist, he has given much attention to the composition of soils in connection with the growth of both American and European grapes, of which last he has about ninety varieties under culture. It is well known to the chemical physiologist, that a large quantity of potassa is annua'ly abstracted from the soil in which grapes are grown, to constitute the base of the bitartrate of potassa found in their juices. A deficiency of this alkali has a marked influence on the wine produced, as when in sufficient proportion so large an amount of acid is removed as to render the wine dryer and more mellow and agreeable, whilst, when deficient, the free acid, not being precipitated from ihe forming wine, like the potassa salt, it is retained, and gives it acerbity. Mr. Rehfuss has experimented successfully by using wood ashes as a manure, and his guests were gratified in comparing wines of the same grape and year, the one produced from ashes manured soil and the other from the same soil without that addition: the former being more bland and mellow than the latter, though equally spirituous. The hilly character of the country around Cincinnati appears to adapt it admirably for the vineyard, and much soil, for this reason, ill-suited to agricultural purposes, has been rendered available and valuable. The grape crop of the present year will be much influenced by the late spring frosts; and a species of mildew, probably the oidium, has made in some vineyards extensive inroads on the grapes after they have attained half their growth. Mr. Rehfuss finds the application of a dilute solution of sulphuret of potassium to stop the progress of this blight when timely applied. From the results of his experiments he anticipates much success in the production of tartar, and in the manufacture of pure brandy. After duly availing themselves of the elegant hospitality of their hostess, and not forgetting the Pure Catawba of their host, the Association returned to the Hall highly gratified with their visit.—ED. *Amer. Jour. Pharm.*]

EVENING SESSION, EIGHT O'CLOCK, P.M.

After the organization of the meeting and the reading of the previous minutes, Dr. Guthrie offered the following resolution, which was unanimously adopted:

Resolved, That the thanks of the Association are due and are hereby tendered to Mr. Lewis Rehfuss for the many interesting and valuable facts furnished in connection with the culture of the grape, and for his generous hospitality.

John Scott, of Cincinnati, having been recommended and endorsed by the Credential Committee, was duly elected, and signed the constitution.

There being no further business, the Secretary read the general minutes, which, after amendments, were adopted as a whole, and the Association adjourned.

The Cincinnati College of Pharmacy provided an elegant entertainment at the Burnet House, that the medical fraternity and the pharmaceutists of the city and Association might cordially unite in sympathy with the efforts of the Association. Seventy persons, invited guests, sat down at nine, P.M. The following officers of the Cincinnati College of Pharmacy had charge of the entertainment:—Dr. W. B. Chapman, President; W. C. Arons, Recording Secretary; E. S. Wayne, Corresponding Secretary; W. J. M. Gordon, Treasurer; W. S. Merrell, Theodore Marsh, J. V. Whetstone, A. H. Stevens, W. H. Coolidge, and John Parr, Trustees.

After the removal of the cloth, toasts and sentiments were given, with speeches from Dr. Lawson, Dr. Mendenhall, Dr. Graham, Dr. Bakhaus, and others of the medical faculty, approving of the object of the Association, and wishing prosperity to the enterprize.

In response to a toast by Dr. Guthrie to the *Cincinnati Gazette*, for the publication of the proceedings of the convention, a reply was made by Colonel Schouler. Mr. Bruen and Mr. McCormick were also called out, and answered for the press. Professor Proctor replied to toasts complimentary to the Philadelphia College of Pharmacy, and Mr. Colcord, of Boston, to those complimentary of the Massachusetts College of Pharmacy.

The absent members were toasted, and the company parted at twelve o'clock.

ON OSMOTIC FORCE.

Abstract of the Bakerian Lecture.

BY PROFESSOR GRAHAM.

This name was applied to the power by which liquids are impelled through moist membrane and other porous septa in experiments on endosmose and exosmose. It was shown that with a solution of salt on one side of the porous septum and pure water on the other side (the condition of the osmometer of Dutrochet when filled with a saline solution and immersed in water,) the passage of the salt outward is entirely by diffusion, and that a thin membrane does not sensibly impede the molecular process. The movement is confined to the liquid salt particles, and does not influence the water holding them in solution, which is entirely passive. It requires no farther explanation. The flow of water inwards on the other hand affects sensible masses of fluid, and is the only one of the movements which can be correctly described as a current. It is osmose and the work of the osmotic force to be discussed.

As diffusion is always a double movement, while salt diffuses out, a certain quantity of water necessarily diffusing in at the same time in exchange, diffusibility might be imagined to be the osmotic force. But the water introduced into the osmometer in this way has always a definite relation to the quantity of salt which escapes, and can scarcely rise in any case above four or six times the weight of salt, while the water entering the osmometer often exceeds the salt, leaving it at least one hundred times. Diffusion, therefore, is quite insufficient to account for the water current.

The theory which refers osmose to capillarity appears to

have no better foundation. The great inequality of ascension assumed among aqueous fluids is found not to exist, when their capillarity is correctly observed; and many of the saline solutions which give rise to the highest osmose are indistinguishable in ascension from pure water itself.

Two series of experiments on osmose were described, the first series made with the use of porous mineral septa, and the second series with animal membrane. The earthenware osmometer consisted of the porous cylinder employed in voltaic batteries, about five inches in depth, surmounted by an open glass tube 0·6 inch in diameter, attached to the mouth of the cylinder by means of a cup of gutta percha. In conducting an experiment the cylinder was filled with any saline solution to the base of the glass tube, and immediately placed in a large jar of distilled water; and as the fluid within the instrument rose in the tube, during the experiment, water was added to the jar, so as to prevent inequality of hydrostatic pressure. The rise (or fall) of liquid in the tube was highly uniform, as observed from hour to hour, and the experiment was generally terminated in five hours. From experiments made on solutions of every variety of soluble substances, it appeared that the rise or osmose is quite insignificant with neutral organic substances in general, such as sugar, alcohol, urea, tannin, &c.; so also with neutral salts of the earths and ordinary metals, and with chlorides of sodium and potassium, nitrates of potash and soda, and chloride of mercury. A more sensible but still very moderate osmose is exhibited by hydrochloric, nitric, acetic, sulphurous, citric and tartaric acids. These are surpassed by the stronger mineral acids, such as sulphuric and phosphoric acid and sulphate of potash, which are again exceeded by salts of potash and soda possessing either a decided acid or alkaline reaction, such as binoxalate of potash, phosphate of soda and carbonates of potash and soda. The highly osmotic substances were also found to act with most advantage, in small proportions, producing in general the largest osmose in the proportion of one quarter per cent. of salt dissolved. Osmose is indeed eminently the phenomenon of weak solutions. The same substances are likewise always chemically active bodies, and possess affinities which enable them to act upon the material of the earthenware septum. Lime and alumina were accordingly always found in solution after osmose, and the corrosion of the septum appeared to be a necessary condition of the flow. Septa of other materials, such as pure carbonate of lime, gypsum, compressed charcoal, and tanned sole leather, although not deficient in porosity, gave no osmose, apparently because they are not acted upon chemically by the saline solutions, capillarity alone was manifestly insufficient to produce the liquid movement, while the *vis motrix* appeared to be chemical action.

The electrical endosmose of Porrett, which has lately been defined with great clearness by Weidemann, was believed to indicate the possession of a peculiar chemical constitution by water, while liquid, or at least the capacity to assume that constitution when water is polarized and acting chemically upon other substances. A large but variable number of atoms of water are associated together to form a liquid molecule of water, of which an individual atom of oxygen stands apart, forming a negative or chlorous radical, while the whole remaining atoms together are constituted into a positive or basylous radical, which last will contain an unbalanced equivalent of hydrogen, giving the molecule basicity, as in the great proportion of organic radicals. Now, it is this voluminous basylous radical which travels in the electrical decomposition of pure water, and resolves itself into hydrogen gas and water at the negative pole, causing the accumulation of water observed there, while the oxygen alone proceeds in the opposite direction to the positive pole. Attention was also called to the fact that acids and alkalies, when in solution, are chemically combined with much water of hydration; sulphuric acid, for instance, evolving heat when the fiftieth equivalent of water is added to it. In the combination of such bodies, the disposal of the water is generally overlooked. Osmose was considered as depending upon such secondary results of combination, that is, upon the large number or voluminous proportions of the water molecules involved in such combinations. The porous septum is the means of bringing out and rendering visible, both in electrical and ordinary osmose, this liquid movement attending chemical combinations and decompositions.

Although the nature and *modes operandi* of the chemical action producing osmose remains still very obscure, considerable light is thrown upon it in the application of septa of animal membrane. Ox bladder was found to acquire greatly increased activity, and also to act with much greater regularity when first divested of its outer muscular coat. Cotton calico also impregnated with liquid albumen, and afterwards exposed to heat, so as to coagulate that substance, was sufficiently impervious, and formed an excellent septum, resembling membrane in every respect. The osmometer was of the usual bulb-form, but the membrane was supported by a plate of perforated zinc, and the instrument provided with a tube of considerable diameter. The diameter of the tube being one-tenth of that of the mouth of the bulb or the disc of membrane exposed to the fluids, a rise of liquid in the tube, amounting to 100 millimetres, indicated that as much water had permeated the membrane and entered the osmometer, as would cover the whole surface of the membrane to a depth of one millimeter, or 1-25th part of an inch. Such millimeter divisions of the tube become degrees of osmose, which are of the same value in all instruments.

Osmose in membrane presented many points of similarity to that in earthenware. The membrane is constantly undergoing decomposition, and its osmotic action is exhaustible. Further, salts and other substances capable of determining a large osmose, are all chemically active substances, while the great mass of neutral monobasic salts of the metals, such as chlorides of sodium, possess only a low degree of action, or are wholly inert. The active substances are also relatively most efficient in small proportions.

When a solution of the proper kind is used, the osmose or passage of fluid proceeds with a velocity wholly unprecedented in such experiments. The rise of liquid in the tube with a solution containing 1-10th per cent. of carbonate of potash in the osmometer, was 167 degrees or millimeters, and with one per cent. of the same salt, 206 deg. in five hours.

With another membrane and stronger solution, the rise was 863 millimetres, or upwards of thirty inches in the same time, and as much water, therefore, was impelled through the membrane as would cover its whole surface to a depth of 8·6 millimetres, or one-third of an inch. The chemical action must be different on the substance of the membrane at its inner and outer surfaces to induce osmose; and according to the hypopothetic view which accords best with the phenomenon, the action on the two sides is not unequal in degree only, but also different in kind. It appears as an alkaline action on the albuminous substance of the membrane, at the inner surface, and as an acid action on the albumen at the outer surface. The most general empyrical conclusion that can be drawn is, that the water always accumulates on the alkaline or basic side of the membrane. Hence, with an alkaline salt, such as carbonate or phosphate of soda, in the osmometer, and water outside, the flow is inwards; but with an acid in the osmometer, on the contrary, the flow is outwards, or there is negative osmose, the liquid then falling in the tube. In the last case the water outside is basic when compared with the acid within, and the flow is, therefore, still towards the base. The chloride of sodium, chloride of barium, chloride of magnesium, and similar neutral salts, are wholly indifferent, or appear only to act in a subordinate manner to some other active acid or basic substance, which last may be present in the solution or membrane in the most minute quantity. Salts which admit of dividing into a basic subsalt and free acid exhibit an osmotic activity of the highest order. Such are the acetate and various other salts of alumina, iron, and chromium, the protochloride of iron, chloride of copper and tin, chloride of copper, nitrate of lead, &c. The acid travels outward by diffusion, superinducing a basic condition of the inner surface of the membrane, and an acid condition of the outer surface, the favorable condition of a high positive osmose. The bibasic salts of potash and soda again, such as the sulphate and tartrate of potash, although strictly neutral in properties, begin to exhibit a positive osmose, in consequence, it may be presumed, of their resolution into an acid supersalt and free alkaline base.

The following table exhibits the osmose of substances of all classes:

Osmose of One per Cent. Solutions in Membrane.

Oxalic acid	— 148 deg.
Hydrochloric acid	— 92
Terchloride of gold	— 54
Bichloride of tin	— 46
Bichloride of platinum	— 30
Chloride of magnesium	— 3
Chloride of sodium	+ 2
Chloride of potassium	18
Nitrate of soda	2
Nitrate of silver	34
Sulphate of potash	21 to 60
Sulphate of magnesia	14
Chloride of calcium	20
Chloride of barium	21
Chloride of strontium	26
Chloride of cobalt	26
Chloride of manganese	34
Chloride of zinc	54
Chloride of nickel	88
Nitrate of lead	125 to 211
Nitrate of cadmium	137
Nitrate of uranium	234 to 458
Nitrate of copper	204
Chloride of copper	351
Protochloride of tin	289
Protochloride of iron	435
Chloride of mercury	121
Protonitrate of mercury	356
Pernitrate of mercury	476
Acetate of sesquioxide of iron	194
Acetate of alumina	280 to 393
Chloride of aluminum	540
Phosphate of soda	311
Carbonate of potash	439

It may appear to some that the chemical character which has been assigned to osmose takes away from the physiological interest of the subject, in so far as the decomposition of the membrane may appear to be incompatible with vital conditions, and that osmotic movements must, therefore, be confined to dead matter; but such apprehensions are, it is believed, groundless, or, at all events, premature. All parts of living structures are allowed to be in a state of incessant change, of decomposition and renewal. The decomposition occuring in a living membrane, while effecting osmotic propulsion, may possibly, therefore, be of a reparable kind. In other respects chemical osmose appears to be an agency particularly adapted to take part in the animal economy. It is seen that osmose is peculiarly excited by dilute saline solutions, such as the animal juices really are, and that the alkaline or acid property which these juices always possess is another most favorable condition for their action on membrane. The natural excitation of osmose in the substance of the membranes or cell-walls dividing such solution seems, therefore, almost inevitable.

In osmose there is further a remarkably direct substitution of one of the great forces of nature by its eqnivalent in another force—the conversion, as it may be said, of chemical affinity into mechanical power. Now, what is more wanted in the theory of animal functions than a mechanism for obtaining motive power from chemical decomposition as it occurs in the tissues. In minute microscopic cells the osmotic movements being entirely dependent upon extent of surface, may attain the highest conceivable velocity. May it not be hoped, therefore, to find in the osmotic injection of fluids the deficient link which certainly intervenes between muscular movement and chemical decomposition?—Proceedings of the Royal Society, June 15, 1854, in *Pharmaceutical Journal*, July 15, 1854.

ON THE DIFFERENT SPIRITS OF TURPENTINE.

BY M. MARCELLIN BERTHELOT.

The object of the author is to distinguish and characterize the species or permanent varieties which have been up to this time confounded with spirits of turpentine. This essence is constituted by a carburet of the formula $C^{20} H^{16}$. It forms a crystalline hydrate; it unites directly with one equivalent of hydrochloric acid to form a compound both liquid and solid (artificial camphor). These characters are common to many essences of the *coniferæ*, and connect them thus together by a common bond. Yet these essences are not completely identical, their physical properties, and, above all, their action on polarized light, appears to vary with the nature of the trees which furnish them. Thus the French essence, the extract of the *pinus maritima*, shows polarity to the left, (lævogyration,) while, according to the experiments of MM. Bouchardat and Pereira, the English essence, the extract of the *pinus australis*, shows polarity to the right (dextrogyration). Thus, again, the rotatory power of many lævogyrous essences examined by Bouchardat varies with the species of conifer which produces them. These essences are then molecularly distinct, while of an uniform composition, and up to a certain point of a chemical constitution exactly alike. Is this difference carried out in the compounds and similar conbinations to which each give rise? This is precisely the question which Berzelius resolved in the case of white and red phosphorus, and which occurs very often in the case of the organic acids.

It may be remarked of the spirits of turpentine, that not only does each tree furnish an essence distinguished by certain properties from that of other trees, but that the extract from a single species of pine is not homogenous, that is to say formed of a single hydrocarbon. From numerous observations it is found that the boiling point is not a fixed one, and that the spirits drawn at various stages of the distillation, does not present the constancy of properties which characterizes the physical and chemical unity of an individual substance.

Do these differences result from an alteration which the spirit has undergone during distillation, as Bouchardat supposed, or rather do they indicate the existence of many isomeric hydrocarbons existing in the spirit as they do in the natural exudation? Do these multiple hydrocarbons preserve their distinctness even in the combinations? Finally, does the formation of two hydrochlorates, one solid the other liquid, when the French essence is treated with hydrochloric acid, authorize us to suppose, as M. Thenard has done, that there pre-exists two distinct oils in this substance?

Viewed in this light, the study of spirits of turpentine presents the two following problems:

1st. Do the spirits produced by the various species of pines constitute radical and permanent varieties, susceptible of preserving that distinctness in the combinations into which they enter?

2d. Is the essence contained in the resinous liquid of one pine formed of a single hydrocarbon or of a mixture of various isomeric hydrocarbons? In this last hypothesis, do these hydrocarbons preserve themselves distinct in their carbinations?

To proceed methodically to the study of these two important questions, it is necessary first to give a distinct character to a single hydrocarbon furnished by one species before being able to compare by contrast the spirits yielded by the different pines. For this purpose the author procured, in Sologne, from the turpentine of the *pinus maritima*, as it flowed from the tree, and after being saturated with acids in the cold, he submitted it to distillation in a vacuum. The same process of purification was applied to the English essence.

We cannot follow the author into the detail of the numerous experiments to which he was conducted. We will only state his conclusions, which show:

1st. That the natural essences, having the formula $C^{20} H^{16}$, are, at least in the circumstances examined, a mixture of many isomeric hydrocarbons which constitute permanent varieties in the produce of the same tree, and capable of preserving its identity in its after combinations.

2d. That the spirit of turpentine varies with the nature of the tree which yields it.

In fact, Berthelot has separated the hydrocarbons contained in spirits from the *pinus maritima* and the *pinus australis*, and found that they differ in their physical properties, in the value of their rotatory power, and in the artificial camphors produced from them.

The following are the numbers stating the rotatory power of the two definite hydrocarbons obtained in a vacuum, and of the two artificial camphors which they furnish:

Spirits from the *pinus maritima*,	aj	= — 36·6
Its artificial camphor,	(a) r	= — 23·9
Spirits from the *pinus australis*,	aj	= + 18·9
Its artificial camphor,	(a) r	= + 9·0

If, as a term of comparison, there be added to these numbers those which belong to the essence of the *pinus australis*, which is an isomeric body, modified by heat, and its artificial camphor—

Spirits from *pinus australis*, modified by heat,	aj	= — 11·0
Its artificial camphor,	(a) r	= — 11·2

It may be observed that this last is a modified artificial product which has preserved the fundamental characters of the molecular type of the spirit of turpentine while it acquired an individual peculiarity.

Not only does the artificial camphor of each essence differ from the natural camphor of other essences, but it is also the same with their hydrates. These last compounds are recognized from each other by their solubility, in water, which is determined in this way—each hydrate is purified by two new crystallizations in distilled water, each one followed by washing; then saturated solutions of these bodies being prepared and placed in test glasses, in contact with an excess of the crystals for a week, so that normal saturation may occur. Then ten cubic centimetres of this solution is taken up with a pipette and placed in the capsule. Two distinct capsules being thus filled, with each of the solutions saturated at 15° cent. This operation is performed with all. The capsules are then evaporated together in a vacuum, without ebullition, and left twenty-four hours under a glass full of air saturated with moisture, so as to absorb the two equivalents of water lost by the hydrate in the vacuum. The capsules are then weighed. These determinations have been made with the essence of citron, the Swiss spirit of turpentine, and the spirit from the *pinus maritima*. With this last, Berthelot has made three pairs at once for determination, the one with the layers of hydrate formed first in the preparation, the other with the layers last, the third with the layers last formed many months after the first.

The 10 centimetres of the solution contained—

	Grains.
With the hydrate of the essence of citron, first capsule,	0·038½
Second ditto,	0·038½
With the hydrate of the Swiss spirits turpentine, first capsule,	0·036½
Second ditto,	0·036½
With the hydrate of the French spirit (superior layer formed at the last,	0·040
Ditto, (middle layers,) first capsule,	0·041¼
Ditto, (middle layers,) second ditto,	0·041¼
Ditto, (inferior layers, the oldest,) first capsule,	0·040
Ditto, (inferior layers, the oldest,) second ditto,	0·041

From these numbers it appears there is a different solubility of the hydrates formed by different essences. As for the hydrate formed by the same essence, at successive periods, the differences are almost unperceivable.

Thus the individuality of each essence is maintained, not only in the artificial camphor, but also in the hydrate. The isomerism of the different spirits of turpentine does not appear to imply, between the rotatory power of these hydrocarbons, any relation of symetry such as exists between the different tartaric acids.—*Jour. de Pharm.*, April, 1854, from the *Ann. de Chimie.*

THE METAL ALUMINIUM, ITS PROBABLE USE IN PHARMACY.

BY W. HAMILTON, M.B.

Some years have elapsed since an addition was made to the multitude of our metallic substances, by the discovery made by M. Wöhler in 1828 and 1846, of the metallic basis of clay, which, unlike that of the alkalies, appears to be permanent in all the ordinary states of the atmosphere, and to possess other properties which elevate its intrinsic value, for domestic and other purposes, nearly, if not altogether, to the same level as that of gold, silver, or platina.

To this new metal the name of *Aluminium* has been given, from the earth, or, perhaps, more correctly speaking, the oxide from which it is obtained by a process which does not appear to be either difficult or expensive.

Led by analogy, Mr. Brande, in his lectures at the Royal Institution, expressed an opinion, thirty-five years ago, that the earth alumina would prove like that of lime, &c., a metallic oxide: but it does not appear that any steps were taken, or at least none that I have heard of, to verify the justice of this conjecture, or divest the metal of these adventitious substances which disguised its nature and obscured its splendor. Like Newton's wonderful hypothesis respecting the combustibility of the diamond, and the inflammable nature of water, the metallic nature of the earth of alum was suffered to sleep in unbroken repose from the year 1819, in which Mr. Brande first launched his hypothesis, to the years 1828 and 1846, in which the researches of Wöhler converted the theory into fact. But it is to the successful experiments made in France by M.

Deville that the world is indebted for the practical results of the hypothesis of Professor Brande and the researches of M. Wöhler, for it was the former gentleman (M. Deville) who first produced it in any quantity, and explained the method by which it might be obtained.

Following M. Deville, M. Chapelle repeated his experiments with equal good fortune. Introducing pulverized clay, mixed with common salt and powdered charcoal, into a common crucible, he exposed the mixture to the heat of a reverberatory furnace produced by coke, but not raised to a white temperature. On being suffered to cool, the crucible was broken, when a multitude of minute metallic globules of the color of silver, but not exceeding half a millimetre, or about the fiftieth of an inch, in diameter, were found dispersed through the mass within. M. Chapelle, without determining the purity of these globules, ascertained that, while they resisted the action of cold nitric acid, they were soluble in muriatic acid. The globules, thus obtained, admit of being formed into a mass by melting together, their point of fusion corresponding nearly with that of silver. The mass thus formed is said to equal, if not exceed, silver in the brilliant whiteness of its color; it approaches iron in its tenacity; its density, or specific gravity, does not exceed 2·56, or that nearly of glass or flint; it may be melted and cooled in contact with the air, without undergoing any perceptible amount of oxidation; it acts well as a conductor of heat, and no doubt of electricity too, which, with the power of resisting the action of the air, whether dry or humid, seems to adapt it peculiarly for the purposes of the electric telegraph; it equally resists the action of sulphuretted hydrogen, rendering it preferable to silver in situations exposed to the action of that gas; it is not acted upon by water, either hot or cold, nitric acid, whether concentrated or dilute, or weak sulphuric acid; muriatic acid alone appearing to be its proper solvent, at a temperature of 60°.

Such are the more prominent characteristics of this new metal, as far as I have been able to collect them from the *Mining Journal*, in which the only notices I have been fortunate enough to stumble upon may be found at pages 112 and 187 of the current (xxiv.) volume. From the peculiar properties of this new metal, properties in some degree approaching to those of the costly and intractable platina, and especially from its facility of resisting oxidation at the ordinary temperatures to which it is liable to be exposed, from its insolubility in most of the vegetable and mineral acids, with the exception of the muriatic, and then not under a temperature of 60°, from its ductility and malleability, this metal, if obtainable at a moderate cost, either in a state of purity, or alloyed with other metals, appears peculiarly adapted for chemical and pharmaceutical purposes, and merits more consideration than has been hitherto paid to it. Mr. Willich, in a letter of the 13th of last March, published in the *Mining Journal,* for the 25th of that month, from which the foregoing facts have principally been borrowed, acquaints us that M. Deville is engaged in further experiments to ascertain the possibility of obtaining aluminium in sufficient quantity for use in the arts and manufactures, and as the substance from which it is procured is so widely diffused throughout the world, and of such easy attainment, there can be no doubt that the discovery of a cheap and simple method of reducing the metal from its oxide would, as Mr. Willich justly observes, "open the way to fame and fortune for the discoverer." Mr. Willich further observes, that he feels "sanguine that M. Chapelle's experiment," [detailed above,] "may be repeated with better success *on a large scale*, and by additional portions of salt and charcoal being intimately mixed with the powdered clay. Both soda and chlorine," he continues, "have considerable action on alumina and its metallic base. Why should not carbonic acid be formed by the burning carbon absorbing oxygen from the alumina in its transition state, thereby leaving the metal at liberty? I hope those who have the means at their disposal will not fail to try the reduction of the metal from clay in large furnaces. *I cannot doubt of ultimate success.* That success will open a vast field to the industrial energies of the country, and far exceed in real utility the golden treasures of California and Australia. The useful application of such a metal I need not point out to your readers. In fact, the metal is superior to silver, on account of the unchangeable character of its in-influence. Why may we not have aluminized iron for our roofs and general new work, instead of the galvanized iron?"

Such are the concluding remarks of Mr. Willich's valuable communication; and as the subject, although one of considerable importance to the pharmaceutical chemist, has hitherto been unnoticed in the pages of the *Pharmaceutical Journal*, I thought it would be doing an acceptable service to science to call the attention of practical men to it. Although making no pretensions to originality, this notice may not be without its use in promoting more extensive experiments, and bringing us more fully acquainted with the properties and uses of this new and promising substance, the introduction of which, from its singularly low specific gravity, cannot lead to any deterioration of the metals hitherto applied to the fabrication of plate, or the purposes of a circulating medium.—*Pharm. Journal* (London).

GAS COOKING—GALVANIC BATTERY.

At the stated monthly meeting of the Franklin Institute, Philadelphia, on June 15th, 1854, among other business the following matters were noticed:

Dr. Rand, Chairman Committee Meeting, exhibited several forms of apparatus for cooking and heating by gas. Among them was the *Atmopyre*, a gas stove, in which the gas is mixed with air in a cylinder or frustrum of a cone made of baked clay; the mixture is passed through numerous small perforations and burned. The clay becomes intensely heated, is surrounded by a cylinder of sheet iron with a tube to carry off the products of combustion, and gradually warms the air of the room.

Also, an apparatus for broiling, in which the gas is admitted into a hollow disk and burned in numerous small jets on its under surface, the meat being placed on a gridiron beneath. The whole is surrounded by a short sheet iron cylinder. There is a circular opening in the centre of the disk, so that air is drawn in beneath and around the meat, and carried off above, along with the products of combustion. The meat is thus cooked by radiant heat alone, not being exposed to the gases arising from combustion, or to any free gas which may accidentally escape being burned.

Dr. Rand also exhibited Mr. Andrew Mayer's self-regulating gas nipple. This is a small cylinder, screwed on the branch, and to which the burner is attached. It contains metallic valves or washers, so arranged that only a certain quantity of gas can pass. It is varied in size according to the capacity of the burner, so as to allow the maximum quantity to pass to attain an economical effect, after which no increase of pressure causes any additional flow of gas. Mr. Mayer claims as new, the peculiar mode of packing these valves in the cylinder, and his invention is at present under consideration by the Committee on Science and the Arts. Dr. Rand had used one of these on a patent Argand burner, which was very troublesome from its constant fluctuations with those of pressure, due to the proximity of large public buildings. He had found it entirely effectual, but had not had it in use long enough to be satisfied as to its results during a long trial. He had noticed one remarkable effect from its use. Owing, he presumed, to the retardation of the flow of the gas, the flame of the burner took a different form after its application. Instead of presenting the appearance of an inverted cone with a flaring base and somewhat unsteady character, the flame became elongated and entirely steady, resembling that of a Carcel lamp, or of an ordinary Argand.

Dr. C. M. Wetherill exhibited an improved modification of Hess' apparatus for organic analysis, in which he makes use of a peculiar form of gas jet for heating the combustion tubes.

Dr. Turnbull brought before the meeting "a model of a new form of telegraph battery, for which a patent was applied for by C. T. Chester, Esq., of New York, Feb. 10, 1854. Dr. Turnbull remarked that this battery, while it does away entirely with local action, employs the cheapest materials and most convenient arrangement of parts. Its cells are large, of strong glass, and they are insulated from the shelves by a partial coating with electrophorus. Its metals are amalgamated zinc and a peculiar platinized and peculiarly insulated plate, the result of much study and experiment. The plates are supported by metal clamps and thoroughly insulated wood. The construction is such as to secure perfectly against any cross-fire. The plates can be removed and cleaned separately, without stopping the working of the battery. The solution used to excite it is a dilute sulphuric acid. How free it is from local action may be inferred from the fact, that it has been in constant use for five months without being taken down, and that the zincs last such an unprecedented time. The relative cost of working these three batteries, without taking local action into consideration, supposing each equally free from local waste, is as follows; and the estimate is made up from actual experiment, by computing the destruction of battery material in each, necessary to accomplish a given equal amount of work—say the deposition of a pound of silver in the decomposition trough. To accomplish this—

Grove's consumes:	
1½ pounds nitric acid, at 12c. - -	18 cents.
1¼ pounds zinc, at 10c. - - - -	12½ "
1 pound sulphuric acid - - - -	2 "
	32½
Daniell's consumes:	
4 pounds sulphate copper, at 11c. - -	44 cents.
1½ pounds zinc - - - - -	15 "
1 pound sulphuric acid - - - -	2 "
	61 cents.
The new battery:	
1½ pounds zinc - - - - -	15 cents.
3 pounds sulphuric acid - - - -	6 "
	21

[*Journ. Franklin Institute*, July, 1854

THE MODE OF DINTINGUISHING QUININE FROM QUINIDINE.

TO THE EDITOR OF THE PHARMACEUTICAL JOURNAL.

SIR—Your last number contains a report of a lecture delivered at Liverpool, before the Liverpool Chemists' Association, by Dr. Nevins,* in which the lecturer throws doubts upon the results obtained by previous observers with quinine and quinidine. The subject is not necessarily involved in obscurity, and in order to show the real origin of his difficulties I beg to submit a few observations.

It is difficult to adapt these experiments to a lecture-room; for instance, to ascertain the extent to which sulphate of quinine is soluble in cold water requires some time. If the water is cold, the process of solution goes on extremely slowly when the solution is nearly saturated. Mr. Barry's plan is a better one: he heats the liquid till solution is effected, and then by cooling obtains a cold saturated solution, with a few minute feathers of crystalization. I think we must, therefore, leave the solubility of sulphate of quinine in water as it has been previously settled. A more important question is the tests for quinine and quinidine, founded upon their relative solubility in ether, or in water as sulphates.

Dr. Nevins appears to have taken as the material for his experiments a substance which was not pure quinidine. He found it soluble in ten parts of ether. No wonder, therefore, that the tests recommended by others failed or only partially succeeded. In order to obtain satisfactory results, we must have a pure article as the basis of experiments; for this purpose, quinidine should be crystallized twice out of ether; and any one who will take the trouble to do this will find the old observations tolerably accurate.

It is much easier to obtain sulphate of quinine free from

---

*See *New York Journal of Pharmacy*, p. 345.

quinidine, than sulphate of quinidine free from quinine. Two or three crystallizations will leave the quinidine in the mother-liquors as the more soluble salt; but if we now attempt to crystallize out the sulphate of quinidine, it will, even after repeated crystallizations, contain sulphate of quinine, a difficulty familiar enough to chemists in purifying a more soluble salt from a less soluble.

Consequently, commercial sulphate of quinidine always contains some quinine, more or less, or may happen to contain a good deal, though of course the manufacturer will not purposely sell the more valuable article under the name of the chaper. Even a small quantity of quinine will considerably alter the reactions of quinidine, especially as to solubility, and will of course give proportionate results under the microscope. But Dr. Nevins' results indicate so large a proportion of quinine, that I suspect some mistake somewhere. I am the more inclined to this opinion, because, in procuring a sample of the maker referred to, (Messrs. Herrings, of Aldersgate street,) I found that ʒ ij of ether dissolved the precipitate from 1 gr., but did not quite dissolve it when 2 grs. were used; the solubility of this is, therefore, between 60 and 120 parts. This differs so widely from ʒ ij. dissolving 15 grs., that I suspect that some sort of inferior sulphate of quinine must have been accidentally substituted.

Yours very respectfully,

Robert Howard.

Stratford, June 22d, 1854.

MANUFACTURE AND CONSUMPTION OF QUININE IN THE UNITED STATES.

TO THE EDITOR OF THE PHARMACEUTICAL JOURNAL.

Sir—Although Mr. Robert Howard has written a reply to the article under the above title, which appeared in your May number, yet I think there are still several points requiring notice, the original communication being full of errors.

Quinine was not originally classed in the list of free articles in the new American tariff, and subsequently excluded. The proposed tariff enumerates certain articles to be admitted free, and all others to pay an *ad valorem* duty of 25 or 100 per cent., thus abolishing the present great variety of duties. Quinine would thus come under the lowest duty of 25 per cent.—it now pays 20 per cent.; but it must not be forgotten that bark pays a duty of 15 per cent. There is no probability of the new tariff passing this year.

There are certainly only two manufacturers of quinine in the United States, but we have only two in England, and the same in France and Germany—each country giving a preference to its own manufactured article. Whether they are growing rich in the business depends very much on the skill and capital employed.

Jobst, of Germany, has not rejected the New Granada barks, nor can quinine, containing a certain per centage of quinine, be admitted into the United States. Foreign quinine rejected at New York has been on sale in the London market this spring. Quinine, if intended to pass as quinine, must be pure.

There ought to be no question about the use of New Granada barks for the manufacture of quinine. Has there ever been an objection to the use of Carabaya bark? As Mr. Howard says, "The quinine contained in them is identical in all, from whatever species obtained." The monopoly of Bolivian bark has proved an universal blessing, by stimulating the importation of other kinds. What would have been the price of quinine if manufacturers had depended solely on the use of Bolivian bark?

We imported last year 17,000 serons of New Granada, and 1,500 serons of Bolivian. The New Granada all sold; but the Bolivian, being held for a monopoly price, is still in the market, proving that this kind has very little demand.

Delondre, in his new work on quinine barks, gives an analysis of a New Granada bark containing quite as much quinine as Bolivian Calisaya. If the Calisaya of Sante Fé or Fusagasuga and Pitaya barks of New Granada had been introduced into the market before the Bolivian, there would be no question about the quality of the alkaloids they yield.

I am, yours obediently,

W. H. COLE.

16, *George street, Mansion House.*

ON THE DETECTION OF BLOOD SPOTS.

BY J. LÖWE.

For the recognition of spots of blood upon linen and other fabrics formed of non-azotized filaments, the author recommends the production of ferrocyanide of potassium from the nitrogenous animal matter. By the author's method, a fragment of the linen which has been soaked in blood is moistened with distilled water in a porcelain cup until the dried red mass is completely dissolved, and the linen appears nearly colorless. The linen is then taken with a pair of forceps, folded up, and pressed between two glass plates; it is then well washed with distilled water, the whole of which is added to the red contents of the cup. Carbonate of potash is then added to this, and the whole evaporated to dryness at a temperature of 221° F.; a higher temperature must be carefully avoided. The anhydrous residue thus obtained is put into a longish glass-tube, which is drawn out into a point at the bottom; it is then covered with a layer of carbonate of potash, in order, as far as possible, to prevent the access of the air, which would readily produce a conversion of the cyanide of potassium into cyanate of potash during the fusion; the latter salt is entirely useless in the formation of ferrocyanide of potassium, so that a negative result might readily be obtained in this way. The fusion may also be effected in a small narrow iron crucible, closed, like a platinum crucible, with a tight, overlapping lid.

The mass in the glass-tube is exposed to a strong melting

heat, assisted by the blowpipe, and allowed to cool; the tube is then cut through by a file in the neighborhood of the dark mass, the part containing which is thrown into a test-glass, in which there is a little warm water and iron filings or sulphuret of iron. The production of ferrocyanide of potassium is facilitated by the application of a gentle heat; the solution is filtered away from the metallic residue into another test-glass, the alkaline filtrate slightly acidulated with muriatic acid in order to decompose the carbonate of potash, and two or three drops of chloride of iron are then added to it. The fluid immediately acquires a yellowish-green color, the resulting Prussian blue being suspended in consequence of its finely-divided condition in the solution, which is of a yellow color from the excess of the iron salt. After standing a short time, the blue precipitate settles to the bottom of the tube, and may then be recognized by its characteristic properties. A great number of experiments, performed with very small pieces of linen impregnated with blood, always gave a positive result, whether the blood had been a long or a short time attached to the linen; and the author is firmly convinced that this method would be applicable even after an interval of several years. Linen impregnated with sweat was fused with carbonate of potash, in order to ascertain whether the ammoniacal compounds contained in the cutaneous secretion might assist in the formation of cyanogen, which would, of course, in many cases, render the experiment doubtful; but not the least traces of any blue flakes were to be seen on the addition of chloride of iron and long standing. The solution of the iron salt was repeatedly filtered before being used, in order to avoid all chance of mistake, and the tube afterwards closed with a cork. Moreover, it is more probable that ammoniacal com pounds would have been decomposed and volatilized in the presence of alkalies at a lower temperature, than that the cyanogen should have been produced from the constituents of the ammonia at the high temperature required for the formation of the former substance. The great richness of the blood in proteine substances is favorable to the formation of cyanogen, even when operating upon very small quantities; the author is of opinion that this experiment is sufficiently characteristic to prove the presence of a fluid so complicated as the blood in doubtful cases.

When the similarity of organic pigments with the coloring matter of the blood gives rise to some doubt, this may readily be removed by the well-marked behavior of the former with ammonia, hypochlorite of lime, soda or free chlorine; and as regards rust-spots, whether upon stuffs or upon the blades of cutting instruments, they never can produce cyanide of potassium by fusion with carbonate of potash.—*Archiv. der Pharm.*, l xvii. p. 56, in *Chem. Gaz.*, June, 1854.

ON THE PRODUCTION OF WINE, BRANDY, AND TARTAR IN THE VALLEY OF THE OHIO.

BY W. PROCTOR, JR.

During a recent visit to Cincinnati, we had several opportunities of inquiring into the progress of the grape culture in that neighborhood, and were gratified at the very considerable progress that has been made in that branch of industry. The hill-sides around the city are thickly spotted with vineyards, and the culture of the vine is spreading from farm to farm; the excess of produce, beyond the demand of the table, finding a ready market at the wine presses of the large growers and wine-makers. The difficulties and discouragements incident to all new enterprizes are being gradually overcome, the kinds of grape best adapted to the soil and climate have been ascertained, and the wine-growers now look forward to an annual increase of their crops.

Many foreign varieties of the grape have been experimented with, and several of native origin, but none has proved as well suited to the production of wine as the native *Catawba.* Major Adlum, of Georgetown, D. C., has the credit of being the first to bring the Catawba into notice as a wine grape; and, "in view of its present and prospective importance as the yet unrivalled wine grape, for a native superior to which Mr. Longworth has offered a reward of five hundred dollars, he has declared that in bringing this grape into public notice he has rendered his country a greater service than he would have done, had he paid off the national debt."

Mr. Longworth, of Cincinnati, the pioneer in this enterprize, has been experimenting for thirty years on the foreign grape, both for table and for wine, and has imported vines from Paris, Bordeaux, the Jura Mountains, and from Madeira, but all failed; Mr. Longworth's experiments were first made at the vineyard, well known under the name of Baldface, now about twenty-eight years old. Since Longworth's pioneer enterprize, the Cincinnati Horticultural Society and the American Wine-Grower's Association have fostered the grape culture, and have repeatedly awarded prizes to successful competitors.

In 1846, there were 83 vineyards in the neighborhood of Cincinnati, containing 248 acres under cultivation, and 114 acres bearing, and 24,000 gallons of wine were made. In 1852, 1200 acres were in culture, and 750 bearing, and the yield was calculated to be 500,000 gallons. That portion of this wine crop, called the sparkling (or champagne) Catawba, alone was worth $175,000.

A bushel of grapes will yield from three to three and a half gallons of juice. Mr. Buchanan commenced planting his vineyard in 1843; in 1850, he realized, besides the cuttings, 1,640 gallons of wine. In 1853, he obtained from five acres 4,236 gallons, or 847 gallons per acre. In particular spots, there has been obtained 800 gallons from an acre, but 650 gallons is considered a large yield.

The demand for Catawba wine is far ahead of the supply, and the quality is constantly being improved, both by the cultivators and by those who prepare it for market.

The Wine-Growers' Association, of which Mr. Lewis Rehfuss is the President, hold their meetings monthly, alternately at the vineyards of the members.

The last of these meetings was held in July, on the grounds of Mr. Werk, in Green Township, four miles from Cincinnati where the vineyards of Mr. W. cover fifty acres, one-fifth of which is planted with the Catawba grape. On this occasion, thirty varieties of native wines were examined by the members; but, as usual the prevailing opinion was in favor of the "sparkling Catawba," for which Mr. Werk's is noted. The wine vaults of this gentleman are equal to many of the champagne establishments of France. The deep arched cellars are ninety-eight feet by twenty-seven feet, and contain about sixty-five thousand bottles of wine, with all the conveniences for bottling.

We had the pleasure of visiting the wine cellar of Messrs. Longworth and Zimmermann, of a similar character. The main apartment was an immense stone arched vault, twenty-feet deep, and, perhaps, twenty-five by one hundred in area, on either side of which was arranged a series of wine vats or casks, each of which, we were told, held near three thousand gallons; besides these there were a number of smaller dimensions, the whole probably containing near 100,000 gallons. Opening into this, was the wine cellar for storing bottled wine, large stacks of which were piled horizontally along the sides, to improve by age. The temperature of this vault is about 66°, and, we were informed, is about two degrees warmer in mid-winter than in mid-summer—a temperature highly favorable to the slow fermentation necessary to the maturation of the wines.

We also examined some pure Catawba brandy, made by Messrs. L. and Z., which possessed, in a high degree, the true aroma and flavor of distilled wine.

In looking at this new enterprize, in a pharmaceutical point of view, there are several features of great interest. The item of cream of tartar alone has become so important in medicine and the arts from the numerous products derived from it, or uses to which it is applied, that the scarcity of the salt, from the repeated failure of the grape crop in Europe, has very materially influenced the prices of its derivative products.

It is well known that pure brandy in this country is not *always* to be found, and when met with commands so elevated a price that it is rarely employed as a menstruum when appropriate. These two items alone render the wine growing enterprize extremely interesting to American pharmaceutists, apart from the ameliorating influence which the substitution of pure native wines for crude distilled liquors will probably have in promoting the cause of rational temperance. Mr. Rehfuss has already prepared tartar of excellent quality from his own wine vats, and there can be but little doubt, from the data now ascertained, that a few years will enable the wine-makers of the West to supply almost wholly the domestic demand for this valuable salt.

Mr. R., as we have already noticed at page 399, has turned his attention to the application of chemistry to the grape culture, and finds that manuring with wood ashes, in some soils, greatly improves the resulting wine, by increasing the deposit of tartar at the expense of the acid of the grape.

As brandy is frequently made from weak wines, which retain much of the tartar, the residue of the brandy still is another source of cream of tartar, which will be rendered available. From Mr. Rehfuss's experiments, he believes that grape juice will yield *one* per cent. of tartar. This gentleman has been made chairman of a committee to report on the subject of the production of wines and tartar, to the next annual meeting of the American Pharmaceutical Association, and we may anticipate an interesting account of the whole matter from his able pen.—*Amer. Journ. Pharm.*, September, 1854.

THE PREPARATION OF SUGAR OF MILK IN BAVARIA.

In the portion of the Bavarian Alps, known under the name of Allgau, .where Alpine industrial economy is worthily carried on, excellent cheese is not only made, which equals the best kinds of Swiss cheese, but in a recent period milk-sugar has been also prepared there for medical purposes. The following is a description of the method by which the milk-sugar is manufactured. By means of rennet the caseine of the milk, heated to a certain temperature, is coagulated, and thus the cheese is obtained. For this purpose either milk as it is, that is, such as still contains the butter, or such as has been churned to separate the butter, is taken. The latter affords less and poor cheese. From the former the cheese is obtained fatty and good, in which the butter and cheese are intimately combined. Only a certain portion of butter remains behind in the residual liquid after the cheese has been separated. A little acid is mixed with the liquid, which causes the butter to separate and float on the surface as a scum, which is removed. The heating is continued, more acid added, and now a coagulum forms, which is skimmed off. From that which remains in the vessel, namely, the whey, the milk-sugar is made.

To purify the whey from accidental impurities, it is strained through a clean linen cloth into a well-tinned vessel, then boiled, and the scum constantly removed from its surface. Its evaporation is continued until when a spoonful of it is taken out; it does not pour away in fluid drops, but seems tenacious as a thin syrup. This mass is poured into a wooden vessel, and allowed to remain therein two or three days, by which it becomes thick, feels sandy, exhibits a brown color, and tastes sweet. This mass is now purified by means of fresh spring water, which is poured in rather large quantities into the vessel; the mass is often stirred and then allowed to remain quiet for some time until it is deposited on the bottom of the vessel. The dirty water is then poured off and fresh added, and the dirty water poured away from time to time until a fine white powder is obtained. The first water poured off may be used for fattening pigs, and the latter ones, which have rather a white color, and contain much milk-sugar dissolved, are evaporated as the whey. The white powder is milk-sugar, and must be converted into certain forms. It is thus crystallized. The pure white powder is dissolved in boiling water, poured into a well-tinned vessel, and allowed to stand there for eleven to fourteen days. It forms fine crystalline sticks in the form of a cake. To obtain the crystals in the form of a sugar-loaf, wooden rods are introduced into the vessel about which the milk-sugar crystallizes. After the time named the sugar is taken out and dried, when it is fit for use.

The water remaining in the vessel is further evaporated, purified, and yields very fine milk-sugar, which is made into tablets by pouring moist powder on a wooden table covered with linen, allowing it to stand twelve hours, then cutting the mass into tablets and drying them.—*Ann. of Pharm.*, July, 1854, from *Buch. Repert.*

PREPARATION OF CUBEBIN.

W. Englehardt* has examined a crystalline deposit from an ethereal infusion of cubebs, which had been kept for some months in a well-closed vessel, and found it to consist of cubebin. However, as cubebin is almost insoluble in ether at the ordinary temperature, it was very probably dissolved by the oils extracted by the ether. In the preparation of this substance, according to the general method, there would consequently be a considerable loss resulting from the extraction with ether previous to dissolving the cubebin in alcohol.—*Pharm. Journ.*

---

* *Neues Repertorium für Pharmacie*, No. 1, 1854.

Varieties.

On some Peculiar Reductions of Metals in the Humid Way.—By Professor Wöhler.—The following experiments were made for Professor Wöhler by Hiller. The observation first made by Bucholdz, that long crystals of metallic tin are formed when a rod of that metal is inserted in a solution of protochloride of tin, and the latter carefully overlaid with water, was first of all further tested. It appeared that, for the production of large crystals, the solution of chloride of tin must be acid. Of the tin immersed in the solution there was always more dissolved than was made up by that which crystallized. In one experiment the proportions were as 7 : 6.

These crystals are formed at the point of contact between the two fluids. If the solution be neutral, they appear below this in the solution of the protochloride, and remain bright.

Copper, inserted into a neutral solution of nitrate of copper, covers itself entirely with brownish-red crystals of protoxide of copper, and afterwards with sharp crystals of metallic copper. The copper is dissolved, especially at the point of contact of the fluids. The same phenomenon is produced, but in a less degree, with sulphate of copper. In solution of perchloride of copper, the copper is covered with crystals of the protochloride.

A rod of zinc, under similar circumstances, covers itself with grey granules of metallic zinc, especially at its lower end. In this case also the zinc is dissolved at the point of contact of the fluids.

Cadmium behaves in a similar manner in the solution of its nitrate; the reduced metal is more purverulent, and, therefore, much more readily oxidized in the air than the reduced zinc.

Lead, in a solution of neutral nitrate or acetate of lead, furnishes small shining crystals of lead.

Bismuth precipitates the metal from a solution of protochloride of bismuth, if the latter has been overlaid first with muriatic acid, and afterwards with water.

On silver, immersed in a concentrated solution of nitrate of silver overlaid with water, metallic silver is deposited in a dendritic form, always originating from a few scattered points of the surface of the silver.—*Ann. der Chem. und Pharm.*, lxxxv., p. 253.

Prof. Tiedemann.—The *Fête Jubilaire* of the celebrated anatomist, Frederick Tiedemann, who was made Doctor of Medicine in March, 1804, and who has resided at Frankfort four years, has just been celebrated in that town. He was Professor at Heidelberg more than forty years, and he retired from the University in

1849, in consequence of a great domestic affliction—namely, when his son was shot by the Prussian soldiers. The Universities of Heidelberg, of Giessen, of Frieburg, and of Wurtzburg; the Imperial Society of Naturalists and of the Academy of Sciences at Munich; the Medical Corporation of Mayence; the Learned Societies of Frankfort; and the Municipality of the town of Heidelberg sent envoys to give him their felicitations. The Society of Natural History of Frankfort opened a subscription for a gold medal, executed at Munich, to be presented to this celebrated anatomist. On one side is a portrait of the Professor, and on the other a star-fish, the subject of his first great monograph, which was rewarded by the Institute of France.—*Gaz. Hebd.*

Syrupus Calcis Phosphatis.—By Thomas S. Wiegand.—In the twenty-fifth volume of the *American Journal of Pharmacy*, p. 411, a formula for a syrup of phosphate of lime was published by Mr. A. Durand, which, being prepared by means of phosphoric acid, is so thoroughly in accordance with the chemistry of the salt used, that it challenges the respect of the profession; but, while so chemically correct, it has been found in practice that the free use of phosphoric acid in many cases is not unattended with disadvantage; the more so, as the class of persons intended to be benefitted by the syrup in question cannot endure the slightest diarrhœa without being much injured.

Yet the use of the phosphates of iron, lime, soda and potash has proven satisfactory in the hands of several of our first physicians, and, in view of these facts, it was thought that a formula avoiding free phosphoric acid might be of use:

℞. Calcis phosphatis precip,	℥j.
Acidi chlorohydrici	f. ʒ iv.
Aquæ q. s. ft.	f. ℥ vii.
Sacchari q. s. ft.	f. ℥ xiiss.

Dissolve the phosphate of lime, previously mixed with an ounce of water by means of the acid, filter, then add the remaining water. To this add the sugar, until the bulk is increased to twelve fluid ounces, and strain.

Adulteration of Castor Oil.—It is hardly possible to conceive that any person can be base enough, for the sake of enriching himself, to be guilty of adulterating articles intended for food or medicine; yet we have abundant proof that such transactions are of common occurrence in this, as well as in other cities and towns. It is unnecessary for us at this time to make an *expose* of all articles which are known to be more or less sophisticated, as we have repeatedly alluded to the circumstance before; but we will simply allude to the fact of the extensive sophistication of castor oil, by the use of *lard oil*. It is true there is nothing deleterious to health in this adulteration; nevertheless, it is excessively annoying, both to the physician and patient, to be obliged to make use of large quantities of the oil in order to obtain the desired effect. Much of this adulterated oil is sold by the grocers, and it would, therefore, be advisable for consumers to purchase only of responsible druggists and apothecaries.—*Boston Med. and Surg. Journ.*

COST OF THE ELECTRIC LIGHT.—M. Regnault, director of the telegraph on the Rouen Railways, who has established the lighting of the "Napoleon" Docks by electricity, has calculated the cost at which they are lighted. The apparatus has been worked regularly for four months consecutively with regularity, and consists of 50 Bunsen cells of large size:

	fr.
Labor, per day,	4·50
Mercury,	5·
Zinc,	4·50
Charcoal cylinders,	1·40
Nitric acid,	1·80
Sulphuric acid,	1·84
Total,	19·04, or $3 75.

The cost for burners for 800 workmen amounts to 38fr. 08 each evening, or about 4½ centimes (less than 1 cent.) per man. The process is unaccompanied with danger, and the light is produced with more regularity than by any other method.—*Rep. de Pharm.*, May, 1854.

CHEAP SUBSTITUTE FOR DAMP BLUE.—M. Grüne proposes to substitute sulphuric acid for the expensive tartaric acid, in the preparation of damp blue. For this purpose great exactness should be observed in the proportions of acid and salt, as an excess of the former would injure the cloth; the proper proportions would be, one pound of prussiate of potash, and 222 grains of oil of vitriol, mixed with one-half to one quart of water. The prussiate should not be powdered, but introduced in pieces about the size of a nut into the cold dilute acid, and stirred about until complete decomposition has ensued, which takes place very rapidly. A white sediment of fine crystallized sulphate of potash is deposited, and a clear greenish-yellow solution formed, which, with the addition of boiled starch, or dextrine, and the necessary quantity of ferro-cyanide of tin, may be employed for printing, &c.—*Polytech. Jour.*

EDITORIAL.

M. Ortlier, Pharmacien, at St. Marie, Upper Rhine, recommends the use of the fuming or nordhaussen oil of vitriol for the manufacture of collodion as preferable to the common sulphuric acid, the latter being difficult to find always of the desired strength. The cotton when once dipped in a mixture of nitrate of potassa and this acid dissolves rapidly in ether, to which a little absolute alcohol has been added. There is never any necessity to repeat the dipping.

At the trial of the Queen *v.* the Pharmaceutical Society of Great Britain, after the verdict was rendered, the following conversation occurred upon the proper pronunciation of the word "pharmaceutical."

Lord Campbell said there appeared to be one vexed question which he should like to have decided, as some gentlemen pronounced the "c" in the word soft, but others treated it as hard. He would ask the Attorney-General what he said it was?

The Attorney-General said, in his opinion, it was soft. It came from the Greek: but when it became English it must be subject to the English rules; but he had been cautioned by some of his learned friends as to the mode of pronouncing it.

Sir F. Kelly said, of course, he should bow to the opinion of his learned friends, who were so much superior to him in learning as in everything else.

The Attorney-General said, that was rather too bad, as Sir. F. Kelly had himself cautioned him.

Sir F. Kelly said, whatever his lordship should say it was, that would be the mode to be adopted.

Lord Campbell—Then let it be soft. Be it so.

This, we believe, is rather an unusual mode of determining the pronunciation of the word. In this country the *c* is universally soft in this as well as many other words used in medicine and surgery—such as cyst, hydrocephalus, cephalites, encysted, which are in England as often sounded hard as soft.

We have given *in extenso* the proceedings of the American Pharmaceutical Association, the commencement of which was given in the August number. On reviewing its transactions, we cannot perceive that much was accomplished by the Society for the benefit of Pharmacy.

NEW YORK

JOURNAL OF PHARMACY.

FOR NOVEMBER AND DECEMBER, 1854.

EXTRACT CINCHONÆ RUBRI FLUID.

BY JOHN CANAVAN.

Having been called upon by a physician for a "fluid extract of cinchona" for a patient of his who could not take the "compound tincture," in the absence of a formula in any of the Pharmacopœias, I prepared some according to a formula which I give below, and it has so far answered an admirable purpose in every case in which it has been tried, and they have been many. In some cases where the Sulph. Quinin. had failed to have the effect, or could not be borne by the patient, the physician has succeeded in breaking up the disease with it alone.

Another advantage which it has is, that it is a very beautiful and palatable preparation, which is a great deal in favor of an "Allopathic" preparation in these days of NICE DOSES of our "Homeœpathic" friends. Knowing this, and also having been called upon for a supply of the article from other "Apothecaries," I, therefore, make it public, for the benefit of the profession at large:

℞ Pulv. Cinchon. Rubr. ℥ viij (Troy)
Acid. Sulph. Dilut. q. s.
Alcohol. Dilut. q. s.
Sacch. Alb. ℥ viij (Troy).

Digest the "cinchona" in four pints of "alcohol dilut." for

24 hours, then filter, and displace the dregs that remain in the filter with "alcohol dilut.," acidulated with "acid sulph dilut.," until the liquor comes away nearly tasteless; then mix the two liquors together, and evaporate to one pint, and filter; to this add the sugar, and dissolve without heat, which will make it measure about twenty fluid ounces, consequently one drachm will represent about twenty-five grains of the "cinchona," about the usual dose for an adult. During the evaporation, the coloring matter of the "cinchona" is nearly all precipitated along with the "resin," to which may adhere a small quantity of the alkaloids, scarcely sufficient to taste, and not enough to be considered of any consequence.

[Translated for the N. Y. Journal of Pharmacy, by Professor Torrey, M. D.]

ON THE ANALYSIS OF RAIN WATER.

BY M. MARTIN.*

The numerous analyses of rain water made by many chemists, and the very important report of Arago on a memoir of M. Barral, having impressed me with the importance of such researches, I have thought that a series of analyses made at Marseilles might—in view of its favorable position—enable me to determine whether the presence of certain bodies in such water was constant or accidental. The *present* inquiry relates only to the water which fell at Marseilles on the morning of 27th of May, 1853. The analysis was made upon about 14 *litres*.

I am indebted to M. Valz, who was good enough to place at my disposal the water which was collected in the rain-guage of the observatory, which he so successfully directs. Not having at my command other vessels than those of glass or porcelain, I was compelled, for the reasons given by M. Barral, in

---

* From *Annales de Chimie et de Physique*, *Mai*, 1854.

his second memoir, to confine myself to the determination of *Iodine*, of *Chlorine*, of *Ammonia*, and of *Nitric Acid.*

Before describing the analysis, I will say a word upon the principal reagents employed.

1st. The Distilled Water used was obtained in the following manner—The alembic giving twelve *litres* of distilled water, at each operation, I reserved for use all between the fifth and the ninth.

2d. The Caustic Potash was procured from the bitartrate, crystallized many times, then calcined in a porcelain crucible, and finally rendered caustic by pure Lime.

3rd. The Hydrochloric acid was prepared by treating common salt, twice recrystalized, with twice its weight of distilled sulphuric acid, with all the precautions proper to ensure its purity.

EXAMINATION FOR IODINE.

I evaporated to dryness over a water-bath, in a porcelain basin, four kilogrammes of the water to which I had previously added about one gramme of pure Carbonate of Soda.

The residue was treated with twenty cubic centimetres of water, and the solution divided into two equal parts, which were placed respectively in test-glasses, marked No. 1 and No. 2.

Alongside of No. 1 was placed a glass, No. 3, containing, in ten cubic centimetres of water, 0.00005 grammes of Iodine, in the state of Iodide of Potassium.

To each of them were added a few drops of a fresh solution of starch, two drops of dilute nitric acid, and a single drop of dilute hydrochloric acid. No. 3 exhibited a very sensible blue tint, while No. 1 showed not the least color.

Alongside of No. 2 was placed a glass, No. 4, which, like No. 3, contained 0.00005 grammes of Iodine. To each of these were added a few drops of the same starch solution, as above, and three or four drops of a fresh and weak solution of *chlorine.* No. 4 assumed a blue tint, more marked than that in the preceding experiment, while No. 2 did not change in color.

From these experiments, I infer that this rain water contains no Iodine, either free or combined, at least in appreçiable quantity.

DETERMINATION OF CHLORINE.

A simple preliminary trial upon only 100 cubic centimetres of the water having shown the presence of chlorine, three kilogrammes, in which about one gramme of pure Carbonate of Soda was dissolved, were evaporated to dryness, over a very slow fire, in a glass-flask, which had been thoroughly washed with water, rendered slightly sour by nitric acid, containing no traces of chlorine or hydrochloric acid. The residue was treated with fifty cubic centimetres of water, and the flask with a similar quantity. The whole liquid was evaporated to dryness in a porcelain basin, and that residue, after being exposed to the temperature of 40° C. for one hour, and then of 120° C. for two hours, was raised to a low red heat for half an hour, to insure the destruction of organic matters. The residue was dissolved in fifty cubic centimetres of water—the solution filtered: the capsule and the filter each washed with a similar quantity of water—and thus 150 cubic centimetres of the mixed liquids were obtained.

Fifty of these were placed in a test-glass, and an equal quantity of nitric acid added. The determination of the chlorine was made by means of a solution of Nitrate of Silver, containing, in 500 cubic centimetres, 3.048 grammes of pure silver, so that each cubic centimetre would correspond to one milligramme of chlorine, and by employing a *burette*, giving seventeen drops to the entire centimetre, the chlorine could be determined to within one-seventeenth of a milligramme. Four centimetres and five drops were required, the effect of the last drop being somewhat uncertain. The experiment lasted three days.

One hundred cubic centimetres were next employed, and likewise acidulated with nitric acid. For this quantity, eight cubic centimetres and eleven drops of the silver liquid were required. The experiment lasted fifty hours. It is needless to say that the flasks were kept in a dark place. These analysis prove then the presence of 4 5-17 milligrammes of chlorine, or of 7 6-100 milligrammes of chloride of sodium in each kilogramme of the water, a quantity which is much greater than that found by M. Barral, in July, 1852. The difference is I suppose due to the fact that the water which I analysed fell during a violent south wind.

DETERMINATION OF THE AMMONIA.

Considering the large mass of the liquid in which I had to determine a very small quantity of ammonia, I could use no other method than that which M. Boussingault has so happily employed in ascertaining the quantity of this alkali in running waters. I, therefore, employed a normal liquor, of which each cubic centimetre contained 5 milligrammes of SO^3, a quantity of sulphuric acid, corresponding to 3 25-100 milligrammes of ammonia, assuming the formula of the latter to be NH^4O.

A normal alkaline liquid was also prepared, in which, instead of using a solution of lime in sugar, as is commonly done, I employed, in preference, ammonia itself.

This normal liquid was such that for neutralizing ten cubic centimetres of the acid liquid. there were required 382 divisions of the alkaline liquid, measured in a *burette*, giving one-tenth of a cubic centimetre. In three successive trials there were required, 1st, 382 divisions; 2d, 383; and 3d, 382.

I adopted 382 divisions, which give for the quantity of alkali, 32.5 milligrammes, or 85-1000 of a milligramme for each division.

Before proceeding to the direct determination of the ammonia, I was desirous of verifying, not the method, for of that its authorship is a sufficient guaranty, but my own method in using it. For this purpose, I introduced a little more than three *litres* of distilled water into the flask destined for use in my subsequents. After boiling this slowly for a quarter of an hour, and when it had become completely cold, I added to it 100 divisions of the normal alkaline liquid and five cubic centimetres of potash. From this mixture there were drawn, by distillation, 150 cubic centimetres into a receiver which contained 10 cubic centimetres of the normal acid liquid. To produce neutralization, 334 divisions of the normal alkaline liquid were required.

The distillation being still kept up, to the next 150 cubic centimetres of product were added ten cubic centimetres of the acid liquid. Neutralization now required 331 divisions of the alkaline liquid. Continuing the distillation, obtaining again 150 cubic centimetres of product, and adding as before 10 cubic centimetres of the acid liquid, 381 divisions of the alkaline liquid were required for neutralization. The ammonia added to the water had thus entirely come over with the first 300 cubic centimetres, and I had obtained 99 per cent. of the alkali employed.

I then put in the flask three kilogrammes of the rain water with five cubic centimetres of potash. When the distillation commenced, the product was received in a vessel containing five cubic centimetres of the acid liquid until there was an amount of 150 cubic centimetres. The receiving vessel was replaced by another containing five cubic centimetres of the acid liquid, to the extent of making a new amount of 150 cubic centimetres. The same thing was done a third time. I should have had then, if the distilled product contained no ammonia, to employ, for the neutralization of the acid, three times 191 divisions of the normal alkaline liquid. I had only used 129 divisions for the first vessel, 143 for the second, and 189 for the third. The difference is about 110 divisions of the alkaline liquid, which were not employed. This corresponds to 9 35-100 milligrammes for 3 kilogrammes of water, or 3 116-1000 milligrammes for each kilogramme.

In the same flask were placed three kilogrammes of the water under examination, to which were added five cubic centimetres of potash, and the distillation proceeded with. As before, the operation was continued until 450 cubic centimetres of distilled product were obtained, which was distributed in equal portions into three vessels, each containing five cubic centimetres of the normal acid liquid.

To the first of these three vessels were added 126, to the

second 152, and to the third 184 divisions of the alkaline liquid. The sum of the differences is 111 divisions of the alkaline liquid, corresponding to 9 5-10 milligrammes of ammonia, which is equivalent to 3 17-100 milligrammes of ammonia to each kilogramme of the water. The mean of these two results is 3 144-1000 milligrammes to the kilogramme.

DETERMINATION OF THE NITRIC ACID.

Being sure that not the slightest quantity of nitric acid had been introduced into the water which had been used for determining the ammonia, I reduced this liquid by evaporation to the volume of half a *litre.* The evaporation was then carried to dryness over a water-bath, and the residue, having been exposed for one hour to a heat of 110° C., and for two hours to that of 120° C., was heated to a low red heat for half an hour, for the purpose of destroying organic matter. The residue obtained was dissolved in 60 cubic centimetres of water, forming a solution which should contain all the nitric acid present in six kilogrammes of the water. This solution was maked A. This having been done, another solution was prepared of Permanganate of Potash, of such strength as to require 217 divisions for converting into perchloride one decigramme of iron.

Two trials made under all the conditions required in the analysis of the nitrates, and in each of which I employed 5 milligrammes of nitric acid, by means of its equivalent quantity of Nitrate of Potash dissolved in 100 cubic centimetres of water, required, for producing the perchloridizing effect, no more than 184 divisions of the permanganic liquid. Hence 33 divisions of this last liquid represent 5 milligrammes of nitric acid.

This being done, one decigramme was dissolved in hydrochloric acid, and the solution added to 10 cubic centimetres of A, representing one kilogramme of the water. The conversion of the iron into perchloride required 218 divisions of the permanganic liquid.

In a second trial, 20 cubic centimetres of A were employed, and these required 215 divisions of the permaganic liquid.

In the third trial, the remainder of the solution A, that is

30 cubic centimetres, representing 3 kilogrammes of the water, was employed, and required 217 divisions.

I give these results simply as I have observed them, leaving each reader to interpret them in his own manner. As concerns myself, I am induced to believe that nitric acid was not present, at least in sensible quantity, in the water I analyzed.

It might be supposed that nitric acid had, perhaps, disappeared during the calcination at a low red heat, by the combustion of the minute quantity of organic matter which I sought to destroy.

To remove this doubt, I evaporated four *litres* of water, which contained a very considerable quantity of organic matter, so as to reduce it to 100 cubic centimetres. The liquid was then filtered, and divided into two portions, A and B. To B only were added five milligrammes of nitric acid, and the evaporation was continued as before. A yielded me 1 5-10 milligrammes of nitric acid, and B 6 3-10 milligrammes. Meanwhile, as I propose to analyze the rain water falling every month, I will soon ascertain whether my results express a constant fact with regard to sea winds, or whether they show a faulty analysis.

SUMMARY.

In pursuing, in the analysis of this water, the ordinary methods, I have sought only to determine four bodies, viz., Iodine, Chlorine, Ammonia and Nitric Acid.

In treating it by comparison with a liquid containing a very small quantity of iodine, I have not found the slightest indication of the presence of this body. The determination of chlorine, made by the volumetric method, afforded 4 29-100 millimetres of chlorine, corresponding to 7 6-100 millimetres of common salt, a quantity much above that heretofore found.

The determination of ammonia by the process with which M. Boussingault has enriched chemical analysis, gives 3 144-1000 milligrammes of that alkali to the kilogramme of water.

As regards nitric acid, I have been unable, in spite of the most sedulous care, to detect its presence.

The analyses which I shall hereafter make will prove whether my results are the expression of a constant fact with regard to rain falling with a sea-wind or whether they are faulty. I hope, meanwhile, that some one more capable would assume a task much above my ability, and, why should I not say it, much above my means.

[Translated for the N. Y. Journal of Pharmacy,
by Professor Torrey, M. D.]

ON THE FILTRATION OF AIR CONSIDERED AS A MEANS OF PRESERVING ORGANIC SUBSTANCES FROM PUTREFACTION.

BY MM. H. SCHRÖDER AND TH. DE DUSCH.*

An organic substance recently boiled with water is preserved from putrefaction by a current of air properly filtered through cotton.

This interesting fact has been proved by the following experiments.

Fresh meat was introduced with water into a flask, hermetically closed with a waxed cork, which was traversed by two tubes, bent at right angles. The first passed into the interior to within a short distance of the meat, and was connected externally with a gasometer, acting as an aspirator and filled with water. The second communicated with a horizontal tube, three centimetres in diameter and sixty long, filled with cotton. The anterior extremity of this tube was closed by a cork, giving passage to a small tube, through which the outer air entered the apparatus.

Another and similar flask received the same quantities of fresh meat and of water, which were left exposed to the free action of the atmosphere.

Things being thus arranged, the water contained in both

---

* From "*Annales de Chimie et de Physique,*" *Juin*, 1854.

flasks was boiled for some time, to expel the air and effect the complete coagulation of the juices of the meat. Then, by opening the stop-cock of the aspirator, the water was allowed to escape, drop by drop, so as to draw the air slowly through the tube filled with cotton. The experiment was commenced February 9th, 1853, and was continued without interruption to March 6th. During the second week, the meat and the accompanying liquid, contained in the open flask, entered into putrefaction, and gave out an insupportable odor. In the other, whose contents had been exposed to the current of filtered air for twenty-three days, they were found on examination to be perfectly fresh. No smell was remarked, but, when warmed, they gave out the peculiar odor of fresh and hot soup. Another experiment was made, extending from April 20th to May 14th, with a similar result. We are, therefore, justified in the conclusion that fresh boiled meat and fresh soup are preserved without change in a current of air filtered through cotton. We arrived at the same result in operating upon the wort of beer, whose disposition to ferment is so well known. Exposed during twenty-three days to a current of filtered air, it lost neither its aroma, its sweet taste, nor its slight acid reaction. On the other hand, some experiments were made, under similar conditions, for the purpose of preserving boiled milk and fresh meat, simply heated in a water-bath, without the addition of water. It was found, however, that in these cases the materials entered as rapidly into putrefaction as they do in open vessels.

Another experiment was made at a hotter season of the year with fresh beef and soup, but whether the boiling was incomplete, or from some other cause, these materials were not preserved without alteration. This last experiment does not, however, invalidate the positive results which the first ones gave.

It appears to the authors that certain spontaneous decompositions of organic substances do not require for their commencement and completion anything beyond the access of atmospheric oxygen. Such is the putrefaction of fresh meat, of the caseine of milk, and the transformation of lactine into lactic acid. In other phenomena of fermentation and putrefaction, it is not alone oxygen that is concerned, but certain other unknown matters in the air, which can be eliminated by heating it, as has been done by M. Schwann, or by filtering it through cotton.

ON THE ESSENTIAL OIL OF OSMITOPSIS ASTERISCORIDES.

BY M. GORUP BESANEZ.*

OSMITOPSIS ASTERISCORIDES is a *composita* growing in Africa. It possesses tonic and anti-spasmodic qualities which entitle it to a place in the Materia Medica. Dr. Thunberg has employed it with great success in paralysis. The plant abounds in an aromatic essential oil, which, according to M. Gorup Besanez, is isomeric with Borneo camphor, oil of cajeput, &c. He gives it the formula—

$$C^{20} H^{18} O^{2}.$$

The essential oil of osmitopsis has a slightly greenish-yellow color, and a penetrating, disagreeable odor, which re-calls that of camphor and oil of cajeput.

It possesses a caustic taste, but is without action upon vegetable blues; its density at 13° R. is 0.931. It is insoluble in water; dissolves iodine with facility, and is browned by sulphuric acid. Cold nitric acid does not attack it, but when heated violent action commences, and the oil thickens.

The ammoniacal solutions of silver are only reduced by it after long continued boiling.

---

* *Ann. der Chem. und Pharm.* New Series, vol. xiii., p. 215.

THE IDENTITY OF PEUCEDANINE WITH IMPERATORINE.

BY M. WAGNER.*

M. Wagner has established the perfect identity of peucedanine with imperatorine by the study of their chemical and physical properties and their metamorphoses. Treated by an alcoholic solution of potash, these two substances each form angelate of potash and oreoselone—

$$\underbrace{C^{24}H^{12}O^{6}}_{\text{Peucedanine.}} + KO\,HO = \underbrace{C^{10}H^{7}KO^{4}}_{\text{Angelate of Potash.}} + \underbrace{C^{14}H^{6}O^{4}}_{\text{Oreoselone.}}$$

Angelic acid, discovered by M. M. Meyer and Zenner in the root of Angelica Archangelica, appears to exist in many Umbelliferæ. It is probable that it has often been confounded with valeric acid, from which it at most only differs by two equivalents of hydrogen.

ON THE ACTION OF SOLANINE UPON THE ANIMAL ORGANISM.

BY M. FEAAS.†

Solanine is very generally considered as a dangerous narcotic poison. M. Desfosses, the discoverer of this alkaloid, was the first to make known its poisonous effects, and his observations have since been verified by a great number of chemists and toxicologists. If one may judge from the results obtained in a recent investigation by M. Feaas, it is probable that those who experimented previous to this physiologist, employed a

* *Jour. fur Prakt. Chem.*, vol. lxi., p. 503.

† *Neues Repert. fur Pharm.*, vol. il., p. 529.

different solanine from that used by the latter. M. Feeas is director of the veterinary school at Munich. An epizoon, which appeared periodically upon the swine in some districts of Bavaria, having been considered as the effect of poisoning by solanine, proceeding from the potatoes which had begun to germinate, M. Feaas was asked to investigate the subject, and funds were furnished by the Government enabling him to prosecute the research under the most favorable conditions.

Experiments were made with swine, dogs and hares. Solanine being introduced into the stomach and veins, the following are the general results of these researches. Pure solanine introduced into the stomachs of swine produces no poisonous effects, even in doses of about two grammes. The same result followed with the alkaloid in saline combination. No effect was produced upon dogs, except in doses of about 8 decigrammes. Hares were killed by a dose of one decigramme. Horses did not appear affected by it.

Solanine acts more energetically when introduced into the circulation. One decigramme thus employed sufficed to kill small dogs.

ANALYSIS OF THE SHELL OF HELIX POMATIA.

BY M. WICKE.*

According to M. Joy, the shell of this mollusk is composed of 98.5 per cent of carbonate of lime, and of 1.5 per cent. of organic matter.

The operculum of this shell is covered with little points, soluble in dilute acetic acid, without effervescence. This caused M. Wicke to suppose that this part of the calcareous envelope was different from the rest, and he accordingly submitted it to analysis, taking care previously to remove the adhering organic matter, by washing with potash water.

---

* *Annales de Chimie et de Pharmacie*, vol. lxxxvii., p. 224.

One hundred parts gave—

Phosphate of lime (Ph. O^5 3 CO) - -	5.73
Carbonate of lime - - - - -	94.24
Oxides of iron and manganese - -	traces.

The operculum of a *trochus*, from the Mediterranean, gave, upon analysis—

Carbonate of lime - - - - -	98.72
Organic matter and phosphate of magnesia,	traces.

ON RED AND BLACK SULPHUR.

BY G. MAGNUS.

The author made some observations on sulphur which have led him to the discovery of a few more allotropic forms of that body, and which may be included under the following divisions.

1. If well melted sulphur be rapidly cooled, part of it is converted into sulphur insoluble in bisulphuret of carbon. The flowers of sulphur contain nearly one-third of this insoluble sulphur.

2. By repeated fusing, at a high temperature, and rapidly cooling, the sulphur assumes a red-brown color, in which state it has been called "red sulphur" by Deville. The author proposes for this the name of "re-melted" sulphur, in order to distinguish it from the proper red sulphur. It contains sometimes one-third of insoluble sulphur, which, although of a yellow color, consists partly of yellow, partly of black, insoluble sulphur.

3. If this insoluble residuum be heated in a water-bath, it becomes soft and viscid; when cool, bisulphuret of carbon dissolves a part of it, viz., the yellow sulphur, because it is easier converted at 212° into the soluble modification than is the black sulphur. If the insoluble residuum be repeatedly acted on at 212° F., it becomes of a chocolate-brown color.

4. Fusing the preceding at 570°, and abruptly cooling, a quite black viscid mass is obtained, which hardens only after some time, when it assumes a glassy appearance. This black sulphur is insoluble, or at least very slightly so, in bisulphuret of carbon, alcohol, ether, benzole, oil of turpentine and chloroform.

5. If the black sulphur be kept for a length of time at the temperature of boiling water, it is converted into soluble sulphur. The solution contains much yellow, besides a little red sulphur.

6. If the black sulphur be exposed to a heat between 280° F. and 400° F., for a very short time only, it is, after cooling, of a brown color and crystalline structure, and is soluble in bisulphuret of carbon. The solution contains much red and but little yellow sulphur.

7. When the solution is concentrated, by evaporation, crystals of yellow sulphur appear, which assume a red color as the evaporation progresses, the intensity of the color increasing as the solution becomes more concentrated. The mother-liquor forms at last a stiff, red mass.

8. This hardened mass is again soluble in bisulphuret of carbon, and, if properly treated, granular, and of a carmine-red color.

9. This sulphur, the red sulphur of the author, fuses at a temperature between 280° and 325° F. into a red mass of crystalline structure, part of which is soluble in bisulphuret of carbon.

10. Heated to 570° F., and suddenly cooled, the red sulphur is converted into black sulphur.

Hence the author distinguishes the following modifications of sulphur.

1. Soluble prismatic yellow sulphur.
2. " octaëdric " "
3. Insoluble " "
4. " red "
5. Soluble " "
6. Black sulphur.

Often fused and suddenly cooled sulphur contains soluble

yellow, insoluble yellow, black and soluble red sulphur.—*Pogg. Annalen*, Bd. xcii., p. 308–323.

[Translated by Benjamin Canavan.

ARSENIC EATERS.

BY DR. J. J. TSCHUDI.

In the report of a remarkable trial of one Anne Alexander, for poisoning, which took place before a jury at Cilli, it was stated that three of the witnesses were interrogated as to whether the deceased, Lieutenant M. Wurzel, was a "poison eater" or not? The affirmative was not proven, and the only testimony (of little weight) which could have rendered the supposition probable was that of First Lieutenant M. J., who declared that, in 1828, he found in the drawer of Wurzel a small box, containing little substances, of the size of a grain of maize, which could not have been aught but white arsenic. The testimony of the other witnesses was based merely on hearsay.

Poison eating being for the medical public a phenomenon more or less unknown, I have thought of publishing some facts and observations on this matter. In some countries of Lower Austria and Styria, particularly in the mountains which separate it from Hungary, there is met with amongst the peasants the remarkable habit of "arsenic eating." They purchase it under the name of *hedri*, (*hedrich*, *huttegruuch*,) from herb peddlers, &c., and they in their turn obtain it from the workers in Hungarian glass, veterinarians, quacks, &c.

The arsenic eaters have a double object; *firstly*, to give themselves a *fresh* and *healthy* air, and also a certain degree of *plumpness*. They are consequently (!) very frequently young peasants who have recourse to this expedient through coquetry and a desire to please; and it is really surprising with what success they attain their wish, for the young poison eaters are eminently distinguished by their freshness of color, and an appearance of buxom health. I will cite only a single case among many within my knowledge. A milk-maid, good-looking, but thin and pale, living on a farm in the village of H——, having a lover whom she wished to attract more strongly by her charms, had recourse to the afore-mentioned means, and took arsenic many times a week. The desired result was not slow to appear, and after a few months she became plump, buxom, blythe, a belle of the first water. In consequence of augmenting imprudently the dose of arsenic, she fell a victim to her coquetry. She died poisoned, and her end was deplorable. The number of deaths by the abuse of arsenic is not insignificant, particularly amongst the young. Every ecclesiastic in those countries can enumerate many victims; and the results of my inquiries amongst pastors are very curious. Through fear of the law, which renders illegal the possession of arsenic, or that the "small, still voice" reproaches them for their crime, the poison eaters conceal as much as possible the use of this dangerous remedy. Usually, it is only a death-bed confession which raises the veil of secrecy. The *second* advantage which poison eaters have in view is, to become brisk ("volatil"), that is to say, to facilitate respiration while making an ascent. At each long excursion on the mountains, they take a little morsel of arsenic, which they allow gradually to dissolve in the mouth. The effect is surprising: they ascend *easily* heights which they could not surmount except with the greatest difficulty without this practice. I will add here that, based on this fact, *I have administered Fowler's Solution in asthma with signal success.*

The quantity of arsenic with which the arsenic eaters commence, according to the acknowledgment of many of them, is rather less than half a grain. They stop at this dose, which they swallow many times a week, in the morning at breakfast, for some time, "to habituate themselves;" then they increase the dose insensibly and cautiously, and according as the usual dose loses its effect. The peasant R., of the commune Ag——, a sexagenarian, enjoying very good health, took actually each time a piece equal to nearly four grains. For forty years he maintained this habit, inherited from his father, and bequeathed to his son.

It is worth noting, that no trace of arsenical cachexy is visible in this individual any more than other arsenic eaters; the symptoms of chronic arsenical poisoning never appearing in those who know how to apportion the dose to their constitution and idiosyncracy (tolerance). It must, however, be remarked, that the suspension of the use of arsenic, whether through want of the poison or for any other reason, is always followed by morbid phenomena which resemble those of arsenical poisoning (intoxication) in a milder degree; for instance, there is observed great uneasiness, with indifference to surrounding objects, solicitude for their persons, indigestion, anorexy, sensation of fullness of stomach, glairy vomitings, with pyrosis, spasmodic constriction of the pharynx, griping, constipation, and above all *dyspnœa.* Against these phenomena, there is no remedy save the immediate return to arsenic. From information the most accurate, received from the inhabitants of this country, poison eating never degenerates into a passion, as opium eating in the East, the use of betel in India and Polynesia, and of coca in Peru, but becomes rather a necessity for those who are addicted to it. This abuse of arsenic is in other countries simulated by that of corrosive sublimate. I recollect a case known and authenticated by the English ambassador in Turkey, that of an opium eater of Broussa, who swallowed, daily, with his opium, the enormous quantity of *forty grains* of corrosive sublimate. In the mountains of Peru, I have often met similar individuals; and in Bolivia, the use of corrosive sublimate is so extensive that the article is openly sold in the provision market.

It is useless to mention the common use of arsenic, even in Vienna, particularly by the grooms and coachmen of the great. They mix a good portion with meal, a piece of which, the size of a pea, they wrap up in a piece of linen, and fasten it to the bridle when harnessing. The glossy, round, and elegant appearance, equal to that of the most choice horses, and above all, the white foam at the mouth, arise generally from arsenic, which has the effect of increasing salivation. The charioteers, in mountainous districts, put often a dose of arsenic in the forage which they give their horses previous to a laborious ascent. The jockeys often supply themselves with little leaden pellets, for the short winded horses which they take to market. They cause them to swallow from a quarter to half a pound. These pellets are made with one part of arsenic to one hundred of lead, and it appears the effect of them, which lasts some days, is due to the arsenic which they contain. The quantity of arsenic which is found on those gentlemen of the stable is sometimes considerable. A brewer, R—— A——, sent to an apothecary of his neighborhood, Mr. B. Sch——, a piece of arsenic, three-quarters of a pound weight, which he found in his servant's trunk. The past winter, a peasant poisoned himself in my vicinage, with a piece of arsenic the size of a pear, which he pulverized and swallowed with water; he died in half an hour. This practice is continued for years without accident; but when the horse passes to an owner who does not use arsenic, he sickens, loses spirit, becomes lean, and, despite the most abundant food, never regains his good appearance.

These sketches of "poison eaters" will show how useful it is to physicians and jurists to be aware of this wide-spread abuse in some of the countries of Austria. The judicial investigation, of which mention is made at the beginning of this letter, has not established the fact that M. Wurzel was an "arsenic eater;" but the supposition is allowable. If the autopsy and chemical examinations had not been conducted with unpardonable negligence; if the accused (endowed with a quick genius) had been embarrassed by cross questions, and been led into contradictions and inaccurate declarations, it is probable that the verdict of the jury would have been less favorable for the woman, Alexander, despite her innocence.

[Another letter containing further statements to the same effect, from the same hand, is connected with this, and followed by this—

Note du Redacteur. It is desirable that men of science, residing in the localities where are said to be found the "*arsenic eaters,*" should confirm or deny the statements of M. Tschudi.] —*Jour. de Chimie Medicale.*

NEW VARIETY OF BALSAM OF COPAIBA.

BY MR. CHARLES LOWE,

Assistant in the Royal Institution Laboratory, Manchester.

An organic fluid was lately placed in my hands by Mr. Crace Calvert for examination, which he had received from an oil merchant of this city, who stated that all he knew of the substance was, that it was obtained by the incision of a certain tree growing on the coast of *India*. From the characters it presents I have ascertained it to be a balsam of copaiba, but as it differs in some of its properties from other balsams that I have examined, I forward you the following notice, in hopes that it may prove interesting to some of your numerous readers.

In appearance this balsam of copaiba is dark colored and turbid. Its turbidity is due to a greenish, resinous matter, held in suspension, which is, however, easily separable, either by filtration or deposition, leaving a brown transparent liquid, of sp. gr. 0.970. When the latter fluid is submitted to a careful distillation it yields:

Essential oil - - - - -	65	per cent.
Resin - - - - - - -	34	"
Acetic acid and water - - -	1	"
	100	

I find that the essential oil in its various reactions with potassium, iodine, nitric acid, &c., and moreover in taste, exactly corresponds with those presented by pure essence of copaiba. The resin left by distillation of the balsam, either with or without water, is, if deprived of the whole of the essential oil, extremely hard. Its entire solubility in coal naphtha proves the absence of any of the soft resin which exists in most of the copaiba of commerce. This hard resin (copaivic acid) being most probably the active principle of balsam of copaiba, I am induced to think its quantity and purity in the one I have examined is indicative of its superior value as a medicament. The dark color of the balsam may, perhaps, limit its employment, but the large quantity of copaivic acid it contains renders it valuable, as the latter may be made available by heating the filtered balsam to the boiling point with a small quantity of caustic potash or soda lye, of sp. gr. 1.34, and separating the resinate of potash or soda from the essential oil. The alkaline resinate may then be dissolved in water, giving a colorless solution, (similar to Frank's specific,) or the balsam may be treated with magnesia to form the ordinary copaiba pill.

I have in conclusion remarked:

1st. That the essential oil obtained by the distillation of balsam of copaiba has, like several other hydrocarbons, the property of dissolving indigo.

2dly. The new variety of balsam above described presents the curious property of becoming gelatinous (so much so that the tube may safely be inverted,) if heated to 230° F., even if a *sealed* tube be employed. This character being dissimilar to the one given in the same circumstances with such other balsams as I had at my disposal, I am induced to attribute it to the large amount of "*hard* resin" it contains.

3rdly. Balsams of copaiba, in general, give, on distillation with two per cent. sulphuric acid, a beautiful blue volatile oil. Chlorine, hypochlorite of lime, and bichromate of potash, give a similar character with the balsam, which appears to me to be due to the oxidation of the hard resin, as I have been unable to obtain but a small proportion of the blue-colored oil when I employed a balsam containing "*soft* resin," comparatively to when I made use of the one above described, which, as I have already remarked, contains only "hard resin." A further support of this view is, that pure essence of copaiba assumes no blue coloration when distilled as above.

4thly. That cold sulphuric acid produces a purple coloration with balsam of copaiba, similar to that obtained by its action on cod-liver oil. Such being the case, it is probable that a small quantity of it mixed with olive, or some other oil, may be sold by unprincipled persons as genuine cod-liver oil.—*London Pharmaceutical Journal.*

ON A NEW PROCESS OF PREPARING POWDER OF IRON.

BY ARTHUR MORGAN, L.A.C.,

Apothecary to Sir Patrick Dun's Hospital.

This preparation, known also as the "Fer Reduit," or Quevenne's iron, from the name of the gentleman who introduced it, has obtained a place both in the last Dublin Pharmacopœia and in that of the United States. On the continent and in America, practitioners speak highly of its effects as a chalybeate and tonic; in this country its use has not been sufficiently extensive as yet to justify a decided opinion. I may mention, however, that in several cases in which it has been lately used at Sir Patrick Dun's Hospital, its good effects were well marked.

In the formulæ which have been published in the two Pharmacopœias already mentioned, the process is difficult and uncertain; it consists of passing a stream of hydrogen gas over oxide of iron heated to redness in an iron tube. The chief difficulty consists in regulating the heat, for if the heat is not sufficiently high, the product will be a pyrophorus, taking fire immediately on exposure to the air; and on the other hand, if the heat be too high, the powder will become agglutinated. These difficulties cause this preparation to fetch a high price, and afford temptations to the substitution of spurious imitations.

By the process which I propose, these difficulties are overcome, and an opportunity will be afforded of determining by extensive use whether the remedial effects of this preparation justify its addition to our already over-stocked Materia Medica.

To prepare powder of iron according to my plan, the steps to be pursued are as follows:

Eight ounces of yellow prussiate of potash are to be heated in an oven till the water of crystallization is driven off, reduced to a very fine powder, then thoroughly mixed with four ounces of red oxide of iron (previously well washed and finely pulverized) and three ounces of pure dried carbonate of potash. This mixture is then to be introduced (a small portion at a time) into a crucible previously heated to low redness. The heat must be kept up till all appearance of effervescence has ceased. The crucible is then allowed to cool, the mass scooped out, powdered, and having been introduced into a large bottle, repeatedly washed by agitation and decantation with distilled water, till the washings cease to precipitate with solution of nitrate of silver. The powder is then to be turned out on a filter, and dried as rapidly and with as little exposure to air as possible. It may now, if necessary, be passed through a fine sieve to separate any particles which may have agglutinated, owing to the application of too high a heat. The powder should be preserved in a well-stopped bottle. With this process, and the quantities mentioned, the product obtained will weigh about three ounces and a half.

As thus obtained, the reduced iron is a fine powder, of a dark grey color, not feeling gritty or coarse under the fingers; it dissolves completely in muriatic acid with considerable effervescence, and the solution thus obtained yields with potash or ammonia the greenish gelatinous precipitate indicative of a protosalt. If the precipitate be reddish, it shows the powder to contain oxide of iron. Water digested on the powder should not precipitate with solution of nitrate of silver; that would indicate that all the cyanide of potassium had not been washed out.

The chemical decompositions which take place in this process I believe to be as follows:—Two atoms of ferrocyanide of potassium 2 (2 K Cy + Fe Cy), and two atoms of carbonate of potash 2 (KO, CO^2), being fused together yield five atoms of cyanide of potassium 5 (K, Cy), one atom of cyanate of potash (K O+Cy O), two atoms of metallic iron, and two atoms of carbonic acid gas, which are given off in effervescence. The five atoms of cyanide of potassium thus formed now acting on three atoms and one-third of the peroxide of iron, decompose the peroxide, giving rise to five atoms of cyanate of potash 5 (KO, CyO), and setting free the iron in a finely divided condition, thus we obtain all the iron contained in the materials used, both that of the ferrocyanide and that of the peroxide.

The proportions in the process detailed above do not exactly agree with the atomic quantities just mentioned. According to the above explanation, the quantity of peroxide of iron required should be 2144 grains instead of four ounces, or 1750 grains, directed to be used. But as Wittstein has remarked (in speaking of Liebig's process for obtaining the mixed cyanide of potassium and cyanate of potash, by fusing ferrocyanide of potassium and carbonate of potash together in the proportions adopted in the process which has been detailed) that some of the cyanide is decomposed during the exposure to heat, the product instead of being five atoms of cyanide of potassium to one atom of cyanate of potash, as by theory should be the result, consists of cyanide and cyanate in the proportion of seven of the former to five of the latter; it was, therefore, necessary to allow for this decomposition, and also further to reduce the amount of oxide used, so as to maintain a considerable excess of cyanide of potassium to protect the metal already reduced from oxidation by exposure to the heat and air.

This process, affording an easy and certain method of preparing an article which promises to be of some value as a therapeutic agent, and of obviating the use of a difficult and uncertain procedure, I have been induced to make known in the hopes that it may turn out of some value to the pharmaceutic chemist.—*Dublin Medical Press.*

ON A NEW VARIETY OF FLAXSEED.

BY WILLIAM PROCTER, JR.

During a recent visit to Cincinnati, Mr. Edward S. Wayne showed me, in the cabinet of the College of Pharmacy of that city, a specimen of flaxseed, differing in appearance from the common brown seed, it having a greenish yellow color instead of the well marked deep brown of the ordinary drug. In size, shape and lustre they appear to be quite alike. The history of this variety of flaxseed is clearly traced, and Mr. Wayne has kindly given it to me, as follows:

Mr. E. Everingham, who resides about fourteen miles east of Piqua, Miami County, Ohio, in 1846, observed in his field of brown flaxseed *one stalk* with white blossoms, and taller than the rest of the field. He carefully marked the place, and on gathering the seed, when ripe, found it, to his surprise, to be entirely different from any he had ever seen. Next season he sowed it in his garden, but the plants were nearly destroyed by worms, yet he succeeded in gathering about a teacupful of the seeds. From that time it succeeded well, and proved to be more productive than the brown seed. The first seed sold was to Messrs. Sawyer and Jackson, of Piqua, for $3 per bushel, and another lot at Urbana, Champlain County, at $4 the bushel. Messrs. Sawyer and Jackson, who have had considerable experience in manufacturing oil from it, still give it the preference over the brown seed.

At the State Agricultural Fair, held in Cincinnati, in 1850, a premium was awarded for it as a new and valuable variety. The crop of seed this year is estimated at about fifty thousand bushels, which speaks well for its productiveness. Mr. Wayne was informed that it takes three pecks of brown seed to sow an acre, and of the white variety but two pecks is required, the product being equal.

At first sight this variety of flaxseed might readily be taken for canary seed, but on closer inspection it will be found to be lighter in color, flatter and not so pointed. When bruised in a mortar with a little water they afford a stiff, ropy, mucilaginous paste, having very little color, with the peculiar odor of ordinary flaxseed. One hundred parts of the powdered seeds afforded to ether 32 parts of oily residue. Macerated in cold water they communicate a mucilaginous consistence to it, and the mucilage affords precipitates with alcohol and subacetate of lead precisely as that of ordinary flaxseed mucilage. In fact from the slight examination to which it has been subjected, the absence of the brown coloring matter appears to be the only difference. The absence of color is an advantage in favor of its use in medicine, as the meal produced affords a cataplasm less repulsive in appearance. It is probable that the oil it contains is less colored, which is a desideratum to the painter.—*Amer. Journal of Pharmacy.*

ON THE CHANGES PRODUCED IN THE BLOOD BY THE ADMINISTRATION OF COD-LIVER OIL AND COCOA-NUT OIL.

BY THEOPHILUS THOMPSON, M.D., F.R.S.

The author has found that during the administration of cod-liver oil to phthisical patients their blood grew richer in red corpuscles, and he refers to a previous observation of Dr. Franz Simon to the same effect. The use of almond-oil and of olive oil was not followed by any remedial effect, but from cocoa-nut oil results were obtained almost as decided as from the oil of the liver of the cod, and the author believes it may turn out to be a useful substitute. The oil employed was a pure cocoa oleine, obtained by pressure from crude cocoa-nut oil, as expressed in Ceylon and the Malabar coast from the *Copperah* or dried cocoa-nut kernel, and refined by being treated with an alkali and then repeatedly washed with distilled water. It burns with a faint blue flame, showing a comparatively small proportion of carbon, and is undrying.

The analysis of the blood was conducted by Mr. Dugald Campbell. The whole quantity abstracted having been weighed, the coagulum was drained on bibulous paper for four or five hours, weighed and divided into two portions. One portion was weighed and then dried in a water oven, to determine the water. The other was macerated in cold water until it became colorless, then moderately dried and digested with ether and alcohol to remove fat, and finally dried completely and weighed as fibrine. From the respective weights of the fibrine and the dry clot, that of the corpuscles was calculated. The following were the results observed in seven different individuals affected with phthisis in different stages of advancement:

		Red Corpuscles.	*Fibrine.*
First stage, before the use of cod-liver oil	Female	129.26	4.52
	Male	116.03	13.57
First stage, after the use of cod liver oil	Female	136.47	5.00
	Male	141.53	4.79
Third stage, after the use of cod-liver oil	Male	138.74	2.23
Third stage, after the use of cocoa-nut oil	Male	139.95	2.31
	Male	144.94	4.61

—*Chem. Gaz.* July 15, 1854.

ON THE PREPARATION OF CALOMEL IN THE HUMID WAY.

BY PROFESSOR WÖHLER.

It has long been known, from Vogel's experiments, that protochloride of mercury is precipitated from the solution of the perchloride by sulphurous acid. This behavior appears to me to be available in the practical preparation of calomel. It is obtained in this manner as a very delicate powder, of a dazzling white color, which glitters in the sunlight. The difficult process of sublimation and the tedious preparation would thus be avoided; and its preparation in the laboratory would be a very easy matter. It would be obtained immediately in the finely divided state in which the pulverulent sublimed colomel is produced, without any necessity for an operation of so much danger as the preparation of calomel by sublimation, which, moreover, can only be performed on a large scale. As the calomel formed by sulphurous acid is crystalline, and, therefore, in the same condition as the sublimed, there can also be no doubt that it will not differ from this in its medicinal efficacy. The crystals may be distinctly recognized, even with a magnifying power of only 100 diameters; they are generally united, forming regular crosses.

For its preparation it is only necessary to dissolve commercial perchloride of mercury in water, heated to about 122° F., until this is saturated, and afterwards to pass sulphurous acid gas into the hot solution. The gas is evolved by heating coarse charcoal powder with concentrated sulphuric acid. The separation of the calomel commences immediately. When the solution is saturated with gas, it is digested for some time, then left to get cold, and filtered from the calomel, which is afterwards washed. The filtrate usually still contains some unchanged perchloride, which may be converted into calomel, either by heating to boiling, or by a fresh introduction of sulphurous acid and heating. It still remains to be ascertained what temperature is the most proper for the conversion of the whole of the perchloride into calomel.—*Chem. Gaz.*, July, 1854, from *Ann. der Chem. und Pharm.*, xc., p. 124.

ON THE TINCTURE OF ARNICA.

BY M. V. GARNIER.

For some years back I have prepared, by different ways, the tincture of arnica, and the formula that I have constantly adopted appears to deserve a preference over those of M. Monchon, as well on account of the proportions as the process itself.

M. Monchon takes 4 parts of bruised arnica flowers, 8 parts of water, 8 of alcohol, makes two infusions, presses out and adds the alcohol to the watery infusion. This process does not appear to me rational, and is in opposition to his own remarks. I do say that is not rational, for the alcohol is never found in contact with the flowers, from which it can dissolve so much.

It appears, in the process of M. Monchon, not to be employed, but for the chief preservation of the infusion, from which he removes a portion of its principle whilst he occasions in it a very abundant precipitate, and takes up none of it.

The contradiction of which I have spoken is found in this observation, "This alcohol only marks 16 degrees, but should it not weigh but 14, it would be at least of as much use, alcohol dissolving so much more of the soluble portions of the arnica as it is more watery." Therefore, if alcohol, weak as this, is capable of dissolving one portion of the arnica, why not use it altogether in the outset of the above process. This appears to me an incontestible objection.

To establish a comparison I have treated arnica by this process of Monchon, and have obtained a tincture much less aromatic than that I have up to now.

I have also made one, observing the proportions pointed out by Monchon, by infusing 1 part of arnica with 8 of water. After having expressed strongly, I passed 8 parts of alcohol upon the arnica in a displacement apparatus; I united the two liquids and obtained a more agreeable and aromatic tincture.

Lastly, the process which I have used this long time back, only differs from the last in the proportions.

In place of passing the arnica through only six times, I passed it through ten times, which is more in conformity with our decimal system. For instance:

Bruised arnica flowers . . .	100 parts.
Boiling water	500 parts.
Alcohol, of 34 degrees . . .	500 parts.

Infuse in a close vessel, and express after being cooled, then put the arnica into a displacement apparatus, and pass through the alcohol. Displace it with a little water to remove all the alcohol, besides the water of the infusion which remained in the arnica. Unite the liquors and filter after 24 hours lying together.—*Repert. de Pharm.*, June, 1854.

ON TINCTURE OF ARNICA.

BY M. PICHOU.

With respect to the process of M. Monchon for preparing tincture of arnica, I may say that each time that I have had to renew my stock of this tincture, I have never followed any other but his for the last two years, the time when I first became acquainted with it while occupying myself with the alcoholic digestion of arnica (tincture of the fresh plant).

I ought not to omit remarking here what I have more than once done, and to which I think it worthy to call the attention of pharmaceutists. When applying to the fresh plant of arnica, in a mode of treatment analogous to that pointed out by Monchon, for the preparation of the tincture, we obtain an alcoholic liquid preserving the well marked odor, *the characteristic aroma of the flower*, which we look in vain for in the "tincture," for it disappears, or is converted into resin, in the drying of the plant. This peculiar balsamic principle ought to have given to it but a small degree of therapeutic value, yet it appears to us sufficiently remarkable to engage the operators to employ the alcoholic digestion in preference to the tincture in localities where the fresh plant can be collected.—*Ibid.*

Aromatic Vinegar.—Strong acetic acid, 16 ozs., camphor, 1 oz. When dissolved, add one ounce each of essential oils of cloves, lavender, and lemon.—*Beasley.*

APPLICATION OF MUREXIDE AS A COLORING MATTER FOR WOOL.

The beautiful researches of Liebig and Wöhler upon uric acid, and its derivatives, made us acquainted with a peculiar substance, to which they gave the name of alloxan. This body is obtained by adding very gradually one part of the uric acid to four parts of nitric acid, of a specific gravity of from 1.45 to 1.5. The uric acid is dissolved with evolution of nitrogen and carbonic acid, accompanied by a considerable rise of temperature, which must be prevented as much as possible; on cooling, the mass becomes nearly solid, from the deposition of white granular crystals of alloxan. If these crystals be drained and dissolved in a very small quantity of water, and exposed to spontaneus evaporation in a moderately warm room, large, brilliant, colorless crystals, in the form of short right rhombic prisms, will be obtained. Alloxan is remarkable for the facility with which it undergoes changes when treated with different substances, and for the number of curious compounds thereby produced. Thus, if sulphuretted hydrogen gas be passed through a solution of it, sulphur is precipitated and a new body formed, to which the name of alloxantine has been given, or if its solution be slightly acidulated, and a slip of zinc placed in it, the same body will be produced under the influence of the nascent hydrogen evolved during the dissolution of the zinc. Alloxantine being sparingly soluble in cold water, readily separates in crystals, which may be obtained pure by solution in hot water, for, unlike alloxan, it is not decomposed by continued boiling. If 4 parts of alloxantine and 7 of alloxan be dissolved in 240 parts of boiling water, and 80 parts of carbonate of ammonia be added, a very peculiar body will be formed, which will crystallize on the liquor cooling. These crystals are of a beautiful garnet red color, by transmitted light, and have a beautiful iridescent green by reflected light. To this body the name murexide was given, from the murex or shell-fish, from which it was supposed the Tyrian purple was formerly procured. Previous, however, to the experiments of Liebig and Wöhler, Dr. Prout had described the same substance under the name of purpurate of ammonia, but obtained in a somewhat different way. So readily is this body formed, that a solution of alloxan will stain the skin purple in consequence of its production. This fact led its second discoverers to imagine that, like the Tyrian purple, it might be employed as a dye stuff. The difficulty, however, of obtaining it, and of fixing it upon the fabric when formed, prevented, for that time, the idea from proving fertile.

Some time since, however, Dr. Sacc turned his attention to the subject, and led by the fact abovementioned, that a solution of alloxan stained the skin, came to the conclusion, that by impregnating a piece of woollen cloth with that substance, he might be able to produce the murexide directly in the tissue. He tried the experiment, and succeeded in dying a piece of cloth of an amaranthus tint far more beautiful than that produced by cochineal. He communicated the results of his first experiments, still incomplete, to M. Albert Schlumberger, who has succeeded, by modifying and completing the experiments of Dr. Sacc, to render the process, merely indicated by the latter, perfectly practicable.

His process is simple enough: he prepares a solution of alloxan, formed of 30 grammes of alloxan to each litre of water, and soaks the tissue to be dyed in it, the excess of liquid being then squeezed out in the ordinary way, or by pressure between rollers. The cloth is then dried at a gentle temperature, and after an ageing of 24 hours, the color is brought out by passing the cloth over a roller heated to 212° F. For this purpose the drying machines, composed of several drums, would answer perfectly, the cloth being successively passed over each, the greatest care being taken to avoid folds; woollen yarn and wool should be put in a stove heated by steam. According as the heat is communicated to the cloth, a magnificent purple tint, far more beautiful than any thing hitherto produced by the ammoniacal preparation of cochineal, or by red dye woods, makes its appearance as if by magic. The intensity varies according to the strength of the solution of alloxan which has been employed. It is only necessary to wash the cloth in cold water to give to the shade its full brilliancy.

M. Sacc found that the finest and most vivid shades could only be communicated to the tissues mordanted with salts of peroxide of tin, and M. Schlumberger has confirmed this observation. Cloth not mordanted did not give very satisfactory results, even after a prolonged exposure to warm and damp air. He obtained the most satisfactory results by soaking the cloth in a solution composed of equal parts of perchloride of tin and oxalic acid, of a specific gravity of 1.006. In this solution, at a temperature of about 100° F., the cloth is to be allowed to remain for an hour, then rinced and dried, and is then fit to be treated with alloxan. If stronger solutions of the mordant be employed, there is a considerable loss of coloring material, and a deterioration of the shade. This may be attributed to the presence of too great an excess of stannic acid, which from its opacity may mask the murexide, or by its acid reaction may decompose it. This is especially the case if chloride of tin be employed instead of stannate of soda. Experience has shown that fabrics freshly mordanted give better results than those which have been mordanted for some time; the depreciation in purity and brilliancy of tint in the latter may even amount to 20 or 30 per cent.

Murexide, as we have already remarked, being produced by the action of heat and ammonia, it occurred to M. Daniel Dollfuss, and the other members of the committee for the chemical arts, appointed by the *Societé Industrielle* of Mulhouse, to report upon the memoirs of M. Schlumberger, to try the effect of exposing a piece of cloth, treated with alloxan, to the vapor of ammonia. The result confirmed their anticipations, for the color was immediately produced, without the necessity of ageing the cloth after its impregnation with the alloxan. There can therefore be no doubt that the best results will be obtained in future by the employment of ammoniacal vapors, for, besides the saving of time, there will also be a saving of alloxan. This substance is very liable to decompose, especially in the presence of even minute traces of reducing agents, such as protochloride of tin or sulphurous acids; traces of the latter substance always remain in the cloth after the operation of bleaching, no matter how well washed it may be, and would be quite sufficient to prevent the formation of the murexide.

As yet all the attempts that have been made to communicate the murexide purple to cotton or silk have failed, that substance having an affiinity apparently only for wool, to which it gives a very durable and permanent dye. Sun light, so destructive to other purples, appears to have but little action upon that of the murexide; a piece of cloth dyed of a rose color, had its tint scarcely altered by exposure to the full action of the strongest sunshine during two days, and the color was only fully discharged by an exposure of more than two months. Boiling water and steam completely destroy the color produced upon cloth mordanted with salts of tin; the decoloration commences in boiling water at a temperature of about 153° F. and augments with the increase of temperature. This destruction of the dye is caused by the action of the mordant, for cloth dyed without the use of a mordant, not only supports to a certain extent the action of boiling water, but even acquires an uniform and perhaps a more beautiful and deeper tint than that given by prepared woollen fabrics. Further experience may show that hot water and the application of ammonia alone may be advantageously substituted for the mordanting and the passage over heated cylinders.

Cold alcohol or ether have no action upon murexide purple; the former liquid destroys it at boiling temperature, without being colored purple as water is. Alkalies, especially in a caustic state, are very destructive to it; if a piece of cloth dyed with murexide be dipped into a solution of caustic soda, it assumes a violet blue color, and is then decolorized. Soap, acting as a weak alkali, after a time alters it. Chlorine has no immediate action upon it, at least not in weak solutions. Acetic and oxalic acids are not sufficiently energetic to immediately discharge the color. Hydrochloric, nitric and sulphuric acids act as decolorizers, nevertheless the latter acts less quickly than the first two, and, what is singular, the color almost destroyed by sulphuric acid reassumes a rose violet by immersing the tissue in ammonia.

Bichromate of potash, chlorate of potash, acetate of lead, acetate of alumina, are without action upon murexide. This is not the case, however, with reducing compounds, such as proto-chloride of tin, sulphuret of ammonium, proto-sulphate of iron, which destroy the rose tint very rapidly; the proto-chloride of tin produces a blue tint before it decolorizes it. The reduction of the murexide gives birth to a new substance, which, in its turn may reproduce that substance by a properly conducted oxidation.

From these reactions it is evident that the rose, amaranthus, and purple shades produced with the murexide, and which exceed those produced by all other means in richness and brilliancy of tints, have also the advantage of being the most solid and durable, an advantage which will no doubt be soon appreciated.

We have now to speak of the sources from whence the supply of uric acid may be obtained, should the employment of murexide become general. At present the price of that substance, which has never hitherto become an article of commerce would be so high, that the murexide purple would be far more expensive than that produced with cochineal. But, if we recollect, that independent of the excrements of serpents, from which hitherto uric acid has been made, those of pigeons, and especially of all carnivorous birds, silk worms, &c., and, above all, Peruvian guano, which may be obtained in immense quantities, are very rich in uric acid, and it may be produced from them at a very moderate price as soon as it becomes an article of commerce. No doubt, if necessary, fowl might be so fed as to produce it in much larger quantities than they do naturally.

Connected with this part of the subject we may mention, that in the making of the alloxan from the uric acid, a considerable quantity of the former remains in the acid mother liquid, from which the crystals of alloxan separate. This portion could not be used to impregnate tissues in consequence of the nitric acid present, and would cause a considerable loss of material, and a considerable enhancement of the cost of the dye, unless it could be utilized. If a piece of zinc be introduced into the acid mother liquid, alloxantine will be formed, which may be recovered by evaporating the liquid and allowing it to separate out. This substance, as we have before remarked, will also produce the purple color, and a mixture of it with alloxan will afford the best conditions for its production.

M. Schlumberger has indulged in some curious speculations relative to the existence of this coloring matter ready formed in nature which it may be interesting to notice. M. Sacc has found that poultry, and especially birds with very brilliant plumage, such as the different paroquets, do not produce sensible traces of uric acid during their period of moulting, whilst the quantity is very large when their feathers are fully developed. The question naturally suggests itself, what becomes of the uric acid in the former case? May it not be transformed by some, as yet unknown, metamorphosis in the animal body into a substance like alloxan, capable of coloring the feathers? Murexide, as we have observed, is green by reflected light, a substance then which gives violet (red and blue), and green (yellow and blue), can undoubtedly produce all shades of colors, which are made up of those three colors. How curious if it should hereafter be found that murexide was indeed the source of all the varied hues of birds' plumage! Still further, it is chiefly those animals which have but one means of exit for their excrements, and who produce large quantities of uric acid, that exhibit a display of coloring. Thus, for example, we have the skin of the serpent and lizard, the scales of fish, the wings of butterflies, often colored in the most gorgeous manner, whilst the skins of the mammalia are dull, and without that iridescence and metallic lustre which is so characteristic of the coloring of some of the classes of animals mentioned. These are, however, mere speculations, but they nevertheless lead to a very unexpected supposition. The ancients were acquainted with a process for dyeing wool of a fine purple, which has been lost to our days, or at least is only practiced in the ast. Tradition, however, tells us that this beautiful purple nt was produced by pounding a quantity of small shell fish, and adding to the mass either a quantity of urine in the state of putrefaction, or water in which some of the same shell fish had been allowed to putrify. The cloth soaked in the liquid produced by these mixtures, only developed the beautiful purple color after long exposure to the air, and probably to heat. This mode of producing the color, so strikingly resembles that by which the new color of murexide is produced, that one is tempted to believe that the Tyrian purple was produced by that substance; and that many centuries before the beautiful discovery of Liebig and Wöhler, murexide was formed by the action of ammonia in the putrid matter employed upon substances derived from the uric acid which must exist in the intestines of the shell fish pounded up.—*See the Bulletin de la Société Industrielle de Mulhouse, No.* 123, *p.* 242, *for Dr. Schlumberger's Memoir.*

INTRODUCTORY LECTURE,

DELIVERED BEFORE THE PHARMACEUTICAL CLASS OF THE COLLEGE OF PHARMACY, NEW YORK, NOV. 1854.

In appearing for the first time as a lecturer, you will readily believe me when I say that I do so with no inconsiderable amount of trepidation. The initiative in all undertakings is, generally, the most difficult part of the whole affair, but it is peculiarly so where inexperience of one's own powers disables you from estimating what probable amount of success may attend your labors. The modesty of others better qualified than myself has in this instance caused to devolve on me the duty which we, this evening, proceed to perform, and, according to the result, will this our trial be an encouragement or a warning.

It is usual at the commencement of a course of lectures to embrace the opportunity, which is not so well afforded at any other period, of addressing some observations to the students explanatory of the nature and extent of the instruction which is to be communicated to them, and of their obligations in relation thereto, together with whatever general remarks circumstances of any sort may render necessary or proper.

It is known to you that an alteration has been made in that department of the instructions of this college which falls to our lot, by which the course of Materia Medica, to which the medical portion of the lectures has been hitherto chiefly confined, shall be extended so as to embrace a series of instructions in Practical Pharmacy. This arrangement will render it necessary to restrict the remarks on Materia Medica to those of a more practical character: and while each article of the list will be examined and demonstrated, with a full attention to the source whence it is obtained, and the manner in which this is done, its sensible, chemical and distinctive properties, together with the characteristics of goodness of quality and the tests whereby to detect adulterations, and all the other points of practical value—all far-fetched and abstrusely scientific disquisitions, which frequently leave the learner, at least, about as wise as he was before, will be excluded, as being subjects better adapted to more advanced study, and which those who may desire to become conversant with the mere literature of their art will find treated of in the various works relating to them.

In following this design, it is not to be expected that we shall be able to present you with much that is new. Our task is to teach what is already known, not to add to it—a privilege accorded to few—nor, were it in our power to do so, would this be the place, or, pardon me for saying so, you the persons to reap benefit from such efforts.

Our duty will be, therefore, to inculcate the chief principles, the salient points, which it is indispensable you should know, in the most condensed, impressive and intelligible manner, so that they may be readily understood and easily retained; and although it may be said with some truth, that you will learn little here that you might not, if you would, be able to acquire by judicious reading at home, yet are there many advantages attending the *viva voce* or oral method of conveying instruction which render the lecture-room the very best place to acquire knowledge, even though it may be merely retailed.

You do not require to be told what a change comes over the crude drug when submitted to the nice manipulations of the expert pharmaceutist—decayed portions are separated, foreign matters rejected, the less useful and efficient parts removed, and the whole is purified, redeemed, invigorated, when, lo! the medicine emerges from the drug.

Some such process is that adopted by the lecturer, and, as is frequently the case, with the drug, that a small proportion only is available for curative purposes—so, frequently, does a lecture of an hour's duration give you more sound and genuine information than would the desultory reading of ten-fold the extent. That this private study would be performed is also very questionable. The mind, especially the youthful one, however naturally eager for knowledge, seeks, without compulsion of some sort, that only which is easiest of acquisition, and is often powerfully reluctant to apply itself to what is most necessary. For this reason, principally, it seems to me, the system of lecturing has been adopted in colleges, and is indispensable, in order that, by a regular attendance thereat, it is made certain that what is absolutely necessary to be known should be at least once heard and understood, that you have been taught, at least, what you must know, not, indeed, all you should be master of.

Let not, then, the promptings of indolence, or, it may be, the disappointment of some unwarrantable expectation of novelty or entertainment, induce you to suppose that because you cannot listen to the learning of a Pereira or the researches of a Liebig, that you shall not be the gainers by the short attendance necessary in the lecture-room, leaving out of the question the concentrated form of the materials of the lecture, and the competency or otherwise of the lecturer. The new (to us at least) application of a familiar fact, or its mere revival in the memory, by an accidental allusion, and a thousand suggestions which will be the offspring of the moment, will not seldom abundantly reward the attentive and regular listener. But, remember that you come here to be instructed not entertained, and that those who have the care of your education have provided for that purpose the best means within their power, and which they consider sufficient if fully availed of.

Be careful, then, how you slight their efforts, and bring your unfledged opinions into collision with those of men of riper years, whose experience has taught them the duty of insuring to you the opportunities which were denied or unprovided for them.

These remarks have been suggested by the frequency of such expressions of dissatisfaction as have been alluded to, which, believe me, are insidious temptations to divert you from that which will prove highly beneficial, and the want of which can never afterwards be compensated for.

The first division of the course will be devoted to Materia Medica; afterwards we will review the Pharmaceutical Preparations preparing before you, as many of them as may be necessary to demonstrate the necessary manipulations, or where they may be attended with any peculiarity.

It shall be our endeavor, in this department, to inculcate the strictest accuracy and minute attention to the directions of the Pharmacopœia, which shall always be our text, except where experience may have suggested an evidently necessary alteration or improvement, in which case we shall be careful to note it, so as to prevent you confounding that which is officinal with that which is not, as is often done; and at the conclusion some useful instruction will be given in compounding and dispensing.

It is also our intention to make a series of periodical examinations during the progress of the course, in order to incite to the proper attention and exertion of the memory, exposing negligence, and holding up to emulation and applause the industrious and attentive.

The monotonous and homely, but useful, avocations of the apothecary afford little scope for the indulgence of the imagination or the display of eloquence. Enchained as it were to a constant routine of unostentatious duties, his lot, to the superficial observer, seems little envious, and is more apt to provoke a sneer than to excite a note of admiration. Pass on ye votaries of pleasure and devotees of fashion, your's are not the minds to appreciate usefulness in any of its aspects; but, perchance, a pause will come in your career of dissipation, the grasp of disease may arrest your steps, and then, when every medicament that issues from the laboratory of the oft-despised practitioner of the pharmaceutic art is hailed as the harbinger of restored health, may you learn to estimate the real value of him on whose care, accuracy and scientific knowledge depends, in an eminent degree, the fruition of your eager desires. Men of the highest order of genius, whose labors have acquired a world-wide reputation, have not disdained to busy themselves with the very implements which seem to you the badges of a despicable employment. The pestle, scarcely less indispensable in the laboratory than the shop, which has felt the honored grasp of a Humboldt, a Davy, a Newton, and the class of great men which those names represent, need cause no blush on the cheek of him who wields it, although it may not be considered quite so gentlemanly (because more useful) a weapon than the sword-cane or the duelling pistol.

We are no new claimants brought into existence by the whim of the enthusiast or the delusion of the imposter. The birth of Pharmacy is anterior to that of science itself, for in the preparation of charms and in the form of incantations the superstitious origin of the art may be found in the remotest ages of antiquity.

In the absence of knowledge and cultivated reason, the instinct of the human mind, the voice of Nature, taught it to seek aid and support in the creations of the imagination, a portion of our mental constitutions, which seems to be, most invariably, in full development in the natural man; but, according as experience and observation gradually withdrew the veil from the face of natural truth, did the art of pharmacy forsake the amulet and the cauldron, and we behold then the collector of simples, the "mere concoctor of villainous drugs," who is, perhaps, very nearly represented by the herb doctor of our own day.

In China, where the civilization of a very ancient period has been stereotyped, as it were, by the exclusiveness and self-sufficiency of its inhabitants, and transmitted to us in all its barbarous perfection, we shall find preserved for us what may be called, perhaps, an apothecary's shop of the second age of pharmacy, when the herbalist succeeded the sorcerer.

We have lately been informed that a veritable Chinese apothecary has located himself in the good city of Sacramento, a description of whose shop, although many of you may have already perused it, I hope I may be pardoned for reading, as peculiarly appropriate in this place:

"The sign, in the present instance, must have cost the artist who executed it considerable labor. All of the complicated Chinese characters were deeply graven in the wood of which it was composed; gold and bright vermilion appeared in abundance, and a rich silk drapery, arranged in a tasteful manner, hid the edges from view.

"The inscription, when translated, read, '*Tung Fuk Tung*,' and was the name of the '*Teacher*' with whom the proprietor of the shop had studied for a term of years.

"On entering we were struck with the absence of fluid preparations, and throughout our examination we discovered but one article of this kind, and not a single mineral preparation.

"A narrow but very high counter, a range of gaudily painted drawers, wide shelving, and sundry Chinese stools, constituted the shop furniture. The shelves were mainly occupied with bundles, containing roots, herbs, &c.; and it will astonish many when they learn that we counted over eleven hundred bundles, each marked with a different character, and all brought from the Celestial Empire, thus proving that the '*Materia Medica*' of the Chinese is in nowise deficient in the number of remedies. The drawers were divided into six compartments; unique porcelain '*galley pots*' occupied the shelving immediately over them; and above, ranged in regular order, were fancy packages, containing very diminutive bottles of strong ol. mentha piperita, and a peculiar kind of musk artificially manufactured. We also saw various compounds with long written papers attached, the true nature of which we were unable to determine, but from the remarks of our companion we strongly suspected that even the '*Celestials*' were not free from the '*cure alls*' and '*patent nostrums*' which flourish so greatly in the United States. The *mortars* used in compounding are composed of porcelain and iron, the shape being somewhat different from those manufactured by the English.

"For powdering an exceedingly uncouth instrument is used; it is made of iron, about four feet long, and the inside resembling a whale boat, with a depressed centre and elevated ends. A heavy iron wheel, hung on a wooden axis, is made to revolve in the channel, the motive power being the feet of the *operator*. This quickly and easily reduces most substances to a powder.

"Various sizes of knife blades, arranged on the end of an elevated trough, in a similar manner to the old style of *straw cutters*, are in use for cutting up roots and barks; also large shallow baskets for drying purposes.

"The *scales* show the great antiquity of the people. They still disdain to use other than those which have been in use for centuries. These have but a single plate and long beam, the weight sliding on this last, similar to the old-fashioned *steelyard*. Many, however, are of fine workmanship, and in the hands of a skilful person prove very accurate."—G. L. Simmons, "On Chinese Pharmacy," in *Amer. Pharm. Journal*, March, 1854.

Such, gentlemen, is the other extreme brought into juxtaposition with its latest improvement, in this most progressive age of the world; such, too, is the selfishness of human nature that it can entomb nations in their own overweening pride to make them the butt and lesson of after ages; and here, also, may we see the irresistible and universal power of gold, which can draw even the human snail from his shell and make the Chinaman a citizen of the world.

You will observe that minerals are entirely absent from Ancient Pharmacy, for it was not until our necessities or curiosity had exhausted the treasures of the surface of our globe that we were induced to look beneath it, and penetrate even to its centre.

Much prejudice has always existed against this class of medicines, and it was natural and even useful. It was natural for man, in the aboriginal state, to place more confidence in the simple substances, (which were almost forced on his notice by Nature herself, and formed the food of the animals around,) the herb and flower of the field, than to trust to those mysterious products drawn from the hidden bosom of Nature, and compounded by the skill of selfish man into multitudes of forms It was useful that some check should be placed to a system which would otherwise have taught us to appreciate a remedy only according to the depth at which it was found from the surface.

A prejudice of the same sort still exists, and, no doubt, as naturally and usefully as ever, teaching us not to despise the things "which grow at our own doors," while at the same time we reject nothing that may be good from whatever source it emanates.

From these two divisions of pharmacy, viz., botanical and mineral, sprang, respectively, the sciences of Medicine and Chemistry; for, strange as it may seem, that Art, which is now only regarded as the handmaid of those sciences, has been, in reality, their parent. This is necessarily so, for it could only have been in watching the effect of the remedy that we obtained the knowledge of symptoms, and it must have been by observing the peculiarities of the mineral that we arrived at its chemical properties, for chemistry was at first inorganic; that relating to organized matter is of comparatively recent date.

In the progress of the art to the high importance with which it is invested at the present day, especially in the most highly civilized countries, it has extended its researches into the other kingdoms of Nature, and been, in its turn, enriched by the sciences to which it has given birth. Not only has the animal, in many cases, been compelled to surrender to its use the most costly products, but the elaborate and minute investigations of organic chemistry have enabled it to transmute one substance into another, and, in many cases, (there is no reason to suppose that, at some future period, it shall not be in all,) has stolen a march on the tardy operations of Nature, by forming at will, from a few universal and inexhaustible elements, several substances, of which those elements were discovered to be the component parts. Thus valerianic acid, a product of valerian root, is now generally obtained from fusel oil, in which the elements of the acid are found to exist, and are only required to be made to undertake a different arrangement to produce it. Thus, also, is benzoic acid, metamorphosed from hippuric, abundantly existing in the urine of the horse.

Many other examples of this are known, and so great are the expectations excited by these wonderful achievements of science, that a prize has been offered, and is still, I believe, unwon, by the French Academy of Sciences, for the manufacture of quinine from its ultimate elements.

Why, then, should we not have reason to despise, in our turn, the vulgar-minded and ignorant who know not, nor can understand, who we are or whence we came?

So important a bearing has the practice of pharmacy on the health and happiness of mankind that in all countries it has been more or less the cherished *protege* of the legislators thereof, and in some the very great care which is sometimes lavished on it seems to us here very much like oppression. The narrow limits of education, however, in those places renders it highly necessary that the poorer and illiterate people should be protected by stringent laws from imposition or injury; but here it seems, at least so far, that some other means than the protection and encouragement of the Government must be relied on to aid the advancement and protect the integrity of our art. The difficulty and odium of enforcing laws which restrict the liberty of individual action would render, as it has done, the interference of legislation practically null and void. Nor is this interference necessary in a community where education is as free to all as the very air we breathe. Yet is there a need that something should be done to guarantee the faithful administration of his office by the pharmaceutist. This, it appears to me, cannot be attained by adopting the systems which, although they have been found to produce some good results under very different circumstances, are not only worthless but inefficient and impracticable here; but it will depend mainly on the increased enlightenment of the community and a just appreciation of our services which will lead them to make a most necessary distinction between him who is properly qualified and him who is not.

That this will result, I do not doubt, and we shall then see to what perfection our ancient art shall attain under the auspices of freedom, where there is nothing to restrain but the "still small voice" within and the enlightened discrimination of our fellow man.

The recent growth and rapid progress of pharmacy, within the small circle of our own observation, gives good promise of a hopeful future.

Until within comparatively a few years, many, if not most, of our physicians were in the habit of compounding their own prescriptions, and we are not yet quite rid of the evil of the amalgamation of the practice of medicine and pharmacy.

The laws which have been made in our regard have been as "dead letters," but yet, from the increased amount of labor which the advancement of science has rendered necessary to fulfil its requirements, a division of the burden has pretty generally been obtained, and the result is best told by comparing the present with the past.

At the period to which we have adverted the pure apothecary was unknown. The "wholesale and retail" druggist supplied the physician with his remedies, and his patients with the more ordinary articles which it was inconvenient for him to dispense. The druggist was seldom, if ever, a man very deeply read in Materia Medica, but a good deal in price currents; he bought and sold, and made his profit; and, it is to be hoped, that, in those primitive times, the vigilance with respect to the quality of his wares, which the "cuteness" of the present day renders necessary, was scarcely required, for if it were it was "*non est inventus*"—"a change came over the spirit of the dream"—and then were seen apothecary shops owned, though not ostensibly, by one or more physicians, to which was transferred the business previously confined to the office. This was convenient and profitable, but it met not with general approval. Many persons imagined that such a system offered too great a temptation to extortion, and so, at last, after many foul suspicions, the matured apothecary was fully fledged, and has since rapidly spread himself over the extent of the city and its suburbs. We cannot, however, flatter ourselves that we have now reached the "*sine qua non*" of perfection, for, alas! there are many drawbacks. The integrity of the art has been sacrificed to the spirit of Mammon, and, with the exception of a few who do a legitimate business, we daily witness the most unworthy annexations made to the apothecary shops, from the domain of the bar-room, the tobacconist, the confectioner, and the quack, and to such an extent sometimes as to obscure the very identity of the place and to deprive us of the innocent amusement which we formerly derived from some absurd enquiry for an article which was then altogether foreign to our business. This is no longer an absurdity, for there is scarcely anything, from an assafœtida pill to a tooth-pick, that you cannot obtain at the apothecary's, either at the present moment or eventually if you ask for it often enough.

This is an evil, however, which a little experience will correct, for the same necessity which separated the physician from the apothecary will also detach the apothecary from the general retailer; and the day is approaching when a degree of competency will be required in us that will require the devotion of all our time to the study and practice of our own peculiar business exclusively.

There is a subject which, though it may not be exactly "apropos" in addressing a class of students, still, as it is rarely too early to inculcate good principles, its importance may justify its introduction here—I allude to the enormous traffic in nostrums or patent medicines.

It is quite useless to expect that these preparations can be wholly expurgated; but a good deal depends on us to abate the nuisance. These articles supply a want very generally felt in the more remote and thinly settled portions of the country, where medical aid is difficult or impossible to be had, and it is chiefly from this cause that they derive their support and surreptitious characters. The wonderful cures which they are believed to have been instrumental in producing under those circumstances are related and listened to with avidity by the sufferer, and it is fair to suppose that, in the absence of better means, they may have proved useful, nay, sometimes, just what was required, and this, if no attempt were made to promote their abuse in the most shameful manner, might, for the moment, furnish some slight excuse for their toleration. But even this want might be much better satisfied in a more legitimate way, and one not open to the many objections to those preparations, as well on the score of morality as their utter worthlessness, when compared with the regular officinal preparations.

If a system were adopted by which persons residing in localities inconveniently situated for the procuring of medical assistance could be supplied with the usual medicines, plainly labelled, and accompanied with simple directions for their use, in the ordinary complaints, of which the treatment is pretty uniform, a much safer and more effectual means of enabling them to relieve their sufferings would be provided, and then, when the only apology I can think of for the use of nostrums is thus removed, would the work of repudiating them entirely be more successful.

There would still be a class of persons, it may be said, and truly, whose prejudice and folly would not thus be gratified; but their number will gradually diminish in proportion to the advancement of science and general education. *Our* difficulty with regard to this matter is that we are supposed to be governed by interested motives in our opposition. This should not deter us. Without waiting to repel such accusations, which, if true, would still not diminish the laudability of our efforts, insomuch as the grievance we seek to remove is a real one, and not our's alone but that of all—we should firmly adopt whatever means prudence and justice may prompt to remove this reproach to morality and common sense.

An undue regard for public opinion causes many well disposed apothecaries to accede by little and little to the requirements of the populace, and, from time to time, one after another of those vile compounds is introduced to his shop, until, at last, he finds himself surrounded by such an assemblage of trash, as would excite our indignation, did we not compassionate his weakness.

I am borne out in these remarks by the Report of the Committee on Quack Medicines presented to the American Pharmaceutical Association, at its last meeting; but, in the same report is made the following announcement, "the tendency to take medicine, *ad libitum*, is a feature of the Anglo-Saxon race, duly inherited by the American people, which, whatever may be its faults, is as much their nature as is their love of political and personal freedom." If by this is meant that that portion of the human race designated is addicted to dissipation with medicine, it is a grave charge, and to me a new one, although I have heard them often accused of beer-drinking and gluttony; but if, as I suppose, it is intended to mean merely a dislike of personal restraint, then I should say that this is a quality eminently possessed by the whole American people, as well as that portion of them who are descended as stated. And herein lies the great difficulty; but, if men will not be dissuaded from error, even let it be so.

On your parts, I hope, neither "features of character" nor mistaken notions of freedom may induce you to do what your conscience disapproves.

Before concluding, another important matter deserves, from its practical importance, to be impressed upon you as strongly as may be. This is, the subject of adulterations. No duty you may have to perform is more incumbent than to qualify yourselves as perfectly as possible to detect falsifications and impurities in the articles you use or purchase. The means of doing so is best to be acquired by the assiduous cultivation of the senses of smell, taste and touch, and a familiarity with the visible properties every drug presents. Many may be tested by chemical means, and those you should not only know but familiarize yourselves with; but, so wonderful is the tact which great experience gives, that a mere glance is sometimes sufficient to enable the old apothecary to estimate the quality of an article with an accuracy which further examination will verify.

I have heard of a chemist's assistant who, from habitually tasting almost everything he met with, acquired so great a nicety of that sense that he has been known to detect, by this means, the presence of some poisons in such minute quantity as to be scarcely more than appreciable by a chemical test.

That you may be fully successful in acquiring such a power of discriminating as may enable you to distinguish the quality of medicines, it will be our desire to devote as much attention as practicable to this object; but this department of pharmaceutical knowledge is the least communicable of any, and the most will depend on yourselves.

With an earnest request that you will be regular in your attendance, for your own sake as well as our's, we will bring these observations to a close, and at our next meeting we will commence the practical part of our duties.

PHARMACEUTICAL NOTES AND GLEANINGS.

Hydrocyanate of Iron.—It has been stated in the medical journals, that "hydrocyanate of iron" had been used advantageously in epilepsy. Having been applied to for the salt, and being at a loss to determine what compound was intended, we consulted several authorities without satisfaction.

The dose, one or two grains, would indicate a more active substance than prussian blue. Hydrocyanate of potassa is synonymous with cyanide of potassium. Why not hydrocyanate of iron then be *cyanide of iron?* Gmelin says, (Handbook, vol. vii., p. 432,) that "When aqueous cyanide of potassium is mixed with a ferrous salt free from ferric oxide, a light red brown precipitate is obtained, which dissolves in acids. The composition of this precipitate requires further investigation, but it is, perhaps, the true protocyanide of iron C^2 N Fe." In attempting to dry this precipitate it assumes the color of prussian blue, by contact with the air during the process. By washing this precipitate with boiled water, and afterwards displacing most of the water from the particles by alcohol, and then drying, the same result occurred, viz., the whole mass gradually assumed a blue color, but not so deep as prussian blue. Hydrocyanic acid shaken with solution of carbonate of iron, in carbonic acid water, forms a greenish oxide of iron, which turns blue by exposure to the air. There is a white cyanide of iron formed when aqueous sulphuretted hydrogen is agitated with finely-powdered prussian blue, which converts it into protocyanide of iron; it, however, becomes blue by exposure. There is also a permanent cyanide of iron obtained when the ferrocyanide of ammonia is boiled in close vessels till the hydrocyanate of ammonia all sublimes, but it is insoluble in acids. It is to be regretted that medical writers, in referring to the therapeutic powers of new remedies, do not take more pains to identify the substances they have employed where any doubt may arise. We supplied the compound obtained by double decomposition between cyanide of potassium and protosulphate of iron, partially washed with alcohol, and dried in a jar over sulphuric acid, but have not yet learned whether it had the desired effect.—Ed. *Amer. Journ. of Pharm.*

Sulphate of Quinidinia.—Last year, Dr. William Pepper, Physician to the Pennsylvania Hospital, published an account of the results of substituting sulphate of cinchona for sulphate of quinia in intermittent fever, and so successful did it prove that he has since continued to use it in his hospital practice. In April last, at the suggestion of Dr. Conrad, Dr. Pepper made a trial of *sulphate of quinidin*, (the third alkaloid in cinchona bark,) in several cases of intermittent, with such decided success that he is disposed to believe that quinidin is more active than either of the other alkaloids. These results corroborate a similar trial in two obstinate cases of intermittent, by Dr. Helfrick, of this city, which had a like result. If these observations are supported by other testimony, we shall not hear of the rejection of cinchona barks because in the aggregate of alkaloids there happens to be *less than one per cent. of quinia.*—*Ibid.*

AMERICAN PHARMACEUTICAL ASSOCIATION.

B.

REPORT ON STANDARDS OF QUALITY FOR THE GOVERNMENT OF SPECIAL EXAMINERS OF DRUGS, &C.

The Committee appointed in Boston, 1853, "to consider that part of the report of the Committee on the Inspection of Drugs relating to the fixing of Standards of Quality for those drugs capable of it, together with the appropriate tests for detecting adulterations, when practicable," report that they have given due consideration to the subjects referred to them.

The serious difficulties in the way of accomplishing the objects aimed at in the above resolution, were so fully appreciated by the last Committee that they felt best satisfied to ask the direct action of the Association regarding the feasibility of standards for those drugs liable to come under the notice of examiners. In not adopting that recommendation, the whole difficulty was thrown on this Committee, with the liberty of inviting the co-operation of the Colleges of Pharmacy should they deem it best. The Committee determined not to seek this collateral aid, but to prepare the report from the best means within their reach, and let the Association decide at its next meeting on any ulterior course that may be necessary to carry on the work should they deem it necessary.

The object of recognized standards attached to particular drugs is two-fold—as a guide to the inspector, giving him a well-defined basis for his examinations, and as a means of comparison for the analytical chemist when subsequently referred after rejection. A large number of substances cannot be judged by chemical analysis, as to medicinal strength, because they cannot be analyzed in a quantitative manner so as to decide what constitutes a proper per centage of their active principles. Hence standards based on chemical analysis apply only to inorganic drugs, and to such organic drugs as contain well-defined and insoluble principles. Analysis in its proximate sense may be employed to establish the identity of a drug without its being sufficient to determine its actual strength.

When analysis fails, the judgment of the inspector must be based upon the pharmacological characteristics of taste, smell, feel and conformation, including its botanical characters, if of vegetable origin, and its appearance under the microscope. The parallelism of external sensible properties with regular chemical constitution is in most instances sufficiently accurate to be relied upon. For instance, rhubarb, that is strongly odorous, has a good color, and the decided bitterness and peculiar taste of the root, rarely fails to be active as a medicine; and where the pharmacological knowledge of the inspector is full and practical we would prefer trusting to his judgment in such cases than to the opinion of a chemist, at least until proximate organic analysis is more perfect than at present. In judging a bale or cask of senna, the examiner will first satisfy himself that it is senna and not a sophistication, which he does by the botanical characteristics of the leaf; next its freedom from an excessive proportion of accidental substances; third, that its color, odor and taste are correct. In the case of digitalis, where the leaves of the second year are preferable, accurate acquaintance with structural botany will afford essential service to the inspector.

Again, when a test standard is affixed to an organic drug requiring a certain amount of an active principle to be present, it would be more satisfactory if the law would define in what way the drug should be treated to yield it. For instance, a manufacturing chemist, skilled in the difficult processes of proximate analysis, will obtain a larger product from a given specimen than a chemist who is not specially familiar with that department. In the case of opium, an instance occurred where that drug was condemned for deficient morphia, when it really contained an overplus.

The absolute strength of organic drugs cannot be fixed—the natural variation in the proportion of the constituents of vegetables, arising from climate, soil and season, is so great that the range of strength in genuine specimens of a drug may be quite wide. All such, as a general rule, will have to be overlooked; yet in a few cases the law should be made to exert its influence, as for instance in the cinchonas, where every proportion of quinia from 0.1 to 3.0 per cent. exists, owing, as has been alleged, chiefly to the location of the trees above the sea level; and in opium, where in some locations narcotina appears to be secreted to a large extent instead of morphia (in certain varieties).

When the law declares that a certain per centage of active matter must be present to enable a drug to pass the examiner, it is necessary to the effectual carrying out of the ordinance that a practical means of demonstrating the fact, *pro* or *con*, be known. To say, for instance, quoting from Secretary Guthrie's circular, that "Jalap root, whether in root or powder, shall afford 11 per cent. of pure jalap resin," is wanting in clearness of meaning. There are two resins in jalap, both equally resins of jalap. One of these is the active principle, and is *insoluble* in ether, the other inert and soluble in ether. The instructions should, therefore, expressly state that a certain per centage of jalap resin (*jalapin*) insoluble in ether should be yielded by the drug, else, in the case of the powder especially, other inert resins might be introduced with fraud. Again, in the case of benzoin, the instructions should say by what process this drug should be tested to prove the absence of 12 per cent. of benzoic acid, in order to cause its rejection, as the process of sublimation and precipitation afford very different results, the latter being the most productive.

In reference to the purity of medicinal chemicals there should be a clear understanding. To say that they shall be pure in the chemical sense is preposterous, as ninety-nine hundredths of all that are imported are not so. There is a generally recognized degree of purity in chemicals, manufactured on a large scale, which is understood by competent druggists, and while it is not easy to fix a rational per centage standard of purity beyond which such accidental extraneous matter shall not exist, any system of inspection based on positive or quantitative examination should embrace at least the more important chemicals, the standard being fixed by careful trials of commercial chemicals in good esteem.

In carrying out the last recommendation a provision should be made for the importation of chemical substances for the manufacturing chemist in the shape of raw material, else our own manufacturers will be unable to compete with those of other countries. *Crude Iodine*, for instance, is now virtually excluded by the construction put upon the law.

As the Committee have not been able, for want of time, and material necessary to accomplish the objects of the resolution under which they were appointed, to make but a partial report, they have determined to classify the more prominent items of the materia medica as regards their susceptibility of being tested, and afterwards to give the standards recommended by them for adoption.

1*st.—List of substances which may be quantitatively examined in reference to their active principles or purity by analysis, viz.:*

Salts of Ammonia,
Ammoniacum,
Salts of Antimony,
Assafœtida,
Balsam of Peru,
Balsam of Tolu,
Benzoin,
Bromine,
Salts of Lime,
Camphor,
Catechu,
Cinchona barks,
Copaiba,
Creasote,
Elaterium,
Ext. Cannab. Ind.,
Galbanum,
Gamboge,
Guaiac resin,
Salts of iron,
Iodine,
Jalap.

Salts of Lead,
Lactucarium,
Lupulin,
Salts of Magnesia,
Manna,
Myrrh,
Piperin,
Nicotina,
Veratria and its salts,
Strychnia and its salts,
Opium,
Salts of lead,
Salts of potassa,
Scammony,
Sagapenum,
Salts of Soda,
Storax,
Flowers of sulphur,
Salts of zinc,
Arsenious acid,
Acetic acid,

Benzoic acid,
Citric acid,
Gallic acid,
Prussic acid,
Tannic acid,
Tartaric acid,
Valerianic acid,
Aconitia,
Conia,
Cinchonia and its salts,
Atropia, " "
Codeia,
Caffeina,
Delphinia,
Morphia and its salts,
Brucia,
Veratria,
Quinia and its salts,
Quinidinia and its salts,
Beeberin, " "
Salicine,

2d.—*Drugs which may be examined by external and sensible properties and characters, but the genuineness of which may be corroborated by chemical tests:*

Aloes,	Ergot,	Valerian root,
Aconite root and leaves,	Extract of liquorice,	Saffron,
Belladonna root and leaves,	Galls,	Rhubarb root,
Cantharides,	Gum arabic,	Buchu,
Cardamoms,	Helleborus,	Canella,
Angustura bark,	Ipecacuanha,	Capsicum,
Allspice,	Kino,	Krameria,
Cloves,	Nux Vomica,	Cascarilla,
Cocculus Indicus,	Volatile oils,	Gentian,
Cochineal,	Black pepper,	Pyrethrum,
Colchicum root and seed,	Burgundy Pitch,	Quassia,
Colocynth,	Sabadilla,	Scilla,
Columbo,	Pareira,	Serpentaria,
Conium leaves,	Savin,	Veratrum album,
Cubebs,	Dulcamara,	Hyoscyamus,
Digitalis,	Cetraria.	

3d.—*Substances which may be examined by external and sensible characters only.*

Castor,	Carum,	Lavender flowers,
Maranta,	Cassia fistula,	Flaxseed,
Musk,	Carthamus,	Mace,
Sarsaparilla,	Chondrus,	Nutmegs,
Senna,	Cinnamon,	Mezereon,
Ginger,	Contrayerva,	Cowhage,
Garlic,	Fennel seed,	Papaver,
Althaea flowers and root,	Liquorice root,	Rosa Gallica,
Aniseed,	Pomegranate root bark,	Rosmarinus,
Chamomile,	Pomegranate fruit rind,	Santalum,
Arnica flowers,	Elecampane,	Simaruba,
Orange peel,	Orris root,	Tormentilla,
Calamus,	Juniper,	Matricaria,

Essay towards a list of standards or tests for the guidance of the examiners of drugs in carrying out the law against the importation of adulterated or deteriorated medicinal substances.

Ammoniacum should possess the proper sensible properties, should yield at least 90 per cent. of soluble matter to alcohol and water, at least 60 per cent. of which should be ammoniac resin; and should be free from designed impurities.

Assafœtida should contain at least 45 per cent. of bitter resin soluble in ether, and three per cent. of volatile oil when distilled with water.

BALSAM PERU should yield 60 per cent. of cinnamein or odorless volatile oil, heavier than water, when treated with alcohol, potassa and water, and should afford at least five per cent. of cinnamic acid.

BALSAM OF TOLU should yield, by careful distillation, *per se*, in a glass retort, at least ten per cent. of cinnamic acid, after the empyreumatic oil is separated; and should possess the proper sensible properties of this drug according to its age.

BELLADONNA ROOT should be sound; and its syrupy, alcoholic extract when mixed with an excess of solution of potassa, should readily yield atropia to chloroform when agitated with that fluid.

BENZOIN should contain 70 per cent. of resin and at least 12 per cent. of crude benzoic acid, when boiled to exhaustion with milk of lime and the filtered solution precipitated with muriatic acid.

CHLORINATED LIME should afford 25 per cent. of chlorine as indicated by the sulphate of iron test.

CANTHARIDES should be sound. They should yield at least —— per cent. of oily extract to ether, which, when treated with liquor potassæ, should afford —— more grains of cantharidin as a residue.

CARDAMOMS should be mature and sound, and should afford at least 15 per cent. of oily ethereal extract, one-fourth of which is volatile oil.

CARYOPHYLLUS. Cloves should yield *at least* 11 per cent. of volatile oil, by distillation, of not less than 1.04 sp. gr.

CINCHONA. *Calisaya* bark should yield at least 2½ per cent. of sulphate of quinia. Other Peruvian and Columbian barks should yield at least 2 per cent. of alkaloids, all told.

CONII FOLIA should possess a uniform green color, decided narcotic odor, and when powdered and macerated in liquor potassæ should evolve a decided odor of conia.

COPAIBA, if of thick consistence, should, when boiled with water till the oil is driven off, leave a brittle resin. When the copaiba is thin and limpid, it should afford more volatile oil without any terebinthinate odor.

CUBEBS should yield at least 16 per cent. of fluid oleo-resinous extract to ether.

DIGITALIS should be of the second year's growth, free from stalks, of uniform green color, and fully developed in size, odor and taste.

ELATERIUM should yield at least 20 per cent. of elaterin when its syrupy, alcoholic extract is thrown into hot liquor potassæ.

ERGOTA should be free from insects, strongly odorous, should yield 34 per cent. to ether, and when its alcoholic extract is distilled with potassa in solution, the distillate should be strongly odorous of secalin.

GALBANUM should yield 60 per cent. of resin and 5 per cent. of volatile oil as a minimum.

GAMBOGIA should yield 60 per cent. of its weight to ether, and the ethereal extract should possess the properties of gambogic acid.

GUAIAC should contain not less than 80 per cent. of guaiac resin, known by its insolubility in oil of turpentine, and by its reactions with nitric acid and alkalies.

HELLEBORUS should have the taste and odor of the root strongly developed, and should not exhibit the cruciform structure when sliced transversely.

IODINIUM, if re-sublimed, should be pure—if of the variety called *commercial* it should not contain beyond 5 per cent. of water or other impurities, unless specially admitted for manufacturing purposes on bond.

IPECACUANHA should, in addition to the usual external evidence of soundness, etc., be found when necessary to contain —— per cent. of colored emetia obtained by precipitation.

JALAP should contain at least 7 per cent. of resin insoluble in washed ether, (or rhodeoretin,) which should not be precipitated from its solution in hot liquor potassæ by acids.

MANNA should contain 95 per cent. of matter soluble in water, of which at least 37 per cent. is mannite.

NUTMEGS at least three per cent. of volatile oil.

MYRRH should contain 25 per cent. of bitter resin, and yield 2 per cent. of volatile oil when distilled with water.

Nux Vomica should be sound and afford at least 0.3 per cent. of strychnia.

Oils fixed and volatile should be commercially pure, and should withstand the best tests stated in pharmacological authorities.

Opium should contain at least 7 per cent. of morphia, purified by ether from narcotina, &c., unless admitted under bond for manufacturing purposes.

Bitartrate of Potassa should not contain more than 3 per cent. of tartrate of lime, and should require 18 parts of boiling water for solution.

Rhubarb Root should be sound, strongly odorous, decidedly bitter, and should contain at least 10 per cent. of oxalate of lime. A strict adherence to those points will exclude the European rhubarb, which is deficient in the oxalate of lime, and in odor and bitterness.

Sagapenum should yield 3 per cent. volatile oil, and fifty per cent. of resin possessed of the properties described in the Dispensatories.

Sarsaparilla. The several distinct varieties of this drug should be examined by their external characters and taste, rather than by chemical analysis.

Scammony. Two varieties of scammony should be recognized. Amorphous or Virgin scammony, which should yield to ether 70 per cent. or more of resin, and Cake scammony not less than —— per cent. of resin, possessing the proper characters of scammony resin, in not being precipitated from its solution in *hot* liquor potassæ by an acid.

Senna should be botanically true, of good color and odor, and should yield at least —— per cent. of dry extract to alcohol of 20 per cent.

Pyroxylic Spirit should not become milky on the addition of water, and should dissolve chloride of calcium without separating into two layers.

Flowers of Sulphur and Milk of Sulphur should be wholly volatile when placed on a red hot coal.

It will be seen that this sketch of standards is in many places imperfect—several blanks remain to be filled. The

Committee have been unable to find the time necessary to carry out the work as it should have been done to be complete, and submit the above sketch for the consideration of the Association, that it may decide on the propriety of proceeding in the work. So much depends on the character and qualification of the examiners, that, it seems to us, a movement of the Association that would place the inspection of drugs in qualified hands would do more for the drug market than the most accurate and scientific system of standards will effect if its execution is to be placed in charge of political favorites but little fitted for the post.

WILLIAM PROCTER, JR., } Committee.
GEO. D. COGGESHALL, }

C.

Report on the Circular of Instructions issued by the Secretary of the Treasury, under date of June 4, 1853.

The Committee to whom the Circular of Instructions, issued by the Secretary of the Treasury, was committed at the last meeting, report that they have examined that document, and offer the following critical remarks on some of its items, viz.:

1st.—"ALOES when affording 80 per cent. of pure aloetic extractive," is not sufficiently explicit as a guide to the examiner. If the *aloesin* of Robiquet is meant, the figure is too high, and applies only to the best socotrine aloes. If the matter soluble in cold water is alluded to, it is also too high. We think the standard for this drug should recognize cape and socotrine aloes under distinct heads.

2d.—The standard for ASSAFŒTIDA is fair.

3d.—The standard for CINCHONA will do well, provided the second clause, "or *two* per cent. of all the alkaloids combined," be construed to mean all the alkaloids collectively without regard to the proportion of quinia. If the first clause is insisted upon, all the pale and other *cinchonia* barks will be excluded.

4th.—The standard for BENZOIN should indicate in what way that drug should be treated to yield 12 per cent. of benzoic acid, whether by sublimation or precipitation.

5th.—The standard for COLOCYNTH is incorrect, as no colocynth contains 12 per cent. of colocynthin. According to Vauquelin 100 parts of the *pulp* contains 14.4 parts of the principle, and on the average the best colocynth yields but one-third of its weight of pulp; hence about *five per cent.* would be nearer the correct amount.

6th.—ELATERIUM is required to have 30 per cent. of elaterin. This figure is too high, as the best commercial elaterium will rarely yield over 25 per cent., which is quite high enough.

7th.—GALBANUM is required to have more volatile oil than the average yield of the two published analyses. It should not be higher than the average, else the objeet of the inspection will be defeated; 4 or 5 per cent. is an ample average.

8th.—GAMBOGE, the requiring of 70 per cent. of resin will exclude all but the pipe gamboge, the best quality, both the cake and coarse varieties not reaching that degree of richness in resin. It may be wrong to exclude these.

9th.—The standard for the GUAIAC at 80 per cent. of resin is proper.

10th.—AMMONIAC is required by the treasury circular to contain 70 per cent. of resin, and 18 per cent. of gum. As it often happens that this gum resin, when of good quality, contains some easily separable impurities, as capsules, etc., and as the per centage of resin above noted is the highest that has been published, it would be more appropriate to put the per centage at 60, or, what is better, to require a certain amount of matter soluble in alcohol and water, say 90 per cent., at least 60 per cent. of which must be ammoniac resin.

11th.—JALAP. If by pure jalap resin the circular intends the jalapin or active resin insoluble in ether, it is erroneous, as very little of the commercial root will afford more than 7 or 8 per cent. If the crude resin is intended the figures are about right in the circular.

12th.—MANNA. The proportion of 37 per cent. of mannite as a minimum is a very proper ratio for this drug.

13th.—MYRRH. The standard for myrrh is based on the proportion of resin and gum. The quantity of myrrh depends much on the proportion of the volatile oil. A better means of judging myrrh is from the amount of semi-fluid oleo-resin resulting from the evaporation of the ethereal tincture of myrrh.

14th.—OPIUM. To require 9 per cent. of pure morphia from opium is too high for a standard. Eight per cent. is ample, and much opium contains not more than 7 per cent. without being specially adulterated. It is understood that pure morphia means morphia deprived of narcotina and codeia.

15th.—RHUBARB. The item under this head in the circular requires that "rhubarb root should contain 40 per cent. of soluble matter, whether in root or powder," without indicating the menstruum to be used, or the nature of the soluble matter, and then declares "none admissible but the articles known as East India and Turkey, or Russian rhubarb."

We think this method of judging rhubarb entirely erroneous. The odor and bitterness of the drug, and the presence of a certain proportion of oxalate of lime are far better criteria than the ratio of soluble matter.

16th.—SAGAPENUM. Three per cent. of volatile oil, and 50 resin, is correct.

17th.—SCAMMONY. If but one variety of scammony is adopted, the proportion of 70 per cent. of resin is too high, as the so-called virgin scammony of commerce does not reach that proportion on the average. If a practicable standard is desired, *sixty* per cent. is about a full ratio.

18th.—SENNA. The test of senna is based on its ability to yield 28 per cent. of soluble matter, without noting the menstruum. This is not a safe or dependible standard to judge by, as it relates to only a particular quality of the drug.

19th.—The clause of the circular in reference to the condition of vegetable drugs is good.

20th.—The clause in reference to the essential oils is hardly to be relied on, as the means of judging the purity of these liquids is not yet sufficiently understood and described to enable any one, who is not thoroughly versed in their behaviour with tests, and with their changes by time and exposure, to arrive at positive conclusions.

21st.—The clause respecting "patent medicines and secret preparations," throws the passing of them through the Custom House entirely upon the judgment of the examiner as regards their safety "to be used for medicinal purposes." The power thus delegated to the examiners is very extensive, and liable to be arbitrarily applied. If the Drug Law delegates this power to the Secretary of the Treasury, and through him to the examiner, its proper enforcement may produce wholesome results, yet there are many who, deeming the law to be aimed at excluding adulterated and deteriorated drugs, chemicals, and medicinal preparations, doubt the right of the examiner to exclude these medicines unless adulterated or made different from what they profess to be.

22d.—The clause relative to appeal requires the importer to make known his intention within ten days after the rejection of his goods, which is well. That section making it obligatory on the analytical chemist to make a full qualitative and quantitative report under oath appears to have been introduced to prevent chemists from substituting *opinion* for *analysis*, and so far is good, but its strict construction is in most instances as useless as it is unnecessary, and may in some hands defeat the right of appeal.

The last clause of the circular, giving the examiner power to appeal from the results of the analytical chemist may occasionally detect fraudulent intent, yet the law expressly declares the report of the chemist to be final, and not to be reached by any subsequent action of the examiner.

Wm. Procter, Jr., on behalf of the Committee.

THE LEAVES OF THE MAGNOLIA TRIPETALA AS A DRESSING FOR BLISTERS.

BY JOHN STAINBACK WILSON, M.D., OF AIRMOUNT, ALA.

As this journal is eminently practical, it is hoped that a brief notice of the remarkable species of Magnolia which heads this article will not be unacceptable.

The M. tripetala is known by the common names of "umbrella tree" and "wild cucumber," the latter being, we think, the most common in Alabama, where it grows abundantly; although it seems that this name is most generally applied to the M. acuminata.

The species of Magnolia under consideration is one of the most remarkable productions of the United States, and will not fail to attract the attention of the most unobservant, by the wonderful size of its leaves and the beauty of its flowers: "the former are eighteen or twenty inches long, by seven or eight in breadth," and even larger than this: while the latter are of corresponding magnitude, being "seven or eight inches in diameter." We are informed that "this species of the Magnolia extends from the northern parts of New York to the southern limits of the United States," but we have never seen it in any part of the State of Georgia. Still, as it is no doubt a common production of the rich lime lands of the South Western and Western States, its "medical properties and uses" should be known to the physicians of that region; and it should not suffer unmerited neglect like too many of our useful indigenous remedies. The M. tripetala (the bark) is highly esteemed by the common people as a tonic, and some of them even consider it an infallible specific in dropsies; this, of course, cannot be conceded, but the estimation in which it is held is, at least, an evidence that it is not by any means destitute of medicinal virtues. And in addition to this, we have the higher evidence of our Dispensatory that it has been found useful in chronic rheumatism, and intermittent and remittent fevers. We have had no experience with it in the treatment of the above diseases; but we have used the leaves as a dressing for blistered surfaces with satisfactory results, and the main object of this article is to commend this application to the attention of the profession.

We will simply, in conclusion, mention why we think this dressing should be considered worthy of notice: 1st. The leaves of the Magnolia are not officinal, and it may, therefore, be presumed that their uses are unknown. 2d. We think that they are equally as good as the collard or cabbage leaves, so much used, while they are often more readily obtainable, much larger, and less offensive in smell.

Before using, we scald them, but think it possible that they would answer every purpose, if applied in the natural state.—*Southern Med. and Surg. Journal*, July, 1854.

DECOMPOSITION OF PHOSPHATE AND SULPHATE OF LIME BY HYDROCHLORIC ACID.

BY M. CARI-MANTRANET.

A mixture of equal parts of bone ashes and wood charcoal powder, heated to redness in a porcelain tube, through which gaseous muriatic acid is passing, furnishes phosphorus, which condenses in the cool portion of the tube, while oxide of carbon goes off. This decomposition probably takes place in accordance with the following equation:

$$PO^5\ 3\ Ca\ O + 8\ C + 3\ H\ Cl = 8\ CO + 3\ Cl\ Ca + 3\ H + P.$$

No trace of phosphoric acid was found in the residue. The hydrogen of the muriatic acid is passive in this operation, but the same result is obtained by the employment of dry chlorine. This, when its evolution is well regulated, is completely absorbed, forming chloride of calcium and phosphorus, and the action is still more rapid than with muriatic acid. Sulphate of lime mixed with charcoal, and treated in a similar manner with a current of muriatic acid gas, furnished chloride of calcium, oxide of carbon, sulphur, and a little sulphuretted hydrogen.

Even without any addition of charcoal, sulphate of lime allows sulphuric acid to escape, when heated in muriatic acid gas, a portion of it is decomposed into sulphurous acid, and oxygen and chloride of calcium is formed.—*Comptes Rendus*, 38, p. 864, in *Chem. Gaz.*, July, 1854.

ON THE INFLUENCE OF BELLADONNA IN COUNTERACTING POISONOUS EFFECTS OF OPIUM.

BY THOMAS ANDERSON, M.D.

Dr. Graves had first suggested that, in continued fever, with protracted pupils and coma, if an agent, administered internally, would occasion dilatation of the pupils, it might also relieve the other symptoms of cerebral derangement. Dr. Anderson, acting on this theory, administered large doses of belladonna in two cases of poisoning by opium, which he related as follows:

"A patient of whom I had charge, and laboring under delirium tremens, having received an overdose of a solution of the muriate of morphia, became comatose. He had taken, in thirty-six hours, two ounces of the solution of the muriate of morphia, and it had been continued by the attendant after sleep was procured. When I saw him he was in profound coma, his breathing was stertorous, amounting to no more than four or five per minute, and his pupils were contracted to mere points. His pulse was excessively weak, and rather slow; it was quite impossible to rouse him. I ordered him, immediately, the following mixture:—Tincture of belladonna, six drachms, in five and a half ounces of water, of which an ounce was to be given every half hour. Three ounces of the mixture were administered with great caution, after which his pupils began to dilate. The six drachms of the tincture of belladonna were taken, and in four and a half hours after the first dose of it was given, the patient was in the following condition:—The coma was entirely gone, respirations were between twenty-two and twenty-five per minute, the pupils were much dilated, the pulse had risen to nearly one hundred and twenty in the minute, and was also increased in strength. His countenance, also, from being cold and pallid, had become much flushed, and the whole body was much warmer. He replied, readily and coherently, to all my questions. He continued to improve for three days after, when, rising suddenly to stool, he fainted, and before the assistance of the nurse could be procured, he was dead.

A fortnight afterwards, a woman about fifty, took, at four P. M., two drachms of laudanum, and, at half-past five P. M., three drachms more. She was brought to the infirmary at eight P. M. After making vain attempts to rouse her from the coma, by walking her about, &c., the stomach-pump was used at a quarter-past eight P. M. By this means her stomach was thoroughly evacuated, but no trace of opium was detected by smell or sight. It had, probably, been all absorbed. A current of electricity was then applied to her hands for nearly ten minutes, but without rousing her. I saw her at a quarter to nine P. M., for the first time, and on being told that she had been poisoned by laudanum, I determined to try the effects of belladonna.

At that time her pupils were contracted to mere points, her respiration was stertorous, ten per minute, the pulse was feeble, and the extremities rather cold. Between nine and half-past nine, I gave her one ounce of tincture of belladonna in three ounces of water, which was all swallowed, but with difficulty. In the course of the next half hour, two drachms more were administered. At eleven P. M., the first alteration on the size of the pupil was observed; the respirations had also then increased to twelve or thirteen in the minute, and the pulse was much stronger. The symptoms continued to improve till two A. M., when all indications of opium poisoning had disappeared. The woman was then sitting up in bed talking to the nurses, with pupils dilated to a little more than their natural size, and still slightly sensible to light. The extremities were quite warm, the pulse about 100, and of good strength.

She gave me a coherent account of her motives for taking the poison, of the amount of money she had spent in purchasing the laudanum, and the names of the druggists where it had been procured. She also replied sensibly to questions about her family, and the ages and occupations of her children. She continued awake till nearly four A. M., after which she slept till nine A. M. In the morning I found her pretty well, her pupils being no more dilated than they were four hours after the first administration of the belladonna. She complained, however of nausea, but unaccompanied with vomiting. This symptom along with the dilated pupils had entirely disappeared in the course of two days. She was kept in the hospital, under observation, for ten days after the accident, at the end of which time she was dismissed, perfectly well. The tincture of belladonna, used in both these cases, was of the strength of four ounces of the leaves to two pints of rectified spirit, and prepared by percolation. Half a drachm is considered a full dose. I have seen dilatation of the pupil produced by a drachm given at once.

The committee on Dr. Anderson's communication reported that they had designed to test Dr. Anderson's views by experiments on animals, but had found, on inquiry, that the animals commonly used for experiments were almost entirely insusceptible of the poisonous action of opium or belladonna. Where the effects were so different from those observed in man, it is obviously impossible to pursue the investigation which they had intended; the committee, therefore, while recognizing that Dr. Anderson's views require more extended observations in order to confirm them, deemed them worthy of the attentive consideration of the society.—*Edin. Monthly Jour.*

SODA AN ANTIDOTE FOR SNAKE BITE AND THE STING OF POISONOUS INSECTS.

A correspondent in the south writes us as follows:

An article in the *Memphis and Arkansas Christian Advocate*, copied from the *St. Louis Medical Journal*, has just fallen under my notice; and among other things it is said that alcohol, if brought in contact with the venom of serpents, is, to a certain extent, an antidote. As every one is liable at some time or other to come in contact with, and be bitten by, serpents, such facts as this article contains are of general interest. I am, therefore, induced to send you the following statement, in hopes that if it possesses any value it may be further tested.

Some short time since, while in conversation with a friend, he informed me that a small piece of soda* applied to the sting of a wasp, hornet, or bee, would immediately relieve the pain, and prevent swelling. I have tried the remedy in two instances, and, in both cases, with the best result.

Some time since, I had a negro who was bitten by a snake, about dark; he did not, however, let me know it until the next morning. I then had the leg (which was much swollen) bathed in warm water, and soda applied to the wound, and in two days the pain and swelling both were entirely relieved. The soda should be moistened a little with water before being used.

If this matter should be of sufficient importance to claim the attention of scientific men, it may possibly lead to important results. Respectfully,

A Farmer.

NEW MODE OF PREPARING OINTMENT OF NITRATE OF MERCURY.

We copy the following note from Mr. Wilder's recently published treatise on the *Diseases of the Ear* :

There is no other medicine in the whole Materia Medica so frequently prescribed by the practitioner which presents the same differences, both in appearance and effects, as the ointment of the nitrate of mercury. Prepared as directed in any of the Pharmacopœias of the three kingdoms, it is impossible to procure it alike in any four establishments. It is found of all shades of color—straw-colored, gray, green, yellow, orange, and of every degree of consistence, dry and hard, or soft and

* We presume the bi-carbonate of soda is here meant.

pasty. If mixed with almond oil, as in diluting it into an eye-salve, it soon becomes green, and gets a very unpleasant smell, whether covered up or not; and in this state it is often very irritating.

Many apothecaries in Dublin do not adhere to the Pharmacopœial formula, but make it up according to a form of their own; some use fresh butter instead of lard, and others different kinds of oil, as from habit or experience they find best.

On explaining my difficulties, some years ago, to Mr. Donovan, he procured me a citrine ointment of a very dark orange or brown color, soft, perfectly and equally smooth, and which does not alter in any way by keeping, by exposure to light, by mixing with oils, or even by being gently heated to the point of fluidity; and it never acquires an acid smell. Its therapeutic effects I have had long experience of, and they are decidedly superior to those of the ointment in common use. Mr. Donovan has not made its constituents, nor its mode of preparation.

Mr. Nicholls has made for me a citrine ointment precisely similar in color, smell, consistence and effects; and he informs me that he uses rape oil instead of olive oil, and does not let the heat employed during the preparation exceed 200 deg.

Mr. John Evans has employed cod-liver oil, and also seal oil, and the preparations thus produced are exceedingly elegant and useful ones. Mr. Carroll likewise uses cod-liver oil in the composition of this unguent.

Messrs. Bowley have obtained for me a brown citrine ointment, somewhat like those already mentioned, and they inform me that it is by using only the very pure olive oil. I find this ointment a very decided improvement on the old preparation, and its composition should be investigated by those engaged in the preparation of medicines and pharmacopœias. When about to be used, it should be melted to the consistence of cream by placing the vessel containing it in hot water. It forms an admirable application in ophthalmic tarsi, as well as in various diseases of the ear.—*N. Y. Med. Jour.*

IODINE INJECTIONS IN LEUCORRHŒA.

BY DR. RUSSELL.

It is not my design, in this communication, to enter into any theoretical inquiries respecting the nature of leucorrhœa, or the *modus operandi* of the remedy I propose for its cure; my object being simply to give the results of my experience in relation to iodine as a remedial agent in this obstinate, and in many cases intractable disease; and in doing which I shall record facts, well assured that one well-attested fact contributes more to the advancement of the science of medicine than three-fourths of the theories to which the press has ever given publicity.

I consider this disease to consist in inflammation of the vagina or the internal cavity of the uterus, or of both; and in the majority of those cases which have continued for a number of years, and resisted the ordinary modes of treatment, ulceration to a greater or less extent will generally be found to exist. For this condition, I have found no remedy equal to iodine; and, in illustration of its effects in my hands, I will briefly detail several cases from a number that have come under my observation.

CASE I.

In July, 1848, I was requested, by Mr. W——, to visit Grace, a favorite mulatto servant, aged forty-eight years, who, he informed me, had leucorrhœa of twelve years' standing had been under the care of a number of physicians during this period, and had been subjected to a great variety of treatment, but without avail. I found her confined to bed, very much debilitated and emaciated, face cadaverous, pulse quick and feeble, skin cool, urine scanty, severe pains in the lumbar and pelvic regions, and œdema of the lower extremities. The vaginal discharge, often escaping by gushes, was excessive, and her general health had become seriously involved from the effects of this long-continued drain to the constitution. Upon examination per vaginam, the vagina, os, and cervix uteri were found to be in a sub inflamed condition, and denuded of epithelium. The os was partially everted, and when deprived of its adherent mucus presented a vermilion color. The external cervix was enlarged, indurated, and ulcerated. The body of the uterus was sensibly enlarged, and descended within two inches of the os externum. The secretions from these several parts varied essentially in character, and when discharged externally resembled somewhat, in quantity, consistence and color, the yolk of an egg intermixed with purulent and sanguinolent matter, and all blended in a thick, opaque, tenacious plasma.

Ascertaining that she had never used iodine in any form, and believing it would afford her relief, I ordered the aqueous solution of the following strength to be thrown upon the vagina twice daily, and retained several minutes, the parts being previously well syringed with warm water and Castile soap, and the patient placed in a horizontal position, with the hips elevated:

℞. Iodini, gr. i; potass. iodid., gr. ii; aquæ pluvialis ℥i. M.

As this solution ceased to create any sensation of warmth or excitement in the parts, it was gradually increased to treble its strength. The muriated tincture of iron, in the proportion of twenty drops three times daily, was given as a tonic.

Under this treatment, with a nourishing diet, she soon began to improve; the irritated condition of the parts gradually subsided, the muco-purulent discharges by degrees ceased, the cervical ulcers regularly healed, and at the end of three months from its commencement she had regained her health and strength to such an extent as to enable her to resume her occupation as cook to the family. I may add, that her mammæ, which was very small and flaccid, became full and enlarged while under the influence of this medicine, and for several weeks secreted rather copiously a brownish watery fluid. This secretion being tested with starch, produced the characteristic blue color, showing that the iodine was absorbed.

CASE II.

August, 1848. Mrs. W—— consulted me; she was aged nineteen years; small and delicate figure; had been married four years, and dates the commencement of her present "weakness" to an abortion which occurred about six months subsequent to her marriage. Prior to marriage was remarkably healthy and active. At the time I saw her, she was anemic and emaciated, countenance chlorotic, eyes sunken, pulse feeble, menstruation painful, and either scanty or profuse. The vaginal discharge was constant and copious, muco-purulent, slightly streaked with blood, and very offensive. An examination, with the speculum, revealed an irritated condition of the vagina, with relaxation and loss of its natural rugæ, and accompanied by a partial displacement of the uterus. The cervix was enlarged and indurated, with several ulcers upon its external surface. She had never submitted to medical advice, contenting herself with the use of some simple domestic remedies. Correcting the torpid condition of her liver by means of the usual remedies, I prescribed the aqueous solution of iodine and the muriated tincture of iron, as above, recommending a nourishing diet, with free exercise in the open air.

She gradually improved under this plan of treatment, and in a few months her general health was re-established. She has, I understand, continued well ever since.

CASE III.

October, 1850. Mrs. G——, aged about twenty-seven years, large frame, mixed temperament, five years married, but has never been pregnant. Says that she was never "sick" previous to marriage, but subsequent thereto has always been in "delicate health." Has enlargement and induration of the liver and spleen, sequelæ of the intermittent fever, menstruation irregular and profuse. She was sallow and exsanguined, and exhibited, in a great degree, that long train of symptoms consequent upon an obstinate and protracted leucorrhœa. The vaginal discharge was constant, but variable in quantity and quality. Occasionally it was thin and acrimonious, often viscid and scanty, but usually purulent or muco-purulent, and excessive. The cervix was soft and tender to the touch, and, when seen by the speculum, was found enlarged and presenting a dark greyish appearance. The os was patulous, with tumefied edges, and of a reddish tint. A slight abrasion was found on the posterior lip.

Astringent vaginal injections—as the nitras argenti, acetas plumbi, &c.—were advised, and to relieve the enlarged and indurated condition of the liver and spleen, I prescribed the following:

℞. Prot. iod. mer., scrupulus i; pulv. aloes, scrupulus iss; ext. hyoscyami, ℥ i. M. Div. in pilulæ xxiv.

One pill to be taken every night; at the same time five drops of nitro-muriatic acid in a wine-glassful of the infusion of gentian, three times daily, was administered.

Under this treatment, the visceral derangements totally disappeared in about eight weeks, and her general health was greatly restored.

The leucorrhœa still continuing, (no benefit having resulted from the use of astringent injections,) and no amelioration in the condition of the parts being found on a second vaginal examination, which was now made, I ordered the aqueous solution of iodine and the muriated tincture of iron as above recommended. In six weeks after using these remedies, she declared herself well; shortly afterwards became pregnant, and was in time delivered of a fine healthy child.

Other cases could be adduced to prove the remedial powers of iodine as a local remedy in leucorrhœa, but as they are somewhat similar to the above in all essential particulars, it is unnecessary to introduce them here. Regarding the disease as being essentially a local one, our mode of treatment is principally local, and applied by means of a proper syringe to the parts affected. The preparation should at first be made weak, and gradually strengthened as the parts become accustomed to its application. The mildest preparation is frequently disagreeable, and sometimes painful, but these sensations are only momentary.

We have used it varying in strength from one to four grains of iodine with double the quantity of the iodide of potash to an ounce of water. It may be applied once or twice a day, or once every second or third day, as occasion may require. In some of the severer forms of this complaint, attended with considerable abrasion and ulceration, the diluted tincture may be used with great advantage.

Its curative powers are far greater than the nitrate of silver—which, in our hands, often seemed to exasperate the complaint—or any other remedy with which we are acquainted.—*Charleston Med. Jour. and Review.*

THE SALTS OF MANGANESE.

BY E. H. DAVIS, M.D., PROF. OF MATERIA MEDICA, ETC.

It is quite curious to observe how rapidly some remedies have attained a wide-spread reputation, and after a short-lived popularity, have lost it as soon. But such has not been the case with the various salts of manganese; for although some of them, at least, possess intrinsic value, they have been very tardily adopted by the profession.

It was observed, many years since, that the workmen in the manganese mines of Macon, in France, were uniformly cured of scabies and other cutaneous affections during their stay at the works. This led, at the time, to the use of the oxide for such cases elsewhere.

But we do not purpose, in this article, to chronicle the rise and progress of this metal as a medicinal agent, but merely to call the attention of the profession to some of its preparations.

Having recommended for years the use of the principal salts of manganese, such as the carbonate, sulphate, malate, tartrate, phosphate, and iodide, we were much surprised on a recent occasion, when sending a prescription containing the phosphate of manganese, to learn that the article could not be found, although some half-dozen of the best shops in the city were visited. The, patient, of course, was compelled to wait until the salt was produced in the laboratory.

The French have paid special attention to this remedy within a few years, in consequence of the discovery, by M. Millon, of the presence of this metal in the blood.* M. Hannon has experimented on himself and others, proving conclusively the power of manganese to improve the color of anæmic patients, as iron has long been known to do. The result has been the development of important therapeutic resources, fully equal, and in some respects superior, to those of the ferruginous compounds so long familiar to the profession.

It is stated among the prominent advantages of manganese over iron, that its preparations may be combined with all the vegetable tonics and astringents without risk of chemical incompatibility.

The *carbonate* has often been prescribed, but is considered too bulky—four to ten pills, of four grains each, being necessary daily for chlorotic patients.

Honey or syrup should be used in the preparation of these pills, as saccharine matter tends to prevent further oxidation. Mitchell recommends also the addition of fresh charcoal for the same purpose.

The *malate* is easily procured by acting upon the carbonate with malic acid. It is a desirable preparation, and can be given, in the form of pill, in quantity of from two to five grains at a dose. A syrup, which is generally the best form of exhibition, may be made thus:

℞. Mal. Mangan. ℥ ss.
Ess. Limon. ʒ i.
Syrup Simp. ℥ viii.
Dose, tea-spoonful three or four times a day.

* Transactions of the Académie des Sciences of Paris.

The *tartrate* is made just as the malate, merely substituting tartaric for malic acid, and may be dispensed in like manner. A highly tonic syrup can be formed with it as follows:

℞. Syrup Tolu. ℥ vii.
Ext. Rhatan.
Tart. Mang. āā. ʒ i.
Mix well. Dose, tea-spoonful four or five times daily.

Phosphate of Manganese is produced by adding a solution of phosphate of soda to a solution of sulphate of manganese. After the precipitate is dried, pills may be made, in the proportion of a drachm and half combined with half a drachm of Peruvian bark, and sufficient syrup of catechu or other syrup to make a mass. Pills to be divided into four grains each. A syrup is thus prepared:

℞. Phosph. Mangan. ʒ ss.
Syrup Tolu. ℥ iij.
Syrup Cinchon. ℥ v.
Ess. Limon. ʒ iss.
Pulv. G. Arab. scrupulus i.
Mix quickly—keep in a well-closed bottle. Dose, tea-spoonful.

The *iodide* may be administered in form of pill, or in combination with syrup of sarsaparilla.

These preparations have been highly recommended for the anæmic state resulting from tubercular disease.*

Hannon proposes to combine the two metals, where iron alone is not successful. It is also suggested to use first the insoluble preparations—as the carbonate, phosphate, and oxide—and afterwards the more soluble, as the tartrate, malate, &c.

The salts of manganese are more easily assimilated than those of iron, and, consequently, a shorter period is required for their exhibition. They are considered valuable in the depraved state of the blood consequent upon intermittent fever,

* Braithwaite's Retrospect, part xx.

and it is thought their use will prevent a return of the attacks. Enlargement of the spleen is speedily reduced by the iodide with syrup of cinchona.—*Amer. Med. Monthly.*

PURIFICATION OF SPIRITS BY FILTRATION.

BY MR. W. SCHAEFFER.

Instead of resorting to repeated distillations for effecting the purification of spirits, Mr. Schaeffer proposes the use of a filter. In a suitable vessel, the form of which is not material, a filtering bed is constructed in the following manner:—On a false perforated bottom, covered with woollen or other fabric, a layer of about six inches of well-washed and very clean river sand is placed; next about twelve inches of granular charcoal, preferring that made from birch; on the charcoal is placed a layer of about one inch of wheat, boiled to such an extent as to cause it to swell as large as possible, and so that it will readily crush between the fingers. Above this is laid about ten inches of charcoal, then about one inch of broken oyster shells, and then about two inches more of charcoal, over which is placed a layer of woollen or other fabric, and over it a perforated partition, on to which the spirit to be filtered is poured; the filter is kept covered, and, in order that the spirit may flow freely into the compartment of the filter below the filtering materials, a tube connects such lower compartment with the upper compartment of the filter, so that the air may pass freely between the lower and upper compartments of the filter. On each of the several strata above described, it is desirable to place a layer of filtering paper.

The charcoal suitable for the above purpose is not such as is obtained in the ordinary mode of preparation. It is placed in a retort or oven, and heated to a red-heat until the blue flame has passed off, and the flame become red. The charcoal is then cooled in water, in which carbonate of potash has previously been dissolved, in the proportion of two ounces of carbonate to fifty gallons of water. The charcoal being deprived of the water, is then reduced to a granular state, in which condition it is ready for use.—*Annals of Pharmacy*, August, 1854.

NEW PROCESS FOR PROCURING PHOSPHORUS.

BY M. CARI-MONTRAND.

M. Dumas read to the Academy of Sciences, at Paris, at their session of 15th May, a letter from a young chemist, M. Cari-Montrand, in which he proposes a new mode for the preparation of phosphorus on a practical scale, the usual process being slow, complicated, yielding but little product, and giving an educt of no value. The process proposed consists of passing over a thorough mixture of equal parts of finely-powdered charcoal and bone-earth, at a red heat, a quantity of dry hydrochloric acid, or, still better, of dry chlorine. The end of the porcelain tube in which the experiment was performed was attached to a glass tube, dipping under water. Phosphorus, carbonic oxide and water are given off, and chloride of calcium is left in the tube. On analysis, no trace of phosphoric acid, or any other compound, was found in the tube; the decomposition is, therefore, complete, and, as no phosphorus passed off, the whole amount contained in the earth was obtained as a product. The following equation explains the reaction, when hydrochloric acid is used:

$$3\ Ca.O,\ PO^5 + 5\ C + 3\ H\ Cl. = 5\ CO + 3\ HO + 3\ Ca.\ Cl. + P.$$

The same letter contains a notice interesting to chemists, of the entire decomposition of gypsum, and the procuring of its sulphuric acid, by treatment of a mixture with charcoal by dry chlorine, or hydrochloric acid gas. A good deal of excitement appears to have been caused among some of the would-be scientific papers, by the announcement of this process, which, it was asserted, would materially reduce the price of sulphuric acid. But it will be easily seen that, as at least the equivalent of hydrochloric acid (dry weight 36) must be used for each equivalent of oil of vitriol, (weight 49,) the process would be more expensive than at present. This is clearly stated by M. Cari-Montrand, who had the process tried on a large scale by M. Kühlmann, but found that the expense of making and drying the hydrochloric acid was an insurmountable obstacle to its introduction into the arts.—*Journal of the Franklin Institute.*

POLYTRICHUM JUNIPERINUM.

This name is given to a species of moss called hair-cap moss or robbins rye, which grows abundantly in some parts of the Northern States, and to which Dr. Wood, of Connecticut, attributes the most extraordinary diuretic powers.

It may be given in almost any quantity, however large, without danger of bad effects, and is said to act with great certainty and power upon the kidneys, causing very profuse discharges of the urine, and relieving hydropic affections, even of long standing, in a very few days.

If the one-half is true of what is related of its diuretic qualities, it is by far the most certain remedy of this class known, and ought to be found in all our apothecary shops.—*Memphis Med. Recorder.*

Varieties.

ON THE DETECTION OF ALCOHOL IN JUDICIARY INVESTIGATIONS.

BY DR. ED. STRAUCH.

Thomson has recommended the use of chromic acid for the detection of alcohol. The author confirms the distinctness of the reaction by reduction, formation of aldehyde, &c., but points out the inaccuracies which may arise from the reduction being also caused by many other bodies, although these affect less the distillate.

The essential portion of the author's communication is the following description of a method of determining alcohol by means of platinum-black, which enables us to decide within a quarter to half an hour whether the distillate of the substance under examination for alcohol contains that body or not.

The part of the body to be examined for alcohol is to be finely divided immediately after it has been taken out of the corpse; or, if the test cannot be immediately applied, it must be placed in a well-closed vessel, in order to prevent the volatilization of any alcohol that may be contained in it. If the substance under investigation have an acid reaction, a few drops of very dilute solution of potash are carefully added to it until a piece of litmus paper dipped into the mixture is no longer reddened. The substance is then put into a tubulated retort, either by means of a funnel or a pair of forceps. This may be of such a size as to hold about one pound of water. For smaller quantities smaller retorts may be made use of, but it is always well to use as much as possible of the substance to be tested. If it be desired to detect alcohol in the lungs, the retort must only be half filled, as the lungs when heated froth up very much, and by this means a portion of the mass in the retort may boil over. The retort is placed in a water-bath, and so arranged that its neck may be but little bent down. This is broken off so far up that a tray of platinum, fine silver or glass, of about one-third of an inch in breath and two inches long, may be slipped into it. Into this tray some platinum-black is put, and at each end of it is placed a piece of blue litmus paper, moistened with distilled water, which must be partially in contact with the platinum-black. The tray is now pushed, by means of a wire hook, to the place where the neck of the retort passes into its belly, and the water-bath is heated by means of a spirit-lamp. The operation may be facilitated by filling the water-bath with a solution of chloride of calcium or sodium, instead of water. As alcohol boils at a lower temperature than water, it, of course, is the first to be driven off. As soon, therefore, as the first water-drops begin to condense in the neck of the retort, that portion of the litmus paper which is in contact with the platinum-black becomes reddened, whilst that portion which is turned towards the belly of the retort still remains blue, and thus at once shows that the acid did not come out of the retort, but was only formed in contact with the platinum-black. When the heat has been applied for some time, and single drops begin to run from the neck of the retort, without any reddening of the litmus paper, we may conclude with certainty that no trace of alcohol was contained in the substance under examination. But if, on the contrary, the litmus paper is quickly and strongly reddened, and it be desired to produce further proof of the presence of alcohol, the tray is again to be drawn out of the retort; the latter is then bent down a little more, a receiver is attached to it, and distillation is continued until the distillate amounts to several drachms, during which the receiver is cooled by a cloth soaked with cold water. The distillate is then transferred into a small retort, and about the same quantity of fused chloride of calcium; or, if this be not at hand, well-dried chloride of sodium is added to it. This retort is then put upon the water-bath in pure water, a receiver is attached to it, and distillation continued as long as anything passes over. A few drops of this second distillate may now be added to a mixture of bichromate of potash and sulphuric acid, to obtain the alcohol reaction. The remainder of the distillate may be made use of to ascertain the specific gravity; but this, when operating upon such small quantities, not only requires fine apparatus, but also much skill, and must, consequently, often remain undone. A portion of the fluid may afterwards be poured into a metallic or porcelain capsule, when its ignition, by means of a burning match, may be attempted. If this does not succeed, the capsule may be heated by a spirit-lamp, when the alcohol contained in the water is the first to evaporate, and may be ignited by a burning match. A portion of the distillate may be set aside; and, if a considerable quantity still remains, the following experiment may be made with it. The neck of a small glass funnel is loosely closed by means of a small glass rod; some platinum-black is then put into the funnel, moistened with a few drops of distilled water, and the alcoholic fluid is then allowed to flow upon it in a very slow stream by means of a cotton thread, which may act as a siphon. A fluid, with an acid reaction, then drops from the funnel; this is carefully neutralized by a few drops of very dilute solution of potash, and evaporated to perfect dryness on the water-bath. A portion of the residue may be added to some very dilute chloride of iron, to obtain the ordinary reaction of the acetates; another portion may be triturated with a small quantity of arsenious acid, and heated in a small test-tube, when the characteristic strong odor of oxide of kakodyle is produced. These two latter tests, however, require rather larger quantities of acetic acid before they will succeed; as a general rule, the test with the platinum-black, to which the reaction with chromic acid and the test of combustibility may be added, is quite sufficient.

The platinum-black employed for this purpose is precipitated from a very dilute solution of chloride of platinum by means of zinc; it is washed first with muriatic acid, then with nitric acid, and lastly with potash. The author concludes with a series of experiments, which sufficiently prove the applicability of the method.—Strauch's Inaugural Dissertation, Dorpat, 1852, in *Chemical Gazette.*

The treatment of cholera by castor oil continues to be the fruitful topic of discussion in the professional and non-professional journals of London. If we read but one side we might be easily convinced.—*Amer. Med. Monthly.*

METHOD OF RAPIDLY BLEACHING WAX, AND PURIFYING TALLOW, OILS, &c.

Wax, properly speaking, consists of pure wax and a coloring matter; there are several kinds of wax, distinguished commercially by the relative amount of coloring matter which they contain. Formerly it was supposed that wax could only be bleached by the action of sunlight; to effect this object, the operations could only be commenced in the month of May, when the fine season has set in, and the sun attained sufficient altitude to send its rays more directly, for a longer period and with more force; and these conditions continue only at most for three or four months. To bleach wax by this process, it must be made into ribbons of great tenuity, or feathered as zinc is by being poured into water; an operation which must be repeated at least three times, whilst the duration of the exposure to the sunlight must occupy from one month to six weeks, in order to destroy the coloring matter to which we have alluded. To do this requires a considerable space, which is often very expensive, and a heavy outlay in plant, such as bleaching frames, canvas, &c.; this primitive condition of the wax industry renders the bleaching not only embarrassing, but uncertain and variable according to the weather.

In order to diminish the amount of capital which was required to be sunk in this branch of trade, and above all to shorten the time required to bleach the wax, M. Cassgrand, some years ago, patented a process in France, which has now passed nto the public domain, and which, it appears, has been very successful.

This process consists in melting the wax by means of steam until it becomes very liquid, and then passing it, along with the steam, through a kind of serpentine or worm, by which a large surface becomes exposed to the action of the steam. After traversing the worm, it is received in a pan with a double bottom, heated by steam, where water is added in order to wash it; from this it is elevated by a pump, kep t hot by steam, into another pan similarly heated, and where it is also treated with water, and is again passed through the serpentine. This operation is repeated twice, thrice, or four times, according to the quality of the wax; during the passage with the steam through the worm, it becomes denser by, it is said, absorbing water, (per-mechanically?) and deposits in the upper pan. It is allowed to repose in this for about four or five minutes after each passage; and after the last one, about one or two hours, according to quantity, in order to allow of any impurities to subside. The wax is then granulated in the ordinary way by means of cold water, is allowed to dry during two or three days, and the action of light and air does the rest, for which one person is sufficient. The whole of the operations do not require more than a few days, are perfectly certain, and are attended with no danger. Independent of the advantage which such an apparatus has for bleaching wax, it has also that of enabling its qualities, according to relative whiteness, to be distinguished; for this purpose it is only necessary to present the wax in mass to the end of the worm, and in a second or two the vapor determines the relative color which it will yield.

This process is also applicable to the purification of tallows and of oils; even fish-oil, when passed through the apparatus of M. Cassgrand, and washed as just described, is completely deprived of its disagreeable smell; and if it be set aside in a place where the temperature only reaches from 59° to 68° F., a fresh deposit will form, and the oil will become perfectly clarified and nearly colorless.

This process has considerable analogy with one which Mr. Dixon, of Dublin, patented some time since for bleaching palm-oil, the principle of which was exposing the oil to the action of steam. Cassgrand's apparatus might, no doubt, be applied to the same purpose, and appears to us to have certain advantages over that of Dixon, especially in exposing a larger surface to the action of the steam, and varying that surface oftener. If not already known here, the process is worthy of the serious attention of soap-boilers. Such a method would evidently be much more effective than the present system of purifying oils, especially where sulphuric acid is used, which is almost universally the case. As that acid is scarcely ever effectively removed, many samples of trottor, rape, and other similar oils, are usually quite acid; where the former is used for the manufacture of hair-oil, it is very destructive to the hair, and the latter destroys the lamps when used for burning, &c. The only modification required for the purification of oil would be to divide the oil as much as possible by means of a diaphragm of copper, pierced with holes, in the first steam-vessel, and thus expose the largest possible surface to the action of the steam in flowing through the pierced diaphragm.—*Dublin Journal of Industrial Progress.*

ON THE RECOGNITION OF BLOOD-SPOTS UPON LINEN AND COTTON STUFFS.

BY C. WIEHR.

In the course of last year the author had to examine some pieces of stuffs which bore red spots; these were a dirty old piece of coarse unbleached linen and a blue and white checked pillow-cover. The object was to ascertain whether the red spots upon them were produced by blood.

With this object, a red fragment was cut out of each piece of stuff, and each fragment extracted separately with distilled water. The spots on the coarse cloth had already begun to decompose, as it had lain a long time buried in dung. The filtered fluid from it had a dingy brownish-red color. By the employment of the reagents, such as liquid chlorine, ammonia, nitric acid and tincture of galls, which are particularly adapted for the detection of albumen, the proper reactions were certainly obtained; but as the fluid was not of a pure red color, they were not so distinct as to enable the presence of blood to be determined with perfect certainty. With the second fluid from the pillow-cover, which had a dark violet color, from the bad blue which was produced by logwood, these reagents could not be employed. The author endeavored to produce cyanide of potassium with the supposed blood-spots of these stuffs. For this purpose, having first ascertained, in the well-known manner, that the stuff contained no wool, he roasted a red fragment of the coarse linen in a porcelain crucible until it could be rubbed to powder; this powder was mixed with some carbonate of potash, and strongly heated to redness. The calcined mixture was extracted with distilled water, and a little solution of a salt of protoxide, and another of peroxide of iron, mixed with the filtered fluid, by which means a precipitate of indeterminate color, consisting of protoxide and peroxide of iron, precipitated by the excess of carbonate of potash and protopercyanide of iron, was produced. A little dilute sulphuric acid was now added, by which the oxides of iron were dissolved; whilst, on the other hand, the protopercyanide of iron, which is insoluble in sulphuric acid, made its appearance with its blue color. The same result was obtained with a piece of the checked stuff on which red spots existed, but not with fragments of the stuffs which presented no appearance of blood-spots.

The experiments were also frequently repeated with other blood, and furnished satisfactory results even with the smallest quantities.

The operation also succeeds when a piece of stuff spotted with blood is boiled with solution of caustic potash, the fluid evaporated to dryness and calcined, and then treated with iron salts and sulphuric acid. This method may also be employed when blood-spots are found upon metallic objects; the spots are dissolved from the metal by solution of potash.—*Archiv der Pharm.*, lxxviii. p. 21.

Experimental Investigation of the Poisonous Quality of the Oil of Bitter Almonds when Freed from Hydrocyanic Acid.—A servant girl having been poisoned by half a drachm of essential oil of almonds, taken by mistake, Dr. Douglas Maclagan has been led to investigate the poisonous quality of the simple hydruret of benzule, which constitutes, with more or less of hydrocyanic acid, the commercial essential oil of almonds. The following are the conclusions:

1. The marked difference between rectified and unrectified oil of bitter almonds shows that the poisonous character of the latter is essentially due to the hydrocyanic acid which it contains.

2. That the oil, really free from hydrocyanic acid, in doses of a few drops, does not act as a poison on animals generally; and that the instances of fatal effects on man and animals of such doses of the unrectified oil, must be referred entirely to the hydrocyanic acid.

3. That experiments on rabbits with quantities of half a drachm, and under, invariably show, that, if quite free from prussic acid, such doses do not cause fatal effects. That in larger doses (a drachm and upwards) it does, even when quite free rom hydrocyanic acid, prove fatal to rabbits, but with great variation as regards the rapidity of the death, which variation is due to the physiological peculiarities of these animals.

4. That on dogs, whose organization renders them much better subjects for testing the probable effects of the substance on man, doses even so large as three drachms of the oil, entirely or nearly free from prussic acid, produce no other effect than a little vomiting, and do not cause death, or even dangerous symptoms.

5. That experiment shows that if this substance is to be called a poison at all, it must be regarded as one of no great activity; but that, in reality, it cannot, even on the ground of its effect on rabbits, be styled a poison, without including under this denomination many other substances, such as oil of cloves, which cannot be regarded as poisonous, in the common sense acceptation of the term.

6 That the use of the purified oil to make flavoring condiments is open to no objection which would not apply to ordinary aromatic volatile oils; and that the spi-

rituous solutions sold for this purpose, if made of properly purified oil, are not dangerous.

7. That since, by due care, the oil can be so entirely freed from hydrocyanic acid as to deprive it of active poisonous properties, great culpability will attach to the sale of preparations made with unrectified oil.

The author has given a short notice of the opinions of different toxicologists on the properties of this oil, with the details of his own experiments; forming a very valuable contribution to toxicological science.—*Edin. Month. Jour. Med. Science.*

Poisoning attributed to Vapor of Cyanide of Potassium.—The bodies of four individuals were found dead in a cottage in the village of Elscar, in Yorkshire. On the inquest, it was stated that the cottage abutted on the foundation of a smelting furnace, and it had been discovered that there were cracks in the wall of the furnace. Death was attributed to the vapor of cyanogen having escaped, and having been inspired by the inmates after they had retired to bed. The symptoms and circumstances of their death could not be known, as all four had evidently been several hours dead when the catastrophe was discovered. According to the report of the inquest in the daily papers of December 6th, there does not appear to have been any scientific investigation to ascertain whether cyanogen, or carbonic acid gas, had escaped through the fissure in the wall of the furnace.

Recovery after taking a Large Dose of Prussic Acid.—Mr. W. H. Burman, of Watch-upon-Dearne, has communicated a very interesting history of the recovery of his father from accidental poisoning by prussic acid. We regret that our limits compel us to confine our notice of this instructive case to a short abstract. Mr. Burman, sen., took, by mistake, a drachm of Scheele's acid instead of diluted acid. In a few seconds he perceived by the bottle the mistake he had made; he immediately swallowed half an ounce of aromatic spirit of ammonia, with a little water, and then called to his son, and told him what had occurred; he spoke hurriedly, breathed deeply. Mr. W. H. Burman immediately administered some solution of crystals of sulphate of iron, trusting to the ammonia swallowed previously for the formation of an insoluble compound of the acid with the oxides of iron. This was two minutes after the poison had been swallowed; from this time, for twenty minutes, Mr. Burman had no recollection of anything that was taking place. Respiration became deeper and slower. Four minutes after taking the poison, cold douche was freely employed, and more solution of sulphate of iron with spirits of ammonia administered. Vomiting took place; a slight convulsive shudder occurred; the cold effusion was persevered in, with the occasional administration of spirits of ammonia. In twenty minutes he began to exhibit signs of returning consciousness. In about fifteen minutes later he was able to walk up stairs to bed. Perfect recovery took place. The patient was of about sixty years of age, and of a strong constitution.

By chemical analysis, Mr. W. H. Burman found that the quantity of the acid which his father had taken contained 2.4 grains of anhydrous acid. Mr. Burman observes that this is the largest recorded quantity taken and followed by recovery. It is also a matter of interest in this case that the time at which insensibility came on is so exactly known, viz., two minutes after the poison was swallowed.—*Lancet.*

Poisoning by Darnel Seeds.—The *lotium temulentum*, or darnel grass, when taken in sufficiently large doses, exerts a local action upon the alimentary canal, with remote action on the brain and nervous system. There is heat, pain in the stomach, nausea, vomiting, diarrhœa, followed by languor, loss of vision, ringing in the ears, and vertigo. There is, however, no recorded instance of their having proved fatal to man.—(Taylor on Poisons, p. 745.) These effects have usually arisen from the accidental mixture of the seed with food grain. The following newspaper paragraph records an instance of this kind:

"The town and neighborhood of Roscrea was thrown into the greatest consternation on Christmas Day, during Divine Service, by intelligence having been communicated to the police that several families had been poisoned by having eaten whole-meal bread at breakfast. Medical assistance was immediately rendered the unfortunate sufferers, when it was ascertained that they labored to an intense degree, under the violent symptoms produced by the seeds (flour) of the bearded darnel, rye-grass, commonly called ryley, which was mixed with the whole-meal. Over thirty persons received medical aid, and presented symptoms as if from intoxication. Remedies having been applied, on the following morning all the sufferers were found convalescent, but much debilitated."—*Leinster Express* (Ireland).

It appears from experiments made by Alvaro Reynso upon the effects of the inhalation of ether and chloroform that other phenomena than insensibility follow their use in man and animals. One of the results newly arrived at is that sugar appears in the urine after anæsthesia. This fact, the knowledge of which is due to Reyneso, in most cases occurs after the use of chloroform, and this too when the individual is otherwise in good health, and is always constant after the insensibility following the administration of the liquid. This discovery of Reyneso just now is very interesting, as Bernard has been directing attention to the appearance of sugar in the blood, both from injury of the base of the brain and from lesion of function in the liver. Reyneso shows its connection with disordered respiration and inefficient action of the lungs. The Academy of Sciences, Paris, have granted him 500 francs as an encouragement for the research bestowed upon his labor.

In a paper communicated to the same body upon the metals accompanying platina in its ore, by Fremy, he divides them into three classes, viz., ***dust***, compound of iridium and rhodium; ***scales***, formed of iridium, ruthenium, rhodium and osmium; and ***grains***, containing rhodium, osmium and iridium.

The *Journal de Pharmacie* for April last publishes a list of the members of the Society of Pharmacy of Paris, which it may be interesting to give a short account of here. The society consists of resident members, honorary members, free associates, home correspondents, and foreign ditto. The number of residents is fixed at 60; free associates, at 20; home correspondents, 100; and foreign correspondents, 60. The number of honorary members is unlimited. The resident members must be regularly qualified pharmaciens; the free associates are chosen out of those resident in Paris, not practising pharmacy and distinguished in the natural or medical sciences. Corresponding members are chosen from home and foreign pharmaciens and *savans*. The business of the society is conducted by a president, a vice-president, and a secretary, who are chosen annually; a treasurer for three years, and a "general" secretary for six years. The vice-president passes each year *by right* into the office of president, and then re-elected until after ten years. The general secretary and treasurer may be elected immediately, vote by ballot, the absolute majority electing. Election each December; the society meets the first Wednesday of the month, at two, P.M. Among the general rules is one which will not admit, nor allow to remain in the society, any pharmacien who has committed "reprehensible acts," particularly by his announcement of medicines which would compromise the dignity of the society. The only foreign corresponding members in this country are Messrs. Kane and Durand, both of Philadelphia.

ARTESIAN WELLS.—They have sunk an Artesian well in St. Louis 2,200 feet, and are still boring. It is to get pure water for a sugar refinery. At the depth of 700 feet a vein of salt water was struck, and at 1,500 feet an immense vein of sulphur water burst forth, which has been running ever since its discovery in a large stream from the mouth of the well.

This water is the same as that of the Blue Lick Springs in Kentucky, and possesses a purity and freshness of taste quite superior to that which reaches us in barrels and casks. It is carried off by a large sewer leading to the river.

It seems too wasteful that such profuse quantities of this celebrated water should be permitted to flow away, but the refinery needs the clear, unadulterated element, and it must have it and nothing else. Other medicinal waters have been discovered, we believe, but they have been of little consequence.

In Charleston, S. C., a sinking for an Artesian well has been made. The tubing has now been let down to the depth of 1,200 feet, the total depth of the boring exceeding that amount slightly.

UNIVERSITY OF EDINBURGH.—Professor Edward Forbes has been appointed to the Chair of Natural History in this Institution, long filled by the late Professor Jameson. This is an excellent appointment. Professor Forbes is one of the most eminent and zealous naturalists of the age.

Obituary.

The following tribute to the memory of the late Dr. Enderlin, whose name has appeared on this Journal as one of its collaborators, is extracted from a contemporary, the "American Medical Monthly," and supplies us with terms to join in the regret for his loss:

"It is with heartfelt regret we take our pen to record the decease of the illustrious chemist, Dr. Charles Enderlin, by whose indefatigable labors in the laboratory the pages of physiological chemistry have been so greatly enriched. His loss will be deeply deplored by the scientific men of both hemispheres, as he ranked among the pioneers.

"Through the kindness of an intimate friend, we learn that he was born at Steinbach (Baden), Germany, April 16th, 1813; that he pursued the study of pharmacy, under Geiger, at Heidelburg, that of medicine in the same city and in Würzburg, and completed his chemical course under Liebig at Giessen.

"His contributions to physiological chemistry appeared in a series of communications in Liebig's Annalen.

"In 1843, 'On the Acids of the Gastric Juice;' in 1844, 'Physiologico-Chemical Investigations on the Constitution of Human Blood and the Blood of different Herbivorous Mammalia;' in the same year, 'On the Constitution of *Bile* and of *Saliva*;' in 1847, 'On the Constitution of the Blood of Birds and Fishes;' also, two analysis of the blood of frogs.

"All of the above investigations referred especially to the mineral constituents of the liquids, and was sustained by long series of analysis of their ashes.

"In 1848 appeared a oontinuation of his investigations of the blood of birds, fishes, etc.; in 1850, 'Special Researches on the Quantity of Potash in the Blood, and the relative proportions of potash and soda;' in the same year, 'On a Specific Metamorphosis of the *Bile* of the *Ox*, as a contribution to the knowledge of the chemical constitution of bile in general;' and again, 'A Communication on *Human Bile* and *Biline*;' also one 'On the presence of *bile* in the *blood*.'

"Although the greater part of his investigations were devoted to the highest department of his favorite science, chemistry as applied to physiology; yet, after his arrival in the United States, October 8, 1850, and his successful establishment of a laboratory in this city, agricultural chemistry and mining operations attracted his attention. In fact, it was on his return from a mining excursion in Canada, while at the railroad depot in Hamilton, C. W., that he was struck senseless, and died a week after, on the morning of September 16th, the immediate cause of his decease being pronounced by the attending physicians as compression of the brain. His remains were interred in Hamilton.

"His gentlemanly bearing, manly character, and warm heart, as well as his profound erudition, endeared him to all who enjoyed his acquaintance or called him friend. For those who claimed him by the more endearing ties of husband and father, we offer our sincere expressions of sympathy.

"We trust that the numerous and valuable unpublished papers of Dr. Enderlin may not be lost to the scientific world.

"R. O. D.

NEW YORK

JOURNAL OF PHARMACY,

EDITED BY

THOMAS ANTISELL, M.D.,

AIDED BY

PROFESSOR TORREY, M.D., CHARLES ENDERLIN, M.D.,

BENJAMIN CANAVAN.

Vol. III.

NOS. 11 & 12

NOVEMBER and DECEMBER, 1854.

New-York:

PRINTED BY CHARLES SHIELDS,

CORNER OF PLATT AND GOLD STREETS.

TERMS, THREE DOLLARS PER ANNUM, IN ADVANCE.